Race and

in the Classical

World

RACE AND ETHNICITY IN THE CLASSICAL WORLD

AN ANTHOLOGY OF PRIMARY SOURCES IN TRANSLATION

Selected and Translated by

Rebecca F. Kennedy, C. Sydnor Roy,
and Max L. Goldman

Hackett Publishing Company, Inc.
Indianapolis/Cambridge

25 24 23 22   3 4 5 6 7

For further information, please address
        Hackett Publishing Company, Inc.
        P.O. Box 44937
        Indianapolis, Indiana 46244-0937

        www.hackettpublishing.com

Interior design by Elizabeth L. Wilson
Composition by Innodata-Isogen, Inc.

Library of Congress Cataloging-in-Publication Data

Kennedy, Rebecca Futo, 1974–
  Race and ethnicity in the classical world : an anthology of primary sources
in translation / Selected and Translated by Rebecca F. Kennedy, C. Sydnor
Roy, and Max L. Goldman.
     pages cm.
  ISBN 978-1-60384-994-4 (pbk.) — ISBN 978-1-60384-995-1 (cloth)
  1. Ethnicity—Rome—History. 2. Ethnicity—Greece—History. 3. Race—
Social aspects—Rome—History. 4. Race—Social aspects—Greece—History.
5. Ethnicity in literature. 6. Race in literature. 7. Civilization, Classical. 8.
Rome—Civilization. 9. Greece—Civilization. I. Title.
  DG78.K46 2013
  305.800938—dc23   2013013529

CONTENTS

CONTENTS   vii

THE PEOPLES OF THE ANCIENT WORLD

ACKNOWLEDGMENTS

We would like to acknowledge the people who have supported the production of this volume. Thanks go out, first, to Rick Todhunter and Liz Wilson, our editors. Rick had the foresight to take on the project and the faith that we would see it to fruition. After three years and 225,000 words translated, Liz took up the work of seeing it through production. We owe thanks as well to Monica Cyrino, who introduced us to Rick and believed that this was a text worth pursuing. If she (or anyone, really) ever wants to teach a course with the book, we have syllabi you can borrow. We are aware that no selection of passages will please all teachers and we hope that those who use the book will share with us their experiences, good and bad.

Thanks also must go out to a number of anonymous brave souls such as the reviewers, who were not frightened of the very large manuscript that confronted them and who spent time and effort evaluating the clarity of the translations and the editorial choices we made for the selections. Thanks also to the copyeditor for dealing with dozens of different types of texts and citation systems from dozens of different authors and for dealing with the wonderful variety of names and spellings on display in the ancient geographers and ethnographers. Also, to Becky Woods, administrative assistant in the Dept. of Classics at Denison University, our thanks is owed for typo-hunting the first draft of the manuscript.

Importantly, we should acknowledge the students at Denison University and Temple University for reading and discussing many of the texts as we selected and translated them. This project is as much about them as it is about our research and love of antiquity and its variety. It is in part because we wanted to offer courses on the history of race and ethnicity as concepts instead of on "barbarians" that this book emerged. Sydnor would like to especially thank Dan Tompkins and Eric Kondratieff, her colleagues at Temple who developed Temple's course on Race, and her research assistant Rick Powanda.

Finally, I (Rebecca Kennedy) want to offer a deep and sincere thank-you to my co-translators, Sydnor Roy and Max Goldman. When I asked you to join me on this project, I don't think any of us knew how long and how much endurance it would take. Nor do I think either of you were really sure even what you had signed up for. That it is finished and finished so well is a testament to your hard work. Sydnor and I would especially like to thank Max, who joined us at the midway stage of the project. His generous help allowed us to finish on time.

ACKNOWLEDGMENTS

INTRODUCTION

The past is a foreign country: they do things differently there.
—L. P. Hartley[1]

RACE AND ETHNICITY: MODERN CONCEPTS, ANCIENT TEXTS

The title of this book is an intentional anachronism. The ancients would not understand the social construct we call "race" any more than they would understand the distinction modern scholars and social scientists generally draw between race and "ethnicity." The modern concept of race is a product of the colonial enterprises of European powers from the 16th to 18th centuries that identified race in terms of skin color and physical difference. In the post-Enlightenment world, a "scientific," biological idea of race suggested that human difference could be explained by biologically distinct groups of humans, evolved from separate origins, who could be distinguished by physical differences, predominantly skin color. Ethnicity, on the other hand, is now often considered a distinction in cultural practice within the same race. As a result, a "white" person from Eastern Europe is racially identical to a white person from England, but they are ethnically distinct. Likewise, a "black" person from the United States is racially identical to a black person from Nigeria, but they are ethnically distinct. Such categorizations would have confused the ancient Greeks and Romans.

The Greeks and Romans, like us, struggled to understand the varieties of humanity in the world as they knew it. Some people, for example, had pale skin with fine, red hair and freckles. Others had dark skin with coarse, curly hair. How did such differences arise among the peoples of the world? Their theories for difference, while not the same as our concepts of race and ethnicity, suggest that they considered similar causes. The ancient origin myths of humanity in Greece and the Near East tended to posit a single source for all humans. The first humans were shaped from clay by Prometheus (Chapter 2, Selection 12), and after the destruction of the earth in a great flood, the next generation of humans was born of rocks thrown over the shoulders of Deucalion and Pyrrha (Chapter 2, Selection 13). The "races" of mankind imagined by Hesiod (Chapter 1, Selection 9) and other Greek mythologists were generations of people, born and then destroyed; they were not the origins of distinctive groups of humans. Born from the same

---

1. L. P. Hartley, *The Go-Between* (New York: Knopf, 1954), 17.

original source, humanity somehow diverged into groups with distinctive physical features, languages, and customs. Greek and Roman myth had no Tower of Babel. There were no sons of Cain or Abraham. Unlike the ancient Hebrews, the Greeks had multiple and competing explanations for human difference.

If all humans came originally from a single source, external factors must have altered them into different forms. Theories arose to meet this problem. The scientific awakening of the Greeks and developments in medicine in the Hippocratic schools gave rise to theories of geographic and climatic determinism. Philosophers and early ethnographers speculated with theories of biological or genetic determinism. Some ancient peoples even developed theories of separate human origins. They claimed to be autochthonous, born from their own land and not by evolution from the humans created by Deucalion and Pyrrha. Theories based on the mixing of peoples from these autochthonous origins through mythic conquests accounted for both human differences and similarities. But it was not always clear what counted as a distinguishing characteristic: Were people to be distinguished by physical features, by language, by religious practices, by choice of government, or by funeral rights? Were these a result of nature or nurture?

These multifarious theories were not always distinct, nor did they develop chronologically, one theory building upon another. Rather, these theories often competed with each other, sometimes within a single text (e.g., the Hippocratic *Airs, Waters, Places* or Herodotus' *Histories*). The Greeks and Romans were obsessed with understanding human difference, but they never could seem to agree on what differences mattered or what caused the differences. They could not even agree on what words they would use to discuss the differences: *genos, ethnos, ethnê, phulê*—all were used variously to denote a race, an ethnic group, a political unit, or some other social or cultural unit.

The aim of this book is to introduce readers to the wide variety of theories from the ancient Greeks and Romans concerning human difference as well as to broaden access to these foundational ideas. This book focuses on what the ancient Greeks and Romans wrote. Archaeology can provide many insights into ancient racial and ethnic identities, but the material can be difficult to present and to interpret,[2] thus we leave it up to instructors and scholars to engage with the visual and material evidence elsewhere. We hope these translations of ancient writings will be useful to anyone interested in the ancient world and its legacy—archaeologists, historians, philologists, anthropologists, philosophers—anyone seeking to understand how the ancients understood human difference and how their ideas continue to impact our world today. These theories are explained in the ancient written sources left by the Greeks and Romans, though it is our earnest hope that students, teachers, and scholars will view material remains along with these texts to understand better the everyday "ethnographic way of

2. On the use of material remains in the study of race and ethnicity, see S. Jones, *The Archaeology of Ethnicity: Constructing Identities in the Past and Present* (Routledge, 1997).

thinking" experienced by the ancients. There are hundreds of sculptures, paintings, and household objects that show different ways of representing race and ethnicity that suggest thinking about human difference was a part of popular as well as intellectual life in antiquity.

In recent years, the study of these differences has been confined mostly to discussion of texts that reflect a structuralist and postcolonial approach to the barbarian "other" as found in the Greco-Roman sources, the primary exceptions being B. Isaac's *The Invention of Racism in Classical Antiquity* and M. Sassi's *The Science of Man in Ancient Greece*. But for the Greeks and the Romans, the barbarian was only one construct of difference, a culturally based one, that even the Greeks and Romans themselves recognized as constructed and flexible: one could *become* a barbarian, and a barbarian could *become* Greek or Roman. The theories represented in this book include the concept of the barbarian, but do not privilege it as the only theory. We give space to the other theories, such as those represented in the ancient scientific and technical writers, especially the geographers and ethnographers. Although the ancient discussions of the barbarian were influential in the development of modern colonial concepts of race and ethnicity (beginning with its impact on the way the New World was understood in the wake of its discovery in 1492),[3] the ancient genetic and environmental theories influenced and contributed most to modern scientific theories of race such as Darwinian evolution, polygenism,[4] craniometry,[5] and eugenics.[6] These theories were the foundation of the modern field of anthropology and have their roots in the tradition of the classical education of the men who developed them and the thinkers who influenced them (Hegel, Locke, Kant, Voltaire, and Montesquieu, among others).

The ancient theories may not directly correlate to our terms "race" and "ethnicity," but both the modern concepts and the ancient texts share the principle that human difference is a product of both internally determined and externally produced influences.

ORGANIZATION AND STRUCTURE

The first part of the book introduces the ancient theories, in order to give readers a framework for examining the subsequent ethnographic and geographic texts. We start with the works of Homer and Hesiod, the earliest attempts to grapple with "otherness." These attempts are then followed

---

3. Grafton 1992.

4. The idea that there are distinct genetic histories among human groups that originated and developed separately. These theories were used to support miscegenation.

5. The theory that the moral character, intelligence, and race of a person could be distinguished through measuring his or her skull. Although this seems like an absurd notion to most people now, it was one of the hallmarks of modern anthropology well into the 20th century. Many of the skulls gathered at the Smithsonian Institute were subject to craniometric examinations.

6. The theory strongly associated with the racial theory of typologies, the most well-known of which is Aryanism.

by genealogies and origin stories. These genealogies are concerned with the origins of the Greeks and Romans themselves and reflect their own attempts to understand what distinguished them from and made them similar to non-Greeks or non-Romans. Next come the three major theories from antiquity: environmental, genetic, and cultural. These theories are not mutually exclusive, but the texts often emphasize one theory over another; for example, an author may emphasize closed descent to preserve certain characteristics of superiority instead of the notion that the choice of monarchy over democracy was the primary influence in the character of a people.

The second part of the book, "The Peoples of the Ancient World," presents a series of ethnographic texts, both fictional and non-fictional. The first chapter includes texts that describe the organization of the world in general or include references to numerous peoples at once. Following this are nine geographical chapters arranged according to the order of Pomponius Mela's *chorography* (counterclockwise from Rome beginning with Egypt and ending with the Gauls, Germans, and Celts). These texts enact or manifest the various theories presented in the first half of the book. We have not included separate chapters on Greek and Roman views of their own ethnicity here. Instead, we included texts throughout the first part of the book, "Theories," that reflect Greeks and Romans exploring their own identities, since it is in genealogies, myths of autochthony, and other similar moments of self-definition that they were most explicit about how they viewed themselves and their place in the world.

Within each chapter, the texts are organized chronologically by author.[7] Since authors often use much earlier material, the order of presentation may not necessarily represent intellectual developments. Some stories, like the story of Europa and the bull, may have been in circulation as early as the 7th or 6th centuries BCE, but the sources we use for the story come from the 2nd and 3rd century CE authors Hyginus and [Apollodorus], who compiled summaries of ancient myths. In some cases, it is easy to see the influence of one text upon another—Herodotus is frequently cited by later sources, like Aristotle or Strabo, and corrected or supported by them. In other cases, even if the texts are contemporary, the stark contrasts between the representations of a people suggest different theoretical approaches, a lack of knowledge of other theories, or even different ideas about who exactly dwelt in a region. For example, Herodotus and the Hippocratic *Airs, Waters, Places* both give extensive descriptions of the Scythians, but offer different portraits of the Scythian people.

Citations for the ancient texts are given in full at the beginning of each selection so that anyone who wishes to consult the original texts may do so easily. We provide details of the Greek and Latin texts we used for the

---

7. The exception is Chapter 10, on the Persians and Parthians. Although the Romans often conflated the two and the Parthians were descended from the Persians, they were distinctive cultures with distinctive practices and were confined to different periods.

translations at the back of the book. The selections in this volume are not exhaustive but are intended to be representative of materials from a large variety of genres that have been especially influential over time. We include texts spanning over a millennium, from the 8th century BCE to the 3rd century CE. We also include works from many different ancient cities in hopes of moving beyond the dominant voices of 5th-century Athens and Imperial Rome. We hope this variety will enable readers to understand more thoroughly the various ways the ancients approached and puzzled over the world they lived in.

We have included as well a series of maps reconstructed from ancient descriptions of the world. These maps show how the ancients may have imagined the geographic space that the various peoples of classical antiquity occupied or were thought to occupy. These maps present a progression of Greco-Roman knowledge of their world. Geography has always been intimately bound to theories of race and ethnicity. For the ancients, the world was first and foremost a place of peoples, and the description of the people was tied to the understanding of the landscape and plant and animal life surrounding them. If a land was not known to be inhabited, the Greeks especially had no qualms about imagining people to occupy the land. Such fantasies and inventions can sometimes tell us even more than descriptions of real people and practices can about how human diversity was understood. Environmental theories in particular were premised on the way geography, topography, and climate shaped the people who lived there. Thus the maps help us to understand the context for the peoples who occupied the Greco-Roman reality and imagination. Where did they imagine the boundaries of the world lay? What waters fed the various lands and created their internal boundaries? What happened to a fantasy people found on one map once their land had been explored and they were not found to live there? Seeing how the map of the world changed from Homer to Ptolemy can help us understand the changes in approach to human difference.

This book provides students and scholars alike with the resources needed to explore how the ancient Greeks and Romans engaged the questions surrounding race and ethnicity. Although much of this material proved influential in the development of modern race theory, many of the ancient answers may still strike modern readers as strange or even absolutely *foreign*. As L. P. Hartley reminds us in the epigraph opening this introduction, we encounter difference not only in space but also in time: they do things *differently* there. This volume was created to show the ancient Greeks and Romans thinking about foreignness, about human diversity. As we examine their search for ways to understand and explain their world to themselves, we can reflect on our ways of explaining our own world.

NOTES ON THE TRANSLATIONS

All translations are by the authors. Initials at the end of each citation indicate the translator: Rebecca Kennedy (RFK), Sydnor Roy (CSR), and Max

Goldman (MLG). We have chosen in the translations to privilege clarity and meaning over a strict adherence to the grammar and syntax of the original Greek or Latin. We have also attempted to make the translations readable and consistent. For this reason, we have chosen a prose format for poetic texts. We have also tried, however, to maintain readability without sacrificing the fundamental characteristics of an individual author's style. In some cases, it is difficult to render into the most polished English the Greek or Latin of an author without losing something important in the structure and style of the text. We have also converted ancient measurements and distances to modern ones wherever possible.

The following symbols appear throughout:

[Author]	denotes a doubtful attribution of author.
[text]	denotes material supplied by the translator.
< . . . >	denotes a lacuna in the text.
. . .	denotes text has been elided by the translator.
<*italics*>	denotes text supplied by the editor of the edition of the text used as the basis for the translation.
Italics	denotes a foreign word.

Map 1. **World according to Homer and Hecataeus.** From *Ginn and Company's Classical Atlas*, map 4 (Boston, 1894). Maps attributed to W. & A. K. Johnston.

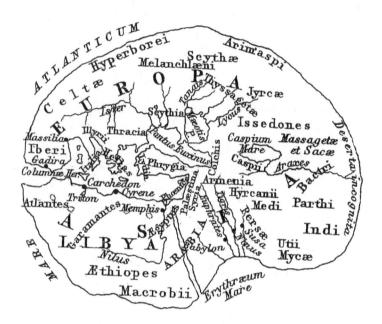

Map 2. World according to Herodotus. From *Ginn and Company's Classical Atlas*, map 4 (Boston, 1894). Map attributed to W. & A. K. Johnston.

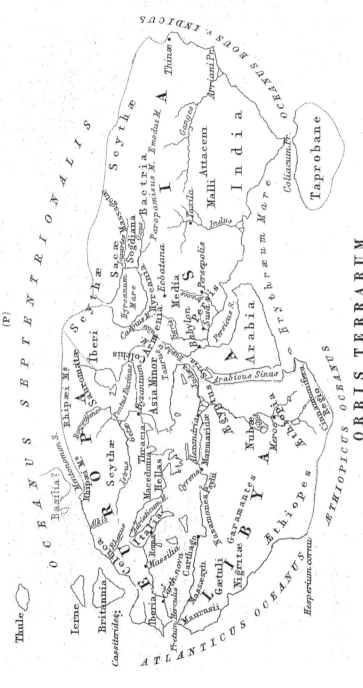

(P)

Map 3. World according to Strabo and Eratosthenes. From *Ginn and Company's Classical Atlas*, map 4 (Boston, 1894). Map attributed to W. & A. K. Johnston.

ORBIS TERRARUM

ex sententia Eratosthenis et Strabonis circa 200 ante Christum usque ad 20 post Christum

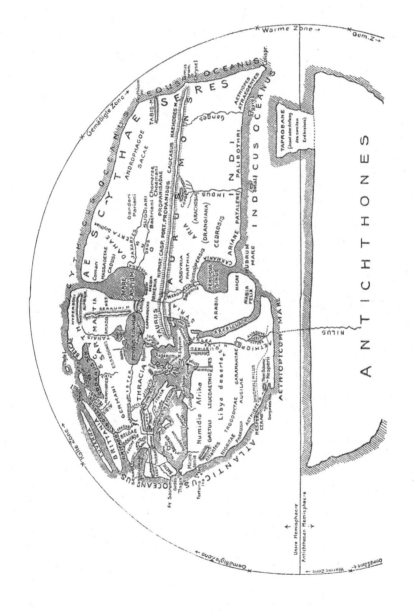

Map 4. World according to Pomponius Mela. From Philipp, H. (ed), *Pomponius Mela: Ozeanländer* (Leipzig, 1912). Map attributed to H. Philipp.

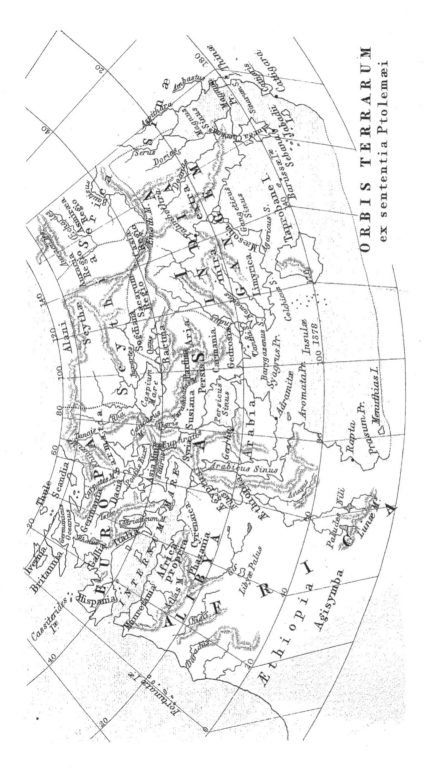

Map 5. World according to Ptolemy. From *Ginn and Company's Classical Atlas*, map 4 (Boston, 1894). Map attributed to W. & A. K. Johnston.

THEORIES

CHAPTER 1

HOMER AND HESIOD: EARLY THEORIES OF FOREIGNNESS

One of the earliest notions of how the Greeks viewed foreign cultures and how they identified themselves in relationship to those cultures assumed that people outside of the boundaries of the known Greek world were marvelous or monstrous. Homer's Odyssey *(8th century BCE) is our earliest example of Greek encounters with "others." Hesiod's "Races of Man" myth, part of his* Works and Days *(7th century BCE), is a foundation story for later Greek genetic theories.*

1. Homer, *Odyssey* **1.22–26 (8th century BCE).** *An early mention of the Ethiopians associates them with the gods and the eastern and western ends of the earth. (CSR)*

But Poseidon was visiting the Ethiopians, who live far away. Indeed, the Ethiopians, who are the most far-off of men, are divided in two. Some live where the sun sets, and some dwell where it rises. Poseidon went to accept a hecatomb of bulls and sheep. And while there he enjoys the feast.[1]

2. Homer, *Odyssey* **4.77–89 (8th century BCE).** *Menelaus describes to Telemachus his journey home from the Trojan War. This narrative reveals an early conception of the Mediterranean world that is at times miraculous. (CSR)*

Dear children, no mortal could compete with Zeus: his homes and property are immortal. A man might compete with me in wealth, or not. Indeed, I returned after eight years, carrying wealth in my ships, after great suffering and much wandering. I roamed to Cyprus and Phoenicia and to the Egyptians; I reached the Ethiopians and the Sidonians[2] and the Erembi and

---

1. Poseidon's visit to the Ethiopians is also mentioned at *Od.* 5.282–284, when Poseidon spies Odysseus on the sea leaving Calypso's island.

2. The Sidonians are also noted for offering hospitality and proper guest-friend gifts to Menelaus at 4.615–619.

Libya, where the lambs grow a full set of horns quickly. The ewes there bear lambs three separate times in a full year. There neither lord nor shepherd lacks cheese or meat or sweet milk, but always the ewes give enough milk to drink.

3. Homer, *Odyssey* **4.219–232 (8th century BCE).** *After tales of Odysseus have saddened Menelaus and Telemachus, Helen brings down special drugs from Egypt to ease their sorrows. The earliest references to Egypt by the Greeks associate it with medical knowledge.*[3] *(CSR)*

But Helen, the daughter of Zeus, planned otherwise. [220] Straightaway she threw a drug into the wine, and then they drank. It was a drug that negates pain and anger, causing them to forget all their sorrows. Whoever drinks this down, when it is mixed in the wine bowl, would not let tears pour down his cheeks for one whole day, not even if his mother and father died, not if someone should, right in front of him, kill his brother or his dear son with a bronze weapon, and he watches it with his own eyes. Such were the helpful drugs the daughter of Zeus had (they were good drugs), which were given to her by Polydamna, the wife of Thon, [230] a woman from Egypt, where the fruitful land offers the most drugs, many that can be mixed into something healthful, and many that are ruinous. Each man in Egypt is a doctor, the most knowledgeable of all mankind. For, the Egyptians are the offspring of Paion.[4]

4. Homer, *Odyssey* **7.22–36, 7.77–132 (8th century BCE).** *Odysseus and Athena (disguised) talk about the Phaeacians. Odysseus displays typical Greek worries about what he might encounter in foreign lands. (CSR)*

7.22–36. Odysseus: "O child, could you not guide me to the house of the man Alcinous, who rules among these men? I am a much suffering stranger here and I have come from afar, a distant land. Thus, I do not know anyone who lives here, who inhabits this city and land." And the goddess, grey-eyed Athena, answered him: "Indeed, kind old stranger, I will show you the house that you ask me about, since the house of my blameless father is nearby. But go in silence, and I will show the way, [30] and do not look on any of the men nor ask them questions. For these men don't like foreigners very much. No, they do not care for or love a man who comes from

---

3. Egypt is mentioned further in the *Odyssey* as a place of incredible wealth (4.126–127), where gods dwell (4.351–570), and of consistent hospitality. The river Aegyptus itself (the Nile), is "fallen from Zeus" or "from heaven" (4.477). Egypt is also portrayed by Odysseus as a place where suppliants are recognized and treated properly (14.272–288).

4. In Homer, the physician who healed the gods. Used more generally in Classical Greek to denote one who frees others from pain.

elsewhere. But rather they trust in their swift ships that are indeed speedy, and they traverse the great gulf of the sea, since the Earth-shaker [Poseidon] granted them that their boats be swift as if they were winged and travel as quick as thought.

The Phaeacians are a marvel and provide one model for what Greeks hoped to find in foreign lands.

7.77–132. Once she finished speaking, grey-eyed Athena went away across the unfruitful sea and left charming Scheria. She came to Marathon and Athens, which has wide streets, and she entered the well-built house of Erechtheus. [80] But Odysseus went to the splendid house of Alcinous. He contemplated many things in his heart as he stood there, before he stepped up to the bronze threshold. A shimmer, like from the sun or the moon, danced over the high-roofed house of great-hearted Alcinous. For the walls all around were bronze, all the way into the innermost rooms from the threshold, and there was cyan[5] around the eaves; [90] golden doors shut in the well-built house, and silver doorposts stood in the bronze threshold, and the lintel of the door was silver, and the handle was gold. On each side there were gold and silver dogs, which Hephaestus had fashioned with his knowledgeable skills so that, immortal and undecaying for all time, they guard the house of great-hearted Alcinous. Within the hall thrones were set around the walls from here to over there, right through from the threshold to the inner rooms, and on these thrones fine, well-spun robes were placed; the robes were the work of women. And there the leaders of the Phaeacians had seats. There they would drink and eat, for they had more than enough. Golden boys stood on the well-built altars [100] holding burning brands in their hands, which brighten the nights for the diners in the house. There are fifty slave women in the house. Some grind apple-colored grain on millstones, and others sit weaving on looms and spinning wool on distaffs. They make fabric similar to the leaves of the tall poplar tree. Flowing olive oil drips from fine linen cloths. As much as the Phaeacian men are skilled above all men at driving a swift ship on the sea, with the same skills the women work at their looms, for Athena gave to them the knowledge to accomplish [110] the most beautiful weaving, and she also gave them good sense. Outside of the courtyard and near the door lies a great garden laid out over four measures of land with a hedge that runs around it on both sides. There great blooming trees produce everything, pear trees and mulberries and bountiful apple trees and sweet figs and luxuriant olive trees. The fruit of these trees is never lost nor abandoned in winter or summer, but they bloom and fruit year-round. For at all times the warm west wind causes some to bud and others to ripen. Pear grows upon pear, apple on apple, [120] and also bunches on bunches of grapes, and fig on fig. His vineyard, rich in fruit, stands there as well: one part of this vineyard has grapes drying in the sun on a sunny spot of level ground, other grapes men

---

5. A dark-blue enamel.

gather, still more the men crush with their feet. In front there are unripe grapes just letting their bloom fall, and other grapes are beginning to redden. There also by the last row of vines an ordered garden plot of all kinds of plants is in bloom, looking bright all the time. Within this area there are two springs, one of which sends out its water to the whole garden, the other goes under the threshold [130] of the courtyard to the high-walled house, from the house citizens fetch it. Such were the shining gifts of the gods in Alcinous' house.

5. Homer, *Odyssey* 9.105–139, 9.171–298 (8th century BCE). *Unlike the land of the Phaeacians, the land of the Cyclopes lacks laws or craftsmanship. The Cyclopes are presented as one of many monsters at the edges of the world. Their island produces all the necessities of civilization, as a Golden Age land[6] might, but the Cyclopes do not have the skills or desire to cultivate them. (CSR/RFK)*

9.105–139. From there we sailed further on, grieving in our hearts, and we came to the land of the Cyclopes, an arrogant and lawless race, who neither plant with their hands nor plow, but rather put their trust in the immortal gods. Everything grows there, but unsown and unplowed. [110] There is wheat and barley and vines that produce a wine from fine red grapes, which the rain of Zeus nourishes. But the Cyclopes have no advisory councils or laws; instead, they inhabit the peaks of high mountains and live in hollow caves. Each sets the rules for his own children and wives; they do not trouble themselves about one another. Neither near nor far from the land of the Cyclopes, a fertile, wooded island stretches out from the harbor. On the island are countless wild goats. [120] No steps of men keep them off, nor are their woods entered by hunters, hunters who endure grief in woods while wandering through the towering mountains. The land is not occupied by flocks nor is it cultivated, but is unsown and unplowed. It is devoid of men day in and day out and feeds only the bleating goats. For the Cyclopes have no ships with red prows, nor any ship-builders who could construct well-decked ships that could succeed in transporting every necessity by traveling to the cities of men, and traversing the seas between other cities as men often do. [130] Such men would have wrought for the Cyclopes a well-tilled land since the island is not poor at all, but bears everything in its season. On the island are well-watered and lush meadows along the coast of the grey sea. The vines especially would be undying. On the island are level fields for plowing that especially would continually yield deep crops in season, since there is much fecundity in the earth. On the island is a harbor with good anchorage, where there is no need of cables, nor need either to cast anchor or fasten the stern cables. Rather, beached, it is possible to remain

---

6. A perfect land of abundance that required no labor, similar in conception to Eden.

in the harbor until such time as the heart of the sailors urges them to leave and the winds blow.

> *Odysseus and his men enter the harbor and disembark upon the nearby shore. Odysseus decides to investigate the Cyclopes' island.*

9.171–298. And then I, establishing an assembly, spoke among all my men: "The rest of you should remain here for now, my faithful companions, but I, with my ship and my own crew, will go and make a trial of these people, whoever is here. I want to find out whether they are violent and wild and unjust, or loving of strangers and respectfully god-fearing." Thus I spoke and boarded my ship. I commanded my companions to embark as well and to loose the stern cables. They went on board quickly and sat upon the benches, [180] and, sitting in rows, they beat the grey sea with their oars. But when we arrived at the nearby land, there we saw on a remote cliff beside the sea a lofty cave covered with laurels. There, many livestock, both sheep and goats, passed the night. Around it a lofty courtyard had been built from massive stones embedded in the earth and mighty pines and oaks. There also a gigantic man, who shepherded his flock alone and apart from others, passed the night. He did not engage with others but dwelt far away and was without law. [190] For he was built like a monstrous marvel, nor was he like any bread-eating man, but was like a lofty peak in the high mountains, which appears separate from the rest.

Indeed, I ordered the rest of my faithful companions to remain there with the ship and to guard it while straightaway I chose the twelve best of my companions and went toward the cave. I had with me a goatskin-sack of sweet dark wine, which Maron gave to me. Maron was the son of Euanthus, priest of Apollo, who protected Ismarus. He gave me the wine because we, revering him, guarded him along with his child and wife. [200] He dwelt in a dense forest sacred to Phoebus Apollo. He gave me splendid gifts: Of gold he gave me seven talents and an all-silver, well-wrought mixing bowl. In addition, he gave me wine, sweet and unmixed, a godly drink, to the amount of twelve two-handled amphorae. None of his household servants or attendants knew of it. Only Maron, his dear wife, and a single housekeeper. When he would drink the honey-sweet red wine, filling a single cup, he would pour it out in twenty measures of water, and a sweet, [210] amazing scent would waft from the mixing bowl. At that point, no one could hold back from it. I carried a sack filled with this wine and also provisions in a bag. For my manly heart considered that soon this man, wrapped in great strength, would come home, fierce and ignorant of justice and law.

We arrived quickly at the cave but did not find him inside. He was tending his fat flock in the fields. Going into the cave, we marveled at each thing: crates heavy with cheeses, [220] pens packed with lambs and kids. Each pen held them separated: the first-born were in their own pen, the summer lambs in theirs, and the newborns in their own. All the handmade milk-pails and bowls into which he milked, were flowing with whey. Then, immediately, my companions, begging, asked that I take cheeses and come back once again and then quickly drive the lambs and kids onto our swift ship and sail away over the briny sea. But I was not persuaded by them (though truly it would have been better had I been) because I wanted to see this man and see if he would give me guest-gifts. [230] Nor truly, when he appeared, would he be a pleasure for my companions.

Then, starting a fire, we made a sacrifice. Then we grabbed cheeses and ate them. We sat and waited for him inside the cave until he returned with his flocks. He carried a heavy burden of wooden logs, which would be of use to him in preparing dinner. Throwing them down in the cave, he made a great crashing noise. We, frightened, moved toward the innermost part of the cave. He drove all the members of his fat flock, the ones he milked, into the cave and left the male animals out of doors in the deep courtyard, both the rams and the goats. [240] Next, he lifted up a great stone and set it in place as a door. Not even twenty-two excellent, four-wheeled wagons could heave it from the earth, he put such a massive stone in the entrance to the cave. Then, he sat down and milked the sheep and bleating goats. He milked each in their turn and, beneath each, he set a newborn lamb. Immediately after, he curdled half the white milk and collected it in woven baskets and put it away. The other half of the milk he placed in bowls so that he could drink it and have it for his dinners.

He accomplished these tasks quickly [250] and then lit the fire again. That's when he saw us. He asked us, "Oh strangers, who are you? What watery paths did you sail over? Have you wandered here for business? Or wantonly, as pirates roaming over the seas, risking your lives and bringing evil to strangers?" Thus he spoke and our own hearts broke in fear at his deep and monstrous voice. But even as he spoke, I answered him and said, "We are Achaeans, driven from Troy [260] by all the winds beyond the great gulf of the sea. Though heading homeward, we came here by a different path, a different route, just as, it seems, Zeus wished to contrive it. We boast that we are of the army of Agamemnon, son of Atreus, whose glory is now, indeed, the greatest under the heavens, since he sacked so great a city and destroyed many troops. Now, however, we are supplicating you, taking your knees, if somehow you might offer us hospitality or give some sort of guest-gifts. This is the right of strangers. But, revere the gods, most noble one. We are supplicating you. Zeus, god of Guests, avenges suppliants and strangers, [270] Zeus who at times even accompanies revered strangers."

Thus I spoke and straightaway he replied with a ruthless heart, "You are a fool, stranger, or you come from very far away if you call upon me either to fear or flee the gods. For the Cyclopes don't care about aegis-bearing Zeus or the blessed gods. We are by far greater than they are. I would not spare you and your companions to avoid the enmity of Zeus unless my own heart urged it. But, tell me so that I might learn it, where did you leave your well-wrought ship when you came here? Is it somewhere far off? [280] Or maybe nearby?"

Thus he spoke, prodding me, but his attempt didn't escape my notice— I have experienced much. Instead, I responded to him with subterfuge,

"Poseidon the Earth-shaker smashed my ship by casting it upon the rocks on the limits of your land, driving it upon the cape. The wind then carried the wreck out to sea. But I fled with my companions here from utter destruction."

Thus I spoke and he, with his ruthless heart, did not reply. Instead, he lunged forward and flung his hands at my companions. He seized two of them and, as if they were little puppies, smashed them against the ground. [290] Their brains poured out of their heads and soaked the ground. Then, cutting them limb from limb, he made them into his meal. He ate them just as a mountain lion eats its prey, leaving nothing. He ate their entrails, flesh, bones, and even marrow. We cried out and raised our hands aloft toward Zeus as we witnessed these wicked deeds. Despair filled our hearts. But the Cyclops, when he had filled his great belly with his human meal and then washed it down with pure milk, he laid down inside the cave, stretching out among his flocks.

6. Homer, *Odyssey* 10.1–19, 10.87–124 (8th century BCE). *As in Book 9, Homer provided examples to his audience of proper and improper customs and conduct. Odysseus and his men leave the island of the Cyclopes and land on Aeolia, the home of the demigod Aeolus. (RFK)*

10.1–19. We arrived at the island of Aeolia, where Aeolus, son of Hippotas, dear to the immortal gods, lived on a floating island. Around the entire island was a wall made of indestructible bronze. The cliff upon which it sat was sheer. Aeolus has twelve children in his halls. Six are daughters and six are sons in their youthful prime. The daughters he offered to his sons as wives. Always, they feast beside their dear father and excellent mother. And before them lie a myriad of tasty dishes. [10] The halls are filled with the scent of these meals and the courtyard too is filled all day. At night, however, they lie beside their honored wives on coverlets and carved beds. We arrived, then, at the city and beautiful halls of Aeolus and his family. For an entire month, he welcomed me and asked about each thing in turn: Troy, the ships of the Argives, the homecoming of the Achaeans. I recounted the entire tale for him. And when indeed I asked about the journey home and urged him to send us on our way, he did not refuse me anything but made preparations for the journey.

> *Aeolus presents Odysseus with a bag filled with adverse winds, which his men believe is a treasure and open while Odysseus sleeps. As a result, their ships are blown back to Aeolia. When Aeolus refuses to help a second time, Odysseus and his men set off again and land on the island of the Laistrygonians.*

10.87–124. We arrived in the glorious harbor, encircled by a continuous towering rock face on both sides. The capes projected opposite each other just forward [90] at the mouth of the harbor to form a narrow entrance. All our curved ships rested inside this harbor. The ships anchored near each other inside the hollow harbor where never did waves increase, either a great deal or even a little, but a splendid calm was all around. I alone kept my black ship outside the harbor, there at the edge, fastening my cables to the rocks. I stood watch after going up upon a rugged peak. There we saw works of neither oxen nor men, only smoke rising from the earth. [100] I then sent forth companions to go and discover who these men were upon the earth, eating its bread. I chose two men and sent along a third as a herald. They disembarked and went along a level path from the lofty mountains toward a city. Before the city, they encountered a young girl drawing water. She was the mighty daughter of Antiphates, the Laistrygonian. She had come down into the beautifully flowing fount at Artacia. Water was carried from there to the city. [110] They came up to her and addressed her and asked her who was king of this land and over whom was he lord. She immediately pointed to the high-roofed home of her father. When they entered the fine halls, they found a woman who was the size of a mountaintop. They were appalled at the sight of her. She quickly called from the town square to her husband, famous Antiphates, who made a grievous destruction for them. Immediately, he snatched up one of my companions and prepared him as dinner. The other two rose up in flight and arrived back at the ships. But Antiphates made a cry resound throughout the city, and the Laistrygonians, hearing him, came from every direction, [120] thousands of them, seeming more like giants than men. They hurled stones (too heavy for a man to lift) down upon the ships from the rocks above. At once, an evil din arose from the ships, a combination of men's destruction and the breaking of ships. And, as if our men were fish, the Laistrygonians pierced them and carried them off for a joyless supper.

7. Homer, *Odyssey* 11.119–134 (8th century BCE). *As part of his prophecy to Odysseus in the underworld, Tiresias describes what Odysseus must do to finally assuage the anger of Poseidon. (CSR)*

But when you have killed the suitors in your halls, [120] either by a trick or publicly with a bronze sword, then go, taking a well-made oar, and travel until the time when you reach people who do not know the sea, nor do they eat food flavored with sea salt. And they do not know about red-prowed ships nor well-made oars, which act as the wings for ships. And I shall tell you a very clear sign, nor will it escape you: whenever another traveler meets you and says that you have a winnowing fan[7] on your shining shoulders, then stick the well-made oar into the ground, and perform beautiful sacrifices to Lord Poseidon, a young ram and a bull and a boar that mounts sows, and then go home and perform holy hecatombs to the immortal gods who hold wide heaven. Do it for all of them each in order.

---

7. A device used for spreading out grain before grinding it that separates the wheat from the chaff.

8. Homer, *Odyssey* 15.380–453 (8th century BCE). *An exchange between Odysseus in disguise and his swineherd Eumaeus reveals a common perception of the Phoenicians as crafty traders, and also shows the fluidity of society both in terms of origin and social class.*[8] *(CSR)*

And then wily Odysseus answered him and spoke: "O alas, when you were little, swineherd Eumaeus, you were led far astray from your homeland and your parents. But come, tell me and speak truly, whether someone sacked your well-built city of men, there where your father and lady mother lived, or if ill-intentioned men took you on their ships one day when you were wandering with the sheep or cows and sold you as a slave to this man's house, who purchased you for a worthy price." And then the swineherd, that leader of men, addressed him: [390] "Stranger, since you ask me these things and inquire, listen now in silence and relax; drink wine while you are sitting. These nights are incredibly long. There is time to sleep and to listen while one enjoys oneself. Nor is it at all necessary to sleep before it is time; too much sleep is as much trouble as not enough. Whoever of the others may be compelled by his heart or mind, let him go away and go to sleep; and from the beginning of dawn let him eat and then follow our king's swine. But we two will drink and eat in the tent and enjoy the wretched sorrows of each other [400] as we think of them. For, a man enjoys sorrows too after the fact, whoever has suffered much and wandered much. And I will tell you what you inquire and ask about. There is a certain island called Syria, if ever you've heard of it, north of Ortygia, where the sun turns in the sky, it is not excessively large, but it is good: good pastures, good flocks, abundant in wine, rich in corn. Hunger never comes into the home, nor any other plague that is hateful and harmful to wretched mortals. But when the men grow old in this city, [410] Apollo with his silver arrows comes with his sister Artemis and kills them with gentle arrows as he draws near. There are two cities there, and everything is divided between them. My father was king of both. His name was Ctesius, the son of Ormenus, a man who was like a god. And Phoenician men came there, men famous for being swindlers, bringing thousands of delights in their black ship. There used to be a Phoenician woman in my father's house, beautiful and tall and trained in glorious crafts. And the exceedingly crafty Phoenicians seduced her. [420] First one slept with her while she was down washing clothes by the hollow ships. Sex deceives the minds of womanly women, even if they are great do-gooders. He asked her who she was and where she came from, and straightaway she pointed out to him my father's high-roofed house. 'I claim to be from Sidon rich in bronze. And I am the daughter of Arubas, who is abundantly wealthy. But some Taphian pirates snatched me up while I was coming in from the countryside, and they enslaved me and brought me

---

8. Odysseus first characterizes the Phoenicians at 14.288–291 as greedy, evil-doers who are full of guile. He characterizes himself (the character in disguise) no better, however. He acts like a pirate when he describes his initial landing at Egypt. They land and, unprovoked, steal women, food, and wealth from the Egyptians.

here to that man's house, and he paid a worthy price.' [430] The man then spoke to her again, the one who had slept with her in secret, 'Would you now return with us to your home again, so that you might see the high-roofed home of your mother and father and see them too, for they are still around and are called rich?' And the woman addressed him and answered with this speech: 'This may be so, if you would be willing, sailors, to make an oath to return me unharmed to my home.' So she spoke, and they all swore as she bid them. But when they had sworn and accomplished the oath, the woman spoke to them again: [440] 'Now keep silence, and let no one of your companions address me with words, when they meet me unexpectedly on the street, or perhaps by the fountain, so that someone won't go to the house and tell the old man, and he would suspect and bind me in troublesome chains, and plan your destruction. But keep this speech in your minds, and hurry the sale of your wares. But when your ship becomes full of goods for trade quickly send a message to me in the house; for I will bring gold, whatever I can find lying around, and I would willingly give another thing for my fare. [450] For I am rearing up the noble child of the master in the palace, such a crafty boy, always running out of doors. I would take him on the ship, and he will earn a huge sum for you, wherever and to whomever you transport him.'"

9. Hesiod, *Works and Days* 109–181 (7th century BCE). *Hesiod tells a number of stories about the decline of man, including the story of the five races of man, four associated with a different metal.*[9] *(MLG)*

Golden was the very first race of chattering humans. [110] They were constructed by the immortals who have homes on Olympus. They lived under Cronus who was king at that time. They lived like gods, hearts free from worry, and far removed from wretched toil. No terrible old age existed: their feet and hands remained the same, and they rejoiced in feasts, removed from every evil. Their death appeared like falling asleep. All good things were theirs. The fertile land produced fruit on her own and produced it in unstinting abundance. Quietly, just as they pleased, they lived off the many good things from the fields, [120] <*rich in flocks, dear to the blessed gods*>.

But the earth covered over this race; they are spirits through the plans of great Zeus, good spirits who dwell on earth, guardians of mortal men. <*They guard justice and harsh deeds, traveling everywhere on the earth, wrapped in mist.*> They confer wealth, possessing this as their king's prize.

The gods, who have homes on Olympus, made the next race silver, much worse than the previous one, resembling the golden race in neither speech nor mind. [130] Their children were raised by their watchful mothers for one hundred years, playing childish games in the house. But when they finally grew up and reached a measure of maturity, they lived but a short

---

9. Ovid (1st century CE) also provides a "myth of the ages" (Metamorphoses 1.89–150). His version leaves out the heroic age.

time, experiencing pain from their folly. For they were unable to restrain themselves from reckless violence against each other. They were unwilling to revere the immortals and to sacrifice on the holy altars of the blessed ones, as is just for mortals from custom. This race was removed by Zeus, son of Cronus, who grew angry because they did not honor the blessed gods who possess Olympus. [140] But when even this race was covered over by the earth, mortals called them the blessed ones below the earth—second in rank, it is true, but honor also follows even them.

Father Zeus made another race, the third, of chattering men, the bronze race, completely different from the silver, born from tree nymphs, terrifyingly powerful, obsessed with the keening deeds of Ares and acts of violence. They did not eat bread at all, but had powerful hearts of adamantine rock, implacable. Great was their force, and from their shoulders grew stout arms and invincible hands. [150] They had bronze weapons, bronze homes, and they constructed with bronze. Dark iron did not exist. These people were overcome by their own hand and went without any name to the broad house of chilly Hades. Black death seized them, although they were mighty, and they left behind the bright light of the sun.

But when this race was covered over by the earth, Zeus, son of Cronus, made another again, the fourth on wide-nourishing earth, better and more just. A divine race of heroes called [160] demigods, the race before ours on the broad earth. These were destroyed by evil war and terrible battle, some under the seven gates of Thebes, the land of Cadmus, as they fought over the cattle of Oedipus; others were destroyed after traveling in ships across the broad deep of the sea, because of lovely-haired Helen. Some of them were embraced by death, but others were granted customs and a life apart from men by father Zeus, son of Cronus, dwelling at the ends of the earth. [170] These live with carefree minds in the islands of the blessed beyond the deep-eddying Ocean. They are the blessed heroes, for whom the fertile land willingly bears sweet-smelling fruit three times a year.

I wish I did not live among the fifth people! If only I had already died or was born later. For the race now is iron. Never will they cease from miserable toil by day nor from being distressed by night. The gods will give them difficult worries, but they will mix goods with the evils. [180] Zeus will destroy even this race of chattering people when they are born with grey hair.

CHAPTER 2

GENEALOGIES AND ORIGINS

The ancient Greeks and Romans had numerous mythical genealogies or stories of ancient migrations; these served to create their own identities and to explain the distinctions between different peoples. Such differences needed explaining, since the Greeks sometimes envisioned humankind as coming from a single source. Man simply appears in Hesiod without being created (as woman was), and there were numerous stories attributing man's creation to Prometheus and his re-creation after the flood to Deucalion. This chapter provides a selection of genealogies or origin stories for the Greeks and Romans. The ethnographies in the second half of the book, "The Peoples of the Ancient World," provide such stories for foreign peoples written by the Greeks or Romans.

1. Pindar, *Olympian* 9.40–46 (5th century BCE). *Pindar is our earliest extant source for the story of Deucalion and Pyrrha making humanity from stones. (RFK)*

Do not prattle on now about such things. Keep war and battle far from the immortals. Rather, lend your tongue to the Protogeneian city where Deucalion and Pyrrha, by the decree of lightning-wielding Zeus, descended from Parnassus and first established their home. There they asexually created the unified race of man, made from stone, a people [*laos*] named from the stone.[10]

2. Herodotus, *Histories* 7.150 (5th century BCE). *Xerxes attempts to use mythological genealogies to convince the Argives to stay neutral in his conquest of Greece. (RFK)*

This is how the Argives tell the story, but there is another story told throughout Greece that Xerxes sent a herald into Argos before he set his army in motion against Greece. When the herald arrived, it is said that he told the Argives, "Argives, King Xerxes says this to you: We believe that Perses, our ancestor, was the child of Perseus son of Danae and Andromeda daughter of Cepheus. Thus we Persians are your descendants. We think it inappropriate

---

10. A pun on the word *laas*, a stone.

to send an army against our progenitors, and that you give aid to others and become our enemy. Rather, it is fitting that you keep to yourselves. If everything goes as intended, I will esteem no one higher than you."

3. Thucydides, *History of the Peloponnesian War* 1.2–12 (5th/4th century BCE). *As part of his discussion as to why the Peloponnesian War was the greatest war yet to shake the Greeks, Thucydides records an "archaeology" of the Greeks from the time of Minos to his own day. His account of the pre-history of Greece is thoroughly rationalized and addresses the notion of ethnic identity among the Greeks as part of an historical process. The term "barbarian" is used here as it is in other classical authors to denote someone who was not Greek. (MLG)*

1.2. It is obvious that the land now called Hellas was long ago without fixed settlements; instead the people were migratory at first, and each group easily left their own land whenever they were under compulsion by more numerous people. [2] Inter-polis commerce did not exist; inter-tribal dealings were unsafe by land and by sea; each group used its own lands only so much as to sustain life and without producing surplus wealth and cultivating the land, since it was not clear when someone might invade and rob them (they were then without walls). Since they were aware that they could find a daily subsistence anywhere, they had no difficulty migrating. For this reason they had no strength in large cities nor in other resources. [3] There was a constant change of inhabitants in the richest districts, in those now called Thessaly and Boeotia and the majority of the Peloponnesus (Arcadia excepted) and the rest of the best land. [4] It was through the excellence of the land that some men gained power, by creating the internal conflicts through which the communities were destroyed; the fertility of the land also led to frequent invasions from other tribes. [5] Attica, at any rate, was free from internal conflict for the greatest time as a result of its poor soil and was always inhabited by the same people, [6] a not inconsiderable proof of my narrative that migrations prevented the rest of the lands increasing in similar fashion to Attica. In fact, the most powerful men who were banished from the rest of Greece through war or internal conflict came to the Athenians for safety. The men became citizens and right from the start made the city swell in numbers. As a result, they sent colonies even to Ionia because Attica was not sufficient.

1.3. The fact that the weakness of the ancients was not minor is proved to me by the following consideration. Before the Trojan War it is obvious that Hellas engaged in no common action. [2] I am inclined to think there was no universal name as yet. But before Hellen, son of Deucalion, this name did not exist at all; instead, each group took its own name, and the name Pelasgian was general.[11] After Hellen and his children came to power at

---

11. The Pelasgians appear in numerous 5th base-century texts, including Herodotus and Aeschylus' *Suppliants*, as the original inhabitants of Greece.

Phthiotis[12] in Thessaly, they brought aid to the rest of the cities and through this connection more and more began to be called Hellenes. It took some time, however, for this name to win out for all. [3] Homer provides the best evidence: though himself living much later than the Trojan War, he in no way gives this name to all. None are Hellenes except those who came with Achilles from Phthiotis, and they were the first so called. Instead, he uses in his poems the names Danaans and Argives and Achaeans. Homer, in fact, does not mention barbarians because, I am inclined to think, the Hellenes had not yet been brought under a single name in opposition to barbarians. [4] And so those people, as each of them came together city by city and later all became known as Hellenes, did nothing together as a group before the Trojan War because of their weakness and lack of interaction. However, even this common expedition against Troy was only made by way of the sea.

1.4. The earliest person who tradition tells us made a fleet was Minos. He controlled the majority of the sea now called Hellenic, ruled the Cyclades Islands, and became the first of many colonizers, after he drove out the Carians and established his sons as leaders. It seems likely that he cleared the sea of piracy as best as he was able in order to maintain his revenues.

1.5. Long ago the Hellenes and those barbarians who lived on the coast and on islands, as soon as they began to have contact with each other through ships, turned to piracy. The strongest hoped for gain for themselves and sustenance for their weak dependents. Falling upon un-walled communities that were hardly more than a collection of villages, they plundered and in this way made the greatest part of their livelihood because this act as yet held no shame and even brought some glory. [2] The proof of this can be found among some current mainland dwellers for whom plundering brings a certain distinction. Proof can also be found in the earliest of the poets. They represent people regularly inquiring of people who arrive by ship whether they are pirates, and they imply that neither do those asked consider the act unworthy nor do those who are eager to know reproach them. [3] They even ransacked each other by land. Much of Greece (the Ozolian Locrians, the Aetolians, the Acarnians, and the same area of the mainland) even now lives in this old fashion and still retains the habit of wearing weapons because of this ancient practice of piracy.

1.6. All of Hellas used to wear arms because their homes were without protection and their interactions with each other were unsafe. They led their life in arms just like the barbarians. [2] These areas of Hellas still living in this way indicate that the way of life then was once similar for all. [3] The Athenians were the first both to set aside their weapons and to turn to a more luxurious and looser manner of living. The older men of the wealthy class only recently ceased to wear the luxurious linen tunics and to tie up their hair in knots and hold it in place with a golden fastener in the shape of a grasshopper. The custom of the type of adornment long practiced among

---

12. Also frequently called Phthia.

older generations in Ionia comes from a shared kinship with Athens. [4] The Spartans, on the other hand, were the first to wear a moderate and modern style of dress, and those with greater wealth undertook in every other way to lead a lifestyle like the majority. [5] They were the first to train openly while stripped naked, and the first to anoint themselves with oil. But in antiquity even in the Olympic contests the athletes wore loincloths and covered their genitals, a practice that has only recently ceased. In fact, even among the barbarians today, and those in Asia Minor especially, competitions for prizes in boxing and wrestling are undertaken wearing loincloths. [6] In this and in many other ways it may be observed that the ancient Hellenic manner of life was similar to the modern barbarian way of life.

1.7. Among the communities most recently founded and already well suited for navigation, those having a greater surplus of resources were established and fortified with walls on the coastline. The inhabitants occupied the isthmuses for the sake of commerce and for the sake of power against their neighbors. However, the older communities were founded away from the sea because of frequently occurring piracy. This was the case for both the communities on the islands and on the mainland (this was because they stole from one another and from all the rest of the inhabitants living by the sea). Even now they remain established inland, away from the sea.

1.8. No less piratical were the islanders, both the Carians and Phoenicians. In point of fact they inhabited the majority of the islands. This is proved by the following consideration. When the Athenians were purifying Delos during the Peloponnesian War and they took up a number of caskets of the dead on the island, more than half of these caskets were clearly Carian, since they were recognized by the weapons buried with them and by the style of burial that they still use. [2] After Minos had established his navy nautical communication became easier (this is because the malefactors were uprooted from the islands by Minos at the same time as he settled many of them). [3] The coastal peoples were already applying themselves more to the acquisition of wealth and thus lived more securely. Some even constructed walls around their communities since they had become wealthier. Weaker people, since they desire profit, endure slavery to the stronger, and the more powerful men, since they have a surplus of wealth, subjugate lesser communities. [4] In this way, somewhat later in time, they went to war against Troy.

1.9. Agamemnon could gather the expedition, I am inclined to think, because he was superior in power to the men of his time and not so much because oaths bound Helen's suitors to Tyndarus. [2] In confirmation, the Peloponnesians who preserve most clearly the memory of the past relate the following tradition: Pelops first acquired power for himself through the great wealth that he had when he came from Asia into a land of poor people, and thus the land was named for him although he was a stranger. Later, the situation improved even more for his descendants: Eurystheus was killed in Attica by the Heraclids, and Atreus was his mother's brother. Because of this family relationship, Eurystheus, before he would go on campaign, would hand over Mycenae and the rule to Atreus, who, it so happened, was in Mycene to escape his father because of the death of Chyrippus. And when Eurystheus did not return, Atreus took up the kingship from the Myceneans, who were willing because of their fear of the Heraclids, and because Atreus seemed a powerful man and had ingratiated himself with the multitude of Myceneans and Eurystheus' subjects. The Pelopidae became even greater than the Persidae. [3] Since Agamemnon took up this inheritance and at the same time began to make himself stronger than others with a navy, I am inclined to think that it was due less to goodwill than to fear that he gathered and made the expedition. [4] He clearly arrived with the most ships and furnished the Arcadian contingent, as Homer makes clear, if his evidence is accepted. In addition, during the transfer of the staff he calls himself "the ruler of many isles and all Argos."[13] As a mainlander, he would not have ruled these nearby islands (there would not have been many) unless he possessed a navy. One may naturally draw conclusions about earlier expeditions from this expedition.

1.10. Because Mycenae was small or because some of its ancient communities now seem insignificant, one would be using inaccurate evidence to doubt that the expedition was of the size that the poets claim and the tradition relates. [2] For if Lacedaemonia were deserted and the temples and building foundations were forsaken, I think that there would be among future generations as time went on a massive distrust in traditions about their power. And yet, they control two of the five parts of the Peloponnese; they are leaders of the rest and have many allies outside as well. And yet because the community is not concentrated and does not have expensive temples and monuments, but is settled into villages in the ancient manner of Hellas, it would appear inferior. If Athens, on the other hand, were to suffer the same fate, her power would likely seem from the visual appearance twice as great as it is. [3] It is not reasonable to distrust traditions and to examine the appearance of cities rather than their powers; instead, one should consider that this expedition was the greatest of any sent before it, even if it falls short of modern ones. If it is right to put trust in the poetry of Homer, who as a poet may be expected to exaggerate, even so the expedition was clearly inferior to modern ones. [4] He wrote of 1,200 ships. The ships belonging to the Boeotians contained 120 men and those of Philoctetes had 50. He thus showed, I think, the largest and smallest number of ships. At least, he does not record the numbers of the rest in the catalogue of ships. All these men fought and rowed, a fact that he makes clear in the case of Philoctetes' ships, where all rowers were bowmen. It is unlikely that many who were passengers only sailed with the expedition, excepting the kings and officials, especially since they were to sail on the open sea with war supplies on ships that possessed no cargo hold, but were fitted out pirate-fashion in the old way. [5] When we take the mean of the largest and

---

13. Homer, *Iliad* 2.108.

smallest number of ships, it is clear that not many came on the expedition, given that they were composed in common from all of Hellas.

1.11. The reason for the size was less because of scarcity of men than because of lack of money. I say this because the difficulty of supply induced them to reduce the army to a size they expected to feed while making war at Troy. After they achieved a victory in a battle upon arrival (this event may clearly be deduced from the fact that they otherwise could not have fortified their encampment), they clearly did not employ their whole force there. Instead, they were driven to the cultivation of the Chersonese and to pillaging by lack of supply. It is because of this dispersion of their strength that the Trojans were able to forcibly resist for ten years; they were closely matched with those Greeks who were left behind. [2] If the Greeks had arrived with an abundance of supplies and had pursued the war continually and as a whole without farming and piracy, they would easily have won the battle and taken the city. In fact, even dispersed the part of their force that remained at Troy for ongoing fighting was able to match up with the Trojans. Had they maintained the siege, they would have taken Troy in less time and with less effort. But since expeditions before this one were weak because of poverty, so this one was too, although it is the most famous of earlier expeditions, and it shows that it was inferior in fact to its reputation in the currently prevailing poetic tradition.

1.12. Since even after the Trojan War, Hellas was still in a process of upheaval and settlement, there was naturally no peaceful growth. [2] The slow return of the Greeks from Troy caused many revolutions, and there were frequent factional quarrels within communities, which led to exiles founding new cities. [3] The Boeotians, for example, were driven out of Arne by the Thessalians in the sixtieth year after the sack of Troy. They settled the present Boeotia, the land formerly called Cadmeïs (there were formerly some Boeotians in the land, who made up part of the expedition to Troy). On the eightieth year after the war, the Dorians took the Peloponnese with the Heracleidai. [4] It took a considerable amount of time for Hellas to become secure and tranquil, and only then did she begin to send out colonies. The Athenians settled Ionia and most of the islands; the Peloponnesians, the majority of Italy and Sicily and some lands in the rest of Hellas. All these places were founded later than the Trojan War.

4. Thucydides, *History of the Peloponnesian War* 6.2–6 (5th/4th century BCE). *In addition to his "archaeology" of the Greeks, Thucydides provides a similar overview of the ancient Sicilians. The accuracy of Thucydides' account has been questioned, and some scholars think the inaccuracy is intended to display the ignorance of eastern Greeks concerning their western counterparts. (MLG)*

6.2. The following are the ancient settlements and tribes of Sicily. According to tradition, the earliest inhabitants of any part of the land were the

Cyclopes and Laistrygonians. I cannot say what race they were, where they came from, or where they went. Let everyone be satisfied with the tales of poets and their own opinion about them. [2] The Sicanoi were apparently the first to have settled after these races; or rather, according to their own account, they were there earlier because they were autochthonous. In fact, the truth is that they were Iberians driven out by the Ligurians from the Sicanos River in Iberia. The island used then to be called Sicany from them, although earlier it was named Trinacria. Today they inhabit the west of Sicily. [3] After the sack of Troy some Trojans escaped the Achaeans and arrived by ship at Sicily. They settled the lands bordering the Sicanoi and are called as a whole people the Elymoi, and their cities are Eryx and Egesta. Settling along with them were also some Phoenicians whom at that time a storm had carried from Troy, first to Libya, and from there to Sicily. [4] The Siciloi crossed to Sicily from Italy (for that is where they lived). They were escaping the Opicians [Campanians], according to tradition (which seems reasonable) on rafts, waiting for the wind to calm in the straits, but they could perhaps have sailed across some other way. Even now there are Siciloi in Italy, and the land took the name of Italy from some king of the Siciloi called Italos. [5] After they arrived in Sicily as a great army, they defeated the Sicanoi in battle and drove them to the south and west. They compelled the land to be called Sicily instead of Sicany. Since coming over, they have held the best part of the land and did so for 300 years before the Greeks came to Sicily. To this day they hold the middle and the north of the island. [6] Phoenicians[14] also dwell around all of Sicily, having taken the cliffs by the sea and the nearby small islands for trading with the Siciloi. But when many Greeks began to arrive by sea, they abandoned many places and concentrated their presence in Motye, Soloeis, and Panormos near the Elymoi because they put faith in the alliance with the Elymoi, and because from there the ship voyage between Carthage and Sicily is shortest. These are the barbarians living in Sicily.

6.3. Of the Greeks, the first to arrive were the Chalcidians from Euboea, who colonized Naxos with their founder, Thoucles. They built an altar to Apollo Archegetos, which still exists outside the city. On this altar, envoys sacrifice first before sailing from Sicily. [2] Syracuse was founded in the following year by Archias, one of the Heraclids from Corinth. He first drove the Siciloi from the islet on which the inner city stands, although it is no longer surrounded by water. Later, those living outside were brought within the circuit of the walls and the city became populous. [3] In the fifth year after the founding of Syracuse, Thoucles and the Chalcidians set out from Naxos. They drove the Sicels out and founded Leontini, and later Catana. The Catanians themselves made Eurarchon their founder.

6.4. About the same time, Lamis took a colony from Megara and arrived in Sicily. On the river Pantacyas he settled a place called Trotilos. Later, he

---

14. By Phoenicians, Thucydides may mean Carthaginians. The names are mostly interchangeable in 5th-century writings.

left there and joined his community with the Chalcidians at Leontini for a while. Expelled from there, he founded Thapsos. When he died, the rest of his followers were driven out of Thapsos. A certain Sicil king, Hyblon, ceded a bit of land and led them to it. This they settled and named Hyblaean Megara. [2] Dwelling there for 145 years, they were expelled from the city and the land by the Syracusan tyrant Gelon. Before their expulsion, 100 years after the founding, they sent Pamillos out and founded Selinus. Pamillos had come from the mother city Megara to be a fellow colonist. [3] Gela was founded together by Anthiphemos from Rhodes and Entimos from Crete, both leading out colonists forty-five years after the foundation of Syracuse. The community took its name from the river Gela. The space where the city is now and which was first fortified is called Lindii. Their institutions are Doric. [4] The Geloans founded Acragas 108 years after their own foundation. They named the city from the river Acragas and made Aristonos and Pustilos the founders and established Gelan institutions. [5] Zancle was founded at first after pirates arrived from Cumae, the Chalcidian city in Opicia. Later a large number came from Chalcis and the rest of Euboea and populated the land together. The founders were Perieres from Cumae and Crataemenes from Chalcis. At first the name of the place was Zancle, given by the Siciloi because the spot was shaped like a sickle (the Siciloi call a sickle "Zanclon"). Later, however, the inhabitants were expelled by some Samians and other Ionians, who had escaped from the Medes and landed in Sicily. [6] Not much later, the Samians were expelled by Anaxilas, the tyrant of Rhegium. He colonized the community with a mixed population and renamed it Messina from the name of his old homeland.

6.5. Himera was colonized from Zancle by Euclides, Simus, and Sacon. Most of the colonists were Chalcidians, although refugees called Myletidae, who were defeated in a civil conflict in Syracuse, joined them. The language was mixed between Chalcidian and Doric; the institutions were primarily Chalcidian. [2] Arcae and Casmenae were founded by the Syracusans: Arcae seventy years after Syracuse; Casmenae almost twenty years after Arcae. [3] Camarina was at first founded by the Syracusans 135 years after the foundation of Syracuse. The founders were Dascon and Menecolos. The Camarinans revolted against the Syracusans and were forced to leave. Some time later Hippocrates, tyrant of Gela, received the land of the Camarinans as a ransom for some Syracusan war prisoners. He himself became the founder in the resettlement of Camarina. Later, the inhabitants were expelled again by Gelon and the city was founded a third time by the Geloans.

6.6. So many tribes of Greek and barbarian origin inhabit Sicily and against an island of such size the Athenians set their expedition in motion. Their real design was to rule the whole island, but they claimed the fine pretense of desiring to come to the aid of their kin and their allies.

5. Dionysius of Halicarnassus, *Roman Antiquities* 1.89–90 (1st century BCE). *After recounting the founding of the city of Rome,*

Dionysius asserts that Rome is not a barbarian city but a Greek one and gives as proof a genealogy. (RFK)

1.89. This, then, is what I was able to discover about the races of the Romans by reading thoroughly and with much care numerous writings of both Greeks and Romans. Therefore, let someone confidently declare that Rome is a Greek city and let him beware the many stories that make Rome a refuge for barbarians by welcoming fugitives and the homeless and, admitting that Rome is the most public and beneficent of cities, let him ponder that the tribe of Aborigines were Oenotrians, and also Arcadians. [2] Let him also recall that the Pelasgians, Argives by birth who left Thessaly and arrived at Italy, were their co-inhabitants.[15] When Evander and the Arcadians arrived, they dwelt around the Palatine Hill, once the Aborigines offered the land to them. Next, the Peloponnesians arrived with Heracles and settled upon the Saturnian Hill. Last were those driven away from Troy who commingled with those who had arrived before. You would find no peoples more ancient or more Greek than these. [3] Interactions with the barbarians came about in time, through which the city unlearned many of its ancient customs. It may well appear a marvel to many who reckon such things that the city did not altogether become barbarian after accepting Opicians, Marsians, Saunites, Tyrrhenians, Brettians, Ombricans, Ligurians, Iberians, Celts, and others, some from Italy and others arriving from elsewhere, many such peoples as shared neither language nor way of life. The ways of life of such a rabble were greatly disturbed from all this discord, which was likely to cause many innovations from the ancient organization of the city. [4] Many others dwelling among the barbarians for only a short time unlearned all their Greekness, so that they did not speak Greek nor use Greek customs, nor know the same gods or suitable laws, by which the Greek nature especially differs from the barbarian. Nor were there any other shared bonds whatsoever between them. Those of the Achaeans who had settled around the Pontus are sufficient proof-positive of my account: having once been Eleans from a most Greek people, they are now the most savage of all the barbarians.

1.90. The Romans speak a language that is neither completely barbarian nor adequately Greek but is a mixture of both, of which the greater share is Aeolic. A single advantage arises from the mingling of so many, that, while their pronunciation is not clear, there are other indications that their race is of Greek descent as no other peoples made of immigrants preserve. The present is not the beginning of their pleasant life, which holds much fortune and flowing good as a teacher of good things. Nor did it begin from the time when they first reached beyond the sea to destroy the empires of Carthage and Macedon. Rather, it began from the time when they all dwelt

---

15. See Aeschylus' *Suppliants* (Chapter 5, section 1) for Pelasgians as Argives. In Herodotus generally, Pelasgians are a pre–Greek people who either left Greece after the Dorians arrived or became Athenians.

together and lived a Greek life. Nor is there any pursuit now for the sake of virtue that is more distinguished now than was before.

> **6. Livy, *From the Founding of the City* 1.1–4, 1.8–9 (1st century CE).** *Livy's account of the origins of Rome is an attempt to reconcile a number of different stories of Roman origins, including descent from Troy through Aeneas, kinship with the Etruscans, and links to the mythical Latinus, who was of native Italian descent. Later, after the founding of Rome, Romulus opens the city to all comers and, lacking women, contrives to get wives from the neighboring Sabines. (CSR/MLG)*

1.1. First of all it is well established that in the sack of Troy the Achaeans vented their rage against all the Trojans except Aeneas and Antenor. They did not execute the rights of conquerors on these men because of their longstanding hospitable relations and because they had always been the authors of peace and pushed for Helen's return. [2] After various misfortunes, Antenor left with a group of Eneti. They had been driven from Pamphlagonia in a rebellion and were thus seeking a home and a leader (their king, Pylaemenes, had died at Troy). They went into an inner harbor of the Adriatic Sea and expelled the Euganei, who lived in the area between the sea and the Alps. [3] The Eneti and the Trojans held these lands. The place where they first disembarked is called Troy, and the name of the district is Trojan; the whole race there is called Venetian. [4] A similar misfortune put Aeneas to flight, but the fates led him to greater undertakings. First he went to Macedon, and from there he went to Sicily seeking a home, and from Sicily he went to the Laurentine land. [5] This place is also called Troy. There the Trojans disembarked. Because of their great wandering, they had nothing left except their arms and their ships and so pillaged the fields. King Latinus and the Aborigines who lived there at that time armed themselves and ran from their city to the fields in order to resist the force of the invaders. From this point, the story diverges in two. Some say that Latinus was defeated in battle and made peace with Aeneas, agreeing to an alliance through the offer of marriage to his daughter; [6] others say that when the battle lines were drawn up and established, but before the battle signals were sounded, Latinus, with his foremost men, went out and called the leader of the strangers to a parley. [7] He asked them who among mortals they were, from where and by what accident did they leave their home, or what did they seek in coming into the Laurentine land. [8] After he heard that the group was Trojan, that their leader was Aeneas, the son of Anchises and Venus, that they had been driven from their homes after their homeland was burned, and that they were seeking a home and a place to found a city, he admired the spirit of their leader and the nobility of their race, which was prepared for either war or peace. Then, by extending his right hand to Aeneas, he sanctioned the faith of their future friendship. [9] Then a treaty was struck between the leaders, and greetings were exchanged between the armies. Aeneas went to the hospitable house of Latinus as a guest, and there, in front of his household gods, Latinus gave his daughter to Aeneas in marriage, and thereby joined a domestic treaty with a public one. [10] This agreement affirmed the Trojans' hope for a stable and certain rest from their wanderings, which were now at an end. [11] The Trojans founded a town; Aeneas named it Lavinium after his wife. Soon thereafter a male child resulted from the new marriage. His parents named him Ascanius.

1.2. Then war came to both the Aborigines and the Trojans. Turnus was the king of the Rutulians, to whom Lavinia had been promised before the arrival of Aeneas and whose reputation suffered badly because a foreigner was preferred over him. He brought war on Aeneas and Latinus at the same time. [2] Neither side left this battle happy: the Rutulians were conquered; the victors, the Aborigines and the Trojans, lost their leader Latinus. [3] Then Turnus and the Rutulians, lacking confidence in their strength, fled to the flourishing wealth of the Etruscans and King Mezentius, who ruled in the then-opulent town of Caere. He was already hardly happy to see the foundation of a new town, and as it developed he thought that the Trojans had grown greater than was safe enough for their neighbors. So he readily formed a military alliance with the Rutulians. Aeneas was opposed to the horror of so great a war. In order to win over the minds of the Aborigines, and so that they all might live not only under the same law but also under the same name, [4] he gave the name Latins to both races. [5] After that the Aborigines equaled the Trojans in their eagerness and faith toward King Aeneas. Although Etruria was so great in wealth that already the fame of its name filled not only the lands but the sea through the whole length of Italy from the Alps to the Sicilian strait, Aeneas trusted in the spirits of the two peoples coalescing more day by day and led out troops in battle lines once he was able to drive the battle back from his defenses. [6] The battle was favorable to the Latins, although it was the last of mortal deeds for Aeneas. He, whatever it is lawful or right to call him, is buried along the river Numicus: they call him Indigenous Jove.

1.3. Ascanius, son of Aeneas, was not yet ready to rule; nevertheless his position remained safely for him until he reached the appropriate age. In the meantime, it was in the safekeeping of a woman, his mother. Lavinia's character was so great that the Latin government and the kingship of his grandfather and father was kept secure for the boy. [2] By no means will I go into the debate—for who could affirm for certain such an ancient matter— whether this was Ascanius or someone older than him, by which I mean Iulus, Aeneas' child from Creusa, who was born while Troy was unharmed and who was a companion in his father's flight from Troy, and whom the Julian clan claims as the originator of its name. [3] This Ascanius, born wherever and from whatever mother—certainly it is established that he was born from Aeneas—left Lavinium to his mother (or stepmother) when its population was growing and it was already flourishing and wealthy. He established a new city under the Alban mountain. The city was named

Alba Longa for its location stretched out along the mountain's ridge. [4] Thirty years lapsed between the settlement of Lavinium and Alba Longa. Once the Etruscans had been defeated, the people's wealth grew so great that neither Mezentius nor the Etruscans nor any other neighbors dared to attack them [5] after the death of Aeneas or during the woman's rule or at the first beginnings of the boy's kingship. [6] Terms of peace established that the river Albula, which they now call the Tiber, would be the border between the Etruscans and the Latins. [7] Ascanius' son Silvius, so named because he was born in the woods, ruled next; he fathered first Aeneas Silvius and then Latinus Silvius. [8] He established several settlements, and their inhabitants were called Old Latins. Afterwards the cognomen Silvius remained for all who ruled at Alba. [9] After Latinus came Alba, then Atys, Capys, Capetus, and Tiberinus, who drowned in crossing the river Albula and gave the famous name to the river for later generations. Then came Agrippa, Tiberinus' son; and after Agrippa, Romulus Silvius ruled with the authority he received from his father. He was struck by lightning and handed his kingdom over to Aventinus. Aventinus was buried on the hill that now is part of the Roman city; he gave his name to the hill. [10] Proca then ruled. This man fathered Numitor and Amulius. He left the old kingdom of the Silvian race to Numitor, who was the older son. But force was a more powerful thing than the will of their father or respect for age, so Amulius ousted his brother and ruled. [11] He then added crime to crime by killing his brother's sons and making his brother's daughter, Rhea Silvia, a Vestal. This appointment looked like an honor, but in so doing he took away any chance for her to have children because of the requirement of perpetual virginity.

1.4. But the origin of so great a city and the beginning of the greatest empire second to that of the gods was destined, so I think, by the fates. [2] The Vestal was raped and produced twin boys. She named Mars as father of the doubtful offspring, whether because she truly thought this or because it was more honorable that a god be the originator of the fault. [3] But neither gods nor men saved either her or her offspring from the king's cruelty; the priestess was bound and put into custody, and he ordered the boys to be set adrift in the flowing river. [4] By chance and divine intervention the Tiber had overflowed its banks into calm pools and one could not approach the normal course of the river. The men carrying the infants hoped that the floodwater, although slow moving, would be able to bear them away and drown them. [5] Thus they performed the order of the king and exposed the boys in the nearby flood zone where now the Ruminal fig tree is—they say it was called the tree of Romulus. At that time these places felt vast and empty. [6] The story goes that when the still water where the boys had been exposed receded and left the floating basket on dry land, a thirsty wolf turned her wandering course out of the mountains into the region toward the boys' wailing. She offered the infants her teats so gently that the keeper of the royal herd found her licking the boys with her tongue. They say his name was Faustulus. [7] He took the boys from that place to his hut and gave them to his wife Laurentia to raise. There are those who think that

Laurentia was called a she-wolf among the shepherds because her body was communal and that later this story was replaced by the miracle tale. [8] Having thus been born and so raised, when first they matured in age they were not lazy at home or with the flocks but wandered the forests in their hunting. [9] In the forests their bodies and minds grew in strength. They did not subsist on wild animals alone, but also attacked robbers who were overburdened with spoils and divided up what was stolen among the other shepherds. While the flock of young men around them grew day by day, they carried out serious matters and jokes.

. . .

1.8. Romulus attended to the gods and summoned the crowd. Because this crowd could not unite into a single people except through laws, he gave them laws. These laws, he believed, would be a greater object of reverence if he made his person more venerable through the symbols of power. He not only dressed in a more distinguished way, but he also accepted twelve lictors. Some supposed that he took that number from the number of birds who predicted his rule. I follow the opinion of those who think that he took attendants of this sort and their number from the Etruscans, the source also of the curule chair[16] and the toga praetexta.[17] The Etruscans are supposed to have this number because the twelve communities who elected a king in common each gave a single attendant.

In the meantime, the city was growing, gathering more and more places within its fortifications. They were fortifying the space that they hoped would contain the future, and not the current, population. So that the size of the city would not be pointless, Romulus deployed an old strategy for increasing populations used by city founders, who acquire an obscure and lowly multitude and pretend that they had sprung from the earth. He opened up as an asylum the spot that is now enclosed between groves as one descends the Capitoline hill. To this spot fled from their neighbors an indiscriminate rabble, free and slave, who desired a new situation. This was the first step in the greatness of strength that was emerging. Since Romulus was no longer dissatisfied with his strength, he provided direction for that strength. He created one hundred senators, either because that number was sufficient or because there were only a hundred who were the sort who could be made "fathers." The senators, of course, were called "fathers" out of respect and their descendants were called "patricians."

1.9. Rome was then so vigorous that she was the equal in war to any of her neighbors. But a lack of women threatened to limit her greatness to a single generation because there was no hope of children at home nor any rights to marriage with her neighbors. And so in consultation with the senators, Romulus sent ambassadors to their neighbors in order to request

---

16. The chair reserved for use by higher-ranked Roman magistrates.

17. Toga with a two- to three-inch purple border worn by higher-ranked Roman magistrates.

alliances and marriage rights for his new community. Cities, the ambassadors argued, grow like everything else, from the lowest point. From there, the cities that are supported by their own excellence and by the gods become wealthy and famous. They said that they were satisfied that the gods were present at Rome's origin and that their excellence would not fail. For this reason they should not be embarrassed to join their blood and race with fellow men. This message was not well received. Their neighbors simultaneously felt disdain for the Romans and were afraid for their own relations and descendants with so great a power growing in their midst. The ambassadors were often asked after they were sent off if they had opened up their asylum for women too—that was, they said, the way to find suitable marriages. The Roman people took this rejection badly and certainly the matter seemed to be headed toward violence. So that this violence might be focused at a suitable time and place, Romulus concealed his anger and carefully organized the festival dedicated to equestrian Neptune called the Consualia. He ordered that the spectacle be disclosed to their neighbors. They prepared for it with as much magnificence as was in their power and knowledge at that time in order to make the event widely known and anticipated. Many people gathered, eager also to see the new city, but especially the nearest neighbors: the inhabitants of Caenina, Crustumium, and Antemnae, and a whole crowd of Sabines with their children and wives. The Romans graciously welcomed the visitors into their homes and showed them the site and fortifications and the city filled with buildings. The visitors were amazed at how Rome had grown in such a short time. When the time for the spectacle came and their whole attention was directed to it, the prearranged violence began. When a sign had been given, the Roman youth ran in to steal the young unmarried women. A great number of the women were random victims, but some outstanding beauties had been selected for the principle senators, and these specific plebeian men had been given the task of bringing them home. One woman, far more beautiful than the rest, had been seized by a gang belonging to a certain Thalassius. Since many men sought to know to whom she was being taken and in order to avoid violence, they are said to have cried out "to Thalassius!" It is from this that the marriage cry came about.

The celebration broke up in fear and the parents of the young women fled in sorrow. They charged the Romans with violation of their guest rights, and they called on the god to whose solemn festival they had properly and faithfully come only to be deceived. The women who were seized were hopeless on their own account, and their indignation was no less. But Romulus himself circulated among them and informed them that the arrogance of their own parents was to blame, who had denied marriage rights with their neighbors. He said that they would nevertheless be married and partake in all their fortunes and citizenship and children, the most precious possession of the human race. They should soften their rage and suit their minds to the men whom fate had given their bodies. It is often the case that injury can lead to forgiveness and affection. For this reason, they will obtain better husbands because each will strive on his own to both fulfill his duty as husband but also supplement your desire for parents and country. The men added their own enticements: they gave their desire and their love as the excuse for their action, which are just the sorts of excuses likely to appeal to women.

7. Vergil, *Aeneid* 3.94–113, 3.161–171 (1st century BCE). *Before the Trojans finally arrive in Italy, they wander the Mediterranean in their search for a new city. They consult the oracle of Apollo on Delos, who advises them to "seek their ancient mother." They originally interpret this to be the island of Crete, the birthplace of Teucer, one of the founders of Troy. (CSR)*

3.94–113. We fall prostrate on the ground and a voice comes to our ears: "Hardy sons of Dardanus, the land which first bore you from the race of your parents will receive you when you return to its happy breast. Seek your ancient mother. Every shore will be ruled by this house of Aeneas and by his children's children and even by those born from them." Phoebus Apollo said these things, and great joy rose up as the cheers mingled, and everyone asked what these walls were to which [100] Phoebus calls the wanderers and bids them to return. Then Aeneas' father, considering the traditions of ancient men, said: "Listen leaders! And learn what you may hope for. The island of Crete, belonging to great Jupiter, lies in the middle of the sea, where the Idaean mountain is and the birthplace of our race. The people inhabit a hundred great cities; it is a most fertile kingdom, from which our earliest ancestor, if I recall what I have heard correctly, Teucer was first carried onto Trojan shores. He chose the place for his kingdom. Ilium and the citadel of [110] Pergamum had not yet been built; they were living in the lowest valleys. The great mother who dwells on the mountain of Cybele and her bronze dancers and the Idaean grove come from Crete, from here we get the faithful silence in sacred matters, and the lions that we yoke beneath the chariot of the goddess.

The Trojans travel to Crete and lay the foundations for a settlement. Attacked by famine and plague, Aeneas' household gods appear and tell him that he is in the wrong place.

3.161–171. Lares: "You must move your settlements. Delian Apollo did not urge you to these shores or order you to settle on Crete. There is a place, which the Greeks call Hesperia, an ancient land, powerful in arms and in the fertility of its soil, which Oenotrian men inhabit. Now they are called the Italian people from the name of their leader. In that place a site is secured for you. From here Dardanus and father Iasius were born. From this beginning came our race. Come, rise and joyfully bring these words back to your aged father, [170] words that should not at all be doubted: Let him seek Corythus (Cortona) and the Ausonian lands. Jupiter denies you Crete."

8. Vergil, *Aeneid* **12.818–840 (1st century BCE).** *At the end of the Aeneid, Juno agrees to put aside her anger at the Trojans, with the stipulation that the Italians will not have to change their names or customs to match the Trojans. (CSR)*

Juno: "And now I yield and I leave these loathed battles behind. But I have a request of you, a request forbidden by no law of fate. [820] I ask on behalf of Latium, on behalf of the majesty of your peoples, that when they make a peace with happy wedding bonds (let it be so), when they make laws and treaties, do not compel the native Latins to change their name or to become Trojan and to be called Teucrians or to change their language or their clothes. Let Latium be, let them have Alban kings through the ages, let the Roman race be powerful with Italian strength. Troy has fallen, and let it have fallen with its name." Smiling down at her, the maker of men and things said: [830] "You are the sister of Jupiter and the second child of Saturn, you roil such great waves of anger in your heart. But come and release your anger, vain from its beginning. I give you what you wish, and, overcome, willingly I concede to you. The Ausonians will keep the speech and customs of their fathers, their name will be what it is now—Latins; the Trojans, adding only their blood, will fade. I will add a custom and rites of sacred worship, and I will make them all Latins with one language. From them a race will arise, mixed with Ausonian blood, that you will see exceed all men and all gods in piety, [840] and no race will match their celebration of your honors."

9. Ovid, *Metamorphoses* **1.78–88 (1st century CE).** *After describing the creation of the universe, Ovid tells of the creation of man. (MLG)*

A more conscientious animal than these and more capable of deep thought, the sort that could rule the rest, is as yet lacking. A human was born. Either that artisan of the universe created it with his divine seed, or [80] the earth herself did it, freshly removed from the high atmosphere and retaining the seed of kindred heaven. Planting this seed, the son of Iapetus mixed it with rainwater and fashioned it into the shape of the gods who direct all. He gave man a face directed upwards and bid him look at heaven and to lift his upright countenance to the stars. In this way the earth, recently wild and formless, was changed and clothed with the previously unknown shapes of humans.

10. Josephus, *Jewish Antiquities* **12.225–227 (1st century CE).**[18]
Josephus recounts an anecdote that linked the Spartans and Jews through

---

18. Josephus is using as his source here I *Maccabees* 12.8–18, dated to around 100 BCE. The authenticity of such a letter is highly uncertain.

a son of Abraham. The letter is supposedly dated to the reign of King Areus of Sparta (309/8–265 BCE). (RFK)

12.225. After Simon died and his son Onias succeeded him to the high priesthood, the Spartan King Areus sent an ambassador to him with a letter, a copy of which states, 226. "Areus, king of the Lacedaemonians, sends his greetings to Onias. We have happened upon a document that says that Judeans and Lacedaemonians are of the same race and related through Abraham.[19] It is just, then, since you are our brothers, that you let us know if there is anything you need. 227. We will do the same with you and will consider your affairs equal to our own. Demoteles, who bears this letter, will transmit your response. This letter has four sides and bears the seal of a dragon clutching an eagle."[20]

11. Tacitus, *Annals* 11.24.1 (1st/2nd century CE). *The Senate is debating whether to replenish the Senate by allowing men from Gallia Comata, who had long been allies of Rome and possessed citizens' rights, to obtain public office and thus membership in the Senate. Tacitus first includes a vehement speech of opposition, to which the Emperor replies. (MLG)*

The emperor [Claudius] was unimpressed by such arguments as these. He immediately laid out the opposing position when he spoke to the assembled Senate: "The oldest of my ancestors, Clausus, was originally a Sabine. He was adopted at the same time into the Roman state and into the patrician class. These ancestors encourage me to follow similar ideas in governing the Republic, by relocating here anything of excellence. You are not, of course, ignorant of the fact that the family of the Julii come from Alba, the Coruncanii, from Camerium, the Porcii, from Tusculum, and—to pass over ancient history—men have been accepted into the senate from Etruria, Lucania, and the whole of Italy. Then, the very expansion of the state to the Alps united not just individual men but whole lands and tribes under our name. There was a firm peace at home and our influence abroad was strong at the time when the people living beyond the Po were given citizenship, when we accepted the strongest provincials to support our weak empire under the pretext of spreading our legions over the world. Are we truly sorry that the Balbi have come to us come from Spain? That no less remarkable men have come from Gallia Narbonensis? Their descendants are still with us and their love of our country is no less than ours.

---

19. Diodorus recounts a version of the Exodus that connects Cadmus and Danaus to Moses. See Chapter 11, Selection 2.

20. This statement is meant to guarantee the authenticity of the message.

12. Pausanius, *Description of Greece* 10.4.4 (2nd century CE). *Pausanius describes two rocks said to be remnants of Prometheus' first men. (RFK)*

At Panopeus, there is a structure near the road, not large but crudely made. Inside are images made of Pentelic marble. One is surely Asclepius. They say that the other is Prometheus and offer as proof of this identification the following: beside the streambed [near the Panopeus] are two stones, each sufficiently large enough to fill a wagon. Their surface is clay-colored, not an earthy red but like the streambed or a sandy torrent. They also emit a smell very much like that of human skin. They say that these are the remnants of the clay from which the whole of the human race was fashioned by Prometheus.

13. [Apollodorus], *The Library* 1.7.2 (2nd century CE). *An account of the repopulation of the earth after the Great Flood. (RFK)*

Prometheus begat a son Deucalion. Deucalion was king of the land around Phthia and he married Pyrrha, daughter of Epimetheus and Pandora, whom the gods made as the first woman. When Zeus wished to destroy the bronze race, at Prometheus' bidding Deucalion constructed an ark, loaded on provisions, and then embarked with Pyrrha. Zeus destroyed the majority of Greece, inundating it with heavy rains falling from the skies, so that all of mankind was destroyed except for a few who had fled into the nearby mountains. It was at this time that the mountains of Thessaly were divided, and all the land beyond the Isthmus and Peloponnese overwhelmed. But Deucalion was carried upon the seas in the ark for nine days and nights, coming at last to Mount Parnassus. There, when the rains finally let up, he disembarked and sacrificed to Zeus for his salvation. Zeus sent Hermes to him and bid him choose whatever he wished in return. Deucalion chose to beget humankind. On Zeus' advice, he picked up stones and threw them over his head. Whichever stones Deucalion threw became men. Whichever stones Pyrrha threw became women. Whence people are named metaphorically "people" from *laas*, the word for stone.

14. [Apollodorus], *The Library* 2.1.4 (2nd century CE). *The genealogy of the African continent and the Argives from Epaphus, son of Io and Zeus. (RFK)*

Epaphus, while king of the Egyptians, married Memphis, a daughter of the Nile, and founded the city of Memphis after her. They bore a daughter named Libya, after whom the land of Libya is named. Libya and Poseidon bore twin sons, Agenor and Belus. Agenor departed to Phoenicia and ruled. There he became progenitor of great stock (I will defer my discussion of them until later). Belus, on the other hand, remained in Egypt and ruled. He married Anchinoe, a daughter of the Nile, and they bore twin children also, Aegyptus and Danaus (though Euripides says that they also bore Cepheus and Phineus). Bellus established Danaus in Libya and Aegyptus in Arabia. Aegyptus, however, subdued the land of the Melapods and named it Egypt as well after himself. Fifty sons were born to Aegyptus from many wives, while fifty daughters were born to Danaus.[21] After the brothers later fought on account of Egypt, Danaus feared the sons of Aegyptus. On Athena's advice, he prepared a ship, boarded his daughters, and fled. Landing first at Rhodes, he set up a statue to Lindian Athena. Next, he arrived at Argos where King Gelano handed rule over to him.[22] Danaus then became king and renamed the inhabitants Danaans after himself.

15. Hyginus, *Genealogies* 178 (2nd century CE). *This Latin summary from Greek sources tells of the descendants of Europa and the founding of Thebes. (RFK)*

Europa was the Sidonian daughter of Argiope and Agenor. Jupiter turned himself into a bull and carried her from Sidon to Crete. In Crete she bore him Monis, Sarpedon, and Rhadamanthus. Her father Agenor sent forth his own sons, Phoenix, Cilix, and Cadmus, to bring their sister back or never to return to his sight. Phoenix went to Africa, where he remained. Thus the Africans are called Phoenicians.[23] Cilix gave his name to Cilicia.[24] While Cadmus was wandering, he inquired at Delphi. There he received an oracle that he should buy a cow from a shepherd, a cow with a moon mark on her rump, and drive her before him. In the spot where she lay down to rest, he was fated to build a city and to rule. Cadmus, when he heard his fate, did what he was ordered. Afterwards, while seeking for water, he came to the Castalian fountain, guarded by a dragon, a son of Mars. The dragon killed Cadmus' companions. Then Cadmus killed it with a rock. Minerva then advised Cadmus to plough the dragon's teeth into the earth. The Sparti [Sown Men] then sprouted up. They fought among themselves until only five survived: Chthonius, Udaeus, Hyperenor, Pelorus, and Echion. Boeotia, however, took its name from the cow [*bovis*] that Cadmus had followed there.

---

21. It is unclear if Danaus also had many wives. A common opposition between Greeks and foreigners was polygamy versus monogamy, so it would be interesting to note whether Danaus, a founder of Greek cities, had multiple wives.

22. See *Aeschylus' Suppliants* (Chapter 5, Selection 1) for an earlier variant of this myth.

23. The Africans referred to here are the north Africans west of Egypt, in what was called in both ancient and modern times Libya.

24. This was the ancient name for the southeast coastal region of modern Turkey, which lies near Syria.

CHAPTER 3

ENVIRONMENTAL THEORIES

Environmental theories focus on the way geography, nature, climate, or physical environment shape physique and character. There are many manifestations of this theory, and it often combines with theories of descent or genealogy. Variations on the environmental theme appear in texts ranging from geographers and astrologers to medical writers and architectural texts.

/1. **Hippocratic Corpus,** *On Airs, Waters, Places* **12–24 (5th century BCE).** *This text is the longest exposition of the environmental theory of race and ethnicity. It was written as a handbook for physicians as they headed out into the world to practice their craft. After a detailed discussion of how various climates can cause different sorts of illnesses or medical conditions, the author shows how climate dictates facial features, physique, and even the character of peoples in various regions outside of Greece, focusing especially on the Scythians. (RFK)*

12. I want to show now how Asia and Europe differ from each other in all ways, and particularly how the peoples of each place differ physically from one another. I assert that Asia varies most from Europe in the nature of its plant life and inhabitants. Everything grows more beautifully and larger by far in Asia. The land there is less wild than Europe, and the people are also gentler and more even-tempered. The reason for this is a temperate climate. Specifically, the land lies east in the middle of the sun's path and is further away from cold than we are. Such growth and tameness is most frequently a result of no single element (like cold or heat) dominating. Instead, a sense of equality permeates everything . . .

The author describes the climate and plant life of the central portion of Asia Minor.

. . . The men are also well nourished and their physiques very noble. They are extremely tall and differ very little from one another in build and stature. The land is most like spring in its nature and consistency of climate. Courage, endurance, and industriousness would not be able to arise in such a climate, either among natives or immigrants. Thus, by necessity, pleasure reigns < . . . >[25] Among the wild animals, there is a variety of shape and size.

13. The same can be said, as I see it, of the Egyptians and Libyans. They live to the right of the sun's course near Lake Maeotis,[26] the boundary between Europe and Asia. Their condition is as follows: these peoples are more diverse than those in Asia because of the changes in climate and the nature of the land. The land experiences the changes just as the men do. For, where the changes in the seasons are very excessive, the land is also savage and very irregular. You will find massive mountains, woods, plains, and meadows. Where the seasons alter very little, the landscape is very regular. It's the same for men, if someone cares to examine them. The natures of some of them resemble wooded and well-watered mountains. Others resemble airy, dry lands, or marshy meadows, or bare, dry plains. The seasons, which alter the nature of one's physique, differ among themselves. If the differences in the seasons are vast, then the differences between the shapes and sizes will be more noticeable.

14. I will leave out discussion of those peoples who differ from us minimally and will describe instead those peoples who are very different physically and culturally. Let's begin with the Macrocephalai, or Longheads. Their heads are unlike those of any other people. At first, they had long heads through custom, but now it is a combination of custom and nature. The Macrocephalai believe that the longest head is the most beautiful. Their custom concerning this is as follows: whenever a child is born, immediately while the head is still pliant, they use their hands to reshape the head to make it longer and then apply bandages and other appropriate "shapers" to aid in the process. The roundness of the head is thus destroyed and the length increased. Custom worked in the beginning in such a way that it forced nature to follow suit. As time went on, nature itself took over so that custom was no longer needed since one's "stock" comes from every part of the body: healthy stock from the healthy parts and diseased stock from diseased parts. If, then, bald children come from bald parents and grey-eyed children come from grey-eyed parents and deformed children from deformed parents, and so on, would this not be the case with other physical characteristics? What prevents a long-headed child being born from a long-headed parent? Nevertheless, having a long head is now less common than before, since marriages outside of the community are no longer restricted by custom.

15. That is what I have to say about the Macrocephalai. I turn now to those who dwell on the Phasis River.[27] The land is marshy, hot, wet, and wooded.

---

25. There is a large lacuna in the text here in which the author most likely discussed the Egyptians and Libyans in detail.

26. Lake Maeotis is north of the Black Sea to the northeast of the Caucasus Mountains. The Tanais River flows into the lake. See Map 2.

27. The Phasis River is located at the far east of the Black Sea in the Caucasus Mountains.

Frequent torrential storms mark the region year-round. The people dwell in the marshes and construct homes of wood and reeds on the water. They rarely walk around the city and harbor, preferring to sail up and down the water on single logs since there are numerous canals. They drink hot, stagnant water that has been corrupted by the sun and augmented by the rains. The Phasis itself is the most stagnant of all rivers with an almost nonexistent flow. The fruits that grow there are meager, soft, and underdeveloped because of the excessive rains. This also explains why they never ripen. The water also creates a lot of fog over the land. The aforementioned conditions are why the Phasians' bodies are so different from the rest of mankind. They are tall, extremely fat, and neither their joints nor veins are visible. They have pallid complexions as if yellowed by jaundice. Their voices are the deepest of all men because the air they breathe is not clear, but damp and dirty. They are naturally lazy when it comes to physical labor. The seasons do not vary much, neither with heat nor cold. The winds are mostly damp except for one wind particular to the region. This wind blows strong and hot and is called the *chechrona*, the millet wind. The north wind rarely blows there and whenever it does, it is weak and mild.

16. That is all I have to say about the differences in nature and shape between the inhabitants of Asia and Europe. There is more to be said about the faint-heartedness and cowardice of Asians. Asians are less warlike than the peoples of our part of the world. The reason is, of course, the climate. There are no great shifts in the weather, which is neither hot nor cold but temperate. Therefore, they experience no mental anxiety and no physical shocks. Such shocks enflame the temper and increase recklessness and passion more so than constant sameness. As a result, it seems to me that Asian races are feeble. Their laws only add to this condition. Asians live mostly under kings. Where men neither rule themselves nor are autonomous but are subjects to a despot, there is no self-interest in appearing warlike. On the contrary, it benefits them more to seem the opposite, since their dangers are not the same as those who self-govern. It is more likely that subjects under a despot will be forced to suffer and die or to be separated from their families and friends for the sake of the despot. All their famous deeds and courage serve to increase the means and glory of the despot, while all they themselves get are danger and death. Furthermore, the land upon which such men live is necessarily made desert by their enemies and their own laziness. The result is that anyone born with a courageous and bold nature is changed by the laws of the land. I have proof of this: All the Greeks and barbarians in Asia who are not ruled by a despot but by themselves endure hardships for their own sake and are the most warlike men of all. They endure dangers for their own sake, and they alone take home the prizes for courage or infamy for acts of cowardice. You will find that Asians differ from each other as well. Some are superior, some inferior. Changes in the climate are the reason for this, as previously stated.

17. This is how conditions hold for Asians. In Europe, there is a Scythian tribe called the Sauromatai who dwell near Lake Maeotis. They are different

from all other peoples. Their women, so long as they are unmarried girls, ride horses, practice archery, hurl javelins from horseback, and fight tribal enemies. They do not set aside their maidenhood until they have killed three enemies, and even then they do not enter into a marriage until they have made the traditional sacrifices. Once a woman has taken a husband to herself, she stops riding horseback unless there is a tribe-wide military campaign. These women do not have a right breast. While they are still infants, their mothers apply a specially made hot bronze device to their right breast and burn it so that growth stops. The result is that all growth and strength shifts to the right shoulder and arm.[28]

18. Concerning the physiques of other Scythians and how they are similar to others or not, the same principle applies to them as to Egyptians, though Egyptians are afflicted by heat, while the Scythians are afflicted by cold. The so-called Scythian desert is, in fact, a meadow-like plain devoid of trees and moderately wet (there are great rivers that act as drains for the water from the plain). The Scythians who live here are called Nomads. They don't dwell in houses but in wagons. The smallest of these wagons has four wheels, the rest have six. The wagons are covered with felt and are constructed like houses with two or three rooms. These wagons are proofed against water, snow, and winds, and each one is pulled by two or three hornless oxen (they are hornless because of the cold). The women live in these wagons and the men ride alongside upon horseback, followed by all the sheep, oxen, and horses. They all remain in the same place as long as there is plenty of food for the animals. Once the food runs out, they migrate to another area. They themselves eat roasted meat and drink mare's milk. They also snack on a mare's milk cheese called *hippace*.

19. Those are their customs and lifestyles. The climate and physiques of the peoples of Scythia are very different from those of other people and, like the Egyptians, are very uniform among themselves with very little diversity. The land produces very few and very small wild animals since Scythia lies right under the Great Bear and the Rhipaian Mountains,[29] whence the north wind blows. The sun comes nearest them only during the summer solstice and at the end of its journey. It warms them, then, a little and for a short time. The winds blowing from hot regions do not arrive there except very rarely and weakly. However, the cold winds from the north always blow with the snow, ice, and heavy rains. The mountains are continually

---

28. Chapter 14 includes numerous descriptions of the Amazons. Amazons are also said to be one-breasted warriors and to come from the Scythian plains. Supposedly, there is also a tribe of Amazons in Africa. In visual representations, Amazons are often conflated through clothing style with Scythian and Persian warriors.

29. The Great Bear, the constellation Ursa Major, is in the northern hemisphere and is often used by ancient authors for the "north." The Rhipaian Mountains are typically located by ancient geographers near the Caspian Sea (the Scythian Ocean) between the Scythians and the Hyperboreans.

inundated with such weather and are thus made uninhabitable. During the day, dense fog lies upon the plains where they live. Thus, it is always winter, while the summer is nearly nonexistent. The plains are high and barren and are not encircled by mountains, but they are sloped on the northern side. The wild animals there are not large but are of such a kind as can shelter themselves in the barren landscape. The winter and the barrenness of the land stunt their growth because there is no warmth or shelter. The changes in the seasons in this region are neither obvious nor shocking. Instead, the weather is fairly constant with only unnoticeable changes between seasons. Because of this, the people are identical in appearance (men with men, women with women). Because the summer and winter are the same, year-round they wear the same clothes, eat the same food, breathe the same damp air, drink from the same snow- and ice-melted water, and refrain uniformly from labor. It is well known that where there are no strong shifts in climate neither bodies nor souls can endure physical activity. By necessity, then, their bodies are stout, fleshy, jointless, bloated, and flabby, while their lower bellies are the most bloated bellies of all peoples. It is nearly impossible for a stomach to dry out in such a land with a nature and climate of this sort. And, because of their fatness and smooth fleshiness, the bodies of all, male and female, are identical with each other. Since the seasons are constant, the genetic materials undergo no decay or damage when they merge, except through some trauma or disease.

20. I will present an obvious proof of their bloatedness. You will find that the majority of the Scythian Nomads had their shoulders, arms, wrists, breasts, hips, and loins cauterized for no other reason than their soft and bloated nature. Because of the bloating and flabbiness, they are not able to draw a bow with their shoulder or hurl a javelin. When they cauterize themselves, the excess water is dried up from the joints and their bodies become more taut, better nourished, and more defined. Their bodies are flabby and wide, first, because they don't swaddle themselves like the Egyptians do. They think [that pants are better] for horseback riding, allowing them to sit ahorse more easily. Secondly, they are lazy. Male children, until they are old enough to ride horses, spend the bulk of their life in the wagons, and they rarely walk because of the constant migrations. The female children are a marvel of flab and fat. Also, the Scythian race is red-headed and red-faced, though not because of the sun's fierce heat. The cold burns their faces and turns them red.

21. Such a nature does not encourage fertility either, since the men are not all that eager for intercourse given their bloated stomachs and extremely soft and cold lower bellies—a man in this condition is highly unlikely to be able to satisfy his lusts. Furthermore, the constant bouncing on horseback has rendered Scythian men unfit for sex. This is why the men are infertile. The women, on the other hand, are infertile because they are fat and bloated. Their wombs are so wet that they are incapable of absorbing a man's seed. Their monthly purge is also not as it should be, but is infrequent and scanty. Moreover, the mouths of their wombs are clogged by fat and thus the seed is blocked. The women

are fat and lazy and their bellies are cold and soft. Thus, the Scythian race is infertile. Clear proof? The slave girls. They have strong and fit bodies, and the moment they've had sex with a man, they become pregnant.

22. Additionally, the majority of Scythian men become impotent and do women's work, live as women, and converse like women. Such men are called the Anares, the non-men. The natives believe a god is responsible for this condition, and they revere and worship those who catch it, while fearing for their own manhood. It seems to me that these diseases are divine (as all are), but no more than any other disease is divine or more human than another. All are equal and all are divine. Each has its own nature and does not arise without this nature. This particular disease seems to me to happen for the following reason: All that horseback riding causes joint swelling[30] because their feet are always dangling from the horses' backs. In the worst cases, the swelling is followed by the development of lacerated and disabled hips. Their cure is as follows: When the disease first appears, they cut the veins behind each ear. Once the blood stops flowing, light-headedness overtakes them and they fall asleep. When they wake up some men are cured, others are not. As I see it, though, the seed is destroyed by this practice. It is the cutting of these veins, the ones behind the ears, that causes the impotence. Men who try to have sex with a woman after this cure and are unable think nothing of it at first. After two or three or more unsuccessful attempts, however, they start to think they have offended a god and assume that is the cause of the impotence. They then don women's clothes since they believe their manhood is lost. They proceed to act like women and work with the women at their tasks. Only the strongest and most noble among the Scythians experience impotence, not the rabble. It is because they alone ride horses. The poor do not experience it as much simply because they do not ride . . .

> *The author goes on to discuss why the disease would strike the poor more often if it were truly a "divine" disease.*

. . . And such a disease arises among the Scythians for the reasons I already stated. This is how it is for other peoples as well where the majority ride frequently and for extended periods of time. The majority of these peoples are seized by swelling, sciatica, and gout and have very limited libidos. These are common problems for the Scythians, and for the reasons stated above they are the most impotent of men. The fact that they wear pants and are on horseback most of their lives also contributes to their impotence since both of these things limit masturbation. Furthermore, the cold and fatigue cause them to forget about sexual desire so that they are unmanned without ever having been aroused.

23. This is how the Scythian race lives. The other races of Europe differ among themselves in stature and physique on account of changes in the seasons, which are dramatic and frequent. The summer heat is extreme and the winters harsh. There are excessive rains followed by extended droughts and

---

30. The Greek word used here has no clear meaning, but is used with reference to aneurysms and arthritis.

winds, which cause more variations in the weather. As a result of this, it is likely that the development of the embryo[31] varies depending on whether it happens in the summer or winter, in rain instead of drought. This is why I think the physiques of Europeans show more variety than those of Asians, and why their stature changes even from city to city. The thickened semen is more prone to flaws and irregularities when the seasons change more frequently than when they remain constant. The same logic holds for character. In such inconsistent environments, savagery, antisocial attitudes, and boldness tend to arise. The frequent shocks to the mind make for wildness and impair the development of civilized and gentle behaviors. This is why I think those living in Europe are more courageous than those in Asia. Laziness is a product of uniform climate. Endurance of both the body and soul comes from change. Also, cowardice increases softness and laziness, while courage engenders endurance and a work ethic. For this reason, those dwelling in Europe are more effective fighters. The laws of a people are also a factor since, unlike Asians, Europeans don't have kings. Wherever there are kings, by necessity there is mass cowardice. I have said this before. It is because the souls are enslaved and refuse to encounter dangers willingly on behalf of another's power and they withdraw. Autonomous men—those who encounter dangers for their own benefit—are ready and willing to enter the fray, and they themselves, not a master, enjoy the rewards of victory. Thus, laws are not insignificant for engendering courage.

24. This, then, is all there is concerning Europe and Asia. There are in Europe itself tribes that differ from each other in stature, physique, and courage. The differences are the same as those I stated above, but I will now clarify further. Whoever dwells in a mountainous region, a region rugged, high, and damp, and where changes in seasons are dramatic, they likely have large physiques and have become acclimatized to endurance and courage. They are also quite savage and fierce. Whoever dwells in valleys, regions with meadows, stifling heats, winds that tend to be hot instead of cold, and where they use hot water, these people would not be large, nor would they be models of physical perfection. Instead, they would be naturally wide, fleshy, dark-haired, and swarthy rather than fair-skinned. They would also be less phlegmy and more bilious.[32] They would likewise not be by nature courageous or enduring, but with laws and reinforcement of such qualities, they could become so. If there should happen to be rivers in the region to siphon off the stagnant waters and rains from the land, those people would be healthy and bright-skinned. Where no rivers are, the people would drink stagnant, marshy, fenny waters, which would necessarily make their bellies bloated and distended. Whoever dwells in a region with

---

31. A number of ancient Greeks understood the formation of the zygote as a "thickening" of the male sperm in the water of a woman's womb, which was regarded as nothing more than a receptacle for the seed that did not contribute to the genes of the child. The image is of a seed immersed in water until it begins to expand and sprout.

32. This statement relates to the ancient theory of "humors," distinctive fluids that were understood to make up the human body and were the target of medical treatments. Phlegm was watery, while biles were associated with dry climates.

high plateaus, windy and damp, would be tall and fairly homogenous. Their character, however, would be rather unmanly. Those who dwell in a region with thin, dry, bare soil, where the climate is not temperate, here the people are likely to be hard, lean, and muscular, with yellowish skin rather than dark, and a stubborn and independent character and temperament. Where the changes of seasons are most frequent and differ radically from each other, there you will find the most diverse physiques, character, and nature.

Climate, then, is the greatest factor in diversity among people. Next come the land in which one is raised and the waters there. You will find, for the most part, that the physique of a man and his habits are formed by the nature of the land. Where the land is rich, soft, and well watered, and the waters are near the surface so that they become hot in the summer and cold in the winter, and where the climates are nice, there the men are flabby and jointless, bloated, lazy, and mostly cowards. Lack of eagerness and sleepiness are evident among them and they are stupid and witless. But where the land is barren, dry, harsh, and harried by storms in the winter or scorched by the sun in the summers, there one would find strong, lean, well-defined, muscular, and hairy men. By nature they are hard-working, wakeful, stubborn, and independent. They are fierce rather than gentle, more skilled, intelligent, and warlike than others. The things that grow in a land also conform to the climate.

These are the most diverse natures and physiques among men. You will not go wrong if you use these rules as a starting point for further observations.

2. Herodotus, *Histories* 3.12 (5th century BCE). *Herodotus sees what he considers to be a physical or genetic difference between Egyptians and Persians and explains that difference through a description of environment combined with cultural practices. (CSR)*

I saw a great marvel there, which I learned about from the locals. The bones of the people who died in the battle from each side were scattered separately (for the bones of the Persians were lying in one place, where they had been separated at the beginning, and the bones of the Egyptians in another place), and the skulls of the Persians were so weak that, if you wanted to strike one with a pebble, you would pierce through it. The heads of the Egyptians, though, were so strong indeed that you would hardly break through, even if you struck them with a big rock. [2] They say that the cause of this phenomenon is as follows (and they persuaded me easily): The Egyptians, right from childhood, shave their heads and the bone is thickened in the sun. [3] This is the same reason why they do not become bald—Egyptians have the fewest number of bald men out of all mankind. [4] This, then, is why Egyptian men have strong heads. The Persians have weak heads because they wear felt hats from birth to shelter themselves from the sun. This is how things stand now. I also saw other similar things among those who were destroyed at Pampremis together with Achaemenes the son of Darius by Inaros of Libya.

3. Herodotus, *Histories* 9.122 (5th century BCE). *At the very end of his* Histories, *Herodotus relates an anecdote about Cyrus, the first king of Persia, and correlates the toughness of a people with the harshness of their climate. (RFK)*

Artayctes, who was hung up,[33] had a grandfather named Artembares. He introduced the Persians to the following idea, which they took up and proposed to Cyrus: "Since Zeus has given hegemony to the Persians, and to you in particular, Cyrus, once you've destroyed Astyages, let us go! For we possess a meager and rugged land. Let's depart and dwell elsewhere. There are many lands both near and far that, possessing them, we would truly be worth the admiration of all. It is reasonable for men who rule an empire to do such things. Indeed, when will there be a better opportunity than now, since we rule over many men and the whole of Asia?" Cyrus listened but was not impressed by what they wanted to do. Instead, he exhorted them and offered the following comment: "Do it, if you want. But be prepared to rule no longer but be ruled instead. For soft men tend to come from soft lands. It's not common for marvelous fruits and men courageous in war to grow from the same earth." The Persians agreed, defeated by Cyrus' logic, and decided to return home. They thus chose to dwell in a poor land and rule rather than sow rich soil and be slaves to others.

4. Xenophon, *Agesilaos* 1.27–28 (4th century BCE). *King Agesilaos II (444–360 BCE) invaded Persia in 396 BCE, claiming to liberate Greek cities in Asia Minor from Persian control. In this passage, he has gathered his forces together in Ephesus to prepare for a campaign. (CSR)*

1.27. How encouraging would that be to have seen Agesilaos followed by his crowned soldiers marching from the gymnasium to dedicate their crowns to Artemis? For when men revere the gods, train in warfare, and exercise obedience, how is it not likely that everything they do is filled with noble aspirations? 28. Agesilaos, believing that despising one's enemy emboldens men to fight, instructed heralds to sell the barbarians, stripped naked, who had been captured in raids. The soldiers saw how pale their skin was from never

---

33. Artayctes was a Persian noble. When the Greeks were advancing to tear down the Persians' bridge over the Hellespont, he attempted to bribe them to let him and his son live. The Greeks hung him on the bridge and forced him to watch his son be stoned to death.

stripping[34] and saw that they were fat and lazy from always riding in litters. They concluded that fighting a war with them would be little different from fighting against women. Then, Agesilaos announced that he would lead them immediately by a shortcut to the best region in Asia Minor so that they could prepare their bodies and minds for battle as if preparing for an athletic contest.

5. Aristotle, *Politics* 7.5.6 (1327b) (4th century BCE). *Aristotle reflects the tensions found in* Airs, Waters, Places *between environmental and cultural reasons for differences in character and physical features. (RFK)*

Concerning the citizen population, we stated earlier what the maximum number should be. Now, let's discuss the innate characters of that population. One could potentially learn this from observing the most famous cities among the Greeks and how the rest of the inhabited world is divided up among the various peoples. The peoples living in cold climates and Europe are full of courage but lack intelligence and skill. The result is a state of continual freedom but a lack of political organization and ability to rule over others. The peoples of Asia, however, are intelligent and skilled but cowardly. Thus they are in a perpetual state of subjection and enslavement. The races of the Greeks are geographically in between Asia and Europe. They also are "in between" character-wise, sharing attributes of both—they are intelligent and courageous. The result is a continually free people, the best political system, and the ability to rule over others (if they happen to unify under a single constitution).

6. [Aristotle], *Physiognomics* 806b15 (4th century BCE). *Physical characteristics and geography are here linked to determine character in birds and men. (RFK)*

In general, the same holds true among birds—stiff-winged birds are brave and soft-winged birds are cowardly. The same is observable among quails and cocks as well. Likewise, this can be seen among the races of men. For those men who dwell in the north have stiff hair and are courageous, while those who dwell further south are cowardly and have soft hair.

7. Cicero, *On Divination* 2.96–97 (1st century BCE). *Cicero refutes the astrological theory that the stars are responsible for the diversity of peoples by referring to environmental factors. (CSR/MLG)*

2.96. Can there be any doubt that many people who have been born with some unnatural deformity are restored and corrected by nature herself

---

34. Stripping naked for work or exercise was a Greek practice.

(when she comes to her senses), or through some skill or medicine? For example, people whose tongues have become stuck and could not speak are relieved by a cut of the scalpel. In fact, many people have removed a natural fault by careful effort, just as Demetrius of Phaleron has written about Demosthenes. When the orator could not say the Greek letter *rho*, constant practice allowed him to pronounce it very clearly. But if the constellations created and influenced these conditions, no amount of effort could change them. What about the different environments? Don't they produce dissimilar men? Such differences are indeed easy to list—the differences, for example, of body and character among the Indians, Persians, Ethiopians, and Syrians. There is unbelievable variety and differentiation.

2.97. These differences prove that the environmental situation has more influence on birth than the moon's state. Surely the rumor is false that for 470,000 years the Babylonians have taken the horoscopes of children on their birth and tested the results. Really, if that was their custom, then they would not have stopped. But we have no authority to say that it is now performed or know that it ever was!

8. Vitruvius, *On Architecture* 6.1.3–5, 6.1.8–11 excerpted (1st century CE). *In book six of his treatise on architecture, Vitruvius argues that buildings should be appropriate to their environment by comparing how nature adapts the human body to its local environment. (RFK)*

6.1.3. We should observe and examine the effects of environment on buildings and should observe also nature's effects on the limbs and bodies of various peoples. For the sun produces only moderate heat in some places where it maintains temperate bodies. As for those places that advance near the sun, the inhabitants burn and the sun removes the moisture from them. In contrast, in cold regions, the moisture is not taken from the complexions of those who live there because they are far from the south. Instead, dewy-moist air pours down from the sky onto their bodies and gives them larger physiques and deeper voices. These same people who dwell in the north receive from the ample moisture and cool air tall bodies, fair complexions, straight red hair, blue eyes, and a lot of blood. [4] Those peoples who dwell near the southern axis, however, and who live nearer to the course of the sun are shaped by its violence with shorter stature, dark complexions, curly hair, black eyes, strong legs, and a limited amount of blood. On account of this limited supply of blood, they are afraid to stand in a battle line, but, since their bodies are nourished by fire, they endure heat and fevers without fear. This is unlike the bodies of those living in the north, whose bodies are weakened and enfeebled by fever, but who have no fear in battle since they have ample blood to spare. [5] As with the bodies, no less so do the voices of the various peoples differ. . . .

Vitruvius goes on to describe the shape of the world and to explain with comparison to a triangular, stringed instrument known to the Greeks as a sambucê *how its regions differ according to their distance from the sun and equator.*

6.1.8. Indeed, the phenomenon that deeper voices prevail in damper regions while higher-pitched voices occur in hot ones can be observed through an experiment. Take two cups,[35] fired for the same amount of time in the same furnace and that have the same weight and make the same sound when struck. Of these two cups, dip one in water and, after removing it, strike both it and the dry cup. When done, each generates a distinctively different sound as well as has different weight. Similarly, human bodies that are shaped in the same way and that are born in the same world vary according to their specific conditions. Some, under the influence of heat, have high, sharp voices, while others speak very deeply because of the abundance of moisture in the air around them. [9] Likewise, southern peoples are moved rather quickly toward the devising of plans because the dry air renders their minds sharp as opposed to northern people, who have sluggish minds slowed by the thick air and chilling dampness. These same effects can be observed in snakes: they move most quickly when the heat has dried out any chilling dampness in the air, but become motionless and sluggish during the seasons when the weather turns rainy and cold. It should not be surprising, then, if warm air renders the minds of men more astute while the cold slows their wits. [10] Of course, although southern peoples have the keenest minds and infinite cleverness in making plans, when it actually comes time to act bravely on those plans, they fail because the courage has been sucked out of their bodies by the sun. Those who are born in colder regions are more prepared for the violence of battle. Draped in great courage, they know no fear, though due to their slow wits, they rush into battle without thought and are thwarted by their lack of tactics and planning. Since the world, then, is allocated as it is, and since all peoples are distinguished by their varied mixture, truly we can see that it is the Roman people who are positioned in the direct center of the entire world. [11] Regarding the need for bravery, the people in Italy are the most balanced in both their physical build and their strength of mind. For just as the planet Jupiter is tempered due to running its course between the extreme heat of Mars and the extreme cold of Saturn, in the same manner, Italy, located between north and south and thereby balanced by a mixture of both, garners unmatched praise. By its policies, it holds in check the courageousness of the barbarians [northerners], and by its strong hand, thwarts the cleverness of the southerners. Just so, the divine mind has allocated to the Roman state an eminent and temperate region so that they might become masters of the world.

---

35. Vitruvius here assumes a clay cup that unlike most modern ceramics has no glaze or sealant preventing moisture from penetrating it, rather similar in composition to a simple clay flowerpot, though thinner.

9. Manilius, *Astronomica* 4.711–730 (1st century CE). *Manilius links each of the astrological signs with the different parts of the human body as well as different regions of the earth. He sees this astrological association in tandem with environmental determinism. (RFK)*

For that reason, humankind is arranged by various standards and physical qualities, and peoples are fashioned with their own complexion, indicating through their physical appearance, as if by private treaty with nature, the shared society and similar substance of their people. Germany stands tall, with its towering offspring, all of it blonde, while Gaul is slightly dyed with a redness akin to Germans. Hardier Spain is an assemblage of compact, sturdy limbs. Romulus endows the Romans with the face of Mars and, through the union of Mars and Venus, a well-balanced proportion of limbs, while clever Greece announces through its well-tanned people [720] their preference for athletics, especially manly wrestling. Curly hair at the temples reveals the Syrian. The Ethiopians defile the earth and form a people drenched in shadows, while India bears people less burnt. Egypt, flooded by the Nile, darkens its people more gently because of the well-watered fields nearby and makes their complexions only moderately dark by its mild climate. Apollo, the sun god, dries out the people of Africa with dust in their desert sands, and Mauritania contains its name in the people's faces, [730] the title "mauritania" being one with the color itself.[36]

10. Seneca, *On Anger* 2.15 (1st century CE). *Seneca answers supposed objections to his view on anger. (MLG)*

An objection: "You can recognize that anger has something noble in it when you see the free tribes, such as the Germans and the Scythians, who are the most prone to anger." The answer: this happens because a naturally brave and steadfast character is inclined to anger before training softens it. Certain virtues, as you know, are inborn only in better characters, like a vigorous and stout copse of trees created by the earth without human cultivation. Fertile soil makes a tall forest. Therefore, a person with a naturally brave character becomes enraged, and their fiery and ardent personality has nothing delicate or meager. This spiritedness, however, is incomplete as is everything that originates from a natural good alone without any art. If it is not quickly controlled, a personality prone to bravery becomes accustomed to a reckless temerity. Why? Are not the gentler vices, such as pity, love, and modesty, connected to the milder temperaments? Yes. So I shall show you how a good trait also has its own inherent bad qualities. Even if these traits are characteristic of a better nature, they remain nonetheless vices. In addition, all those fierce tribes of yours, like lions and like wolves, can no more be a slave than they can be a general. This is because they do not have the

---

36. Mauretania derives from the Greek *maurousia*, meaning "darkened."

power of human intelligence but the force of an unmanageable beast. No one can rule unless he can also be ruled. The result is that nearly all those people who live in moderate climates live in empires. Those who live in cold climates facing the north have "uncontrolled temperaments," as the poet says, "and very similar to their climate."

11. Pliny the Elder, *Natural Histories* **2.79–80**[37] **(1st century CE).** *Pliny combines environmental theory with astrological explanations for behaviors and characteristics, a common combination among Roman authors. (CSR)*

2.79. Some people observe a day one way, others, another way. The Babylonians measure a day between two sunrises; the Athenians measure it between two sunsets. The Umbrians measure it from midday to midday; the general population measures it from daylight to darkness; the Roman priests and those who keep track of the official day, the Egyptians and Hipparchus likewise, measure it from midnight to midnight. There appear to be shorter intervals of daylight between sunrises around the solstices than around the equinoxes, because around the equinoxes the position of the zodiac is more at a slant, but near the solstice it is straighter overhead.

80. We must add to these observations the connection to heavenly causes. It is not in doubt that the Ethiopians are burned by the heat of the sun, which is nearer to them, and are born like burned people with their beards and hair frazzled. On the opposite and icy side of the world there are peoples with white skin and light-colored hair. The latter races are wild because of the cold, the former lackluster because of the weather's fickleness. We can look to the legs for similar evidence. For those who live in the cold, their humors are drawn into the higher regions of their bodies; for those who live in the heat, it is driven away into the lower parts. In cold regions savage beasts are produced; in the warm regions various kinds of animals, especially birds, are nourished by the heat. In both cases, their size is huge—in the warm climates because of the pressure of the heat, in the cold climates by the nourishment of moisture.

But in the middle of the world there is a healthy mixture of hot and cold. The lands are fertile for all things, and the people's bodies appear moderate in size and color because of this proper mixture. We find gentle customs, clear thoughts, and temperaments open and capable of understanding all of nature. Similarly, empires occur in the middle. Empires have never arisen among the most remote races. Those in remote climates are cut off and solitary because of the force of their savage natures, and they have never been subjugated by the inhabitants of the middle region.

---

37. The text of Pliny has multiple numbering systems due to the many extant manuscripts. For this volume, we have opted to number the selections of Pliny according to the book and paragraph numbers and have excluded the addition "scroll" numbers typically presented in Roman numerals in the various editions. See About the Sources for information on the text of Pliny used for these translations.

12. Apuleius, *Apology* 24 (2nd century CE). *Apuleius, defending himself from charges of using magic, argues from a Platonic notion of the immortality of the soul that environmental theories of race are foolish.*[38] *(MLG)*

Now, concerning my homeland: it is, as you show from my own writings, located on the border of Numidia and Gaetulia. In those writings I openly stated, when I spoke publicly in the presence of the honorable Lollianus Avitus, that I am half Numidian and half Gaetulian. I see no reason why I should feel any shame in that! It was the same for Cyrus the Great, since he was of mixed race: half Mede and half Persian.

Of course we should examine not the place of birth but the moral character of a person. We should weigh not the region but the way a person lives his life. Cabbage-sellers and wine merchants are rightly allowed to recommend cabbage and wine based on the nobility of the soil in which it is grown. For example, Thasian wine or Philisian cabbage. Obviously, the nourishment of the earth provides great support for better flavor, as does the fertility of the region, a wet climate, calm winds, and bright sun and rich soil.

But of course the soul of the man comes from outside to settle in the lodging of the body. So how can even the tiniest bit of virtue or vice be added to it from the place of birth? Although some races have been seen to be remarkable for either stupidity or cleverness, is it not a fact that all races have produced people of differing talents? Was not the philosopher Anacharsis born among the idiotic Scythians? Was not Meletides the idiot born among the clever Athenians? I don't speak this way because I am ashamed of my homeland, although we were once the town of King Syfax. But when he was defeated, the Roman people gave us as a gift to King Masinissa. Recently we have been settled by veteran soldiers and become a most glorious colony. My father was one of the leaders of this colony, a *duovir*,[39] who held every post of honor. As soon as I began to take part in public affairs, I maintained his status in that republic, I hope, with equal dignity and respect. Why have I said all this? So that you, Aemilianus, will after this get less angry with me and instead forgive me if through some chance negligence I did not choose to be born in your Attic Zarat.

13. Ptolemy, *Tetrabiblos* 2.2 (2nd century CE). *Ptolemy distinguishes two types of astrology: universal astrology for entire peoples, countries, or cities, and individual. In the following, he links the character and physique of a people to their location on the zodiac circle. (RFK)*

Concerning the Characteristic of Peoples According to General Region: The differentiation of ethnic character is determined according to the general

---

38. Cf. Plato, *Timaeus* 24, Chapter 7, Section 1, where he suggests Athenian superiority is linked to their environment.

39. Title granted to one member of a dual magistracy.

parallels and angles, by their position in relation to the circle at the center of the zodiac and the sun.[40] For while our region is in one of the northern quarters, those who dwell under more southerly parallels—and I am speaking here of those from the equator up to the summer tropic[41]—who have the sun directly overhead and burn as a result, have black skin, wooly, thick hair, compacted bodies, and wasted, slender physiques. Their natures are hot and their character is generally savage since their homes are continually oppressed by the heat. These people we bring together under the name "Ethiopians." Not only are we all witness to this state among them, but even the other animals and the plants of the region show evidence of baking.

Those who dwell in the more northerly parallels—I mean those who have the Bears directly overhead—they are far from the center of the zodiac and the sun's heat. As a result, they are chilled. They live in a moisture-rich region, which is especially nourishing and not desiccated by the heat of the sun. Because of this, the people are white-skinned, straight-haired, and have large and well-nourished physiques. Their natures are cold. They, too, are savage, as a general characteristic, because their homes are constantly cold. It thus follows that the wintry climate affects the size of their plants and the wildness of the animals the same way it affects the people. We tend to give these people the general name "Scythians."

Those who dwell between the summer tropic and the Bears, because the sun neither appears directly overhead nor far off from the vertical during its midday course, partake of a balanced climate and, though the weather does vary, it fluctuates only a little. In this region, the people are medium-skinned, have middling height, and are mild-mannered, sociable, and civilized. Of these peoples, those further south are generally wittier, more ingenious, and more adequately versed in divine matters because of their proximity to the zodiac and the stars revolving around it. This proximity gives them active souls that are contemplative, curious, and particularly good at grasping that field of study we call mathematics. Of those people, those to the east are healthier, have more vigorous souls, and are transparent in all ways. This is likely because those in the east receive a passionate nature from the sun. That region follows a solar cycle, is masculine, and right-handed. For this reason, we see that the right sides of animals there are stronger and more vigorous. Those to the west are more womanly, softer-souled, and secretive in all ways, since, again, this region is lunar—always the moon rises first here and makes its way from the direction of the southwest wind. On account of this, it seems a nocturnal region, womanly, and, contrary to the east, left-handed . . .

---

40. Parallels are positions north and south; angles, east and west.
41. The Tropic of Cancer, which runs through northern Africa.

*✎ **14. Vegetius, *On Military Matters* 1.2 (5th century CE).** In his discussions of Roman military practices, Vegetius includes a discussion of the composition of the army and the use of foreign auxiliaries. (CSR)*

The proper order of things demands that we should treat in the first part of this tract the provinces or peoples from which recruits ought to be picked. It is, of course, agreed that cowardly and brave men are born everywhere. Nevertheless, one race surpasses another in war. Climates have a great influence not only on the strength of bodies, but also of minds. We will not omit the places where these things occur, which have been verified by the most learned men. The dryness caused by excessive heat affects all tribes living near the sun. They are said to be quick-witted, it is true, but they have less blood and therefore lack the steadfastness and confidence to fight hand to hand, because people who know that they have little blood fear wounds. On the other hand, the northern peoples, who are remote from the fires of the sun, deliberate less but overflow with blood and so are most eager for war. Therefore, recruits ought to be chosen from more temperate climates. These people possess a good supply of blood for wounds and thus also contempt for death. Furthermore, they cannot lack good sense, which preserves moderation in war camps and is more than a little useful in arguments in the assemblies.

CHAPTER 4

GENETIC THEORIES

Genetic theories reflect an understanding of inherited physical characteristics. In some cases, moral characteristics were also considered heritable. One major strand in genetic thought dealt with the idea of autochthony—the idea that a people were born from the earth and were somehow more "pure" than others. These genetic theories are inextricably bound up with cultural theories, since the Greeks and Romans believed the moral qualities of the people would give rise to certain types of political or social arrangement. They also appear in conjunction with environmental theories (e.g., the Hippocratic Airs, Waters, Places *14 concerning the Macrocephalai).*

1. Athenian Citizenship Law of 451 BCE (from Plutarch, *Life of Pericles* **37.1–5).** *The Citizenship Law was passed at the height of Athenian power in the Aegean and restricted citizenship to children born of two Athenian citizen parents. This passage is the fullest description of the law and its details. (MLG)*

After the community put the remaining generals and leaders on trial for their conduct in the war,[42] there was clearly no one left who had the requisite authority or required dignity for such leadership. They longed for Pericles and called him to the speaker's platform to accept the generalship. Pericles at the time was lying depressed at home because of his sorrow, but he was persuaded by Alcibiades and the rest of his friends to come forward.[43] [2] After the people had apologized for their foolish behavior toward him, he once again took up public affairs and was elected general. He then asked that the law about children with only one Athenian parent be repealed. Although he himself had introduced this law, he now did not want his name and family line to be completely wiped out through lack of descendants. [3] The following circumstances surrounded the law. Many years earlier when Pericles was at the height of his political power and had legitimate children (as was said), he proposed a law that only children born from two Athenian parents were to be Athenian.

---

42. Plutarch inserts the note on the Citizenship Law into his description of events in 429 BCE.

43. Pericles lost both of his citizen-sons in the plague.

It happened that the king of Egypt sent 40,000 measures of grain as a gift, and it was necessary to divide it up among the citizens. Many private lawsuits sprang up from this law against illegitimate citizens, who had till then escaped notice or been overlooked. Very many suffered from the prosecuting informers. [4] As a result of the scrutiny, a little less than 5,000 were convicted and sold into slavery; 14,040 were judged Athenian citizens and remained in the polity. [5] And so it was terrible that a law, which had powerfully affected so many, be repealed by the very man who proposed it. However, the present misfortune of Pericles' family, seeming a sort of penalty for his contempt and arrogance, moved the Athenians to pity. Since they considered that he was suffering retribution and that his request was only human, they allowed him to enroll his illegitimate son in the *phratry* and give him his name.[44] And it was this son who later won a naval victory against the Peloponnesians at Arginusae and whom the people put to death along with his fellow generals.

2. Herodotus, *Histories* **3.101.2 (5th century BCE).** *In the course of his description of the peoples of India, Herodotus refers to an ancient theory on the relationship between the color of skin and the color of semen. (RFK)*

The Indians have skin nearly identical to the Ethiopians. The semen of the Indians, the seed they ejaculate into their women, is not white like that of other men, but is black like their skin. This is the same as the semen of the Ethiopians.[45]

3. Euripides, *Suppliants* **219–225 (5th century BCE).** *Theseus, king of Athens, condemns Adrastus, king of Argos, for marrying his daughters to foreigners, thus corrupting his city with non-Argive blood. (RFK)*

Theseus: You, Adrastus, appear to me to be among this company, a fool. You followed the oracles of Apollo and gave your daughters to foreigners to marry, as if gods, not mortals, decided marriages. But doing so, you have mingled your clear line with a muddy one and sorely wounded your house.

---

44. Scholars debate whether the exception was made only for Pericles' son or if the law was suspended for others as well. A *phratry* was a kinship group around which local governments were often formed. Athenian citizens often had their sons registered both in their kin group and with the city, through registration with their local government (the *deme*). While it was necessary that a citizen be registered in a *deme*, it does not seem to have been necessary that they be registered with a *phratry*.

45. Cf. Aristotle, *History of Animals* 3.22 (523a17–18), "The semen of all animals is white. Herodotus was utterly deceived when he wrote that Ethiopians ejaculate black semen."

4. Euripides, *Ion* 57–75, 260–272, 289–296, 585–594, 1295–1305, 1569–1594 (5th century BCE). *Euripides' Ion tells the story of the reunion of Creusa, princess of Athens and descendant of Erechtheus/ Erichthonious,*[46] *the autochthon (born from the earth), with her lost son by Apollo, Ion. The play's numerous plot twists are enabled by the focus on the Athenians' autochthonous birth and xenophobia. (RFK)*

57–75. Hermes: Creusa, the one who bore him, was married to Xuthus under the following circumstances: A wave of war crashed over Athens and the Chalcidians, who hold sway in Euboea. Xuthus was deemed worthy of being Creusa's husband through his efforts in the war even though he was foreign born, an Achaean, the son of Zeus' son Aeolus. Now, although they have planted many a seed in their marriage bed, Xuthus and Creusa have long been childless. For this reason, they have come to the oracle of Apollo, longing for children. Little do they know that Apollo Loxias was who had driven them to this fate, nor has he been unaware of them, so it seems. For when they enter the oracle, Apollo will give Xuthus this child [Ion], claiming that it is Xuthus' natural-born son. Later, Apollo will arrange for Creusa, the child's true mother, to recognize that the boy entering her household is, in fact, the child she bore to Loxias. Everyone will win! Loxias' rape will remain concealed and the boy will receive his proper birthright. Apollo will also ensure that the boy, the founder of Asian lands, will be called Ion throughout Greece.

260–272. Creusa and Ion meet in the temple, where Creusa has gone to pray concerning her lost child and where Ion works as an attendant.

Creusa: Creusa is my name, Erechtheus, my father, the city of Athens, my fatherland.

Ion: You amaze me, lady. You live in a famous city and are born from noble ancestry.

Creusa: I am fortunate in this regard, stranger, but in nothing more.

Ion: By the gods, tell me truly, as the story is told among mortals . . .

Creusa: What is it, stranger, that you want to learn? Ask it.

Ion: Did your ancestors really sprout from the earth?

Creusa: Erichthonious did, yes; not that my race benefits me at all.

Ion: And did Athena really take him up from the earth?

Creusa: Yes, and right into her virgin hands; she didn't give birth to him.

Ion: And then she gave him, as paintings usually show . . .

Creusa: . . . to the daughters of Cecrops to keep safe and hidden.

---

46. There is much confusion in Athenian mythology about these figures. By 412 BCE, the genealogy has settled: Erichthonious is the first autochthon, while his descendant Erechtheus is king of Athens and father of Creusa. Erichthonious is half-man, half-serpent—common among autochthons and similar to the non-Athenian autochthon Cecrops. It is Erechtheus who fights the battle against Poseidon's son and is killed by Poseidon at the spot on the Acropolis now marked by the Erechtheum.

289–296.

Ion: Who of the Athenians married you, lady?

Creusa: He isn't a citizen, but an import[47] from another land.

Ion: Who is he? He must be of noble race.

Creusa: Xuthus, born of Aeolus and descended from Zeus.

Ion: And how did this foreigner get to marry someone as well-born as you?

Creusa: There is a city in Euboea, which is near Athens . . .

Ion: Separated by only a watery boundary, they say.

Creusa: Well, he attacked this city as an ally of the Cecropidae.[48]

Ion: He came as a mercenary and was then married to you?

Creusa: Yes. He took me as a war-won dowry and a spear-prize.

> *585–594. Xuthus is told by the oracles that Ion is his son and announces to Ion that he will return to Athens and become his heir.*

Ion (to Xuthus): Matters don't look the same from far off as they do seen close up. I welcome the fate that led me to find out you're my father. But, father, listen to what's on my mind. It's said that the famous Athenians are autochthonous, born from the earth, not an immigrant race. Thus I'll be showing up there with two black marks against me. First, my father is a foreigner. Second, I'm a bastard by birth.

> *1295–1305. When she learns that Xuthus intends to bring Ion (whom she believes is Xuthus' son by a foreign woman) home, Creusa tries to murder Ion to prevent him from inheriting the Athenian kingship.*

Creusa: You were intending to live in my house, taking it from me by force.

Ion: So you were trying to kill me in fear of what I intended?

Creusa: Why wouldn't I kill you unless this wasn't your intent?

Ion: Are you jealous because you are childless and my father found me?

Creusa: Are you trying to steal the house of those without children?

Ion: Look, my father is giving me his land.

Creusa: How does the race of Aeolus have a share with the race of Pallas?[49]

---

47. The Greek term used here is typically used for mercenaries and emphasizes the view of Creusa that she is a war prize.

48. Cecropidae are descendants of Cecrops; it is another way of naming the Athenians.

49. Inheritance is by birth only, thus Creusa asks by what right Ion, whom she does not know is her son, inherits the land of *her* ancestors from someone not related to her family by birth. Further, the phrase "to have a share in" implies citizenship, which, based on the Citizenship Law of 451 BCE, was from two citizen parents only, though some scholars argue that citizenship was opened to some inhabitants with only one citizen parent during the years 430-403 BCE because of heavy losses during the Peloponnesian War.

Ion: He earned your house by arms, not words.

Creusa: The mercenary is nothing but an inhabitant, a colonist, of the land.

Ion: And there is no share in my father's land for me?

Creusa: His spear and shield—that's the full extent of your share of *this* land.

> *After Ion attempts to murder Creusa in turn and the situation has reached an absurd peak, Ion and Creusa recognize their relationship through tokens left with him when she abandoned him at birth. Athena descends to further put things right. The genealogy she establishes for the Dorians and Achaeans is inconsistent with earlier mythological genealogies and seems to reflect Athenian propaganda.*

1569–1594. Athena: But now listen to what I have to say, so that I may bring this business to an end and fulfill the god's oracles, which is why I harnessed my chariot. Creusa, you are to take this child with you to Cecrops' land and establish him on the royal throne. As a descendant of Erechtheus, he has a right to rule over my land, and his fame will spread throughout Greece. His sons—four from the one root—will give their names to the land and to the native tribes of the land, the inhabitants of my cliff. The firstborn will be Geleon, then the second < . . . > the Hopletes and the Argades, and the Aegicores, named after my aegis, will constitute a single tribe. Then in due course of time the children of these four will found communities on the islands of the Cyclades and the coastal mainland, whose might will support my land. They will also colonize opposite sides of the straits on the two continents, Asia and Europe. They will be named Ionians, after your son here, and they will win great renown. You and Xuthus will have children together: Dorus, whose descendants, the Dorians, will be celebrated throughout the land of Pelops. The second son, Achaeus, will be king of the coastland near Rhion, and a people named after him will be marked with his name.

5. Euripides, *Phoenician Women* 818–821, 931–944 (5th century BCE).

Euripides' play, performed in Athens some time between 411 and 408 BCE, is set after the events recounted in plays such as Sophocles' Oedipus the King. *In the play, Oedipus and Jocasta are still alive and in Thebes while their sons, Eteocles and Polyneices, are disputing rule of the city. Polyneices, denied his turn to rule, marched upon the city with an army from Argos. In order to save the city, Creon, brother of Jocasta, is told he must sacrifice his son Menoiceus. The Theban royal family is autochthonous. (RFK)*

818–821. Chorus: O Gaia, you bore, you bore once, as I heard, as I learned from a barbarian long ago back home, I learned that you bore a people from the cut teeth of the dragon, a beast nourished on beasts and blood-crested, this birth a most noble reproach to the Thebans.

931–944. Tiresias: It is necessary to offer Menoiceus as a sacrifice, pouring out his blood in the chamber where Dirce, the earth-born dragon, was born and served as a watchman over the sacred spring. His sacrifice will be an appeasement for the ancient wrath of Ares, who seeks vengeance against Cadmus for the murder of his earth-born serpent. If you do this, you will gain Ares as an ally in battle. And if she receives fruit for fruit, mortal blood for dragon blood, Gaia will be well-minded toward you, Gaia who once sent forth to us the Sparti, gold-helmeted men sown in the earth. One must die who is descended from the dragon. You are the only remaining descendant of the Sparti, the Sown Men, pure of blood on both the mother's and father's side.

6. Euripides, *Bacchae* 538–544 (5th century BCE). *The* Bacchae *(405 BCE) tells the story of the god Dionysus' return to his mother's home city. The anger of his nephew King Pentheus is linked to his autochthony. (RFK)*

Chorus: Such, such rage, Pentheus, of the earth-born race, once born of the dragon, shows forth. Pentheus, whom Echion, the earth-born, bore. He is not a mortal, but a savage monster, like a blood-thirsty giant[50] rivaling the gods.

7. Plato, *Timaeus* 18d–19a (4th century BCE). *Socrates and Timaeus discuss the creation of the universe, beginning from the nature of the ideal city and how people in such a city would be allotted to particular roles according to their "nature." (RFK)*

18d. Socrates: "What about the issue of child-rearing? Or is this easy to remember on account of the novelty of our conclusions? We concluded that everything pertaining to marriage and children should be estab-lished as communal, shared by all, thus ensuring that no parent would recognize their own particular offspring at any point. The reason for this would be so that everyone would consider everyone as family—those of similar age with a person would become sisters and brothers, those older would be parents or grandparents according to age, and those younger would be as children or grandchildren."

Timaeus: "Yes, as you say, that is easy to recall."

------

50. The giants are another group of monsters classified as autochthons. Others include the gorgons and the venomous snakes of Libya (see Sallust Chapter 8, Selection 4, and Lucan Chapter 8, Selection 8).

18e. Socrates: "Well, then, do you not also recall what we said concerning the rulers, male and female alike, how they would be brought to their fullest natural potential? To the best of our ability, it was considered necessary to contrive secretly through some sort of mating lottery that inferior people and noble people mated separately from each other, like with like, but they must believe that it was chance, not contrivance, that allotted them in this way lest some enmity arise between the groups over the mating issue."

Timaeus: "Yes, we recall all this."

19a. Socrates: "And further we said that the offspring of noble people were to be reared while those of inferior people were to be assigned secretly to another polis. As these children grew up, those charged with keeping constant watch over them would need to bring back to the city those deemed worthy while taking back to that other land in exchange those deemed by them unworthy."

> **8. Plato, *Republic* 414d–415c, 459a–e (4th century BCE).** *In the first selection, Socrates is being asked to relate what "Phoenician tale"[51] he would tell to the people in his ideal city-state in order to convince them that the hierarchical social structure they lived under was rooted in their very natures and should be followed. The second selection is a conversation with Glaucon on the proposed proper marriage practices for the ideal city. (RFK)*

414d–415c. Socrates: "Indeed, I'll tell you—I don't really know, though, what sort of daring or what sort of words I'll use. First, I will try to persuade the rulers and generals, then the rest of the polis, that everything we raised them to and taught them, everything they experienced or that happened to them, was nothing more than a dream. During that time, they were actually encased below the earth and were being shaped and nourished there while they, their weapons, and the rest of their necessities were being created. When they were altogether brought to perfection, the earth, their mother, gave birth to them,[52] and now if anyone should attack her, it is necessary that they take counsel and defend the land as if their homeland were their mother and their nursemaid. They consider the rest of the citizens to be their brothers and children."

Glaucon: "Well, it's not without reason, Socrates, that you were ashamed not too long ago to tell us this lie."

---

51. A Phoenician tale is an unbelievable story told for the benefit of others, a noble lie.
52. A variation of the autochthony theme.

Socrates: "Of course I was! Nevertheless, listen to the rest of the story. For while all are brothers in the city, as we will tell it in our tale, the god, when he created those fit to rule, mixed gold into their generation. Thus they are the most honored. Those who help them are mixed with silver. Iron and bronze make up the farmers and craftsmen. Although everyone is related by birth and you only breed with those like yourself, there is a chance that a silver child may be born from gold and from a silver father comes the occasional gold, and so on and so forth from the rest. And so, the god, first and foremost commands that the rulers keep a vigilant eye upon the offspring in case there is an intermixing among the groups in their souls. And if their children are ever born tainted with bronze or iron, they are to show no manner of pity and cast the children out and assign them to the place appropriate to their status among the farmers and craftsmen. And if the opposite happens and a child of gold or silver is born to a bronze or iron parent, honor the child and raise it up among either the guardians or the helpers. Tell the people that there is an oracle that explains that should an iron or bronze guard ever serve as guardian, the city would be destroyed. Do you see any way to persuade the people to believe this story?"

459a–e. Glaucon and Socrates discuss marriage.

Socrates: "How then will they be most useful? Tell me this, Glaucon: I see that you have in your house a great many hunting dogs and pedigreed cocks. Do you give much thought to how they couple and breed?"

Glaucon: "Sure I do." Socrates: "Okay. Firstly, among your animals, though all pedigreed, don't certain ones produce the best offspring?"

Glaucon: "They do!" Socrates: "Well, then, do you breed them equally? Or are you especially intent on breeding from the best stock?"

Glaucon: "From the best, of course." Socrates: "And how about the youngest or the oldest? Or do you prefer to use those in their prime?"

Glaucon: "Those in their prime." Socrates: "And if they aren't bred this way, do you suppose your dogs and cocks would be the worse for it? The stock pedigree diminished?"

Glaucon: "They would, yes."

Socrates: "What about horses, and other animals? Does the same go for them?"

Glaucon: "It would be odd if it didn't."

Socrates: "Well, then, let me tell you, dear friend. Obviously it is of the utmost importance that our chief leaders also take care of breeding if the principle holds the same with humans."

Glaucon: "It does apply. What of it?"

Socrates: "It means that it is necessary for them to use many remedies, I said. We decided before that a less qualified doctor was sufficient for treating a body not in need of medicine, but wanting only diet and exercise. But whenever prescribing medications is needed, we know that a more exceptional doctor is necessary."

Glaucon: "This is true. But what's your point?"

Socrates: "My point is this: our leaders will need to use many and altogether convincing lies for the sake of the ruled. We said, I believe, that in the case of medicines, all such tricks were useful."

Glaucon: "So right."

Socrates: "Well, in marriage and childbearing, it would seem that there is no small need for this kind of 'right' action."

Glaucon: "How so?"

Socrates: "Given this fact, it is necessary that the best breed with the best as often as possible and the worst breed with the worst as infrequently as possible. It is also necessary that the children of the best be raised and those of the worst not be. Additionally, if our flock is to be at its peak, everything we have done to make it so needs to remain hidden from everyone except the rulers themselves. This is so especially if the herd of guardians is to be as free from unrest as possible."

9. Plato, *Menexenus* 237b–238b, 238e–239a (4th century BCE). *Plato's version of an Athenian funeral oration emphasizes the Athenian focus on their unusual origin. The theory of autochthony expands to include not only the descendants of Erichthonious but also any Athenian. Plato explicitly links Athenian autochthony to Athenian customs and culture. (MLG)*

237b–238b. I begin with their excellence of birth: The origin of their ancestors was not foreign. That origin revealed that their descendants were not immigrants come into this land from elsewhere, but were born from the soil and were living and dwelling truly in their fatherland. They were not nursed by a stepmother like other peoples, but by their mother, that is, the land where they live. They now lie dead in the very native lands that bore them, nourished them, and received them. It is most just to praise this mother first. In this way the men's excellence of birth also happens to be praised.

It is appropriate that the land be praised not only by us, but also by all mankind. This is the case for many reasons, but first and foremost because this land is dear to the gods. This fact is confirmed in the stories of how the gods contended for the land and how they judged her. How could a land praised by the gods not justly be praised by absolutely all mankind? A further praise for this land would be the following: At that time when the rest of the world was producing animals both wild and tame, this land of ours did not produce nor was it inhabited by wild beasts. Instead she chose from among all living creatures to give birth to man, an animal that surpasses the rest in intelligence and alone esteems justice and the gods.

A powerful proof can be found in the following story: The land herself gave birth to our ancestors and the ancestors of those buried here. This is because every child receives suitable nourishment from whoever gave birth to it, and by this fact a woman can be proved a true mother or not. If a mother has no fount of nourishment for the child, then she may have only pretended the child is hers. In this very way our land and mother provides sufficient proofs that she has given birth to humans. She alone at that time was the first to produce nourishment for humans in the form of wheat and barley. It is through these fruits that humans are best nourished because, in fact, the earth herself bore this human animal. Proofs of this sort should be more acceptable in the case of a land even than of a woman because the land does not imitate a woman in conception and birth, rather the woman imitates the land. Nor was the land stingy with this fruit, but distributed it to the rest of humanity. After this, she brought forth for her descendants the olive, a help for toils. After rearing and caring for her children up to the time of their youthful prime, she supplied gods to be leaders and teachers for them. The names of the gods we must pass over in this speech—we know them in any case. They ordered our lives not only with regards to our daily routines (they first taught us arts and skills), but they also taught us the procurement and use of weapons for the defense of the land.

238e–239a. The cause of our form of government lies in our equality of birth. Other communities are composed of an irregular and diverse people. As a result, their governments are irregular, both tyrannies and oligarchies. Thus, the inhabitants consider some slaves and some masters. But we in our community are all brothers from a single mother and think it is unworthy to be slaves and masters to one another. Instead, our natural equality of birth compels us to seek equality in law and to give way to no one except in reputation for excellence and intelligence.

10. Plato, *Laws* 3.692e–693a (4th century BCE). *Plato's Athenian connects mixed descent with slavery and unhappiness. (CSR)*

Athenian: Should someone say that Greece defended itself during the Persian Wars, they would be speaking incorrectly.[53] For if the intention of the Athenians and the Spartans in common had not been to ward off the oncoming slavery, then indeed all the races of the Greeks would be mixed up with each other now. And barbarians would have mingled with Greeks and Greeks with barbarians, just as the Persians rule over people now who are dispersed or gathered together and live unhappily.

11. Aristotle, *Politics* 5.2.10–11 (1303a25–40) (4th century BCE). *Aristotle discusses the nature of civil strife and how it has a tendency to*

---

53. The speaker is pointing out that Greece was not united in its resistance to Persia.

appear in cities where colonists do not share the same tribal or kinship descent,[54] though harmony can emerge when differences of tribe are set aside. (RFK)

Civil strife also results from a lack of shared tribal descent until a state of agreement or harmony is achieved. For just as a city does not emerge from a random group of people, it also does not emerge at a random time. In the past, most cities have admitted either new colonists from their home city, or even additional colonists from another Greek city, and factions then formed. For example, the Achaeans colonized Sybaris with the Troezians but then later on, since they increased in numbers, they ejected the Troezians from the city. The result was a curse on the Sybarites. At Thurii,[55] the Sybarites caused problems by claiming a larger portion of the land as their own and were expelled. At Byzantium, the colonists who had been admitted, but who were not from the same home city as the others, plotted against the other citizens and had to be expelled by force. The people of Antissa opened up their city to Chian exiles, who later had to be expelled by force. The Messinians were themselves expelled from their own city after they admitted Samian colonists. And the Apollonians who live on the Euxine fell into a state of faction after allowing colonists from outside their kinship circle.

12. Aristotle, *Politics* 1.1.5 (1252b), 1.2.7, 1.2.12–14, 1.2.18–19 (1254a–1255a excerpted) (4th century BCE). *Aristotle elaborates upon his theory of natural slavery, a theory that critics in ancient Greece and Rome countered with theories of custom. Like Plato does in* Menexenus, *Aristotle here attributes culture and custom to the innate characteristics of a people. (RFK)*

1.1.5. Among barbarians, the female and the slave have the same rank. The reason for this is that the barbarians do not have a concept of natural hierarchy,[56] but marriage is between a female slave and a male slave. Thus the poet says, "It is fitting that the Greek rules over the barbarian," which suggests that the barbarian and the slave are the same.[57]

. . .

---

54. The term used for shared tribal descent is *homophulos*. Although of different tribe or home city, they are all Greeks.

55. Unlike other colonies founded by the Greek poleis, Thurii was a Panhellenic colony, not a colony composed of people all from a single polis.

56. In the previous sections of *Politics*, Aristotle asserts a series of relationships that are premised in nature as being between a superior and an inferior: human and animal, man and woman, ruler and subject, master and slave.

57. This is a quotation from Euripides' *Iphigenia at Aulis*. The full line reads, "Mother, it is fitting that Greeks rule over barbarians but not barbarians over Greeks, since barbarians are slaves and Greeks are free" (1400).

1.2.7. From what we have said before, then, it is clear what a slave's nature is and what its capabilities are. For any human who does not belong to itself by nature, but to another, is a slave by nature. One qualifies as a human being belonging to another if he or she is the possession of another. By "possession" I mean someone used, a tool separable from the owner. We need to consider, however, whether such a person exists by nature or not, and whether there is justice or advantage to being a slave or if, on the contrary, all slavery is unnatural.

. . .

1.2.12–14. Again, in humans and animals it is the same—tamed animals are better by nature than wild ones, and for all such creatures it is better to be ruled by mankind since there is a benefit from being secure. Additionally, between man and woman, man is the stronger while woman is the weaker, thus men rule and women are ruled. The same must hold true among all humans. Men who differ from their fellow humans in the same way as a human soul is different from a human body or a man differs from a beast are slaves by nature. Those who fall into this category are those whose function is to provide physical labor, and that is the best they can do. For these people, being ruled over by an authority is better, just as it is for tame animals, and they engage with reason only to the extent that they understand it but do not actually possess it. Other animals do not understand reason but are slaves to their emotions.

. . .

1.2.18–19. Generally speaking, some people cling as much as possible to some principle of justice (for custom is an aspect of justice) wherein enslaving prisoners of war is just. However, at the same time they deny this possibility, since it is possible that the origin of a war is unjust and so those enslaved in an unjust war would not rightly be a slave. Otherwise, it might happen that those of the noblest blood become slaves or the descendants of slaves when they are captured in war and then sold. For this reason, they do not mean to say that Greeks are slaves but only barbarians. And yet, whenever they say this, they are, in fact, seeking nothing other than the idea of natural slavery about which we spoke earlier. For they are forced to say that some people are entirely slavish while others never are. The same principle applies to well-born nobles. They consider themselves noble not only at home but also when abroad and away from their own people, while they consider barbarian nobles to be "noble" only when they are at home among their own kind. The implication is that there is an absolute type of nobility and freedom [for Greeks] and a relative type of each [for barbarians]. . . .

CHAPTER 5

CUSTOM OR CULTURAL THEORIES

Cultural theories, or theories involving custom, reflect a belief among the ancient Greeks and Romans that religious practices, social and political institutions, language, and even clothing were aspects of ethnic or racial identity.

> **1. Aeschylus, *Suppliants* 234–294 (5th century BCE).** *This play (c.458 BCE) is the first in a trilogy that tells the tale of the Danaids, the fifty daughters of Danaus, who were forced to marry their Egyptian cousins. First they fled as suppliants to Greece, and then, after being forced to marry anyway, killed their husbands on their wedding night (all except one, that is). Here we see Pelasgus, the King of Argos, seeing them for the first time. The play considers what it means to be Greek—is it shared descent? Or is it shared customs and culture? This myth of the Danaids is also a focal point of discussion concerning the kinship of ancient Mediterranean peoples. (MLG)*

King Pelasgus: This group that we address is un-Hellenic, luxuriating in barbarian finery and delicate cloth. What country do they come from? The women of Argos, indeed of all Greek lands, do not wear such clothes. [240] It is astonishing that you dare to travel to this land, fearlessly, without heralds, without sponsors, without guides. And yet here are the branches of suppliants, laid out according to custom next to you in front of the assembled gods. This alone would assert your Greekness, but would cause only confusion, if your voice was not here to explain.

Chorus: You have spoken truly about our clothing. But for my part, how should I address you? As an official with holy staff of office or as the leader of the city?

King Pelasgus: As far as that goes, respond and answer me with good heart. For I am Pelasgus, the leader of this land, [250] offspring of the earthborn Palaechthon. The race that farms this land logically takes its name—Pelasgoi—from me, the leader. The whole land, through which the holy Strymon runs, to the setting sun, is my kingdom. It contains the land of the Perraiboi, and beyond the Pindos near the Paeonians, the mountains of Dodona. The wet sea is the border of my land. These are the boundaries of my rule. [260] The ground here before you, this very land, long ago took its name Apias from a healer. Apis, a man gifted with divine insight into illness, a child of Apollo, came from the borders of Naupactia. He purged this land here of man-destroying wild beasts. The earth, stained by the pollution of ancient blood-guilt, delivered these very beasts, children of wrath, a hostile brood of monstrous snakes, to dwell with us. After his decisive surgical intervention removed them, [270] Apis blamelessly earned a memorial in our prayers as a reward in the land of Argos. Having now such evidence from me, you may declare openly your origin. And yet the city has no love of long speeches.

Chorus: Short and clear is our story: Argive by race is our claim, offspring of the child-blest cow.[58] I shall confirm the whole truth of this.

King Pelasgus: Strangers, what you say is hard to believe, that you are of Argive descent. It is hard to believe because you look rather more like Libyan women and [280] not at all like women from our lands. The Nile might breed such fruit as you. You are dark like a Cypriot coin, hammered into a female-shaped mould by male craftsmen. I hear that there are nomadic women of India, dwelling beside the Ethiopians, who ride horse-like camels through the land. If you held bows, I would have compared your appearance rather to the unwed, flesh-eating Amazons. But I would better understand this situation if I were instructed [290] how your descent and seed are Argive.

Chorus: It is said that Io was once a priestess of Hera's temple here in Argos.

King Pelasgus: She was indeed. That is widely accepted tradition.

2. Antiphon, *On Truth, Oxyrhynchus Papyri* 1364 and 3647 (5th century BCE). *Theories such as that of Aristotle's on natural slavery (see above) were not universally accepted, and Sophists like Antiphon seemed especially critical of ideas concerning innate character. (RFK)*

1364. . . . . we understand and respect those who live close by but neither understand nor respect distant peoples. In this way then we have been barbarized in our relations with each other, since by nature we are all born with an equally inherent capacity to be both barbarians and Greeks.

3647. We can see this regarding those things that are necessary to all human beings by nature and with regard to those things provided to all according to their abilities; in these particular ways none of us are distinguishable as barbarians or Greeks. For we all breathe in air through our mouths and noses. We all laugh when we are joyful and cry when we are filled with grief. We receive sounds with our ears and see with our eyes in the light. We work with our hands and walk on our feet < . . . >

---

58. Io, who was loved by Zeus and driven to wander the world by Hera's anger. She eventually settled in Egypt.

each group agreed upon what was pleasing to them . . . and made laws [accordingly].

3. Herodotus, *Histories* 1.56.2–57.3 (5th century BCE). *Herodotus addresses the idea of language as an identifier of race or ethnicity. One can be born as part of one group, but can become part of another through the adoption of a new language. (RFK)*

1.56. Doing some research, Croesus discovered that the Athenians and the Lacedaemonians were preeminent among the Greeks. The Lacedaemonians were preeminent among the Dorian race, the Athenians among the Ionian. They were the foremost peoples in antiquity as well—the Athenians among the Pelasgian peoples, the Lacedaemonians among the Hellenes. The Pelasgian Athenians had never moved anywhere, but the Dorian Lacedaemonians wandered a great deal. [3] In the time when Deucalion was king, they inhabited the land of Phthia. Under King Dorus, son of Hellen, they dwelt under Ossa and Olympus in a land called Histiaea. They were then driven from Histiaea by the Cadmeans and moved to Pindus, now called Macedon. From there again they moved to Dryopia and from Dryopia to the Peloponnese where they became known as Dorians.

1.57. I do not know for certain what language the Pelasgians spoke. If we consider the current language spoken by Pelasgians still living—those living above the Tyrrhenian city of Crestos, those who once lived in what is now called Thessaly, adjacent to the Dorians, those dwelling at Placia and Scylace on the Hellespont, [2] those who arrived at some point in the past and merged with the Athenians, and many others who lived in towns that were Pelasgian but changed names later—if we consider what all of these Pelasgians speak, then the ancient Pelasgians spoke a barbarian language. [3] And so, if the Pelasgian language was common here and the Attic people were once Pelasgian, then it seems clear that they changed their language at the same time as they became Hellenes. For indeed neither the Crestians nor the Placians, who share a common tongue, were in any way similar to their neighbors. Their language, which they brought with them when they moved from one land to another, they have preserved distinctly. It is the same language as they have used continually from their origins.

4. Herodotus, *Histories* 3.16, 3.27–29, 3.38 (5th century BCE). *Herodotus develops his argument for a type of cultural relativism. Cambyses is an example of an individual who does not respect laws or customs, not even his own. (CSR)*

3.16. Cambyses arrived from Memphis into the city of Sais, since he wanted to do something, which he did indeed do. When he arrived at the house of Amasis, he ordered straightaway that the corpse of Amasis be taken out of his tomb and brought outside. After this was done, he ordered that the corpse be whipped and its hair torn out and that it be stabbed and mal- treated in all other ways. [2] The men doing this became exhausted for the corpse had been embalmed and so it resisted and did not fall apart. So Cambyses ordered that the body be burned, a command contrary to divine law. [3] The Persians think that fire is a god. Indeed, to burn corpses is not at all legal for either Persians or Egyptians: It has been said already why this is so for the Persians—they say it is not right to give the corpse of a man to a god. As for the Egyptians, they think that fire is a living wild beast that completely consumes everything it takes, and having been filled with food it dies along with what it has eaten. [4] It is not at all lawful for them to give a corpse to an animal. This is why they embalm, so that the body lying there will not be eaten by worms. Thus Cambyses ordered them to do something considered lawful by neither people. [5] The Egyptians, how- ever, say that it was not Amasis who suffered these things, but another one of the Egyptians who had the same stature as Amasis, and that the Persians, in maltreating this corpse, thought they were mistreating Amasis. [6] They say that Amasis learned from an oracle the things that were going to hap- pen to him once he had died, and so as to avoid this he buried the dead man who was whipped in the doorway of his tomb and he commanded his child to put him in the innermost recess of the tomb. These commands from Amasis to have the man in the tomb do not seem to me to be true. Rather, the Egyptians embellish the story.

. . .

3.27. When Cambyses had returned to Memphis, Apis appeared to the Egyptians, whom the Greeks call Epaphus. When the appearance occurred the Egyptians immediately put on their best clothes and had a celebration. [2] Upon seeing the Egyptians doing these things, Cambyses thought that they were rejoicing because his expedition against the Ethiopians had gone badly, and he called the governors of Memphis to him. When they had arrived before him he asked why the Egyptians had done nothing like this before when he was in Memphis, but rather now, when he was here again, and had lost some large number of his army. [3] They explained that the god had appeared and that it would be a long time until he next appeared, and so when he appears, all the Egyptians celebrate and have a festival. After hearing these things Cambyses claimed that they lied and punished them with death as liars.

    3.28. After killing these men he then called the priests before him. When the priests said the same thing, Cambyses said that it would not escape his notice if some tame god had arrived and was in Egypt. Having said such things he ordered the priests to bring Apis to him. They went out and complied. [2] This Apis or Epaphus is a calf born from a cow, which having birthed him no longer can bear to carry young in her belly. The Egyptians say that a ray of light comes down upon the cow from heaven and from this light she gives birth to Apis. This calf called Apis is marked as follows: it is black with a white diamond on its forehead, and on its back there seems to be an image of an eagle, and on the tail the hairs are double, and there is a beetle mark under its tongue.

3.29. When the priests led in Apis, Cambyses, who was close to the point of insanity, brandished a dagger and, wishing to strike Apis' belly, hit his thigh. He laughed and said to the priests, [2] "O fools, are your gods of such a sort, of blood and flesh and able to be struck by iron? This god is worthy of the Egyptians, but in your rejoicing, you will not get away with making me a laughingstock." After he said these things, he ordered those whose job it was to beat the priests and to kill any of the other Egyptians who were captured while celebrating. [3] The festival was ended for the Egyptians, and the priests punished, and Apis lay in the temple struck in the thigh and dying. And after he died from his wound, the priests buried him in secret from Cambyses.

. . .

3.38. It is completely clear to me that Cambyses was very insane, since he would not otherwise have enjoyed mocking the priests and the laws. For if someone should put laws before all men and order all men to choose the most beautiful of all the laws, upon examination, each would choose his own laws. Thus each thinks that his own laws are the most beautiful by far. [2] It is not likely then that anyone other than a crazed man would suggest that such things are laughable. This is what all men think about their laws, and proof for this judgment is present in many other examples, but this one in particular: [3] During his reign Darius called some of the Greeks who were present and asked them what he could pay them to eat their fathers who had died. The Greeks replied that they would not do this for any amount of money. [4] Then Darius called some of the Indians who are called Callatiae, who eat their parents, and asked them while the Greeks were present (he learned their response from an interpreter) what amount he could pay them to burn their dead fathers on a pyre. The Indians let out a great cry and begged him to say something more auspicious. These practices have become customary among them, and it seems to me that Pindar rightly said that custom is king of all.

5. Herodotus, *Histories* 5.22 (5th century BCE). *Herodotus addresses the status of Macedonians, whether they are considered Greek or not. (RFK)*

That those descendants of Perdiccas[59] are Greek, according to what they say, I happen to know for certain and will show later in my history.[60] Additionally, the Hellenodicai, who govern the Olympic games, judged them so. [2] For, when Alexander[61] elected to compete in the games and entered the lists

---

59. Perdiccas was a Macedonian king and ancestor of Philip and Alexander.

60. At 8.137–139, Herodotus recounts the story of the earliest member of the Temenids, the Macedonian royal family, describing them as descendants from an Argive exile, thus the "proof" that the Macedonians are Greek.

61. Not Alexander "the Great" but an earlier Alexander.

to do so, the Greeks who ran against him prevented him from competing, saying that the games were not for barbarian contestants but Greeks only. Alexander then demonstrated his Argive descent, was deemed a Greek by the judges, and competed in the foot race and finished in first place.

6. Herodotus, *Histories* 8.144 (5th century BCE). *Herodotus has the Athenians explain to the Spartans why they will not ally with the Persians by evoking the concept of Panhellenism, which is here explained through cultural practices rather than genetic heritage or geographic proximity. (RFK)*

Athenians: "It was quite natural for the Spartans to fear that we would come to an agreement with the barbarian. Nevertheless, we think it disgraceful that you became so frightened, since you are well aware of the Athenians' disposition, namely, that there is no amount of gold anywhere on earth so great, nor any country that surpasses others so much in beauty and fertility, that we would accept it as a reward for medizing and enslaving Hellas. [2] For there are a great many things preventing us from doing this even if we wanted to. First and foremost are the images and temples of the gods that were burned and destroyed—necessity compels us to avenge this destruction to the greatest extent possible rather than come to agreements with the one committing the acts. Second, it would not be fitting for the Athenians to prove traitors to the Greeks with whom we are united in sharing the same kinship and language, together with whom we have established shrines and conduct sacrifices to the gods, and with whom we also share the same mode of life."

7. Euripides, *Andromache* 155–180 (5th century BCE). *An example of anti-barbarian rhetoric that suggests that barbarian peoples are inherently inferior to Greeks, but also have customs that reflect and nurture this inferiority. (RFK)*

Hermione, daughter of Menelaus and Helen and wife of Neoptolemus (the son of Achilles), to Andromache, the former wife of Hector of Troy and now the slave (and mistress) of Neoptolemus.

You are a slave and a spear-won woman and yet you want to drive us out and lay hold of the household for yourself. Because of your poisons, I am loathed by my husband. My belly is barren and shriveling because of you. The minds of Asian women are clever at these things. [160] I will prevent you from doing this. The halls of the Nereids will not save you, neither their altars nor inner sanctum.[62] You will die. If some mortal or god should want to save you, you must put aside your delusions of grandeur, cower down low in fear, and fall upon my knees. Sweep my halls! Sprinkle the pure waters of

---

62. Andromache has fled to the temple of the Nereids to seek refuge from Hermione and her father, Menelaus.

Achelous from golden vessels with your hand! Learn where you are in this world. There is no Hector here. No Priam and his gold. This is a Greek city. [170] Wretched woman! You are a fool if you think you can sleep with the man who murdered your husband and bear children with his murderers. That's so like the barbarian race. Fathers have sex with daughters, sons with mothers, sisters with brothers. The closest kin use murder to change places with them. There is no law to prevent it. Don't introduce such customs to us. It's no good for a man to bridle two women. Rather, anyone who wants to live a life free of evils looks to a single wedded Cypris for love.

8. Euripides, *Cyclops* 11–26, 113–128, 275–304, 316–346 (5th century BCE). *Euripides'* Cyclops *is the only extant complete satyr play. The Chorus, a group of satyrs led by Silenus, have washed up on the shores of Sicily and become slaves of Polyphemus, the Cyclops. Odysseus and his men have just landed there during their journey home from Troy. (RFK)*

As the play opens, Silenus recounts how he and the satyrs arrived there.

11–26. Silenus: When Hera stirred up the race of Tuscan pirates against you [Dionysus] to sell you abroad as a slave, I learned of it and sailed off with my children in search of you. I myself stood at the stern and guided the double-oared ship. My children manned the oars and turned the silvery sea white with waves as they sought you, Lord. But an east wind blew down upon us as we were sailing near Cape Malea[63] [20] and threw us onto rocky Aetna, where the one-eyed children of the sea god, the murderous Cyclopes, dwell in their desolate caves. One of them, Polyphemus, caught us and enslaved us. He's the one we serve. In place of our Bacchic revels we herd the flocks of this unholy Cyclops.

113–128. Odysseus asks Silenus about the island.

Odysseus: What land is this and who lives here?
Silenus: This is Mount Aetna, the highest point in Sicily.
Odysseus: Where are the walls and the ramparts of the city?
Silenus: There aren't any. These lands are devoid of people, stranger.
Odysseus: Then who holds this land? A race of wild beasts?
Silenus: The Cyclopes. They live in caves, not halls.
Odysseus: Whom do they obey? Or is power shared by all?
Silenus: They are loners. No one listens to anyone about anything. [120]
Odysseus: Do they sow Demeter's grain? If not, how do they live?
Silenus: On milk and cheese and the meat[64] of sheep.

---

63. Malea is the easternmost promontory on the tip of the Peloponnese.
64. The Greek word used for "meat" here, βορά, is typically used with reference to cannibals, which the Cyclopes are.

Odysseus: Do they have the drink of Bromius? The juice of the grape vine?

Silenus: No! Not in the least! They lead a sad, danceless life.

Odysseus: Do they love guests? Do they tend to the god who watches out for strangers?

Silenus: They say that the flesh of guests is the sweetest of all.

Odysseus: What?! They enjoy the flesh of murdered men?

Silenus: There isn't anyone yet who's come to this island and not been eaten.

> 275–304. *Odysseus attempts to convince Polyphemus not to eat him by call-ing upon certain characteristics that were thought to bind Greeks together in their identity (see Herodotus,* Histories *8.144 above).*

Cyclops: I want to ask you something. Where have you sailed from, strang-ers? From what country? What city raised you up?

Odysseus: We are Ithacans by birth. We arrived upon your shores from Troy. After we sacked the city, we were driven here by sea storms, Cyclops.

Cyclops: Were you among those who avenged yourselves upon Ilium beside the Scamander [280] for the kidnapping of that absolutely awful Helen?

Odysseus: Indeed. We endured that terrible labor.

Cyclops: Well, that was a shameful campaign—sailing to Phrygian[65] lands for the sake of a single woman.

Odysseus: It was a godly deed. Blame no mortal. But we are supplicating you, true-born son of Poseidon, and we openly reproach you: Don't you dare kill those headed home to their friends and families and make of them an unholy meal for your jaws. [290] We defended the temples of your father, Lord, in every corner of Greece. Because of us, the sacred harbor of Tainarum[66] is unharmed. Because of us, the high sanctuaries of Malea are safe. Because of us, silver-rich Cape Sounion, beloved of Athena, and the Geraistian[67] havens are preserved. We did not surrender Greek possessions to the Phrygians, a grievous disgrace that would have been. You share in these events since you dwell in Hellas (on its edges) under the fire-streaming rock Aetna.

If you reject these reasons, consider that among mortals [300] there is a law that you welcome as suppliants those wrecked at sea. You offer them hos-pitality and provide clothing. <*It is just that we receive such treatment from you, lord,*> as opposed to being put on a spit and roasted for you to eat . . .

316–346. Cyclops: Little man, wealth is a god to the wise. The rest is just blatherings and fancy speeches. Go ahead and celebrate the watery crags where my father has his sacred seats. Why do you rattle on about them

---

65. In poetry, Phrygia is frequently used interchangeably for Asia Minor or the Persian Empire.

66. On the central peninsula of the Peloponnese.

67. The cape on the southern tip of Euboea near Carystus.

to me? [320] I'm not intimidated by Zeus' thunderbolts, Stranger, nor do I know a way in which Zeus is a stronger god than I. <*If I ever gave him any thought before this,*> he certainly isn't on my radar for the future. Listen why: Whenever he sends his rain down from above, I cozy up inside my waterproof cave here and snack on either a roasted calf or some other wild beast and I feast my upturned belly to its delight. Then I drink a jar of milk and bang on it creating a clamor as loud as Zeus' thunder. And when the north wind dumps snow down upon me from Thrace, [330] I throw an animal skin around my body and build a fire. I don't bother about the snow. The earth automatically supplies grass to fatten up my flocks, whether it *wants* to or not. I don't sacrifice to anyone but myself and that greatest of all divinities, my tummy (and certainly not to "the gods"). To drink, to eat, and to cause oneself no grief—this is Zeus to the sensible man. You people, who make laws and complicate your lives so? [340] That's your problem. I'm not going to stop doing what makes my life enjoyable, like eating you! But, so you don't have cause to reproach me, I'll show you some "hospitality." Here's a fire and some salt from my father and a big kettle. Once it's boiling, it will serve to cover your currently poorly covered flesh. Just walk yourself inside my cave now and arrange yourself around the altar and entertain me!

9. Anonymous, *Dissoi Logoi* 2.9–18 (5th/4th century BCE). *The author offers arguments for relative definitions of what is proper and what is shameful. After discussing it in relation to individuals, he turns to relative customs among different peoples. (RFK)*

2.9. I will go on to what cities and peoples consider shameful. To begin with, it is proper to the Lacedaemonians that girls exercise in the nude and move about bare-armed and without tunics, while this is shameful to the Ionians. [10] Also, the Lacedaemonians consider it shameful that children learn music and letters, whereas the Ionians think it shameful *not* to learn these things. [11] To the Thessalians it is proper for a man to take a horse from the herd and break it himself, and the mules as well, and to also take cattle himself and slaughter it, skin it, and cut it up. In Sicily, this is considered shameful and the work of slaves. [12] To the Macedonians it seems proper that girls love and have sex with a man before marrying him, but they deem it shameful to do so after the wedding. [13] To the Thracians it is proper that their girls tattoo themselves, but to others tattoos are a mark for criminals. The Scythians think it proper after killing a man to scalp him and dress the brow of their horse with the front of the scalp and then to gild or silver the skull and use it as a drinking cup or for libations to the gods. Among the Greeks, no one would enter the home of a person who did such a thing. [14] The Massagetai cut up their parents and eat them. In Greece, someone doing this would be driven out from Greece and would die badly because they did such shameful and terrible things. [15] The Persians think it proper for men to adorn themselves as women do and also to have sex with daughters, mothers, and sisters. The Greeks consider these behaviors both shameful and contrary to law. [16] It seems proper to the Lydians that girls prostitute themselves and earn money and then marry. No Greeks would marry a girl who had done this. [17] The Egyptians do not consider the same things proper as any other people. For Greece it is proper that women weave and labor, but in Egypt men do such work and the women do what men here do. Also, kneading clay with hands and dough with feet is proper, but we do the opposite. [18] I think that if someone should order all people to compile into one list what each thinks shameful and then to remove what each considers proper, nothing would be left, but everyone would remove everything. For not everyone thinks the same way.

10. Isocrates, *Panegyric* 50 (4th century BCE). *Isocrates praises Athens as a "school of Hellas." (MLG)*

Our city has so far outstripped the rest of humanity in intelligence and literature that students of Athens are the teachers of the rest. The city has caused the name, Hellenes, to seem to belong less to a race than to intelligence itself, and people are called Hellenes more for taking part in our culture than sharing our blood.

11. Demosthenes, *Third Philippic* 30–32 (4th century BCE). *Demosthenes gave a series of speeches against Philip II of Macedon. Here he is attempting to persuade the Athenians (and the other Greeks) to resist Philip's inroads into Greece. In this part of the argument, he points out that Philip is not even Greek. (CSR)*

30. And know this, too, that however much the Greeks suffered because of the Spartans or because of us, at least they were wronged by legitimate sons of Greece, and someone could understand it in this way—even if a legitimate son who was born into a wealthy house pursues something not honorably or not rightly, he is understood to be worthy of blame and accusation so far as it goes, but he who does these things must be related or be an heir. 31. If a slave or an illegitimate child had thrown away and destroyed things that did not belong to him, by Heracles, everyone would have claimed that it was much more terrible and worth their anger. But concerning Philip and the things he is doing now, they do not act in this way, although he is not only not Greek and does not belong to the Greeks, but he is not even a barbarian from anywhere considered good; rather he is a pestilent Macedonian, where it is not even possible to buy a good slave.

32. Furthermore, what last hubris remains for him? Beyond destroying the cities, does he not preside at the Pythian games, the common gathering of the Greeks? And, if he is not himself present, does he not send slaves

to organize them? And is he not the lord of the Gates[68] and the entryways to Greece, holding these places with guards and foreigners? And indeed, does he not have the right to consult the oracle first, pushing us and the Thessalians and the Dorians and the other members of the Amphictyonic League aside from a thing that is shared by all Greeks?

12. Polybius, *Histories* 6.47 (2nd century BCE). *Book 6 of Polybius'* Histories *contains his analysis of constitutions. In the analysis, Polybius connects the success of a people to the nature of their laws and customs. (CSR)*

I think that there are two governing principles for every state. On account of these things it follows that their power and constitution are either adopted or shunned. These things are its customs and its laws. [2] The ones that should be adopted make men holy and harmonious in their private lives and render the common character of the city civilized and just. The ones that should be shunned create the opposite result. [3] Therefore, just as when we see that the customs and laws fall to the side of good, we confidently claim that the men from these states and the constitution of these states are good. [4] And likewise, when we observe that the men are grasping in their private lives and that their common practices are unjust, it is clearly true to say that their laws, their particular customs, and their whole constitution are cheap.

13. Cicero, *Academica Posteriora* 1.9 (1st century BCE). *Cicero is concerned with the forging of Roman philosophical writing in emulation of and competition with Greek culture. He places the scholar Varro's many works in this context, describing the effect of Varro's* Antiquities *(1st century BCE) on his contemporaries. Investigations into Roman history and culture can define for the Romans (or as Cicero imagines it, reveal) who they are. (MLG)*

We were, you know, foreigners in our own city, wandering lost like strangers, and it was your books that led us back home, as it were. As a result we were able to recognize who and where we were. It was you who revealed the age of our country, the historical chronology, religious and priestly rules, civil and military customs, the location of districts and regions, in sum the causes, duties, types, and names of every human and divine matter. At the same time, you shone a bright light on the history of our poets and in general on Latin writers and Latin language. You yourself have composed elegant and multifarious poems in nearly every meter and began the

---

68. Thermopylae.

study of many branches of philosophy well enough to provoke their study if too little for a complete training.

14. Josephus, *Jewish Antiquities* 12.239–241 (2nd century CE). *Josephus describes an instance in the process of Hellenization among the Jews in Judea (c.170 BCE). (RFK)*

12.239. This Jesus changed his name to Jason, and Onias was called Menelaus. Jason, as former high priest, revolted against Menelaus, who had been established as priest after him. The people were divided in their loyalties. The children of Tobias threw in their lot with Menelaus. 240. The masses backed Jason. Thus Menelaus and the sons of Tobias were distressed and fled to Antiochus.[69] They made it clear to him that they wished to abandon their ancestral customs as Jews and follow the king's constitution and have a Greek way of life. 241. They called upon Antiochus to begin the building of a gymnasium in Jerusalem. After Antiochus consented, they took measures to hide their circumcised genitals, so that even when naked they would be Greek. They also abandoned all and every ancestral practice and imitated those of other peoples.

15. Plutarch, *Life of Lycurgus* 4.5, 27.3–4 (2nd century CE). *Plutarch recounts cultural similarities between the Spartans and Egyptians and accounts for Spartan xenophobia. (CSR)*

4.5. The Egyptians also think that Lycurgus came to them and was especially impressed at the division of the warriors from the other tribes. They conclude that he moved the system to Sparta, and, by separating out the craftsmen and artisans, produced a constitution truly elegant and pure. Some of the Greek writers even bear witness to what the Egyptians assert. But the claim that Lycurgus went to Libya and Iberia and that in his travels around India he spent time with the Gymnosophists, no one we know except Aristocrates the son of Hipparchus, a Spartan, has said so.

. . .

27.3. Lycurgus did not allow those who wanted to leave and wander to do so, in case they would acquire foreign habits and mimic uneducated lives and different constitutions. He drove out those crowding in for no purpose and sneaking into the city, not, as Thucydides says, because he feared that they would become mimics of his constitution and discover something useful about virtuous living, but rather so that the teachers would not adopt any bad practices. For by necessity foreign ideas come in together with foreign people, [4] and new ideas generate new disputes, from which by

---

69. Antiochus IV Epiphanes, king of the Seleucid Empire 175–165 BCE.

necessity emotions flare and policies appear that are discordant with the established constitution or the harmony of the society. Therefore, Lycurgus thought it more important to guard the city so that it would not be infected with worthless habits than to guard against people coming in who got diseased abroad.

16. Plutarch, *Life of Alexander* 45, 47.3–4, 50.4–51.3, 71.1–3, 74.1 (2nd century CE). *As Alexander passed further into Asia, he is represented in many sources, including Plutarch, as having increasingly embraced barbarian practices and "become" the barbarian. (CSR)*

45. From there Alexander moved his camp into Parthia and, since he had the opportunity, he put on barbarian clothes for the first time. He did this either because he wished to connect himself to the local customs, thinking that shared custom and shared race lends to the humanizing of men, or he did it because this was a trial of the custom of prostration set for the Macedonians, who were being gradually accustomed to accepting his change and shift in habits. [2] He did not, however, venture the Median style, which is wholly barbaric and unusual. He did not take up the pants, Median cloak, or tiara, but rather he blended something of Persia and of Media together. It was less arrogant than the Median style, and more impressive than the Persian. At first Alexander wore the outfit when he was entertaining barbarians or his companions at home, but he was also seen in it by many while he was out riding or conducting business. [3] To the Macedonians the sight was offensive, but they admired his character and thought that it was necessary to concede something to his pleasure and his reputation. Indeed, in addition to all his other affairs, Alexander had just recently taken an arrow in his calf, because of which pieces of his tibia had fallen out from the fracture. Also, he had been hit on the back of the neck with a stone, resulting in clouded vision that lasted for some time. [4] All the same, he did not stop putting himself in danger willingly, and he even crossed the Orexartes River (which he thought was the Tanais River), defeated the Scythians, and pursued them 1.5 miles despite being troubled with diarrhea.

. . .

47.3. And so Alexander changed his way of life to be even more like the natives, and he brought their ways closer to the customs of the Macedonians. He thought that matters would stabilize by intermixing and engaging them with goodwill rather than by force, even when he had gone far away. Because of this he chose out 30,000 boys and ordered them to learn the Greek language and to be trained in Macedonian weapons, and he appointed many teachers for them. [4] His relationship with Roxane, whom he had seen, beautiful and young, dancing at a drinking party, was loving and seemed to harmonize with his other aims. For the barbarians derived confidence from the marriage and they loved him to excess because he acted most tactfully in these matters and did not dare to touch the only woman who had, without following custom, overcome him.

. . .

50.4. Cleitus did not finish sacrificing but went straightaway to the dinner party of King Alexander, who had sacrificed to the Dioscuri. After some high-spirited drinking had occurred, poems by a certain Pranichus, as some say, or Pierio, were sung to shame and mock the generals who had been recently defeated by the barbarians. [5] The older men there annoyed and reproached the poet and the singer, but Alexander and those around him listened delightedly and bid him to keep speaking. Cleitus, who was drunk, and harsh by nature, as well as stubborn, became especially angry, and he kept on claiming that it was not good to insult the Macedonians, who were better by far than those who were mocking them, in front of barbarians and enemies, even if they had experienced misfortune. [6] When Alexander said that Cleitus was pleading on his own behalf when he defined cowardice as misfortune, Cleitus stood up and said, "This cowardice, however, saved you, though born from a god, when you turned your back to Spithradates' spear, and it is by Macedonian blood and these wounds that you have become so great that you renounce Philip and make yourself the adoptive son of Ammon."

51. Alexander felt provoked and said, "So, vile man, do you think that there will be no repercussions when you speak about me thus on all occasions, causing strife among the Macedonians?" And Cleitus replied, "Not even now are we safe since we are provided such ends to our labors as this. We consider lucky those who were already dead before seeing Macedonians beaten with Median staffs and begging Persians to go to see our king." [2] Cleitus boldly said these things, and those around Alexander jumped up and rebuked him. The older men tried to control the chaos. Alexander turned to Xenodotus of Cardia and Artemius of Colophon and said, "Don't the Greeks seem to you to walk among the Macedonians like demigods among wild animals?" [3] Cleitus did not give up, but bid Alexander either to say to the group what he wanted or not to call free and frank-speaking men to dinner, living instead with barbarians and slaves, who prostrate themselves before his Persian belt and white tunic. Alexander no longer controlled his anger. He threw one of the apples lying around and struck Cleitus and then sought for his dagger.

. . .

71. The 30,000 boys, whom he had left behind to train and learn, grew to manhood with good-looking physiques. Furthermore, they showed dexterity and an amazing lightness in their drills. Alexander was pleased, but despondency and fear accompanied the Macedonians, for they thought that the king would pay less attention to them. [2] On account of this, when he sent the weak and incapacitated down to the sea, they thought that it was outrageous and abusive that he should use up the men in everything and

now put them aside with shame and toss them back to their homelands and parents, no longer the strong men he had taken from them earlier. Therefore, they ordered him to send them all away and to consider all Macedonians useless, since he had these young dancers of war, with whom he could go and gain possession of the inhabited world. [3] Alexander was disturbed at these things and greatly reproached them in his anger. He drove them away and handed the position of his guards to the Persians, from whom he appointed bodyguards and staff bearers. Upon seeing him accompanied by these men while they were kept from him and treated badly, the Macedonians were humbled. Thinking logically, they began to realize that they had not been far from becoming enraged by jealousy and anger.

. . .

74. After he heard this, Alexander had the man removed, as the seers bid him. But he lost heart and was despondent in regard to the divine and suspicious toward his friends. He was especially afraid of Antipater and his sons, of whom Iolas was his primary cupbearer, and Cassander had recently arrived. When Cassander saw some of the barbarians prostrating themselves, he laughed uncontrolledly, since he had been reared in the Greek manner and had never before seen such a thing.

17. Achilles Tatius, *Leucippe and Cleitophon* 5.5.2 (2nd century CE). *When asked by Leucippe about the story behind a painting, Cleitophon explains that it represents the myth of Tereus, a barbarian, and the Greeks Procne and Philomela, who had been changed to birds. (MLG)*

The hoopoe is the man, and of the two women, Philomela is the swallow and Procne the nightingale. The women come from Athens. The man is named Tereus. Procne is Tereus' wife. For the barbarians, it seems, one wife does not satisfy sexual desire, especially when there is an opportunity for rape.

18. Achilles Tatius, *Leucippe and Cleitophon* 8.2.1–4 (2nd century CE). *Having been punched in the face by his rival Thersander in a temple of Artemis, Cleitophon declaims a tragic screed against this tyrannical abuse. (MLG)*

Where should we go to escape from violent men? Where should we run for refuge? To some god other than Artemis? In the temple itself I was struck! Before the veil of the sanctuary I was beaten! Such things happen in trackless deserts where there is no human witness. But you, you behaved tyrannically in the sight of the gods themselves! [2] Although the guilty receive refuge in the safety of temples, I, who have done no wrong, I, who am a suppliant

of Artemis, I am beaten before the altar itself as the goddess—alas!—looks
on. The punches were against Artemis! [3] His drunken madness surpassed
simple punches but extended to face wounds, as in war and battle, which
have defiled the ground with human blood. Who pours such libations to
the gods? Is it not the barbarians, the Taurians, the Scythian Artemis? Only
their temple is so bloodied. You have turned Ionia into Scythia! Taurian
blood flows in Ephesus! [4] Take up a sword against me! But what need of
iron? Your hand has done the work of a sword! This slaughtering and pol-
luting right hand has behaved like a murderer.

THE PEOPLES OF THE ANCIENT WORLD

CHAPTER 6

THE INHABITED WORLD

The Greeks and Romans often included within their works lengthy references to the scope and size of the oikoumenê, *the inhabited world. These references frequently compare peoples from different regions or provide a verbal map of the known world. Greece or Rome is generally placed in the center.*

1. **Pindar,** *Olympian* **3.1–41 (5th century BCE).** *Pindar includes an early description of Heracles' journeys to foreign lands in his ode celebrating the victory of Theron, tyrant of Acragas, in the Olympic chariot race in 476 BCE. (CSR)*

I profess to praise the hospitable Tyndarids[70] and beautiful-haired Helen as I award a prize to glorious Acragas, raising the Olympic victory hymn to Theron, the finest hymn of tireless-footed horses. Therefore, a Muse stood by me as I devised a shining new way to blend the song of lovely celebration to the Dorian dance. For, crowns bound to Theron's hair divinely require an appropriate mingling of the tuneful lyre and cry of flutes with well-crafted words for the child of Ainesidamos. Such also Pisa proclaims, whence [10] come divinely ordained songs to mankind, whenever, fulfilling the prior mandates of Heracles, the precise Aetolian judge should place around his hair above his brow the greyish ornament of the olive branch that Heracles brought from the shaded springs of the Danube, the loveliest memorial of the games in Olympia. He persuaded the Hyperborean people, attendants of Apollo, with words. Faithfully minded, he asked of Zeus a shady plant for the all-welcoming grove and a common crown of great deeds for men. For already, with altars dedicated to his father, the mid-month moon [20] blazed forth her whole eye from her golden chariot in the evening, and he had established the sacred trial of the great games during their quadrennial celebration on the holy banks of the Alpheus. But the land of Pelops in the glens of the Hill of Cronus was not flourishing with lovely trees. To him the garden, bare of these, seemed to withstand the piercing rays of the sun. Then his heart stirred him to go to the Istrian land,[71] where Leto's horse-driving

---

70. Castor and Pollux, the twin sons of Tyndareus of Sparta.

71. The upper Danube.

daughter[72] had welcomed him arriving from the ridges and the twisting valleys of Arcadia, when by the decrees of Eurystheus[73] his father's compulsion urged him to lead back the golden-antlered hind,[74] [30] which Taÿgeta[75] ordained as a holy offering for Orthosia,[76] While chasing it, he saw also that land beyond the blast of cold Boreas. Standing there, he marveled at the trees. A sweet desire took him to plant some of them around the turn of the twelve-lap racetrack. And now he comes to the festival with the godlike twin sons of deep-bosomed Leda, for when he went to Olympus he gave it to them to oversee the wondrous games of the excellence of men and racing chariots. And so my spirit urges me to tell to the Emmenidae and to Theron that glory has come, given by the horsemen, the sons of Tyndareus, [40] because they, most of all mortals, ply them with hospitable feats, and with pious intention they keep the rites of the blessed gods.

2. [Aeschylus], *Prometheus Bound* 786–815, 829–843 (5th century BCE). *Prometheus recounts the journey of Io around the world and to its edges. Io was the human lover of Zeus, whom he turned into a cow to hide her from Hera. Hera, seeing through the disguise, sent a gadfly to drive her into madness. (RFK)*

786–815. Prometheus (to Chorus): Since you are eager, I will not refuse to tell all that you ask. First, to you, Io, I will tell about your much-driven journey. Inscribe it in your memory. [790] When you have crossed over the stream that marks the boundary between the continents,[77] travel toward the rising of the flaming sun across the sea without waves.[78] You will arrive at the plains of Cisthene, home of the Gorgons, where the Phorcides dwell, three ancient maids shaped like swans. They share a single eye among them and have only one tooth between them all. Neither the sun with its rays nor the moon at night have ever beheld them. Nearby are their three-winged sisters, the mortal-hating, snake-haired Gorgons, [800] whom no mortal has ever gazed upon and breathed another breath. I tell you this for your protection. But hear of another vexing spectacle: Be on guard against the unbarking sharp-toothed dogs of Zeus, the griffins. Look out as well for the one-eyed horsemen, the Arimaspians, who live near the gold-flowing stream of Pluto. Avoid these creatures and men. You will come also to a

---

72. Artemis.

73. Heracles' cousin, the king of both Tiryns and Argos, who commanded the famous Twelve Labors.

74. The Ceryneian Hind, sacred to Artemis; Heracles' third labor was to capture it alive.

75. One of the Pleiades.

76. A Spartan cult-name of Artemis.

77. The Tanais River.

78. The Scythian Plain.

remote land near the Ethiops River at the source of the sun's course where dwell a black race of men. [810] Walk beside the banks of this river until you arrive at the cataract,[79] whence the Nile's sacred stream flows from the Bibline Mountains. This path will guide you to the triangular land of Nilotis.[80] Indeed, it is here, Io, that you and your children are fated to establish a far-off colony.

To prove his prophetic powers, Prometheus next recounts Io's earlier journey to find him in the Caucasus.

829–843. For when you came to the Molossian land and the high mountain-ridge around Dodona, [830] where the mantic seat of Thesprotian Zeus lies and where is that unbelievable marvel, the speaking oaks, by which you, who would become the famous wife of Zeus, were addressed clearly and not in riddles. Do these words resonate with you? From there, driven to madness by the gadfly, you journeyed along the seacoast to the great bay of Rhea. You were again driven from there, this time forced inland by a storm. [840] Know well that this corner of the sea will be called from this time on the Ionian Sea by all mankind in memory of your journey. These words are proof of my mind's ability to perceive more than is evident.

Prometheus then tells Io that she will finally end her journey in Egypt and give birth to Epaphus.

3. Herodotus, *Histories* **4.36–45 (5th century BCE).** *Herodotus describes the shape of the earth and the division of the continents. The map he criticizes is likely Hecataeus' (see Map 1). (CSR)*

4.36. I am not telling the story about Abaris, who was said to be a Hyperborean, how he carried an arrow across the whole earth while not eating. But if there are people living in the extreme north, then there are others living in the extreme south. [2] I laugh when I see the many people drawing charts of the earth and not one showing reason in them. They draw the Ocean flowing around the earth, which is circular as if from a compass, and make Asia equal to Europe. In a few words I will make clear the size of each continent and what each of them should be on a map.

4.37. Persians live extending to the southern sea called the Red Sea, the Medes live above them to the north, the Saspeires live north of the Medes, and the Colchians live north of the Saspeires extending up to the northern sea, into which the Phasis River feeds. These four races live between the seas.

4.38. From there toward the west, two peninsulas extend into the sea, which I will describe. [2] The one peninsula begins to the north from the

---

79. Near Aswan and Elephantine on the Nile River. This was considered by the ancients to be the boundary between Egypt and Ethiopia.

80. The Nile Delta.

river Phasis and stretches into the sea by the Pontus and the Hellespont until it reaches Sigeum at Troas. And the same peninsula starts in the south and stretches into the sea until the cape of Triopium from the Myriandic Bay, which lies by Phoenicia. Thirty races of men live on this peninsula.

4.39. The other peninsula starts from Persia and extends into the Red Sea. Persia, Assyria, and, after Assyria, Arabia are taken up by it. The peninsula comes to an end only by convention in the Arabian Gulf, to which Darius built a canal from the Nile. [2] Up to Phoenicia from Persia the land is wide and great, but after Phoenicia the peninsula passes forth into this sea of ours past Palestinian Syria and Egypt, and it ends there. Only three races are on this peninsula.

4.40. These are the areas from Persia and to the west in Asia. Next are the lands beyond the Persians, Medes, Saspeires, and Colchians, and the lands rising to the east and the sun. They are between the Red Sea to the north, the Caspian Sea, and the river Araxes, which flows toward the east. [2] Asia is inhabited as far as India; from there it is empty to the east, and no one is able to say anything about what sort of land it is.

4.41. This is the size and extent of Asia. Libya is on the other peninsula, since Libya comes next after Egypt. At Egypt the peninsula is narrow, for from our sea[81] to the Red Sea is 10,000 fathoms, or approximately 125 miles. From this narrow space it widens out to the peninsula that is called Libya.

4.42. I am amazed at those dividing and setting apart Libya,[82] Asia, and Europe. For the differences between them are not small ones. Europe stretches along the length of both, and there seems to me to be no comparing their widths. [2] For Libya is clearly surrounded by water, except where it meets with Asia. Necho the Egyptian king was the first known to have discovered this, when he stopped digging the trench from the Nile to the Arabian Gulf, and instead sent Phoenician men with ships, commanding them to sail through the Pillars of Heracles until they reached the northern sea and thus returned into Egypt. [3] The Phoenicians hastened on and sailed from the Red Sea into the southern sea. Whenever it was autumn, they would land and cultivate the land, wherever in Libya they happened to sail, and then wait for the harvest. [4] Once they had reaped their harvest, they sailed. Thus after two years and into the third year, they turned into the Pillars of Heracles and arrived in Egypt. And they said something that seems untrue to me but might ring true to someone else, that when sailing around Libya the sunrise was on their right.

4.43. Thus was Libya first perceived. The Carthaginians say the following: Sataspes the son of Teaspis, an Achaemenid man, did not sail around Libya, although he was sent to do this. Instead, fearing the length of the sea voyage and the solitude, he came back, and thus he did not complete the task his mother commanded of him. [2] He had raped the virgin daughter

---

81. The Mediterranean.

82. Herodotus uses Libya as the name for both a part of north Africa to the west of Egypt and as the name for the entire continent of Africa.

of Zopyrus, the son of Megabyzus. When he was about to be impaled by King Xerxes because of this crime, Sataspes' mother, who was the sister of Darius, pleaded on his behalf. [3] She said that she would give him a greater punishment than Xerxes would. She said that she would force him to sail around Libya so far that, by sailing around he would return back into the Arabian Gulf. Xerxes agreed to these conditions, and so Sataspes went to Egypt, took a ship and sailors and sailed for the Pillars of Heracles. [4] He sailed through and rounded the extreme point of Libya, which is called Soloeis, and then sailed south. He passed through a great sea for many months, but since there was always more, he turned back and sailed to Egypt. [5] Returning from there to King Xerxes, he said that at the furthest point where they had sailed there were little men wearing palm leaves for clothes, who, whenever they landed their ship, would flee to the mountains leaving their cities behind. But they did not harm them when they arrived but took only some meat from them. [6] He said that the reason for not sailing around Libya entirely was that his ship was not able to go further but was held fast. Xerxes did not think that he was speaking truthfully and impaled him for the original crime since he did not complete the proposed punishment. [7] A eunuch of this Sataspes ran away to Samos as soon as he learned that his master had been killed and took a large amount of money, which a Samian man took from him. Although I know this man's name, I am leaving it out on purpose.

4.44. Darius, who wanted to know about the Indus River, which is the second of all rivers to have crocodiles, especially where this river gives out into the sea, discovered many things about Asia. He sent other men with ships whom he trusted to speak the truth, and especially a Caryandan man named Scylax. [2] They set out from the city of Caspaturos in the Pactyican land and sailed toward the sea down the river east to where the sun rises. Sailing through the sea to the west, on the thirtieth month they arrived at the land whence the king of the Egyptians had ordered the Phoenicians to sail around Libya as I mentioned before. [3] After those men sailed around Libya, Darius subjugated the Indians and made use of the sea. Thus the rest of Asia, except the part in the east, has been discovered to be similar to Libya.

4.45. Europe is not clearly known to anyone, neither to the east nor to the north, nor if it is surrounded by water. It is known that it stretches lengthwise across both the others. [2] I do not know why the earth, though united as one landmass, has three names, each named for a woman, or why the Nile River is set as one boundary while the river Phasis in Colchis (or some say the Tanais River at Lake Maeotis and the Cimmerian Strait) serves as another, nor have I learned the names of those who divided it, and for what reason they established the names. [3] Libya is said by many Greeks to derive its name from a native-born woman named Libya, and that Asia is named for Prometheus' wife. The Lydians claim the name also, saying that Asia is so-called from Asies, the son of Kotys the son of Manes, and not from Prometheus' Asia. From this Asies, they say that the people in

Sardis are called Asians. [4] It is unknown by any man if Europe is surrounded by water, nor where the name was taken from, nor is it clear who
named it, unless we say that the land took the name of Europa from Tyre,
and that before it was unnamed as were the others. [5] But it is clear that
Europa came from Asia and did not reach the land now called Europe by
the Greeks. Rather she only traveled from Phoenicia to Crete, and from
Crete to Lycia. I have said enough about these matters since I will be using
the established names for the continents.

4. Apollonius, *Argonautica* 1.922–954 (3rd century BCE). *This is
the beginning of the journey of the Argo from Argos into the unknown
regions of the north. (RFK)*

From Samothrace, rowing across the depths of the black sea,[83] they held
course between the land of the Thracians and Imbros to their north. Just
as the sun was setting, they reached the Cheronesan peninsula. There, a
swift wind blew for them, and tacking their sails to the fair wind, they
entered the swift stream of the Athaman maid.[84] The sea to the north was
left behind at dawn. During the night, they crossed a second sea within the
headlands of Rhoeteum, [930] keeping the Idaian land to the right. Leaving
behind Dardania, they continued to Abydos. Next, they passed by Percote,
the shady shores of Abaris, and sacred Pitueia. And, indeed, throughout
the night, while the ship moved ahead in two ways,[85] they arrived at the
Hellespont swirling with whirlpools.

Within the Propontis is an island, high and steep, a little way from
the fertile Phrygian mainland. It slopes down to the sea and projects out
just off an isthmus washed over by water and sloping down to the sea.
[940] On the island are two promontories; they lay beyond the Aesepus
River. Those dwelling around the island call it the "Island of Bears." The
Gaiagenes [earth-born], savage and violent, dwell there. They are a great
marvel for their neighbors to see. Six hands of tremendous strength hang
from each, two from their massive shoulders and four joined underneath to
their dread torsos. The Doliones dwell round the isthmus and the plain. The
hero Cyzicus, son of Aeneus, ruled among them, whom Aenete, daughter
of godlike Eusuras, bore. [950] The Gaiagenes, though violent, did no harm
to them at all by the aid of Poseidon. For the Doliones were his descendants.
To this place, the land of the Doliones, the Argo pressed forward, driven by
Thracian winds.

---

83. This is not the modern Black Sea, which the Greeks called the Euxine. It is a
smaller sea in the northern Aegean.

84. The Hellespont, named for Helle, daughter of Athamas who fell in while flying
over on the golden ram.

85. Using both sail and oars.

5. Catullus, 11.1–16 (1st century BCE). *Catullus bids two of his friends to take a message to his hated ex-lover. His friends are described as willing to go to any length for him, perhaps ironically. (CSR)*

Furius and Aurelius, companions of Catullus, whether Catullus goes to the land of the far-off Indians, where the shore is beaten by waves by the far-resonating east, or travels among the Hyrcani and soft Arabs, or the Scythians or the arrow-bearing Parthians, or where the seven-fold Nile colors the sea; whether he climbs across the high Alps [10] to look at the monuments of great Caesar, or the Gallic Rhine and the terrible Britons who are the most distant of all, you two, prepared to attempt all these things, and whatever else the gods will you, together give these few not-nice words to my mistress.

6. Catullus, 29 (1st century BCE). *Like Catullus 11 above, this poem reveals Catullus' knowledge of military activity on the edges of the empire. (CSR)*

Who is able to see this, who is able to endure it, unless he is shameless and greedy and a gambler, that Mamurra has that thing which Hairy Gaul and far-off Britain used to have? Romulus you catamite, will you see these things and allow them? And that man, now proud and wealthy, wanders around the bedrooms of everyone, like a little white dove or Adonis? Romulus,[86] you catamite, will you see these things and allow them? [10] You are shameless and greedy and a gambler. Is it for this reason, one-of-a-kind commander, that you were on the furthest island to the west, so that your fucked-out little prick could consume it 200 and 300 times? What is this other than immoral liberality? Has he squandered too little? First his good inheritance was mangled, then his Pontic booty, then third his Spanish booty, which the gold-bearing river Tagus knows. [20] Now he is feared in Gaul and Britain. Why do you nurture this evil man? What can he do other than devour rich inheritances? Is it for this reason, father-in-law and son-in-law,[87] that you have destroyed everything in a most extravagant fashion?

7. Vergil, *Aeneid* 8.655–662, 8.685–713, 8.720–728 (1st century BCE). *Aeneas' mother, Venus, brings him a shield made by Vulcan that depicts several scenes from Roman history. The first scene represents the sack of Rome by the Gauls, the second describes Antony and Cleopatra before and during the battle of Actium. (CSR)*

8.655–662. And here flitting about the golden porticos the silvery goose was singing that the Gauls were on the threshold. The Gauls were near at

---

86. Likely a reference to Julius Caesar.
87. Caesar and Pompey.

hand, coming through the thickets and holding the citadel, defended by the darkness and the gift of shadowy night. Their hair is golden; their clothes, golden. [660] They shine in their wicker-woven cloaks, and their milky-white necks are circled with gold; two Alpine javelins shake in each hand, and their bodies are protected by long shields.

8.685–713. On this side is Antony, surrounded by barbarian wealth and various arms; a victor over the people of dawn and the shores of the Red Sea, he brings Egyptian and Oriental forces and the people of furthest Bactria with him, and his Egyptian wife follows (O the shame!). They all rush as one and the whole sea foams, churned up [690] by their back-paddling oars and the triple beaks of their ships. They seek open seas; you would have thought that the Cyclades had been torn out and were swimming and that the high mountains were ramming against mountains, just so the men attack the towering sterns in such a great mass. Golden flames and iron set to flight by bows are scattered by force. Neptune's fields grow red with the fresh slaughter. In their midst the queen organizes the troops with her homeland's *sistrum*;[88] she does not yet see the twin snakes at her back. Gods of all shapes, and especially barking Anubis, brandish weapons against Neptune and Venus and [700] Minerva. Mars rages in the middle of the battle, engraved in iron, and the Furies rain down sorrow from the air, and, wearing a torn cloak, Discordia wanders and rejoices; Bellona follows her with a bloody whip. Seeing these creatures, Actian Apollo stretches his bow from above. All of Egypt and the Indians, all the Arabs, all the Sabaeans begin turning their backs to this terror. The queen herself can be seen giving her sails to the winds she prayed for and letting go now of already-loosened ropes. Amidst the slaughter carried on the waves and the northwest wind, [710] the master of fire made her pale while facing her future death. The Nile mourns with its great body and opens its capes and with all its garments calls the conquered into its sea-blue lap and secret streams.

8.720–728. Caesar sits on the snow-white threshold of shining Apollo and acknowledges the gifts of the peoples and fastens them to the high doors. The conquered races process in a long line, as varied in their languages as in their clothes and arms. Here Vulcan fashioned the race of Nomads and the Africans with their clothes unbelted; here he fashioned the Leleges, the Carians, and the arrow-bearing Gelonians, the Euphrates now going more softly with its waves, the Morini from the farthest-away zones, the two-channeled Rhine, and the unconquered Dahae, and the river Araxes, indignant at his bridge.

---

88. A sacred instrument used in Ancient Egypt that produced a rattling sound.

8. Strabo, *Geography* 17.3.24 (1st century BCE/1st century CE).
Strabo ends his work with a description of the extent of Roman control in the world. (RFK)

These are the various parts of our inhabited world and how they are situated. Since, however, the Romans control the best and most well-known share, and have surpassed all earlier world leaders (of whom we know), it is worthwhile to mention briefly their territories. It has already been noted that the Romans began with only a single city and came to rule the whole of Italy through conquest and diplomacy. After Italy, they incorporated the lands surrounding Italy through the same arts. Of the three continents, they hold almost all of Europe, except the lands beyond the Ister and those bordering Ocean between the Rhine and Tanais Rivers. Of Libya, the entire coastal region bordering Our Sea[89] is under Roman control. The regions on the continent not under Roman control are either uninhabitable or are inhabited only scarcely and by nomads. Likewise, the entire coastal region of Asia touching upon Our Sea is under Roman dominion, unless someone should consider the lands of the Achaei, Zugi, and Heniochi, who all lead lives of piracy and nomadism in small, impoverished towns. Of the interior of Asia, part is controlled by the Romans, part by the Parthians. Of the lands beyond the Parthians, they are controlled by barbarians who dwell there. To the east and north are the Indians, Bactrians, and Scythians. Next are the Arabians and the Ethiopians. Parts of their lands, however, are always being acquired by the Romans. Of all these lands, some are ruled by client-kings, others the Romans control directly and call provinces. The Romans send governors and tax-collectors to the provinces. Some of Rome's lands are even made up of free cities that approached Rome first in friendship. Still others were freed by the Romans themselves as a way of honoring them. The Romans also dominate various royal dynasties, chieftains, and priests.

9. Horace, *Carmen Saeculare* 37–60 (1st century BCE). *The* Carmen Saeculare *was composed by Horace for Augustus' great Secular Games in 17 BCE to announce the beginning of a new hundred-year cycle in Rome's history. The poem sounds many of the themes behind Augustus' policies, including the rise of the Roman Empire. (CSR)*

If Rome is your work and if the Etruscan shore is held by a Trojan band, a remnant ordered to move Lares and city [40] in a safe journey, for whom pure Aeneas, survivor of his homeland, actually paved a road to freedom through burning Troy, Aeneas, who was fated to give more than what he left behind. Gods, give fitting manners to youth willing to learn; Gods, give rest to quiet old age, give wealth and offspring and every glory to the race of Romulus. And whatever the famous offspring of Anchises and Venus [50] begs of you

---

89. The Mediterranean Sea, encompassing as well the Ionian Sea, Aegean Sea, and so on. "Our Sea" was a common designation used by both the Greeks and Romans.

with the sacrifice of white cows, let him achieve it, superior against a warring enemy, lenient against an enemy cast down. Already the Mede fears our troops, who are powerful on sea and land, and our Alban axes; already the Scythians, proud until recently, and the Indians seek pronouncements from us. Now faith and peace and honesty and ancient modesty and neglected courage dare to return, and blessed Plenty appears with a [60] full horn.

10. Horace, *Odes* 3.4.29–36, 3.8.17–24, 4.14.41–52 (1st century BCE/1st century CE). *Horace frequently mentions Rome's enemies and foreign threats in his poetry. (CSR)*

3.4.29–36. Whenever you are with me, willingly as a sailor I will attempt the raging Bosphorus and as a traveler try the burning sands of the Assyrian shore; unable to be harmed, I will look upon the Britons, fierce toward foreigners, and the Concani, who rejoice in drinking horse's blood, and I will gaze upon the quivered Gelonians and the Scythian River.

3.8.17–24. Let go your civic concerns for the city; the army of Dacian Cotiso has fallen; the Mede, harmful to himself, is sunk down in lamentable arms; our old enemy from the Spanish shore, Cantaber, is enslaved, conquered finally by a chain; now the Scythians, with their bows relaxed, are considering yielding their plains to us.

4.14.41–52. You, O present protection for Italy and mistress Rome, are admired by Cantaber, once unable to be tamed, and by the Mede, by the Indian, and by the Scythian in flight. The Nile, which hides the origins of its flow, and the Ister, and the rapid Tigris, the Ocean abounding in monsters, which roars at the remote Britons, and the land of the Gauls who are not fearful of death, and the land of the troublesome Iberians, and the Sygambri who delight in slaughter, having now laid aside their arms, they all venerate *you*.

11. Pomponius Mela, *Description of the World* 1.3–8, 1.11–14, 1.18–19, 1.22–23 (1st century CE). *Pomponius opens his description of the world with an overview of the general shape and arrangement of the continents and seas and the various peoples who inhabit each continent. (RFK)*

1.3. All this, therefore (whatever it is to which we attach the name of world and sky), is a single thing within a single circumference. It embraces itself and all things, though it differs in its parts. The space whence the sun rises is called the "orient," or east. Where the sun sets is the "occident," or west. The south is where the sun runs its course, while the north lies opposite the south.

1.4. In the center, the raised earth is surrounded on all sides by Ocean. In the same way, by an east-west line, the earth is divided into two halves called hemispheres, and then these hemispheres are separated further into five zones. Heat makes the middle zone uninhabitable, and the zones on the farthest edges are uninhabitable because of cold. The two remaining habitable zones have similar annual seasons, but not at the same time. The Anticthones[90] inhabit one of these zones, while we inhabit the other. The chorography of the other landmass is unknown because of the zone between us and because it is rendered uninhabitable by heat. Our chorography, however, is as follows: 5. This zone extends from east to west and, because it is oriented this way, it is longer than it is at its widest point. It is entirely surrounded by Ocean, and from Ocean it receives four seas: one from the north, two from the south, and a fourth from the west. These will be discussed in their own sections. 6. This last sea is at first narrow, nor does it ever widen more than ten miles wide, then it cleaves open the land and penetrates it. It spreads far and wide and repels the deeply receding shores. When the same shores join together from the opposite end, the sea becomes so narrow that it opens less than a mile wide. From there, it spreads out again, but very moderately, and then recedes into a space even narrower than before. When the sea has been received there, it expands out again and is joined to a large marsh but with a tiny opening. All this sea, where it comes in and where it spreads, is called by a single term, "Our Sea."

1.7. We call the narrows and the entrance the Strait.[91] The Greeks call it the Channel. Where the sea extends, it receives other names in other places. Where it first contracts itself, it is called the Hellespont. Then it expands again as the Propontis, and then narrows again as the Thracian Bosphorus. When it widens again, it is called the Pontus Euxine.[92] It connects to a marsh at the Cimmerian Bosphorus. The swamp itself is called the Maeotis.[93] 8. The whole landmass is divided into three parts by two famous rivers, the Tanais and the Nile. The Tanais flows down almost into the middle of the Maeotis, flowing north to south. The Nile flows from the opposite direction into the Sea. Whatever land lies between the Strait and those rivers is called, on the north side, Europe, and on the south side, Africa. Africa ends at the Nile, Europe at the Tanais. Everything beyond those rivers is Asia.

. . .

---

90. Those who live in "opposite land." Pomponius here envisions a landmass in the southern hemisphere that mirrors the one known in the north.

91. The Straits of Gibraltar.

92. The Black Sea.

93. Sea of Azov.

1.11. We understand that the first humans in Asia, from east to west, are the Indians, the Seres,[94] and the Scythians.[95] The Seres inhabit nearly all the central part of the East, while the Indians and the Scythians inhabit its edges, both spreading out and extending to the sea, not only in a single location. For the Indians look also southward and have continuously occupied the coast by the Indian Sea as a nation, despite part of it being uninhabitable because of the heat. The Scythians also look northward and have settled the coastal regions around the Scythian and Caspian Seas, except where they were prevented by the cold. 12. Near the Indians are the Arianae, the Aria, Cedroses, and Persians, who reach up to the Persian Gulf. The Persians surround this Gulf; the Arabs, the other. From the Arabs to the edge of Africa dwell the Ethiopians. To the north, the Caspiani encircle the Caspian Sea. It is said that the Amazons dwell beyond the Caspiani and the Hyperboreans beyond that.

1.13. A great variety of peoples inhabit the interior of Asia. Beyond the Scythians and the Scythian deserts are the Gandari, Pariani, Bactri, Sogdiani, Pharmacotrophi, Chomarae, Choamani, Propanisadae, and Dahae. Beyond the Caspian Sea are the Comari, Massagetai, Cadusi, Hyrcani, and Hiberi. Beyond the Amazons and Hyperboreans are the Cimmerii, Cissianti, Acae, Georgili, Moschi, Cercetae, Phoristae, and Rimphaces. Where the land extends into our seas are the Matiani, Tibarani, and the more well-known Medes, Armenians, Commogenes, Murrani, Vegeti, Cappadocians, Gallo-Greeks, Lycaones, Phrygians, Pisidae, Isauri, Lydians, and Syro-Cilicians.

1.14. Again, from these peoples who look south < . . . >[96] and the same people hold the interior coast up to the Persian Gulf. Beyond here are the Parthians and the Assyrians. Beyond the Persian Gulf are the Babylonians; beyond the Ethiopians are the Arabs. The Egyptians reside on the banks of the Nile River and near our sea. Then Arabia, with narrow shoreline, touches the neighboring shores. As we related above, Syria covers the land from Arabia to the bend in the land. In the bend itself is Cilicia, as well as Lycia and Pamphylia, Caria, Ionia, Aeolis, and the Troad right up to the Hellespont. From there are the Bithynians all the way to the Thracian Bosphorus. Around the Pontus are any number of peoples called as a whole "Pontic" but with a variety of borders. Near Lake Maeotis are the Maeotici and the Sauromatai, who dwell near the Tanais.

. . .

1.18. The first peoples of Europe are Scythians (different from the ones mentioned before). They stretch from the Tanais to about the middle of the Pontus. From here, Thrace reaches into part of the Aegean and touches upon Macedon. Then Greece protrudes and divides the Aegean

---

94. The Chinese.

95. There are people in both Europe and Asia called Scythians.

96. It is thought that the missing text refers to the Caspian Sea.

from the Ionian Sea. Illyria occupies the Adriatic coast. Italy extends in between the Adriatic and Tuscan Seas. Gaul is in the heart of the Tuscan Sea, while Spain is on the far edge. 19. Spain itself advances west for a great distance and also to the north with multiple coastlines. Then Gaul again continues for a long distance until it reaches our shores. The Germans extend from Gaul to the Saromatai, who themselves extend as far as Asia.

. . .

1.22. In the part of Africa adjacent to the Libyan Sea near the Nile is a province called Cyrene. Then comes Africa, named after the term applied to the whole continent. The Numidians and the Mauritians hold the rest of the region; the Mauritians are exposed to the Atlantic. Beyond these peoples are the Nigritae and Pharusians, who extend to the Ethiopians. The Ethiopians settled the rest of the continent and the entire coast, which looks south as far as Asia. 23. But, beyond the shores nourished by the Libyan Sea are the Libyan Egyptians and the White Ethiopians and the Gaetuli, a very populous nation. Next is a region devoid of people and entirely uninhabitable. Then, to the east, we hear first of the Gamarantae, the Augilae, the Trogodytai, and, farthest to the west, the Atlantes. In the interior of this region, if one puts faith in such stories, are the hardly-human and mostly-savage Goat-Pans, Blemyes, Gamphasantes, and Satyrs. They "possess" more than inhabit the land, since they don't have houses or settlements but just wander about.

12. Propertius, *Elegies* 3.11 (1st century BCE). *Propertius discusses the character of foreign peoples through their famous women. (MLG)*

Why are you surprised that a woman controls my life, binds and herds her man under her own laws? Why do you contrive sordid charges against my person because I cannot break free of ball and chain? A sailor best knows how to predict the habits of the wind; a soldier has learned fear from his wounds. I made the same boasts as you in my lost youth. Now you learn fear from my example.

The woman from Colchis yoked flame-breathing bulls to adamant [10], sowed the land with violent battles and shut the savage maw of the guardian dragon so that the golden fleece might go to Aeson's home. Once upon a time, savage Penthesilea from Maeotis boldly attacked the Greek fleet, shooting her arrows from horseback. Her shining beauty conquered her conqueror after her golden helm revealed her countenance. Omphale, a Lydian girl, dyed by Gyges' lake, obtained such recognition of her beauty that the man who pacified the globe and held up its pillars [20] took to weaving soft wool with his brutal hands. Semiramis built the Persian city of Babylon, raising up a structure of solid brick so large that two chariots, racing in opposite directions on the wall, would not touch axles in passing. She even diverted the Euphrates through the middle of the citadel she built and ordered Bactria to bow its head to her power. Well, why am I putting heroes and gods on the witness stand? Jupiter convicts himself and his house of infamy.

What about the woman who recently defamed our army and, [30] after screwing her own slaves, demanded a price for her lewd union—the walls of Rome and the senate bound to her own kingdom? Criminal Alexandria is a land best suited to treachery, and Memphis has been so often bloodied to our disadvantage. There, the sand removed three triumphs from Pompey. No day shall wipe out this stain from you, Rome. It would have been better, Pompey, for your funeral to travel along the Phlegrean fields, or if you would have given your neck to your father-in-law. Of course, the whore queen of promiscuous Canopus—[40] the single stain burned on Philip's blood—boldly set barking Anubis against our Jupiter and compelled the Tiber to endure the Nile's threats. She dared to replace the Roman trumpet with the rattling *sistrum*, to pursue Liburnian galleys with barge poles, to cover the Tarpeian rock with dirty mosquito nets, and to give legal judgments between the statues and arms of Marius! What pleasure now in having broken the axes of Tarquin, whose arrogant lifestyle inspired his arrogant name? Sing your triumphal hymn, Rome, and [50] offer a prayer to live a long, safe life under Augustus! Then you fled, Cleopatra, to the meandering stream of the timid Nile; your wrists received Romulan fetters. You watched as your arm was bitten by a sacred serpent and your limbs were poisoned by that secret path to torpor. "You need not have been afraid, Rome, since you had such a citizen!" Thus she spoke, her tongue constantly buried in strong wine. The lofty city of seven hills, which controls the whole world, <endures and no human hand can destroy it.>[97]

Gods established these walls; the gods will also preserve them: Rome hardly needs fear Jupiter while Caesar lives. Where now is the fleet of Scipio? The standards of Camillus? Or you, Bosphorus, recently captured by Pompey? The spoils from Hannibal? The monument for the conquest of Syphax? Pyrrhus' glory, which was shattered before our feet? Curtius filled the hole to create a monument and Decius drove his horse to break the battle line. The pathway still bears witness to Cocles' removing of the bridge. One received his name from the raven. Leucadian Apollo shall memorialize the enemy in flight: [70] a single day has removed so great a work of war. But you, sailor, when you arrive at and leave the port, remember Caesar all over Ionia.

13. Pliny, *Natural History* 7.6, 7.9–32 (1st century CE).[98] *Pliny introduces his book on human diversity. Variety, he says, is the nature of things. He then continues on to describe the strange and unusual*

---

97. The text is corrupt here.

98. The numbering of the chapters for Pliny's *NH* are varied. We have rendered the various systems as Book, chapter, subchapter.

peoples beyond India, Ethiopia, and the other fringes of the known world. (RFK/MLG)

7.6. We have spoken about humanity in general at great length in relation to the tribes of men.[99] Nor will we recall again the numerous rituals and customs of men, which are almost as varied as the people themselves. Nevertheless, I think certain peoples can hardly be omitted, especially those dwelling beyond the sea. I doubt very little that some of what I recount about them will appear unnatural and absolutely unbelievable to many. For who believed in stories about Ethiopians before he saw them? Or what is not considered a miracle when it first becomes known? How many things are judged impossible before they happen? Truly, the power and majesty of the nature of things lacks believability at all times if someone embraces in their minds only a portion of the universe and not the whole. I need not mention peacocks, nor the spots and stripes of tigers and panthers, nor the embellishment of so many animals—little things to speak of, but immeasurable in their extent. So many languages among people! As many languages as there are tongues. There are so many varieties of ways of speaking that an outsider is often hardly considered human to someone in the next town over! Already in form and face, where there is scarcely more than ten distinctive parts to combine, there exists no two men among a thousand who share the same features—a feat no art could strive to surpass in a majority of instances even among a few men only. Nevertheless, I will not swear by the stories, but rather in questionable cases I will ascribe them to the authors who rendered the accounts. May it not be distasteful[100] that in some cases I follow those Greeks whose diligence and care in this study is by far greater than my own.

. . .

7.9. I have earlier pointed out[101] that there are types of Scythians, and many at that, who eat human flesh. This fact would seem unbelievable unless we reflect that in the middle of the world there used to be monstrous races of this sort such as the Cyclopes and the Laistrygonians. In our own time there are tribes beyond the Alps who are accustomed to perform a thing not much different from cannibalism.

7.10. Next to the northward-facing Scythians and near to the cave where the north winds rise (a place called Ges Clithron) the land produces the Arimaspi, whom we mentioned earlier. These people are distinguished by a single eye in the middle of their forehead. They wage continual war around their mines with griffins, a type of wild flying beast. As is the common report, these snatch gold from the mines and try to protect it from the Arimaspi, who try to steal it. Many have reported this, but the most

---

99. He does this in the geographical books elsewhere in the *Natural History*.

100. To the Roman audience, some of whom disdained the Greeks and Greek culture.

101. In 4.88 and 6.50, 6.53.

illustrious were Herodotus and Aristeas Pronnensius. 11. Beyond the rest of the Anthropophagoi[102] Scythians, there is a region called Abarimon, in a certain large valley of the Imavus Mountains.[103] In this region there is a forest people whose feet face backwards and who are outstandingly fast and who traverse vast spaces with wild animals. Baeton, Alexander the Great's surveyor, reports that these people do not breathe in other climates and thus have not been displayed before the neighboring kings nor before Alexander himself.

7.12. Those Anthropophagoi, whom we just mentioned as living toward the north, are ten-days journey past the river Borysthenes,[104] according to Isigonus of Nicaea, and drink from human skulls and wear on their chest scalps with hair as napkins. The same author reports that in Albania there exist certain people who have sharp-sighted grey eyes and who are bald from youth. They see better at night than in the day. Isigonus also reports that thirteen-days journey beyond the Borysthenes live the Sauromatai, who always eat every other day.

7.13. Crates of Pergamum says that in the region of Parium on the Hellespont there was a race of people whom he calls the Ophiogenes. These were accustomed to relieve snakebites by touch and then draw the poison from the body with their hand. Varro says that even now there are a few people whose saliva can heal snakebites. 14. According to the writings of Agatharchides, there was a similar tribe in Africa, the Psylli who are named for their king Psyllus. His tomb is located in the region of the greater Syrtes. Their bodies produce a poison deadly to snakes, and their smell puts snakes to sleep. In fact, it is their custom to expose their newly-born children to the most savage snakes in order to test the fidelity of their wives, since snakes do not flee from a child born with adulterous blood. This tribe was indeed massacred and nearly annihilated by the Nasamonians, who now control those regions. Nevertheless, that race of people still exists in places, since they fled or were absent during the fighting. 15. Even in Italy this race of human remains, the Marsians, who are supposed to be descended from the son of Circe and to have on this account an inborn natural power. In point of fact, all humans have an internal poison against snakes. It is said that snakes flee from spit as from boiling water, and if it gets in their mouths, they even die, especially if the spit comes from a fasting person. Beyond the Nasamones and bordering them are, according to Calliphanes, the Machlyae Androgyni [men-women], who have characteristics of each sex and take turns coupling. Aristotle adds that their right breast is male and their left female.

7.16. Isigonus and Nymphodorus report that there are certain families in Africa that practice magic and whose speech of praise destroys fields, dries up trees, and kills infants. Isigonus adds that this race exists among the Triballi and the Illyrians, who can bewitch with a look and who kill those

---

102. This word means "man-eating."

103. Perhaps part of the Himalayan range.

104. The Dnieper River, which flows through modern Russia, Belarus, and Ukraine toward the Black Sea.

they gaze upon for any period of time, especially when their eyes are angry. He says that adults are more easily affected by their witchcraft, and that they are most remarkable for having two pupils in each eye. 17. Apollonides describes women of this race in Scythia called Bitiae. Phylarchus reports of a race in Pontus, the Thibii, and many others of the same nature. He says that some are known from the double pupil in one eye and others from their horselike appearance, and that they cannot sink in water, not even weighed down by clothing. Damon reports a similar race in Ethiopia, the Pharmaces, whose sweat relieves illness when it touches the skin. Indeed, all women everywhere with double pupils cause harm by their gaze, according to the Roman author Cicero. 18. Thus nature, when she has produced in humans the custom of eating human flesh like wild beasts, also decided to produce poisons in their entire bodies and in the eyes of some in order that every evil everywhere would also be in humans.

7.19. In the territory of the Faliscans, not far from Rome, are a few families called the Hirpi. During the annual sacrifice to Apollo performed at Mount Soracte, they walk across burning coals without being burned. Because of this they have an exemption by perpetual senatorial decree from military service and all other duties. 20. Certain people have been born with miraculous body parts. For example, the right big toe of King Pyrrhus could cure inflammation of the spleen with a touch. This toe, it is said, would not burn when he was cremated and was deposited in a chest in a temple. 21. India and the territories of Ethiopia especially abound in marvels. The largest animals are born in India. For example, their dogs are larger than other dogs. There are reports of trees of such height that one cannot shoot over them with an arrow. The richness of the soil, the mildness of the climate and the abundance of water cause, if one wants to believe it, that a single fig tree can shelter cavalry squadrons. The reeds are of such height that a single section can at times make a canoe capable of carrying three people. 22. It is agreed that many men there are taller than 7.5 feet, never spit, and never suffer from any ailments of head, teeth, or eyes, and rarely in any other part of the body. They are toughened by the moderate warmth of the sun. Their philosophers, whom they call Gymnosophists [Naked Wise Men], stand from sunrise to sunset gazing upon the sun with unmoving eyes and shift all day from one foot to another because of the hot sand.

7.23. In a mountain called Nulus are men with backward feet and eight toes on each, according to Megasthenes. He reports that on many mountains, there is a race with dog heads, dressed in animal skins, who use barks as language, and who live by hunting and fowling with their fingernails. He claims that when he wrote their population was around 120,000. Ctesias writes that in a certain Indian tribe the women give birth only once in their life and after birth immediately go grey. The same authority speaks of a type of men called Monocoli who have only one leg but jump surprisingly swiftly. The same people are called Sciapodae, because in hot weather they lie on their backs on the ground and use their foot to shade themselves. They do not dwell far from the Trogodytai. Not far from these to the west are certain people who have no neck and eyes on their shoulders.

24. There are even satyrs in the eastern mountains of India in a region called Catarcludi. These are very fast animals who run at times on four legs and at times upright in human fashion. On account of this speed, only the old and the sick are captured. Tauron calls a forest tribe the Choromandae, who have no language but a horrifying hissing, hairy bodies, grey eyes, and teeth like dogs. Eudoxus says that in the south of India the men have feet eighteen inches long, and the women have feet so small that they are called Struthopodes [sparrow-foot].

7.25. Megasthenes reports that there is a tribe among the Indian nomads called the Sciritae who have only holes in place of a nose like snakes and who are bowlegged.[105] He also reports that at the farthest eastern border of India near the source of the Ganges is a tribe, the Astromi, who have no mouths, who have hair over all their bodies, who dress in fuzz scraped from leaves, and live only on breath and on the smells that their noses extract. They have no food and no drink, simply the diverse aromas of roots and flowers and wild apples, which they take with them on longer trips in case they run out of odors. He adds that a somewhat stronger smell can kill them. 26. Past these in the farthest region of the mountains it is said that the Trispithami and Pygmies dwell. These grow to three spans, that is, twenty-seven inches and no more. The climate is healthy and perpetually spring, because it is protected from the north wind by mountains. Homer also reports that these Pygmies are attacked by cranes. There is a story that in spring they mount on the backs of rams and goats, arm themselves with arrows, and descend to the sea in a single battle line, where they eat these birds' eggs and young chicks. This campaign takes three months, and they would not be able to resist the future flocks if they did not destroy the young. Houses there are said to be constructed with mud, feathers, and eggshells. 27. Aristotle recounts that the Pygmies live in caves but agrees with other authorities in other respects. Isigonus reports that a race of Indians, the Cyrni, live for 140 years, and he judges that the same is the case for the Macrobioi [long-lived] Ethiopians and the Seres and the men who live on Mount Athos, because they eat snake flesh and therefore their heads, clothes, and bodies are safe from harmful creatures.

7.28. Onesicritus says that in some regions of India where there is no shade, the bodies of the people grow to a height of around eight feet and they live for 130 years without growing old and die in middle age. Crates of Pergamum called the Indians who live beyond a hundred years the Gymnetes, but there are no small number of authorities who call them the Macrobioi. Ctesias mentions a tribe who are called the Pandae, who dwell in a valley and live 200 years and whose hair starts out white in their youth and turns black as they age. 29. There are others, we hear, who only live forty years, neighbors to the Macrobioi, whose women only give birth once. Agatharchides also reports this, adding that they eat locusts and are swift. Clitarchus gives these people the name Mandi, and Megasthenes

---

105. Or, who have holes in place of nose and feet twisted like snakes.

numbers their villages at 300 and reports that their women give birth at seven years old and old age is forty. 30. Artemidorus says that on the island of Taprobane people live very long lives without any weakening of their bodies. Duris says that some Indians have sex with wild animals and give birth to mixed and semi-wild beings. He says that among a certain Indian tribe, the Calingi, the five-year-old women get pregnant and only live for eight years. In other areas, he says, an amazingly fast people are born with hairy tails. He also mentions some who are entirely covered by their ears. The river Arabis divides the Oritae from the Indians. The Oritae know of no other food except fish, which they cut up with their fingers and roast in the sun; in this way they make bread from fish, as Clitarchus says.

7.31. Crates of Pergamum claims that the Trogodytai, a people beyond Ethiopia, are faster than horses. He also says that there are Ethiopians taller than twelve feet; he calls this tribe Syrbotae. Along the river Astragus is a north-facing tribe of Ethiopian nomads called the Menismini who are twenty-days journey from the ocean. They live on the milk of an animal we call Cynocephali [dog-head]. They pasture herds of these, killing the males except for breeding. 32. In the African deserts, the shapes of men suddenly appear before the traveler and disappear a moment later. These and such races of humans have been created by clever nature to amuse herself and to amaze us. Who could list the separate races she makes daily and nearly hourly? To have presented the tribes among her monsters should be enough to reveal her power.

14. Martial, *Epigrams* 7.30 (2nd century CE). *Martial highlights the multicultural nature of Rome. (MLG)*

You give it up for Parthians, for Germans, and for Dacians, Caelia. You don't spurn the beds of Cilicians and Cappadocians. A fellow who sails from Memphis in Egypt or a black Indian from the Red Sea fucks you. You don't run away from the cocks of circumcised Jews. One of the Alani doesn't pass you by on his Sarmatian horse. Why is it, when you are a Roman girl, that no Roman cocks please you?

15. [Apollodorus], *The Library* 2.5.11 (2nd century CE). *The journey of Heracles to fetch the apples of the Hesperides. (RFK)*

His labors were finished in eight years and one month. Eurystheus, however, would not accept the Augean stables, so he ordered an eleventh labor—to bring back the golden apples of the Hesperides. They were not in Libya as some say, but were in the land of the Hyperboreans on Mount Atlas. Gaia had presented them to Zeus upon his marriage to Hera. An immortal dragon, a child of Echidna and Typhon, guarded them. This dragon had one hundred heads, which each used a different voice. Along with the dragon, the Hesperides also stood as guards—Argyle, Erytheia, Hesperia, and Arethusa. Wandering, Heracles arrived at the Echedorus River. There, Cucnus, the child of Ares and Pyrene, challenged him in single combat. Because Ares took sides in the combat and fought for his son, Zeus hurled a thunderbolt between the combatants and parted them. Heracles then walked through Illyria and rushed to the Eridanus River, where he came upon nymphs born to Zeus and Themis. The nymphs revealed Nereus to him, whom Heracles seized while he was sleeping. He held him tight, though Nereus kept changing form, and did not release him until he learned from him where he might happen to find the apples and the Hesperides. Learning their location, he crossed Libya. Antaeus, a son of Poseidon, was ruling there. He used to kill foreigners by compelling them to wrestle. When Heracles was forced to wrestle him, he killed Antaeus by wrapping him in a bear hug, lifting him off the ground, and breaking him. For Antaeus happened to gain strength when he touched the earth, a mysterious result, some say, because he was the child of the earth.

After Libya, Heracles traveled to Egypt. Busiris, son of Poseidon and Lysianassa, daughter of Epaphus, was king there. He used to sacrifice foreigners upon the altar of Zeus in accordance with an oracle.[106] So the story goes, for nine years drought had seized Egypt, and Phrasios, a trustworthy seer, came from Cyprus and said that the drought would end if they slaughtered a foreign man each year. Busiris started by killing the seer and then sacrificed foreigners as they arrived. Thus, when Heracles arrived, he was seized and dragged to the altar. He broke his bonds, however, and killed both Busiris and his son Amphidamus.

Traveling across Asia, he arrived next at Thermydrae, the harbor of the Lindians. There he released a bull from a cart belonging to a cowherd, sacrificed it, and ate it. The cowherd was powerless to protect his goods from Heracles and so, instead, stood on a mountain and cursed him. For this reason, even today the Lindians curse while they are sacrificing to Heracles. Passing near Arabia Heracles now killed Emanthion, son of Tithonus. Then, traveling across Libya to the outer sea, he received the goblet from Helios.[107] He crossed the Ocean to the opposite shore and there shot down with arrows Caucasus the eagle, child of Typhon and Echidna, who was continually eating the liver of Prometheus.

---

106. The sacrifice of foreigners was a common motif in Greek stories about mythical barbarians. See also *Iphigenia among Taurians*.

107. Apollodorus later (2.107) recounts the story of the goblet. Heracles shot arrows at Helios for making him too hot. Helios admired his daring and granted him a goblet, which was so large that Heracles used it as a boat to cross the Ocean.

16. [Apollodorus], *The Library* 3.5.1–3 (2nd century CE). *Dionysus' journeys and the spread of his cult. (RFK)*

3.5.1. Dionysus, after discovering the vine and being driven mad by Hera, wandered around Egypt and Syria. First, Proteus, king of Egypt, received him gladly. Soon after, he arrived at Cybele in Phrygia, and there was purified and initiated into the rites of Rhea.[108] He began to wear the garb associated with her cult and marched through Thrace against the Indians. Lycurgus, son of Dryas, was king of the Edonians, who dwell near the Strymon River. Lycurgus was the first to commit an outrage against Dionysus and expel him. Dionysus himself fled to the sea to Thetis, daughter of Nereus. His Bacchae and many of his satyr companions were imprisoned. Miraculously, though, his Bacchae were freed and Dionysus drove Lycurgus mad. . .

3.5.2. After traveling across Thrace and all of India, where he set up monuments, he arrived at Thebes.[109] There he compelled the women to leave their homes and join the Bacchanal on Mount Cithaeron. Pentheus, child of Agave and Echion, had become king after Cadmus. He sought to prevent Dionysus' worship and went to Mount Cithaeron to spy on the Bacchae. He was torn apart by his mother Agave, who thought he was a wild animal. Once Dionysus had thus shown the Thebans that he was a god, he went to Argos. In Argos, he once again drove the women to madness because he was not appropriately honored. The women were made to eat their children, infants still held to their breasts.

3.5.3. Dionysus then wanted to travel from Icaria to Naxos and so hired a ship from Tyrrhenian pirates. The pirates boarded his ship and then set sail past Naxos and headed toward Asia to sell him there as a slave. Dionysus, however, turned the mast and oars into serpents and filled the ship with vines and the sound of the *aulos*.[110] The pirates went mad and threw themselves into the sea where they became dolphins. Thus men honored Dionysus as a god.

17. Ptolemy, *Tetrabiblos* 2.3.59–72 (2nd century CE). *The* Tetrabiblos *is an astrological work. In this section, Ptolemy links geography and astrology to show how the peoples living under certain stars resemble in national character the character of the astrological sign associated with those stars. Ptolemy begins by defining the four triangles of the zodiac*

---

108. The cult of Cybele, or Magna Mater. Dionysus is frequently associated in classical myths with eastern cults and as a result was long considered by modern scholars to be a late, foreign "import." Inscriptional evidence from the Bronze Age (c.1300 BCE), however, shows that he was worshipped very early on the Greek mainland.

109. Greek Thebes, not Egyptian.

110. A Greek flutelike instrument associated with reveling.

into which the sky is divided. These triangles are then overlaid upon the disk of the oikoumenê, *the inhabited world. (RFK)*

2.3.59. This is how the triangles are arranged. The inhabited world[111] itself is divided into four quadrants, equal in number to the triangles. The world is divided along its width by Our Sea from the Straits of Heracles up to the Gulf of Issus and the ridged mountains next to it to the east. The southern and northern regions created by this line are separated heightwise by the Arabian Gulf, Aegean Sea, the Pontus, and Lake Maeotis.[112] [60] The eastern and western sections are thus separated, and the four quadrants emerge similar in position to the four triangles of the zodiac. The first quadrant lies in the northwest of the world and includes the Celto-Gauls. We typically call this quadrant Europe. Lying opposite Europe to the southeast is the next quadrant encompassing the eastern Ethiopians,[113] which we would refer to as the southern half of Asia Major.[114] Again, to the northeast of the world, including Scythia, is the northern quadrant made up of the northern half of Asia Major. Opposite this quadrant toward the southwest wind is what is commonly called Libya, where the eastern Ethiopians dwell . . .

Ptolemy next describes how the quadrants all meet near the center, and how this intersection of the quadrants binds each quadrant to both its triangle of the zodiac and its opposite quadrant. This binding results in those peoples closer to the intersection point at the center sharing characteristics with their opposites. Hermes, the god of boundaries and travelers, governs in the center as a go-between.

2.3.61. From this arrangement, the remainder of the first quadrant—and I mean here Europe—lying to the northwest of the world cohabitates with the northwestern triangle containing Aries, Leo, and Sagittarius, and is ruled, of course, by the masters of the triangle, Zeus and Ares western. The nations within this region are Britain, Galatia, Germany, Bastarnia,[115] Italy, Gaul, Apulia, Sicily, Tyrrhenia, Celtica, and Spain. Of course, it happens, because of the dominance of the triangle and its associated co-ruling stars, that in general these people are characterized as freedom-loving, fond of weapons, hard-working, and warlike with elements of leadership, cleanliness, and courage. [62] However, because of the western orientation of Zeus and Ares, and more so because of the associations of the earlier noted

---

111. Ptolemy uses the Greek *oikoumenê* throughout, which was the common designation for the earth and represents a view of the world as always "people-centered," not space-centered.

112. In both divisions, Ptolemy exemplifies the Greek preference to use natural bodies of water as the primary method of creating boundaries. See Map 5.

113. The Indians.

114. A designation among the geographers for the landmass of Asia that stretches east from the Euphrates.

115. The southwestern region of Russia.

regions of the triangle, the people in this part of the quadrant are manly, while those in the other part are womanly. These nations are uninterested in women and think poorly of the arts of love. They prefer and are more satisfied by relationships with men.[116] Neither do they consider the act shameful for those "on top"[117] nor, truly, do they become soft or unmanly by virtue of the act because they are not disposed to take the sexual role of the woman.[118] Thus they retain their manly spirits, sense of camaraderie, faith, love of family, and call to service. Of these same lands, Britain, Galatia, Germany, and Bastarnia are more strongly associated with Aries and Ares. Thus they are generally more savage, more daring, and more fierce. Italy, Apulia, Gaul, and Sicily are closer to Leo and the sun. Accordingly, they are more leadership- and service-oriented and cooperative. Tyrrhenia, Celtica, and Spain are ruled by Sagittarius and Zeus, and so they are freedom-loving, simple, and fond of cleanliness.

2.3.63. Those parts of Europe that are positioned near the center of the world—Thrace, Macedon, Illyria, Greece, Achaea, Crete, the Cyclades, the Asia Minor coast, and Cyprus—and that lie near the southeast part of the quadrant, have an affinity with the southeast triangle that contains Taurus, Virgo, and Capricorn and is ruled jointly by Aphrodite, Cronus, and Hermes. Thus the inhabitants of this land are brought into conformity with the signs and are mixed in body and soul. They are leaders because of Ares, freedom-loving, autonomous, democratic, law-abiding, lovers of learning and contests, and clean in their daily habit because of Aphrodite, and are social, fond of strangers, lovers of justice and literature, and well-practiced in public speaking because of Hermes. They are also especially accomplished in the mysteries[119] because of Aphrodite's western orientation. Further, within the quadrant those who dwell near the Cyclades, the Asia Minor coast, and Cyprus are more closely associated with Taurus and Aphrodite. Thus they are on the whole very decadent, clean, and careful of their bodies. Those living in Greece, Achaea, and Crete are closer to Virgo and Hermes. For this reason, they are more logical and learned and exercise their minds instead of their bodies. [64] Those living in Macedon, Illyria, and Thrace are ruled by Sagittarius and Cronus, thus making them lovers of gain, less mild-mannered, and with unsocial customs.

In the second quadrant, the one containing the southern portion of Asia Major, those regions including India, Ariana, Gedrosia, Parthia, Media, Persia, Babylonia, Mesopotamia, Assyria, and the area positioned near the southeastern part of the world, obviously cohabitate with the southeastern triangle, which consists of Taurus, Virgo, and Sagittarius, with Aphrodite and Cronus ruling in their eastern orientation. [65] On account of this, one would likely find that the natures of the people living in those regions reflect

---

116. The Greek term here is *sounousîa*, the term used for sexual relationships.

117. The active sexual partner, i.e., the one who penetrates.

118. Ptolemy says they do not act *pathêtikôs*, meaning the passive or penetrated partner.

119. Ritual cults in which members were initiated through secret rituals.

the natures of the ruling elements. And, indeed, they revere Aphrodite as Isis and Cronus as Mithras Helios. The majority of these people are diviners of the future. They also deem their genitals sacred because the orientation of their stars is generative by nature. In addition, they tend to be rash, salacious, and inclined toward sexual pleasure. They are also suited to dancing and leaping and love adornment—all because of their affinity with Aphrodite. They are decadent because of their closeness to Cronus. They have sexual relations with women in the open instead of behind closed doors because of their eastern orientation, but loathe sexual relations with men. Accordingly, it happens that the majority of their children are begotten with their own mothers and, because of the morning rising of the planets and the leading position of the heart (similar in power to the sun), they perform *proskynesis*[120] to the breast.

The other regions are generally effeminate in their clothing, adornments, and all-over condition of their bodies because of Aphrodite. In their souls and principles of life, they are generous, noble, and warlike on account of their affinity with Cronus in his eastern orientation. Further, Parthia, Media, and Persia are more closely aligned with Taurus and Aphrodite. As a result, those who dwell there use embroidered cloth, which covers their entire bodies except one breast, and they are generally clean and decadent. Babylonia, Mesopotamia, and Assyria, because of their nearness to Virgo and Hermes, are especially inclined to mathematics and the observation of the five planets. With Capricorn and Cronus are India, Ariana, and Gedrosia, whence the ugliness, uncleanliness, and savagery of those who dwell there.

The remaining sections of the quadrant, those positioned near the center of the world—Idumaea, Coele-Syria, Judea, Phoenicia, Chaldaea, Orchinia, and Arabia Felix—which are situated in the northwest of the quadrant, dwell also in the northwestern triangle. Aries, Leo, and Sagittarius influence them, and they are ruled by Zeus, Ares, and Hermes as well. Accordingly, they are fonder of commerce and trade than others. They are also more cunning than others, are insolent cowards, scheming, have the souls of slaves, and are altogether fickle. Further, from this group, Coele-Syria, Idumaea, and Judaea are more closely aligned with Aries and Ares. [66] On account of this, they are generally bold, godless, and scheming. Phoenicians, Chaldaeans, and Orchinians are closer to Leo and the sun, thus they are without wealth, are humanitarians, lovers of astrology, and more than all others revere the sun. Those who dwell in Arabia Felix are aligned with Sagittarius and Zeus, whence the fertility of the land that gives them their name, and the abundance of spices, accommodating nature of the people, and their free attitude toward daily living, commerce, and work.

2.3.67. The third quadrant, which contains the northern part of Asia Major and includes Hyrcania, Armenia, Matiana, Bactria, Casperia, Serica, Sauromatica, Oxiana, Sogdania, and the place lying to the northeast of the world, is aligned with the northeastern triangle, namely, Gemini, Libra, and

---

120. See Herodotus *Histories* 1.134 (Chapter 10, Selection 4) on Greek interpretations of *proskynesis*. This view is a misinterpretation of Persian practice.

Aquarius, and is ruled by Cronus and Zeus in their eastern orientations. Accordingly, those who dwell in these lands revere Zeus and Cronus, are extremely wealthy in gold, are clean and pleasant in the way they live, and are both wise and are expert in divine matters. They also have just and free dispositions. They have great and noble souls, hate ne'er-do-wells, are affectionate, and are ready to die for those closest to them in a good and sacred cause. Regarding sexual intimacy, they are solemn and pure. They dress extravagantly, are gracious and confident. All these characteristics result from the eastern orientations of Cronus and Zeus. Of these nations, Hyrcernia, Armenia, and Matiana are more closely aligned with Gemini and Hermes. Accordingly, they are more easily roused and somewhat wicked. Bactria, Casperia, and Serica are aligned with Libra and Aphrodite, thus the inhabitants are very wealthy, lovers of music, and rather effeminate. Sauromantica, Oxiana, and Sogdania are influenced by Aquarius and Cronus. [68] For this reason, the nations are rather wild, harsh, and savage.

The remaining parts of this quadrant, including the part lying near the center of the world—Bithynia, Cappadocia, Lydia, Lycia, Cilicia, and Pamphylia—because they are located in the southwestern of the quadrant, share affinity with the southwestern quadrant opposite it. Here, Cancer, Scorpio, and Pisces lie, with Ares, Aphrodite, and Hermes ruling. [69] The result is that the inhabitants of these regions revere Aphrodite as mother of the gods,[121] granting her a variety of local names. They also revere Ares and Adonis, again, by other names. They surrender themselves to certain mysteries through lamentation. They are a thoroughly evil people, are slaves in their souls, difficult, and wicked. When they serve as mercenaries, they steal and kidnap. They make their own people slaves and engage in destructive types of warfare. This is because of the eastern orientation of Ares and Aphrodite. Since Ares is with Capricorn, a sign of Aphrodite's triangle, and Aphrodite is with Pisces, a sign in Ares' triangle, wives there are altogether well-minded toward their husbands; they are affectionate, domestic, industrious, servile, and entirely hard-working and obedient.

Those who dwell in Bithynia, Phrygia, and Colchis are more akin to Capricorn and the moon. As a result, the men are generally circumspect and submissive, while the majority of women, because of the eastern and masculine orientation of the moon, are manly, commanding, and warlike. An example are the Amazons, who flee sex with men, love weaponry, and from early childhood make masculine all their female qualities; for military purposes, they cut off their right breasts and bare this part of themselves when arrayed for battle as a way of showing their unfemale nature. The inhabitants of Syria, Commagenes, and Cappadocia are aligned with Scorpio and Ares. Accordingly, they are particularly bold, wicked, scheming, and difficult. Those dwelling in Lydia, Cilicia, and Pamphylia are closer to Pisces and Zeus. They are, therefore, more wealthy, mercantile, commercial, free, and trustworthy in contracts.

---

121. Magna Mater, the Great Mother.

2.3.70. The remaining quadrant contains the region called Libya as well as Numidia, Carthage, Africa,[122] Phazania, Nasamonia, Garamantia, Mauritania, Gaetulia, Metagonitis, and those places located in the southwest of the world. These are aligned with the southwestern triangle of Cancer, Scorpio, and Pisces, and are ruled, of course, by both Ares and Aphrodite in their western orientation. The majority of inhabitants of these regions, because of the junction of the stars, tend to be ruled by husband and wife who are siblings of the same mother, with the brother ruling the men of the nation and the sister ruling the women and with such a succession preserved over time. The peoples are very passionate and fond of sexual intercourse with women, so that even marriages are made through rapes. Often, the kings share "first rights" with the bride. Among some inhabitants, the women are shared by all. These peoples tend to love beautifying themselves and dressing themselves up with womanly adornments because of Aphrodite. They are also manly in their souls, wicked and magical, but also charlatans, deceitful, and reckless because of Ares.

Of these peoples, the Numidians, Carthaginians, and Africans are more aligned with Cancer and the moon. Accordingly, they happen to be communal and commercial and live their lives entirely prosperously. Those who dwell in Metagonitis, Mauritania, and Gaetulia are akin to Scorpio and Ares. [71] As a result, they are rather savage, very warlike, carnivorous, extremely reckless, and so contemptuous toward life that they don't even spare each other.

Those who dwell in Phazania, Nasamonia, and Garamantia are linked with Pisces and Zeus. As a result, they are both free and easy in their manners, industrious, smart, clean, and independent. They are also generally devoted to Zeus under the name Ammon. The rest of the quadrant, located in the center of the world—Cyrenaica, Marmarica, Egypt, Thebais, the Oasis, Troglodytica, Arabia, Azania, and central Ethiopia—which is oriented toward the northeast of the whole quadrant—also partake of the nature of the northeastern triangle of Gemini, Libra, Aquarius, and its rulers Cronus, Zeus, and Hermes. Whence the inhabitants, sharing nearly five planets as rulers in their western orientations, are devoted to the gods, superstitious, very religious, and lovers of lament. They hide their dead in the ground and make them invisible on account of the western orientation of the region. They use all types of customs, habits, and rituals for all types of gods. When serving others, they are humble, cowardly, soft-spoken, and patient. [72] When leading, they are courageous and proud. But they are polygamous and polyandrous and inclined even toward marrying their sisters. The men are very potent, the women extremely fertile, just as the land is fertile. Many of the men are unsound and womanly in their souls. Some even despise their generative parts because of the orientation of the evildoing stars with western Aphrodite.

---

122. The Roman province, not the continent, which they often called Libya.

Of these people, those dwelling in Cyrenaica, Marmarica, and especially those in Lower Egypt are more closely aligned with Gemini and Hermes. As a result, they are intelligent and wise and shrewd concerning everything, especially in the discovery of wisdom and divine things. They are magicians and accomplished in secret mysteries. They are also altogether competent at mathematics. Those who dwell in Thebais, the Oasis, and Troglodytica are aligned with Libra and Aphrodite, whence they are more passionate and mutable and have a lifestyle marked by abundance. Those dwelling in Arabia, Azania, and central Ethiopia are aligned with Aquarius and Cronus. Accordingly, they are carnivorous, fish-eating, and nomadic. They live a savage and harsh life.

CHAPTER 7

AFRICA: EGYPT

Egypt was ancient even to the most ancient of the Greeks and was a crossroads of many peoples. The power and uniqueness of the Nile was the subject of many texts and was considered the greatest determining factor in defining Egyptian culture. The Macedonians (as the Ptolemaic dynasty) ruled Egypt for 300 years after Alexander's conquest and the establishment of Alexandria. The Romans too were fascinated with Egypt's antiquities and culture. The Roman civil war and subsequent establishment of the principate by Augustus entwined Cleopatra, the last Ptolemaic ruler, in Roman affairs and brought Egypt at last under Roman control.

> **1. Herodotus, Histories 2.2–5, 2.13–18, 2.28, 2.30–32, 2.35–42, 2.46–48 (5th century BCE).** *Herodotus dedicates nearly all of Book 2 of his* Histories *to describing in great detail the land, people, and culture of Egypt, which had been incorporated into the Persian Empire under Cambyses in the 6th century BCE. (CSR)*

2.2. The Egyptians, before Psammetichus became their king, thought that they were the oldest of all men. But once Psammetichus was king, he wanted to know who the first people were. As a result of his inquiry, the Egyptians think that the Phrygians are older than they are and that after the Phrygians they are older than everyone else. [2] Since Psammetichus was not able to discover the answer to who the first people were by asking around, he devised this test. He gave two newborn children from the same parents to a shepherd to raise in the countryside in the following way: He commanded that no one who met them would utter a sound, and that the shepherd should settle them in a remote homestead by themselves and bring them a goat for their care, feeding them goat's milk and managing their other needs. [3] This is what Psammetichus did. He wished to listen to the children, once they had left off from meaningless wailing, so he ordered the people to tell him what their first sounds were. This is what happened. For two years the shepherd carried out the king's commands, and eventually, whenever he opened the door and came in, both children would rush headlong toward him stretching their hands, shouting "bekos." [4] Indeed, upon first hearing these things the shepherd was undisturbed, but this word was said so often to him as he was visiting and tending to them, that, after he made this known to the king and was ordered to bring them in, he took the children to the king. Once Psammetichus himself heard it, he sought out someone who used the word *bekos*, and, as a result of his inquiry, he discovered that the Phrygians call bread *bekos*. [5] Thus the Egyptians yielded, for they judged from this experiment that the Phrygians are older than they are. I heard about this event from the priests of Hephaestus in Memphis. The Greeks say many silly things about this story, the silliest being that Psammetichus made a home for the children with women whose tongues he had cut out.

. . .

2.3. Such things are said about the rearing of the children, and I heard other things in Memphis, when I conversed with the priests of Hephaestus. Indeed, I went into Thebes and the city of the Sun to have these conversations, for I wanted to know if the priests there agreed with the stories told in Memphis; for the Heliopolitans are said to be the most informed of the Egyptians. [2] I am not eager to explain the stories I have heard about the gods, except for their names, since I think that all men have equal knowledge about them. I will mention them when I am forced by my narrative to do so.

   2.4. As for human affairs, the priests agree in their stories that the Egyptians were the first of all mankind to invent the yearly cycle, dividing up the year into the twelve seasonal units. They said they learned these things from the stars. They act more wisely in such a thing than the Greeks do, it seems to me, because the Greeks add in an intercalary month every third year to accord with the seasons, but the Egyptians take twelve months of thirty days and add five days to every year beyond the allotted days, and thus the cycle of the seasons once completed coincides again with the calendar. [2] They said that the Egyptians were the first to conceive of the names of the twelve gods and that the Greeks took these from them. They are also said to have first assigned altars and statues and temples to the gods and to have carved figures onto stone. They proved to me that this is how it happened. They said also that the first human king of the Egyptians was Min. [3] In his time all of Egypt was a swamp, except for the region around Thebes, and there was nothing visible below what is now Lake Moeris, which is seven days sailing from the sea on the river.

   2.5. And they seem to me to have spoken accurately concerning their land. It is clear even to one who has not heard it in advance, but sees it, if he has any intelligence, that the Egypt to which the Greeks sail is a newly deposited gift of the river to the Egyptians. And the same is true for the land south of the lake for a three-days sail. The priests said nothing more about this, but there is more proof. [2] The nature of Egypt is that it is new land, for if you sail out on a steady course for one day from land and send down a sounding line, you will bring up river mud even if you go down sixty-six feet. This shows how far out the river deposits mud.

. . .

2.13. The priests shared with me a great proof about the nature of this land, that during the kingship of Moeris, the river would rise to at least 12 feet and in this way would water Egypt below Memphis. Not quite 900 years had passed since Moeris died, when I heard these things from the priests. But now, if the river does not rise at least rise 22.5 to 24 feet, it does not overflow into the land. [2] Those Egyptians living north of Lake Moeris seem to me to be inhabiting different lands—the Delta is especially strange—for if the land grows in height and in width to the extent that it has in the past, then the Nile will no longer flood and the Egyptians will suffer for all time what they say the Greeks suffer, drought. [3] For when they learned that the whole of Greece was watered by rain, not by rivers like their own land, they said that the Hellenes would be cheated of their great hopes and would suffer badly. The meaning behind these comments is as follows: if the god does not want to send water for them, but wants instead to destroy them with a drought, the Greeks will be in the grip of famine since there is no other way for them to get water except from Zeus alone.

2.14. What the Egyptians say about the Hellenes is right. But now let us move on and I will tell you how it is among the Egyptians. If the land north of Memphis (for this is what is increasing), as I said before, should continue to increase in height over time, then what else would happen except that those of the Egyptians inhabiting this place would go hungry, if their land is not rained upon or their river is not able to flow over into the fields? [2] For indeed right now these men transport their grain with the least amount of toil compared to all other men and the rest of the Egyptians, for they do not have to work at breaking up the land with a plow nor do they have to hoe or do any other work that other men do as they labor over their crops. When the river, of its own accord, comes through and waters the fields and recedes again after watering them, then each man sows seeds on his own land and releases pigs into it. The seeds are trampled down by the pigs and only the harvest remains to be done. The pigs also thresh the harvest and so that too is taken care of.

2.15. If we wish to consult the opinions of the Ionians about Egypt, who say that Egypt is the Delta alone, according to them it extends from what is called the Look-out of Perseus along the sea and up to the Pelusian works and measures 182 miles. From there it stretches from the sea into the middle of the land up to the city of Cercasoros, where the Nile splits and flows into Pelusia and Canopus. The Ionians say that some parts of Egypt are actually of Libya, and others of Arabia. If we use this definition we can point out that earlier the Egyptians did not have this land at all. [2] For indeed the Delta is alluvial and appeared just recently, as the Egyptians themselves say and so it seems to me too. If, therefore, there was not at least some land for the Egyptians at the beginning, why did they go about thinking that they were the first men? For then it would not have been necessary for them to go through the experiment with the children to discover the first language. [3] But I do not think that the Egyptians came into being together with the land which the Ionians call the Delta, but that they always were from the time when the race of men came into being. While the land was forming down the river many of them stayed behind but many of them moved down with it. Thus long ago Thebes was called Egypt, the perimeter of which was 695 miles.

2.16. So if we are right in our thinking about these things, then the Ionians are incorrect about Egypt. But if the opinion of the Ionians is right, then I will show that the Greeks and the Ionians themselves do not know how to reason clearly if they say that there are three parts to the whole earth: Europe, Asia, and Libya. [2] For, in this case, it is necessary for them to consider that the Delta of Egypt is a fourth part if it is not Asian or Libyan. According to their reasoning, the Nile creates the boundary between Asia and Libya. The Nile breaks around the top of the Delta, so that the Delta is between Asia and Libya.

2.17. Let us leave the opinion of the Ionians behind and talk about our thoughts concerning these things—that all Egypt is the land occupied by the Egyptians just as Cilicia is occupied by Cilicians and Assyria by Assyrians, and that we know that there is no boundary for Asia and Libya, if we are thinking correctly, than the boundaries of the Egyptians. [2] But if we follow the opinions of the Greeks, we would think that all of Egypt, beginning from the Cataracts of the Nile and the city of Elephantine, is divided in two and has two eponymous halves. For one side would be part of Libya, the other part of Asia. [3] Indeed, the Nile, starting from the Cataract, flows through the middle of Egypt and cuts it in two as it flows down toward the sea. The Nile flows as one river up until the city of Cercasoros, and from that city it splits into three channels. [4] One of these turns to the east and is called the Pelousian mouth; another of the channels heads west and this is called the Canopic mouth. And indeed there is the mouth of the Nile, which goes straight. It moves on from this city and reaches the point of the Delta, then it cuts through the middle of the Delta and flows into the sea, carrying not the least volume of water nor is it less famous; it is called the Sebennytic mouth. [5] There are two other mouths that have split off from the Sebennytic mouth and flow to the sea: one is called the Saitic mouth and the other the Mendesian. [6] The Bolbitinic mouth and the Boucolic mouth are not naturally formed but rather constructed.

2.18. There is a witness to my opinion that Egypt is as I describe in my account: the oracle of Ammon. I learned about this oracle after I formed my opinion about Egypt. [2] The people from Mareia and Apis, who live on the border of Egypt and Libya, thought that they were Libyans and not Egyptians and so were upset about the religious rules concerning sacrifices they had to follow that said that they should not sacrifice cows. They sent to Ammon and said that there was nothing common between them and the Egyptians; they lived outside the Delta and did not get along with them at all, thus they wanted to be able to eat everything. [3] The god did not allow them to do these things, saying that the land that the Nile waters in its flow is Egypt, and the Egyptians are those who live downstream from the city of Elephantine and drink from the river. These things were prophesied to them.

. . .

2.28. Let these things be as they are and have been from the beginning. Not one of the Egyptians, Libyans, or Hellenes I asked claimed to know the sources of the Nile except a man in Egypt in the city of Sais, a scribe of the holy treasury of Athena. [2] This man seemed to me to be teasing when he claimed that he knew exactly. He said this: There are two mountains that taper off into narrow peaks and lie between the cities of Syene in the Thebaid and Elephantine. The names of the mountains are Crophi and Mophi. [3] The sources of the Nile are without bottom and flow from between these mountains. Half of the water flows to Egypt and toward the north, and the other half flows to Ethiopia and the south. [4] As for the bottomless sources, he said that Psammetichus, the king of Egypt, put them to a test. He dropped a woven rope many thousands of feet long down into the source, and the rope did not reach the bottom. [5] This scribe, if what he said really happened, proved, as I understood him, only that there were strong whirlpools and back currents, so that a sounding line would not be able to reach the bottom.

. . .

2.30. Sailing from Meroë for an amount of time equal to the length of time it took to get to Meroë from Elephantine, you will come into the land of the Deserters. The name for these deserters is *Asmach*, a word that means in the Greek "those standing on the left hand of the king." [2] These 240,000 Egyptian warriors deserted to the Ethiopians for this reason: Some guards were stationed by King Psammetichus in the city of Elephantine against the Ethiopians, others in Pelousian Daphnae against the Arabians and the Syrians, and more still were stationed in Mareia against the Libyans. [3] Even in our time Persian guards were stationed there as they were in Psammetichus' time, since the Persians keep guards both in Elephantine and in Daphnae. For three years no one released those Egyptians guards from their stations. They took counsel and planned together to rebel from Psammetichus and go over to Ethiopia. [4] When he learned about this, Psammetichus pursued them. After he caught them, he spoke to them for a long time and asked them not to abandon their ancestral gods or their children and wives. But it is said that one of these men showed his private parts and said, "Where this is, there I will have children and wives." [5] Then these men went into Ethiopia, and gave themselves to the king of the Ethiopians, who rewarded them as follows. Since some men born in Ethiopia were hostile to him, he bid the Egyptians to go out and settle their land. Since they settled among the Ethiopians, the Ethiopians became more civilized once they learned Egyptian customs.

2.31. The Nile is known to extend for a four-month journey by sail and by foot from where it flows into Egypt; that is how many months someone would count who set out from Elephantine until he reached these desert-ers. The Nile flows from the west and the setting of the sun. But beyond this distance no one is able to know clearly, for the land is deserted because of the burning heat and sun.

2.32. I heard these things from Cyrenian men who claimed that they went to the Oracle of Ammon and conversed with Etearchus, the king of the Ammonians. They told of how they went from other topics into a debate about the Nile, how no one of them knows its sources, and Etearchus said that once some Nasamonian men came to him. [2] This is a Libyan tribe, and they inhabit Syrtis and the land to the east not far from Syrtis. [3] The Nasamonians talked and were asked if they had something more to say about the wastelands of Libya, and they said that there were some brash sons of powerful men with them, who, since they were grown up, had devised some uncommon plan. Indeed, they selected five of themselves by lot to go check out the wastelands of Libya and to see if they could learn more than what was already known. [4] For the Libyans live everywhere along the northern sea starting from Egypt up to the Soloentian promontory, which is the end of Libya. Libya extends along the whole area, and there are many tribes in Libya, except wherever the Hellenes and Phoenicians have settled. In the areas away from the sea and away from the men who live near the sea, Libya is full of wild things. In the area south of the wild animals it is sandy and terribly dry and empty of everything. [5] After the youths were sent off by their peers, well equipped with water and food, they first went to inhabited places, and then they arrived at the land full of wild animals. From there they went through to the desert once they discovered a road heading west, [6] and after they had gone through a great sandy area for many days they saw trees growing on a plain. They went there and grabbed fruit hanging from the trees, and little men attacked them who were smaller than most men. The men captured them and led them away. There was no common language between those who were Nasamonian and those who had captured the Nasamonians. [7] They took them through great swamps and then they came to a city where everyone was equal to their captors in size and black-skinned. Beside this city a great river flowed from west to east, and in it crocodiles appeared.

. . .

2.35. I am going to extend my account of Egypt, since it has more wonders than any other land and monuments beyond description. Because of these features, I will talk more about it. [2] The Egyptians, since their climate is different from ours and the nature of their river is different from other rivers, have established many customs and laws that differ altogether from other men's laws. Among these, the women go to sell in the market while the men stay in the house and weave. And while other people weave upward by pushing the woof up, the Egyptians push it downward. [3] The men carry burdens on their heads, the women on their shoulders. The women urinate standing up, the men do it sitting down. They relieve themselves in their houses, but they eat out in the streets, saying that shameful and necessary things are done in secret, but things that are not shameful are done in public. [4] No woman is a priestess of a male or female deity; the men are priests of all deities. There is no need for sons to take care of their parents if they do not want to, but daughters must do so regardless.

2.36. Priests of gods in other lands wear their hair long, but in Egypt they shave their hair. It is the custom for other peoples in mourning to cut their hair especially close, but after a death Egyptians let their hair grow out both on their heads and chins before cutting it in mourning. [2] Among other peoples animals are kept apart in separate shelters, but the Egyptians share a living space with their beasts. Others live by eating wheat and barley, but the Egyptians think eating these is a great shame. They make their food from spelt, which some call *zeias*. [3] They knead dough using their feet, but they lift up mud and dung with their hands. Others leave their genitals as they are, except for those who learned from the Egyptians to follow their practice of circumcision. Each man has two sets of clothes, and each woman has one. [4] While others attach the rings and lines of their sails on the outside, the Egyptians do it on the inside. The Hellenes write letters and do their reckonings by carrying their hand from the left to the right; the Egyptians write from the right to the left, and in doing these things they say that they do it "rightly," and the Hellenes "leftly" [wrongly]. They use different scripts—one belongs to the priests, the other is called demotic.

2.37. They are the most exceedingly devout of all people and use the following laws. They drink from bronze cups and wash them every day; all of them do this, not just one man or another. [2] They always wear freshly-washed linen garments, this they are especially fastidious about. They circumcise their genitals for the sake of extreme cleanliness, thinking it better to be clean than to be more attractive. The priests shave their whole body every third day, so that no louse or other abomination gets on them when they worship the gods. [3] The priests wear only linen clothes and papyrus sandals; it is not permitted for them to take other clothes or other sandals. They wash twice each day in cold water and twice each night. They complete thousands of other religious rites, so to speak. [4] They enjoy not a few good things, for they do not pay anything for the expenses of their households. Their food is sacred and prepared for them, and there is an abundance of beef and goose for each day, and they receive wine from grapes. They are not allowed to taste fish. [5] The Egyptians do not really sow beans in the ground; they do not eat raw the ones they have, nor do they eat them after cooking them. The priests cannot abide looking at them, for they think that the beans are unclean. There are many priests for each of the gods, not just one, and one of these is the head priest. When he dies, his son takes over in his place.

2.38. They think that male cows belong to Epaphus and on account of this they examine them in this way: if they see one black hair, he is not thought to be clean. [2] One of the priests appointed to this purpose examines the hairs both while the bull is standing upright and when it is upside down.

The priest also examines the tongue to see if it is clear of signs; I will tell about these things in another story. He looks over the hairs of the tail to see if they have grown naturally. [3] If it is clean of all these things, he marks it by twisting papyrus around its horns, and then he stamps his ring on it with clay. After all of this they lead it away. The penalty for sacrificing an unmarked bull is death.

2.39. They sanction the sacrifice in this way, and then the sacrifice proceeds as follows. After they lead the marked victim to the altar where they sacrifice, they light a fire. Then they pour wine on the victim and the altar and cut its throat while calling on the god. Finally, they cut off the head. [2] They skin the body of the sacrificial victim, and, having brought down many curses on its head, they take it away. Where there is a market and Hellenes as residents and merchants, they carry the head into the agora and the Hellenes buy it from them. For those who do not have Hellenes around, they throw it in the river. [3] They say these curses to the heads so that if something bad is about to happen either to those sacrificing or to all of Egypt, it will fall on the head. [4] All Egyptians follow the same laws concerning the heads of sacrificial victims and the offerings of wine, in all their rituals, and because of this custom no Egyptian will eat the head of any living thing.

2.40. The removal of the entrails and how they are burned is different according to the each victim. I will talk about the goddess whom they think to be the greatest and who has the greatest festival they celebrate. [2] When they skin the bull, they pray over all the intestines they took from it, but they leave its guts and the fat in the body, and they cut off the legs and the tip of the hips and the shoulders and the neck. [3] Once they have done these things they fill the rest of the body of the cow with purified bread and honey and raisins and figs and frankincense and myrrh and other good-smelling things and then they burn it up, while continuously pouring out oil. [4] They sacrifice after fasting, and while the offerings are burning they all beat their breasts. Once they have beaten their breasts, they set out the remaining meat of the victims for eating.

2.41. All the Egyptians sacrifice pure male cows and male calves; they are not permitted to sacrifice the females, since they are sacred to Isis. [2] For the image of Isis is a woman with cow horns, in the way the Hellenes fashion Io, and all the Egyptians honor female cows more than all animals. [3] On account of this no Egyptian man or woman will kiss a Greek on the mouth, or use the knife of a Greek man, or his skewers or his pot, and they will they not eat the flesh of a pure cow sacrificed by a Greek knife. [4] They bury their cows who have died in this manner: They throw the female ones into the river, but they bury the male ones in their neighborhood with one or both of the horns showing as a mark of its grave. After the flesh has rotted it is time to collect the rotted flesh. Barques[123] come to

---

123. A single-masted, oared ship used by the Egyptians and considered to be important religious artifacts; they were thought to be the mode of transportation to the afterlife. Models of barques have been found in numerous tombs.

each city from an island called Prosopitis. [5] This island is in the Delta and its perimeter is four miles. There are numerous other cities on this island of Prosopitis, but the one from which the barques come and take the bones of the cows, is called Atarbechis. There is in this city a holy sanctuary dedicated to Aphrodite. [6] Many people travel from this city to other cities. Once they have dug up the bulls' bones they take them and bury them all in one area. They bury other animals that have died similarly. They do not kill these animals either, for it has been established by custom.

2.42. Whosoever has established a sanctuary of Theban Zeus or is from the Theban nome[124] [district], he avoids sheep and sacrifices goats. [2] The Egyptians do not honor all the gods equally or in the same way, other than Isis and Osiris (whom they say is Dionysus). These two they all worship in the same way. Whosoever has a sanctuary of Mendes or is of the Mendesian nome, avoids goats and sacrifices sheep. [3] Now the Thebans and whosoever avoids sheep say that this custom was established for them. Heracles wanted to see Zeus, but Zeus did not want to be seen by him; finally, since Heracles persisted, Zeus devised this plan: [4] after skinning a ram and cutting off its head, he held it before him, donned the fleece, and showed himself. Because of this story, the Egyptians make ram-headed statues of Zeus. The Ammonians, who are colonists of Egyptians and Ethiopians and use a language that is a mixture of both, also think this practice comes from the Egyptians. [5] It seems right to me that the Ammonians get their name from this story and use an eponym. For the Egyptians call Zeus Ammon. Also because of this story, the Thebans do not sacrifice rams but think that they are holy. [6] On one day of the year, at the festival of Zeus, after they have cut up one ram and skinned it, they clothe the statue of Zeus in the ram skin and bring before it a statue of Heracles. Once they have done these things, they all beat their breasts in mourning for the ram and then bury it in a holy tomb.

. . .

2.46. The Egyptians mentioned earlier do not sacrifice goats and especially male goats on account of what follows. The Mendesians reckon Pan to be one of the eight gods, and they say that the eight gods were earlier than the twelve gods. [2] Painters and sculptors depict and carve the image of Pan (like the Hellenes do) as goat-headed and goat-shanked. They do not, however, think that this god looks like this; rather, they think he is similar to the other gods. Why they paint him in such a way is not a pleasure for me to say. [3] The Mendesians worship all goats, and the male ones more than the female, and the herdsmen have great honor here. They pick one especially from among these goats, who, when he has died, causes great lamentation to come upon the entire Mendesian nome. [4] Both this goat and Pan are called Mendes by the Egyptians. A sign occurred in this nome in my time:

---

124. See Strabo this chapter, Selection 4 for a description of the nomes.

a goat had sex with a woman in public. This happened as part of a show in front of men.

2.47. The Egyptians think that the pig is an unclean animal. For one example, anyone who touches a pig or is around them then goes to the river and throws himself in with all his clothes. For another, even swineherds who are native Egyptians do not go into any holy place in Egypt, nor does anyone want to give his daughter to them nor marry one of his daughters; therefore, the swineherds give and take daughters with one another. [2] The Egyptians do not think it just to sacrifice a pig to any other gods, but they do sacrifice one to Selene and Dionysus at the same time, that is, at the full moon. After they sacrifice the pig, they eat the flesh. As to why they abhor pigs at other festivals where they perform sacrifices, the Egyptians provide a reason. It is not, however, very appropriate to say out loud although I have learned it. [3] The sacrifice of pigs to Selene is done in this way: When someone sacrifices, he holds together the tip of the hip, the spleen, and the caul of the entrails; then he hides them all together in the fat around the belly and then dedicates it in the fire. They eat the rest of the meat at the full moon in the place where they made the sacrificial offerings; on any other day they would not even taste it. The poor fashion dough pigs, bake them, and then sacrifice these.

2.48. At the festival to Dionysus, in the evening each man, having sacrificed a young pig in front of the dogs, gives the pig to one of the swineherds who sold it to be taken away. [2] The Egyptians celebrate the rest of the festival to Dionysus, except for the dancing, in nearly all the same ways as the Greeks do; in the place of *phalloi* something like puppets have been devised that can be moved by strings with the fingers. The women carry them around through the villages and nod the genitals, which are not much smaller than the rest of the body. A flute player leads, and women follow hymning Dionysus. [3] As to why the genitals are big and are the only things on the body that move, there is a sacred story told about this.

> **2. Plato, *Timaeus* 21e–24d (4th century BCE).** *Critias recounts to his dinner companions, including Socrates, the story of Solon's visit to Egypt, where a priest informed him of Athens' great antiquity. In this chronology, the Athenians, not the Egyptians, are the oldest of all peoples, and Egypt's culture is a continuation of the ancient order established by Athena in both ancient Athens and Egypt, though the Athenians have forgotten their own distant past. (RFK)*

21e. "There is a certain place in Egypt," Critias said, "in the Delta around where the head flow of the Nile splits its course. The region is called the Saitic. Its greatest city is Sais and claims King Amasis as its own. The supposed founder of the city was a certain god named Neith in Egyptian, but in Greek, so the story goes, Athena. They say that the people who dwell there are especially fond of Athens and are in some fashion our kinsmen.

Indeed, Solon said that when he traveled there, he was honored greatly by them. 22a. Also, while questioning the priests among them who were most knowledgeable about antiquity, he realized that neither he nor any other Greek knew anything at all about anything pertaining to antiquity, so to speak. At one point, he wanted to lead them into a discussion concerning antiquity, so he tried telling our most ancient stories—about Phoroneus, said to be the first man, and Niobe, followed by the story of the flood and Deucalion and Pyrrha, how they survived it. [b] He then tried to calculate the time periods based on tracing their descendants and how many years each period spanned. At that point, one of the priests (a very elderly fellow) said, 'Solon! Solon! You Greeks are always children! No Greek is old.' Hearing this, Solon replied, 'What do you mean?' 'Your souls,' he said, 'are young. For in them you have no ancient opinions handed down from antiquity and no knowledge grey with age. [c] The reason for this is that there have been many and will continue to be many different catastrophes for humanity, the greatest being fire and flood, with other less significant kinds. Truly, the story you told, also, how Phaethon, son of Helios, yoked the chariot of his father and, because he was unable to drive it along his father's path, burnt up the earth and was himself killed by lightning, this tale has the appearance of a myth, [d] but its truth is found in the course of the celestial bodies moving around the earth and the destruction that comes intermittently to everything upon the earth through great fires. At those times, as many people as dwell in the mountains and in lofty dry regions perish at a higher rate that those residing near rivers and the sea. The Nile is our savior here (as in other ways) because it saves us and frees us from calamity by fire. However, whenever the gods flood the earth and cleanse it with water, herdsmen and shepherds in the mountains are preserved while those of you in the cities are carried into the sea by rivers. In Egypt, though, neither during great floods nor at other times did water flow over our land from the skies. Instead, all water has risen up naturally from below. Thus whatever is preserved here is found to be most ancient.

"'Truly, in every region where excessive cold and heat are kept away, the races of humans always exist, in greater or smaller numbers at various times. 23a. And such things as we know of by report either in our land or in another land (whether something noble or great has happened or even something particularly distinctive), all of this has been written down here in our temples and preserved from ancient times. But you and other peoples, so it happens, have to learn anew writing and the other requirements of a city after each catastrophe. Whenever, like a plague, a flood again bears down in its regular cycle upon you from the heavens and leaves behind only the illiterate and crude among you, [b] once again you become as children who know nothing of ancient times either here or in your own lands. At any rate, Solon, the genealogy you just now recounted concerning your people is little different from a children's story. For, first, you recalled one catastrophe only while there have been many over the years. Further, you don't know that the noblest and best race of mankind was born in your own land, a race from which both you and your entire city derive [c] from some tiny seed they left behind. This descent has escaped your notice, however, since for many generations your people were voiceless because they lacked writing. For, indeed, Solon, at one point in time, before that greatest watery catastrophe, there was, where now rests the city of the Athenians, a people bravest in war and the most well-ordered in all other ways. They say that in this city were the most beautiful works and the noblest constitution of all those cities ever under the heavens about which we have received reports.' [d] Hearing this, Solon said that he was amazed and was altogether eager to learn from the priests everything about these ancient citizens precisely and in exact order. The priest then said, 'I won't refuse you, Solon. For your sake and your city's, I will tell you. Mostly, though, I tell you for the sake of the goddess who obtained your land and ours by lot and who nourished and reared us both, you first for 1,000 years [e] after receiving your seed from Gaia and Hephaestus, and our own land later. From that point, our priests have written down 8,000 years of our own history.[125] Of those citizens who lived 9,000 years ago, I will make clear to you briefly their laws and the noble deeds done by them. 24a. We will discuss the exact details concerning all of this later when we take up in order the writings themselves about this.

"'So, then, look toward the laws here in Egypt if you want to know their laws. For you will find here now many examples of the laws used by your ancient ancestors. First, the class of priests is set apart from others. Next, comes the class of craftsmen—each one practices a trade separately from the others and does not mix with other craftsmen. This is followed by the separation of the classes of shepherds, hunters, and farmers. [b] In addition, you likely notice that the military class is separated off from all the other classes. Nothing else matters by law for those men except that they concern themselves with preparing for war. Furthermore, regarding the nature of their weapons, the shield and spear, we were the first people in all Asia to arm ourselves with them because the goddess showed them to us, just as she had shown them to you Athenians first in the other land. Again, concerning wisdom, [c] you see how the law here favored study of the cosmos from the beginning by encouraging discovery of all things sent from the divine to humanity up to and including the practice of divination and the art of medicine, an art concerned with health. We obtain all sorts of learning that follow from such arts. Indeed, when the goddess established your people and arranged your city in its well-ordered and regimented way before she did so all other cities, she selected a location for your birth where she perceived the climate would yield the wisest men. [d] Because the goddess was a lover of war and of wisdom, she first established Athens and chose the land most likely to yield men most like herself.'"

---

125. Thus, the priest dates the generation of autochthonous Athenians to 9,000 years before Solon's time (7th/6th century BCE).

3. Plato, *Laws* 2.656d–657a (4th century BCE). *Plato's Athenian stresses the unchanging nature of Egyptian society through a discussion of hieroglyphs. (CSR)*

2.656d. Athenian: It is wonderful even to hear about. Once, long ago, so it seems, this rationale, which we were just now speaking about, was decided upon—that it was necessary for the young people in their society to practice beautiful dance postures and songs in their daily interactions. They established what these forms and songs were and what they were like and depicted them in their temples. [e] It was not permitted for painters or anyone else who works on forms or likenesses to innovate or contrive anything other than what was customary either in these arts or any musical form. Upon looking you would discover there that something written or 2.657a. carved 10,000 years ago is no better or worse than what is being practiced in the present, but is completed in an identical manner with the same art.

4. Strabo, *Geography* 17.1.3, 17.1.19, 17.1.39–40, 17.1.44, 17.1.52–53, 17.2.5 (1st century BCE/1st century CE). *Strabo gives an extensive account of the land of Egypt, its people and its history, including a tour of Alexandria. He quotes frequently from earlier Greek authors, especially from the Hellenistic period, and makes corrections to Herodotus' account where he sees fit. (RFK)*

17.1.3. From the beginning, the Egyptians have lived in a civil and cultured manner and have dwelled in well-known lands, thus allowing their system of organization to be remembered. Further, they are worthy of respect, at any rate, for how well they seemed to utilize the good fortune their land provided them and for having properly distributed and tended the land. For when they appointed a king, they also divided the people into three groups: the soldiers, the workers, and the priests. These last were in charge of sacred matters, while the other two tended to secular matters, the soldiers to military affairs, the workers to peacetime ventures. They worked the land and practiced trades from which were gathered the king's revenues. The priests trained in philosophy and astronomy and served as companions to the king.

The land was divided first into districts called nomes. There were ten in the region around Thebes, ten in the Delta, and sixteen in between (some say that the number of nomes was equal to the number of halls in the Labyrinth, but there were fewer than thirty halls). The nomes were further divided into sections called *toparchies*, and the majority of these were divided once again into smaller sections. The smallest sections were called *arourae*.[126] There was a need for accurate and detailed division of the land because of the confusion caused by the repeated destruction of the boundaries by the flooding of

---

126. Plots of land equal to about 150 square feet. Soldiers in Egypt were granted twelve *arourae* to farm tax-free.

the Nile. When the Nile rises, land is added and subtracted and the shape of the land altered. All markers used to distinguish personal property are also lost. The repeated need to measure the land provided the framework for the development of geometry, just as, so some say, accounting and arithmetic arose from Phoenician needs associated with their trade activities.

Just as with the total population, the population of each nome was divided into three, mirroring the equal distribution into three equal parts. Hard work and careful attention in matters surrounding the river allow the people to overcome nature, since by nature the land bears an abundance of crops, even more so when the land is irrigated. By nature, the greater rising of the Nile waters the land extensively, but oftentimes, due diligence succeeds where nature does not by providing water for the land even in a low rising. Through canals and dykes, as much water is provided during low risings as is provided even in the greater rising of the Nile.

. . .

17.1.19. In the heart of the country beyond the Sebennytic and Phatnitic mouths of the Nile is Xoïs, both an island and city in the Sebennytic nome. Also, here are the cities of Hermus, Lycus, and Mendes, where they honor Pan and, among the animals, goats. As Pindar says, the goats there have sexual intercourse with women. Close by Mendes are the city of Dios, the lakes around it, and Leontopolis. Eratosthenes says that the expulsion of foreigners is common for all barbarians, and the Egyptians in particular are accused of this based on stories told about Busiris in the Busiritic nome, because later people wished to charge the Egyptians with being xenophobic. But, by Zeus, there was never a king or tyrant named Busiris.[127] He also quotes, "to Egypt is a treacherous and painful journey." That Egypt was harborless aided this view. Not even its harbor at Pharos was accessible since it was guarded by shepherd-pirates who attacked any who came to anchor there. The Carthaginians also used to throw into the sea any foreigners who were sailing to Sardo or the Pillars. On account of this, many tales of the west are doubted. Even the Persians maliciously led ambassadors by roundabout roads and impoverished lands.

. . .

17.1.39. After the Arsinoïtic and Heracleontic nomes is the city of Heracles where the Egyptian mongoose is honored—the opposite of the Arsinoïtes, who revere the crocodile and, accordingly, their canal and Lake Moeris are full of crocodiles because the Arsinoïtes revere them and lay no hands on them. The Heracleans, however, worship the mongoose, the most dread foe

---

127. Although Busiris is associated with Egypt in mythological stories, Attic vase paintings typically represent him as Nubian or Ethiopian, not Egyptian. This points to a common confusion in ancient Greece about the borders of the various north African states and peoples. There are numerous myths, such as the story of Andromeda's birth, that reflect attempts to fit Ethiopian, Nubian, Phoenician, Egyptian, and Carthaginian peoples all together in a single geographic region.

of the crocodile, as well as of the asp, since they eat both the eggs and the animal itself. To do this, they armor themselves in clay by rolling around in the mud and letting it bake hard in the sun.[128] Then, they seize the heads and tails of the asp and pull it into the river where they kill it. When attacking crocodiles, they lie in wait until the crocodile is basking in the sun with its mouth open and then they rush inside and eat through the innards and stomach until they finally emerge from the dead body.

17.1.40. The nome of Cynopolis is next along with the city of Cynopolis. Anubis is worshipped here and dogs are granted honors and holy foods. On the further side of the river are the nome and city of Oxyrynchus. They honor the oxyrynchus, the sharp-snout fish, and have a temple dedicated to it. The oxyrynchus is worshipped commonly by all Egyptians, just as many animals are worshipped in common by all Egyptians. For example, there are three land animals common to all, the ox, the dog, and the cat; two birds, the hawk and the ibis; and two water animals, the scale fish and the oxyrynchus. Individual groups among the Egyptians also worship specific animals: the Saitaians and Thebaitians honor the sheep; the Latopolitans, the latus fish of the Nile; the Lycopolitans, the jackal; and the Hermapolitans, the dog-faced baboon. The Babylonians who live near Memphis worship the nisnas monkey. This monkey has a face like a satyr and in other ways is a cross between a dog and a bear. They originate in Ethiopia. The Thebans honor the eagle; the Leontopolitans, the lion. The Mendesians honor both the wild goat and the domesticated goat, while the Athribitans honor the field mouse. Other groups honor other animals, though they do not all agree on the reason for this.

. . .

17.1.44. In Abydus, they honor Osiris. In the temple of Osiris it is not possible for singers, flute-players, or harpists to make offerings to the god, as is the custom with other gods. After Abydus is the small city of Dios, and then the city of Tentyra. There the crocodile is dishonored and believed to be the most hateful of all creatures, contrary to the beliefs of all other Egyptians. Despite knowing the evil of these creatures and their destructiveness for humans, the majority of Egyptians worship them nevertheless and keep their distance from them. The Tentyritans, however, track them and kill them in any way they can. Some say that, just as the Psylli[129] have a certain natural antipathy toward reptiles, so the Tentyritans have antipathy toward the crocodile. The result is that they suffer no harm from crocodiles and even dive in and swim among them without fear. No other people are so fearless. The Tentyritans even accompanied crocodiles to Rome when an exhibition was made of them. A holding tank was built for them, and along one side was a platform for them to sunbathe upon. The Tentyritans would from time to time drag the crocodiles out of the tank with nets onto the platform so

---

128. The clay armor serves as a form of camouflage.

129. See also Lucan's description of the Psylli. Chapter 8, Selection 8, lines 890–937.

that the spectators could see them, and then pull them back into the tank again. The Tentyritans honor Aphrodite and have a temple of Isis behind their temple to Aphrodite.

. . .

17.1.52. Both Herodotus and others talk a great deal of nonsense when they attach fantastic stories, as if adding music, or dance movements, or seasoning, to their accounts of Egypt. For example, the statement that the islands near Syene and Elephantine (there are many of them) are the source of the Nile River, and that at this location, the river is bottomless. The Nile has many, many islands scattered about in it. Some of them are completely submerged when the river rises, and others are only partially submerged. On these islands, the highest points are irrigated by screws.[130]

17.1.53. Egypt, then, was peaceful for the most part from its beginnings because of the land's self-sufficiency and because of its inaccessibility to outsiders. From the north, it was guarded by a harborless shoreline and the Egyptian Sea. To the east and west it was protected by desolate mountains, as with the Libyans and Arabians. The rest of the country to the south is inhabited by Trogodytai, Blemmyes, Nubians, and Megabari—in other words, all the Ethiopians beyond Syene. These people are nomads, few and unwarlike, despite what the ancients thought, because they often attacked unarmed travelers like pirates. The Ethiopians who dwell down toward the south and Meroë are also not many, and they do not dwell together as a people since they only live in a very narrow strip of riverfront land. They are not well-prepared either for war or a different way of life.

. . .

17.2.5. It is true what Herodotus says about the Egyptian practice of mixing clay with their hands and mixing suet[131] into bread with their feet. They also have a particular kind of bread called *kakeis* that freezes the bowels and *kiki*, a fruit sown into the earth[132] from which oil is pressed. The oil is used by nearly everyone in Egypt for lamps, but it is also used by the poor and working-class as an ointment, men and women alike. There is also *koïkina*, an Egyptian plaited material made from some plant or other that is similar to textiles made elsewhere of rushes or date palms. Egyptian barley beer is made in a peculiar manner by the Egyptians. It is a drink common to all of them, but each group brews it in its own unique way. One of the things that is common to all Egyptians and that they are especially zealous about is

---

130. The irrigation screws referred to by Strabo are sometimes called the Archimedes screw or the screwpump. It is a watering system consisting of a screw inside a hollow tube that rotates to pick water up at one point and funnel it to another. This was used in antiquity both for irrigation and to remove water from mines.

131. A beef fat used in place of oil or shortening in making pastries. It is commonly used today to make meat pies.

132. As opposed to growing on trees. It is the castor berry.

raising all children born to them[133] and circumcising male and female children alike, a practice also common to the Jews, who, as I noted previously, are Egyptian by origin.[134]

5. Pomponius Mela, *Description of the World* 1.57–59 (1st century CE). *Pomponius discusses the inhabitants of Egypt. (RFK)*

1.57. The inhabitants of Egypt live very differently from others. They mourn the dead while smeared with manure and think it sacrilege to cremate or bury the dead. Indeed, they place the dead in enclosed chambers after they have been preserved by medical arts. They write their letters in the wrong direction. They grind mud down between their hands, but grind flour by trampling on it. Women tend to the forum and business, while men take care of the spinning and the home. Women carry heavy burdens on their shoulders. Men carry them upon their heads. Parents in need must be taken care of by the women. The men are required to raise the children. They eat in public and out of doors, but assign private physical activities[135] to inside the home.

1.58. They worship representations of numerous animals, and even more so the animals themselves, though different people worship different animals. They even go so far in their worship as to make it a crime punishable by death to kill certain animals, even by accident. When the animals die (from disease or by chance), it is considered a sacred duty to bury and mourn them. Apis is considered a divinity common to all Egyptians. He is a black bull distinguished by particular markings and by a unique tail and tongue. Rarely is Apis born, and he is not born through the mating of cattle. The Egyptians say that his birth is divine and he is conceived in a heavenly fire. The day of his birth is the greatest festival day for the Egyptians.

1.59. As the Egyptians state, they are the oldest of all humans, and in their annals they indicate 330 kings prior to Amasis and a span of more than 13,000 years. They preserve in official records evidence that the stars have changed their course four times and the sun has set twice from the direction whence it now rises during the Egyptians' existence.

---

133. The Egyptians did not expose children, the practice of leaving unwanted infants in a deserted location to die or to be claimed by another. The Spartans are supposed to have exposed deformed or unhealthy infants, and classical myth is full of stories of exposed infants, such as Oedipus and the brothers Remus and Romulus.

134. At *Geography* 16.2.34, Strabo comments on the "mixed" nature of the people living in Judea but says that in the temple they are represented as being Egyptian. This is likely a reference to the Exodus, though without knowledge of the story of the children of Abraham's original journey into Egypt.

135. Pomponius uses *obscena*, which seems to imply not only bowel movements but also sexual activity.

6. Horace, *Odes* 1.37 (1st century BCE). *Frequently referred to simply as the "Cleopatra Ode," Horace at first describes the Egyptian queen with the typical negative qualities that the Romans associated with the East. (CSR)*

Now there must be drinking, now must our feet freely beat the ground. The time has come to decorate the god's couches with pontifical feasts, friends. Before this it was wrong to bring the Caecuban wine from our ancestral cellars—when the queen was preparing mad ruin for the Capitoline and death to the Empire with her contaminated flock of men. [10] Shamed by disease and vice, drunk off sweet fortune, out of control, she hoped to gain all she wanted. But a lone ship safe from the flames scarcely diminishes her fury. Caesar compels her mind to true fear, her mind frenzied by Mareotic wine. Caesar closely pursues her by ship as she flees from Italy, just as a hawk pursues a soft dove, [20] or as a swift tracker hunts a hare on the snowy plains of Thessaly. He pursues her, to put a deadly monster in chains. But she, seeking to die more nobly and fearing not the sword as women do, seeks not again with her swift fleet the hidden shores. She dared to look upon her fallen palace with calm countenance. Bravely she dared to bring near her the cruel serpents, to drink in their black poison with her body. Fiercer was she when she resolved to die. [30] Dying she denied to those savage Liburnians[136] the right of triumph over her, no longer a queen but not a humbled woman.

7. Lucan, *Civil War* 10.20–135, 10.172–331 (1st century CE). *Lucan's epic poem describes Caesar's meeting with Cleopatra in Egypt. (MLG)*

10.20–135. There lies the fortunate plunderer, Alexander, the mad son of Philip of Pella, destroyed by a fate avenging the whole world. Men have placed his limbs in sacred shrines—they should have been scattered over the whole globe. Fortune spared his ghost, and the fate of his rule lasted to the end. If freedom were ever to return the world to independence, it would have been to mock the preservation of his corpse and not to provide the faulty lesson that so many lands could submit to a single man. He left the borders of Macedon, his lair, and despised the Athens his father conquered. Impelled by the driving fates, he rushed through the peoples of Asia, bringing carnage with him and running his sword through every tribe. [30] He caused unfamiliar rivers to run with blood: the Euphrates with Persian blood; the Ganges with Indian blood. He was a deadly pestilential lightning bolt, striking equally all the peoples of the world, and a disaster-bringing star for all tribes. He was preparing to launch his fleet against Ocean by way of the external sea. There was no obstacle to him, not flames, not waves, not sterile Libya, or Ammon of the Syrtes. He would have traveled west, following the curve of the world; he would have circled

---

136. A reference to Roman warships modeled after those of the pirates of Liburnia.

the globe and drunk from the source of the Nile. [40] But the end of his life stood in his way—nature could set only this limit on the mad king. This man enviously took his imperial power with him, a power with which he had taken the whole world. Having left no successor, he offered up the cities to be torn apart. He died in Babylon, an object of fearful veneration to the Parthian. For shame! The eastern peoples had more fear of Macedonian *sarissae*[137] than they now have of Roman spears. Although we rule all the way to the north, and we oppress the homes of the west wind and the lands behind the back of the hot south wind [50], we yield in the east to the domination of the Arsacids. Parthia, so unfortunate for Crassus, was a peaceful province of tiny Pella.[138]

Now the child-king, having traveled from the mouth of the Nile near Pelousion, calmed the wrath of his unwarlike people. With this hostage guaranteeing peace, Caesar was safe in the Macedonian court. Without Caesar's knowledge, however, Cleopatra bribed the guard to loosen the chain blocking the port of Pharos and sailed in a little skiff to the Thessalian court. Cleopatra! The shame of Egypt! A wild avenging spirit against Latium! [60] A slut who brought suffering to Rome. As much suffering as Spartan Helen brought to Argos and the homes of Troy with her destructive beauty, so much did Cleopatra stoke the flames of Italian rage. She terrified the Capitol (impious!) with her Egyptian *sistrum*[139] and attacked Roman legions with unwarlike Nile-dwellers, thinking to lead a captured Caesar in Alexandrian triumphs. At Actium the outcome was in doubt: Would the world become the possession of a matron who was not even one of us? This idea came to her on that night when for the first time an incestuous daughter of Ptolemy entered the bed of our generals. [70] Who could fail to forgive your mad desire, Antonius, when the burning raged in the hard heart of Caesar too? In the midst of violent rage, in the midst of madness, in the court haunted by the shades of Pompey, spattered with the gore of the Thessalian slaughter, the adulterer let love join his cares and mixed war with forbidden bed and bastard offspring. For shame! He forgot about Magnus and gave you brothers, Julia, from an obscene mother. He allowed the defeated factions to unite in strength in the far-flung kingdoms of Libya and [80] shamefully squandered his time on a romance by the Nile, since he preferred to give Egypt as a gift, not to conquer it for himself.

Cleopatra put her trust in her beauty and approached him sadly but without tears. She adorned herself, as suited her, with a phony grief and disheveled hair. She began her speech in this way: "Greatest Caesar, you are supplicated by me, a queen. If there is such a thing as high birth, I—the

---

137. The Macedonian spear, approximately 13–20 feet long, that replaced the shorter spears (8–10 feet) used by Greek hoplites as the standard infantry weapon in a phalanx.

138. The Arsacids were the ruling family of Parthia. Crassus died trying to conquer Parthia. Pella refers to the Macedonians.

139. A sacred rattle-like percussion instrument common in Egyptian worship and associated especially with the cult of Isis.

most illustrious offspring of Egyptian Lagus—was driven from my father's power, an exile forever unless your right hand restore me to my ancient destiny. Stand by our peoples, [90] for you are an astrological sign of equity. I am not the first woman to rule the cities along the Nile. The Egyptian makes no gender distinction and knows how to endure a queen. Read the last words of my departed father, who gave me the common rights of rule and a common marriage bed with my brother. The boy himself loves me, his sister, if only he was given his freedom. His feelings and his soldiers lie under the control of Pothinus. Personally, I do not seek access to any of my paternal rights. Only cleanse our home from so much crime and shame! Remove those deadly weapons from the parasite and command the king to rule himself. How swollen is the head of that [100] domestic slave! He removed Pompey Magnus' head and now (may the fates turn this far away!) threatens you. It was enough of a dishonor to you, Caesar, and to the world that the crime and reward for killing Pompey belongs to Pothinus."

Her temptation of Caesar's austere ears would have been all in vain. But her face supported her prayers and her unchaste demeanor gave a powerful peroration. She spent an unspeakable night with her corrupted judge. When the leader's favor was gained and acquired with massive gifts, a great feast followed the pleasures. With a lively commotion, Cleopatra laid out her luxuries, [110] the sort that had not yet found their way to Rome. The place was the image of a temple that a more corrupt age would hardly build. Riches hung from the paneled ceiling and thick gold concealed the rafters. The house was covered with marble, and not simply a facade but whole pieces of stone flashed brightly. Agate and the purple porphyry were not simply decorative but functioned architecturally. Alabaster was spread out over the whole courtyard to be stepped on. Ebony from Meroë didn't simply cover the grand doorframe but took the place of cheap wood, not simply decoration for the house but the very structure. The entry hall was clothed in ivory, [120] and the leaves of the doors were inlaid with dyed Indian tortoise shell, its spots adorned with many emeralds. The cushions shone with inlaid jewels, and the tawny jasper dishes <filled the tables and the couches and> twinkled from the <cloth> coverings.[140] The greatest part of these took their color from repeated washings in Tyrian dye. Part sparkled from enwoven gold, and part was dyed fire-red, as it is the Egyptian custom to entwine different threads into the weave. In addition, there were many house slaves and attendants for the crowd of people. Different colors marked them off by their race, and others were of diverse ages. This group had African hair, another was so fair-haired [130] that Caesar asserted that he had not seen such red hair in any Rhinish fields. A part was dark-skinned[141] with curly hair and receding hairlines. There were also the unfortunate soft youths who had their manhood cut off with iron. Opposite them

---

140. The text is difficult to render here. Supplemental text added by A. E. Housman.
141. Literally, "burned blood."

were boys of greater age but whose cheeks were without any darkening facial hair.

Caesar, as with previous conquerors of Egypt such as Cambyses and Alexander, is fascinated with the Nile and seeks to understand its origins and power.

10.172–331. After pleasure had been satisfied and a limit set on feasting and drinking, Caesar began to pass the night with long speeches, and he addressed Acoreus, who was dressed in linen and seated on the other couch, with flattering words. "Elder, as you are devoted to the sacred and (your age proves it) not neglected by the gods, expound on the origins of the Egyptian people, its geographical location, the character of the common folk, and the rites and forms of the gods. [180] Reveal whatever has been inscribed in your ancient temples and report on those gods who are willing to be known. If your ancestors taught your sacred affairs to Athenian Plato, was there ever a guest more worthy of listening to or more capable of comprehending the universe? The rumor of my son-in-law, it is true, brought me to the Egyptian cities, but the reputation of the Egyptians also played a part. Even in the middle of battles, I gave my spare time to the movements and zones of the stars and heaven. The Julian year shall conquer the calendar of Eudoxus. But because so much valor resides in my heart, so much love of the truth, there is nothing that I would like to know about more than [190] that river that has concealed its nature and source for so many generations. Were there a real hope of seeing the source of the Nile, I would abandon civil war." After he finished, the priest Acoreus rose and made the following speech. "I am permitted, Caesar, to reveal the secrets of our great ancestors, secrets that have remained unknown to the profane peoples up to this age. Let others consider it piety to cloak great mysteries in silence. For my part, I believe the heaven-dwellers are grateful that knowledge of their work pass to all and that diverse peoples learn their sacred laws. The primal laws of the universe have provided different powers to the stars, [200] which direct the movement of Olympus and run opposed to the pole. The sun divides the units of time, changes day to night and forbids the stars to travel with its powerful rays, and maintains the wandering planets in place. The moon mixes the sea-goddess Tethys with the land. Freezing ice and the snowy region belongs to Saturn; Mars holds the wind and unpredictable lightning. Moderate temperature and undisturbed air is under Jupiter. But fertile Venus retains the seeds of all things; Mercury is the ruler of the great sea. [210] When he is retained by that part of the heaven where the stars of Leo are mixed with Cancer, where Sirius kindles swift flames and the circular alteration of the varied year holds Capricorn and Cancer—here hides the secret wellspring of the Nile. When it is struck by the lord of waters with vertical fire, then the Nile opens its source and flows just like Ocean with the waxing of the moon. The Nile appears under orders and does not restrict his expansion before night has regained the summer hours from the sun. Erroneous was the belief of the ancients who claimed that Ethiopian snows assisted the Nile to flow over the fields. [220] There is no north star, no Boreas in those mountains. Witness the color of the people, burned by the sun, and their steamy, warm south wind. In addition, every river's source that is driven by melting ice swells with the onset of spring, with the first melting of the snow. The Nile never expands its waves before the rays of the Dog-star. It never limits its flow to its banks before the Sun is equal to the night under the judgment of Libra. Furthermore, the Nile is ignorant of the laws that govern other waters: it does not swell in winter, when the sun is remote and [230] water is free from responsibility. The Nile, under orders to moderate the weather when heaven is uneven and summer is at its height, travels under the burning zone. In order to protect the earth from being rent by flame, the Nile appears to the world and swells to counter the burning mouth of Leo. The Nile appears in answer to prayers when Cancer burns his Syene. He does not free the fields from his waters until Phoebus slips into Autumn and Meroë lengthens its shadow. Who can explain the reasons? Thus did Mother Nature order the Nile to flow. The world needed this. Erroneous also is the old view that [240] credits the West wind with this flood. The blowing of this wind continues daily during certain seasons and controls the air. There are two reasons for this: First, the winds drive the clouds from the western sky across the south, compelling the clouds to devote themselves to raining. Or, they constantly beat against the waters as they often crash over the shores of the Nile, compelling the waters to resist with a flood. By this delay and by the blockage of the opposed sea, the river's course is agitated, spreading over the plains. Some believe that the lands have vents and great gaping holes. Here the water travels secretly through silent meanders and is recalled from the frozen north down under the Equator [250] when the sun is above Meroë and the scorched earth directs the waters in that direction. The Ganges and the Po are pulled below the silent earth. Then the Nile spews from one source all the rivers and carries them on with many a stream. There is a rumor that the Nile bursts violently from the overflow of Ocean, who encircles all the lands, and that the salt water becomes fresh because of the distance the river travels. We also believe that the Sun and the poles feed on Ocean. The Sun snatches Ocean when he reaches the arms of hot Cancer, [260] and more water raises than the air can dissipate. The night returns this surplus, which overflows the Nile. But in my view, Caesar, if it is right for me to resolve so great a quarrel, certain waters burst forth in the later stages of the world's creation from veins opened in earthquakes (it was not a god's doing) and their origins coincide with the construction of the universe. These waters are compelled to submit to a fixed fate by that maker and creator of everything. Roman, you desire to understand the Nile. So did the Pharaohs, the Persians, and the Macedonian tyrants. [270] No generation lacked the will to pass on this knowledge to the future. But they have been to this day defeated by the secrecy of nature. The greatest of kings, Alexander, though loved by Memphis, was jealous of the Nile. He sent select Ethiopians to the farthest edges of the world, but they were halted by the ruddy zone of the burning pole. They saw the Nile boiling. Sesostris reached the western extreme of the world and yoked his Egyptian chariot to the necks of kings. Nevertheless, they drank from your rivers—the Rhone and the Po—before the Nile's source. [280] Mad Cambyses went east and reached the long-lived peoples. Bested by a lack of food and feeding on the corpses of his men, he returned without learning of you, Nile. Mendacious gossip dared not speak of your source. Wherever you appear, you raised questions. No nation boasts that it rejoices in containing the Nile. I shall make known as much of your course, Nile, as the god who conceals your waters allowed me to know you. Arising from the Equator, you boldly raise your stream against burning Cancer and your waters travel due north toward the middle of the Bootes. [290] The course bends its twisting path east and west, flowing toward the Arab peoples at times and at times toward the Libyan desert. The Seres catch the first glimpse of you, although they also wonder at you. You strike the plains of Ethiopia with foreign waters, but the world knows not who is responsible for you. Nature has not revealed the hidden source to anyone. It has not allowed any people to see you when you are small, Nile. Nature has concealed your source and preferred that people wonder at your origin rather than know it. It is lawful for you to rise on the solstice, to flood in an alien winter, [300] and to bring your own winter weather. It is permitted to you alone to wander through both hemispheres. In one hemisphere the source is sought; in the other, the end. The stream breaks in two and surrounds fertile Meroë and her black inhabitants. The land rejoices in the leaves of its ebony trees. Although the trees are rich in foliage, no shade relieves the heat since Leo strikes the land in a direct line. Running on past the Zone of Phoebus without loss of water, you make the long path through the sterile desert, [310] at times collecting all your strength into a single stream, at times wandering and splashing the yielding riverbanks. The lazy channel recalls the many streams at the point where the gates of the Egyptian kingdom divides its fields from the Arab peoples. At the spot where trade joins the Red Sea to ours, you cleave the desert, gently flowing. Who, seeing you flow so smoothly, could imagine, Nile, the massive rage of your violent vortex? But when your sweep runs into broken courses and high falls, you resent any cliff that bars your previous free flow, [320] and your spray reaches the stars. The waters rumble loudly and the mountains echo back. The river foams white with constrained waves. The land that our venerable antiquity calls Abaton is the next spot to perceive itself battered by the maelstrom. Here are cliffs that have been called the river's veins, because they give the first clear sign of the Nile's new flood. From this point, nature has surrounded the meandering river with mountains that forbid you, Nile, to Libya. The water flows in a deep valley between these mountains, regaining its customary silent flow. [330] Memphis is the first city to provide open plains and fields to you and to forbid the riverbanks from limiting the flood.

8. Juvenal, *Satire* 15.1–13, 15.27–93, 15.100–131 (2nd century CE).
Juvenal describes an atrocity in Egypt. (MLG)

15.1–13. Who is ignorant, Volusius of Bithynia, of the sort of monsters that insane Egypt worships? One group idolizes the crocodile; another reveres the ibis, fattened on snakes. A golden image of the sacred monkey shimmers where the magic chords resound from the broken statue of Memnon and where ancient Thebes with its hundred gates lies in ruin. All the cities worship cats in one place, a river fish in another, dogs everywhere, but nowhere Diana. It is a religious offense to violate the leek or the onion by biting into them. [10] (Oh, you saintly nations whose divinities grow in gardens!) Every table refrains from woolly animals. It's a crime there to kill a goat's kid. One may feed on human flesh. Even Odysseus couldn't convince people that such mythical cannibals existed, especially since he lacked corroborating evidence.

. . .

15.27–93. But I will relate a recent marvel (it happened when Iuncus was consul)[142] that occurred in the walled town of hot Coptus. It is a crime of the mob and more horrific than all the tragedies together. [30] Should you review every tragic ensemble from Pyrrha on, there is no people as a whole who committed a crime in tragedy. Consider the following example from our own time that issued from savage ferocity.

Between the neighboring towns, Omboi and Tentyra, there raged an old, long-standing feud, an undying hatred, a wound that would never heal. There was a general rage on each side because each loathed the gods of their neighbors. Each man believes that the only true divinities are the ones he worships. When one people was celebrating a festival, all the leaders and generals of the enemy decided to take the opportunity [40] to prevent their foes from enjoying a pleasant holy day and from enjoying a great communal feast, which is set out on tables at the temples and shrines with all-night couches, on which they recline day and night until the seventh day. (Egypt is obviously savage, but in luxuriousness its barbarian horde at least matches renowned Canopus, as far as I myself have observed.) An additional consideration is that it would be an easy victory over people sloshed, stuttering, and stumbling in their cups. On one side, men were dancing to the black oboe, doused in various [50] perfumes and flowers and wearing many wreathes on their heads; on the other, an abstemious hatred. First began resounding quarrels. As tempers flare, a shouting match is the call to arms. Next they clash, shouting on each side, and savage each other with bare hands instead of weapons. Few faces lack wounds. Nearly everyone has a broken nose. Throughout the whole battle lines, you would have seen faces torn in half, unrecognizable countenances, shattered bones visible from lacerated cheeks, fists dripping with blood from eyes. Nevertheless,

---

142. 127 CE.

the combatants believed they were playing and [60] childishly practicing fighting, because no one trampled on corpses. And obviously what's the point of thousands rioting if everyone survives? And so the conflict becomes sharper, and now they reach down to pick up stones laying on the ground and begin throwing: rocks are the domestic weapons for riot. These rocks were not like those of Turnus and Ajax. They did not weigh as much as the rock that Diomedes used to break Aeneas' hip. They are the sorts that the right hands of our contemporaries—so unlike those heroes—have the strength to throw. For the human race was already degenerating in Homer's lifetime. [70] The earth now produces wicked and weak humans. And so whatever divinity sees us laughs and despises us. To return to my narrative from its digression: After they were enlarged with reinforcements, some dared to draw out iron weapons and to renew the fight with hostile arrows. The Ombi hotly chase the retreating Tentyres, who inhabit the neighboring region of shady palms. In his headlong and fearful flight, someone slips and is captured. He is cut up into many bits and pieces in order that one dead man provides for many [80]. The victorious mob eats every bit of him, gnawing on his bones. Nor do they boil him or roast him. It seemed a long and tedious delay to wait for a fire; they were content with a raw corpse. One may be happy in this fact: the act did not defile fire, which you stole from the upper heavens, Prometheus, and gave to the earth. I congratulate that element and think that you rejoice. But the man who tolerated chewing on a corpse never ate anything more willingly than this meat. In so great a crime, don't ask or wonder whether [90] only the first throat felt pleasure. The last man standing, after the whole body was consumed, dragged his fingers over the ground to taste some of the blood.

. . .

15.100–131. A Spanish tribe, the Vascones, was driven to cannibalism during a siege [100], which is a forgivable sin. Even the Stoics agree that self-preservation is an excuse, though the Spanish did not then know that philosophy. Of course, now fancy Greek [110] and Roman learning reaches from Britain and Gaul to Thule. Self-preservation in extremes is noble.

Is there any such excuse for Egypt, more savage than the altar at Maeotis?[143] Indeed, that Taurian inventrix [Diana] of the wicked rite simply sacrifices people (if you think that the poetic tradition is worth believing). The victim fears nothing further or grimmer than a knife. What crisis compelled these Egyptians? [120] Was it great hunger? Was it arms intimidating their defense that forced them to dare so abhorrent an atrocity? Could they find no other method to shame the unwilling Nile to rise when the fields of Memphis were parched? Never have the terrifying Cimbri or Britons, the savage Sauromantai or ferocious Agathyrsians, rampaged with the same

---

143. A reference to King Thoas of the Taurians. See Euripides, Chapter 14, Selection 6. It may strike some readers as odd that Busiris, the Egyptian king, is not mentioned in this context, but the myth of human sacrifice had relocated from Egypt to the Black Sea by the late 5th and early 4th centuries BCE.

frenzy as this useless and unwarlike mob, whose custom it is to raise little sails on clay boats and to row tiny oars in painted shell boats. You will discover no punishment for the crime. [130] You will prepare no suitable atonement for this people, in whose mind anger and hunger are one and the same.

9. Athenaeus, *Deipnosophists* 7.299e–300b (2nd century CE).
While at dinner, conversation turns to eels, the delicacy they are currently being served, and other animals worshipped in Egypt. (RFK)

Antiphanes said in mockery of the Egyptians in *Lycon*:

"They say that the Egyptians are clever at other things, like how they consider eels equal to the gods since they are more honored by far than the gods. We can pray to the gods, for certain, but some people pay as much as twelve drachma or even more just to catch the scent of an eel, so holy is this creature to them."

Anaxandrides extends the conversations about the Egyptians in *Cities*:

"I would not be able to ally with you. Neither are our manners similar nor are our customs. They are really very far apart. You worship a cow, I sacrifice mine to the gods. You think the eel is the greatest of divinities, while I find it to be by far the most delectable of dishes. You don't eat pigs, while I take a special pleasure in eating them. You revere dogs, while I tend to beat them when I catch them eating my meal. The custom here is for priests to be whole, while in your land, they seem to cut parts of themselves off. If ever you see a cat in a poor state, you cry. Me? I'd just as soon kill it and skin it. The field mouse has power in your estimation. Not so much in mine."

Timocles says in *Egyptians*:

"How could an ibis or dog save you? How could an altar to a cat destroy anyone when not even those who disrespect the commonly-believed-in gods receive immediate justice?"

10. Achilles Tatius, *Leucippe and Cleitophon* 4.3–5, 4.11.3–4.12, 4.18.3–19 (2nd century CE). *The characters in Achilles Tatius' novel are in Egypt, where they ponder its marvels. (MLG)*

On the hippopotamus and the elephant.

4.3. Then the general summoned us to see the spectacle. Leucippe was present with us. Thus while we gazed upon the wild hippopotamus, the general gazed upon Leucippe and was immediately overcome. [2] He wished us to remain as long as possible so that he might be able to feast his eyes on her. He thus sought for a long-winded discourse. He first catalogues the nature of the animal and then its manner of hunting. The animal is very gluttonous, he said, and makes whole fields its food. Trickery is used to hunt it. [3] After the hunters observe the animal's routine, they dig a ditch and cover over it with reeds and dirt. Below this reed "trap," they place a wooden cage with doors open on top. They then lie in wait for the animal to fall in. [4] When it steps on the trap, it falls right in and is welcomed into the cave-like cage. The hunters leap up and close the top doors. The hunt proceeds in this way because no one can overcome the animal by force. [5] "For the rest," he said, "it is incredibly strong, as you see, and its skin is rough and does not allow it to submit to a wound from a weapon. It is, so to speak, the Egyptian elephant. In fact, it is clearly second in strength to the Indian elephant.

4.4. Menelaus replied, "Have you indeed ever seen an elephant?" "Yes, indeed," Charmides answered. "And I have heard from careful witnesses the marvelous nature of its birth." [2] "Up to this day," I said, "we have not seen one except in pictures." "I would describe it to you," he replied, "especially since we are at leisure. The mother is pregnant for a very long time. For ten years she shapes the seed.[144] After this long run of years, she gives birth when the child has become old. [3] This is the reason, in my opinion, why it becomes huge in size, invincibly powerful, long-lived, and slow to die. For it is said that it lives longer than Hesiod's crow.[145] [4] The elephant's jaw is like the head of an ox. For should you see it, you would say that it has a double horn coming from its mouth. These are the curved teeth of the elephant. Between these teeth emerges the proboscis, in appearance and size like a trumpet. It obeys the elephant's will. [5] Using this, it forages for nourishment and anything edible it finds at its feet. If this should be an elephant delicacy, it takes it immediately, folds it up to its jaws and serves the food to the mouth. If it should see one of the more tasty morsels, it pounces on this, tightly encircles it, and raises the whole thing up and stretches the gift up to its master. [6] For this master is an Ethiopian man sitting upon it, a strange elephant equestrian. This man is flattered and feared by the elephant, who listens to his voice and endures the whip, in this case an iron axe. [7] I once saw a novel spectacle: a Greek man placing his head within the animal's head. The elephant opened its mouth wide and exhaled on the man within. Two things astounded me in this: the man's audacity and the elephant's philanthropy. [8] The man claimed that he even paid the animal since its breath was no less aromatic than Indian spices and was also a cure for headache. The elephant knows this treatment and does not open his mouth freely, but he is a traveling doctor and first demands payment. If this is given, the elephant is persuaded and provides the favor. He spreads wide his jaw and receives in his yawning mouth as much as the man wishes since he knows that he has sold his breath.

4.5. "How," I asked, "does such an ugly animal have such a lovely fragrance?"

---

144. See Pliny, *Natural Histories* 8.28.

145. About 200 to 300 years, according to Plut. *Moralia* 415c7.

"Because," Charmides replied, "of its diet. India, you know, is a neighbor of the sun, and the Indians are the first who see this god rising. A warmer light saturates them, and their bodies preserve the color of the fire. [2] Among the Greeks there grows a flower of Ethiopian color, but among the Indians every flower has petals the size of leaves among our people. The plant hides its odor and does not reveal its perfume. This is either because it is ashamed to boast of its pleasure before spectators, or because it begrudges it to its citizens. But if the plant migrates a small way beyond its land and crosses the border, it reveals the pleasure of its hidden smell and becomes a flower instead of a bush and puts on its fragrance. [3] This is the black Indian rose. The elephant eats this like cows eat grass among us. Considering that they eat this from birth, their whole body smells like their food, and their breath, coming from within, is the most fragrant of all. This is the source of its breath."

> *The lair of the Nile bandits; Cleitophon describes the village of the Nile bandits, called "Herdsmen."*

4.11.3. The situation of the village is as follows. The Nile flows down from Egyptian Thebes maintaining its size up to Memphis and remains small further down. Near the end of the great river is the village called Cercasorus. [4] From that point the single river divides its flow into three branches. Two branches flow off to each side and one branch, flowing as it did before the division, transforms the land into the shape of deltas. [5] But none of these rivers continues to flow all the way to the sea. They keep branching off here and there around cities, and even the branches are bigger than the rivers of Greece. The water, although dividing everywhere, is not exhausted but remains navigable, drinkable, and usable for irrigation.

4.12. The mighty Nile is everything to the inhabitants: river, land, sea, lake. It makes an unusual spectacle. A ship is also a mattock, an oar is also a plow, a rudder is also a scythe. It's the same habitation for sailors and farmers, for fish and for cattle. You plant where you have sailed, and what you plant is a cultivated sea. [2] The river makes regular visits, which the Egyptian awaits calmly, reckoning the number of days. The Nile never lies but keeps its appointed time, and by measuring its flow the river avoids a late-payment charge. [3] The rivalry between the river and land can be seen. Each strives with the other: the water to flood so much land, and the land to contain so much sweet sea. The two conquer equally, and no spot appears conquered, since the water stretches out with the land. [4] Around the villages of the Herdsmen, the Nile always flows abundantly. Whenever the Nile floods the whole land, it also makes lakes in that place. And if the Nile recedes, the lakes remain, with less water and more silt. [5] On these marshes they march and sail. But only single-person boats can navigate them. The silt overpowers anything foreign to the place. Their boats are small and light and a little water is enough for them. But if there should be absolutely no water, they hoist the boats on their backs and carry them until they reach water. [6] Scattered in the middle of these lakes, some islands have been constructed. Some islands lack buildings and have been planted with papyrus reeds. The rows of papyrus have been planted at intervals just large enough for a single person to stand between. The foliage of the papyrus covers the top of this close arrangement. [7] Running under these, the inhabitants plot, they lie in ambush and hide. They use the papyrus as protective walls. Some of the islands have huts and imitate an improvised city-state, fortified by a wall of marshes. [8] These are the residences of the Herdsmen. One of the nearer islands is larger and has more huts than the rest (they call it, I believe, Nichosis). That is the place where they all gather, considering that they are running to the most secure place in size and location. A narrow passage connecting it to the mainland prevents it being an island. It is 600 feet long and its width is 72 feet, and a lake surrounds the city.

The water of the Nile and the crocodile; Cleitophon travels along the Nile.

4.18.3. After the long interruption in sailing, the whole river was filled with ships and there was much pleasure in the sight: sailors' shanties, the applause of passengers, a ballet of ships. The whole river was a festival, and we sailed like a river on parade. For the first time I drank the Nile unmixed with wine, because I wished to judge the river's sweetness. Wine, you know, hides the nature of water. [4] After I scooped it up in a clear glass cup, I saw the water compete in clarity with the cup and win. It was sweet drinking and cold in measure of pleasure, since I know that some Greek rivers even cause harm by their cold and I compared them to this river. [5] For this reason the Egyptian is not afraid to drink the water unmixed, as it has no need of Dionysus. I marveled at the water and the manner of drinking. They are unwilling to scoop up the water to drink with cups. They have a personal cup: their hand. [6] If one of them should become thirsty while sailing, he sticks his face out from the boat and directs it to the water; he then moves his hand toward the water. Cupping his hand, dipping it in, and filling it with water, he shoots the drink toward his mouth and accomplishes his aim. The gaping mouth awaits the shot, receives it, and closes, not allowing the water to fall back out.

4.19. I also saw another Nile animal, one to be praised for strength beyond the hippopotamus. It is called the crocodile. It alternates in form between a fish and a land animal. It is long from head to tail, but its width is not equivalent in size. [2] Its hide bristles with scales; the skin of its back is rocky and black; its belly is white; it has four legs, gently curving from the sides like a land tortoise; its tail is long and thick like a solid body. [3] This is not decoration as with other animals—it is the completion of the spine and part of the whole. On the top, the tail bristles with cruel spikes like the ridges of a saw. [4] The same tail becomes a whip for hunting, since it uses it to strike the prey it wrestles with and with a single blow makes many wounds. Its head is knit into its back and makes a single alignment, since nature concealed its neck. The head is more fearful than the rest of the body. It stretches its jaws very wide and opens them completely. [5] Whenever the beast has its mouth closed, it is a head; whenever it opens up for prey, it is all mouth. It opens the upper jaw, but the lower does not move. The distance between them is large, and the opening reaches to the jaw—a direct route to the belly. [6] It has many very long teeth. They say that the number of teeth is equivalent to the number of days the gods illuminate in a whole year, so large a barrier encloses the plain of the jaws. If it should crawl up on land, you would not believe how much power it has when you see it dragging its body.

CHAPTER 8

NORTH AFRICA: LIBYA, CARTHAGE, AND NUMIDIA

In the earliest maps from antiquity, the continent of Africa was called Libya and was thought to extend only to the edge of the Sahara Desert. Libya was both the name of the continent and the name of the kingdom to the west of the Nile. The Egyptians were typically confined to the region around the Nile. For the Romans, the continent was called Africa, but they still did not know its extent and generally placed the sub-Saharan Africans at the edges of the world. There was, however, much confusion, and the name Libya was used inconsistently, as Herodotus makes clear. The people who inhabited Libya, Carthage, and Numidia were thought to be of Phoenician descent, while the Egyptians were a race of their own. The Ethiopians and other sub-Saharan peoples were also considered distinctive, though both Greeks and Romans often represent peoples of north Africa in writing as of Phoenician decent, but in images as Ethiopian.

> **1. Herodotus,** *Histories* **4.168–197 (5th century BCE).** *Herodotus devotes a large section of Book 4 to describing the various tribes along the coast of northern Africa as well as the peoples he knows of who live inland. For the most part, these tribes practice similar customs, but variations among the tribes give us an idea of what constituted group-defining customs in Herodotus. (CSR)*

4.168. The Libyans live according to these customs. Starting from Egypt, the first Libyans you meet to the west are the Adurmachidae, who practice mostly Egyptian customs but wear clothes similar to other Libyans. Their women wear bronze anklets around each leg and grow their hair long. Whenever one catches lice, she bites it and throws it away. [2] These are the only Libyans who do this, and they alone present their young women who are about to be married to their king. Whoever pleases the king loses her virginity to him. The Adurmachidae live in an area that stretches from Egypt to a bay named Plynus.

4.169. The Giligamae come next. They inhabit a territory that extends all the way to the west up to the island of Aphrodisias. Off the coast in the middle of their territory lies the island of Plataea, where the Cyreneans founded a city. On the shore there is the bay of Menelaus and also Aziris, where the Cyreneans later lived. The silphium growing region begins here and [2] stretches from the island of Plataea to the mouth of the bay of Syrtis. They practice essentially the same customs as other Libyans.

4.170. Heading west, the Asbystai are next to the Giligamae. They live inland from Cyrene. The Asbystai do not live by the sea because the Cyreneans inhabit the land along the coast. They are the greatest drivers of four-horse chariots among the Libyans. They try to imitate most of the customs of the Cyreneans. 171. To the west of the Asbystai are the Auschisai. They live inland from Barca, and their area stretches down to the sea at Euesperides. In the middle of the Auschisai's territory live the Bacales, a small tribe whose land stretches down to the sea at Taucheira, a Barcaean city. The Auschisai practice the same customs as those who live inland from Cyrene.

4.172. The Nasamonians live to the west of the Auschisai. They are a large tribe. In the summer they leave their herds by the seashore, go up into the land of Augila, and gather fruit from date palms. Many palms grow there in abundance, all of which bear fruit. Whenever they hunt locusts, they dry them in the sun and grind them up; then they pour the powder over their milk and drink it. [2] It is their custom that each man has many wives, but they share responsibility for sex with their women, just like the Massagetai. Whenever a staff is set up in front of their tent, they are having sex. When a Nasamonian man marries for the first time, it is the custom for the bride to have sex with all the guests on that first night, going through them one by one. Each of the men she has slept with gives her a gift, which he brought from home. [3] They make oaths and practice divination this way: They swear by the men who were said to be the most just and noble among them while they are touching their tombs. They get prophecies by going to the graves of their ancestors and falling asleep there after a prayer. They consider the visions, which they see in these dreams, prophetic. [4] They make contracts as follows: each man offers the other man a drink from his own hands; if they do not have anything to drink, they pick up dust from the ground and lick it.

4.173. The people next to the Nasamonians are the Psylli. These people were completely destroyed in this way: The south wind blew through and dried up their water reservoirs. The whole land, which lies near the bay of Syrtis, became desert. After agreeing on a common action, they marched against the south wind (I am saying what the Libyans say). When they came to the sandy desert, the wind blew and covered them over. Ever since they were destroyed, the Nasamonians have controlled their land.

4.174. Further inland to the south, in a land full of wild animals, the Garamantes live. They avoid meeting any men or interacting with them. They do not possess weapons, nor do they know how to defend themselves. 175. The Garamantes live inland from the Nasamonians. The Macae hold the land to the west of them along the coast. The Macae wear their hair in crests—they leave the hair in the middle and let it grow long, but they shave down to the skin on both sides of the head. In war they carry shields made from the skin of the ostrich. [2] The river Cinyps flows through their territory, which starts from the hill called the Hill of the Graces and flows into the sea. This Hill of the Graces is thick with trees, but the rest of Libya that I have described is bare. There are 22.5 miles between this hill and the sea.

4.176. The Gindanes are the neighbors of the Macae. Each of their women wear many anklets made of leather as follows (so it is said): They tie an anklet on for each man they have had sex with. Whoever has the most is thought to be the best woman since she has been loved by the most men. 177. The Lotus Eaters live on a promontory that sticks out into the sea from the land of the Gindanes. They live off of the fruit of the lotus. The fruit is as big as a sea onion. Its sweetness is similar to that of a date. The Lotus Eaters make wine from it as well. 178. Along the coast from the Lotus Eaters live the Machlyes. They also use the lotus, but less than the Lotus Eaters do. Their land stretches to a great river called the Triton, which runs into a giant lake called Tritonis. On this lake there is an island called Phla. They say that the Lacedaemonians received an oracle telling them to colonize this island.

4.179. There is a story told that Jason, after the Argo had been built near Mount Pelion, put on board a great sacrificial offering, including a bronze tripod, and sailed around the Peloponnese, since he wanted to visit Delphi. [2] As he was sailing near Cape Malea, a north wind carried him to Libya. Before he even saw land, he was in the shallows of Lake Tritonis. The story claims that Triton appeared to him while he was unsure of how to get away and ordered Jason to give him the tripod. Triton said that he would show him the channel out and send him away unharmed. [3] Jason obeyed, so Triton showed him the passage out and then set the tripod up in his own sanctuary. He then made a prophecy over the tripod and made all of it known to Jason and his men. He said that if one of the descendants of the men who sailed on the Argo took away the tripod, it was completely inevitable that the Greeks would found one hundred cities around Lake Tritonis. When the Libyans nearby heard this, they hid the tripod.

4.180. The Ausees hold the land next to the Machlyes. These people and the Machlyes live all around Lake Tritonis. The river Triton divides them. The Machlyes grow their hair long down the back of their heads; the Ausees grow it long at the front. [2] In a yearly festival to Athena, their young women split into two groups and fight each other with stones and sticks. They claim that they are performing the ancestral rites of their native deity, whom we call Athena. They call those young women who die from their wounds false virgins. [3] Before they send them off to fight, they do this: they dress up the young woman who is the most beautiful among them in a Corinthian cap and a full set of Greek armor, put her in a chariot, and drive her around the lake. [4] I am not able to say how they used to dress up their young women before the Greeks settled near them, but I think they dressed them in Egyptian armor, for I think that the shield and the helmet came to the Greeks from Egypt. [5] They claim that Athena is the daughter of Poseidon and Lake Tritonis, but she blamed her father for something and gave herself to Zeus. Because of this, Zeus made her his daughter. That is what they say. They share their women for sex. They do not live together as couples and they have sex like animals. [6] When a woman's baby grows strong, the men gather together in its third month and the man they agree the child belongs to takes the baby into his house.

4.181. These groups of nomadic Libyans live along the sea. Further inland, Libya is full of wild animals, and further beyond this area a sandy ridge extends from Egyptian Thebes to the Pillars of Heracles. [2] On this ridge, at about a ten-days journey from one to the next, there are chunks of salt in great piles. At the top of each pile, cool, sweet water springs up from the middle of the salt. Men live around them who are closest to the desert and furthest from the area filled with wild animals. The first people you meet there on a ten-days journey out of Thebes are the Ammonians, who keep a satellite sanctuary to Theban Zeus. As I have said before, the statue of Zeus in Thebes has a ram's head. [3] There happens to be another spring of water there. It is lukewarm at dawn and colder at mid-morning when the marketplace has filled up. It is especially cold at noon. [4] They water their gardens at that time. As the day ends the coolness lessens, and by the time the sun has set the water has become lukewarm again. It gets warmer as it nears midnight, and then it boils and bubbles. As night progresses to dawn it gets cooler. This spring is named the Spring of the Sun.

4.182. After another ten-days journey along the sand ridge past the Ammonians, there is a spring and hill of salt similar to the Ammonian one. Men live around there also. The name of this area is Augila. The Nasamonians travel to this area and gather the fruit of date palms. 183. Another ten-days journey from Augila there is another hill of salt and water and many fruit-bearing date palms, just like the other places. The men who live here are called Garamantes, who are a very big tribe. They have put earth over the salt so that they can plant it. [2] The Lotus Eaters are closest to them, and they are thirty days away. The cattle graze backwards here because they have horns that curve down in front. [3] They are not able to go forward without their horns sticking into the ground. Otherwise, they do not differ at all from other cattle except that their hide is very thick and firm. [4] The Garamantes hunt the cave-dwelling Ethiopians with four-horse chariots, because these Ethiopians are the fastest of all the men we have ever heard tell about. The cave-dwellers eat snakes and lizards and other sorts of reptiles. Their language is like no other language—it sounds like bats shrieking.

4.184. After another ten-days journey past the Garamantes there is another hill of salt and a spring, and the men who live there are called the Atarantes. They are the only men we know of who do not have names. As a group they are called Atarantes, but individuals do not have names. [2] They call down curses on the sun when it is excessively hot and abuse it terribly, since its burning afflicts both themselves and the land. A ten-days journey away from them leads to another hill of salt with a spring and the men who live around it. The mountain near this salt hill is called Atlas. It is narrow and round. It is said to be so high that the peak cannot be seen because the clouds never leave it in summer or winter. [4] The locals say that it is the pillar of heaven. These people, who are called Atlantes, get their name from the mountain. It is said that they never eat meat or see things in their dreams.

4.185. I am able to say the names of the people living on the ridge up to the Atlantes, but not beyond them. The ridge extends to the Pillars of Heracles and even beyond those. [2] There are salt pits after every ten-days journey and people living around them. The houses of all these people are built out of salt, for these are the rainless areas of Libya. The walls, since they are made of salt, would not be able to last if it rained. [3] The salt mined here is white and purple. Beyond this ridge, the area to the south and into the middle of Libya is an empty land—waterless, lifeless, rainless, and without growth. There is no moisture there.

4.186. From Egypt up to Lake Tritonis the Libyans are nomads who eat meat and drink milk. They do not eat cows, just as the Egyptians do not, nor do they raise pigs. [2] The women of Cyrene refuse to eat cows because of the Egyptian goddess Isis; they undergo fasts and celebrate festivals for her. The women of Barcae do not eat pigs or cows. 187. That is the way things are done there. To the west of Lake Tritonis the Libyans are no longer nomads, nor do they practice the same customs. They habitually do something to their children unlike anything the nomads ever do. [2] These Libyan nomads (I am not able to say for certain if it is all of them, but many of them at least) do as follows. When their children reach four years of age, they burn the blood vessels on the tops of their heads with the grease from sheep's wool, and for some of them they burn the vessels on the sides of their foreheads. They do this so that phlegm that flows down from their heads will never harm them. [3] They say that they are very healthy because of this, and it is true that the Libyans are the healthiest of all the peoples we know of. I am not able to say for certain if they are the healthiest because of this procedure, though. Should a convulsion come over the child while they are burning him, they have found a cure for it. They treat him by sprinkling him with goat's urine. I am saying what the Libyans themselves say.

4.188. These are the sacrifices performed by the nomads. They offer the ear of their animal sacrifice first and throw it over their home. After they have done this they twist back the victim's neck. They only sacrifice to the sun and moon. All Libyans sacrifice to these, but the ones who live around Lake Tritonis also sacrifice to Athena particularly and Triton and Poseidon as well.

4.189. The Greeks borrowed the clothing and aegis on the statues of Athena from Libyan women. The clothing of the Libyan women is the same except that it is made of leather and the tassels that hang from their aegises are not snakes but leather strips. Everything else is arranged the same way. [2] Also, the name proves that the apparel on the statues of Athena comes from Libya, because Libyan women wear goatskins without the hair that are dyed red outside their other clothes. The Greeks named this the aegis after these *aigeai* or goatskins. [3] Also, it seems to me that the ritual cry to Athena first came from the holy rites in Libya, because the Libyan women make this cry and do it well. The Greeks also learned to yoke four horses together from the Libyans.

4.190. The nomads bury their dead like the Greeks do, except for the Nasamonians. These men bury their dead sitting up. They also make sure that a man dies while sitting up and so does not die while lying down. Their homes, which are portable, are constructed from asphodel woven around reeds. These are the customs these people practice.

4.191. There are some Libyans who work the land and have houses to the west of the Triton River near the Ausees. They are called the Maxyes. They let the hair on their right side grow long and shave the left side. They stain their bodies with red earth. They say that they are descendants of Trojan men. [2] Their land, and the rest of Libya to the west, is filled with many more wild animals and has more vegetation than the lands of the nomads. [3] The eastern part of Libya, where the nomads live, is low-lying and sandy as far as the Triton River; beyond this to the west the land is hilly and has a lot of vegetation and wild animals. [4] There are oversized snakes and lions and elephants and bears and asps and donkeys that have horns, and dog-headed creatures and animals without heads that have eyes in their chests (so it is said by the Libyans), and savage men and savage women and many more wild animals that are not just made up.

4.192. None of these are in the area lived in by the nomads, but there are other animals, such as white-tailed antelope, gazelles, African antelope, donkeys (which do not have horns and never drink), antelope who are as big as bulls and whose horns are used to make the crosspieces for a lyre, [2] little foxes, hyenas, porcupines, wild sheep, birds of prey, jackals, panthers, screw-horn antelope, land crocodiles as long as five feet that look very much like lizards, ostriches, and tiny snakes that have one horn. These are the wild beasts that are only there, in addition to those that also appear elsewhere. The stag and the wild boar, however, do not appear anywhere in Libya. [3] There are three kinds of mice there: one kind is called two-footed, another is called *zegeries* (the name is Libyan, they may be called hill mice in Greek), and the third is bristly-haired. Weasels, similar to the ones in Tartessus, live in clumps of silphium. These are the many wild animals that the land of the nomadic Libyans contains, or, at least, as many as I could learn of by inquiry.

4.193. The Zaueces hold the land next to the Maxyes; their women drive their chariots in battle. 194. The Gygantes live next to them. Bees make a lot of honey there, but it is said that their farmers produce even more of it. They all paint themselves red and eat apes that live in the hills in large numbers. 195. The Carthaginians say that an island lies near the Gygantes called Curauis. It is nearly twenty-three miles in length but narrow in width. You can walk there from the mainland, and it is full of olives and grapevines. [2] There is a pool on the island from which local young women bring gold dust up out of the mud using bird feathers that have been covered with pitch. I do not know if this is true, but I write what was said. It might all be true, since I myself have seen pitch brought out of a pool of water in Zacynthos. [3] There are more pools there, the largest of which is seventy feet in diameter and ten feet deep. The Zacynthians tie myrtle branches onto the end of a pole and dip it in, and then they bring up the pitch stuck in the myrtle branch. It has the smell of asphalt, but in other aspects it is better than the pitch from Pieria. They pour the pitch into a pit they have dug near the pool. When they have collected a lot of it, they take it from the pit and pour it into amphorae. [4] Whatever happens to fall into the pool travels under ground and appears in the sea, which is a half mile away from the pool. It is likely that these facts about the island near Libya are true.

4.196. The Carthaginians talk about a land in Libya beyond the Pillars of Heracles and the men who live there. They say that when they travel there and unload their trade goods, they put them in a row along the beach, board their ships, and build a smoky fire. The locals see the smoke and go down to the shore; they leave gold for the goods and then move away from them. [2] Then the Carthaginians disembark and examine the gold; if the gold seems to them to be worth the value of the goods, they take it and sail away. If, however, it is not enough, they go back onto their boats and wait. The locals then come back and offer more gold until the Carthaginians are won over. [3] No one is cheated. The Carthaginians do not take the gold until it is equal in worth to the goods, and the locals do not take the goods before the Carthaginians have accepted their payment.

4.197. These are the people of the Libyans we are able to name. Most of them do not worry about the Persian king in the present nor did they earlier. [2] I am able to say this much about the land: There are four tribes that inhabit Libya and no more than that. That much I know. Two of them are indigenous, and two are not. The Libyans, who live in the north, and the Ethiopians, who live in the south, are indigenous; the Phoenicians and Greeks are immigrants.

2. Pseudo-Aristotle, *On Marvelous Things Heard* 84, 100, 132 (4th or 3rd century BCE). *These short "notebook entries" about various marvelous islands under the control of the Carthaginians reflect a strong anti-Carthaginian or Phoenician bias and the longstanding prejudices against them as untrustworthy pirates. (RFK)*

84. In the sea outside the Pillars of Heracles, they say that a desert island was discovered by the Carthaginians. The island held all kinds of trees and navigable rivers. It is also a marvel of fruit varieties and is only a few days sail away. Since the Carthaginians often visited the island because of its wealth and some even settled there, the leader of the Carthaginians declared that

anyone sailing to the island would suffer death. He also announced that they would slaughter all the inhabitants so that they might not tell anyone and so that they might not migrate to the island and take away such wealth from the Carthaginians.

100. On the island of Sardinia, they say that there are buildings set in the ancient Greek manner. There are many beautiful structures, including rotundas carved with extravagant forms. They say these buildings were made by Iolas son of Iphicles when, taking along the Thespians descended from Heracles, he sailed to those lands to settle them, since Heracles was master over all lands west and since Iolas claimed the land through his kinship with Heracles. The island itself was, so it seems, once called Ichnussa because its circumference is most like a man's foot [*ichnus*] in shape. It is said that the island was wealthy and productive up to this day. They say that Aristaeus, who was supposedly the most skilled farmer in ancient times, ruled over them in a region previously dominated by large birds. Now, the island no longer bears anything because it was conquered by the Carthaginians, who cut down all the fruits useful for nourishment and then ordered death for any inhabitants if they again let anything grow.

132. On one of the so-called Aeolian Islands, they say there exist a plethora of date-palms [*phoeniceios*], whence the island is called Phoenicodes. What Callisthenes says cannot be true, that the tree took its name from the Phoenicians of Syria who dwell by the seashore. But some say that the Phoenicians themselves were called such by the Greeks because they first sailed the seas and, wherever they disembarked, killed and slaughtered everyone. In the tongue of the Perrabi, the word for murder is *phoenixai*.

3. Polybius, *Histories* 6.51–52, 6.56 (2nd century BCE). *Polybius' history of Rome gives an extensive account of the Carthaginian Wars, including numerous assessments of why Rome was able to overcome this powerful enemy. (CSR)*

6.51. In the beginning, the constitution of the Carthaginians seems to me to have worked well when considering its distinctions as a whole. [2] They had kings ruling over them, the Elders had aristocratic power, and the many were in control of what was appropriate to them. In general it had an arrangement similar to that of the Romans or the Spartans. [3] But in the time of the Hannibalic war, the Carthaginians had a worse constitution and the Romans a better one. [4] For since there is naturally a time of growth for every physical body, constitution, and action, followed by a peak, and finally a wasting away, and as everything is at its most powerful at the peak, for these reasons the constitutions of these states differed from each other. [5] And as much as the power and good fortune of the Carthaginians was earlier than Rome's, by that much the Carthaginian state was in decline at that time. Rome was especially at its peak at that time in terms of the arrangement of the constitution. [6] The people had the most power in the Carthaginians' decision-making, while the Senate was supreme among the Romans. [7] Thus, since the many deliberated in one state and the best deliberated in the other, the Romans' decisions about common affairs were better than that of the Carthaginians. [8] And so the Romans, although they suffered setbacks in battles, won the war against the Carthaginians in the end because of the excellence of their deliberations.

6.52. Beyond those particular features, such as the affairs of the war, the Carthaginians are better trained and prepared for seafaring because this experience is something their ancestors did from the beginning, and they practice seafaring more than all other people. [2] In land warfare the Romans are much better trained than the Carthaginians. [3] For the Romans make this the focus of all their energy. Although the Carthaginians completely look down on their infantry, they give some brief attention to their cavalry. [4] The reason for this is that they use foreign and mercenary power, but the Romans use native and citizen power. [5] In this particular feature, therefore, it is necessary to claim that the constitution of Rome is better, for the Carthaginians always put their hopes of freedom in the courage of mercenaries, whereas the Romans put their freedom in the hands of their own excellence and in the support of their allies. [6] As a result, even when they fail in their initial tries, the Romans recover from their defeats in the end, whereas the Carthaginians experience the opposite. [7] For the Romans fight on behalf of their homeland and their children and are never able to let their anger go; rather, they remain and fight spiritedly until they overcome their enemies. [8] Although the Romans do not have much experience in sea power, as I said above, on the whole they are successful because of the courage of their men. [9] For even though sea power is not a small skill in the dangers of the sea, it is the courage of the fighting men that offers the most weight to the victory. [10] All the Italians differ in nature from the Phoenicians and the Libyans in terms of bodily strength and daring courage, and, in part, through their customs they make the ambition of their youths great. [11] One remark should be a sufficient sign of the eagerness of the state to make the sort of men who will submit to anything for the sake of gaining fame in their country for courage.

. . .

6.56. The customs and laws about money-making are better among the Romans than among the Carthaginians. [2] For at Carthage nothing about the getting of wealth is shameful, but at Rome nothing is more shameful than to accept bribes and to gain improper advantage. [3] It is considered just as excellent to make money from the best source as it is reproachful to profit excessively from improper sources. [4] Here is a proof: in Carthage they take power and give bribes in the open, whereas in Rome the penalty for this is death. [5] As a result, since the rewards for excellence are opposite in each case, so indeed the preparation for these things in each situation is dissimilar. [6] It seems to me that the greatest difference the Roman constitution has that is better is their treatment of matters about the gods. [7] And it seems to me that the thing that is reproached among other men, I speak of religious feeling, holds together the Roman state. [8] There is so much exaggeration and such extravagant introduction of religious matters into their private lives and the common affairs of the city that nothing excessive is left to be done, which would seem amazing to many. [9] I think they have done this for the sake of the many. [10] If, however, Rome was a state made up of wise men ruling together, such a practice would not be necessary. [11] But since all common people are thoughtless and full of lawless desires, irrational anger, and violent hearts, all that is left is to control the commons by unknown fears and such performances as these. [12] Because of this, the ancients do not seem to me to have brought among the common people these thoughts about the gods and these fears about the things in the underworld without planning and by happenstance; rather, I think that the people of the present day throw these beliefs out without planning or rational thought. [13] As a result, apart from other things, those who conduct public affairs among the Greeks, even if they should be trusted with only one talent, are not able to guard the public trust even though they have ten scribes and as many seals and double the number of witnesses. [14] But among the Romans, those who rule and are advisors who deal with a large amount of money act appropriately because they have pledged their faith through an oath. [15] It is rare to find among other people a man who keeps away from what belongs to the people and who has a clean record about these things. Among the Romans, on the other hand, it is rare to find someone who has been caught doing such a deed as stealing public funds.

4. Sallust, *War with Jugurtha* 6–13, 17–19, 89–91 (1st century BCE). *The Roman war with Jugurtha, illegitimate king of Numidia in North Africa, lasted from 112 to 104 BCE. Sallust includes in his history of the war descriptions of the character of the Numidians as well as ethnographic and geographic passages on North Africa. (MLG)*

6. As soon as Jugurtha grew up, he showed himself a young man with abundant physical strength, with a charming appearance, but above all with an energetic intelligence. He did not permit himself to be defiled through luxury and idleness; instead, following the practice of his people, he rode horses, practiced the javelin, competed with his coevals in races, and, although he surpassed everyone in glory, he was nevertheless esteemed by all. In addition, he spent much time hunting, being the first, or among the first, to hit a lion or some other wild animal. He accomplished very much, but spoke very little of himself. [2] Micipsa was at first quite happy with this behavior. He judged that the excellence of Jugurtha would be a source of glory for his reign. However, after he realized that he himself was aging and his children were still small, all the while the young man was constantly growing in

influence, he became very disturbed and brooded over the matter often. [3] He was afraid of human nature, which is greedy for power and inclined to gratify its desires. Most of all, he was afraid that his advanced age and his children's youth provided an opportunity, which leads astray even mediocre men through hope for gain. In addition, there was the Numidians' enthusiasm for Jugurtha. He was anxious lest this enthusiasm, if he were to kill such a man deceitfully, lead to some sedition or war.

7. He was distressed by such difficulties: he saw that such a popular man could not be removed by violence or treachery. Because Jugurtha was physically active and eager for military glory, he determined to subject him to dangers and in this way to try his luck. [2] And so during the Numantian war, Micipsa put him in charge of the troops he sent to the Romans in Spain as foot and cavalry auxiliaries, hoping that he would die easily either through his desire to display his valor or through the savagery of the enemy. [3] But the affair turned out far differently than he expected. [4] Jugurtha was active and clever. He recognized the nature of the Roman commander, Publius Scipio, and the character of the enemy. Through great effort and exertion, through self-effacing obedience, and by frequently confronting dangers, he reached in a brief time such renown that our troops were passionately attached to him and the Numantians intensely feared him. [5] And certainly it is a particularly difficult accomplishment to be both an active fighter and a wise counselor. The latter often tends to produce hesitation through forethought; the former, rashness though aggressiveness. [6] Therefore, the general used Jugurtha in nearly all difficult matters. He considered him a friend and daily became more and more attached to him, especially since Jugurtha's advice and undertakings all succeeded. [7] In addition, Jugurtha was generous and intelligent, aspects that united him with many of the Romans in fast friendship.

8. At that time, our army had many new men and nobles who took more notice of wealth than honesty and excellence. They were factious at home and influential among the allies. They were kindling the by no means small spirit of Jugurtha by promising that if King Micipsa were to die, he might obtain the sole power in Numidia. He had the greatest excellence, they said, and at Rome everything could be bought. [2] After Numantia was destroyed, Publius Scipio decided to release the auxiliaries and to return home himself. He gave Jugurtha gifts and praised him splendidly before the army. He then led him into his tent and there advised him secretly to cultivate the friendship of the Roman people as a whole rather than of individual Romans, and not to become accustomed to bribing them. It is a dangerous thing, he said, to buy from a few what belongs to many. If he were willing to continue with his habits, he would spontaneously reach renown and a kingdom; but if he pursued it too precipitously, he would ruin himself with his own money.

9. After this advice, he dismissed him with a letter for Micipsa. The substance of the letter was as follows. "Your Jugurtha displayed the greatest excellence in the Numantian war, a fact that I am certain is a source of joy for

you. His merits made him dear to us. We shall put forth all our effort that he be dear to the senate and people of Rome. I congratulate you on the basis of our friendship. Really, you have a man worthy of you and your grandfather Masinissa." [2] When the king learned from the general's letter that rumors of Jugurtha were true, he was greatly moved by the man's excellence and influence. He changed his mind and set out to win over Jugurtha with kindness. He immediately adopted him and made him an equal heir with his sons. A few years later, weakened by age and sickness, he perceived that the end of his life was near. Among his friends and relatives, and Adherbal and Hiempsal, the king is said to have addressed Jugurtha in something like the following words.

10. "I took you into my royal household, Jugurtha, when you lost your father as a child and were without hope and resources. It was my belief that you would cherish me no less than a father because of my kindness. [2] The events have not proved me wrong. To pass over your many remarkable deeds, you most recently brought renown to me honorably and my kingdom on your return from Numantia and your valor has vastly increased Rome's friendship with us. The reputation of our family has been renewed in Spain. Lastly, you have accomplished a mortal's most difficult task: you have overcome envy through acclaim. [3] Now nature is making an end to my life. By this right hand, by your loyalty to the kingdom, I advise and implore you to cherish these young men, who are related to you by blood and who are your brothers thanks to me. Do not prefer to join with others rather than keep to those to whom you are joined by blood. [4] The defense of the kingdom is not the army, it is not the treasury, it is friends. Friends cannot be compelled by weapons nor won by money; they are produced by duty and trust. [5] Moreover, who friendlier to a brother than a brother? What trust in others will you find if you are an enemy to your family? [6] For my part, I am handing over to all of you a kingdom that is stable, if you are good men; but if you are bad, it is weak. Concord causes small things to grow; discord causes great things to fall apart. [7] However, it is right that you, Jugurtha, take the lead in ensuring that things do not happen differently. You are the oldest and the wisest. In every contest the more privileged man, even if he is the injured party, still appears to be aggressor because of his greater power. For your part, Adherbal and Hiempsal, cherish and respect such a man as this. Imitate his valor and strive to show that I did not adopt better children than I fathered."

11. Jugurtha responded to this speech politely as suited the occasion; he was aware that the king's speech was a sham and his own view was different. [2] A few days later Micipsa died. The princes, after they performed spectacularly the customary regal funeral rites, met to discuss the rest of the business among themselves. [3] Hiempsal, the youngest of the three, was arrogant and despised Jugurtha's inferior nobility (his mother's side was of lower status). He therefore sat at the right of Adherbal so that Jugurtha could not sit in the middle of the three, the place of honor among Numidians. [4] However, when his brother implored him to give way to

priority in age, he took the other place with bad grace. [5] There, while they discussed many aspects of governing authority, Jugurtha proposed, among many other things, that they ought to repeal the last five years of decrees and laws, since Micipsa had been weakened by age and was hardly vigorous in mind. [6] Thereupon, Hiempsal replied that the idea was very agreeable to him, since Jugurtha himself had come into the royal house through adoption within the last three years. [7] That statement lodged in Jugurtha's heart more than anyone knew. [8] From that moment he was plagued by anger and fear. He began to plot and plan and consider the means by which Hiempsal might be dishonestly removed. [9] Since his plans proceeded rather slowly and his fierce spirit was not mollified, he determined to finish the job anyway he could.

12. During the first meeting of the princes mentioned above, they decided that, due to disagreements, the treasury should be divided and their own districts of rule established. [2] And thus a time for both events was decided, but the division of money was first. The princes, meanwhile, arrived by different routes to the lands near the treasury. [3] Hiempsal was by chance using a home in the city Thirmida, which belonged to a lictor quite close to Jugurtha, a man whom Jugurtha had always esteemed and prized. Since chance had brought him this man as an agent, Jugurtha loaded him up with promises and convinced him to return home as if just to inspect the house and to prepare spare keys for the gates (the first set were given to Hiempsal); for the rest, he said that when the time was right, he himself would come with a huge band. [4] The Numidian completed the task quickly and, as he had been instructed, let in Jugurtha's soldiers at night. [5] After these men broke into the house, they spread out to search for the king. They killed some men in their sleep and some just as they were waking up. They examined all the hiding places, broke the doors, and threw everything into a great noisy tumult. Hiempsal was discovered hiding in a maid's room, where he had at first fled in fear and ignorance of the place. The Numidians, just as they had been instructed, brought his head to Jugurtha.

13. The story of so great a crime quickly spread through all of Africa. Adherbal and everyone who was a former subject of Micipsa were seized by fear. Numidians split into two factions. The larger number followed Adherbal; but those following Jugurtha were better warriors. [2] So Jugurtha armed as many as he could, and he subjugated cities to his control, some by force and some by consent, and prepared to wield authority over all Numidia. [3] Although Adherbal had sent ambassadors to Rome to inform the senate of his brother's murder and his circumstances, he nevertheless was relying on his superior numbers and preparing for armed struggle. [4] When the affair came to the test, he was conquered and fled from the battlefield into the province and, from there, to Rome. [5] When Jugurtha had accomplished his plans and was in control of all of Numidia, he had the leisure to reconsider his acts and began to fear the Roman people. He felt that he had no hope against their anger unless in the greed of the nobility

and his own wealth. [6] And so within a few days he sent ambassadors to Rome with a great deal of silver and gold. He instructed them first to bury his old friends with gifts and then to acquire new friends, and lastly to hurry to arrange whatever they could by bribery. [7] When the ambassadors reached Rome, they followed the king's instructions and sent great gifts to his contacts and to anyone else who possessed great authority in the senate at that time. So great a change of opinion took place that the massive enmity for Jugurtha became the goodwill and favor of the nobility. [8] Some changed position from expectations, others from rewards. They canvassed individual members of the senate, imploring them not to vote harshly against Jugurtha. [9] And so when the ambassadors felt sufficiently confident, a day was appointed to hear both positions in the senate.

Ethnography and geography of Africa.

17. The subject seems to require a brief exposition of the geography of Africa and a short mention of the peoples with whom we have either made war or friendship. [2] I cannot report with any ease on those places and peoples that have been less visited because of the heat, the rough country, or lack of inhabitants. I will discuss the rest as briefly as I can. [3] In the division of the world, most situate Africa in the third part. A few think that there are only two parts: Asia and Europe. They situate Africa in Europe. [4] The borders of Africa extend westward to the strait between our sea and Ocean; it extends eastward to the sloping plateau that the inhabitants call Catabathmos. [5] The sea is violent and lacking in harbors. The land is productive of grain and good for pasture but not suitable for trees. There is little rain and few rivers. [6] The peoples there are healthy in body, fast, and hard-working. If they do not die from war or animals (there are many dangerous wild animals), they die from old age. This is because sickness brings very few down. [7] I shall briefly report the story of who were the first human inhabitants of Africa, who came later, and how they intermixed. My version is different from the common story; it comes from the Punic books said to be by King Hiempsal and translated for us. It is also the view of the native inhabitants. The accuracy of the tradition lies with them.

18. Africa was first inhabited by the Gaetuli and the Libyans, harsh and uncultivated peoples, who ate the flesh of wild animals and fodder from the earth like beasts. [2] They were governed by neither customs, nor law, nor authority. They wandered about and made their home where each night found them. [3] After Hercules died in Spain (as the Africans think), his army, which was made up of many different peoples, quickly broke up. It had lost its leader and many were seeking the command for themselves. [4] From that number, the Medes, Persians, and Armenians crossed to Africa in ships and occupied the lands nearest to our sea. [5] The Persians moved rather nearer to Ocean and turned the hulls of their ships over and used them for huts. They found materials in the area because they could not get any from Spain either by purchase or trade. [6] A large sea and incomprehensible language stood in the way of commerce. [7] These men mixed with

the Gaetuli over time because of intermarriage. Because they often changed locations in search of land, they called themselves Nomads. [8] To this day the dwellings of Numidian peasants (they call them *mapalia*) are oblong with curved sides and constructed like the hulls of ships. [9] The Libyans were added to the Medes and the Armenians. These people dwell nearer the African sea while the Gaetuli were farther south, close to the torrid zone. These peoples had towns earlier because they were divided from Spain only by a strait and instituted trade with them. [10] Over time the Libyans corrupted the name of these peoples, calling them Mauritanians instead of Medes in their barbarian language. [11] The Persian settlement increased in a short time. Later a group under the name Numidians left because of population pressure. They occupied the lands nearest Carthage called Numidia. [12] Each of these groups, relying on the other, subdued their neighbors to their authority by force of arms or by fear, providing themselves with glory and reputation. The most successful were those who had advanced to our sea, because the Libyans were less aggressive that the Gaetuli. Nearly all of the lower part of Africa was controlled by the Numidians. All of the conquered people mixed with the rulers and took their name.

19. The Phoenicians arrived later. Some came in order to relieve population pressure at home. Others were common people and those searching for adventure; they were influenced by a desire for power. The Phoenicians founded Hippo, Hadrumetum, Leptis, and other cities on the coast. These cities grew considerably in a short time. Some protected the interests of their mother cities while others brought glory. [2] As far as concerns Carthage, I think it better to remain silent than to say too little, since my subject reminds me to hasten on. [3] Therefore, starting along the coast of Catabathmos (this land divides Egypt from Africa), the first city is Cyrene, a colony of Thera. Next are the Syrtes and Leptis between them. Following this are the altars of the Philaeni, a place that the Carthaginians consider their empire's boundary with Egypt. After this are other Punic towns. [4] The rest of the lands as far as Mauritania are controlled by the Numidians. The Mauritanians are nearest to Spain. [5] South of Numidia we hear of the Gaetuli, some of whom dwell in huts while others have a more uncultivated, wandering lifestyle. [6] Beyond these are said to live the Ethiopians; beyond them are lands burnt up by the heat of the sun. [7] Therefore, at the time of the war with Jugurtha, the Romans and their administrators controlled most of the Punic towns and the territory held most recently by the Carthaginians. Jugurtha controlled a great part of the Gaetuli and the Numidians up to the river Muluccha. King Bocchus ruled all the Mauritanians. He knew only the name of the Roman people and was unknown to us as well, either in peace or war. [8] Enough has been said for our purpose about Africa and its inhabitants.

The capture of Capsa by Marius.

89. As he had planned, the consul approached the towns and fortresses and wrested them from the enemies, some by force, others by fear or promising rewards. [2] At first he kept his actions moderate because he believed that

Jugurtha would fight to protect his men. [3] When he learned that Jugurtha was far away and intent on other business, he felt it was time to pursue greater and more difficult tasks. [4] In the vast desert was a large and powerful city, Capsa, whose founder was said to be the Libyan Hercules. This city was not subject to tax or oppressive authority under Jugurtha. For this reason the citizens were considered to be the most loyal. They were protected not only by walls, by arms, and by men, but also even more by the harshness of the location. [5] In addition to the area near the town, the country is deserted, uncultivated, lacking in water, and infested by snakes. The snakes' ruthlessness, like all wild animals, increased because of the lack of food. In addition, the snakes' malevolent nature is even more intensified by thirst than anything else. [6] A huge desire to possess this town took hold of Marius, not only because of its strategic use but because it was a difficult endeavor, and because Metellus had earned great renown when he took the town of Thala. Thala was similar to Capsa in its aridity and fortification, with the exception that Thala had a few springs of water not far from the city walls. Capsa had one spring within the city and used rainwater for the rest. [7] Thirst was more easily endured there, and in all the less cultivated areas of Africa from the sea, because the Numidians often consume milk and wild animals. They use no salt or other incitements to appetite. Food for them is only a means to hold off hunger and thirst, not a source of licentiousness and luxury.

90. Thus the consul, after careful reconnaissance, put his trust (I believe) in the gods. This is because planning could only accomplish so much in so difficult a situation. In addition he was assailed by lack of food because the Numidians put more effort into grazing animals than agriculture, and because the food nature provided had been carried into the fortified places at the king's order. The fields, moreover, were dry and empty of grain in that season—it was the height of summer. Nevertheless, he carefully prepared for the situation. [2] All the cattle that had been plundered earlier he gave to the horse auxiliaries to lead. He ordered Aulus Manlius, his legate, to go with the light-armed troops to the town of Laris, where he had placed his funds and supplies. He said that he would go to the same place to forage in a few days. [3] He thus concealed his venture and hastened to the river Tanais.

91. On the march he daily distributed the cattle equally among his army's foot soldiers and cavalry and ensured that water-containers were constructed from their hides. He thus simultaneously mitigated the lack of grain and provided for future needs. And then on the sixth day they arrived at a river and the great effectiveness of the water-containers was shown. [2] After the encampment had been lightly fortified, he ordered the soldiers to take food and to be prepared to depart with the setting of the sun, leaving behind all their baggage and loading themselves and their pack animals with only water. [3] Then, when the time seemed right, he left camp and marched all night before stopping. He did the same on the next night. Then on the third night, long before dawn, he reached a hilly spot about two

miles from Capsa. Here he waited with all his troops, hiding as best he could. [4] When day broke and the Numidians, since they feared no attack, left the city in large numbers, he ordered all the cavalry and the fastest foot soldiers to hasten to Capsa and besiege the gates. Then he himself followed quickly and eagerly and did not allow his troops to pillage. [5] When the townspeople realized what was happening, the confused situation, their immense fear, the unforeseen misfortune, and their follow citizens outside the wall in the power of the enemy, all compelled them to surrender. [6] Yet the city was burned, the adult Numidian men killed, all the rest sold into slavery, and the booty divided among the soldiers. [7] This act, contrary to the law of war, was not committed because of the consul's greed or vicious nature, but because the spot was useful to Jugurtha and difficult for us to approach. Also, because people of this sort were faithless and changeable, they could not be controlled by kindness or fear.

5. Strabo, *Geography* 17.3.7, 17.3.15 (1st century BCE/1st century CE). *As part of his description of the land of Libya, Strabo describes the lifestyles of the Maurusians (Mauritanians) and Pharusians. (RFK)*

17.3.7. Although the Maurusians live their lives inhabiting a land that is blessed for the most part; nevertheless, even up to this day, the majority of them live as nomads. Despite this nomadic lifestyle, they still beautify themselves by braiding their hair and beards, by wearing gold, by cleaning their teeth, and by trimming their nails. Rarely would you see them touch one another while walking. In this way, they insure that their hair adornments remain in place. They fight from horseback predominantly with javelins and use reins made of twisted rushes and ride bareback. They also carry sabers. Their infantry carry elephant hides as shields. They dress and sleep in the skins of lions, leopards, and bears. These people and their neighbors, the Masaesylians, and the Libyans in general are all more or less similar in other ways too. They all use small horses, which are so ready to obey that they are steered by the use of only a little rod. The horses' collars are wooden or made of hair, from which the reins are hung. Some of the horses follow without being controlled, like dogs. The Maurusian infantry bear small leather shields, small broad-headed spears, and ungirded cloaks with a broad stripe upon them. And, as I said before, they also wear mantels and shields made of animal skins.

The Pharusians and Nigritae, who dwell beyond the Maurusians and near the western Ethiopians, are archers like the Ethiopians. They also use scythed chariots. The Pharusians rarely interact with the Maurusians while passing through the desert because they carry skins full of water hanging upon their horses. There are times when they make their way as far even as Cirta by passing through marshy lands and lakes. They say that they are cave-dwellers, digging into the earth. It is also said that where they live summer storms are frequent and the winters are marked by drought. Some of the barbarians there use skins made of serpents and fish as clothing and as bed coverings. Some say that the Pharusians[146] are the Indians who traveled here with Heracles.

Strabo recounts the founding of Carthage and the people who remained in the territory after its destruction by the Romans.

17.3.15. Carthage was a colony of Tyre, founded by Dido. The colony began so successfully for the Phoenicians, both the city itself and the territory as far as Spain (the land both beyond the Pillars and the rest), that the Phoenicians even now inhabit the best land in Europe on the mainland and the nearby islands. They also controlled all of Libya, at least the region one can dwell in without being a nomad. From this power base, they built a city that rivaled Rome and even engaged in three great wars with the enemy. . . .

As a way of demonstrating how powerful Carthage was, Strabo describes the size of the city and its military strength, including the amount of armor and weaponry it still had at the end of the siege and the number of ships and skilled workmen it had.

So powerful was Carthage, and yet it was taken and destroyed. The Romans declared the part of the region that had been under the control of the city a province and appointed Masanasses and the descendants of Micipsa as guardians, since Masanasses was especially respected by the Romans on account of his courage and friendship. It was Masanasses who organized the nomads into civic units and introduced husbandry to them. He also trained them as an army in place of their earlier piracy. A rather peculiar thing had happened to these men. Although their land was prosperous (except for a superfluity of wild animals), they were prevented from destroying the animals and working the land without fear. Instead, they turned upon each other and handed the land over to the wild beasts. Thus it happened that these people led a life of wandering and instability no less so than those driven to a life best avoided by want and a poverty of the land and climate. Such was the life of the Masaesylians that they earned the peculiar name of "Nomads." It is necessary for such men to be thrifty in their way of life, to eat roots more than meat, and to rely on milk more than cheese for food.

6. Pomponius Mela, *Description of the World* 1.41–48 (1st century CE). *Pomponius describes the peoples of north and central Africa, beginning with those closest to the shore and ending with those furthest away. Some of the peoples also appear in the descriptions of far-off, exotic*

---

146. The text says "Maurusians" here, but see Sallust, *Jug.* 18 and Pomponius Mela 3.10.

peoples in authors like Pliny, though they are not necessarily in the same geographic location. (RFK)

1.41. The shores are inhabited by people acculturated for the most part to our customs, except that they differ in language and in gods worshiped as ancestral and revered using ancestral customs. As for the neighboring territories, no cities stand there, although there are dwellings called *mapalia*. The way of life for those who live in them is harsh and lacks elegance. The leaders of the people dress in rough woolen cloaks, while the common folk wear pelts from wild beasts and livestock. Sleeping and feasting takes place on the ground. Dishes are made of wood and bark. They eat mostly the flesh of wild beasts so as to spare their flocks as much as possible. 42. The flocks are the only source of wealth to these people. They live scattered about as separate family units and make no decisions as a united people. Despite this, because each man has several wives at the same time and many children, legitimate and not, these people are never few in number.

1.43. Of those people documented as living beyond the desert, the Atlantes curse the sun at its rising and setting because it is a bane to both themselves and their crops. They do not have individual names nor do they eat animal flesh. They do not see in their sleep what other mortals see in their sleep. 44. The Trogodytai have no wealth and hiss more than speak. They climb around in caves and are nourished on serpents. 45. Among the Garamantae are horned cattle that feed at an awkward angle since their horns hinder them when pointed down toward the ground. No man has a wife of his own. Of the children born in the random chaos that constitutes their parents' sexual practices, parents raise those who seem to share the same physical features with them.

1.46. The Augilae believe that only spirits of the dead are gods. They swear oaths by them, consult them as oracles, and pray to them for the things they want. When they lie down on grave mounds, the spirits send them dreams as oracles. On the night of their marriage, women are religiously obligated to open themselves up to the lusts of any man who comes bearing a gift. At this time only is it appropriate to have intercourse with many men. At all other times chastity is expected.

1.47. The Gamphasantes live in the nude and know nothing of weaponry, not even how to throw or avoid a spear; for this reason, they flee encounters and do not endure engagements or conversations with others not of their own kind. 48. The Blemyes do not have heads. Their faces are in their chests. There is nothing human about the satyrs except their faces, and the Goat-Pans are famous for their shape. This is Africa.

7. Livy, *From the Founding of the City* 21.1, 21.39–44, 22.59 (1st century BCE/ 1st century CE). *Livy introduces the main part of his history of the Hannibalic War. (CSR)*

21.1. In this part of my history I am allowed to say as a preface what many writers of history have stated openly at the beginning of their entire works, that the war I am about to write of is the most memorable of all wars ever waged, the war that Carthage waged against the Roman people while Hannibal was their leader. [2] For never have any states or peoples stronger in wealth come together in war, nor did they ever have so much in terms of men and strength, and they were coming to war not at all ignorant of the arts of war against each other but expert at it because of the First Punic war. Also, the outcome of the war was so doubtful and Mars so wavering that those who conquered had been nearer to danger. [3] They fought with hatred almost greater than their strength, since the Romans were indignant that the conquered should bring war against their conquerors, and the Phoenicians were indignant because they believed that the governing of the conquered was done arrogantly and greedily. [4] There is also a story that Hannibal, just about nine years old, was boyishly begging his father Hamilcar that he be taken to Spain, while his father, who had just finished the African war, was preparing to lead his army to Spain. Hannibal was taken by his father to the altars, and his father forced him, with his hand on the sacrificial victim, to swear an oath that as soon as he could he would become an enemy to the Roman people. [5] The losses of Sicily and Sardinia were choking the man's great spirit, for, to him, Sicily had been conceded in too hasty desperation over the matter and Sardinia had been taken in passing by a trick of the Romans, and, in addition to all this, they had imposed a tribute during the upheaval in Africa.

Hannibal has crossed the Alps. The Carthaginians and the Romans prepare to fight a battle near the river Ticinus. Their leaders encourage the men.

21.39.7. The armies were already nearly in sight of one another. The leaders had arrived, and even though they were not well known to each other, each one was already filled with a sort of admiration for the other. [8] The name of Hannibal was already very famous among the Romans even before the destruction of Saguntum, and Hannibal thought that Scipio was an outstanding man since he had been chosen above all others to lead the Romans against him. [9] They raised their opinions of the other—Scipio because, although he had been left behind in Gaul, he had come to meet him after Hannibal had crossed over into Italy, and Hannibal because of his daring plan and the accomplishment of crossing the Alps. [10] Scipio, however, was the first to cross the Po River. He moved the camps to the river Ticinus and, before he led them out in their battle formation, he began a speech to exhort the soldiers:

21.40. "Soldiers, if I were going to lead into battle the army that I had with me in Gaul, I might have passed over speaking to you. [2] For, what good would it do for me to exhort those horsemen who so excellently defeated the cavalry of the enemy at the river Rhone, or those legions with whom I pursued the enemy here as they were fleeing and had the contest acknowledged as a victory because of the enemy's withdrawal and conduct? [3] Now, because that army, which was conscripted from the Spanish province, carries out its campaign with my brother Gnaeus Scipio under my auspices where the Senate and the Roman people wished it to act, [4] I myself have come to this battle voluntarily, so that you would have a consul as your leader against Hannibal and the Phoenicians. A fresh commander should say a few words to his new soldiers. [5] So you will not be ignorant of the kind of war this is or of your enemy, you are to fight, soldiers, with men whom you have beaten on land and sea in an earlier war, from whom you have taken a tribute for the past twenty years, and from whom you have taken Sicily and Sardinia as prizes in that war. [6] Therefore, in this battle there will be a spirit in you typical of the victor and in the enemy, a spirit typical of the conquered. They are going to fight now not because they dare to, but because it is necessary for them to do so. [7] Unless you believe that those who withdrew from the fight while their army was unharmed, and now have lost two-thirds of their infantry and cavalry in their crossing of the Alps, have found more hope. [8] However, although they are few, they are strong in mind and body; scarcely any force would be able to stand up to their strength and energy. [9] No, not at all. But this is an illusion. They are shadows of men, plagued by hunger, cold, filthiness, and squalor. They have been beaten and crippled by the rocks and crags, their limbs frostbitten, their sinews stiffened by snow, their limbs numbed by the cold; their weapons are broken and their horses are lame and beaten down. [10] That is how it is with the cavalry. The infantry with whom you are going to fight are the last remnants of an enemy, not a true enemy. I fear nothing more than that, once you have fought, it will be the Alps that will seem to have conquered Hannibal. [11] But perhaps it is fitting that the gods themselves should, without any human assistance, bring about and settle a war with a leader and a people who are breakers of treaties, and perhaps it is fitting that we, who were dishonored second after the gods, should complete this war that was already begun and settled.

21.41. "I am not afraid that anyone will think that I speak optimistically for the sake of encouraging you but feel differently in my mind. [2] I had the chance to go with my army into Spain, my province, where I was already going and where I had a brother to participate in my plans and be an ally in danger, and where I had Hasdrubal rather than Hannibal as an enemy and, without a doubt, a less difficult war. [3] Nevertheless, while I was traveling by ship along the shore of Gaul, because of the story of this enemy, I landed, sent the cavalry ahead, and moved the camp to the Rhone River. [4] In the cavalry battle (for it was with this part of the troops that fortune had given me to join in battle) I routed the enemy. Because I was not able to follow the infantry on land that was heading away rapidly in the manner of men who are fleeing, I returned to the ships and I was able to follow with as much speed as I could by a roundabout way on land and sea. Thus I have come to meet this frightening enemy here near the foothills of the Alps. [5] Do I seem like I have come here without the gods' support and to avoid battle, or do I seem to have come up on his footsteps to provoke and drag him into a decisive battle? [6] It pleases me to see whether the land has produced different Carthaginians unexpectedly after twenty years, or if they are the same men who fought near the Aegatian Islands and whom you sent away from Eryx after demanding a ransom of eighteen denarii each. [7] It also pleases me to see whether this Hannibal is one to rival the wanderings of Hercules, as he himself thinks, or if he is a payment, a tribute, and a slave of the Roman people left behind by his father. [8] If the atrocity at Saguntum did not drive him, then assuredly he would respect—if not his conquered homeland—his home, father, and the treaties written by Hamilcar's hand. [9] Hamilcar, who, ordered by our consul, led his garrison away from Eryx; who, raging and lamenting, accepted the burdensome laws imposed upon the conquered Carthaginians; who withdrew from Sicily and agreed to pay tribute to the Roman people. [10] Because of this, soldiers, I would wish you to fight not only with that spirit with which you are accustomed to use against other enemies, but also with a certain indignation and rage, as if you were seeing your slaves suddenly use weapons against you. [11] It was possible for those shut up near Eryx to die from hunger, that last resort for men; it was possible for our victorious fleet to cross over to Africa and destroy Carthage within a few days without any battle. [12] We granted a favor to those who begged us, we sent them out of the siege, we made peace with the conquered, and then, when they were oppressed by the African war, we considered them to be under our protection. [13] In payment for these things that we have given them, they come, following a raging youth, to attack our homeland. Would that this were a fight just for your honor and not your safety. [14] You must fight not just for the ownership of Sicily and Sardinia, about which we were fighting then, but for Italy. [15] There is no other army at your back who will stop the enemy if we do not win; there are no other Alps, which, while they stand in the way, allow new defenses to be built. This is where we stand, as if we were fighting in front of the walls of Rome itself. [16] Let each one of you know that you protect not your own body but your wife and your little children with your weapons. Do not worry over only domestic problems, but at the same time think on this: Our hands now guard the Senate and people of Rome. [17] As our strength and valor will be, so then will be the fortune of that city and Roman power." The consul said these things to the Romans.

21.42. Hannibal decided that his soldiers should be encouraged by observing matters before being encouraged by words, so he circled the army around to watch and placed the men who had been captured in the mountains in the middle bound with chains. He tossed Gallic weapons before their feet and ordered an interpreter to ask whether, if they were released from their chains and the victor should receive weapons and a horse, they would be willing to fight each other to the death. [2] When every last one asked for a sword and a fight, lots were thrown and each man hoped that fortune would choose him to fight. [3] Whosoever's lot came out happily leapt with joy, doing a dance that is customary among their peoples as they were congratulating him, and then he immediately took up the weapons. [4] Indeed, when they were fighting, the inclination not only among the men who shared their situation but also among the spectators in the crowd, was that the fortune of the ones who were victorious would not be praised more than the fortune of those who died well.

21.43. Then, after he had dismissed his men, inspired by watching several pairs, he called together an assembly and it is said that he spoke as follows: [2] "If you will have the same spirit as you witnessed by the example of another's fate only a little while before while considering your own fortune, we will win, soldiers. For that was not simply a spectacle just now, but a metaphor for your own condition. [3] I do not think that fortune has encircled you with greater chains or greater necessity than she did our captives. [4] Two seas on the right and the left enclose you, and you do not have a single ship for flight. The river Po is around you, a larger and more violent river than the Rhone. The Alps constrain you at your back, which you barely crossed when you were whole and healthy. [5] Here you must conquer or you must die, soldiers, where you have first met the enemy. It is the same fortune which imposes the necessity of fighting on you and offers these prizes for you if you win, prizes greater than what men are not accustomed to even hope for from the immortal gods. [6] If we are going to take back only Sicily and Sardinia, stolen from our parents, by our own courage, then they would be ample payment. [7] But now, however much the Romans possess, won and piled up in triumphs, all of that will be ours, along with its masters. For this rich prize then, come! Take up arms while the gods are supporting us! [8] For long enough now you have seen no profit in your great labor and the many dangers you faced while attending flocks in the vast mountains of Lusitania and Celtiberia. [9] It is the time now for you to carry out rich and splendid military campaigns and earn great prizes from so great a journey through so many mountains and rivers and the many armed races that we have passed through. [10] Fortune has given this end of labor to you: Here it will pay a worthy price when your tributes are earned. [11] Do not think that a war of so great a name will be as difficult to win. Often an enemy who is looked down upon has made a bloody battle, and famous peoples and kings have been conquered in a trifling moment. [12] If this one shining name, Rome, is taken away, what is there that explains why they should be compared to you? [13] Let me be silent about your service of twenty years with that courage and that fortune. You have come here as conquerors from the Pillars of Hercules and from the Ocean and the final ends of the earth through so many of the fiercest people in Spain and Gaul; [14] you will fight with an untried army who, this summer, were cut up, conquered, and beset by Gauls, and who are still as unknown to their leader as they are ignorant of him. [15] Or do I, who was nearly born and certainly raised in the tent of my father, that most famous general, the master of Spain and Gaul, the victor over not only the Alpine tribes but over the Alps themselves, which is a much greater thing, compare myself to this six-months-long leader who abandoned his own army? [16] If anyone should today show him the Phoenicians and the Romans after taking away their standards, I think he would be uncertain over which army he was consul. [17] I do not think it a little thing, soldiers, that there is not one of you before whose eyes I myself have not accomplished some soldierly act, or for whom that I have not been a spectator and witness to your courage, whose well-known acts I am not able to tell of together with their time and place. [18] I go to battle with all of you who have been praised and given gifts by me, I, who was your pupil before I was your commander. I will go into battle against men who are unknown to and ignorant of each other.

21.44. "Wherever I turn my eyes, I see everything full of your strength and spirit, a veteran infantry, bridled and unbridled cavalry from the most eminent tribes, you, [2] who are the most faithful and bravest of allies, and you, Carthaginians, who are about to fight both on behalf of your homeland and because of your most righteous anger. [3] We bring on the war and we, with dangerous standards, descend into Italy, we who are so much more daringly and bravely about to fight than our enemy, since our hope is greater and the spirit of the one bringing down force is greater than the one holding it off. [4] Moreover, grief, harm, and indignation fire up and arouse our spirits. They demanded that I, your leader, come begging to them first, and then all of you who had attacked Saguntum. They were going to afflict those of us who surrendered with the worst tortures. [5] That most proud and cruel race thinks that everything belongs to it and is under its sway. That race thinks that it may impose in equal measure whom we may have war with and whom peace. [6] They limit and enclose us in boundaries of mountains and rivers that we may not go out of, but they do not heed the boundaries that they have set for us. 'You may not cross the Ebro! There may be no issue between you and the Saguntines!' [7] But Saguntum is free. 'You may not move anywhere from your path!' Is it too little that you have taken my longest-standing provinces Sicily and Sardinia? Do you take Spain also? If I should go from there, will you cross into Africa? Do I say that you will cross? They sent this year's two consuls, one into Africa, one into Spain. [8] There is nothing anywhere left for us, except for what we claim with our weapons. It is all right for those who have a refuge to be timid and inactive, those men who will be received by their own land and fields while they are fleeing over safe and peaceful roads. It is necessary for you to be brave men who cast off everything between victory and death in certain desperation and either conquer or, if fortune will be uncertain, to see death in battle rather than in flight. [9] If you have all set your minds to it, if it is set fast in your hearts, I'll say it again, you have won. No weapon given by the immortal gods for the defeating of men is sharper than scorn for death."

> *The Romans have suffered a disastrous defeat at the Battle of Cannae—nearly 50,000 Romans were killed and many of the survivors taken as prisoners. In what follows, a representative of these prisoners attempts to convince the Roman Senate to pay to get them back by recounting a history of Rome's military losses. He is unsuccessful.*

22.59. The Senate was opened by the dictator to the representatives of the captives, whose leader spoke as follows: "Marcus Junius and you, the conscript fathers, none of us are ignorant of the fact that captives are held cheaper by no state more than ours; [2] in other respects, if our cause does not please you more than justice does, then no one else should be neglected by you less than we who have come under the power of an enemy. [3] For we did not surrender our weapons on the battlefield through fear, rather we stood on the piles of slaughtered bodies nearly through the night and dragged out the battle and then took ourselves back to camp. [4] For the rest of the day and the following night we, although tired out by our work and our wounds, guarded the fortifications. [5] On the next day, when we were surrounded by the victorious enemy and kept from water and there was no hope of breaking through the enemy that pressed close to us, we did not think it wrong that, after 50,000 men had been slaughtered from our lines, some Roman soldier remained after the battle of Cannae. [6] Then, finally, when we agreed on a price that we might be paid for and then released, we handed over to the enemy our weapons that were no help to us anymore. [7] We had heard that our ancestors had bought their lives from the Gauls with gold and that your fathers, who were very harsh concerning the terms of peace, had sent legates to Tarentum to ransom prisoners. [8] And yet each fight at Allia with the Gauls and at Heraclea with Pyrrhus was made infamous not by the slaughter but by the terror and the flight from battle. Heaps of Roman corpses cover the plains at Cannae, and we would not have survived the fight if their swords and strength had not failed the enemy because of all their slaughtering. [9] There are certain ones among us who were not even in the battle but were left behind as a guard for the camp; when the camp was surrendered, they came under the enemy's power. [10] I do not envy at all the fortune or circumstances of any citizen or fellow soldier, nor would I be willing to put myself forward by pushing someone else back, but those men, unless there is a prize for swiftness of foot and for running, who were mostly unarmed and fled from the battle and did not stop until Venusia or Canusium, should not put themselves ahead of us in worth or brag that they were defenders of the Republic more than we were. [11] You will employ good and brave soldiers in those men and in us, who will be even more prepared to fight for our homeland, since we will have been ransomed and restored to our country by your kindness. You are recruiting from every age and status; I hear that 8,000 slaves are to be armed. [12] Our number is not less, and we can be ransomed at no greater price than they were bought. If I compare us to them, I do an injury to the name of Roman. [13] I propose that one more matter be attended to by you in this council, conscript fathers: If you are planning to be harsher— which you would do although we do not deserve it—to what enemy are you going to leave us? [14] To a Pyrrhus, perhaps, who considered his prisoners to be among his guests? Or to a barbarian or a Phoenician, of whom it is hardly able to be determined whether they are greedier or crueler? [15] If you should see the chains, the squalor, the baseness of your citizens, surely the sight would move you no less than if you saw your legions lying dead over the plains of Cannae? [16] You are able to see the anxiety and the tears of our relatives standing in the front of the curia awaiting your answer. Since these people are in doubt and anxiety over us and those who are not here, what spirit do you think is in those whose life and liberty are being decided? [17] If, by god, Hannibal, against his own nature, was willing to be kind to us, we would think that our life had no worth since we seemed to you to be unworthy of ransom. [18] Once some captives returned to Rome whom Pyrrhus sent back without a ransom, but they returned with legates, the foremost of the state, who were sent to ransom them. Shall I return to my homeland as a citizen who is not considered worth 300 pennies? Each man thinks his own way, conscript fathers. [19] I know my life and my body are under consideration, but the danger to my reputation moves me more. Do not send us away condemned and rejected by you, for no man would think that you were sparing with the price."

8. Lucan, *Civil War* 9.341–949 (1st century CE). *Cato and his men make their way through the deserts of North Africa after losing at Pharsalia against Caesar. (MLG)*

Far from all the fields, a mound of dry sand, unmolested by water, rises up on the surface of the sea. The wretched sailors are stuck. Although their keel is stuck fast, no shore is visible. In this way the sea destroyed part of the boats. The other part followed the guiding rudder and was saved by their flight. Finding by chance sailors who were familiar with the place, they reached unharmed the sluggish Lake Triton.

According to tradition, this lake is beloved of the god who is heard by the sea as he blows across the shining surface of the water with his windy conch-shell. Pallas loves it too, since after she was born from her father's head [350], she touched down at Libya first—it is the closest land to heaven as its very heat proves. She saw her face in the quiet water of the pool and stepped on its edge. She gave herself the name Tritonis from the beloved water. Next to this lake the river Lethe quietly glides by. According to tradition, this river brings forgetfulness from its subterranean channels. And here formerly under the protection of a sleepless dragon lies the garden of the Hesperides, poor now that its fruit was stolen. Spiteful is the man who refuses to believe antiquity and instructs poets to give true accounts.

Once there was a golden grove [360] where branches were heavy in wealth and golden buds. There a chorus of unmarried girls guards the brilliant grove and a serpent condemned never to close his eyes in sleep twisted himself around trees bent under their golden metal. Heracles removed the prize from the trees and eased the work of the grove. He left the branches without their weight and took the shining fruits back to the tyrant of Argos.

After the fleet was driven toward these lands and out of the Syrtes, they did not wander further beyond the waters of the Garamantes. [370] With Pompeius as their leader, they remained in the more temperate part of

Libya. But the manly valor of Cato was intolerant of inaction, and he boldly led his troops into unknown lands, trusting to their arms. He dared the land march around the Syrtes. Winter, which had closed off the sea, also prompted this course of action.

Rain gave grounds for hope to men who feared excessive heat. They hoped that the savage route might be without difficult heat or cold, that it might be tempered by the season of winter on the one hand and by the climate of Libya on the other. Before they set out on the barren desert, Cato made the following speech: "Men, you have chosen to follow my standards as your only safety, [380] holding your head high without fear of death. Prepare your mind for this great work of manly valor and the greatest labors. We march through barren plains and a scorched world, where the sun is excessive, where the water in springs is meager, and where the dry fields bristle with poisonous serpents. Difficult is the journey to the rule of law and the love of a collapsing government. Let them come through the middle of Libya, and let those who have no desire to defect and for whom is it enough just to march attempt this uncharted course. Of course it is not my intention to deceive anyone and to lead the army by concealing my fear. [390] Let men be my comrades, who are attracted by danger itself, who think it a fine Roman act to endure the worst with me as their witness. But if any man needs a guarantee of safety or is overcome by the sweetness of life, let him go find his master by a better route. So long as I am the first to step upon the sands, the first to put my foot on the dust, let the burning heat beat down on me, let the serpent full of venom block my path. Test your danger beforehand by what happens to me. Let only him be thirsty who observes me drinking. Let only him be hot who sees me seeking the shade of a grove. [400] Let only him feel weariness who sees me riding in front of the infantry. He may complain if there is some mark to show whether I am a soldier or the leader. Snakes, thirst, the heat of the sand—these are sweet to courage. Endurance rejoices in difficulties. Virtue is happier when its existence comes at a great price. Libya alone can prove by her host of calamities that it is no disgrace for men to have fled from a battle." In this way Cato set their trembling spirits afire with courage and with a desire for struggles. They seized the one-way route on the deserted path. Libya acquired the sacred name of Cato, whose fate would be closed in a humble tomb, though Cato cared not. [410] Libya is the third part of the world, if you are willing to believe common opinion in all things. But if you follow the winds and the sky, it is a part of Europe. The banks of the Nile, as you know, are no further distant than the Scythian Tanais is from Cadiz on the western edge. At this point, Europe diverges from Libya and its banks curve to give space to Ocean.[147] The greater part of the globe goes to Asia alone. Since although Africa and Europe send forth the west wind in common, Asia contains the northern wind on its left-hand borders and stretches on its right to the south wind and alone contains the east

---

147. The Straits of Gibraltar.

wind. The fertile parts of Libya incline toward the setting sun [420], but even this land is without any streams. Rarely do the northern winds bring the northern rains, which refresh its fields with our fair weather. The land is not violated for any wealth: it is not smelted for bronze or gold. The land is absolutely pure of any criminal clods.[148] Only the woods of Maurentia were a source of wealth for the people, but they did not know how to use it. They were content to live under the leafy shade of the citron tree. But our axes have come to the unknown wood, and from the end of the earth we sought out fancy furniture and feasts. [430] But the whole shore that embraces the mobile Syrtes extends under too much sun and lies near to the burnt sky. The climate chars the crops and murders Bacchus with dust. No roots hold together the powdery land. A life-supporting climate is absent. The land is of no interest to Jupiter and sits listless under a sluggish nature. The sands are not plowed and do not know the changing of seasons. Nevertheless, this sluggish soil thrusts up a little grass here and there. This grass is plucked by a hard living and naked race, the Nasamonians, who inhabit the lands nearest the sea. These men are nourished on the plunder of the world by the barbarian Syrtes. [440] This is because a plunderer lies ready on the sandy shore and recognizes wealth, although no ship touches the port. So, it is by shipwrecks that the Nasamonians hold commerce with the whole world.

Here his implacable valor bid Cato go. There the soldiers, unconcerned with the winds and fearing no storms on land, endured the terrors of the open sea. For though the shore is dry, the Syrtes is buffeted more violently than Ocean is by the south wind, which does more damage on land. This is because Libya has no mountains or cliffs [450] to break the force of this wind and drive it back and scatter it and weaken its hurricane to a gentle breeze. It does not rush through forests and grow calm twisting around ancient trunks. The whole land lies open. The wind, free in its movement, trains its Aeolian violence on all the sands. The south wind drives a rain-less cloud of swirling dust in circles, lifting most of the land into the air and leaving it hanging and twisting perpetually. The poor Nasamonian watches as the wind sets his kingdom wandering. His home is dashed to pieces as his house reveals the Garamantian when its roof is ripped off and flies away. Fire does not lift its destruction higher. [460] Dust fills the air to the same degree that smoke rises up and violates the light of day.

Then also the south wind attacked the Roman line more violently than usual, and the staggering soldier can nowhere stand firm in the sand, which disappears as they step on it. The south wind would shake the lands and would remove the earth from its moorings, if Libya were solidly con-structed and heavy, and if Libya were to close this south wind up within hollowed out caves. But because the land consists in drifting sand that is easily driven around, it remains stable by offering no resistance. The deep-est part of the land remains stable because the top is mobile. [470] The violent and intense movement of the wind twisted off the men's helmets,

---

148. That is, criminal wealth in its soil.

shields, and spears and carried them off through the large empty sky. Perhaps in some extremely distant land, this armor, falling from the sky, was an omen and terrifies peoples who suppose that the weapons, which had been ripped from men's arms, fell from the gods. In the same way those shields fell from heaven as Numa completed his sacrifice, and now the chosen youth wear them on their Patrician shoulders. It was the South wind or the North that had despoiled the people carrying shields that are now ours. [480] As the wind torqued the land, the Roman youth sunk down in fear of being snatched away. They pulled their clothes tight around them and sunk their hands into the ground. They remained in place not only by their weight but by effort as well. They could almost be moved by the wind alone, which rolled huge piles of sand over them and covered the men underground. A soldier hardly had the strength to lift his limbs since he was covered with such a pile of dust. A great pile of heaped up sand held them standing and immobile as the land surged up. The walls were broken to pieces and the wind ripped up the stones and carried them off. [490] It dropped them far away, a marvelous prophecy of misfortunes: Men who have never seen houses watch houses fall in pieces. The path was utterly hidden and there were no landmarks. They knew the route from the stars. The horizon of Libya does not show the constellations whole but conceals many in the sloping border of the earth. When the heat expanded the air, which had been contracted by the wind, the day became scorching, their limbs dripped sweat, and thirst parched their lips. [500] A trickling rivulet was spotted at a distance. A soldier with difficulty scooped it up from the dust in the broad bowl of his helmet and offered it to his leader. The throats of all were parched with dust, and the leader himself, just holding the tiniest drop of liquid, was a source of envy. "Am I," he said, "in your opinion the only one in this whole crowd, you degenerate soldier? Did I appear so very soft and unequal to the first blast of heat? You are so much more deserving of this punishment: You should drink in front of a thirsty people." In this way he roused himself in wrath and dashed the helmet to the ground. [510] This act was sufficient water for everyone.

They arrived at the temple that the uncultivated Garamantians, alone among the peoples of Libya, possess. There stands an oracle of (according to tradition) Jupiter, but the god is not represented brandishing his thunderbolt or at all like our god, but as Hammon[149] with twisted horns. The peoples of Libya have built there no rich temple nor adorned it with treasures of Eastern gems. Although Jupiter Hammon is the only god of the peoples of Ethiopia and the wealthy peoples of Arabia and India, the god is still poor and maintains a shrine not violated by any riches over time. A divinity of the old ways, [520] he protects his shrine from Roman gold. In this place the only green trees in all Libya attest to the presence of the gods. No leaves are known in all the dry sands that divide the tepid lands of Leptis minor near Carthage from burning Berenicis in Cyrenaica. Hammon alone

---

149. Ammon.

acquires a grove. The reason for the trees is a local spring that binds the crumbling soil, masters the sand, and joins it with water. Even here there is no protection from the Sun when the day is balanced at the zenith. The trees hardly protect their trunks, [530] so small is the shadow when the rays are vertical. It has been determined that this is the latitude where the Tropic of Cancer strikes the zodiac. But in your lands, whatever people you are who are divided from us by the Libyan fire, the shadow falls to the south, which for us falls to the north. You see the sluggish Dog's tail [Ursa Minor] rise from the horizon. You believe that the dry Wain [Ursa Major] sinks into the sea. You have no constellation in the sky that does not sink into the sea. Each axis is far away, and the movement of the constellations seizes all in the middle of the sky. The constellations do not travel obliquely in the sky: The Scorpion does not rise more vertically than the Bull; the Ram does not give any of its rising time to Libra; [540] Virgo does not order Pisces to set slowly. Sagittarius rises as high as Gemini, as does burning Cancer and rainy Capricorn. Leo rises no higher than Aquarius.

Standing before the doors of the temple were men sent from the East to learn new prophesies from the advice of horned Jupiter. They gave way to the leader from Latium, and his officers requested that Cato test the divinity famous throughout Libya and pass judgment on its ancient reputation. The greatest promoter of examining the future from the voice of the gods was Labienus. [550] He said, "Chance and the accident of our march have offered up the voice of so powerful a divinity and the plans of god. So great a leader can we use on our journey through the Syrtes, and we can learn the outcomes of the war. To whom else could we believe that the gods would reveal their secrets and speak more honestly than to sanctified Cato? Surely you have ever directed your life by the laws of heaven and followed the gods. Look! A free opportunity to speak with Jupiter is given. Inquire into the fates of unspeakable Caesar and investigate what the character of our country will be like. Will it allowed for our people to enjoy their own justice and laws? [560] Or has the civil war been in vain? Fill your heart with the holy voice. As a lover of implacable valor at least inquire into the nature of valor and seek the pattern for honor."

Inspired by the god that he carried in his secret heart, Cato released a torrent of speech worthy of the oracle. "What do you bid me seek, Labienus? Whether I prefer to have died in armed freedom or witness tyranny? Whether there is any difference between a short life or long age? Can no violence harm the good man? Does chance threaten in vain against valor? [570] Is it enough to desire praiseworthy things? Does success ever increase honor? I already know the answers. Hammon will not lodge them more deeply within me. We all are connected to the gods and, although the oracle be silent, we do nothing without the will of god. Divinity needs no voice. When we were born the creator has told us once and for all whatever we should know. Did he choose these barren sands in order to chant prophesies to a few men? Did he bury truth in this dust? Does god reside anywhere but in the earth, in the sea, in the air, in the heavens, and in valor? Why ask after the gods any further? Whatever you see, whatever you have set in motion, that is Jupiter. [580] Leave the prophesies for men who hesitate and are ever fearful of life's mischances. Me? It is not oracles but the certainty of death that has made me self-assured. The timid man and the brave both must die. That Jupiter has said this is enough." So he spoke and departed, preserving the reputation of the oracle of Hammon, which he left for others untested.

Cato marches on foot in full view of his panting soldiers, carrying his spear in his own hand. Rather than give orders, he demonstrates how to endure toils. He does not recline and relax while being hoisted on men's shoulders, nor does he sit in a wagon. He sleeps less than anyone. [590] When finally a spring was discovered and the men were forced to gaze upon it in their need, he stood by while even the camp followers drank. Last of all, he took a drink. If a great reputation is created by true good acts, and if we look into valor alone without considering success, everything praiseworthy in our ancestors was the result of chance. Has the favor of the war god and the blood of nations bestowed so great a name on anyone else? I would have preferred to lead this triumphal procession through the Syrtes and farthest reaches of Libya than to ascend the Capitoline hill three times in Pompey's chariot or to break Jugurtha's neck. [600] Behold! A true father of his country, a man who most deserves Roman altars of worship. No one would be ashamed to swear by his name. Rome, you will make him a god if ever you stand tall without the yoke of slavery on your neck.

The heat grew thicker and they stepped into a region that borders the southern limit the gods placed on mortals. Water became even scarcer. A single spring was discovered in the center of the plentiful sands, but a crowd of snakes occupied the spot, which could hardly contain them. The dry asps were standing on the margins; in the middle of the pool the *dipsades* serpents swam thirstily. [610] The leader, when he saw that the men would die if they avoided the spring, spoke to the men. "The image of death that you fear is empty, soldiers. Do not hesitate to drink the water. The venom of snakes is poisonous when mixed with blood. They have poison in their bite and threaten death with their fangs. A drink of the water will not kill." He spoke and gulped down the doubtfully poisoned water. In the whole Libyan desert, that was the only spring that he requested to drink from first.

Our effort and care has been insufficient to discover the reason why the climate of Libya overflows with so many pests and is fertile in deaths, [620] or why hidden nature has mixed into the soil the power to harm. The true reason, however, has been replaced by a story known the world over. On the farthest borders of Libya, where the burning land touches Ocean, which is set to boiling by the sinking of the sun, used to lay the broad and overgrown fields of Medusa, daughter of Phorcys. This land possessed no shady groves; it was not softened by plows; it was sprinkled with stones who had witnessed the countenance of their mistress Medusa. In her body did a harmful nature first bring up violent pests. [630] Out of her jaws poured snakes with tongues vibrating and hissing shrilly. Medusa rejoiced when the snakes lashed around her neck. Vipers stretched down her back and stood up in front as if designed by a hair stylist. Viper venom flows down when she combs her coiffure, and it is the only part of unfortunate Medusa that may be gazed upon by all without penalty. For who has time to fear the monster's gaping grin and face? Who was allowed by Medusa, once he gazed on her directly, to die on his own? She stole the fatal moment as it hesitated and outstripped the chance to fear. Their limbs died while breath remained, and [640] the soul stiffened under the bones before it left the body. The hair of the furies caused madness alone; Cerberus quieted his growling when Orpheus sang; Amphitryon's son gazed on the Hydra as he killed it. But this monster was feared by her father, Phorcys, a god of the sea second only to Neptune, and by her mother, Ceto, and even by her sisters, the Gorgons. Medusa could threaten heaven and the sea with an unusual paralysis and turn the world to stone. Birds suddenly fell from the sky under their weight. Wild animals stood unmoving in their caves. [650] All the peoples of Ethiopia who dwell nearby were turned to marble. No living creature survived looking upon her. Even the Gorgon's snakes turned backwards to avoid her face. She turned the Titan Atlas to stone as he stood under the western pillars. When once heaven feared the Giants who walked with serpent legs on Phlegra, her Gorgon face turned them into mountains and made an end to the massive war of gods as it sat on the breastplate of Pallas Athena.

To this land came Perseus, born from Danae, who was impregnated by the golden rain of Zeus. He was carried aloft by the Parrhasian wings given to him by the Arcadian god, [660] inventor of the cithara and wrestler's oil. And winged Perseus suddenly lifted the Cyllenian scimitar—a scimitar already red with the blood of another monster (for he had killed the guard of the cow beloved by Jupiter). Unmarried Pallas brought aid to her winged brother, Perseus. The head of the monster was her part of the bargain, and she ordered Perseus to turn to where the sun rises when at the end of the Libyan lands, and to plow the Gorgon's kingdom with a backward flight. She put in his left hand a shield that shone with burnished bronze, in which she bid him gaze upon the stone-making Medusa. [670] Medusa slept a sleep that would give her the eternal quiet of death. And yet that sleep was not total, for the greater part of her hair remained awake, and the snakes stretched from her hair and protected her head. The other part lay over the middle of her face and *<poured>* shade over her *<closed>* eyes and *<doubled the shadows of sleep>*.[150] Pallas herself guided the agitated hero and directed the trembling Cyllenian scimitar of Perseus who had turned away. She sliced the broad confines of the snake-bearing neck. What a countenance had the Gorgon then when her head was cut off by a wound from a curved sword! How great a poison must, I should suppose, have breathed from her mouth! How great a death poured from her eyes! [680] Not even Pallas could watch, and the gaze of Perseus, though averted, would have frozen if Athena had not tousled Medusa's thick hair and covered her face with snakes.

---

150. Housman's supplement.

The winged hero fled into the sky after he had taken the Gorgon in this way. He indeed thought to shorten his journey and lessen his flight if he cut through the middle of the cities of Europe. Pallas ordered him not to harm fruitful lands and to spare the people. For who would not gaze up at the sky with such a thing flying by? He turned his wings on the west wind and thus over Libya, an uncultivated land and [690] open to the stars and the sun. The sun orbits directly over it and burns the soil. In no other land does the night fall into the sky from a higher point and obstruct the journeys of the moon if it runs straight on through the Zodiac forgetting its curved path, and does not escape the shadow by turning either north or south. Although that land is sterile and its fields produce nothing good, they were fertilized in venom by the gore dripping from Medusa's head. From the savage blood, the land produced a horrid dew, which the heat rendered potent and cooked into the crumbling sand.

Here the blood clot first lifted its head out of the dust [700] and raised up the Asp who brings sleep with its swollen neck. Blood fell more abundantly here with a drop of congealed poison. In no other snake is the poison more concentrated. It lacks heat and does not cross into cold climes on its own; it traverses the sands as far as the Nile. But (Is there nothing we won't be ashamed to make a profit on?) Libyan deaths are imported to Italy from there and we make the asp an item of commerce. The blood-flow snake [*haemorrhosis*] unwinds its huge scaly coils and will not allow its wretched victim's blood to remain within. The land-water snake [*chersydros*] was born to inhabit the Syrtes, [710] whose nature as land or lake is ambiguous. The tortoise-shell water snake [*chelydrus*] moves with smoking track, and the millet-spotted snake [*kenchros*] glides always in a straight line. Its mottled belly is dyed with many more spots than Theban marble flecked by many veins. The sand-burrower snake [*hammodytes*] is indistinguishable from the burnt sand in color. The horned viper [*cerastes*] travels on its twisting spine. The club snake [*skytale*] alone sheds its armored skin in late winter when the morning frost shimmers. Here is found the dried-up-thirst snake [*dipsas*] and the dangerous two-way snake [*amphisbaena*], who twists toward each of its twin heads. Here also is the swimming snake [*natrix*], defiler of water; the javelin snake [*iaculus*], [720] who can fly; the cheek snake [*parias*], who is happy to furrow its path with its tail; the greedy swollen-jaw snake [*prester*], who opens his foaming mouth wide; the putrefying rancid snake [*seps*], who dissolves its victim's body and bones. The king snake [*basiliscus*] terrifies the other snakes with his hissing; his breath kills before his poison; he drives all the common snakes far away, and he makes his kingdom in the emptied sand. You also, *dracones*, who glitter with golden flashes and as harmless divinities slither in all other lands, become poisonous in the burning heat of Africa. You draw down the birds from the lofty heaven; you pursue whole herds, [730] crushing massive bulls with your coils. Not even the size of the elephant makes it safe. You kill everything without need of poison to cause horrible deaths.

Cato with his hardened army measured his waterless march through this pestilence. He witnessed the sad end of many companions, whose unusual deaths resulted from a small wound. Aulus, the young standard-bearer of Etruscan blood, stepped on the head of a *dipsas*, which turned and bit him. He hardly felt any pain from the bite, the wound lacked the appearance of deadly spite and was not threatening. [740] But look! The silent poison sneaks up, a devouring fire seizes his marrow and kindles his insides with a burning corruption. The poison dried up the moisture surrounding his vital organs, and his tongue began to burn in his dry mouth. There was no sweat to run down his weary limbs, and the tears dried in his eyes. The dignity of the commander and the orders of saddened Cato did not restrain the burning man from tossing the standards aside and madly searching in every field for the water that would quench the poisoned thirst in his heart. [750] Thrown into the Tanais, the Rhone, and the Po, he would continue to burn, even if he should drink the Nile as it flooded the fields. Libya hastened his death, taking some of the deadly fame of the *dipsas* by helping with its desiccated land. Aulus searched deeply in the squalid sand. He then returned to the Syrtes and drank down the salty water. Seawater pleases him, but its moisture is not enough. He did not know the cause of his fate was death by poison—he thought it was thirst. He boldly opened his swollen veins and filled his mouth with his blood. [760]

Cato ordered the army to take the standards and march hastily away. No one was permitted to learn that thirst could do this. An even sadder death met their eyes. A tiny *seps* latched onto the ankle of wretched Sabellus. It clung tenaciously by a barbed fang, but he ripped it off by hand and pierced it with his javelin. Though small, no other serpent has such a power to bring bloody death. The skin broke and shriveled around the wound, revealing the pale bone. The wound was a gaping hole without a body. His limbs swam in corruption, his calves melted, [770] there was no skin on his knees, and all the muscles of his legs rotted and his groin dripped with black discharge. The lining of his stomach burst open and his innards flowed out. His body melts to the ground, but there is not so much of it as should be because the savage poison has boiled his limbs down and death contracts everything into the tiniest pool of corruption. The profane nature of the pestilence reveals the substance of man. Death reveals the sinews, the structure of the lungs, the cavity of the chest, everything concealed by the vital organs. The shoulders and strong arms liquefy, his head and neck ooze to the ground. Snow is not melted quicker by the warm south wind. No quicker will wax soften in the sun. It is saying only a little that his body burned up and dripped in corrupted blood. [780] Even a fire does this. But what funeral pyre burns up the bones? These also disappeared, following the diseased marrow. No single trace of the rapid death is allowed to remain. Among the pestilences found in the land of the river Cinyps,[151] you,

---

151. Africa, between Syrtes.

seps, win the contest for destruction. The rest snatch away life; you alone take even the corpse.

But look! Here appears a form that is the opposite of that flowing death. The burning *prester* bit Nasidius, a farmer from the lands of the Marsians. [790] His face burned red and a massive tumor swelled everything and stretched his skin until his form disappeared. The corruption was larger than his whole body and stretched over his limbs and blew up beyond human measure as the venom spread all over. The man himself disappeared, sinking deeply into his swollen body. [800] His breastplate could not contain his swollen chest. A cloud of steam rises less strongly from a heated cauldron; the sails are not so swollen by the northeast wind. His swollen limbs are no longer contained by the shapeless globular mass and the indistinct bulk of his trunk. The body was untouched by the beaks of birds and would provide no safe feasts for beasts. The soldiers dared not put his body on the pyre and fled from the still swelling cadaver.

The Libyan snakes were preparing even greater spectacles. A savage *haemorrhosis* sunk its teeth into Tullus, a greathearted youth and admirer of Cato. Just as compressed Corycian saffron is accustomed to pour out in equal streams from every statue, red poison and blood flowed at the same time from all his limbs. [810] His tears were blood. Blood flowed abundantly from every opening that moisture knows in the body. His mouth and open nostrils overflowed, his sweat was red, every limb was awash from full veins. His whole body was a wound.

The blood in your heart, sad Laevus, froze because of a serpent of the Nile. You did not mention any pain but met your death with a sudden darkness and descended to your dead comrades in sleep. Death is slower in the cups poisoned by the deadly stalks that seem like Sabaean incense plucked by the death gathering Saitae. [820] Look! A serpent, called by Africa the *iaculus*, twisted savagely and hurled itself from a distant barren tree. It pierced Paulus' head and went through his temple. Venom had no effect here; the wound killed him. It was then discovered how slowly a missile flew from a sling and how lazily the air hummed when a Scythian arrow passed.

What good came of the basilisk pierced by wretched Marrus' spear. The poison ran through the weapon and attacked his hand. He immediately drew his sword and cut it off from the shoulder. [830] He stood by safely and watched while his hand died in the sad pattern that would have been his own death. Who would have thought that the scorpion has the power of quick death? Yet heaven is the witness that the scorpion, threatening savagely with its knotted tail and raised stinger, took the glory of defeating Orion. Who would fear to tread on your hiding places, *salpuga*?[152] Even to you did the Stygian sisters give command over their own threads.

Thus they found no rest in bright day or in dark night. The wretched men mistrusted even the land they were lying on. [840] No bed of piled leaves,

_____

152. A poisonous ant.

no bed of heaped straw; they lie, tossing and turning on the ground, expos-
ing their bodies to death. Their warm breath attracts the snakes, cold in the
chill night. Between the limbs of the men, the snakes warm their gaping
mouths, rendered harmless because of the numbed venom. With the sky as
guide, the men do not know the distance nor limit of their marches. They
often lament and cry out, "Return to us the weapons we fled from! Return
Thessaly! Why do we suffer lingering deaths when we are a band sworn to
the sword? The *dipsades* fight for Caesar and [850] the *cerastae* continue the
civil war. We want to go to the torrid zone and to where the sky is burnt
by the Sun's horses. I would gladly ascribe my death to the sky and the
weather. I do not, Africa, complain about you, nor about you, Nature. You
have taken a monster-bearing region away from men and given it to snakes.
You condemned a soil unfit for grain to no cultivation, and you wished men
to lack poisons. We are the ones who have come into the region of serpents.
Receive our penalty, whatever god you are who hates our commerce and
[860] divided the region with a burning desert on one side and the dangerous Syrtes on the other and who set death in the border between. The civil
war continues its march through the hidden parts of your interior, and the
soldier, sharing the knowledge of your secret region, runs into the barriers of the world. Perhaps even worse things remain for us on our march.
Fires meeting hissing water. The nature of the sky pressed to the ground. No
land lies more remote than the gloomy lands of Juba, known to us only by
reports. Perhaps then we will desire these serpent-filled lands. This climate
has a solace: [870] something at least lives here. I do not require my native
lands, neither Europe nor Asia, which gaze up at different suns. Under what
sky, in what land will I leave you, Africa? Recently at Cyrene, winter froze
the land. Have we overturned the law of the seasons in our short march? We
go to the opposite pole, we slide down the globe, we give our backs to the
north wind to beat. Perhaps now Rome herself is below our feet. We want
this comfort for our fate: let our enemies come, let Caesar follow where we
flee." Thus did their enduring patience unburden its laments. [880] They are
compelled to endure such labors by the supreme valor of their leader, who
keeps guard, lying on the naked sand, and hourly challenges fortune. He
alone is present at every death. He flies to wherever he is called and bestows
a benefit greater than survival: the strength to die. A man was ashamed
to die with a groan when Cato was watching. What dominion could any
calamity have against such a man. He overcame misfortune in others' hearts
and as witness he taught that great pains have no power.

Worn out by inflicting such great danger, Fortune late and reluctantly
gave some aid. [890] Inhabiting these lands are only a single people who
are immune to the poisonous bite of snakes: the Marmarican Psylli. Their
language is equal to a powerful drug, and their blood itself is immune and
able to reject any poison even without chanting. The nature of their lands
compels them to live unharmed among snakes. There was a profit to have
placed their home in the middle of poisons. They have a truce with death
from poison. They put great trust in their blood. Whenever an infant is

born, they test the uncertain offspring [900] (it may have been the result of mixing in a foreign love) by the bite of an asp. The bird of Jupiter turns the featherless offspring, recently hatched from a warm egg, to the rising sun: those who can endure the rays and the direct daylight are preserved for the use of heaven; those overcome by the sun are neglected. [910] Thus does the Psyllus consider the true offspring of his people those who do not tremble at the touch of the snake and who plays as an infant with the serpent he is given. This people, not only content with their own salvation, also watched for guests and aided peoples against the deadly monsters. These were then following the Roman army. As soon as the leader ordered the tents pitched, they purified the sands within the camp with a chant and words that drive away snakes. The boundaries of the camp were encircled by a medicinal fire. Here the elder wood crackles and foreign galbanum bubbles, and the tamarisk, unfruitful in leaves, and eastern costas and powerful panacea, and Thessalian centaury, and sulphurwort, and Sicilian thapsus all sputter in the flames. They burned larch-wood, southern-wood, whose smoke is oppressive to snakes, [920] and the horns of a deer born far away. Thus the night was safe for men. But if any man met his fate from a snake by day, then there were miracles from the magical people and a mighty battle between the Psylli and the poison. He first marks the spot bitten with spittle, which constrains the poison and restricts the trouble in the wound. Then he pours out many incantations from his foaming mouth with a continual mumbling; the speed of the wounding gives no space for breath, and a moment's silence means death. Often the blight that has worked right into the marrow is expelled by an incantation. [930] But if the venom obeys too slowly and refuses to come out though ordered, then he leans over and licks the pale wounds and draws out the poison with his mouth and dries the limbs with his teeth. He spits out in victory the death extracted from a cool body. It is quite easy for the Psylli to know, even from the taste of the poison, which snake it was whose bite he overcame.

And so the Roman youth was at last relieved by this aid and wandered far in the wastelands. Twice the moon lost her light and twice regained it; [940] waxing and waning, she saw Cato wandering over the desert. Then the sand began to harden more and more, and Libya condensed and became solid land again. Here and there in the distance a few trees raised leaves, and simple huts made of piled straw rose up. How much joy did the wretched men feel in this better land when first they saw that only fierce lions faced them! They were nearest to Leptis. Stationed there, they spent a peaceful winter, free from storms and heat.

9. Achilles Tatius, *Leucippe and Cleitophon* 2.14.9–10 (2nd century CE). *Hunting gold in a Libyan river.* (MLG)

The land of India is imitated by a Libyan marsh that contains a secret known to the maidens of Libya: the water contains wealth. This wealth is locked and stored away in the mud under the water. It is a wellspring of gold. And so they smear a long pole with pitch and dip it in the water. This unlocks the door of the river. [10] The pole is for the gold what a hook is for fish, for it catches it. The pitch is the bait for the prey. Any piece of gold that touches this pitch, it simply adheres to it, and the pitch plucks its prey up to dry land. In this way gold is hunted from the Libyan River.

CHAPTER 9

AFRICA: ETHIOPIA AND BEYOND

Ethiopia is a part of the classical imagination as early as Homer (Chapter 1), but it is not until the 5th century BCE that it became a part of the "real" world through exploration by both sea and land. Throughout the Classical era, trade with and travel to Ethiopia and beyond only increased. But the imaginary Ethiopians never really disappeared, and they continued to be a marvelous people in a marvelous land.

1. Hanno of Carthage, *Periplous* **(c.5th century BCE).** *All that remains of Hanno the Carthaginian's description of his attempt to circumnavigate Africa seems to be a Greek translation from a Carthaginian summary, a summary likely dating to around 500 BCE. Although many of the geographic and topographical references are unclear, it seems that Hanno and his crew reached as far south as Mount Cameroon (the "Seat of the Gods") and the Gulf of Guinea before turning back. (RFK)*

This is the "sailing around" of Hanno, king of the Carthaginians, into the part of Libya beyond the Pillars of Heracles, which he set up in the halls of Cronus, declaring the following:

1. It seemed good to the Carthaginians that Hanno sail outside the Pillars of Heracles and found Libyphoenician cities. And so, he sailed sixty fifty-oared ships filled both with a muster of as many as 30,000 men and women and also with grain and other supplies < . . . > 2. After putting to sea, we passed the Pillars, and we sailed beyond them for two days and then established our first city, which we named Thymiaterion; it lay near a great open plain. 3. And then having set sail and headed west, we all came to Soloeis, a Libyan promontory thick with trees.

4. After establishing a shrine to Poseidon there, we set out once again and headed toward the rising sun for half a day until we reached a lake lying not far from the sea, which was full of many giant reeds; there were also elephants and many other wild beasts grazing. 5. Passing by the lake and journeying for many days, we settled the cities Caricon, Teichos, Gytte, Acra, Melitta, and Arumbys near the sea. 6. Setting out from there, we came to a great river, the Lixos, which flows down from Libya. Near the river, a nomadic people known as the Lixitai graze their cattle. We remained with them for some time and became friends. 7. Beyond these men live inhospitable Ethiopians, dwelling in a land infested with wild beasts and

surrounded by great mountains whence they say the Lixos flows, and around the hills dwell the Trogodytai—men with strange forms whom the Lixitai believe are faster than horses on a race course.

8. Taking interpreters from among the Lixitai, we sailed south for two days past the desert < . . . > then again, back toward the sunrise for about a day. We then discovered a small island in the inlet of a bay, the circumference of which was a half mile; this we colonized and named Cerne. We figured that this spot lay on a straight latitude with Carthage, since it seems that the distance from Carthage to the Pillars and from there to Cerne is the same. 9. Afterward, sailing out from along a large river, we came to a lake, the Chretes; the lake has three islands in it all larger than Cerne. Sailing down from here a day's journey, we came into the innermost part of the lake, beyond which a great mountain range stretched. The mountains are full of savage men who wear the skins of animals and who tried to crush us with rocks, thus preventing us from leaving the ship.

10. From there, we sailed to the other side and came upon a vast river filled with crocodiles and hippopotami. We then turned around again and went back to Cerne. 11. From Cerne we sailed south for twelve days, gliding along the coast, the entire extent of which the Ethiopian inhabitants fled from us and went into hiding; they yelled at us words unintelligible to the Lixitai with us. 12. On the last day, we anchored near a great mountain range thick with trees. The wood of the trees was sweet-smelling and colorful.

13. Sailing around these mountains for two days we happened upon an immense opening of the sea, opposite which and near the land there was an open plain. During the night we saw fires on that plain on all sides at intervals, sometimes more, sometimes fewer. 14. Drawing water there, we then sailed in the previous direction for five days along the coast, until we came to a large bay that the interpreters say is called the Western Horn. In this bay was a large island, and on the island was a lake of saltwater, and in this harbor was another island upon which we disembarked. We saw nothing but woods there during the day, but at night many fires burned, and we heard the sound of flutes and the crashing of cymbals and drums and countless shrieking. Fear seized us, and the seers ordered us to leave the island.

15. Sailing away quickly, we passed by a fiery land filled with smoke; very large streams of lava came down into the sea from this land; the land was inaccessible because of the heat. 16. Frightened, we sailed away quickly. Moving along for four days, we saw during the night a land full of fire; in the middle was an enormous fire, larger than the rest, reaching, so it seemed, to the stars. On this day, there appeared the largest mountain we had seen, called the Seat of the Gods. 17. On the third day from that point, sailing around the streams of fire, we arrived at a harbor called the Eastern Horn.

18. In the innermost part, the island had a lake, just like the first, and in this lake there was another island filled with savage men. By far most of them were women, with hair covering their bodies, whom the interpreters called "gorillas." Chasing the men, we were unable to capture them because they all fled, being cliff-dwellers, and because they were throwing rocks at us. Three females bit and scratched at us as we led them, and they were unwilling to follow. We killed them, and then we escaped and carried off their skins to Carthage. < . . . > We did not sail on any farther, though, since we were running low on supplies.

2. Herodotus, *Histories* 3.20, 3.22 (5th century BCE). *Herodotus recounts an embassy sent by Cambyses to the Ethiopians. (CSR)*

3.20. When the Fish-eaters came to Cambyses at Elephantine, he sent them to the Ethiopians with orders for what to say and bearing gifts of purple cloth, a golden linked necklace, bracelets, an alabaster box of perfume, and a jar of Phoenician wine. These Ethiopians, the ones to whom Cambyses sent an embassy, are said to be the largest and the most beautiful of all men. They say that the Ethiopians use different laws, distinct from other men's laws, and especially this law concerning their kingship: their citizens think the man fit to be king is the one they judge to be the largest and to have the strength for a man of such size.

The Ethiopian king sees through the embassy and rebukes Cambyses for wanting to conquer the Ethiopians. He then examines the gifts.

3.22. Then he took up the purple cloth and asked what it was and how it was made. After the Fish-eaters told the truth about the purple and the dye, he said that they were deceitful men, and that their clothes were deceitful, too. [2] Then he asked about the gold, the linked necklace, and bracelets. When the Fish-eaters explained about adornment with gold, the king laughed and, thinking that they were fetters, said that there were stronger chains than these among his own people. [3] Thirdly, he asked about the perfume. When they talked about its manufacture and application, he said the same thing about them as he did the cloth. But when he came to the wine and inquired about its making, he was pleased with the drink, and then asked what the Persian king ate and what was the longest lifespan for a Persian man. [4] The ambassadors said that he ate bread and explained the nature of grains, and they said that a full eighty years was the longest lifespan appointed for a man. In response, the Ethiopian king said it did not amaze him that they lived so few years since they ate shit; for they would not even be able to live that long, if they did not mend themselves with their drink, and indicated to the Fish-eaters the wine. In terms of wine, the Ethiopians are bested by the Persians. The Fish-eaters asked the king in turn about their lifespan and diet, and he replied that many of them reach

120, and some went over this, and that their food was cooked meat and their drink milk.

3. Pseudo-Scylax, *Periplous* 112.8–12 (4th century BCE). *This is one of the earliest extant descriptions of a circumnavigation of the world and is dated to about 337 BCE. The author's description of the Ethiopians shows similarities with earlier texts, such as Herodotus and Hanno. (RFK)*

112.8. There are Ethiopians toward the mainland, and the Phoenicians sell their goods to them. They exchange goods in return for the skins of deer, lions, and leopards, as well as elephant skins and tusks, and the hides of cattle. [9] The Ethiopians wear spotted clothing and drink from cups made of elephant ivory. Their women wear bracelets made of ivory, and they even adorn their horses with ivory. These Ethiopians are the tallest of all humans we know of and are over six feet tall, with some even ranging above seven feet tall. They have beards and long hair and are the most beautiful people of all humanity. Their king is whoever among them is the tallest. They have cavalry, javelin throwers, and archers. Their arrows are hardened by fire. [10] Phoenician merchants sell them perfumes, Egyptian stone, other minerals, and Attic pottery and *chous*, pitchers called such because they are sold at the Athenian festival Choës.[153] [11] These Ethiopians are meat-eaters and milk-drinkers. They consume a great deal of wine from the vine, which the Phoenicians sell them. They have a large city to which the Phoenician merchants sail. [12] Some say that these Ethiopians occupy the land continuously from this city to Egypt, that this sea is continuous, and that Libya is just a peninsula.

4. Diodorus Siculus, *The Library of History* 2.55–60 (1st century BCE). *Diodorus reports the journey of Iambulus to the Islands of the Sun, a mythical island far south of Africa. (MLG)*

2.55. Now I shall attempt to give a brief exposition on an island discovered in the ocean to the south and on the astonishing tales associated with it. I shall start from an accurate account of how it was discovered. [2] There was a certain Iambulus, who had zealously pursued his education from when he was a boy. After the death of his father, a merchant, he likewise took up that trade. Traveling inland through Arabia to the spice-producing region, he and his fellow travelers were captured by some raiders. At first, he and one of his fellow captives were appointed to serve as herdsmen. Later some Ethiopians captured him and his companion and carried them off to the Ethiopian coast. [3] They captured them because they were foreigners

---

153. The Anthesteria, the Athenian festival of wine and the dead.

and could serve to purify the land. There was an ancient custom handed down to the inhabitants of this part of Ethiopia and ratified by divine oracles over twenty generations (or 600 years, since a generation is calculated at 30 years). To prepare for the purification ritual, a two-person boat was constructed, adequate in size, strong enough to endure the winter sea, and capable of being rowed by two. In this boat they placed a six-months supply of food, sufficient for two people. The men then boarded the ship and embarked as the oracle commanded. The men were told to sail to the south. [4] They were told that they would reach a blessed island and an excellent people among whom they would live happily. They claimed that people from their own tribe, if they were sent out and reached this island, would likewise enjoy a peaceful and absolutely blessed life for 600 years. But if, panic-stricken at the sea's distance, they sailed back, they would receive the greatest punishment, being considered impious men and destroyers of the whole tribe. [5] It is said that the Ethiopians hold a large, all-night festival by the sea and then make magnificent sacrifices. They put garlands on the men who are going to seek the island and complete the purification of the tribe by sending them off. [6] These men sailed over the great sea in winter and in the fourth month reached the promised island. The island was round and had a perimeter of about 625 miles.

2.56. The account continues: As they were approaching the island, some of the inhabitants ran out to meet them and helped bring in the skiff. The island inhabitants came together and marveled at the voyage of the foreigners, received them kindly, and gave them a share of the island's products. [2] The island inhabitants differ greatly from the people of our lands in their physical characteristics and way of life. The shape of their bodies are similar and their height reaches to six feet. The bones of their bodies are able to bend to some extent and then be restored like sinews. [3] Their bodies have an excessive softness but are more energetic than ours. When they have grasped something in their hands, no one can pry it from their fingers. They have absolutely no hair anywhere on their bodies except on the head, eyebrow, and eyelid, and also on the chin. The rest of their body is so smooth that not the smallest bit of down appears on it. [4] They are distinguished in beauty, and the whole shape of their bodies is harmonious. Their ear cavities are much larger than ours, and they can close them like the muscular contractions of the throat. [5] They have a certain peculiarity with their tongue, partially the result of nature and partially a deliberate contrivance. The tip of their tongue is forked, which they further divide down to the root so that the whole tongue is forked. [6] The result is very cunning adaptability of voice that can mimic not only all human articulate speech but also the many sounds of birds and, in short, any peculiarity of sound. And most surprising of all, when they happen to meet two people, they chatter perfectly with both at the same time. They both answer and converse appropriately with the bystanders because they talk to one with one tongue and similarly to another with the other tongue. [7] They have the most temperate climate, seeing that they live on the meridian and are not vexed by heat or cold. Late summer blooms all year among them, just as the poet says: "Pear upon pear ripens, apple upon apple, bunch of grape upon bunch of grape, fig upon fig."[154] Day is always the same length as night, and at midday there are no shadows because the sun is directly overhead.

2.57. The islanders are said to live in kinship groups and communities with the collected kin groups being no larger than 400. The islanders pass their time in meadows, since the land provides much for subsistence. Because of the excellent land and gentle climate, food is produced spontaneously in a more than sufficient amount. [2] Nature provides them with a plentiful supply of a reed that abounds in a seed similar to white vetch. This is gathered and drenched in warm water until it increases to the size of a pigeon egg. This then is crushed together and skillfully ground by hand, shaped into loaves, and baked. They eat this bread, which has a remarkable sweetness. [3] There are said to be many freshwater springs: the warm ones are used for washing and relieving fatigue; the cold ones have remarkably sweet water that is beneficial for health. They practice every branch of learning but especially astronomy. [4] They use an alphabet with twenty-eight graphemes that correspond to the significant sounds, but there are only seven characters, each of which can be written in four ways. They compose their lines of writing not horizontally as we do, but vertically from top to bottom. The people are said to have excessively long lives, seeing as they can live up to 150 years, and are generally free from illness. [5] A deformed person or anyone generally inferior in body is compelled to commit suicide according to a severe law. It is customary among them to live for a fixed number of years and, when they have completed this time, to embrace a strange manner of death. Among them there grows a plant of a peculiar nature: whenever someone lies down on it, he imperceptibly and gently nods off to sleep and dies.

2.58. The report continues: They do not marry women but hold them in common, and the children who are born are raised commonly with equal affection. When they are babies, those nursing often exchange the newborns so that the mothers cannot recognize their own children. It is for this reason that there is no rivalry among them, that they lack civil strife, and that they consider harmony the most important thing and preserve it. [2] There are some animals there that are small in size but unexpected in the nature of their body and the power of their blood. They are spherical in shape and very similar to the tortoise, but the surface of their body is crossed with two yellow stripes with eyes and a mouth at the end of each stripe. [3] Therefore they see with four eyes and eat with two mouths, but swallow with a single throat through which nourishment flows into a single stomach. The organs and the rest of the innards are similarly singular. Many feet are set under it in a circle, and it uses them to travel in whatever direction it wishes. [4] The blood of this animal is said to have a remarkable power: It immediately rejoins and makes whole any living

---

154. Homer, *Odyssey* 7.120–121. "The poet" generally refers to Homer in the ancient authors.

body that has been severed. Even if a hand or something similar happens to have been cut off, provided the cut is fresh, it can be rejoined to the body by this blood. And so with the other parts of the body that are not connected to parts that are vital for life. [5] Each community maintains a rather large bird of a peculiar nature, and they use it to test the disposition of the soul in their newborns. They attach the babies to the animals, who then start to fly. The children who patiently endure the trip through the air are reared, but those who become sick and are full of astonishment are rejected. These are seen as unlikely to live a long time and as generally unsuitable because of the disposition of their soul. [6] The oldest man of each community always maintains the leadership role like a king and all obey him. Whenever this first man completes his 150 years of legally allotted life, he commits suicide and the next oldest takes up the leadership. [7] The sea surrounding the island has strong currents and very high and low tides but is sweet to the taste. Many of the stars visible to us, such as Ursa Major and Minor, are generally invisible to them. There are seven islands, similar in size and equally distant from each other. The inhabitants follow the same customs and laws as each other.

2.59. The inhabitants of these islands use with restraint the advantages that nature on her own supplies to them in abundance. Instead they pursue simplicity and take only the food that they need. They prepare meat and other dishes by roasting and boiling in water, but those other sauces cunningly contrived by chefs and diverse seasonings are absolutely inconceivable to them. [2] They revere as divinities the whole surrounding atmosphere, such as the sun and heavenly bodies in general. There is an abundance of all kinds of fish, which are caught in diverse ways, and no small number of birds are hunted. [3] The land naturally produces many fruit trees as well as olives and vines, from which they produce abundant olive oil and wine. The snakes are said to be very large but do no harm to humans and have an edible flesh that is remarkably sweet. [4] They make their own clothes from a certain reed that has in its middle a bright and soft fuzz, which they collect and mix with crushed seashells to produce spectacular purple garments. The nature of the animals is unusual and astonishingly unbelievable. [5] Their whole diet is said to be regimented, and they do not always eat the same food. Instead their diet is divided into fixed days: sometimes they eat fish; sometimes birds; sometimes land animals; sometimes olives and frugal side dishes. [6] They take turns serving each other: some fishing, some engaged in crafts, others occupied in other useful activities. They perform the services in a recurring circle except for the elderly. [7] In the festivals and feasts, they declaim and sing hymns and panegyrics to the gods, but especially to the sun, who gives them and their island its name. [8] They bury their dead in the sand whenever the tide is low so that the spot is recovered by the rising tide. The reeds that provide their sustenance are said to be about nine inches long and to fatten with the waxing of the moon and to decrease similarly with the waning. [9] The water from the hot springs is sweet and healthy. It maintains its heat and never cools even if cold water or wine is mixed in.

2.60. Iambulus and his companion stayed among the inhabitants for seven years before being forcibly expelled for being wicked and having evil habits. Having once again prepared the skiff and filling it with provisions, they were compelled to depart. They sailed for more than four months and came upon a sandy and marshy part of India. [2] His companion died in the surf, but Iambulus reached a certain village. The inhabitants led him to the king at the city of Palinbothra, a city many days journey from the sea. [3] The king was fond of Greeks and a learned man, and so he received Iambulus with great cordiality. He finally traveled under safe-conduct through Persia and at last arrived safely in Greece.

5. Diodorus Siculus, *The Library of History* 3.1–10 (1st century BCE). *Diodorus describes Ethiopia, its people, and culture. (MLG)*

3.1. In this book I shall add to what I have already said and discuss the Ethiopians, the Libyans, and the so-called Atlantians. 2. The historians relate that the Ethiopians were the first humans, and they say that there is clear evidence for this claim. Nearly all sources agree that the Ethiopians did not arrive from elsewhere, but being born from the land they are justly called autochthonous. They add that it is obvious to all that the people who live under the midday sun are probably the first that the earth brought forth. This is because the sun's heat dried up the earth as it was still wet from the genesis of everything and produced life. It is therefore likely, they say, that the place nearest the sun first brought forth animate beings. [2] They add further that these people were the first to discover and reveal the honoring of gods and making of sacrifices, the holding of processions and festivals, and the rest of the ways mortals honor the divine. For this reason everyone has heard of this people's piety, and it is assumed that sacrifices in Ethiopia are the most pleasing to divinities. [3] Evidence for this is provided by the poet who is nearly the oldest and the most honored among the Greeks. This poet in his *Iliad* described Zeus and the rest of the gods visiting Ethiopia for the yearly sacrifices and common feast held among the Ethiopians, "for Zeus had yesterday traveled to Ocean to feast with the blameless Ethiopians and all the gods went along."[155] [4] And they say that because of their piety toward divinity, they clearly received divine grace and have never been captured nor experienced a foreign despot. For they have from the beginning of time remained free and in harmony with each other. Although many powerful peoples have invaded their land, no one has succeeded in taking it.

3.3. Cambyses, for example, invaded with a large force. He lost his whole army and put his whole rule at risk. Semiramis, whose name was widely known for her great projects and achievements, only made it a short way into Ethiopia before giving up her whole campaign against that nation.

---

155. Homer, *Iliad* 1.423–424.

Heracles and Dionysus, in their travels over the inhabited world, left only the Ethiopians beyond Egypt unconquered because of the Ethiopians' piety and the very great difficulty of the attempt. They also claim that the Egyptians were colonists of the Ethiopians and that Osiris was the leader of the colony. [2] For in general they say that what is now Egypt was not land but sea when the universe first took shape. Later, however, the flooding of the Nile carried mud down from Ethiopia, which was slowly deposited. The most visible indication that their whole land is alluvial deposit comes, they say, from what happens at the mouths of the Nile. [3] Each year, as you know, new mud gathers at the river's mouth, and the sea is seen being thrust back from the alluvial deposits and the land thus is enlarged. They say that most Egyptian customs are Ethiopian, just as ancient custom is often preserved among colonists. [4] They give as examples the fact that they consider their kings divine and take the greatest care over burials and many other such actions that are Ethiopian practices. Also, the forms of their statues and the shape of their alphabet are Ethiopian. [5] For the Egyptians have two styles of writing: one is called "demotic" and is known by all; the other is called "holy" and is only known among the Egyptians by priests alone, who learn it from their fathers in secret. Among the Ethiopians, however, everyone uses the "holy" type. [6] The organization of the priests has a similar structure in both nations. They purify all those who attend to the gods, and they similarly shave their faces, wear the same robes, and carry a plow-shaped staff, which the kings have. These wear soft felt caps that have a button on the top and are wound around with serpents they call asps. This is likely a sign to indicate that those who dare to attack the king will suffer death from the bites. [7] There are many other claims about their antiquity and the Egyptian colony, which there is no pressing need to write about.

3.4. We must speak instead about the Ethiopian writing system called among the Egyptians "hieroglyphic" so as not to leave out any discussion of antiquities. There is agreement that the written symbols are similar to animals of all types and to parts of the human body and also to tools, especially trade tools. Their writing system does not express the basic meaning from a combination of syllables but from the metaphorical significance of the image that is held in the memory. [2] They draw a hawk, a crocodile, and a snake, and from the human body, an eye, a hand, a face, and the like. The hawk signifies for them everything "swift," since this animal is just about the swiftest of all winged creatures. The significance is then extended by a proper metaphorical extension to all "swift" things and similar things just as if it had been spoken. [3] The crocodile signifies everything evil; the eye, maintaining justice and the protection of the whole body. The right hand with extended fingers signifies earning a living; a closed left hand, the watchful protection of property. [4] The same reasoning pertains to the other symbols, the ones from the body, from the tools, and all the rest. By following the inherent meaning of each symbol and training themselves and their memory for a long time, they recognize fluently the meanings of each image.

3.5. Many Ethiopian customs appear to differ from the customs of everyone else, but especially those involved in the choosing of kings. First, the priests make a preliminary selection of the best among themselves. Whoever of these men is selected by the god is chosen as king by the multitude as he is carried around in a customary parade. And they immediately venerate and honor him as a god because they think that divine foresight has entrusted him with the rule. [2] The man chosen follows a legally ordained manner of life and behaves in all things according to hereditary custom: He portions out neither benefits nor punishment to any person beyond what has been established by custom among them from the beginning. It is custom there that none of his subjects be put to death, not even if someone is clearly deserving of punishment and is condemned to death. In that case, one of his servants is sent, bringing a sign of death to the transgressor. As soon as he sees the sign, he goes to his own home and commits suicide. It is in no way allowed, as it is among Greeks, to emigrate to a neighboring land and by changing homelands to escape the penalty. [3] They even say that someone once, when the death sign had been brought to him from the king, undertook to emigrate from Ethiopia but was discovered by his mother, who strangled him with her girdle. He did not dare to raise his hand against her in any way but allowed himself to be strangled to death in order to avoid leaving a greater reproach on his family.

3.6. The most unexpected custom concerns the death of the king. The priests around Meroë, who dedicate their time to ministering to and honoring the gods, are the greatest and most powerful order. Whenever the idea comes to them, they send a messenger to the king, ordering him to die. [2] For this, they say, has been communicated to them by the gods, whose commands must in no way be disregarded by a mortal nature. And they pronounce other arguments, such as would be acceptable to a simpleminded personality who was brought up in ancient and inescapable custom and who lacks the mental ability to oppose unnecessary commands. [3] In former times the kings obeyed the priests, having been convinced not by weapons or violence but by their fear of god, which overwhelmed their ability to reason. During the reign of the second Ptolemy,[156] the Ethiopian king Ergamenes, who had a Greek education and training in philosophy, was the first to have the courage to despise the command. [4] Having a spirit worthy of a king, he went with his army to the unapproachable holy place, the golden temple of the Ethiopians, where he killed the priests, wiped out this custom, and emended it according to his own policy.

3.7. The custom regarding the friends of the king, although unusual, is said to have continued even until our own time.[157] They say that the Ethiopians have this custom: Whenever any part of the king's body is mutilated for any reason whatsoever, all his companions similarly and deliberately mutilate themselves. For it is considered shameful for the king to have

---

156. 285–246 BCE.

157. This section also seems to share sources with Strabo.

a maimed leg but his friends to have a healthy one, and for the king to limp in public but his friends not to follow with a similar limp. [2] For they say that it is strange for a firm friendship to share suffering and sorrow, to share good and bad alike but not to have a share in the pain of the body. They say it is even customary for the companions to share death with the king and that this is an honored death and evidence of true friendship. [3] Thus among the Ethiopians conspiracy against the king is not an easy task, seeing that all his friends are equally concerned for his safety and their own. These, then, are the customs of the Ethiopians who live in the capital, who inhabit the island of Meroë, and now live next to Egypt.

3.8. But there are many other kinds of Ethiopians. Some inhabit the riverbanks of the Nile on both sides and on the islands in the river; others inhabit the land bordering Arabia; and still others dwell in the inlands of Libya. [2] Most of these, and especially those living on the riverbanks, are black in color, have flat noses, and woolly hair. Their personality is entirely wild, and they exhibit a bestial character, although less in their temperament than in their manner of living. Their whole bodies are squalid, their nails are long and curved like wild animal talons, and they completely lack human kindness for each other. [3] Their voices are shrill, and they have none of the practices of civilized life found among other peoples. They present a complete contrast to our customs. [4] Their weapons are as follows: Some use untanned ox-hide shields and short spears; others use javelins without the leather slings; at times they use bows six feet long, which they draw by placing them against their foot, but when they are out of arrows, they continue to fight with wooden clubs. They even arm the women, establishing their prime of life for military service. Most women follow the custom of wearing a bronze ring in the lip. [5] Some Ethiopians simply do not wear clothes but go naked for their whole life and contrive from what is at hand a simple protection from the heat alone. Some cut off the tails from cattle and cover themselves from their back around the hips and let it hang forward like the shameful part.[158] Some wear the skin of the herd animals, and others cover themselves up to the middle of the body with a wrap, which is made from hair since their flocks produce no wool on account of the peculiarity of the land. [6] As for food, some collect the reed that grows in the water and which rises natively in stagnant pools and marshlands. Some collect twisting branches of a very soft tree, with which they cover their body to cool off at midday. Some plant sesame and lotus. Others are sustained by the very soft roots of the reeds. No small number of them are experienced with the bow and have skillfully shot many birds, with which they supply their natural needs. But most of them live their whole life on meat, milk, and cheese from their flocks.

3.9. The Ethiopians who live above Meroë hold two views about the gods. They consider some to be eternal and incorruptible, such as the sun, the moon, and the whole universe, but they think that others partake of a

---

158. The Greeks frequently uses this euphemism for the penis.

mortal nature and have a share in immortal honors because of their excellence and their general kindness to humans. [2] For example, they revere Isis, Pan, Heracles, and Zeus as well, since they consider them to have done the most service to the human race. And in general, a few Ethiopians do not believe in gods. These unbelievers hurl curses at the rising sun, which they believe to be exceedingly hostile, and flee to marshes. [3] They pursue differing customs even in regard to the dead. Some throw corpses into the river, considering this the best burial. Others pour a rock-crystal over the body and keep it at home, thinking it right that the appearance of the dead be known to their kin and so that near relations not be forgotten by family clan. Some put dead bodies in clay vessels and bury them in the ground in a circle around the temple. Oaths that are taken on them are considered the strongest. [4] Some put the kingship in the hands of the most beautiful, considering that both monarchy and beauty are gifts of fate. Others give the rule to the best herdsman, on the view that these men alone have the best interests of the ruled at heart. Some assign this honor to the wealthiest, believing these can aid the masses through the availability of wealth. Others choose the bravest as king, judging that those with most power in war are alone worthy to receive the first rank.

3.10. A part of the land next to the Nile situated on the Libyan side is superior in beauty since it produces abundant and diverse food and has well-situated protection from the excessive heat in the marshy retreats. For this reason the land has been a source of conflict for Libyans and Ethiopians, who continuously fight each other over it. [2] Many elephants travel there regularly from the land above because, as some say, of the abundance and sweetness of the pasturage. In fact, remarkable marshes stretch out from the banks of the river, and nutriment grows in great abundance in them. [3] For this very reason, whenever the elephants taste the rushes and reeds, they remain because of the sweetness of the nourishment and destroy the means of life for humans. For this reason the inhabitants are compelled to immigrate to those places and become nomads and tent-dwellers, defining their homeland in general by the most appropriate means. [4] The herds of those animals just mentioned leave the interior because of lack of sustenance, because all the plants quickly dry up. And so because of the excessive heat and the want of spring and river water, it happens that the food is scarce and hard. [5] Some say that throughout the so-called "wild animal land," snakes of miraculous size and number are produced. These attack elephants at the watering holes and, rejoicing in their strength, wrap themselves in coils around the elephants' legs and violently contract and bind them with the coils until the beasts fall foaming under their own weight. Then they swarm upon the fallen animal and eat its flesh, easily overcoming it because of its immobility. It remains puzzling why the serpents do not pursue the elephants, their customary food, into that riverside land already mentioned. Some say that serpents of such size avoid the flatness of the ground and constantly dwell at the foot of mountains in canyons suitable to their length and in deep caves. For this reason they never leave these suitable and customary places because nature instructs all animals about such matters. And so this is the extent of our discourse on the Ethiopians and their land.

6. Strabo, *Geography* 1.2.28 (1st century BCE/1st century CE).
Strabo uses supporting texts from Ephorus and Homer in defining Ethiopia. (RFK)

Ephorus reveals the ancient opinion about the Ethiopians, of whom, he says in his book on Europe, "if the regions of the sky and earth were divided into four sections, the eastern part would hold the Indians; the south, the Ethiopians; the west, the Celts; and the north, the Scythians."[159] He adds that Ethiopia is larger than Scythia, since it seems, as he says, that the Ethiopian people extend from the eastern horizon to the western horizon during the winter, and the Scythians lie in opposite fashion. He says that the poet agrees about this and clearly places Ithaca "toward the darkness" (which is north). . . . Further, he says, "either they go right toward the rising sun or left toward the direction of the murky darkness. . . ." When, therefore, he says, "Zeus went yesterday to the Ocean with the blameless Ethiopians," we must more appropriately understand that the whole of Ocean touches the southern hemisphere and the Ethiopians, given that whatever region of this quadrant we consider, we hit upon Ocean and Ethiopians. . . . Thus he says, also rendering the common opinion about cranes, "when they flee the winter and awful storms, they fly with a cry over the floods of Ocean to carry bloodshed and death to the Pygmies." We must acknowledge also that Pygmies are said to live all over the quadrant since Ocean extends along the whole southern coastline and the cranes fly south in the winter. If later writers restrict the Ethiopians only to those living near Egypt, transferring what is said about Pygmies, it does not mean the same as in antiquity. It is the same as the situation now wherein we say that the expedition to Troy was not made up entirely of Achaeans or Argives, as Homer calls them all. I suggest, then, that this is similar to the situation of the Ethiopians. Although they are separated in two,[160] we must understand as Ethiopians all those who stretch along the coast from sunrise to sunset.

7. Strabo, *Geography* 17.2.1–3 (1st century BCE/1st century CE).
Strabo provides an extended description of Ethiopian customs. (RFK)

17.2.1. Previously, I have written much about the Ethiopians so that what we know of them might be studied along with Egypt. The furthest reaches of

---

159. Ephorus, *Fragmente der griechischen Historiker* (FrGH) 30a.

160. He says later that the Arabian Sea separates the two groups of Ethiopians from each other, but they are all still Ethiopians.

the inhabited world, so it seems, lie along those regions with bad and uninhabitable climates, resulting from either extreme heat or cold. Necessarily,
these regions are nonsustaining and inferior when compared to places with
temperate climates. This is clear from their way of life and from their lack of
basic human necessities. Indeed, they live a hard life, are frequently naked,
and are nomads. Their livestock are small, including their sheep, goats, and
oxen. Their dogs are also small, as well as savage and violent. It is probable
that some have suggested and invented stories of Pygmies as a result of
the smallish nature of the animals. No man worth trusting has recounted
seeing them.

17.2.2. The Ethiopians live on millet and barley, from which also comes
their drink. They use butter and vegetable shortening instead of olive oil.
They have no fruit trees except a few date palms in the royal gardens. Some
of the Ethiopians eat grass, as well as twigs, shoots, clover, and the roots of
reeds. They also eat meat, animal blood, milk, and cheese. They worship their
kings as gods, and the kings generally remain shut up in their houses. The city
of Meroë (on the island of the same name) is the greatest royal center. They
say that the island is shaped like a shield. Its size, probably an exaggeration,
is said to be around 341 miles long and 113 miles wide. The island has numerous mountains and large thickets. Some of its inhabitants are nomads, others
are either hunters or farmers. There are copper, iron, and gold mines as well
as mines for other precious stones. The island is surrounded on the Libyan
side by large sandbanks and on the Arabian side by continuous cliffs. To the
south, three rivers come together: the Astaboras, Astapus, and Astasobas. To
the north is the continuous flow of the Nile as far as Egypt along the aforementioned twists and turns of the river. In the cities of Meroë, the buildings are made either of woven wood from the date palm or of bricks. Salt is
dug from the ground, as with the Arabians. The date palm, *persea*,[161] ebony,
and carob are among the most abundant plants. Of wild animals, there are
elephants, lions, and leopards. There are also serpents, known as "elephant-
fighters," and numerous other wild animals since the land, wet and marshy,
attracts animals fleeing from hotter, drier regions.

17.2.3. Lake Psebo, a large lake with a sufficient number of inhabitants on its main island, lies above Meroë. It happens that the Libyans and
Ethiopians, since they each control one side of the island, alternate control
of the island and lake shores. One or another of them is driven out and
gives way to whichever of them is strongest at the time. The Ethiopians
are archers, and their bows are six feet long and made of wood. Their
women are also armed, and most have bronze rings through their lips. The
Ethiopians wear sheepskins, though they do not have wool because their
sheep have goat's hair. Some Ethiopians go around naked, while others
wrap themselves in small sheepskins or cloth made of well-woven hair.

---

161. A genus of evergreen plants, the most well-known of which is, perhaps, the
persea Americana, or avocado. This is likely the *persea Africana*, a leaf used in herbal
remedies.

Strabo next describes the burial practices and lists the gods worshipped by the Ethiopians using language almost identical to Diodorus. He also recounts the practice, discussed by Diodorus, of the king's companions. This suggests a common source.

8. Pomponius Mela, *Description of the World* **3.85–88 (1st century CE).** *Pomponius' description of Ethiopia is short and contains information known to the Greeks as early as the 5th century BCE. His names for the various tribes in Ethiopia are Greek. He cites Hanno the Carthaginian in 3.90 as a reliable source of information. (RFK)*

3.85. The Ethiopians lie beyond [on the outer coast]. They hold the land of Meroë, which the Nile has turned into an island by surrounding it with its first circuit. One part of Ethiopia is inhabited by the Macrobioi [Long-lived], called such because their lifespan is longer than ours by nearly half. Another Ethiopian people are the Automoles [Deserters], called such because they left Egypt to dwell there. These people have beautiful physiques and venerate the body and strength as others venerate the best virtues. 86. They have a custom of selecting their leader based on appearance and strength. There is more gold there than copper, thus they consider gold of less value. They ornament themselves with copper and make chains for prisoners from gold. 87. The place is always crowded with magnificent feasts. Because it is permitted there to eat as they please, they call the land the "Table of Helios" and claim that any food served there has been generated divinely. 88. There is a lake there that causes anyone immersed in it to glow bright as if oiled. They also drink the same water. The lake water is so transparent and weak at holding up anything that falls or is thrown into it that it does not even bear on its surface a leaf that falls from nearby trees but pulls it down into its depths. The most savage and multicolored creatures dwell there, including wolves and sphinxes (such as we have heard of before). There are also marvelous birds, horned tragopanes [Goat-Pans], and pegasuses with horse ears.

9. Anonymous, *Moretum* **27–35 (1st century CE).** *Moretum is typically translated as "salad," and the anonymous poem is a playfully "epic" description of the making of dinner. In the course of the poem, the hero summons his African slave to help him. It is one of the most extended physical descriptions of an African from the Classical world. (RFK)*

Meanwhile, he calls upon Scybale (she was his only attendant, African by race, her entire body proof of her descent, with her twisted hair, thick lips, dark coloring, broad chest, pendulous breasts, concave stomach, thin legs, and profusely spread soles of feet). He calls her and orders her to put wood on the hearth and boil cold water over the flame.

10. Pliny, *Natural History* 5.43–46 (1st century CE). *Pliny describes the peoples of the African interior. (MLG)*

5.43. Beyond the Gaetuli and the deserts, the first inhabitants of the southern interior of Africa are the Libyan Egyptians and then the white Ethiopians. Beyond these dwell three Ethiopian peoples: the first is called Nigritae from the river Niger, the second are Gymnetes Pharusians, and the third are the Perorsi, who live next to Ocean on the border of Mauritania. To the East of these peoples stretch vast empty spaces up to the Garamantes, the Augilae, and the Trogodytai. The most dependable tradition speaks of two Ethiopias beyond the African deserts. Above all, the tradition reported by Homer[162] speaks of an eastern and western division of Ethiopians.

5.44. The river Niger is like the Nile. It has reeds and papyrus; it supports the same animals; and it floods in the same seasons. Its source is between the Tarraelian Ethiopians and the Oechalicae, whose town is called Magium. Some locate the Atlantians in the middle of the empty deserts next to the half-beast Aegipani [goat-foot men], the Blemmyes, the Gamphasantae, the Satyrs, and the Himantopodes [strap-foot men].

5.45. The Atlantians are not full members of the human community, if we believe the report. They use no names among themselves, and when they see the sunrise and set, they hurl curses at it as a catastrophe for themselves and their fields. In their sleep, they do not dream, as is done by the rest of mankind. The Trogodytai dig caves for their homes. They live on serpent flesh and have no voice, only hissing. Thus they do not interact in speech. The Garamantes do not marry; instead, they live with women at random. Augilae worship only the gods of the underworld. The Gamphasantes wear no clothes and have neither wars nor dealings with foreigners. [46] It is said that the Blemmyes lack heads and have their mouth and eyes on their chest. The Satyrs have nothing human about them beyond their shape. The Aegipani have the form that is seen in paintings. The Himantopodes are strap-footed men whose manner of locomotion is like a serpent. The Pharusians (originally Persians) are said to have been companions of Heracles when he went to the Hesperides. I can think of nothing more to report about Africa.

11. Pliny, *Natural History* 6.182–183, 6.187–195, 6.198–205 (1st century CE). *Pliny gives an extensive description of Ethiopia based on reports from various Greek and Roman military expeditions and adventurers. (MLG)*

6.182. During the reign of Augustus,[163] the governor of Egypt, Publius Petronius, traveled to the south, capturing towns. The farthest point he

---

162. Homer, *Odyssey* 1.22–24: "Poseidon was visiting the distant Ethiopians, men living on the edges of the world, divided in two, some where Hyperion sets, and some where he rises."

163. 27 BCE–14 CE.

reached was 870 Roman miles from Syene [Aswan]. However, it was not Roman armies that turned the land into a desert; it was wars for dominance with Egypt that wore Ethiopia down. It was a famous and powerful land even down to the time of the Trojan War, when Memnon was king. It ruled Syria and the coast along our sea during the reign of Cepheus, as the stories about Andromeda show.

6.183. Various reports have been given about the country's size. . . . In fact, the quarrel about the distance from Egypt's border to Meroë has recently been put to rest, since Nero's expedition measured the distance from Syene to Meroë as 945 Roman miles. The distances en route are as follows: From Syene to Hieran Sycamion is 54 Roman miles; from there to Tama in the region of the Evonymite Ethiopians, 72 Roman miles; from there to Primi, 120 Roman miles; to Acina, 64 Roman miles; to Pitara, 22 Roman miles; to Tergedus, 103 Roman miles. In the middle of the route lies the island Gagaudes. . . . Once past this, parrots were spotted for the first time; once past the other island, called Articula, a sphingion ape was seen; and past Tergedus, the cynocephalus [dog-headed baboon]. After Tergedus the next town, Nabata, is 70 Roman miles. It is a small town and the last before the island Meroë, 360 Roman miles further on.

Around Meroë, they report that they saw a more verdant land, some trees, and the tracks of the rhinoceros and elephants. According to the expedition, the town of Meroë is another 70 Roman miles past the entry to the island. Passing along the right channel of the river, there is another island, Tadu, which makes a harbor. They reported that the town has few buildings and a queen named Candace, a name passed down to queens for many years. There is a temple to Hammon, where worship occurs, and little shrines exist all along the journey. Since the Ethiopians controlled affairs at that time, that island was very famous. They report that it was accustomed to supply 250,000 armed men and 3,000 skilled workers. According to current reports, there are 45 kings in Ethiopia. But the whole people were called Etherians, and then Atlantians, and then Ethiopians from the son of Vulcan.

. . .

6.187. It is hardly surprising that the far reaches of the world produce humans and animals with monstrous shapes, since fire's mobility is skilled at forming bodies and designing shapes. There certainly are reports of peoples from the eastern interior who have no noses and whose whole face is a flat plane, some lacking the upper lip and others a tongue. [188] Some have a fused mouth without nostrils and so breathe through a single hole and drink with an oat straw. They eat the oat grains, which grow wild. Some use nods and bodily motions for speech. Before the reign of Ptolemy Lathyrus in Egypt,[164] some did not know the use of fire. Certain writers have reported that a tribe of Pygmies live between the marshes where the Nile begins. On

---

164. 116–81 BCE.

the shores of a land I will describe later, there is a red mountain range that appears to be on fire.

6.189. The whole territory past Meroë is set between the Trogodytai and the Red Sea. The Red Sea is a three-day journey from Napata, rainwater being preserved in many places for use. The region in between is the best for gold. Further on, the area belongs to the Atabuli, an Ethiopian tribe. Next to Meroë are the Megabarri, whom some call the Adiabari. They hold the town of Apollo. Some of them are nomads, who eat elephants. 190. Opposite, on the African side, live the Macrobioi, and past the Megabarri live the Memnones and the Dabelli and, twenty days further on, the Critensi. Past them live the Dochi and then the Gymnetes, who never wear clothes. Next live the Anderae, Mattitae, and the Mesaches, who are ashamed of their black color and smear their whole bodies with red clay. On the African side are the Medimni and then nomads who live on the milk of the dog-faced baboon, the Alabi and the Syrbotae, who are said to be around thirteen feet tall. 191. Aristocreon reports that on the Libyan side, the town of Tollen is five-days journey from Meroë. From there it is another twelve days to the town of Aesar, which belongs to Egyptians who fled from Psammetichus (it is said that they have dwelled there for 300 years). On the Arabian side, Aristocreon says the town of Diaron belongs to them. This town is called Sapen by Bion, and he says that this name signifies "foreigners." Their capital is Sembobitis, which is located on an island. Their third town in Arabia is Sinat. But between the mountains and the Nile live the Simbarri, the Phalliges, and in the mountains themselves, the many peoples of the Asacae. They are said to live five-days journey from the sea and to live by hunting elephants. An island of the Sembritae in the Nile is ruled by a queen. 192. From this island it is an eight-day journey to the Nubian Ethiopians (their town, Tenupsis, is on the Nile) and the Sesambri, whose four-legged animals (including the elephants) lack ears. On the African side, live the Ptonebari and the Ptoemphani, whose king is a dog. They deduce his commands from how he moves his body. The Harusbi live in a town situated far from the Nile. After them live the Archisarmi, the Phalliges, the Marigarri, and the Chasamari. 193. Bion reports that there are also other towns on the islands. A full twenty-days journey from Semboboti toward Meroë lies the town of the next island. It belongs to the Semberritae and is ruled by a queen. There is another town called Asara. On the second island is the town Darden. The third island is called Medoë, in which lies the town Asel. The fourth island has the same name as its town, Garroë. Along the banks are the towns Nautis, Madum, Demadatin, Secande, Navectabe with the Psegipta territory, Candragori, Araba, and Summara.

6.194. In the region beyond Sirbitum, where there are no mountains, some have reported that the Maritime Ethiopians dwell. These are the Nisicathae and the Nisitae, whose names mean respectively "men with three eyes" and "men with four eyes." The reports say that the reason is not because they have that number of eyes but because they employ their very keen eyesight in shooting arrows. Beside the Nile, as it stretches beyond the Greater Syrtes and the southern Ocean, Dalion says that the Vacathoi live and the Cisoroi, who use only rainwater. Five-days journey from the Oecalices live the Logonporoi, the Usibalchoi, Isbeloi, Perusioi, Ballioi, and Cispioi, but all the rest is deserted. 195. After this is a fictional territory. To the west are the Nigroi, whose king is said to have a single eye in his forehead, the Agriophagi, who live for the most part on the flesh of panthers and lions, the Pamphagi, who eat everything, the Anthrophagi, who eat human flesh, the Cynamolgi, with dog heads, the Tettarabitae who have four legs and move like animals, and then the Hesperioi, the Perorsi, and those whom we have elsewhere mentioned dwelling with the borders of Mauritania. A certain part of the Ethiopians live only on smoked and salted locusts, preserved for a year's use. These people live for a maximum of forty years.

. . .

6.198. Ephorus, Eudoxus, and Timosthenes report that there are very many islands in the Eastern Sea. Cleitarchus says that King Alexander heard reports of an island that was so wealthy that the inhabitants traded hundreds of pounds of gold for horses, and of another where a sacred mountain was discovered whose thick forests had trees that produced a scent of amazing sweetness from their sap. Between the Persian Gulf and Ethiopia is an island called Cerne, whose size and distance from the mainland is disputed. It is reported to be inhabited only by Ethiopian peoples. 199. Ephorus relates that the heat prevents those sailing to this island from the Red Sea to pass beyond certain Columns (as the little islands are called). Polybius states that Cerne lies nearly one mile from the shore on the edges of Mauritania next to Mount Atlas. Cornelius Nepos puts it on line with Carthage about ten Roman miles from the shore and no more than two miles around. There is a report of even more islands around Mount Atlas that are themselves called Atlantes. Sailing from these for two days, one reaches the Western Ethiopians and the headland we call the Hesperu Ceras [West Horn]. From that point the coastline turns itself to the west and to the Atlantic Ocean.

6.200. Beyond this headland there are also reports of the Gorgades Islands, where once upon a time the Gorgons lived, which are a two-days sail from the mainland, as Xenophon Lampsacenus says. A journey to these islands was undertaken by the Carthaginian general Hanno, who reports women with hairy bodies and men who escaped through their swiftness. Hanno placed the skin of two of these Gorgades in the temple of Juno as proof of his amazing discovery. These were visible until Rome captured Carthage. 201. Beyond these islands, there are reports of two more islands of the Hesperides. So unsure are the facts about this area that Statius Sebosus reports that sailing past Atlas from the Gorgons' islands to the islands of the Hesperides takes forty days, but only a single day from these to Hesperu Ceras. The reports of the islands of Mauritania are no more reliable. It is only agreed that Juba discovered a few off the coast of Automoles, where he created a trade in dying Gaetulian purple.

6.202. Beyond these islands, some believe lie the Fortunate Islands and some other islands. The same Sebosus reports on their number and distances. He states that Iunonia is 750 Roman miles from Cadiz, and from there westward is the same distance to Pluvialia and Capriara. In Pluvialia, he states, there is no water except rain. He reports that it is 250 Roman miles from here to the Fortunate Islands, traveling west by northwest, opposite the left side of Mauritania. One is called Invallis from its uneven topography, and another is called Planasia from its flat surface. Invallis is 300 miles around, and its trees grow to a height of 140 feet. 203. Juba's investigations into the Fortunate Islands are as follows: The islands are south and west, 625 Roman miles from the Purple Islands, provided that one sails northwest for 250 Roman miles and east for 375 Roman miles. The first island is called Ombrios and shows no trace of buildings. There is a swamp between mountains, and there are trees like fennel stalks from which a liquid is extracted. The liquid from the black trees is bitter to drink; the lighter-colored trees produce a pleasant liquid. 204. The other island is called Iunonia. It has a temple built out of one single stone. In the same area is a smaller island of the same name. Further on, there is the island Capraria, filled with giant lizards. From this island can be seen cloudy Ninguaria, which takes its name from the perpetual snow. 205. Next to this island is the one called Canaria from the large number of giant dogs (two were brought back for Juba). Traces of buildings can be seen there. The whole land abounds in fruit and all types of birds; it also overflows with palm groves, dates, and pine-tree nuts. There is an abundance of honey, and in the rivers are papyrus reeds and the siluros, a river fish. The island is infested with rotting beasts washed up by the sea.

12. Petronius, *Satyricon* 102.14–15 (1st century CE). *Discovering themselves on a ship belonging to their enemies, Eumolpus, Giton, and Encolpius discuss how best to conceal themselves. (MLG)*

102.14. Encolpius: "Now we must look for some path to safety. Consider the plan I have discovered: Eumolpus (he's a scholar, you know) certainly has some ink. Let us change our skin color from hair to nails with this paint. In the guise of Ethiopian slaves, we will cheerfully serve you without painful fetters. We will fool our enemies with a change of skin color."

102.15. Giton: "Oh really? Why not also circumcise us so that we can seem to be Jews. Pierce our ears so that we imitate Arabs, and whiten our faces with chalk so he thinks that we are citizens of Gaul. As if color alone could hide our looks! Many aspects must correspond in a unity in order for the deceit to work. Even supposing that the ink on our faces could last for a bit, and even imagining that no drop of water would fall on our body and the ink not stick to our clothes (a thing that often happens even without a binding agent applied). Come then! Could we also fill out our lips with a hideous swelling? Could we also twist our hair into curls with an iron? Could we also cut our forehead with scars? Could we make our legs bow out? Could we make our ankles touch the ground? Color artfully applied stains the body; it does not change its shape."

13. Achilles Tatius, *Leucippe and Cleitophon* 3.25 (2nd century CE). *The characters await the arrival of a bird so that the army can march, which leads to the story of the phoenix, one of the wonders of Africa.*[165] *(MLG)*

"What bird is this that is deemed worthy of such an honor? And what sort of burial has it earned?" "The bird is called the phoenix, an Ethiopian species, the size of a peacock. The peacock, however, comes second in the beauty of its plumage. [2] The phoenix's wings mix the colors gold and purple. It boasts that the sun is its master, and its head is proof of this because a shapely circle forms a garland for its head, and this garland is an image of the sun. [3] It is dark blue, resembling roses, beautiful to look at, adorned with rays like a feather sunrise. Its life is apportioned to the Ethiopians; its death, to the Egyptians. [4] The reason for this is as follows: Whenever it dies, which happens only after a long time, its son carries it to the Nile after having improvised the funeral rites. The son digs up with its beak a lump of exceedingly aromatic myrrh sufficient in size for a bird casket. The lump is hollowed out in the center, and the hole becomes the coffin for the corpse. [5] The son arranges and sets the bird into the coffin and covers the hole with an earthen plug. He takes the resulting work and throws it into the Nile. He is followed by a chorus of other birds like royal attendants. The bird corpse is like a king leaving his kingdom. It journeys straight to the city of the Sun [Heliopolis]. [6] This is the emigration of the dead bird. It is set on a lofty overlook and receives the god's attendants. Then an Egyptian priest comes, bringing a book from the inner sanctum, and examines the bird from the description. [7] The bird recognizes the distrust and reveals the secrets of its body. He displays the corpse and holds a sophistic funeral speech. The children of the priests of the sun take up the bird corpse and bury it. And the bird is an Ethiopian while it lives, and it is an Egyptian when dead."

14. Heliodorus, *Aethiopica* 14.3–16.2 (3rd century CE). *The heroine of the novel, Charicleia, has arrived after many adventures to Ethiopia, the land of her parents. She is about to be sacrificed but presents tokens so that she will be recognized by her parents as their daughter. The primary*

---

165. See also Herodotus, *Histories* 2.73, and Pliny, *Natural History* 10.3–5.

issue is that Charicleia is white, whereas her parents are black, and thus her birth is in doubt. (CSR)

14.3. Hydaspes was clearly very troubled. Charicleia said, "These things here may be tokens my mother will recognize, but this ring is special to you." She showed him a *pantarbe*.[166] Hydaspes recognized it, since he had given it as a gift to Persinna during their courtship. He said, "O most noble lady, these are my tokens, but I do not yet acknowledge that you, who are in possession of my things, are my daughter and not someone who came upon them somewhere. Apart from other considerations, your radiant skin is for-eign to an Ethiopian woman." [4] At this Sisimithres said, "When I took the child then, the child I took was white; and furthermore, the amount of time that has passed fits with the girl's current age. She is seventeen, and I took the child seventeen years ago. In my opinion, the look of her eyes is similar, and even the whole character of her face and the extraordinariness of her young beauty. I believe that her present appearance agrees with what I saw then." [5] And Hydaspes said to him: "This is out of the ordinary for you, and something more suitable to advocates than judges. But watch out in case you, by unraveling one part, stir up another terrible dilemma that is not at all easy for my wife to resolve. For how in all likelihood could we, both Ethiopians, give birth to a child who is white?" [6] Sisimithres glared at him and then smiled knowingly. "I do not know what you are feeling, but it is not your usual habit to reproach me for my advocacy, not under-taken lightly. For I define a judge as a lawful advocate of justice. Why do I not seem to be your advocate rather than the girl's? I am going to show that you are a father in the company of the gods. I will not overlook your daughter whom I saved for you while she was in swaddling bands and who has now been preserved into her youth." [7] "But you may think what you want about us, who do not care about this, for we do not live for others' satisfaction, rather we seek our own satisfaction by striving after the beauti-ful and the good. Indeed, concerning the unresolved problem of her skin, this cloth provides the solution. On this very thing here, Persinna admits to having absorbed some images and phantasms from looking at the portrait of Andromeda while having sex with you. If you want further proof, go to the source of the images. See how the Andromeda in the picture shows forth unchanged in this girl."

. . .

15. Once they were ordered to do so, the appointed attendants brought in the portrait. After they set it up near Charicleia, they excited applause and cheers from all. And whosoever had an idea of what was being said and done explained it to the others. And they were amazed and really pleased by the nearness of the portrait, so that even Hydaspes could no longer dis-believe it. He stood still for a long time, held in place by his pleasure and

---

166. A type of precious stone, possibly a ruby.

amazement. [2] And Sisimithres said, "One thing remains, for concerning the kingship and the legitimate succession as it regards her, there is the truth itself, most important of all. Bare your forearm, girl! She is stained with a black mark on her upper arm—there is nothing inappropriate in bearing witness to your parents and your race." Straightaway Charicleia bared her left arm, and something like an ebony ring was staining her ivory arm.

16. Persinna did not hold back anymore, but right away she jumped up from her throne and ran to her. She threw her arms around her and cried while she clung to her. Because of her unbounded joy she howled like she was bellowing (for overwhelming pleasure tends to bring forth tears at times) and she nearly brought Charicleia down with her. [2] When Hydaspes saw her weeping, he pitied his wife and turned his mind to sympathy, but he stood holding his eyes like horn or iron on the scene, for he was fighting back the labor pangs of welling tears. His soul was overwhelmed by waves of fatherly feeling and manly determination, his emotions were conflicted by both. He was drawn from one side to the other, just as if he were tossed on the sea. But he made a resolution and yielded to nature, which conquers all things. Not only was he persuaded that he was a father, but he gave evidence of feeling fatherly emotions too. And he did not forget to lift up Persinna, who had fallen on the ground and was holding her daughter. He openly embraced Charicleia and then, with a great flow of tears, he poured out a drink offering to her as proof of his paternity.

CHAPTER 10

ASIA: PERSIA, MEDIA, BABYLON, AND PARTHIA

The great empires of ancient Mesopotamia were intertwined in the history of ancient Greece and Rome. Interactions began in earnest with the colonization of the Asia Minor (modern Turkey) coastline by various Greeks between the 9th and 7th centuries BCE. The Greeks and Persians, for all their expressed antagonism, shared many cultural traits. The eastern end of the Persian Empire, however, was a land of marvels, the city of Babylon being one of the greatest. As the Greeks continued to spread out in the ancient Mediterranean, conflict with the powers in Asia Minor became inevitable. The Persian Wars of the 5th century yielded to the conquests of Alexander in the 4th century and the establishment of Greek kingdoms throughout Asia from the 4th to 2nd centuries BCE. Rome conquered each of these kingdoms in turn, and controlled much of Asia Minor between the 2nd century BCE and the 2nd century CE. During that period, a number of native dynasties emerged either to ally or to contend with Rome. One such dynasty, the Parthians, were their greatest foe in the east.

This chapter begins with texts on Persia, Media, and Babylon followed by texts on the Parthians. The ancient authors that follow are not in strict chronological order.

PERSIA

1. Aeschylus, *Persians* 1–92, 176–199, 231–245, 249–271, 402–405, 535–597, 623–906 (5th century BCE). *Aeschylus' Persians was produced in 472 BCE, only seven years after the events it dramatized. The play is set in the city of Susa, an imperial capital of the Persian Empire, and is a fictionalization of when the royal court of Persia (made up of elder counselors and Atossa, the mother of King Xerxes) received word of the Persian defeat at the hands of the Greeks at Salamis. (RFK)*

A Chorus of Elders opens the play.

1–92. Chorus: We here are called the counselors of the Persians, gone to Greece, and are guardians of their rich and gold-strewn land; our lord, King Xerxes himself, chose us to watch over the land because of our age. [10]

Our hearts, prophets of evil, are already overly troubled within concerning the homecoming of the king and of his many-manned army. For the entire strength of Asia has gone, and our hearts cry out for the young men. Nor has any messenger come, on foot or horse,[167] to the city of the Persians.[168]

No news about those who departed and left behind Susa, Agbatana,[169] and the ancient walls of Cissia, [20] some setting forth on horse, others aboard ship, and others still as foot soldiers, densely arrayed for war: men[170] such as Amistrês and Artaphrenês, Megabatês and Astapês—rulers of Persia, kings who are subjects of the Great King, ephors driving forward the vast army, unconquerable archers and cavalry, dreadful to look upon and terrible in war with steadfast self-confidence in their souls.

No news about Artabarês the charioteer and Masistrês, [30] and noble Imaios, unconquerable bowman, and Pharandakês. The great and many-nourishing Nile sent others: Susiskanês, Egyptian-born Pegastigôn, and great Arasamês, the ruler of sacred Memphis. Add to this Ariomardos, the governor of ancient Thebes, and his dread and [40] innumerable marsh-dwelling rowers.

A mob of Lydians follows—men living in luxury, a completely land-locked people led by Mitragathes and noble Arcteus (kingly command-ers)—and much-gilded Sardis sent forth upon numerous chariots, both two- and three-poled,[171] a fearful sight to behold.

Those dwelling near sacred Tmolos, Mardon, Tharubis, anvils of the spear and the Mysian javelins, [50] threaten to cast the slavish yoke around Greece. Wealthy Babylon sends a mixed-race mob, straggling behind in a long line, both sailors in ships and those who put their faith in their skill with the bow. A saber-bearing host made from the whole of Asia follows at the dreaded command of the King.

Such a flower of the men of Persia's land has gone! [60] The whole Asian land groans in fierce longing for them! Their parents and wives tremble, counting the days as they stretch on and on.

The Destroyer of Cities, a kingly army, already has crossed into the neighboring land lying opposite us; by means of a bridge of boats bound

---

167. The Persians had a very well-known courier system in place that used foot and horse messengers in relays across Asia.

168. The *polis* here is Susa, one of multiple capitals of the Persian Empire. Susa was the imperial capital furthest west and was the city to which the Ionian Greeks brought their tribute to the king and where the mainland Greeks would have sent any embassies.

169. Variant of Ecbatana, the ancient capital of Media.

170. The following list of men who commanded the Persian forces contains some who are known to be historical and others whom scholars have no knowledge of apart from this list. Some scholars have argued that many of the names in the list are simply Aeschylus' imagination of what Persian-sounding names would be.

171. Chariots were four- or six-horsed. Each pole linked two horses, so a two-poled chariot had four horses while a three-poled chariot had six.

together with flaxen ropes, they cross over the strait [70] called Helle (after Athamas' daughter) tossing a well-bolted yoke round the neck of the sea.

Savage in war, ruling over many-peopled Asia, he drives his extraordinary flock across the whole earth in two ways, [80] entrusting them to his stout, reliable commanders by both land and sea—a godlike mortal of the golden race.

His eyes glare with the dark stare of a murderous snake, and he, speeding his Syrian chariot along, accompanied by many men, drives his war of archers against spear-famous men.

No one is so experienced that he can stand against this great flood of men or keep them off with firm defenses; [90] they are a tsunami force. The Persian army cannot be withstood, the Persian people are stout-hearted.

The Queen and mother of Xerxes, Atossa, has entered and recounts her dream, a clear premonition of Xerxes' defeat at Salamis.

176–199. Queen to Chorus: I've become accustomed to continuously having dreams every night since my son gathered up his army and decided to head off to destroy Ionia.[172] But this last vision was . . . it was as if it was happening right in front of me! [180] I'll describe it to you: Two well-dressed women seemed to appear before my eyes. One was decked out in Persian garb, the other in Dorian.[173] They were much taller than is normal for people today, and their beauty was flawless. They were sisters of the same race. One of the women dwelt in Greece, her fatherland obtained by lot, while the other resided in a barbarian land. It seemed to me that discord arose between the two women. When my son learned of the conflict, he tried to control and quiet them. [190] He yoked them under his chariot and put a leather strap under their throats. One woman stood proudly in the harness and held the reigns in her easy-to-control mouth. The other struggled and ripped the harness from the chariot with her hands. She seized it and dragged it away by force without the bridle. She smashed the yoke in the middle and my son fell. His father Darius stood by, pitying him. And when Xerxes saw him, he tore the robes around his body.

231–245. The Queen and Chorus discuss the war.

Queen: Where on the earth do they say Athens is located?

Chorus: Far to the west where Lord Helios dips his head.

Queen: Why would my son want to capture that city?

Chorus: Then all Greece would become subjects of the king.

---

172. This seems to be an acknowledgment by Aeschylus of the Persian practice of referring to all Greeks as Ionians (*Yaunâ* in Old Persian).

173. The women will be represented here as twins in every way except clothing. Since the differences between Persian and Ionian dress for women was slight, Aeschylus changes to Dorian instead of Ionian. Women in Athens wore both styles of dress in the 5th century, so these similarities and distinctions would have been commonly recognized.

Queen: Do they have a surplus of men available for an army?

Chorus: They have a large enough army; it did a lot of damage to the Medes.

Queen: Besides this, what else is there? Do they have wealth in their palaces?

Chorus. They have a flowing spring of silver, a treasury from the earth.[174]

Queen: Are they good archers, using bow and arrow to good end?

Chorus: Not at all. [240] They use spears in close combat and carry shields for defense.

Queen: Who is the shepherd and rules over the army?

Chorus: They are called slaves of no mortal nor are they subjects.

Queen: How then would the men stand against their enemy?

Chorus: Well enough that they destroyed Darius' large and noble army.[175]

Queen: You say something awful for parents of our young men to consider.

> 249–271. A Persian messenger arrives from Greece to give word to the Queen and her counselors about the defeat at Salamis and its aftermath.

Messenger: Cities of all Asia, land of Persia, [250] vast haven for wealth, how in a single blow your great wealth has been destroyed. Calamity has struck—the flower of Persia is fallen. To deliver first word of evils is evil. But necessity calls! Here's the whole disastrous tale revealed, Persian. Our entire barbarian army? Gone.

Chorus: The horror! The horror! Unheard of and cruel! Ah! Persians weep [260] as you hear of this horror!

Messenger: That's right—everything has been destroyed. I didn't even think I'd make it home alive.

Chorus: We are too old for this—we have lived too long that we should hear of this unexpected woe.

Messenger: I was there, Persians. This isn't secondhand information. [270] I can tell you all about the disaster.

Chorus: Good grief! In vain did our multinational, innumerable weapons leave Asia and march to Greece, Zeus' land.

> 402–405. During his description of the battle at Salamis, the Messenger recounts the Greek battle cry as they attacked the Persian fleet.

(Messenger, imitating the Greeks): "Oh sons of Greece, come on! Free your fatherland, free your children, your wives, the shrines of your paternal gods, the graves of your ancestors! The contest now is for them all!"

---

174. The Chorus is referring to the Athenian silver mines at Laurium, discovered around 483 BCE. Funds from the mines were used to build the fleet used by the Athenians in the Persian Invasion of 480–479 BCE.

175. A reference to the expedition against Athens sent by Darius that culminated in the battle of Marathon in 490 BCE.

535–597. The Persian Chorus and the Queen lament the destruction of Persia upon hearing the Messenger's tale.

Chorus: Oh Zeus, King! Now you have destroyed the army of the boastful, innumerable Persians and darkened the cities of Susa and Agbatana with a murky grief. Many women are tearing their veils with soft hands.

Staining, drenching their robes with tears, [540] the wailing women of Persia who yearn to see their newly-wedded husbands, the soft sheets of their marriage beds, the delight of their luxurious youth, they yearn to give themselves over to grief with insatiable weeping. I myself am greatly grieved and suffer truly for the doom of the departed. For now indeed all the land of Asia groans at its emptiness.

Xerxes led them. (Grief!) [550] Xerxes destroyed them. (Pain!) Xerxes governed all foolishly with his sea-faring ships. Why, tell me, was Darius, lord of the bow, ever so unhurtful toward his citizens? [560] Darius. Dear leader of Susa!

The first to greet their doom, (Alas!) [570] possessed by necessity, (Aye!) they are wrecked near Cynchreia. (Groan) Groan and grieve, cry deeply over our divinely sent fate. (Groan) Raise your sadly wailing, wretched voice!

Torn apart by the dread-filled salt sea (Alas!) they are rent by the silent children[176] of the undefiled sea. [580] Our homes, emptied of men, grieve; parents now childless grieve for their divinely sent doom (Groan). Mourning their old age, they know indeed an all-encompassing pain.

No longer throughout Asian land are they governed by Persian law, and no longer do they pay tribute with kingly necessity, [590] nor do they stand in awe, falling prostrate onto the land; the kingly power has been destroyed.

No longer are men's tongues under guard; for people have been loosed to speak freely, since the yoke of strength was demolished. The sea-girt island of Ajax, having been bloodied, holds the [remains] of Persia.

> *After their initial mourning, the Queen returns from the palace and asks the Chorus to help her raise the ghost of the dead king Darius in order to seek advice.*

623–906. Chorus: Queen, lady revered by Persians, pour the libation upon the grave. We will ask with our hymns that the leaders of the dead under the earth be well intentioned. Pure spirits of the Underworld, [630] Gaia and Hermes and the King of those below, send up his soul from below into the light! For if he knows anything further to aid us in our evils, he alone of mortal men could tell us how to fix things.

Blessed King, equal to a god, hear our barbarian cries! Do you hear me sending forth these varying, sad-sounding, mournful cries? I shall cry out our grievous troubles. Does he hear me from below?

But you, both Gaia and the other leaders of the Underworld, [640] allow that very glorious spirit, the Susa-born god of the Persians, to come to me

---

176. Sharks and other fish.

from your halls. Send him up! The earth of Persia has not ever covered over such a one as he.

Dear was the man! Dear was his burial mound! For, dear was the character of the one it hides. Aidoneus[177] guide him upward, [650] Aidoneus guide the divine ruler Darian[178] to us.

For he never destroyed our men through reckless wastes of war. He was called divine counselor for the Persians, and a divine counselor he was since he controlled the army well.

Shah,[179] ancient Shah come! Come to the highest peak of your funeral mound. Raising your saffron-dyed slippered feet, [660] showing us the peak of your kingly tiara. Come father Darian, innocent of evil.

Come so that you may hear about our troubles, new and shared by all. King of Kings,[180] appear! Some Stygian mist hovers over us; [670] for all our young men have recently been destroyed. Come father Darian, innocent of evil. Woe! Woe!

You who died much lamented by friends, why, why master, master, are we suffering twice over because of this mistake? All our triple-banked ships all throughout the land have been destroyed. [680] No ships, no ships.

Ghost of Darius: Oh faithful of the faithful, companions of my youth, Persian elders! Does the city (*polis*) suffer some grief? The earth groans, mourns, and is angry. I behold my wife near the tomb and am struck with fear; but I received the libation favorably. You wail standing near my tomb and shrieking with soul-guiding groans pitiably; you summon me. [690] However, there is no easy route from Hades since the gods below are altogether better at taking than letting go. Nevertheless, I have come since I have dominion among them. But hurry! I don't want to be reproached for spending too much time here. What new grievous evil has befallen the Persians?

Chorus: We are awe-struck at the sight of you. We are as awe-struck to speak face to face with you as one is of a god because of our ancient fear.

Ghost of Darius: That's fine, but since I was persuaded by your dirge and came up from below, don't give me some long and tedious speech, but set aside your awe at me and, speaking concisely, tell me everything.

---

177. This is a lengthened form of Hades, god of the Underworld. It was customary not to name him on stage.

178. This may be a Greek variant on the Persian name for Darius Dârayava^hus. Some scholars suggest the variant is used to create an authentic Persian character to the play.

179. The Greek word here is *ballên*, a Phrygian word for king. I have borrowed Edith Hall's translation as "Shah," which illuminates the use Aeschylus makes of Near Eastern words or Persian-sounding words to emphasize the location of the drama.

180. This may reflect actual usage of the phrase as a formal title by the Persian Kings in their inscriptions and correspondences.

Chorus: We are afraid to gratify your request. [700] We are afraid to tell you tidings face-to-face that are hard to tell to friends.

Ghost of Darius: Well then, since your ancient fear has blocked your ability to think, you, my aging bed-mate and high-born wife, stop crying and groaning and tell me something clear. It's a part of being human that misfortune befalls mortals. For, men encounter many evils both at sea and on land, and the longer the lifetime the more one experiences.

Queen: Oh, you who were fortunate enough to surpass all mortals in prosperity! You were enviable so long as you gazed upon the sun's light and as though a god, you made life happy for the Persians. I envy you now as well since you died before seeing the depths of our misfortune. The short of it, Darius, is this: [710] the prosperity of the Persians is destroyed absolutely.

Ghost of Darius: How so? Did some plague strike? Or is there civil strife in the city?

Queen: Not quite. The entire army has been wiped out near Athens.

Ghost of Darius: Who of my sons led the expedition there? Tell me.

Queen: Savage Xerxes—he emptied the entire continent.

Ghost of Darius: [720] Was the wretch mad enough to attempt this venture with the army or the navy?

Queen: Both. It was a double front, a two-pronged expedition.

Ghost of Darius: How did such an infantry force succeed in crossing to Greece?

Queen: He engineered a path over the Hellespont.

Ghost of Darius: Did he really manage to close up the great Bosporus?

Queen: He sure did. Perhaps some god drove him to the idea.

Ghost of Darius: It must have been a great god indeed who came upon him that he so lost his senses.

Queen: Clearly—the terrible results are the evidence.

Ghost of Darius: Tell me—what happened to our forces that you are all in such mourning for them?

Queen: [730] The navy was destroyed, and this led to the destruction of the land forces as well.

Ghost of Darius: Was the entire army, then, destroyed by their spears?

Queen: It was, which is why all of Susa groans at its lack of men . . .

Ghost of Darius: (So much for the protection and aid of the army!)

Queen: . . . and why the entire population of Bactrians has perished to a man.

Ghost of Darius: (Poor Xerxes. Such allies he lost! They were in the prime of their youth!)

Queen: They say that Xerxes alone (but with a few men) . . .

Ghost of Darius: Wait. How and where did Xerxes end up? Is he safe?

Queen: . . . he alone had the relief of reaching the bridge that linked the two continents.

Ghost of Darius: So, it's true that he has returned safely to this land?

Queen: On this part of the account, everyone is agreed. Yes, he has returned.

Ghost of Darius: [740] Ah! How quickly were the oracles fulfilled! Zeus has hurled my son toward the realization of the prophecies, although I somehow believed that their accomplishment was far off in the future. Whenever someone is in a hurry, though, a god helps him along. Now all my loved ones have discovered a spring of evils. My child achieved this ignorantly in his youthful audacity, my son who hoped to shackle the sacred flowing Hellespont as a slave, the divine flow of the Bosporus. It was my son who altered the path of the sea and, casting around it wrought iron shackles, supplied a wide road for his vast army. Being mortal he foolishly thought to overcome all the gods, especially Poseidon. [750] Surely, some disease of the mind took hold of my son? I fear that all my gathered wealth will become plunder for whatever man comes first to snatch it.

Queen: Savage Xerxes got the idea from talking with evil men. They told him that, while you had obtained great wealth for our children through your military campaigns, he only played the warrior at home and didn't increase his paternity at all. He often heard these sorts of approaches from those wicked men and so laid the plans for his expedition to Greece.

Ghost of Darius: [760] Instead, he accomplished a great deed! An unforgettable deed! A deed with no precedent, not since the time when lord Zeus bestowed the honor that one man rule over all of sheep-nourishing Asia and wield the scepter of authority! He managed to empty out the city of Susa. Medus was the first commander of the host, but another, his son, first accomplished this work. For his wits guided the rudder of his courageous spirit. Third after him was Cyrus, a man blessed by the spirit, who by his rule brought peace for all those dear to him: [770] he acquired the host of Lydians and Phrygians for the Persian realm and by force drove all of Ionia into subjugation—for the god did not hold him hateful, since he was sound of mind. The son of Cyrus was the fourth to manage the host. Fifth to rule was Mardus, a source of disgrace to his fatherland and to the venerable thrones. Him noble Artaphrenes killed by guile in his own palace, aided by men dear to him who undertook this duty, and sixth was Maraphis; seventh was between Artaphrenes and me, and [780] I obtained the lot I wished for.

Many were the campaigns I fought with my great army, yet I did not inflict such a great evil on my city. My young son Xerxes thinks young thoughts and doesn't recall my advice. For know well and clearly, men of my generation, none of us, had we such authority to wield, would be shown to have brought about suffering such as this.

Chorus: What then, King Darius? [790] What point are you making? What, given the circumstances, would be the best course of action for the Persian people?

Ghost of Darius: Don't make any expeditions into Greece, not even if the Median army is larger. For the land of Greece is itself an ally to the Greeks.

Chorus: What do you mean? How is it an ally?

Ghost of Darius: It starves any excessively large population.

Chorus: But we will gather together a well-equipped, select force.

Ghost of Darius: But the army that is even now in Greece [800] will not find a safe homecoming.

Chorus: What are you saying? Is the entire barbarian army not crossing the Hellespont from Europe?

Ghost of Darius: Few from many. Seeing what has now happened, it is necessary to trust in the oracles of the gods. Every single oracle is coming to pass. If indeed this is so, then Xerxes has been blinded by false hope and has left behind his select force in vain. [810] They wait where the Asopos waters the plain with its flood; a precious enrichment of the soil of Boeotia.[181] The greatest miseries are waiting there for them to suffer, a penance for their hubris and disrespect for the Greek gods. When they entered Greece, they had no qualms about plundering the images of the gods or burning their temples. Altars were annihilated; the shrines of the gods were hurled down to the ground from their foundations in mass confusion. Behaving badly, they suffer in amounts equal to what they have done, [820] nor yet have they reached the end of their woes. Still the cost rises. For the bloody slaughter caused by Dorian spears on the Plataean plain will be tremendous. Heaps of corpses will serve as a silent symbol to the eyes of men for three generations to come that a mortal must not consider himself greater than he is. Hubris flowered and yielded a crop of ruin, and from it a tearful harvest was reaped. See the penalties of such actions! Remember Athens and Greece, [830] lest someone disdain his present fortune, lust after the wealth of another, and so squander his own prosperity. For Zeus, a grievous judge, is charged with punishing the arrogant who think beyond their station. In this light, use sensible warnings and admonish Xerxes to stop offending the gods with his arrogant boasting. But you, aged and beloved mother of Xerxes, go into the house and get a seemly robe for him and greet him when he arrives. Grieved at all his troubles, he has rent from his body the splendid robe he wore. [840] It is in shreds. Comfort him with gentle words. Only your voice, I know, will lift his spirits.

---

181. A reference to the battle of Plataea (479 BCE) where the Greek forces, led by Sparta, defeated the select Persian force under the general Mardonius.

I must return back to the darkness. You, elders, farewell. Despite these evil times, give your lives over to pleasure while the sun shines on you still, [850] since wealth is of no use to the dead.

Chorus: Hearing about the many misfortunes, present and future, of we barbarians was grievous.

Queen: Oh, divinity! How many painful misfortunes afflict me! But the misfortune that stings the most is the disgrace of the robes that cover my son's body. I will go inside and get a robe for him from the palace and try to meet him. [860] For I will not abandon those dearest to me in times of trouble.

Chorus: O woe! What a great and excellent life of civic order we partook of when old, all-powerful, untainted by ills, peace-loving, godlike Darius ruled the land. First, we demonstrated how glorious was our army, then our laws, bulwarks, kept all in order. [870] Homecomings from war, without toil or harm, have led us, well accomplished, home again. And what a number of cities he captured!—without crossing the stream of Halys [880] or even stirring from his own hearth—such as the Acheloan cities on the Strymonian sea located beside the Thracian settlements. And those outside the lake, the cities on the mainland, surrounded with a rampart, obeyed him as their king; those, too, obey who boast that they are on both sides of the broad Hellespont and Propontis, deeply-recessed, and the outlet of Pontus. [890] The sea-washed islands, also, off the projecting arm of the sea, lying close to this land of ours, such as Lesbos, and olive-planted Samos, Chios, and Paros, [900] Naxos, Mykonos, and Andros, which lies adjacent to Tenos. And he held under his sway the sea-girt islands midway between the continents, Lemnos, and the settlement of Icarus, and Rhodes, and Cnidos, and the Cyprian cities Paphos, Soli, and Salamis, whose mother-city is now the cause of our lament. And the rich and populous cities of the Hellenes of Ionian heritage he controlled by his own will; and at his command he had an unwearied strength of men-at-arms and of allies from every nation. But now, defeated completely in war through disasters on the sea, we endure this change of fortune no doubt god-sent.

2. Herodotus, *Histories* Introduction and 1.1–5 (5th century BCE).

Herodotus begins his Histories *with stories from both the Greek and Persian sides about how the conflicts between them first began. (RFK)*

Introduction. Here is the culmination of the researches of Herodotus of Halicarnassus, produced so that the deeds of men not be lost to time. I write especially to preserve the memory of the great deeds performed by the Greeks and barbarians,[182] both in general and specifically with respect to the causes of their conflict with each other.

---

182. In 5th century BCE texts, the term "barbarian" often specified the Persians, though "Persians" itself was an umbrella term for all the various peoples of the Persian Empire.

1.1. The Persian writers say that the Phoenicians are the cause of the disagreement. They came from the Red Sea to the Aegean. After settling there (where they still live today), they set out on great sea voyages carrying cargo from Egypt and Assyria and other lands, and they transported it to Argos. [2] At that time, Argos was preeminent in the land now called Hellas [Greece]. When the Phoenicians arrived, they set out their merchandise. [3] On the fifth or sixth day, when nearly everything had been traded away, a group of women including the king's daughter came to the sea shore. According to the Greeks, Io was the daughter of Inachos. [4] As the women stood at the stern of the ship, looking eagerly at the merchandise, the Phoenicians yelled out and rushed at them. The majority of the women escaped, but Io and some others were captured. The traders then boarded the ship and set sail for Egypt.

1.2. This is how the Persians (though not the Greeks)[183] say Io arrived in Egypt, and this was the first injustice between Greeks and barbarians. After this, some Greeks (they didn't specify which Greeks) landed in Tyre and kidnapped Europa, daughter of the king of Phoenicia. They may have been Cretans.[184] This was considered an equal exchange for Io. [2] After this, the Greeks were then responsible for a second injustice, for they sailed a large ship up the Phasis River to Aia in Colchis. Having accomplished what they had come to do, they then seized Medea, daughter of the king.[185] [3] The king of Colchis sent a messenger into Greece to seek reparations for the crime and to reclaim his daughter. The Greeks replied that the Phoenicians had not returned Io to Argos or paid reparations so they were not going to do it for Medea.[186]

1.3. In the second generation after these events, Alexander, son of Priam, heard these tales and determined to steal a wife for himself from Greece and figured there would be no penalty since no one else had been punished previously. [2] Thus, after he stole Helen, the initial response of the Greeks was to send messengers requesting Helen's return and compensation for her kidnapping. The Trojans, however, threw these requests back at them, citing the snatching of Medea and asked how they could expect such reparations when they themselves had refused to pay compensation or return Medea when asked.

---

183. For the Greek story of Io's journey to Egypt, see [Aeschylus], *Prometheus Bound* 786ff (Chapter 6, Selection 2).

184. In the Greek myth, Europa is taken to Crete by Zeus in the form of a bull and there gives birth to a son, Minos.

185. This refers to the adventure of Jason and the Argonauts, who sailed on the Argo to claim the Golden Fleece. For other Greek versions of Medea's seizure, see especially Apollonius' *Argonautica*.

186. Note the conflation of Phoenician, Egyptian, and Colchian here. This may reflect a story that the Colchians, who reside in the Black Sea region, were descended from Egyptians (Herodotus, *Histories* 2.104), or it may simply be a reflection of the notion that all barbarians were somehow related.

1.4. Up to this point, there was only the snatching of women from one another, but for what came next the Greeks were greatly responsible. For they were the first to start a war by sending an army into Asia, not the Asians into Europe. [2] Now, to steal a woman is considered by the Persians the act of an unjust man, but to take the trouble of avenging it after she has already been abducted is unreasonable. Clearly, the women would not have been kidnapped if they didn't want to be. [3] Indeed, the Persians say that Asians do not take account of women who are snatched in this way, but the Greeks gathered a great army and marched it into Asia and destroyed Priam's power for the sake of a Spartan woman. [4] After this, they always considered the Greeks their enemies. For the Persians believe that they own Asia and the barbarian peoples who live there, while they view Europe and all things Greek as separate.

1.5. This is what the Persians say happened, and they consider the sack of Troy the origin of their enmity with the Greeks. [2] The Phoenicians, however, disagree with the Persians about Io. They say that they did not kidnap her and take her to Egypt. Rather, Io had an affair with the ship's captain and, finding herself pregnant and ashamed of facing her parents, sailed off willingly with the Phoenicians to avoid being discovered. [3] This, then, is what the Persians and Phoenicians say.

3. Herodotus, *Histories* 1.95.2–102 (5th century BCE). *After telling of Croesus, the Lydian king whom Herodotus claims was the first to rule over Greeks, Herodotus tells of the origins of the Medio-Persian Empire with their first king, Deioces. Though scholars have long tried to fit Herodotus' Deioces into the known chronology of the Median Empire, it seems that this story has no basis in historical fact. (RFK)*

1.95.2. After the Assyrians ruled for 520 years, the Medes were the first to revolt from them. And somehow they, fighting on behalf of their freedom, became noble men and, casting off their slavery, were freed. After this, the rest of the peoples did the same thing as the Medes.

1.96. But when they were all autonomous throughout the land, they turned once again to tyranny. There was a wise man among the Medes named Deioces, the son of Phraortes. [2] Deioces did the following because he desired tyranny: The Medes at that time dwelled in villages, and Deioces, who had already attained a certain eminence in his own village, now earned even greater renown by his enthusiastic support for uprightness and for his opposition to injustice, although he knew that injustice is the constant foe of justice, and although he did this when anarchy prevailed in Media. [3] His upright conduct was noticed by his fellow villagers, and they chose him as their magistrate. Deioces, always with his eye on the prize, performed his duties with such integrity and fairness that he received high praise from his fellow citizens. When the Medes in other villages heard of his unique reputation for honesty as a judge, they refused to submit to unjust verdicts as they had before and went to Deioces instead, confident that they would receive a fair trial and judgment. Before long, they would not entrust themselves and their causes to anyone else.

1.97. Always greater numbers of people came to him as they heard how truth prevailed in the trials he conducted. Deioces, perceiving that the people had now become dependent on him for everything, was no longer willing to sit all day long judging and making decisions for others as he had been doing, while his own affairs were neglected and he received nothing for all his labors. [2] And so, when robbery and lawlessness became rife again throughout the villages, and even worse than before, the Medes met together to deliberate and make speeches about the current situation (and I assume the friends of Deioces spoke a great deal): [3] "Since we cannot continue to live in this land under the present conditions, let us appoint a king over ourselves. That way, our country will be well-governed, and we can return to our work without threat of losing our homes to anarchy."

1.98. Saying these things, they persuaded each other to be governed by a king. Immediately, they proposed individuals for election, and since Deioces was proposed and praised repeatedly by every man, they were contented that he become their king. [2] Deioces first ordered them to build him a house worthy of a king and to fortify it with bodyguards. They carried out these orders, constructing for him a monumental and secure palace in the very location he requested and entrusted him to a corps of bodyguards specially selected from all the Medes. [3] Now that Deioces had secured his power, he compelled them to build a single great city for a capital, which they would maintain and take greater care of than their villages; and the Medes obeyed him. He surrounded this city, now called Ecbatana, with a series of massive concentric walls. [4] They built the walls so that each circle is higher by the height of the rampart than the circle beneath it. The hill in this particular location helps with this construction, but it is accomplished more by design. There are seven circles all together. The throne room and treasury are located in the last circle. The largest is about the same distance round as the wall that surrounds Athens. The ramparts of the first circle are white, those of the second black, of the third crimson, the fourth dark blue, and the fifth orange. [6] The ramparts of all the circles are painted in this fashion except the two innermost ramparts, which are covered one in silver, the other in gold.

1.99. Deioces built these walls around his own house only. The rest of the people he ordered to dwell outside around the walls. Once his residence was completed, Deioces established the following court protocols (he was the first to do so): No one was permitted in the presence of the king but they had to relay all necessary requests, information and such through messengers. If the king did approach them, no one was permitted to look at the king, let alone to laugh or spit. Anyone who did so was disgraced. [2] He established such protocols in order to distinguish himself from his former peers with whom he had grown up and who were inferior to him neither in family nor in courage. If they did not see him, he would eventually seem different or superior to them, and thus they would neither resent his position nor plot against him.

1.100. When he had set these things in order and had strengthened himself in his tyranny, he became harsh in his defense of justice. Litigants would write down their petitions outside and send them inside the palace to him. He would then make his ruling and send it back out to the parties. [2] He made his decisions according to the laws, but also passed further regulations. If he should hear of some outrage, he would summon the offender and render judgment according to the severity of the offense. He had eyes and ears,[187] who were scattered through all the land.

1.101. Now Deioces united together the Median people as one and ruled over them. The tribes of Media are the Bousai, Paretakenoi, Stroukhates, Arizanoi, Boudioi, and Magoi.

1.102. Having been king for fifty-three years, Deioces died and his son Phraortes inherited the empire. Not being content to rule over the Medes alone, he made war against the Persians and made them the first subjects of the Medes. [2] Once he ruled both these mighty peoples, Phraortes turned his attentions to Asia, attacking one then another people. He even attacked the Assyrians who held Nineveh and once ruled all of Asia, until their allies revolted and left them isolated. They were, however, still formidable, and Phraortes died while leading his army, much of which perished along with him. He had ruled for twenty-two years.

4. Herodotus, *Histories* 1.131–140 (5th century BCE). *After describing how Cyrus became king of Persia (550–530 BCE), Herodotus relates a number of Persian customs, including religious practices, various social customs, education, and burial practices. (RFK)*

1.131. I know that the Persians use the following customs: they do not set up statues, temples, or altars, but consider those who do so foolish. This is the case, it seems to me, because they do not attribute human qualities to their gods as the Greeks do. [2] They are accustomed to ascend to the highest mountain peaks and to perform sacrifices to Zeus.[188] They even refer to the entire heavens as Zeus. They sacrifice to the sun and moon as well as to earth, fire, water, and the winds. [3] From earliest days, they sacrificed only to these gods, but later learned from the Assyrians and Arabians to sacrifice in addition to Heavenly Aphrodite. The Assyrians call Aphrodite Mylitta, the Arabians call her Alilata, and the Persians call her Mithra.

1.132. Persians perform sacrifices to their gods according to the following customs: They neither set up altars nor are they accustomed to offer burnt sacrifices. Nor do they make drink-offerings, play flutes, wear garlands, or

---

187. These are the overseers and informants used by the Persian king (and the Athenians) in subject cities. The King's Eye was an infamous figure and features comically in Aristophanes' *Acharnians* (Chapter 10, Selection 7).

188. Herodotus associates the Persian god Ahuramazda with the Greek Zeus.

use barley meal. Instead, if anyone wishes to sacrifice to one of the gods, he leads an animal to an unpolluted location while crowned with a tiara, preferably of myrtle. [2] No private individual is allowed to pray just for himself, though. He prays for the king and all Persians (of course, he is himself included in "all Persians"). Then the sacrificer cuts the animal into pieces and boils the meat. Next, he places the meat on a bed of the softest grasses he can find, preferably clover. [3] Once he has made all these preparations, a Magus stands beside the offering and recites the story of the origins of the gods, which the Magi say is the appropriate spell for this. It is not their custom to perform sacrifices without a Magus. After a short interval, the sacrificer carries the meat away and uses it however he chooses.

1.133. The Persians think that the day most important for a person to honor is one's own birthday. On this day, they see fit to lay out a feast larger than on any other day. At this birthday feast, the wealthier serve ox, horse, camel, and donkey, cooked whole over flames. The poorer folks serve goat or sheep. [2] They eat few breads or grains but have many dessert courses. In fact, the Persians say that Greeks stop eating though still hungry because Greeks, unlike Persians, serve nothing worth eating after the dinner courses. But if they did serve something worth eating, the Greeks would also eat and not stop while still hungry. [3] Persians are also greatly devoted to wine. They consider it inappropriate, however, to vomit or urinate in the company of others, so they take precautions against such occurrences while in their cups. They are accustomed, in fact, to make plans concerning the weightiest matters while drunk. [4] Whatever decision they found pleasing while drunk, though, is re-presented to them by their evening's host the next morning when they are sober. If the idea still appeals to them even when sober, they use it. If, however, they find it wasn't such a good idea, they give it up. Just to keep themselves honest, they also reconsider while drunk any decisions they made while sober.

1.134. When Persians happen upon each other in public, one can tell the relative social rank of people by how they interact. If they are equals, instead of saying hello, they kiss each other on the mouth. If one is of slightly lower status, they kiss on the cheek. But if one is of significantly lower status, that one falls to the ground and prostrates himself before the other.[189] [2] They honor the various ethnic groups according to their proximity to Persia: those

---

189. This refers to the practice of *proskynesis*, which the Greek practiced only before a god. There is no actual evidence, however, beyond Greek sources that the Persians practiced prostration. Achaemenid scholars believe the ritual was a kiss-like gesture with the hand covering the mouth and with a slight bow. This particular gesture is depicted on a number of Persian reliefs representing the Persian king in audience. It would also make more sense in a sequence with kissing on the mouth and kissing on the cheeks. It is unclear when this misunderstanding by the Greeks of Persian practice enters the sources. It is possible that the Greeks misinterpreted the image of Darius stepping upon the dead body of his foe in the Bisitun inscription, found on Mount Bisitun in Iran and commissioned by Darius, as the living enemy prostrating himself before the king.

who live nearest come first in honors, second place goes to the next nearest, and so on in an outward progression, with those living furthest away being least regarded. Persians believe that they are the most noble of men in all ways and that the rest of mankind partakes in excellence according to their nearness to Persia, in accordance with the order of the world. Since Persia is at the center, those living furthest away are thus the worst of all men.[190] [3] The Medes ruled their various ethnic groups under a similar structure, exerting rule especially over those nearest them and then depending upon those peoples to rule over the peoples on their own borders. Persian honors are distributed in a similar fashion, and, indeed, their empire and its administration function this way.

1.135. Persians are especially keen to adopt foreign customs. For example, they wear Median clothes because they think Median clothes are more attractive than their own. They also wear Egyptian breastplates into battle. They tend to examine the assorted pleasures of others and pursue some of them—like their borrowing of pederasty from the Greeks. Each Persian also marries many "official" wives and then procures many more concubines for himself in addition.[191]

1.136. A man's masculinity is based, first, on his prowess in war, and second, on his ability to produce many children. Throughout each year, the king sends gifts to whatever man has produced the most sons. They believe there is strength in numbers. [2] From the age of five until twenty, children are trained in three things only: horsemanship, archery, and speaking the truth.[192] Until they turn five, the boys do not enter their father's sight but live among the women. The reasons for this practice is to spare the father grief if a son should die while still nursing.[193]

---

190. Although some scholars have read this statement of Herodotus as transferring Greek ethnocentric tendencies to Persians, the inscriptional evidence as well as the great Apadana at Persepolis seem to order the peoples of the empire in concentric circles around Persia in accordance with both geographic nearness and the principle of prestige.

191. The distinction here seems to be between dowered, contracted marriages with appropriate families for political reasons and other women kept for sexual purposes. The wives would have born legitimate children permitted to inherit, while the concubines would have produced illegitimate children. The Greek text suggests that the concubines here were likely slaves, and so any children would have also been slaves. This practice was not uncommon in the Near East (it appears in the Hebrew Bible with the Patriarchs), but it is unclear how much the Greeks understood of the practice.

192. That the Persian kings prided themselves on their abilities in these three areas is made evident in nearly identical inscriptions found in the names of Darius and Xerxes (DNb/XPl §2g–h). Darius also emphasizes in the Bisitun inscription his championing of the Truth over the Lie of the rebels (§54–64, esp.).

193. In antiquity, infant and toddler mortality was high. If a child reached the age of five, it was more likely that they would survive to adulthood.

1.137. I commend that particular custom, and this other as well: The king does not condemn anyone to death for a single offense, nor does any Persian inflict irreparable harm on a member of his household for a single offense. Instead, everything is added up, and if the crimes outweigh the good service, then the king or master acts on his anger.[194] [2] They say that no one kills their own mother or father. They say that on such occasions when this has occurred, investigations revealed that the murderer was either adopted or a child of adultery, since they say that no parent would be killed by a true-born child of their house.

1.138. It is not permitted for them to speak about things they are not permitted to do. They consider lying the worst of all habits. Being in debt ranks second among offenses. There are many reasons for such thinking, but in particular, they believe it inevitable that a debtor will at some point lie. Citizens with leprosy or "the whiteness" are excluded from the cities and from mingling with other Persians. They say that such a disease marks one as having wronged the sun. [2] The many drive out from the land any foreigner with these conditions, and they consider white doves also to be thus afflicted and also drive them out for the same reason. They consider rivers especially sacred and neither permit others nor themselves to urinate, spit, or wash hands in them.

1.139. There is an additional peculiarity among the Persians, something they themselves have failed to notice, but we have not: their names, which are meant to reflect their physiques and their noble status, all end in the same letter, what the Dorians call *san* and the Ionians *sigma*. If you investigate the matter, you will find that not just some Persian names but all end in this same way.

1.140. I speak of those matters from my knowledge and experience. Further tales, however, are hinted at in whispers. Concerning the dead, specifically, it is said that no Persian man is buried before his corpse has been torn apart by birds and dogs. [2] I know for certain that the Magi do this, for they practice it openly. Persians also cover the bodies of the dead with wax before burial. The Magi are as different from the priests of Egypt as they are from other men. [3] Egyptian priests consider it a religious imperative not to kill any living thing except during a sacrificial rite. The Magi, however, kill everything with their own hands except dogs and men. They make great sport, likewise, of killing ants, snakes, and flaying creatures and other beasts. Well, let us be satisfied with knowing of this custom as it originated. I'll now return to my previous tale.

5. Herodotus, *Histories* 1.178–187 (5th century BCE). *Herodotus continues his description of Cyrus' conquests with a description of the*

---

194. This principle is also reflected in the identical inscriptions of Darius and Xerxes (§2a–d, esp.).

Assyrian city of Babylon, famous throughout the ancient world for its size and splendor. (RFK)

1.178. After Cyrus subjected all the mainland, he attacked the Assyrians. In Assyria, there are many other great cities, but Babylon is the most renowned and strongest of them all. Babylon was founded as a royal capital after the destruction of Nineveh. What follows is a description of the city: [2] Babylon lies on a great plain and is a massive square with sides 13.5 miles long each. The entire circumference is 54 miles. Such is the great size of the city of Babylon, designed as no other city of which we know. [3] First, then, around the city comes a trench, broad and deep, filled with water. Next comes a wall 50 royal feet[195] thick and 200 royal feet high. The royal foot is about three inches longer than a standard Greek foot.

1.179. I feel compelled to speak further about these walls in order to make clear how the earth from the trench was used to make the wall at the same time as they dug the trench. They turned the earth that was removed from the trench into bricks. After they had made enough bricks, they baked them in ovens. [2] Using warmed mud as cement and filling every thirtieth layer of bricks with a wicker-work frame, they built first the edging on the trench. Then they built the wall in the same manner. [3] On top of the wall, they built single-story houses facing one another along the edges. There was space left between the houses for a four-horsed chariot to drive through. In the wall's exterior, there are a hundred gates, made all of bronze, posts and lintels included. [4] There is another city about eight-days journey from Babylon named Is where a small river flows, which shares its name with Is. This river is a tributary of the Euphrates. The Is River provides from its waters many lumps of cementing mud such as was brought to Babylon for use in the walls.

1.180. Now, Babylon was built as a city divided into two where the Euphrates, wide, deep, and swift, wends through the middle, flowing from Armenia into the Red Sea. [2] The walls on each side of the river reach down to the river's edge. The walls then curve from that point and become a wall of baked bricks that runs along the river's edges. [3] The city itself is full of three- and four-story houses set in a grid of straight roads, some of which span the river. [4] At the end of the roads there are gates in the river-side walls, each lane having its own gate that opens to the river itself.

1.181. This, then, is the outer wall. A second wall runs inside it that is almost as strong though narrower. [2] In the center of one section of the city was built a royal palace with a large, strong encircling wall. In the other sections there lies still to this day the bronze-gated precinct of Zeus Belus [Ba'al]. It stretches 1,200 feet on all four of its sides. [3] In the center of the precinct is a solid tower about 600 feet in both length and breadth. From this first tower there arises a second, from the second rises a third, and so on until there are eight total towers stacked upon each other. The path up

---

195. 50 royal feet is about 75 modern feet.

the towers is a spiral that wraps around the exterior of the towers. [4] At the midway point of the path is a landing where there are chairs upon which those ascending the tower may rest. [5] At the very top is a large temple. Inside the temple is a large, well-decked couch with a golden table nearby. There is no image of the god within the space, nor does anyone dwell there at night except a single woman chosen by the god from all those who serve as his priests, so the Chaldeans tell us.

1.182. The Chaldeans also say (and this is unbelievable, in my opinion) that the god frequents and rests upon the couch in the temple, as happens also in Egyptian Thebes, so the Egyptians tell it. [2] (Indeed, a woman sleeps on the god's couch in the temple of Theban Zeus as well, and both the Babylonian woman and the Theban woman refrain from sex with all men.) At Patara in Lycia, the prophetess of the god, whenever a woman becomes such, does the same. Even if there are no oracles, then, whenever a woman becomes prophetess, she is shut up inside the temple every night.

1.183. In the Babylonian temple is another shrine below it where a great golden statue of seated Zeus resides. Close to his side is a great golden table. His throne and footstool are also made of gold. The Chaldeans say that the entire group was made of 800 talents worth of gold. [2] Outside the temple is a golden altar with an additional large altar below it. Upon the large altar, mature cattle are sacrificed, while only newborns from the flocks are permitted to be sacrificed on the golden altar. Upon the larger of the two altars, the Chaldeans dedicate 1,000 talents worth of frankincense each year during celebrations of festivals for the god. Up until the time of Cyrus, there was a solid gold statue of the god that stood over twelve feet high. [3] I did not see it myself, but the Chaldeans discuss it, so I merely repeat what they say. Darius son of Hystaspes considered removing it but did not dare. His son Xerxes, however, not only removed it but also killed the priest who forbid him from doing so. This, then, is how the temple is adorned, though there are additional private dedications within.

1.184. There were many different rulers of the city of Babylon (about whom I'll write in my Assyrian history) who built walls and temples. There are two women among them. The first of them ruled under the name Semiramis and preceded the second by five generations. Semiramis is noted for building the levees along the river (quite an achievement). Before she built them, the river was accustomed to form a lake over the entire plain.

1.185. The second queen was named Nitocritis. She was more intelligent than her predecessor and left monuments, which I'll recount. She saw the great empire of the Medes and its restless energy and saw other cities, even Nineveh, fall to them. Thus she defended Babylon from them as much as she was able. [2] First, she dealt with the part of the Euphrates flowing through the city center. She dug trenches above it and made the river so winding that it passed one particular Assyrian town [Ardericca] three times. Those who now travel to Babylon from our sea sail on the Euphrates for three days and in that amount of time come upon the same village three times. [3] She made the route this way intentionally and built up the embankments on each side of the river—a great and high river's edge that is worthy of admiration. [4] Far up above Babylon, she dug out a reservoir of water that stretched itself out a short distance from the river. She dug all the way to the depth of the groundwater and made the circumference more than forty-seven miles round. Whatever dirt was removed from the trench was used to reinforce the banks of the river. [5] When the entire reservoir had been dug out, she had stones brought and placed as reinforcement of the river-bank. [6] She made the river winding and the trench marsh-like for two reasons: first, so that the river's current, broken up by the turns, would be slower, and second, so that the routes into Babylon would be crooked and travelers would have to pass the reservoir. [7] She focused her attentions in the region where there were invasion routes and the shortest roads from Media. In this way, she sought to prevent the Medes from interacting with her people and from spying on her affairs.

1.186. Indeed, Nitocris surrounded the city with this deep river and made additional improvements from this first one. Because the city was divided in two by the river's course through the middle, in the time of earlier kings, anyone who wanted to cross from one side to the other had to do so by boat. This seems a bit inconvenient to me. But Nitocris took care of this as well, for after she dug out the reservoir, she used it to complete another monument. [2] She cut long stones and when the stones were ready and a new trench dug out, she used them to divert the flow of the river to the new trench. When this trench was filled and the old course of the river was dried up, she built up the edges of the old channel that ran the length of the city down to the river through the gates with baked bricks like those used in the wall. Near the city-center, she built a bridge with stones that had been dug up during the process and bound them together with iron and lead. [3] At the beginning of each day, she had squared-off logs laid across the stones for people to walk on. Overnight the logs were removed to prevent people from using the crossing for thievery. [4] Once the bridge was completed and the channel full, she returned the river to its original course as it flowed down from the lake. Thus Nitocris accomplished what she considered necessary by both making the lake marsh-like and by building a bridge for the citizens.

1.187. The same queen also left behind this clever ruse. Above the most heavily trafficked gate of the city, high above street level and the gate itself, she built her tomb and inscribed upon it the following inscription: [2] "If any future king of Babylon should be in dire need of funds, let him open my tomb and take whatever funds he needs. But if he opens it when not in need, he will be the worse for it." [3] The tomb remained unopened until the reign of Darius. Darius considered it an inconvenience and waste, first, that he could not use the gate, and second, that he could not touch the money though it was just sitting up there and the inscription was asking him to take it. [4] He did not use the gate, you see, because there would be a corpse above his head every time he passed through it. [5] So, he opened the tomb and found no money, just another inscription, "If you were not so greedy for money and insatiable, you would not have disturbed the tombs of the dead." This, then, is the kind of queen she is said to have been.

6. Herodotus, *Histories* 1.192–200 (5th century BCE). *After recounting the capture of Babylon by Cyrus, Herodotus describes the wealth and social practices of the Babylonians. (RFK)*

1.192. I will now show the various manifestation of wealth and power of the Babylonians, though I will start with one in particular: All the land ruled by the Great King[196] is divvied up among himself and his army (this is in addition to the tribute). For four out of the twelve months of the year, the territory of Babylon feeds the king. He is fed off of the rest of Asia for the remaining eight months. [2] Thus Assyria accounts for a full third of the wealth of Asia. Further, the government of this territory, what the Persians call a "satrapy," is by far the most powerful of all such government positions. For example, the daily intake of Tritantaiches, son of Artabazus and appointed by the king as satrap, was a full *artaba* of silver [3] (an *artaba* is a Persian measure worth three *choinikes* less than an Attic *medimnus*).[197] Further, in addition to the warhorses, he owned 800 breeding studs and 16,000 mares for them to breed with, a ratio of about one stud to 20 mares. [4] He also raised so many Indian dogs that four large villages on the plain were assigned to provide food for the dogs and were exempted from other taxes. Such are the resources available to a satrap of Babylon.

1.193. The land of the Assyrians receives a little rain, which nourishes the roots of the grain. It is the water from the river, however, that nourishes the crops and ripens the grain, though not as in Egypt, where the river itself rises to the level of the fields, but by hand-watering and with shadoffs.[198] [2] All of Babylonia, like Egypt, is cut up by canals. The largest of these canals must be navigated by boat and runs where the sun rises in the winter from the Euphrates to another river, the Tigris, where the city of Nineveh once stood. This region is by far the most fertile of any land we know for growing the fruits of Demeter [grain]. [3] It does not support other trees like fig, olive, or grape. It bears so much grain, though, that it yields altogether 200 times the normal yield or even, in peak years, 300 times the normal yield of grain. The leaves of the barley and grain are easily four fingers wide. Of millet and sesame I will not even say how large their trees grow

---

196. The Persian king.

197. About 48 *choinikes* made up an Attic *medimnus*. A *medimnus* was about 48 quarts or 12 gallons.

198. A *shadoff* is a mechanism for moving water from one spot to another. It consists of a frame to which a swinging pole with a bucket of sorts is attached. The pole swings on the frame and lifts the water from the trench below, and then, in a single motion, moves it to another. It is a common form of irrigation still used throughout the world today.

(though I do know). [4] I am well aware that to those who have never been to Babylon, what I have already said about the grain is unbelievable. They use no oil but what they make from sesame. There are palm trees growing throughout the plain, most of them fruit-bearing, from which they make good wine and honey. [5] They tend to the fruits of the palms in the manner one would figs. They bind the non–fruit-bearing "male" part to the fruit-bearing "female" part so that the gallfly can enter inside and ripen the fruit without it falling to the ground. These dates have gallflies in their fruit just as figs do.

1.194. I will next relate what is to me the greatest wonder of all the wonders of Babylon (except the city itself). The boats they use for traveling down the river and into Babylon are round and made entirely of skins. [2] The boats are made north of Babylon by the Armenians. Ribs cut from willows are covered over with waterproof hides. They stretch over the outside to form a bottom. They do not distinguish between sterns and prows but make the boats round like a shield. They then fill the boats with reeds and then set the cargo inside. The most common cargo is palm-wood jars filled with wine. [3] Two men with poles steer the boats. One man draws his pole inward, while the other pushes his outward. Some of the boats are rather large, while others are less so. The largest holds a cargo of 5,000 talents.[199] Every boat has at least one live donkey in it. The larger boats have more. [4] When they arrive in Babylon and have disposed of their cargo, the men advertise the reeds and ribbing of the boat for sale and then place the hides on the backs of the donkeys and drive them back to the Armenians. [5] It is impossible to sail up the river because of the swift current. This is why they make the boats of hides instead of wood. When they have driven the donkeys back to Armenia, they simply make new boats in the same manner. This, then, is what their boats are like.

1.195. For clothing they wear a full-length linen tunic. Over this tunic, they wear a second, wool tunic and then throw a white mantel over these. They wear the shoes customary to the region, which resemble the felt shoes worn in Boeotia. They wear their hair long and bind it up in a turban. They anoint their entire bodies in ointments. [2] Each man also has a seal and a handmade staff. On the staves are various images. Some have an apple, or a rose, or a lily, or an eagle, or some other image. It is not the custom to use an unadorned staff. This, then, is the way they dress themselves. I will next discuss their customs.

1.196. The wisest of their customs, in our opinion, is one that I have learned about through inquiry and was also followed by the Eneti in Illyria. Once a year in each village, they used to do the following: Whatever girls had reached marriageable age were all gathered together in a single place, and the men crowded around. [2] A herald then stood the girls up one at a time, and he sold them starting with the most attractive. After she sold and earned a high price, he then called up the second most attractive girl and

---

199. An Attic talent, similar in weight to the measure used by the Babylonians according to Herodotus, weighs about fifty-seven pounds, or twenty-six kilograms.

so on until all the attractive girls had been sold as wives. The wealthier of the Babylonians who were looking to marry could outbid each other for the fairest of all, while those from the lower classes who were looking for wives, but were uninterested in beauty, could take home the less attractive girls as well as some money. [3] For, once the herald finished selling all the attractive girls, he would ask the least attractive, or maybe a disabled girl, to stand up, and he sold her announcing that she would fall to whoever was willing to take her home to wife with the lowest dowry. The sale continued on until the last girl had been married off. The amount paid to the man along with the girl came from the proceeds of the sale of the attractive girls so that their sales provided a dowry for the unattractive and disabled girls. Further, no man was permitted to give his daughter to whomever he wanted, nor was it possible for a man to lead away the girl he bought without first guaranteeing a marriage contract. [4] This was necessary or, by law, the sale was invalid. It was also possible that someone from a neighboring village would come and buy himself a wife. [5] This, then, was the best custom among the Babylonians, but they do not follow it anymore. Instead, recently they've invented a new custom [in order to prevent their girls from being taken to another city]. Because the submission of Babylon to the Persians caused great financial hardship for the people, everyone who lacks a livelihood now sets his daughter up as a prostitute.

1.197. The second wisest custom is as follows: The Babylonians do not use doctors. Instead, they carry the sick and ailing into the marketplace where passersby, if they have suffered from the same affliction or know someone else who did, offer advice to the sick. They approach the sick and tell them about how they managed their own recovery, or how someone they knew brought about their own, and give comfort. No one is allowed to pass the sick in silence. Everyone must inquire into their illness.

1.198. They embalm their dead with honey, and their funeral dirges are similar to those in Egypt. Whenever a Babylonian man has sex with his wife, they both sit before a burnt offering of incense until dawn, when they bathe. They touch no vessels until they have bathed. The Arabians follow a similar practice.

1.199.[200] This is the worst of all Babylonian customs: They require every local woman to sit in the temple of Aphrodite and have sex with a strange man once during her lifetime. Many women of wealth, who think highly of themselves and consider it beneath them to mingle with the other women, arrive at the temple in covered chariots and stand behind a wall of servants. [2] The majority of women (and there are many coming and going) sit in the sacred precinct with a corded crown on their heads. Pathways are marked allowing the men to wander throughout the crowd of women and choose.

---

200. The following passage relates to a practice known as temple prostitution. The Greeks attributed this practice to a number of Near Eastern peoples, and modern scholars for a long time persisted in believing them. Recent scholarship has demonstrated that the practice (like prostration in Persia) was a figment of the Greek (and modern) imagination and was not actually practiced in the ancient Near East.

[3] Once a woman is seated there, she is not free to return home until some stranger has tossed his money into her lap and she has sex with him outside the temple. When a man throws the money at her, he must say, "I summon you in the name of Mylitta" (Mylitta is the Assyrian name for Aphrodite). [4] The amount of money is irrelevant, nor is it lawful for her to refuse it. This money is sacred. It is also "first come, first serve," and she cannot refuse anyone. Once she has had sex, she is purified by the goddess and free to go home. After this experience, there is no amount of money you would give to her that would be enough to win her affections. [5] Now, there are many great beauties in the temple, and they are typically released from their obligation rather quickly. The unattractive women, however, who are unable to fulfill their obligation, remain in the temple a long time. Indeed, some have remained for three years. There is a custom similar to this in parts of Cyprus.

1.200. These, then, are the established customs of the Babylonians. There are also three tribes among them who eat nothing but fish, which they hunt for and then dry out in the sun. Once dried, they throw it into a mortar and grind it up with pestles before forcing it through linen cloth. Whoever wants can knead the fish pulp into cakes to eat or can bake it into a sort of bread.

> **7. Aristophanes, *Acharnians* 61–125 (5th century BCE).** *The play is set during the Peloponnesian War. The hero, Dicaiopolis, tired of the war and tired of the inaction of the Assembly, decides to make his own peace treaty with Sparta. The visit of the Persian ambassador is the final straw for Dicaiopolis. (RFK)*

Herald: The Ambassadors to the King!

Dicaiopolis: What king? I'm annoyed by these ambassadors and their peacocks and preening.

Herald: Quiet!

Dicaiopolis: Wowzers! Look at that Ecbatana[201] of an outfit!

Ambassador: You sent us to the Great King back when Eutheneus was archon[202] with a pay of two drachma per day . . .

Dicaiopolis (to himself): Oh my! That's a lot of drachmas!

Ambassador: . . . and we wore ourselves out roaming around and camping upon the Caustrian plains.[203] [70] We were just dying, lounging around on soft litters.

---

201. The Median court was known for its extravagant and luxurious manner of dress.

202. 437 or 436 BCE or eleven years earlier.

203. The plain in between the Tigris and Euphrates rivers located at the heart of the Persian Empire. The royal court did not reside in one location at all times but moved from palace to palace at intervals throughout the year.

Dicaiopolis: Geez. And here I thought I was really taking care of myself by living under whatever piece of rubbish happened to float by me.

Ambassador: Being entertained as guests, we were forced to drink only the sweetest wines from crystal and gold goblets.

Dicaiopolis: Oh city of Cranaus![204] Do you hear these jeering, mocking ambassadors?

Ambassador: Barbarians consider the best men only those capable of eating and drinking the most.

Dicaiopolis: The measure of our men is in cocksuckers and ass-lovers.

Ambassador: We finally, three years into our journey, arrived at where the King [80] was. At this point, though, the King had taken off with his army to some far off toilet of a region and spent eight months crapping on the golden hills . . .

Dicaiopolis: And at what point did he tighten up his asshole? Full moon?

Ambassador: . . . and then he came back. He then showed us proper hospitality and set before us as dinner an entire ox in a baking pot.

Dicaiopolis: Who's ever seen an ox in a baking pot? What a load of crap.

Ambassador: I swear by Zeus that he also fed us a bird three times the size of Cleomenes.[205] He called it a "quack."[206]

Dicaiopolis: Sounds about right—[90] you've been cheating us with your two drachma a day.

Ambassador: Now, at last, we have returned! We bring you . . . THE KING'S EYE![207]

Dicaiopolis: Well, throw me down and let a crow peck out my eyes! And the ambassador's too!

Herald: THE KING'S EYE.

Dicaiopolis: Lord Heracles! By the Gods! Man, you look like a battleship at arms! Or are you looking about the next bend for a dock? Do you have a rowlock down under that eye of yours?

Ambassador: Come on, now, Pseudoartabas, and tell the Athenians what the King sent you to say.

Pseudoartabas: [100] Iarta namê xarxana pisona satra.[208]

Ambassodor: Do you understand what he's saying?

Dicaiopolis: By Apollo, I don't.

---

204. Cranaus was an early king of Athens.

205. A politician known for his large physique and love of fine food.

206. The Greek word *phenax*, used for imposters or cheats.

207. The title of the Persian officials assigned to oversee the empire and report back to the King. In this instance, assume a character dressed as a gigantic eye coming onto the stage.

208. A comic rendering of some Persian words and names like "satrap" and "Artaxerxes."

Ambassador: He says that the King is sending us gold. (To Pseudoartabas) Tell them loudly and clearly about the gold.

Pseudoartabas: Not getting gold, you gigantic Ionian assholes.

Dicaiopolis: Well, that was pretty damn clear.

Ambassador: Huh? What is he saying?

Dicaiopolis: What? He says that the Ionians are huge assholes if they are expecting any gold from the barbarians.

Ambassador: No, no, no! He says "many *medimnoi*"[209] of gold!

Dicaiopolis: How many "many *medimnoi*"? You are a big fat liar. Get out of here! I'll put the screws to this "Eye" myself. [110] Come on, tell me clearly (see my stick here?). Don't make me dip you in Sardian dyes. Will the Great King send us a lot of gold? (Pseudoartabas shakes head.) So, in other words, we are being swindled by these ambassadors? (Pseudoartabas nods.) Wait. Hold on! These two men here, the Eye and his companion? They nod like Athenians. They aren't Persian! They're Athenians! This one, the eunuch. I know you! You're Cleisthenes, son of Sibyrtius. Oh, you shaver of your own hot-headed anus. You ape. What a beard you've got yourself! [120] And you come here all decked out like a eunuch? And who's your sidekick? Don't tell me it's Strato![210]

Herald: QUIET! SIT DOWN! The Council invites the King's Eye to dine in the Prytaneum.[211]

---

8. Isocrates, *Panegyricus* 150–152 (4th century BCE). *Isocrates' panegyric (circulated sometime around 380 BCE) was intended to convince the Greeks to stop fighting each other and unite against the "barbarian" menace, Persia. (RFK)*

150. None of these things has happened without reason, but all have resulted naturally. For it is impossible that men nourished and governed as the Persians have been should be able to share the virtues of others or to set up battle trophies over their enemies. For how, given their way of life, is it possible that they produce a clever general or noble soldier? The majority of the Persians are an unorganized mob and have been taught slavishness better than people in our own lands.

151. Those among them with the greatest reputations never live for equality, the common good, or the state. Their whole lives are passed either committing outrages on some men or playing the slave to others. Thus

---

209. The Greek is *axanê*, a Persian measure that equaled about 45 Athenian *medimnoi*.

210. Cleisthenes is elsewhere lampooned on stage as a beardless "pretty boy," and Strato appears to be his lover.

211. The public dining hall where foreign guests, ambassadors, honored citizens, and others dined at public expense.

these men especially would be corrupted in their natures. Because of their wealth, they wantonly indulge their bodies. Because of the monarchy, they have souls humbled and timid. They present themselves before the royal palaces, fall down prostrate before others, and in all ways practice low-mindedness. They bow down before a mortal man and address him as if he were a divinity. They think less of the gods than they do of men. 152. So for example, those among them who come down to the sea, whom they call satraps, they do not disregard their upbringing but maintain these same behaviors abroad—they are untrustworthy to their friends and lack courage before the enemy, they live sometimes humbled but at other times overbearing, and they hold their allies in contempt while flattering their foes.

9. Xenophon, *Cyropaedia* 1.2.2–8, 1.3.2, 4–5, 1.3.18 excerpted (4th century BCE). *The* Cyropaedia *(The Education of Cyrus) is a semi-fictionalized history of the life of Cyrus the Great (c.600–530 BCE). The account begins with a description of Cyrus' early life in Persia and Media. His mother, Mandane, is the daughter of the Median king Astyages. His father, Cambyses, is a Persian king. (CSR)*

1.2.2–8. Cyrus was educated following the laws of the Persians. These laws, in their concern for the common good, do not seem to begin at the time when most states begin. For most states let everyone educate their children however he wants, and the older people live however they wish, and then they command them not to steal or rob, not to enter a house by force, not to hit someone it is not right to hit, not to commit adultery, not to disobey one of their leaders, and other things such as these. If someone should break any one of these laws, they impose a penalty on them. [3] The Persian laws, anticipating this, take care from the beginning that their citizens will not be the kind of people who desire anything bad or shameful. They take care as follows. They have what is called a "free square" where the palace and other government buildings have been built. Markets and seedy sellers, their shouts and tastelessness, are driven away from this place to somewhere else, so that their disorder does not get mixed up in the orderliness of educated men. [4] This square, which surrounds the government buildings, is divided into four parts. One of these is for the boys, one for the adolescents, another for full-grown men, and another for those who have aged out of their military service. By law, each of them must go to their own sections. Both the boys and the full-grown men go at daybreak, the older men go according to each one's own convenience—except on pre-established days when it is necessary that they come. The youths pass the night around the government buildings wearing their light armor, except the married ones. They are not asked after unless they were ordered to come, and it is not good for them to be absent too often. . . . [6] The boys go to school and spend their days learning justice. They even say that they go for this purpose, as among us we say that we go to learn reading and writing. Their leaders

spend most of the day judging for them, for complaints of fraud and robbery and violence and deceit and bad rumors and other things of this sort
happen among boys against each other just as among men. They punish
anyone they learn of who commits one of these crimes. [7] They also punish anyone whom they discover has made an unjust accusation. And they
go to trial for a charge that causes the most animosity between men but
is rarely prosecuted—ingratitude. They punish especially whoever they
learn was able to repay a favor but did not. For they think that the ungrateful are especially negligent of the gods, their parents, their homeland, and
their friends. It seems that shamelessness tends to follow ingratitude, and
shamelessness is a great instigator in all wrongs. [8] They also teach the
boys moderation, and it greatly contributes to their learning moderation
that they see the older men living moderately every day. They teach them
obedience, a lesson greatly enhanced when they see the older men obey-
ing their leaders efficiently. They teach them self-control over their stomach and their thirst, and in this too it greatly helps when they see that the
older men do not leave their duties because of hunger before their leaders
dismiss them. Also, the boys do not eat with their mothers but with their
teacher, whenever the leaders give that order. They bring home grain and
bread, bitter-cress as seasoning, and a cup for drinking water drawn from
the river if anyone is thirsty. Besides these things, they learn to shoot arrows
and hurl javelins.

Cyrus and his mother, Mandane, travel to Media to meet his grandfather,
Astyages, king of the Medes.

1.3.2, 4–5. Immediately upon arriving, Cyrus recognized Astyages as
the father of his mother, and, having such a loving temper, straightaway
embraced him just as someone who had grown up with him and loved him
for a long time would embrace him. And seeing him decked out with eye
liner and face paints and false hair—these things are customary among the
Medes, for this is all Median, as well as purple tunics and coats, and neck-
laces and bracelets on their arms; among the Persians at home even now
clothes are poorer and their lives more thrifty—looking at his grandfather's
clothes and his grandfather himself, he said, "O mother, how beautiful my
grandfather is!" When his mother asked him which of the two seemed to
him to be more beautiful, his father or his grandfather, Cyrus answered
right away, "Mother, my father is the most beautiful of the Persians. Of the
Medes, however, as much as I have seen of them in the roads and at court,
my grandfather here is the most beautiful." . . . [4] When Astyages dined
with his daughter and Cyrus, he wanted the boy to have as pleasant a meal
as was possible, so that he might want to go home less. He set before him
little side-dishes and sauces of every kind and meat. They say that Cyrus
said, "Grandfather, you have a lot of work to do when you eat, if you must
stretch out your hands to get all these dishes and taste all these various
meats!" And Astyages said, "Do you not think this meal better by far than
one you would find among the Persians?" And Cyrus replied, "Grandfather,

it isn't that, but for us the road to filling up is simpler and straighter than it is for you. Bread and meat alone lead us to our fill, whereas you travel on the same road as us, but only after wandering many turns up and down do you come to the place we arrived at earlier." [5] "But, my boy," Astyages said, "it does not bother us to wander around these roads, and you will realize that it is pleasant once you have a taste."

> *Mandane leaves for Persia and Cyrus decides to remain in Media. His mother expresses concern about his education in justice, since Medes and Persians have different ideas of government.*

1.3.18. "My child, the ideal of justice followed at your grandfather's house is not in agreement with how the Persians pursue it. He has made himself the master of all in Media, whereas among the Persians they think that it is just to have equality. Your father is the first to do what is commanded by the state and to accept what is commanded. His measure is not his soul but the law. Take care that you not be beaten and killed when you come home, if you come home having learned tyranny (under which they think it is right that one man have more than everyone else) rather than kingship." And Cyrus said, "but your father, mother, is more clever at teaching someone to have less rather than more. Do you not see that he has taught all the Medes to have less than he does? Therefore, take courage, for your father will not send me forth nor anyone else who has learned to be greedy."

10. Livy, *From the Foundation of the City* 9.17.16 (1st century BCE/ 1st century CE). *Livy describes Alexander's enemy Darius III while assessing how he thinks the Romans would view Alexander. (CSR)*

He would have said that the battle was not with Darius, who dragged a troop of women and eunuchs along with him, and who was weighed down, between the purple cloths and the gold, by the trappings of his own fortune. Darius was more a spoil of war than an enemy. Alexander conquered him without bloodshed by simply daring to disregard what was empty vanity.

11. Philostratus the Lemnian, *Imagines* 2.31.1–2 (3rd century CE). *The* Imagines *is a collection of short descriptions of imaginary paintings. Here is a painting of the Athenian general Themistocles, hero of the battle of Salamis, who went to Persia after his ostracism from Athens. (RFK)*

2.3.1. A Greek among barbarians, a man among non-men (seeing as they are ruined and effeminate), certainly an Athenian judging by his threadbare cloak, he pronounces some wisdom, I think, and tries to change their habits and to woo them away from luxury. Here are Medes, the center of Babylon, the royal insignia—a golden eagle on a shield—and the king here sits on his golden throne decked out like a spotted peacock. The painter does not think it worthy to seek praise for how well he has represented the tiara and royal robe or the Median cloak with its large sleeves or the marvelous animal patterns with which barbarians embellish their clothes. He should be praised, however, for how he draws and preserves the design of the threads upon the gold fabric. He should also be praised, by Zeus, for the faces of the eunuchs! The golden courtyard, may he be praised for that as well—it seems so realistic as to not be a painting at all but a real building. We can smell the frankincense and myrrh with which the barbarians corrupt the air of freedom. One spearman converses with another about this Greek man and marvels at him and what they have learned of his great deeds.

2.3.2. Themistocles son of Neocles has come to Babylon, I think, after the battle at divine Salamis, and when he was at a loss as to where in Greece he could be safe. He is conversing with the king about how he aided Xerxes while still commander of the Greek fleet. He is undisturbed by his Median surroundings but is as bold as if he were standing on a speaker's platform in Athens. His speech is not his native tongue; Themistocles is using the Median language, which he learned while there. If you doubt this, just look at his listeners. They indicate with their eyes that they understand what he is saying. Look at Themistocles also; his head is tilted as if he is speaking, but his eyes indicate a hesitation, as if he is searching for what he wants to say like one who has just learned the language.

12. Hyginus, *Genealogies* 27 (2nd century CE). *After Medea left Colchis with Jason on the Argo, Perses, the brother of Aeetes, killed Aeetes, Medea's father, and seized the kingdom of Colchis for himself. Medea, through her son Medus, avenges her father. (RFK)*

It was told to Perses, son of the Sun and brother of Aeetes, to beware death at the hands of a descendant of Aeetes. Medus, while pursuing his mother, was carried by a storm to Colchis, the kingdom of Perses. There he was seized by attendants and taken before the king. Medus, the son of Medea and Aegeus, when he saw that he had fallen into the hands of enemies, falsely claimed to be Hippotes the son of Creon.[212] The king questioned him carefully and then had him thrown into prison. Now, in Colchis there were currently famine and food shortages. When Medea arrived in Colchis upon her dragon-drawn chariot, she lied to Perses, telling him that she was a priestess of the goddess Diana and that she could rid the land of famine. When she learned that Hippotes was in the king's custody, she thought he had come to take vengeance for the murder of his father, Creon. Then < . . . >, she accidentally betrayed her son. For she persuaded Perses that he was not in fact Hippotes, but was Medus, son of Aegeus, sent by Medea to kill him. She asked Perses to bring "Medus" before her so that she, thinking

---

212. Creon, the king of Corinth, whom Medea had murdered as part of her revenge on Jason.

he was really Hippotes, could kill him. And so Medus was led forth to be put to death for lying to the king. Medea, however, realized that he was not Hippotes but Medus, and declared that she needed to converse privately with him before his execution. She then handed Medus a sword and ordered him to avenge his grandfather Aeetes. Medus, upon hearing her, killed Perses and took possession of his ancestral kingdom. He then changed the name of the land to Media after his own name.

PARTHIANS

13. Horace, *Odes* 1.2.49–52, 1.19.9–12, 1.38.1–4, 2.13.13–20 (1st century BCE). *Horace frequently mentions the Parthians in his poetry, conflating them with the Medes and Persians, known from Classical Greek sources. (CSR)*

1.2.49–52. Enjoy great triumphs here instead, here may you love to be called father and princeps.[213] And do not allow the Medes[214] to ride their horses unavenged by us while you are our leader, Caesar.

1.19.9–12. Venus attacks me in full force, she has deserted Cyprus, and prevents me from singing about Scythians or Parthians, bold on their turned horses, and other such things irrelevant to her.

1.38.1–4. I hate Persian trappings, boy. Crowns woven with linden displease me. Do not chase after where the late rose lingers.

2.13.13–20. A man is never cautious enough, hour by hour, about what he should avoid: a Punic sailor shudders at the Bosporus, but he does not fear hidden doom from any other source; the soldier fears the arrows and quick flight of the Parthian, while the Parthian fears chains and the Italian dungeon; but it is an unforeseen death that has seized, and will seize, all the races of men.

14. Ovid, *Ars Amatoria* 1.177–228 (1st century BCE/1st century CE). *In a discussion of how a triumphal procession would be a good place to find girls, Ovid digresses on a prospective Roman campaign in the East. He specifically addresses the return of the standards taken by the Parthians from Crassus. (MLG)*

1.177–228. Behold! Caesar is preparing to add to our possession the part of the world still unconquered. Inhabitant of the eastern end of the world,

---

213. First man in Rome.

214. Horace refers to the Parthian victory over Crassus at Carrhae in 53 BCE. See Chapter 8, Selection 7.

you will soon belong to us. You will pay the penalty, Parthia. Crassus and son, although you are dead and buried, rejoice! Rejoice, [180] Roman regimental standards—you dislike being handled by barbarian hands. An avenger is at hand and, though young, claims leadership and manages a war not to be waged by a child. But cease, timorous men, enumerating birthdays of gods! Caesars obtain their manly valor early: divinely inspired talent ascends more quickly than its years and will not tolerate any debt to slovenly delay. Heracles was a tiny child when he strangled two snakes in his hands and was worthy of Jupiter even in the cradle. You are still a boy, Bacchus, and how big were you [190] when you conquered India and inspired them with fear of your thyrsus? Under the legitimate authority and age of your father, young man, you will wage war, and you will conquer under the legitimate authority and age of your father. Such is the commencement you owe to so great a family name, since you are already the leader of the youths and will soon be leader of the senate. Since you have brothers, avenge the harm done to brothers! Since you have a father, defend the rights of fathers! Your father and the father of the country puts your arms on you; the enemy has wrenched the kingdom from his own unwilling father. You will wield dutiful spears; he, criminal arrows. Justice and duty will stand in front of your legionary standards. [200] The Parthians' cause is conquered; let them be conquered in arms as well. Let my leader add the riches of the east to Rome. Father Mars and father Caesar, grant your divine favor to him on his journey. One of you is a god, the other one will be.

Behold! I prophesy and shall repay with a promised poem. We shall have to sing of you in grand strains. You will stand firm and encourage the troops in battle array with my words (ah, let my words not betray your spirit!). I shall speak of Parthian backs and Roman hearts and [210] of the weapons that the enemy shoots from his horse in flight. Parthian, since you run away to conquer, what will be left to you when conquered? Parthia, even now your army stands under an ominous cloud. And therefore that day will come when you, Gaius, most beautiful man in the world, will dress in gold and be carried by four white horses. The enemy leaders will walk in front with their necks weighed down by chains. In this way they will be unable to run away as they did before. Young men and girls will gather together and gaze with joy. That day will spread great enthusiasm to all. When some girl asks for the names of the kings, [220] when she asks what are the images of foreign lands, mountains, and rivers carried in procession, reply to her every inquiry—reply, indeed, even if she does not ask. Whatever you don't know, reply as if you know it well: "This here is Euphrates, with his forehead crowned with reeds. That guy there with the sea-blue locks hanging low, he's Tigris." Pretend that these men are Armenians, that this here is a Persian girl descended from Danae. That guy, or that guy, let them be leaders. Some you will name truly, if you can, but if you can't, just give them appropriate names.

15. Lucan, *Civil War* **8.289–308, 8.371–388 (1st century CE).**
Pompey Magnus addresses his followers after his crushing defeat at Pharsalia and suggests places they might escape to. (MLG)

8.289–308. Come, companions, let us hasten to the east. The Euphrates separates the great world with its flood; [290] the Caspian is the gateway to immense and remote lands. A different sky turns across the day and night in Assyria. Their sea is separate from ours, their water a different color, and they have their own encircling Ocean. Their only joy is battle. In encampments their horses run faster; their bows are stronger. No child, no old man bends those deadly bowstrings lazily: death is certain from every arrow. They were the first to break the Macedonian battle line with the bow. They captured Bactra, the seat of the Medes, and Babylon, the Assyrian home, although she was proud of her wall. Our spears are not very terrifying to the Parthians. [300] They come boldly into battle ever since they put their Scythian quivers to the test on the day Crassus died. They shot their arrows without trusting only to their iron tips; the buzzing missiles have been soaked in poison. A small wound kills and a scratch is fatal. Ah, if only I did not believe that these things about the savage sons of Arsaces[215] were true! The fate that drives on the Mede is too similar to our own, and there is many a divinity among them.

Lentulus responds to Pompey.

8.371–388. The Parthian may escape through the lands of Media, between the plains of Sarmatia, on the broad fields in the plain of the Tigris. He is unconquerable because he has the freedom to flee. But where the earth swells up, he will not climb the steep peaks of the mountain, nor will he wage war in the cool shade of ravines and forests, weak in his uncertain bow. Nor will he cross a swiftly-moving river by swimming. When in battle his every limb is drenched in blood, he will not endure the hot sun and the burning dust. He has no battering ram, no war machines, no strength to fill ditches. Anything that can protect against arrows will be a defensive wall to the pursuing Parthian. Their battle is a skirmish, their war is flight, and their squadrons wander far. [380] Their soldier is better at retreating than driving an enemy out. Their arrows are smeared with deceit. Their courage never dares to fight it out hand to hand, but only to shoot from a distance and let the winds take the weapons where it will. A sword has strength as does the race of men that makes war with swords. After the first phase of the battle, the Medes are disarmed and they are forced to retreat with empty quivers.

---

215. The founder of the Parthian monarchy.

16. CIL XI 137 (1st/2nd century CE). *A Parthian recounts the key moments of his life and his aspirations on his sarcophagus, found in Ravenna. (MLG)*

GAIUS JULIUS MYGDONIUS

PARTHIAN BY RACE

born a free man, captured

in his youth, transferred to the land

of Rome. When I was made a Roman citizen by the assistance of fate

I arranged for this coffin [or, I started saving] for when I reached

fifty years old. Since I tried from my youth

to reach old age,

now happily receive me, stone.

With you, I will be free from care.

17. Plutarch, *Life of Crassus* **24–28, 31 (2nd century CE).** *Plutarch describes Parthian customs and practices as part of his account of the Parthian campaign of Crassus and the results. (CSR)*

24. While the Romans were panic-stricken from the noise, suddenly their enemies threw off the coverings on their weapons and appeared to gleam from their helmets and breastplates, the Margianian iron flashing sharp and glittering, and their horses were covered with bronze and iron armor. [2] Surena himself was the tallest and most beautiful, and the effeminacy of his beauty did not match his reputation for courage. He was dressed more in the Median fashion—he had painted his face and parted his hair, whereas the other Parthians wore their hair in long bunches over their foreheads like Scythians. [3] First, the Parthians intended to push and attack with their pikes and thus carry the front ranks by force. But when they saw the depth of the ranks with overlapping shields and the constancy and steadfastness of the men, they went back and seemed to scatter and break up their battle lines, but in secret they circled the square battle formation. [4] When Crassus ordered his light-armed troops to advance, they did not advance far, but after quickly coming under fire from many arrows they retreated and took cover with the heavy infantry. There they caused the beginning of disorder and fear, for the heavy infantry saw the force and strength of arrows that could break armor and that could be sent through every sort of armor, both strong and soft alike. [5] But the Parthians stood at intervals and began to shoot from all sides at once, and not without accuracy (for the dense unbroken line of the Romans would not allow even someone who wanted to miss not to hit a man), but they were making strong and powerful shots from strong and large curved bows so that their arrows had great

force. [6] Immediately, the Roman situation became horrendous; for if they remained in their battle lines they were wounded in great numbers, and if they tried to close the distance and fight, they were equally far from doing anything and suffered just the same. For the Parthians shoot as they flee, and they do this more effectively than anyone other than the Scythians. It is very intelligent to head to safety while still defending yourself, and it lifts the shame of the retreat.

25. As long as the men had hope that their enemies would run out of arrows and hold off from battle or engage in hand-to-hand combat, they remained steadfast. But when they saw the many camels nearby loaded with extra arrows, from which those who first had ridden around them could get new ones, Crassus, seeing nothing more to do, became discouraged. He sent messengers to his son and ordered him to force a fight with the enemy before he was completely surrounded, because their cavalry was attacking and encircling his wing, in particular trying get behind him. [2] Therefore, his son took 1,300 horsemen, 500 of whom had been Caesar's, 500 archers, and 8 cohorts of men with shields who were closest to him and led them in an attack. But, the Parthians surrounding him turned back and ran off either, as some say, because they came upon marshland, or because their strategy was to attack the younger Crassus as far away from his father as they could. [3] Crassus' son, after shouting that the men were not standing their ground, pushed on, and Censorinus and Megabacchus went with him. Megabacchus was known for his bravery and strength; Censorinus had the rank of a senator and was a strong speaker. They were companions of the younger Crassus and near in age. The horsemen followed them, and the infantry did not remain behind because they were filled with eagerness and joyful anticipation. They thought that they had won and were chasing the enemy until they recognized the trick after they had advanced a good way. The Parthians, seemingly in flight, turned around and additional men joined them. [4] The Romans stopped there, thinking that the enemy would fight at close quarters with them since they were so few. But the Parthians arrayed their heavy-armored cavalry opposite the Romans and sent their light-armed cavalry around them. They stirred up the plain and raised huge dust clouds from the earth that reduced the Romans' vision and communications. [5] Thus, the Romans were corralled and shot as they fell on one another. They died neither easily nor quickly, but rather, wracked by spasms of pain and thrashing around the arrows, they broke them off in their wounds and tried by force to drag out the barbed arrowheads that had pierced through their arteries and tendons. The result was repeated tearing and self-mutilation. [6] Many died. And those who lived were useless in a fight. When Crassus' son Publius called on them to attack the heavily armored cavalry, they showed him that their hands were stuck to their shields and that their feet were nailed to the ground making them incapable of either retreat or defense. [7] Publius himself urged on the horsemen and vigorously charged and joined battle with the enemy, but he was unequal to the attack or to defending himself. His men were striking steel- and

hide-covered breastplates with small weak spears. The light-armed and bare-bodied Gallic soldiers were struck repeatedly with long pikes. Publius placed great confidence in these men, and with them he accomplished marvelous deeds. [8] Since the heaviness of their armor weighed them down, they took hold of the spears and wrestled the Parthians from their horses. Many of the Gauls left their own horses behind, dove under the Parthians' horses, and struck them in their stomachs. The horses would rear up from the pain and, as they died, would trample on riders and enemies alike. [9] Heat and thirst especially bothered the Gauls, for they were unaccustomed to both. Most of their horses had been killed, driven onto the enemies' pikes, and so they were forced to retreat to the infantry. They brought a badly injured Publius with them. They saw a sandy hill nearby and retreated to it. They tied their horses in the center and fastened their shields together on the exterior. They thought that they would thus easily ward off the barbarians.[216] [10] The result was the opposite, for, on level ground the men in the front ranks offer some respite for those behind them, but here the unevenness of the ground elevated one man above another and raised up even more the man behind. There was no escape, everyone was being hit equally as they lamented their inglorious and useless deaths.

[11] Two Greek men were with Publius who lived nearby in Carrhae, Hieronymus and Nicomachus. These men assisted in persuading Publius to withdraw with them and flee to Ichnae, a city connected to Rome and not far away. But Publius said that he feared no death so terrible that he would leave those who were dying for him. He then ordered Hieronymus and Nicomachus to save themselves and, after grasping their hands, sent them away. Then, since he was unable to use his right hand (it had been struck through with an arrow), he offered his side to his armor-bearer and ordered him to strike him with a sword. [12] They say that Censorinus died the same way. Megabacchus did the same to himself, as did the noblest of the rest. The Parthians climbed the hill and pierced the remaining fighters with their pikes. It is said that no more than 500 were captured alive. The Parthians cut off the heads of those around Publius and pushed on against Crassus.

26. This is how it went for Crassus: Once he ordered his son to attack the Parthians and someone announced to him that Publius had soundly routed the enemy and was pursuing the enemy vigorously, he saw that they were no longer pursuing him (for most had gone away to fight Publius) and recovered his courage a little. He drew his men together and gathered them on rising ground, expecting that his son would come back from the chase to aid him. [2] The first messengers, sent by Publius to his father to say that he was in danger, died after falling in among the barbarians. The later ones escaped with much effort and pain and announced that Publius was done for unless his father quickly sent reinforcements. [3] Many emotions began to overwhelm Crassus, and he was no longer able to think rationally.

---

216. Plutarch uses the word *barbaros* here, rather than enemy or Parthian.

He did not know what to do: fear for everyone encouraged him not to send reinforcements; longing for his son provoked him to. Finally, he urged his forces to go forward. Then the enemy, ever more frightening, assaulted them with noise and battle cries, and their many drums roared around the Romans who expected the beginning of the next battle. [4] The Parthians, who carried the head of Publius fixed on a spear, rushed forward and displayed it, arrogantly inquiring into his parents and family. They said it was not fitting for Crassus, a most cowardly and base man, to be the father of a son who was so noble and brilliant in his excellence. This sight, more than all the other terrible things they had experienced, exhausted and broke the spirits of the Romans. They were overcome by shivering and quaking rather than a desire for revenge, which would have been fitting. [5] They say, however, that Crassus appeared most brilliant in that time of suffering, for, while riding along the ranks, he shouted: "O, Romans, this sorrow is mine and private; the great fortune and reputation of Roman stands unbroken and unbeaten in you who are saved. If you have any pity for me, robbed of the noblest of all sons, make this clear in your rage against the enemy. Strip them of their joy! Punish them for their cruelty! Do not be laid low by what has happened! It is necessary for those aiming at great things to suffer as well. [6] Lucullus did not bring down Tigranes without bloodshed, nor did Scipio Antiochus. Our ancestors lost a thousand ships around Sicily, and many commanders and generals in Italy. None of them, by being beaten, prevented them from defeating the ones who had conquered them. For the Roman state came to its present power not by good luck but by the endurance and excellence of those who advanced against terrible things in its name."

27. Even after saying such things and encouraging them, Crassus saw that not many men were listening to him eagerly; when he ordered them to shout out together, the dejection of the army was evident, for they made such a weak, small, and uneven shout. The splendid and brave shout of the barbarians overcame them. While they turned to their work, the enemies' light-armored cavalry at their sides circled round them and shot at them, and their front line, using their pikes, drove the Romans into a narrow space except for those who, fleeing death from the arrows, recklessly dared to attack their enemies. [2] They did little harm but died quickly from serious, mortal wounds as the Parthians thrust pikes heavy with iron into their horses, pikes that could, if thrust with sufficient force, go through two men. They fought in this way until night fell and then they withdrew. The Parthians said that they would give Crassus one night to mourn his son, unless he thought better about his situation and was willing to go to Arsaces rather than to be dragged there. [3] The Parthians set up their camp nearby and were in high hopes, but a difficult night took hold of the Romans. They made no plans to bury their dead nor to treat their wounded or dying, rather each cried about his own situation. It seemed impossible to escape if they waited for the day or went into the vast plain at night. Those who were wounded presented a great challenge: Should they take them

and let them impede the swiftness of their flight, or should they leave them to announce their escape with their shouts? [4] As for Crassus, although they considered him at fault for everything, they longed for his face and his voice. But he lay covered in darkness, a paradigm of bad luck to many, and to the wise a symbol of bad planning and ambition. Driven by ambition, he was not content with being first and greatest among so many men. Because he was judged to rank below only two other men, he thought that he lacked everything.

[5] The legates Octavius and Cassius then raised him up and tried to encourage him, but since he had completely given up, they summoned the centurions and captains. When those deliberating decided not to remain, they roused the army without a trumpet call and in silence at first. When the incapacitated realized that they were being left behind, a terrible disorder and confusion of wails and shouts overcame the camp. [6] Then disorder and fear that the enemy was attacking overtook those retreating as they marched. They turned aside often, and often they got into formation. Whosoever of the wounded were following them had to be picked up or put down at intervals. They were wasting time, except for 300 horsemen, whom Ignatius led to Carrhae around midnight. [7] Ignatius called out to those guarding the walls in the Roman language. When they heard him, he ordered them to announce to their leader Coponius that a great battle had occurred between Crassus and the Parthians. Saying nothing else, not even who he was, he rode away to Zeugma, thereby saving his men along with himself, but evil is spoken of him since he left his commander. [8] The message sent to Coponius did, however, benefit Crassus, for Coponius thought that the speed and confusion of the message implied that it announced nothing good. He commanded his army to ready for battle, and when he first learned that Crassus was on the move, he went out to meet him, took over the army, and escorted them into the city.

28. The Parthians realized the Romans were escaping that night but did not pursue them; as soon as it was day they went into the camp and cut the throats of those who were left behind—not less than 4,000 of them—then they rode off and captured many who were wandering in the plain. [2] Also, four cohorts, which broke away with Vargontius while it was still night, were surrounded on a hill as they wandered from the road and were slaughtered as they tried to defend themselves, all of them except twenty men. The Parthians admired these twenty men, who had pushed their way through with their swords, and they let them through. They gave them a clear road to Carrhae as they were leaving. A false report came to Surena that Crassus had escaped along with other noblemen, and that the crowd that flowed into Carrhae was a mixed group of men not worthy of worry. [3] Surena thought that the result of his victory had gotten away, but he was still unsure and wanted to learn the truth so that he might either wait there and besiege Crassus or pursue him and let the people of Carrhae go unpunished. Therefore he sent one of his men who was bilingual to the walls and bid him to call for Crassus or Cassius in the Roman language

and say that Surena wished to meet with them to speak terms. [4] After the interpreter said these things it was reported to Crassus, who accepted the proposal. After a little while some Arabs came from the barbarians who knew Crassus and Cassius well by sight, since they had been in their camp before the battle. These men saw Cassius from the wall and told him that Surena proposed a peace and offered to protect those who were friends of the king so long as they left Mesopotamia. He saw this as more profitable to both forces instead of pursuing an extreme position. [5] Cassius accepted and asked that a place and time be determined for when Surena and Crassus would come together. The messengers said that they would do this and went away.

> *Surena besieges the city and Crassus flees. Surena fears that the Romans will be able to get away and so promises again to come to terms with Crassus. He agrees unwillingly.*

31. Octavius and those around him did not remain but went down the hill with Crassus. Crassus forced back the lictors who had accompanied him. Two Greeks of mixed blood were the first of the barbarians to encounter him. They jumped down from their horses and prostrated themselves before him. They addressed him in the Greek language and encouraged him to send some people ahead who would see that Surena and those around him were coming forward without shields or swords. [2] Crassus told them that if he had even the least thought for his life, he would not have come into their hands. For all that, however, he sent two brothers, Roscians, to find out how many were coming and on what terms. Straightaway Surena captured and held these men and went forward on horseback with his top men and said: "What is this? A Roman commander goes on foot, but we ride?" He ordered a horse to be brought to Crassus. [3] Crassus said that neither he nor Surena was making a mistake, for they were carrying out the meeting in a way typical of each man's country. Surena said that from that moment on there were treaties and peace between King Hyrodes and the Romans, but that it was necessary for the treaties to be written after they reached the river ("For you Romans, indeed, are not completely mindful of agreements") and he held out his right hand. He then said it was not necessary to send for a horse, "for the king has given this one to you." [4] When he said this, a golden-bridled horse stood next to Crassus and the grooms lifted him up, mounted him on the horse, and attended him while hurrying the horse along with blows. Octavius was the first to lay hold of the bridle, and after him it was Petronius, one of the commanders. Then the remaining men surrounded him and tried to stop the horse; they also drove back those who were pressing against Crassus on either side. [5] After some pushing, disorder, and then blows, Octavius drew his sword and killed the groom of one of the barbarians, but then another killed Octavius by striking him from behind. Petronius did not have a weapon, but after being hit in the breastplate he leapt off his horse unharmed. A Parthian named Pomaxathres killed Crassus. [6] Some deny that it was this man and claim that someone

else was the killer, and they say that he cut off the head and the right hand of Crassus as he was lying there. These facts are inferred rather than known, for, out of those who were present, some of the men fighting there around Crassus were killed and others fled back up the hill right away. [7] The Parthians approached them and said that Crassus had paid the penalty, but Surena bid the rest of them to take heart and come down. Some of the men came down and entrusted themselves to Surena, others scattered during the night, and few of these men escaped altogether. Some of them the Arabs tracked, captured, and killed. It is said that 20,000 all told died, and 10,000 were taken alive.

CHAPTER II

ASIA: JUDEA AND THE JEWISH DIASPORA

The Jews do not appear in the accounts of Greeks and Romans until the Hellenistic period, although tales of Jewish interactions with the Greeks (specifically the Spartans) earlier in the 4th century BCE exist. When they do finally appear, it is as a fully distinctive people, already recognized for their unique dietary and religious practices. It was unclear to the Greeks and Romans, however, whether to consider the Jews as a distinctive race or as Egyptian. A number of Jewish apologists, like Philo of Alexandria, wrote eloquent works to clarify and defend Jewish practices to others, and plays like the Exagogia *(The Exodus) presented stories from the Bible for non-Jewish audiences.*

1. **Diodorus Siculus,** *The Library of History* **34/35.1.1–5 (Posidonius, 1st century BCE).**[217] *Diodorus recounts the attempts of the advisors of Antiochus VII Sidetes (d. 129 BCE) to convince him to annihilate the Jewish people. Posidonius (d. c.51 BCE) the philosopher may be his source for this story. (RFK)*

34/35.1.1. Diodorus tells us about King Antiochus' siege of Jerusalem.[218] The Jews resisted for some time. When, however, their supplies were exhausted, they were compelled to send ambassadors to negotiate a cease-fire. The majority of Antiochus' friends advised him to take the city by force and to wipe out the race of the Jews. They alone of all peoples, the advisors said, refused to mingle with other peoples and considered all other peoples their enemies. They pointed out how the ancestors of the Jews were impious and were hated by the gods and had thus been driven into exile from all of Egypt. 2. The Egyptians, as a way of purifying the country, had rounded up and driven into exile anyone who had white or leprous marks on their body, as if they were cursed. Those driven out took up residence

---

217. Both this passage and Diodorus 40.3 come down to us in the *Library* of Photius (d. c.893 CE) as summaries and quotations from Diodorus' own *Library*.
218. 134 BCE.

around Jerusalem.[219] They united as the Jewish people and made hatred toward mankind a tradition among themselves. On account of this, they established altogether contrary customs: to not share hospitality with other peoples, and to not demonstrate any goodwill toward them.

34/35.1.3. The advisors reminded Antiochus also about the earlier hatred of his ancestors toward the Jews. An earlier Antiochus, given the name Epiphanes,[220] when he conquered the Jews, entered into the inner-most sanctuary of the temple of the god, something only the priest could do by law. Inside, Epiphanes found a stone statue of a thick-bearded man sitting upon a donkey and holding a book in his hands. He assumed this was Moses, who had founded Jerusalem and united the people. It was also he who drafted the misanthropic and transgressive laws for the Jewish peo-ple. Epiphanes abhorred their misanthropy toward all peoples and strove to destroy these customs. 4. Toward this end, he sacrificed a huge sow in front of the statue of the founder and the open-air altar of the god. He then poured the pig's blood upon both, altar and statue, and, having prepared the meat, ordered that the sacred books that contained the xenophobic laws be sprinkled with the pig broth. He ordered also that the lamp, which the Jews called undying and that burned constantly in the temple, be snuffed out. He further ordered that the high priest and the rest of the people be forced to eat some of the pig meat.

34/35.1.5. The friends of Antiochus recounted these things and called upon Antiochus to annihilate the entire race, or, if not that, at least destroy their customs and compel them to change their way of life. The king was a magnanimous man and of gentle disposition. He instead took hostages and dismissed the complaints against the Jews. He then collected an appropri-ate tribute and removed the walls from around Jerusalem.

2. Diodorus Siculus, *The Library of History* 40.3.1–8 (Hecataeus *FrGH* F6, 1st century BCE). *This account of the origins of the Jews by Diodorus comes from the* Aegyptica *of Hecataeus of Abdera (360–290 BCE), an idealized account of the nature of Egyptian practices. Diodorus recounts it as part of his description of Pompey's wars in Asia. (RFK)*

40.3.1. Since we are about to write about the war against the Jews, we think it appropriate to recount summarily the origins and customs of this peo-ple from their beginnings. Long ago in Egypt, a plague struck. The rabble thought the cause of this trouble was divine, the cause being the many for-eigners who lived among them and practiced different rituals and sacrifi-cial rites. As a result, the native Egyptian gods were not receiving their due. 2. And so, the native Egyptians decided that they would not be free of their

---

219. In the area around what would be called Jerusalem. The city did not exist when the exiles arrived.

220. Antiochus IV (c.215–164 BCE). This is the Antiochus portrayed so negatively in Maccabees 1–3.

troubles until those foreigners went elsewhere. Straightaway, the foreigners were banished. Their most prominent and energetic men, notable and exceedingly exceptional leaders such as Cadmus and Danaus, so the story goes, united and were storm-tossed to Greece and certain other lands. The majority of the host was shipwrecked upon a land called Judea, not too far from Egypt and at that time an unpeopled land. 3. A man called Moses led the colony, a man renowned for both courage and wisdom. After he seized the land, he founded, among other cities, a city called Jerusalem that is now considered exceptional among cities. He founded as well the temple that they honor most. He introduced the honors and holy rites of their god and established laws and organized their constitution. He divided the people into twelve tribes, because this number was considered the most perfect and in harmony with the number of months in a year.

40.3.4. Moses did not build any statues of their god whatsoever since he did not think that god had a human form. Instead, he thought that only the heavens surrounding the earth were the god who ruled over all. Moses established sacrifices different from those of other peoples. He also established rules for living that differed. For, on account of their exile, he introduced misanthropic and antisocial practices. Choosing the most influential and most capable men to govern the people, he appointed them as priests and arranged that they would pass their time tending to the temple and the honors and sacrifices of the god. 5. He appointed these men also as judges of the most important trials and turned over guardianship of the laws and customs to them. On account of the priests, there has never been a king among the Judeans,[221] and power over the people is granted to the one among the priests who seems to exceed the others in wisdom and excellence. They call this man the high priest and think that he is the messenger of god, delivering god's commands to them. 6. They say that this priest pronounced what had been commanded during assemblies and other meetings. The Jews were so ready to obey for their part that they fell to their knees on the spot and made obeisance to the high priest as he uttered the commands. It is even written at the end of their laws that Moses heard god say these words for the Jews. The lawgiver paid a great deal of attention to military matters and compelled the young men to practice courage, patience, and endurance in the face of misfortune in general. 7. He also made military expeditions against neighboring peoples. He acquired much land in this way and divvied it out in parcels both to private citizens in equal allotments, and in larger allotments to the priests so that, having acquired ample enough incomes, the people could devote themselves to the worship of their god without the distractions of work. It was not permitted for private citizens to sell their private plots in order to avoid some people

---

221. This notion, of course, is countered by the accounts of the kings in the Hebrew Bible. It suggests that the Greeks were unaware of the text. Hecataeus would not have known since it was not translated into Greek until at least the 2nd century BCE, nor should we expect Diodorus to have access to it in the 1st century BCE.

purchasing those plots out of greed, which would result in an oppressed poor and a scarcity of manpower.[222]

40.3.8. Moses compelled those living on the land to raise their offspring.[223] Because rearing children was inexpensive, the Jewish race was always numerous. He established customs concerning marriage and the burial of the dead that were very different from those of other men. When the Jews were later subject first to the Persian Empire and then the Macedonians who had conquered the Persians, many of the ancestral customs of the Jews were changed—a result of their mingling with foreign peoples. Hecataeus of Abdera has recounted these things about the Jews.

3. Cicero, *On Behalf of Flaccus* 67–69 (1st century BCE). *Cicero represents the Jews as a seditious and generally venal people with repulsive religious practices. (MLG)*

67. Since it was customary for gold to be transported yearly in the name of the Jews from Italy and all our provinces to Jerusalem, Flaccus issued an edict to the effect that gold was not to be exported to Asia. Is there anyone, judges, who could not truly praise this act? Not only has the Senate often resolved that gold ought not be exported, but the weightiest resolution to that effect was passed when I was consul. Moreover, it was an act of high seriousness to resist this barbarian superstition, and it was an act of the highest dignity to show disdain on behalf of the state for the mass of the Jews who often disturbed the assemblies. It is true [as the prosecution points out] that Gnaeus Pompey took no spoils from that temple when he captured Jerusalem.

68. First, as in much else, Pompey acted wisely. In so suspicious and slanderous a state, he left no space for the complaints of detractors. I do not believe, of course, that the religious beliefs of the Jews and our enemies was any sort of an impediment to so outstanding a general. It was, rather, propriety. Where is the crime, then? You do not even allege a theft, you approve the edict, you admit it was correctly established, you do not deny it was proposed and passed openly. The very matter itself reveals that it was done by men of the first rank. Nearly a hundred pounds of openly-seized gold was placed before the feet of the praetor in the forum at Apamea by Sextus Caesius, a Roman knight of the greatest moral integrity. A little more than twenty pounds was taken at Laodicea by this Lucius Pedeucaeus here, one of our judges. A hundred was taken at Adramytium by the legate Gnaeus Domitius, and a small amount at Pergamum.

69. There is agreement about the accounting of the gold. The gold is in the treasury. No theft is alleged. They are seeking only to arouse hostility. A

---

222. Note the similarities to the Spartan land distribution under Lycurgus, a connection some ancient authors took to mean they were related.

223. Meaning they were not permitted to expose any infants they did not want.

speaker turns from the judges and lets his voice pour out over the assembled audience. Each state has its own religious beliefs, Laelius, just as we have ours. Even when Jerusalem was standing and the Jews were pacified, still the glory of our empire, the dignity of our name, and the traditions of our ancestors recoiled at the religious practices of such men. But now even more, because that tribe revealed their opinion of our empire when they revolted. The failed revolt revealed how dear they were to the immortal gods since they were conquered, since they became subject to taxation by our tax farmers, and since they were enslaved.

4. Philo of Alexandria, *On Special Laws* 1.1.2–3 (1st century CE).
Philo discusses the virtues of circumcision. (MLG)

1.1.2. I shall begin from the practice that has been mocked by many: the circumcision of the reproductive organs. It is a practice of the highest seriousness among other peoples but most of all among the Egyptians, a people with the highest reputation for being populous, for their antiquity, and for their philosophy. [3] Therefore it would be more fitting to leave off childish mockery and to investigate thoughtfully and solemnly the reasons for this custom's power. People should not jump to condemn great peoples for sinful dissolution. They should consider the likelihood that the many thousands, generation after generation, who have practiced circumcision, painfully and agonizingly submitting their own bodies and the bodies of their closest family to surgery, had many and good reasons to preserve and follow this ancient practice.

5. Philo of Alexandria, *On the Virtues* 134–141 (1st century CE).
*Philo here defends some of the laws of the Jews as handed down by Moses.
(MLG)*

134. Since he wished to sow in their minds seeds of gentleness and fairness in various forms, he established another edict similar to those previously mentioned. He forbade the sacrifice of mother and child on the same day.[224] If a sacrifice must be made, then they are to take place at different times at least. This is because it is exceedingly savage to kill on the same day the source of birth and the one born. 135. Why is this slaughter of mother and child done? Either because of the type of sacrifice or to satisfy the belly. And so if it is done because of the type of sacrifice, then the term is false: it is slaughter not sacrifice. Come now! What altar of a god will accept such impious rites? What fire would not split itself in two in order to escape the union of two things that should not be mixed? I think that the flame would not last even for the shortest moment, but would immediately sputter out

---

224. Not a human mother and child but animal. Leviticus 22.28: "And whether it be cow, or ewe, ye shall not kill it and her young both in one day" (King James).

because of some providence for not allowing the air and the holiest nature of breath to be defiled by rising flame. 136. If the object is not the sacrifice but the following feast, who would not reject these strange and deviant yearnings for unnatural gluttony? Such men pursue unusual pleasures. But what pleasure is it for men eating meat to taste in the same bite the flesh of mother and child? If someone should desire to mix the limbs of mother and child and put them on spits in order to feast on the roasted flesh, I do not think the limbs would remain silent, but they would let loose their voice and complain indignantly of the monstrous novelty and would vociferously abuse the gluttony of those who load their table with a forbidden feast.

137. But the law also forbids from sacred areas all pregnant animals, not allowing them to be sacrificed until they have given birth, reasoning that the contents of the womb are equal to those already born. This is not because what has yet to come out into the light has obtained an equal rank, but to suggest a means of curbing the depraved habit of jumbling everything together. 138. If the life that grows like a plant and is considered part of the mother (still a single being but in the space of months to be separated from this shared life) is to be defended by the protected status of the mother and through its expectation of becoming life and for the sake of avoiding the defilement mentioned above, then how much more so in the case of those already born and endowed with soul and body? For it is the most impious act of all to kill mother and child together on one occasion and on a single day. 139. From this, I believe, some lawgivers have established a law in reference to condemned women that requires pregnant women who have committed offenses worthy of death to be held in custody until they give birth. This is so that the products of their womb not be destroyed along with them.

140. These lawgivers understand these principles for men, but Moses went even farther and extended the principle of justice even to mute beasts, so that by practicing on different species we might employ a much greater abundance of human kindness <even for our own species> and restrain ourselves from causing harm and retaliation. We would not hoard our personal goods but bring them out into the center for everyone everywhere as if for kinsmen and natural brothers. 141. And so let the clever calumniators abuse the people as misanthropic; let them condemn the laws as if they urged unsociable behavior, since the laws so obviously enjoin pity on flocks of animals, and through the guidance of the laws our people adapts any disobedience in our souls to docility.

6. Philo of Alexandria, *Apology for the Jews* (1st century CE).
Philo's Apology *appears in Eusebius (P.E. 8.6.1–5) as part of a discussion of who the Jews were and how their laws were established. Unlike a number of ancient sources, neither Philo nor Eusebius consider the Jews Egyptian in origin. (MLG)*

Eusebius: Come, then, let us examine from the most prominent of their authors the charter established by Moses' laws. I shall start with Philo's discourse on the exodus of the Jews from Egypt, which was accomplished under the leadership of Moses. I will quote from the first writings entitled "hypothetica," where he speaks about the Jews as if defending them in court.

8.6.1. Their ancient ancestor came from the Chaldeans, but the people who had moved from Syria long ago later moved from Egypt when the population swelled to indescribable numbers and the land was insufficient. In addition, they had been raised from a young age for great courage; at the same time, God revealed the exodus to them by visions and dreams. Most of all they had an inspired desire for obtaining their ancient fatherland. It was from there, of course, that this ancestor had migrated to Egypt, either inspired by god or by his own foresight. They prospered so greatly there that from then until the present this people has existed there and remained very populous. [2] Shortly later Philo says: The man who led them in their exodus and journey was no different from any other man. Thus some even abused him as a charlatan and swindler. A fine swindle that! With it his whole people—beset by thirst, by hunger, by ignorance of the route, and by general lack—were preserved as if they had a great abundance of supplies and trading opportunities with neighboring peoples. It also allowed him to protect them from internal strife and maintain their loyalty. [3] He accomplished these things not for a short time but for longer than one expects a well-off family to remain harmonious. Neither thirst, nor hunger, nor bodily deterioration, nor fear for the future, nor ignorance of what was to come roused the deceived and destitute peoples against this swindler. [4] Why do you think this was the case? Shall we claim that this man had such skill, such power of persuasion or intelligence that he naturally overcame so many and such strange events, events that could bring destruction to all? Or was it the case that the nature of the people under his authority were not without learning and not troublesome, but obedient and prepared for the things to come? Or were they themselves wicked, but God softened their disorderliness as if established over their present and future state? Whichever of these explanations you believe to be the truth, it appears to be a powerful source of praise, honor, and admiration for all of them. [5] These are the facts about the exodus.

7. Philo of Alexandria, *Against Flaccus* 53–57 (1st century CE).
Philo reports on anti-Jewish riots that took place in Alexandria in 38 CE when Aulus Avilius Flaccus[225] was the Roman prefect of Egypt. (MLG)

53. Even after Flaccus seized our synagogues without even leaving them their name, he saw that his campaign against our customs was progressing well. He then turned to another plan: the removal of our citizens' rights. After he cut off the customs of our fathers and our participation in political rights, the only safe harbors of our life, his aim was for us to undergo

---

225. This Flaccus is not the same figure as in Cicero's speech.

this final misfortune, leaving us without a safety net. 54. A few days later, he made a proclamation in which he branded us foreign aliens and immigrants, unable to speak in our defense, but subject to immediate condemnation. What greater sign of tyranny could there be? He himself became everything: accuser, enemy, witness, judge, punisher. To these two previous acts he added a third: he permitted the enemies of the Jews to rob them as if sacking a city. 55. What did those who took this opportunity do? There are five districts in the city, two of which are called Jewish because the majority of Jews live in them. No small number of Jews are scattered around the rest of the districts. What then did these enemies do? They expelled the Jews from four districts and herded them into the smallest part of a single district. 56. The Jews were robbed of their property and, due to their numbers, spilled out of the city onto the beaches and the garbage dumps and the tombs. The empty Jewish houses were overrun and pillaged by their enemies, who then distributed the goods like spoils of war. No one stopped them as they stole as much as they could find in the workshops of the Jews, which had been closed for the mourning of Drusilla.[226] There was much to plunder, and they carried it through the center of the marketplace, treating other people's property as their own. 57. Even more burdensome than this theft was the lack of employment that followed. The suppliers lost their merchandise and no one—no farmer, ship-owner, merchant, artisan—was permitted to practice his accustomed business. These two causes resulted in poverty. The theft stripped the Jews of their property in a single day, and they were no longer able to make a living from their customary professions.

8. Strabo, *Geography* 16.2.35–37 (1st century BCE/1st century CE).
In his geography of the Near East, Strabo pauses to discuss the province of the Judeans, describing it through a discussion of their lawgiver, Moses. (RFK)

16.2.35. Moses, who was an Egyptian priest, held a portion of what is called Lower Egypt, but he left there and came here [Judea], since he was unhappy with the state of things in Egypt. Many people who honored his god went with him. For Moses said and taught that the Egyptians were not thinking rightly or properly when they represented god in the forms of wild animals and cattle, nor the Libyans. He said further that the Greeks were also incorrect to represent god as human. God should be this one thing only: a being that surrounds us and the sea and earth, all of it, which we call the heavens and the universe and the nature of all that is. Indeed, since god is thus, who would have the courage of mind to make an image of god similar to anything around us? Instead, we should abandon image-making entirely and establish a sacred precinct and famous shrine to honor

---

226. Julia Drusilla, great-granddaughter of the emperor Augustus and sister of the emperor Caligula. She died on June 10, 38 CE.

him without images. Also, those who experience auspicious dreams ought to sleep in the temple, both for their own sake and for the sake of others. Further, those who live a life of moderation and justness should always expect nobility and always a gift and a sign from god, while others should expect no such things.

16.2.36. Therefore, by saying such things, Moses persuaded not a few well-minded men to join him, and he led them to this place, where the city of Jerusalem now is. He occupied the land quite easily; it is not an enviable land, nor one that anyone would fight for in earnest. For it is rocky, and though well-watered itself, it is surrounded by barren and dry lands. The area within the city, about seven miles square, is also rocky. At the same time, Moses designated that sacred and divine activities would take the place of weapons. He deemed it worthwhile to seek a sacred space for god and promised to provide some sort of worship and ritual practice that would involve little inconvenience by way of money, ecstatic worship, or unusual rituals. Moses was, therefore, held in high repute by the people and, as a result of his personal interactions with them and what he offered to them, was able to establish an unusual type of rule.

16.2.37. Those who succeeded Moses continued in these habits and acted justly and revered god for a time. But later, when superstitious men first were established in the priesthood (tyrannical men), from their superstition emerged the rejection of meat, which even now they practice, as well as circumcision and excision,[227] and other practices such as these. Also, brigandage emerged from these tyrannical practices. Revolutionaries harried the land, both their own and their neighbors, while supporters of the rulers seized upon the property of others and even subdued Syria and much of Phoenicia. Nevertheless, some men behaved decently when it came to their acropolis.[228] They did not connect it to the tyranny, but revered it and worshipped it as holy.

9. Horace, *Satires* 1.4.138–143 (1st century BCE). *Horace comments on a commonplace that Jews in Rome were proselytizers. (MLG)*

Whenever I have any free time, I play around with writing. This fault is one of the lighter faults I was mentioning, but if you should be unwilling to allow me this, the giant crowd of poets would come to bring me aid (for we are very numerous), and like the Jews, we will force you to come over to our side.

---

227. This is likely referring to female circumcision, but the term is also used to refer to castration.
228. The Temple Mount.

10. Petronius, *Carmina* 50 (1st century CE). *A poem attributed to the novelist Petronius mocks the Jews for their dietary restrictions and the Sabbath.*[229] (MLG)

Although a Jew worships his divine pork-head, although he calls upon heaven's highest little ears, unless he trims the boundary of his groin with iron, unless he artfully releases his wrapped up glans, he will be removed from his people, must emigrate from home, and will break the Sabbath with illegal meals.[230]

11. Josephus, *Jewish Antiquities* 14.213–217, 14.223–227 (1st century CE). *Josephus seeks to establish the facts of Jewish goodwill toward other nations and the benefits they have received in return. He does not have access to decrees from either the Persians or Macedonians who had earlier subjected the Jews, but he provides copies of a number of decrees, publically displayed, regarding the friendship and privileges of the Jews under the Romans. (RFK)*

14.213. "Julius Gaius, general and praetor of the Romans, sends greeting to the leaders, assembly, and people of the Parians. The Jewish people in Delos and in surrounding areas, while your ambassadors were present, met with me and declared that you have passed a law to prevent them from following the customs and sacred laws of their ancestors. 214. It displeases me that such laws are affecting our friends and allies and that they are prevented from living according to their customs and from gathering for common meals or sacred rites there when they are not prevented from doing so even in Rome. 215. For even when Gaius Caesar, our general and consul, by his decree prevented the Bacchic revelers from gathering in the city, he did not prevent these people alone from gathering together their goods and sharing their common meals. 216. Likewise, while I prevent other such revelers, I permit these people alone to gather according to their ancestral customs and laws and to hold their feasts. Therefore, you would do well to invalidate any decree you may have made concerning our friends and allies on account of their goodwill and excellence toward us."

14.217. After Gaius' death, when Marcus Antonius and Publius Dolabella were consuls, they called the Senate together and presented the ambassadors of Hyrcanus. They discussed what they thought worthwhile and then

---

229. See Plutarch, this chapter, Selection 19.

230. The text of this line is disputed; the translation captures the sense rather than the literal wording: "he will press down the Sabbath with a non-dry law." According to Courtney ad loc., "Pagan literature regularly but wrongly asserted that the Sabbath was a fast day (Justin 36.2.14 and probably also Strabo 16.2.40.763, Martial. 4.4.7). Shackleton Bailey changes *non* to *nos*, which makes the speaker an observant Jew.

made a "friend of Rome" agreement with the Jews. The Senate then decreed everything to them that they had asked for.

. . .

14.223. Hyrcanus also sent one of his ambassadors to Dolabella, now the governor of Asia, and called upon him to release the Jewish people from military service and to permit them to observe in Asia their ancestral customs and live according to their way of life. 224. This was granted them readily. Dolabella, when he received Hyrcanus' letter, wrote a letter concerning the Jews, without deliberation, to all of Asia, but to Ephesus in particular, the premier city in Asia. The letter is as follows:

14.225. "In the prytany of Artemon, on the first of Lenaion, Dolabella, imperator, sends greetings to the leaders of the Ephesians and the assembly and the people. 226. Alexander, son of Theodorus, ambassador of Hyrcanus, the son of Alexander and the high priest and *ethnarch* of the Jews, discussed with me the inability of the Jewish people to serve in the military since they are unable to bear arms or travel on Sabbath days. Further, they are unable to provide for themselves while on campaign the food their ancestral customs decree for the Sabbath. 227. Therefore, I grant to them, as previous governors have done, release from military service, and I permit them to follow their ancestral customs. I grant them also the right to gather for the sake of their sacred rites in accordance with their laws. I further permit them to take away from sacrifices the choice parts. I want you to write these words to the cities."[231]

12. Tacitus, *Histories* 5.1–5, 5.8 (2nd century CE). *Perhaps the most famous (and influential) discussion of the history of the Jews by an ancient author, Tacitus introduces his history of the year of the four emperors (69 CE) with Vespasian and Titus' war in Jerusalem. (CSR)*

5.1. In the beginning of that same year Titus Caesar, who had been chosen by his father to conquer Judaea and who was famous for his military service when both were still private citizens, was advancing to greater power and fame at that time because of the competition of the provinces and the eagerness of the armies. And Titus, so that he might be thought to exceed his lot in life, was constantly demonstrating his elegance and readiness in war. By his friendliness and encouragement he summoned obedience and work ethic, and mingled in the lines with the common soldiers while not diminishing his dignity as general. Three legions greeted him in Judaea, the fifth, the tenth, and the fifteenth, the old soldiery of Vespasian. He added the twelfth from Syria as well as men from the eighteenth and the third taken out of Alexandria. Twenty cohorts of allied forces accompanied

---

231. Presumably, the Ephesians were to disseminate the decree of Dolabella to the cities under their jurisdiction.

him, and eight divisions of cavalry, and at the same time the kings Agrippa and Sohaemus and the auxiliary troops of King Antiochus and a strong band of Arabs made hostile to the Jews from the hatred common between neighbors, and many people summoned from the city and Italy itself who hoped to catch the eye of the still uncommitted leader. With these troops he entered the borders of the enemy with a well-arranged battle line, exploring everything and prepared to fight. He made camp not far from Jerusalem.

5.2. But since we are about to tell of the last day of a famous city, it seems right to lay bare its beginnings. Some recall that the Jews, having fled from Crete, settled the furthest part of Libya at the time when Saturn ceded his kingdom in defeat at the hands of Jupiter. The evidence for this origin is provided by a name: there is a famous mountain in Crete, Ida, and the inhabitants of it were called Idaeans until the name was lengthened in barbarian fashion and they were called J(I)udaeans. Some others say that while Isis was reigning, the overflowing numbers in Egypt were removed by the leaders Hierosolymo [Jerusalem] and Judas into neighboring lands. Many others say that they are the offspring of Ethiopia, whom fear and hatred drove to migrate when Cepheus was king. There are those who consign them to being Assyrian refugees, a people lacking in lands, who gained possession of a part of Egypt and soon colonized several cities in Hebrew lands and the part nearer to Syria. Others give a famous beginning to the Jews, that they are the Solymi, a race celebrated in the songs of Homer, and they named the city they founded Jerusalem after their own name.

5.3. Most authors agree that once there was a disease that defiled the body that arose throughout Egypt, and that the King Bocchoris, in seeking a cure, consulted the oracle of Ammon and was ordered to cleanse the kingdom and take this race of men hated by the gods into other lands. Thus the people were sought out, collected together, and then left in an empty place. While everyone else was paralyzed by tears, Moses, one of the exiles, warned them not to look for help from gods or men since they had been deserted by both, but to entrust themselves to a heavenly leader, with whose help they might beat back their present miseries. They agreed and began their random wandering, ignorant of everything. Nothing tired them out so much as their lack of water, and already, not at all far from death, they collapsed upon the plains. Suddenly, a herd of wild asses retreated from their pasture to a rock made shady by a grove of trees. Moses followed them suspecting that he would find a grassy spot and, indeed, found a large spring of water. This was a relief. Having measured out a continuous journey of six days, on the seventh they got hold of some lands after pushing out the inhabitants, in which lands a city and a temple were dedicated.

5.4. Moses, so that he might affirm his position over the people in the future, brought in new rites that were different from those of other people. Everything that is profane there is sacred among us, and what is allowed among them is forbidden to us. They consecrated in their inner temple an image of the animal whose appearance drove away their wandering and thirst. They sacrifice a ram as if in reproach to Ammon and a cow because the Egyptians worship Apis. They abstain from pig in memory of their misfortunes, because they once were infected with the mange to which this animal is liable. They acknowledge their great famine long ago with frequent fasts, and the Jewish bread with no yeast is retained as a reminder of the fruits they stole. They say that rest is approved on the seventh day, because this day brought the end of their labors, and then because the rest was pleasing the seventh year was also given to idleness. Others say that the seventh year is kept in honor of Saturn, either from the origins of their religion handed down by the Idaeans (whom along with Saturn we believe were driven out and became founders of the Jewish race), or because among the seven ruling stars, the star of Saturn has the highest orbit and has the greatest power, and most of the heavenly bodies cross the heavens in numerals of seven.

5.5. These rites, in whatever way they were introduced, are defended by their antiquity. Other of their rites are unfavorable and greatly defiled as a result of their depravity. For each of the worst races, having scorned their fathers' religions, brought tribute and gifts to them, whence the affairs of the Jews were increased. Because their faith is fixed among themselves and tenderhearted in public but includes hostile hatred against all others, they remain separate from others at meals and keep their bedrooms separate. Their race is most likely to throw themselves into lust. And, though they abstain from cohabitation with foreign women, among themselves nothing is forbidden. They instituted the circumcision of their genitalia so that they would be recognized by their difference. Those who cross over into their religion practice the same thing, and they take in no one until they learn to condemn gods, reject their homeland, and hold their parents, children, and brothers of little value. Nevertheless, there is care for the increase of their numbers; for it is wrong to kill anyone at birth, and they think that the souls of those taken in battle or as suppliants are immortal. From this belief comes a love of ancestry and contempt of death. They bury bodies rather than cremate them, a practice derived from the Egyptian custom, and they have the same practices and beliefs about the underworld, though they think opposite the Egyptians about the divine. The Egyptians venerate many animals and composite images. The Jews comprehend divinity intellectually as a single being, while they consider profane those who fashion images of the gods in the likeness of men from mortal materials. They believe their god is supreme and eternal and neither imitable nor perishable. Therefore no statues stand in their cities nor even in their temples. This type of fawning is also not granted to their kings, nor is this type of honor granted to our Caesars. Because their priests make music with flute and cymbals and are crowned with ivy and a golden vine found in the temple, some think that they worship father

...ne tamer of the East, although with not at all congruent prac-
...ces. Dionysus established festive and happy rites, and the religion of
the Jews is harsh and dirty.

Tacitus describes the land of Judaea.

5.8. A great part of Judaea is scattered with villages. They also have towns.
Jerusalem is the capital of the people. A temple of great wealth stood
there. First was the city with fortifications, then the palace, and then the
temple enclosed within. The approach to the gates is only for a Jew, and
everyone except the priests are kept from the threshold. While the East
was under the power of the Assyrians, Medes, and then Persians, the
Jews were the most scorned of their slaves. After the Macedonians came
to power, King Antiochus tried to end their superstition and give them
Greek customs, in an attempt to change this most vile race into a better one, but he was prevented from following through by the war with
the Parthians. This was when Arsaces had revolted. Then the Jews chose
kings for themselves since the Macedonians were weak, the Parthians not
yet fully powerful, and the Romans were still far away. These kings were
expelled by the fickleness of the people, but, with their power restored
through recourse to arms, they dared to banish their citizens, overthrow
their cities (murdering brothers, wives, and parents in the process), and
do other such things accustomed by kings. They nurtured the superstition, because they took up the offices of the priests themselves as an affir-
mation of their power.

13. Juvenal, *Satires* 3.10–21[232] (2nd century CE). *Juvenal describes
his friend Umbricius on the day of his departure from Rome. Rome has
become too corrupt and foreign for Umbricius. (MLG)*

While all his possessions were being loaded onto a single cart, he
stopped at the old arch of the damp Porta Capena. We walked down into
the valley of Egeria with its artificial caves. How much more productive
of religious awe for the water spirit would this place be if green grass
encircled the waters and marble did not violate the natural tufa stone!
This is the land where Numa used to tryst with his nighttime girlfriend,
but now this grove with its sacred fountain and shrine is leased out to
Jews with their basket and hay chest. Every tree, of course, is forced to
pay its tax to these people, and the forest throws out its Italian muses
and goes a-begging.

---

232. The ordering of the text is disputed. The translation follows the order of the text
in Braund's translation and orders the lines 10–11, 17–21, 12–16.

14. Juvenal, *Satires* 6.542–547 (2nd century CE). *Juvenal comments on both the proselytizing stereotype of the Jews and their associations with money. (MLG)*

After the Egyptian priest leaves your wife's side, a trembling Jewish woman puts aside her hay and basket to beg at your wife's private ear. She is an expounder of the laws of Jerusalem and a great priestess of the tree,[233] a faithful intermediary of highest heaven. She also fills her hands with cash, but more modestly: the Jews sell dreams of anything you want for the smallest penny.

15. Juvenal, *Satires* 8.155–162 (2nd century CE). *Juvenal's satire on nobility points out the differences between public persona and private behavior. This passage describes a certain Lateranus, whom Juvenal calls a mule-driver consul. (MLG)*

In the meantime, while he sacrifices sheep and a strong ox in the fashion of Numa, he swears before the altar of Jupiter by Epona alone and the faces painted in stinky stables. But, when he decides to celebrate again his all-night bar crawl, a Syrian Jew [*Syrophoenix*], dripping with perfume, runs to meet him. This inhabitant of the Idumaean gate greets him in the manner of a host with the title "my lord and master," with a flagon, and with a blue-eyed prostitute with her skirts lifted.

16. Juvenal, *Satires* 14.96–106 (2nd century CE). *Examples of parents careless of their children's moral education. (MLG)*

Some children get a Sabbath-fearing father. These kids worship nothing but clouds and the divinity of the sky. They think pork, which their father would not eat, no different than human flesh. Soon they even give up their foreskin. Moreover, they are accustomed to despise Roman laws. They learn the Jewish code, preserve, and reverence whatever the secret book of Moses hands down. It enjoins them not to show their way except to fellow worshippers, to take only the circumcised to the desired fountain. But blame the father, who held the seventh day to be a day of laziness and untouched by any part of life.

---

233. The text of Juvenal reads "tree," but perhaps some word for "temple" would make more sense (Courtney, ad loc.). Or, the "tree" refers to the grove referred to in *Satire* 3.

17. Martial, *Epigrams* 11.94 (2nd century CE). *Martial mocks his rival (both in poetry and in love) by referring to the most distinctive feature of the Jews of antiquity, circumcision. (MLG)*

I forgive the fact that you are quite envious and are everywhere mocking my books. You have taste, circumcised poet. So, I also do not care about you stealing from my poems at the same time as you criticize them. Even in this, circumcised poet, you have taste. This is what is driving me insane: You, circumcised poet, born in Jerusalem itself, are fucking my boyfriend. Look at you deny it and swear to me by the temple of thundering Jupiter. I don't buy it. Swear, circumcised guy, by Anchialus.[234]

18. Plutarch, *On Superstition* 169c8–10 (2nd century CE). *Plutarch discusses the strange custom of the Sabbath kept by the Jews. (RFK)*

For god is an impetus to virtue, not an excuse for cowardice. But the Jews, on their Sabbath, even though the enemy had thrown up scaling ladders and had seized the walls, sat down and remained in place as if bound within a single net by their superstition.

19. Plutarch, *Dinner Conversations* 669f–670a, 670d–f, 671c–672c (2nd century CE). *Over dinner, Callistratus, Polycrates, and Lamprias discuss whether the Jews abstain from pork because they revere pigs or loathe them. This is followed by a discussion led by Symmachus and Moeragenes over who exactly the god of the Jews is. (RFK)*

669f. When he had finished these remarks and when it was clear that some wanted to make extended counterarguments, Callistratus evaded another such long speech by interjecting, "What are your thoughts on what is said about the Jews, that they don't eat the meat most appropriate for eating [i.e., pork]?" "I agree with it very much," said Polycrates, "and I raise a further question: Do these men refrain from eating it because they revere pigs or because they loathe the creature? For what they themselves say about it seems like a myth, unless they have some serious reasons they keep from others."

"Well, as I see it," said Callistratus, "the creature must have some place of honor among them. 670a. Certainly, the pig is ugly and filthy, but its appearance is no more strange that that of the dung-beetle, the vulture, crocodiles, or cats, nor is its nature more crude. And yet, each is considered sacred by some group of Egyptian priests or another. They say that the pig is honored for practical reasons, since, so they say, the pig was the first creature to split the earth with its protruding snout and make furrows in the

234. Possibly a well-known, wealthy Roman Jew or a corruption of Archelaus, son of Herod the Great and a ruler of Judea.

earth. This action of the pig introduced the idea of plowing, whence also comes the name for the ploughshare, *hunis*. . . ."[235]

Callistratus mentions numerous other animals revered or loathed by the Egyptians, the Pythagoreans, and the Magi of Persia as support for his logic concerning Jews and pigs.

670d. "I think, then, that Jews, if they were repulsed at the idea of eating pigs, would kill them, just as the Magi kill mice. But now, it is just as forbidden for Jews to destroy a pig as it is to eat one. Perhaps the logic holds that, since they honor the ass, who first showed them sources of water, [e] thus they also revere the pig who taught them about sowing and plowing. Otherwise, by Zeus, someone could say that the Jews refrain from hare as well because they are unable to endure a dirty and unclean creature."

"No, clearly," said Lamprias, taking up the point, "they refrain from hare because of its particular resemblance to the ass, which they honor. For the hare seems to be a lesser ass in both stature and weight. The skin and ears, the shining eyes, and the gluttony of the hare and ass are like each other's in amazing ways. Nothing small has ever resembled something big so much as the hare does the ass. By Zeus, furthermore, speaking as an Egyptian would, they consider as divine the swiftness of the creature and the sharpness of its senses. [f] Its eyes are indefatigable, so much so that it sleeps with them in the open. It seems also to surpass other creatures in the sharpness of its hearing, which the Egyptians marvel at so much they use the hare's ears as the symbol in their sacred writing [*hieroglyphs*] for 'hearing.'

"The Jews, however, seem to consider the pig's skin an abomination. Barbarians more than any other peoples hate whiteness of the skin or leprosy and think that such diseases contaminate humans through contact. . . . "

Lamprias continues to describe the pig's normal skin condition, fondness for dirt, tendency to squeal, and lack of keen eyesight as further causes for Jewish dislike of the creature. They are not animals, he says, to be admired like the hare. During further discussion, Dionysus is mentioned, and Symmachus questions Lamprias about a connection he seems to make between Dionysus and the god of the Jews.

671c. Marveling, then, at the flow of the conversation, Symmachus said, "Lamprias, are you including your homeland god Dionysus, flush with his orgiastic, maenadic honors, and linking him with the unspeakable rites of the Hebrews? Is there some story that demonstrates that the god of the Jews is the same as Dionysus?" Interrupting, Moeragenes said, "Look here. I'm an Athenian and I will answer this. I assert that Dionysus and the god of the Jews are one and the same. Many of the proofs of this, however, are spoken and [d] taught only to those who have been initiated into the great mysteries by us. What I say now, though, is not forbidden among friends,

---

235. Callistratus derives it from the Greek for pig, *hus*.

especially while we are enjoying wine, the gift of the god. If you urge me, I am ready to speak."

Everyone urged him on, begging him to speak. "First then," he said, "of the greatest and most important festival of the Jews, the right time and customs are associated with Dionysus. For when they conduct what is called the 'fast' at the peak of harvest time, they lay out tables and fruits of every kind under tents and huts woven mostly from twigs and ivy.[236] They call the first feast the 'feast of booths.' [e] A few days later, they conduct another feast, called explicitly, not secretly, the feast of Bacchus. This feast involves carrying fig branches and the thyrsus in a procession to the temple. What they do once they enter the temple we don't know, but it is likely a Bacchic ritual since they use small war-trumpets, as the Argives do for Dionysus, to call upon their god. Others play the kithara in the procession. These men are referred to as Levites, deriving either from Lysios [Releaser] or, more likely, Euion.[237]

671f. "I also think that the Sabbath celebration is not altogether unconnected from the worship of Dionysus. For even now many call the Bacchantes 'Sabi,' and they utter this cry whenever they are in the throws of their orgiastic celebration with the god.[238] Confirmation of this is, of course, found in Demosthenes and Menander. Someone would not be wrong to assign the name to a certain type of excitement, which takes hold of those celebrating the mysteries. 672a. The Jews themselves bear witness to what I say— whenever they keep the Sabbath, they are especially likely to invite others to drink with them and indulge in wine. Even when there is something more important to be done that prevents this, they generally, at least, make sure to sip some unmixed wine. Someone might say that these things are only 'likely,' but the high priest himself puts naysayers forcefully to shame when he leads the processions of Jewish festivals wearing a mitre and clad in a gold-threaded fawn-skin. His robe reaches to his feet and he wears high boots. [b] Many bells hang upon his clothes, and they ring beneath his robe as he walks. This is the same as we do in our worship. They also use noise in their nightly festivals and greet nurses of the god as 'brass-sounding.' The carved thyrsus on the face of the temple and the kettle-drum they use also show similarity. For surely all these things belong to no other god than Dionysus.

"In addition, the Jews do not use honey in their sacred rites, because the honey seems to destroy the wine with which it is mixed. Mead, a honey-wine, was once used as a libation, before the grape vine was revealed to man, reducing the sweetness with winelike roots and bitters. Greeks also pour unmixed and honey-wine offerings, since the natural properties of

---

236. Sukkot, the Feast of Tabernacles, a seven-day festival celebrated typically in mid-October.

237. A false etymology. These are both Greek names for Bacchus. Euion Bacchus refers to the cry worshippers utter as part of their procession.

238. Another false etymology connecting the word "Sabbath" with Dionysus' epithet Sabazios.

honey are considered especially antithetical to wine. [c] Proof that they think this is true (and it is no minor bit of evidence) is the fact that of the numerous forms of punishment among the Jews, one in particular they exact from criminals is that they must abstain from wine during the period the judge names for their punishment. . . . "

> *The text breaks off here, so we are left to wonder the reasons why the abstention of criminals is important, nor do we know what further proofs Moeragenes offers that Dionysus and the god of the Jews are one and the same.*

CHAPTER 12

ASIA: ARABIA

Arabia was a place of wonder for both the Greeks and Romans. Most knowledge of Arabia was filtered through Egyptian and Persian sources, places with extensive trade with the peoples of Arabia. Although the Romans did send at least one expedition into Arabia, it is unclear how far they penetrated the peninsula. Attempts to circumnavigate and map Arabia proved successful. Ptolemy's map (2nd century CE; Map 5) gives a somewhat accurate portrayal of its shape and size.

1. Herodotus, *Histories* 3.107–113 (5th century BCE). *Herodotus describes some of the wonders of Arabia, the source of many of the most exotic and desired spices and fragrances in antiquity. (RFK)*

3.107. Again, Arabia is the furthest south of the inhabited lands, and in this land alone are frankincense, myrrh, cassia, cinnamon, and gum-mastic.[239] All of these except myrrh, the Arabians obtain with some difficulty. [2] They gather frankincense by burning storax,[240] which the Phoenicians export to Greece. They burn the storax first and then take the frankincense, because small, winged serpents, of the many-colored variety, guard frankincense-bearing trees. There are many of these serpents around each tree (these are the same serpents that regularly wage war on Egypt), and they are driven away from the trees by nothing except the storax smoke.

3.108. The Arabians also say that the entire land would be full of these snakes, if what I believe happens among vipers did not also happen among the winged serpents. [2] The god, you see, has great forethought, as is to be expected, and has wisely made it so that all creatures that are cowardly and edible are very prolific so that they not go extinct by being completely consumed. Meanwhile, those creatures that are hardy and troublesome to man, the gods makes them less prolific.

Herodotus proves his point with reference to the hare, a notoriously prolific breeder, and the lioness, which tends to produce smaller numbers of offspring than the rabbit.

---

239. Most likely acacia gum from the sap of the acacia tree. Its sap hardens into a gum that is edible.

240. A type of fragrant sap produced by the storax tree.

3.109. Just so, if vipers and winged serpents among the Arabians were born as is natural among snakes,[241] life would be unlivable for men there. But now, when these particular snakes attempt to reproduce, as soon as the male emits his seed into the female snake, she fastens onto his neck with her teeth and clenches without letting go until she had bitten clean through. [2] The male dies in the way just described, while the female is repaid for killing the male in the following way: avenging their father, the offspring, while still in the womb, eat through their mother, devouring her belly as they make their escape. [3] Other serpents, the kind that are not harmful to humans, lay eggs and hatch a great many offspring. Vipers, of course, live in every land, but the winged serpent lives only in abundance in Arabia and nowhere else. Accordingly, they appear to be numerous.

3.110. The Arabians, then, obtain, frankincense in this way. They obtain cassia in the following manner: when they go out to get cassia, they bind together hides and other skins and cover their entire body and face except for the eyes. Cassia grows in a shallow lake around and in which lodge winged creatures somewhat like a bat. They have a terrible shriek and are brave in their own defense. It is necessary to guard one's eyes from these creatures while culling the cassia.

3.111. Indeed, they collect cinnamon in a still more marvelous manner. For where it comes from and what land produces it, they can't say, except that some say it likely grows in those lands where Dionysus was raised. [2] They say that large birds carry the dry sticks, the ones the Phoenicians (and us through them) call cinnamon, and bear them away to nests they make from mud upon sheer cliffs, where it is impossible for a man to approach. [3] The Arabians solve this problem in a clever way: They cut up into pieces as large as possible dead oxen, cows, and other livestock. They then carry them out to where the birds dwell and lay them near the nests and then withdraw far off. The birds fly down from their nests and grab pieces of the meat to carry back to their nests. The weight of the meat is too great for the nests, and they break up and fall down onto the ground. The Arabians then go out from their hiding place and gather the cinnamon sticks. This is how cinnamon is collected and how it makes its way from one land to another.

3.112. But truly, gum-mastic, which the Arabians call lanadon, comes from the most peculiar source. For it is the most sweet-smelling product, but comes from the most foul-smelling. It is found in the beards of he-goats, appearing there as resin does in a tree. It is useful for many perfumes, and Arabians burn it most frequently for fragrance.

3.113. Let us then speak further of the marvels of Arabia. The smell that arises from Arabia is so sweet it is divine. They also have two types of sheep there worthy of amazement, sheep which exist there and nowhere else. The first type have long tails no less than three or four feet in length. If these sheep were to drag their tails behind them, they would develop wounds on their tails from rubbing on the ground. [2] However, every shepherd

---

241. That is, hatched in large quantities from eggs.

knows enough woodworking to make little wagons. They bind the tails of each individual sheep to its own little wagon. The other type of sheep have wide tails that are about a forearm across.

2. Diodorus Siculus, *The Library of History* 2.49–54 (1st century BCE). *Diodorus, like Herodotus, finds Arabia to be a land of marvels. (MLG)*

2.49. The region of Arabia is so different from the waterless desert on its border that it has been called Arabia Felix because of its bountiful produce of fruits and other good things. [2] The land yields an abundance of the reed, the rush, and other spicy plants. In general, the land yields all sorts of plant-derived fragrances and is renowned for the diverse perfumes derived from distilled sap. The most remote areas, for example, produce myrrh and frankincense, which is most dear to the gods and exported to the whole inhabited world. [3] Fields and thickets of costos, cassia, cinnamon, and the like grow there so profusely that they use as fuel for their cooking the incense others place sparingly on the gods' altars, and they use as stuffing for their servants' mattresses material others have in only tiny amounts. The amazingly useful materials called cinnamon, pine-resin, and terebinth grow everywhere fragrantly. [4] The mountains contain not only abundant silver fir and pine but also abundant cedar and juniper and the tree called borbaton. There are many other aromatic fruit-bearing plants that have sap and odors most pleasant to those who approach. In fact this feature of the land has a certain natural exhalation like sweet incense. [5] For this reason, when they dig in some regions of Arabia, fragrant deposits are found that are mined and create quarries of vast size. Gathering material from these, they build their homes. Whenever raindrops fall from the atmosphere, the moisture melts part of the construction, which flows into the joints between stones. When this congeals it unites and compacts the walls.

2.50. Throughout Arabia there is mining of the so-called fireless gold. This gold is not, as elsewhere, smelted from gold dust, but it is found by digging up nuggets the size of chestnuts. It is so much like a flame in color that when artisans make settings of it for the most precious stones it produces the most beautiful adornments. [2] There is so great a number and variety of creatures throughout the land that the many tribes who choose a nomadic life are able to live well, having no need of grain but being well served by the abundance of the animals. The region bordering Syria produces an abundance of valiant beasts. For indeed, the lions and leopards there are greater in number and size and naturally outstanding in valor compared to those in Libya. In addition, there are the tigers called Babylonian. [3] It also produces animals that are double in nature and mixed in form: For example, the so-called ostrich-camels, who embrace, as the name implies, a mixed type from birds and camels. It is similar in size to a newborn camel, fine hair stands on their heads, their eyes are large and black, indistinguishable in shape and color from camels. [4] It has a long neck and a short, sharp beak. It is feathered with wings covered with soft hair. Standing upon two legs with cloven hoofs, it appears at the same time a land animal and a bird. [5] Unable to take to the air and fly because of its weight, it glides swiftly over the ground and, when pursued by horsemen, it hurls the stones under its feel so forcefully that its pursuers often fall from the severe wounds. [6] Whenever it is surrounded, it hides its head in some brush or such protection. It does not do this, as some think, from stupidity and listlessness of soul, thinking it cannot be seen and captured by others if it does not see them. But considering this part of the body to be the weakest, it shelters it to save itself. [7] Nature, you know, teaches every animal well how to save not only itself but its children, and, by engendering a love of life, she leads the generations through the eternal circle of continuity.

2.51. The so-called camel-leopard[242] is a mixture of the two animals that make up its name. In size it is smaller than a camel and has a longer neck. Its head and the arrangement of eyes have been shaped much like a leopard. Although they have a hump on their backs much like a camel, they resemble the leopard in color and coat. They are like this beast also in the length of the tail. [2] There are also goat-stags and boubali[243] and many other types of bi-form creatures who are composites of vastly different animals. So many, in fact, that it would take long to describe them bit by bit. [3] For clearly, the lands near the south breathe in the greatest force of the sun's life-sustaining power. For this reason the land breeds the many beautiful and multicolored animals. This is why crocodiles and hippopotami are born throughout Egypt, why Ethiopia and the Libyan deserts produce many elephants and reptiles of all kinds and the other wild beasts and the snakes of differing size and spirit, and why there are elephants throughout India of surpassing mass, number, and even of spirit.

2.52. In these lands, not only are animals produced whose forms are completely changed by the sun's collaborative power, but there are also diverse rock formations with multiple colors and shining brilliance. [2] It is said that this rock-crystal is composed from pure water that has been frozen not by cold but by the power of divine fire. This causes it to remain uncorrupted and to be dyed many colors by the vapor of breath. [3] There are emeralds and the so-called Beryllium from the copper mines, which takes on the same color from being dipped and bound in brimstone. There is the chrysolith, which is said to derive and receive its color from the smoky vapor produced by the sun's heat. [4] For this reason it is said to be called pseudo-gold, because it is constructed from a mortal fire, kindled by humans who dip in the rock-crystals. It is said that the nature of the red precious stones derives from the power of the light, and the greater or lesser compression of the light accounts for color differences. [5] It is said that the

---

242. A giraffe.
243. A water buffalo.

shapes of birds similarly receive their colors: some appear completely red, others have diverse colors on different parts. Some are flame red, others yellow. One is emerald green. Many take on a golden hue when facing the sun. In short, there are too many colors to adequately describe them all. A similar phenomenon is seen with rainbows in the sky created by the sun's light. [6] The natural philosophers are said to derive from this their explanation for the appearance of that variety of colors just mentioned: the material is dyed by an innate heat when the sun, life's creator, collaborates in each form. [7] In general, they say that the many colors of flowers and the diverse hues of the earth derive from the sun as cause and creator, whose activity is imitated by mortal artisans when they create their many-colored objects, learning from nature. [8] They say that light produces not only the colors but also the smell of fruits and their characteristic juices and even the size of animals and their forms. In addition to these, the sun's heat produces the characteristics of the earth, heating the fertile earth and productive water, becoming the creator of each substance. [9] For this reason, white Parian marble or other marvelous rocks cannot equal Arabian stones, whose whiteness is the most brilliant, whose weight is greatest, and whose smoothness leaves no space for improvement. The reason that parts of this land have this unique characteristic is, as I have said, the power of the sun. It has hardened the land by heat, compressed it by dryness, and illuminated it with brightness.

2.53. Therefore, the race of birds, since it has the largest share of heat, has become winged on account of the lightness, and it has become many-colored because of the collaboration of the sun, and this is especially true of the regions lying near the sun. [2] For example, Babylonia brings forth a multitude of peacocks who are variously and brightly colored. The farthest reaches of Syria produce parrots, purple coots, guinea-fowls, and other animals showing all sorts of mixed and peculiar colors. [3] The same logic pertains to the other regions of the world that are situated in a similar climate. I mean India and the Red Sea, and also Ethiopia and parts of Libya. [4] But the eastern lands are more fertile and so produce larger and more noble animals. The animals of the rest are always produced following the same logic of excellence in proportion to the local conditions. [5] Trees are similar: the palms throughout Libya produce fruit that is dry and small, but the fruits called *caruoti* produced in Coele-Syria are distinguished for sweetness and size as well as for their juice. [6] Fruits much larger than these can be seen throughout Arabia and Babylonia: in size, they reach six fingers long; in color, some are green and some dark red, and a few are purple. As a result they please the eye and charm the palate. The palm's trunk rises high into the air and is smooth all around up to the top. [7] The foliage on the top differs in shape from tree to tree. Some have fronds that spread out on all sides and fruits like bunches of grapes hanging down in the middle from broken bark. Others have fronds hanging from the top on one side, looking like a lamp that has been kindled. Sometimes the fronds hang down on both sides, and by this double layering of branches with leaves all about produce a picturesque impression.

2.54. Of Arabia as a whole, the southern-facing part is called Felix and the interior is inhabited by many Arab nomads who have chosen a life in tents. These pasture great herds of animals, and their encampments spread out over measureless spaces. [2] The land between this and Arabia Felix is desert and waterless, as has been said. The regions of Arabia stretching to the west are divided by sandy deserts as large as the sky. Those who travel through these deserts must direct their passage like sailors by means of the constellations Ursa Major and Minor. [3] The remaining part of Arabia stretches toward Syria and is full of farmers and merchants, who compensate for the deficiencies of both regions by seasonal trade in goods each has in abundance. [4] The region of Arabia that is next to the ocean is situated above Arabia Felix and is divided by many large rivers. Many regions there have stagnant pools and are largely covered in huge marshes. [5]. By irrigating much land with water from these rivers and from the summer rains, the inhabitants are able to produce two harvests a year. This land nourishes herds of elephants and other monstrous land animals and animals evolved into mixed forms. In addition, the land teems with all types of domestic animals, especially cattle and the sheep with long and thick tails. [6] It nourishes the greatest variety of camel species: the short hair and the shaggy-haired, the so-called double hump for having two bulges growing from the spine. Some provide milk and are eaten, furnishing the inhabitants with abundance of meat. Others are raised as beasts of burden who can carry 540 liters of wheat on their back and can lift five men stretched on a couch. Others, slender in build with short legs, are dromedaries. They can cover a great distance, especially in journeys across the waterless desert. [7] These same animals are used in war, carrying into battle two bowmen seated back to back. One resists enemies in front and the other protects the rear. This concludes my discourse on Arabia and its ecosystem. Even if I have gone on too long, I have nevertheless recorded many facts that lovers of reading will delight to hear.

3. Strabo, *Geography* 16.4.22, 16.4.25–27 (1st century BCE/ 1st century CE). *Strabo describes Arabia in detail—its geography, topography, and people—based directly on the reports from a recent expedition of Aelius Gallus, Prefect of Egypt (26–24 CE). (RFK)*

16.4.22. A very recent expedition by the Romans into Arabia, made during our own lifetime, has taught us much of the peculiar character of the land. Aelius Gallus led the expedition. Augustus Caesar sent him to obtain evidence of the peoples both of this region and of Ethiopia, because Caesar saw that the land of the Troglodytai,[244] the one next to Egypt, also bordered the Arabians, while the Arabian Gulf, which completely divides the Arabians from the Troglodytai, was narrow. Caesar intended either to coexist with

---

244. Although other texts refer to them as Trogodytai, Strabo uses Troglodytai. We assume they are the same peoples.

the Arabians or to subjugate them. Another motivating factor was the eternal report of their great wealth; they sold aromatic herbs and spices as well as costly gems to outsiders for gold and silver, but never spent the wealth they took in with anyone outside their land. Thus, he expected in Arabia either to deal with wealthy friends or to overpower wealthy enemies . . .

. . .

16.4.25. Now, then, they divide the aromatics-producing world into four parts, as we have said. Of the aromatic herbs and spices, they say that frankincense and myrrh come from trees, and cassia comes from shrubs. Some say that the most cassia comes from India, but the best frankincense is from near Persia. According to another division, they split the whole of Arabia Felix into five kingdoms. The first region holds the warriors who fight on behalf of all the others. Another contains farmers who produce the food for all of the people of Arabia. The next region contains the lowly manual laborers, the fourth is the myrrh-producing region, and, finally, the frankincense-producing region. Both of these regions also produce cassia, cinnamon, and spikenard.[245] One does not exchange one occupation for another in Arabia, but each person remains in the occupation of his father. Most of the wine in Arabia is made from palm.

Brothers are more honored than offspring. The descendants of the kings rule according to seniority and control other offices as well. Possessions are common to all kin, and the eldest family member is the head of household. There is one wife for everyone in the household. Whoever enters her room first has sex with her and leaves his staff outside her door (custom dictates that each man carry a staff), but she spends the nights with the eldest. As a result, the children are all brothers. They also have sex with their mothers.[246] Death is the punishment for adulterers, but an adulterer is only someone from a different clan . . .

> Strabo next recounts the story of a king's daughter who tricked her fifteen brothers into leaving her alone by keeping a different staff in front of her door at all times.

16.4.26. The Nabataeans[247] are wise and so skilled in the art of gathering possessions that a public penalty is laid upon anyone who lessens what they have, while honor is paid to those who increase it. They have few slaves and so are served by family members more than by others or themselves. This custom extends even to the kings. They eat in a common mess hall in groups of thirteen men. There are two female singers at each symposium. The king has many symposia in his great hall, but nobody drinks more than eleven cups of wine, each from a different cup. The king is so democratic

---

245. Possibly a type of lavender.

246. These are all male children. There is no mention of the role of female children in the household.

247. A people located on the Arabian peninsula in what is now Jordan.

that he serves not only himself but even at times others as well. Often the king gives a formal accounting of his rule to the people and sometimes even his manner of living is scrutinized. Their homes are expensive because they are made of stone, but their cities are without walls because of peace.

Arabia has many fruits, but no olives. They use sesame instead. The sheep there are white-woolen, the oxen are large, and the land does not support horses. Camels supply the services horses typically render. Nabataeans go outside without tunics. Instead they wear girdles wrapped around their loins and little slippers. Even the king dresses this way, though his girdle is purple. Some items are entirely imported, others not entirely, such as items that are produced locally like gold, silver, and many herbs and spices. But bronze, iron, and even purple cloth, storax, saffron, costas, carved artworks, paintings, and molded works are not locally produced.

Arabians consider dead bodies no different from manure, just as Heracleitus says, "Corpses are more disposable than manure." Accordingly, they bury even their kings near manure piles. They honor the sun and dedicate altars on top of their houses. They pour libations on them and burn frankincense daily.

16.4.27. When the poet says, "I came to the Ethiopians, Sidonians, and Erembi,"[248] writers have doubts concerning the Sidonians, whether they should speak of those dwelling on the Persian Gulf, from whom come the Sidonian colonists we are familiar with. This is similar to those who inquire whether some Tyrian islanders are also Arabians, from whom they say those near us are colonists, or whether they are Sidonians. But, further, concerning the search for the Erembi, whether one ought to say those forcing the etymology of Erembi from *"eis tên eran embainein"* ("to go into the earth"), or whether they are Arabians. Zeno changes Homer's text thus: "Sidonians and Arabians." Posidonius plausibly writes, with minor changes only, "Sidonians and Arambians," because that is what the poet called Arabians in his own day. Posidonius says further that there were three Arab tribes, each located and mingled with the others, that seem homogenous with each other. On account of this, they have been called by names all closely resembling each other, such as Armenians, Aramaeans, and Arambians . . .

4. Pomponius Mela, *Description of the World* 3.75, 3.81–84 (1st century CE). *After describing the geography and topography of the Arabian and Persian Gulfs, Pomponius describes some of the peoples who inhabit the region. It is unclear whether some of the peoples he describes are actually "people." (RFK)*

3.75. The land from the region I just described to the Persian Gulf is uninhabited except where the Turtle-Eaters dwell. On the Gulf itself, located on the right side as you sail in, are the Carmanii, who wear no clothes, have no

---

248. Homer, *Odyssey* 4.84.

fruit, flocks, or homes, and clothe themselves in fish skins. They eat meat of the fish and are covered entirely in shaggy hair except for their heads.

Pomponius next describes the topography and geography on the opposite bank down to where the Arabs dwell.

3.81. Beyond the Arabian Gulf, but nevertheless still on the bay of the Red Sea, part of the land is infested with beasts and so uninhabitable. The Panchai inhabit the other part. They are called the Snake-Eaters because they eat snakes. Further inland were once the pygmies, a little people who have since gone extinct due to a war with cranes over their crops.[249]

3.82. There are many varieties of flying beast and snake there. The snakes most worthy of note are tiny but ready with their venom. At a certain time each year, they emerge from the muck of thick swamps and invade Egypt in a giant swarm. As soon as they cross the border, however, they are met by a competing swarm made up of birds called ibises, who form their own battle line and fight the snakes.

3.83. Of the flying creatures, the phoenix, always unique, is worthy of recounting. For it is not conceived through sexual reproduction nor given birth to. Instead, when it has lived for a lifespan of 500 years, it lays itself down to sleep upon a funeral pile heaped up with various aromatics and dissolves. 84. Next, it reconstitutes from the moisture in its decomposing limbs and conceives itself. Thus it is born again from itself. When it grows to maturity, it carries the bones of its former self to Egypt wrapped in myrrh to a city called the City of the Sun. There, it places its bones on a burning altar and dedicates them in a funeral service.

5. Babrius, *Fables* 57 (possibly 1st century CE). *Many of Babrius' fables are derived from Aesop's fables, some of which Babrius put into iambic verse. Thus, the original prose version of this fable could date back to Aesop in the 6th century BCE or could derive from any time up until Babrius' own. It is therefore uncertain how far back this type of characterization of Arabs dates. (RFK)*

Hermes filled up his wagon with lies, many tricks, and all sorts of roguery and traveled throughout the world. He walked from one tribe to another, handing out a little bit of his goods to each people. But when he reached Arabia, they say, and was passing through, his wagon broke and he got stuck there. The Arabians then snatched up all Hermes' goods as if they were the precious cargo of a merchant, nor did they allow the wagon to move on to the remaining peoples. This, then, is the reason why Arabians are liars and cheats (as I've experienced myself). Never did a word of truth grace their tongues.

---

249. There are numerous images of the battle, a favorite story dating back to Homer (*Iliad* 3.3–6). Domitian apparently staged it in the Colosseum (Statius, *Silvae* 1.61–63).

CHAPTER 13

ASIA: INDIA, CHINA, AND THE EDGES OF THE WORLD

India was known to the Greeks through the Persians as early as the 5th century BCE. It was not until the 4th century, however, with the invasion of India by Alexander, that firsthand accounts of India are produced by Greeks. The accounts of Alexander's generals and officials are preserved in large part in Strabo and other later geographers. India was both a place of wonder and strangeness as well as familiarity. While the Indians shared marvelous qualities with the Ethiopians, and the land of India contained marvelous animals, natural phenomena, and plants, the Indian Wise men, considered by the sources to be cousins of the Ethiopian Wise men, seem to share many philosophical views with Greek philosophers such as Pythagoras and even the Skeptics. While barbarians in the general sense of "not Greek," the Indians are presented in the sources as a noble, wise, and cultured people, like the Egyptians.

1. Herodotus, *Histories* **3.98–105 (5th century BCE).** *Herodotus turns from his description of Arabia to tell his audience about the strange method by which the Indians acquire large amounts of gold. (RFK)*

3.98. The Indians obtain a large amount of gold, from which they provide the previously mentioned gold dust to the king, in the following manner. [2] There is sand to the east of Indian territory, for of all of the peoples of whom we have knowledge who dwell in Asia (even those of whom something accurate is reported), the Indians are closest to the dawn and the rising sun. Thus, to the east of India is a land made desolate by sand. [3] There are many tribes of Indians, and none of them speak the same language. Some are nomads, others are not. Some live in marshes on the river and eat raw fish, which they catch, working from reed boats. Each boat is made from a single reed joint.[250] [4] These particular Indians wear clothes made of water plants. Whenever they cut and harvest an abundance of reeds from the river, they plait them as one does a mat and don them as corselets.

---

250. Herodotus refers here, most likely, to a class of giant reed known to grow up to twenty feet tall.

3.99. Other Indians, those who dwell east of the river folk, are nomads and eat raw flesh. They are called the Padaeoi. They are said to follow these customs: Whoever falls ill, whether it be a man or woman, is killed by their closest friends. If a man, the men kill him, saying that wasting away from a disease destroys the person's usefulness as meat. The sick person completely denies that he is ill, but the others disagree, kill him, and eat him. [2] If a woman falls ill, the women closest to her do the same thing the men do to a man who falls ill. They also sacrifice and eat anyone reaching old age. Not many people arrive to old age, however, since most fall ill earlier and are killed.

3.100. There is a different way of dealing with food among another group of Indians. They neither kill any living creature, nor do they cultivate anything, nor are they accustomed to having houses. Instead, they eat grass and they gather, boil, and eat a large husked grain (and its husk) similar to millet, which grows naturally from the earth. If one of them falls ill, he simply walks off into the desert and lies down. No one knows then whether he dies or is just sick.

3.101. Sex among these Indians is conducted out in the open in the manner of cattle. They also have skin nearly identical to the Ethiopians. [2] Their semen, which they ejaculate into their women, is not white like that of other men, but is black like their skin. This is the same as the semen of the Ethiopians.[251] These Indians dwell far off from the Persians and to the south of other Indians and were not ruled by King Darius.

3.102. Other Indians neighbor on the city of Caspatyrus and the land of the Pactyicae and dwell further north than the rest of the Indians. They have a way of life nearly identical to that of the Bactrians. They are the most warlike of the Indians and are the Indians dispatched for the gold, for the region where the gold is has been made desolate by sand. [2] In this sandy desert are large ants, slightly smaller than dogs but bigger than foxes.[252] Some of these creatures were caught and are at the court of the Persian king. These ants make their homes underground and dig up the sand in the same manner that Greek ants do among the Greeks. They have the exact same body shape as Greek ants, too. The sand that they dig up contains gold-dust, and [3] the Indians make expeditions into the desert for this sand. Each person harnesses three camels together, two males who ride along

---

251. See note on Chapter 4, Selection 2.

252. Although the story has been considered nonsense for thousands of years, the French ethnologist Michel Peissel said that his team discovered marmots that do, in fact, dig up gold-laced sand along with a local Indian tribe that sifted the sand for the gold. The Persian word for marmot was the equivalent to "mountain ant" and could have caused Herodotus, who did not understand Persian and only heard the story third-hand, some confusion (*The Ants' Gold: The Discovery of the Greek El Dorado in the Himalayas.* New York: Harper-Collins, 1984). The Greek word for "ant," *murmex,* is also close to the etymologically derived marmot. It is possible that misunderstanding in translation from Persian to Greek to Latin to English explains the confusion concerning these creatures.

on either side of a female camel in the middle. The rider himself rides the female, which, after he has trained her, he harnesses her and takes her away from her children when they are at as young of an age as he possibly can. These camels are as fast as horses, and besides are more capable of carrying heavy burdens. 103. I'm not going to describe the general characteristics of camels since Greeks know what they look like, but I will describe what they don't already know. For example, camels have four thigh bones and four leg joints in their hind legs. Also, their genitals point backward through their hind legs toward the tail.

3.104. The Indians, with the camels thus harnessed and arranged, drive them forward toward the gold, taking into account for their raid the time of day when the heat will be at its hottest, since the ants escape underground from the burning heat. [2] The sun is hottest among the Indians in the early morning from sunrise to market closing,[253] not at midday as it is for other men. During this time, it burns there by far more than Hellas does at midday, so that it is said that the men douse themselves with water at this time of day. [3] The midday sun burns the Indians almost the same as it does other men. As midday gives way to evening, their sun becomes as the early morning sun for others. As it moves away from morning, the day becomes cooler until sunset when it is extremely cold.

3.105. When the Indians arrive at the location holding their sacks, they fill the sacks up with sand and dash back to their camels as quickly as possible since the ants smell them and, so the Persians say, pursue them. They say that nothing is equal to the ants for speed, so that no one of the Indians would escape if they did not have a head start. [2] Now, the male camels are cut loose as they start to lag (though not both at the same time), since they run slower than the females. The females, recalling their offspring left behind back home, do not slack at all. The Indians obtain the majority of their gold in this way, so the Persians say. Another, though less abundant source of gold, is mining the land.

2. Ctesias, *Indica* Fragment 1 excerpted (Photius, *Library* 72.45a–50a, 4th century BCE). *A summary of the lost work of Ctesias, the* Indica, *in which he gathers together anecdotes and observations (based on Persian accounts mostly, not personal observation) on the land, people, and creatures of ancient India. (RFK)*

72.45a. I also read the same author's *Indica* contained in one book and written more so in the Ionic dialect [than the *Persica*].

He says concerning the Indus river that it is 4.5 miles wide at its narrowest point and 23 miles at it broadest point. He says of those living in India that they are almost as numerous as the population of the whole rest of the world combined. Concerning a worm living in the river, he notes that it

---

253. Around 10:00 A.M. This theory makes sense if Herodotus assumed that the world was flat, a likely scenario.

is the only creature to be born in the river. He says that men do not dwell beyond India.

He says that it does not rain in India but that it is watered by the Indus. He writes about elephants that can knock down walls, of little monkeys with six-foot-long tails, and of extremely large roosters. He tells of a parrot as large as a hawk that has a human tongue and voice, a purple beak, and a black beard. Its feathers are dark blue up to the neck, which is red like cinnabar. Ctesias says that the bird speaks Indian as does a native speaker and, if taught Greek, would also speak it as a native speaker would . . .

72.45b. Ctesias says that Indian dogs are so large that they attack lions. The mountains are also large, and the Indians mine sardonyx, onyx, and other stones used in signet rings.

He says that it is very hot and that the sun is ten times larger than it seems to be in other lands. Many people there suffer from the stifling heat. He says also that the sea there is no smaller than in Greece, but that the surface and the water to a depth of four fingers is so hot that the fish don't live there near the heat but spend their lives down below.

Ctesias says that the Indus River flows through the mountains and plains where the bamboo is said to grow so wide that two men joining their arms together would be unable to wrap their arms around it. The wood is as big as the mast of a merchant ship . . .

He tells also of the *martichor*, a wild animal found in India that has a human face. It is as large as a lion and its skin is red like cinnabar. It has three sets of teeth, ears like a human's, and grey eyes similar also to a human's. Its tail is similar to a land scorpion's and has on it a barb more than eighteen inches long. It has barbs on both sides of the tail and on the top of its head, as does a scorpion. If anyone approaches it, the barbs kill him—being stung always leads to death. [46a] If someone is in front of the *martichor* and attacks from far away, the *martichor* sets up its tail and, just as from a bow, hurls its barb. If attacked from behind, it extends its tail straight back and hurls its barbs in a line as far as a hundred feet. Everything hit by it, except elephants, dies. The barbs are about a foot long and as wide as a reed. In Greek, the *martichor* is called a man-eater, because it carries off and eats a great many humans, though it eats other creatures as well. It fights with its talons and barbs. The barbs, Ctesias says, grow back again after they have been shot. There are many *martichors* in India. They are killed by men riding on elephants who hurl spears at them from atop.

Concerning the Indians, Ctesias says that they are very just. He also writes of their habits and customs. He writes about a sacred land in an uninhabited region where they worship in the name of the sun and moon. It is about a fifteen-day journey from Mount Sardus. The sun there is cool for thirty-five days of the year, which allows them to hold a festival and return home again without being burnt by the sun. He further states that in India there is no thunder, lightning, or rain, but there are frequent winds and many tornadoes that snatch up whatever they happen upon. After the sun rises, it is cool for half a day, but the rest of the day is exceedingly hot as in the majority of India.

Ctesias says that Indians are not black because of the sun[254] but by nature. He says that there are very pale men and women among them, though few. He himself saw such Indians, including two women and five men . . .

He says that in the middle of India are black men called pygmies, who speak the same language as the other Indians. They are very small. The tallest of them is three feet, but the majority are just over two feet tall. [46b] They have very long hair all the way down to their knees and even longer. Their beards are the longest of all men. When their beards grow to great length, they no longer wear clothes, but their hair, which hangs down from their head to the knees, and their beards, which drag near their feet, wrap around their bodies in place of clothes. They then gird themselves with leather thongs. They have large genitals that hang to their ankles and are thick. They have flat noses and are ugly. Their sheep are as small as lambs, and their donkeys and oxen are the size of rams. Their horses, mules, and other pack animals are also the size of rams. Because they are exceptional archers, 3,000 pygmies escort the king of the Indians. They are a most just people and follow the same customs as the other Indians. They hunt hare and fox not with dogs, but with ravens, martens,[255] crows, and eagles.

There is a lot of silver there and silver mines, though not deep ones. The mines of Bactria are said to be deeper. There is also gold in the land of India, it is not found in the rivers and washed as it is in the Pactolus River, but in numerous lofty mountains where griffins live. Griffins are four-footed birds as big as wolves. Their legs and claws are like those of lions. They have black feathers covering all their body except for their breast feathers, which are red. Because of the griffins, a large amount of gold there is difficult to obtain . . .

72.47a. Ctesias says there is a river of honey that flows from a rock. He says much concerning how just the Indians are, their goodwill toward their king, and their contempt for death. He says that there is this mountain and the water from it when drawn congeals like cheese. If three obols[256] worth of the curdled substance is ground down and drunk in water, whoever drinks it speaks out about everything they have done, because the person becomes deranged and mad for a day. The king uses this water when he wants to find out the truth about those who are accused of a crime. If the person confesses, they are ordered to commit suicide by starvation. If they do not say anything, they are acquitted.

---

254. This is a refutation of environmental theories as reflected in authors such as Vitruvius, Pliny, and Manilius (see Chapter 3, Selections 8, 9, and 11).

255. A mammal related to the weasel and ferret.

256. The common silver coin of ancient Greece. There were approximately six obols in an ancient *drachma*. In Classical Athens, the average pay of a day laborer or member of the navy was around two to three obols per day.

They say that no Indians are subject to headaches, ophthalmia,[257] tooth-aches, mouth sores, or any sort of degeneration of their strength. They live 120, 130, even 150 years. Most Indians even live up to 200 years . . .

> Ctesias then describes a number of medically beneficial roots and seeds found in the region.

In these mountains,[258] men with dog heads dwell. They wear clothes made from wild animal skins and have no language at all except barking just as dogs do. They communicate to each other through this barking. Their teeth are larger than a dog's, and their fingernails are similar to a dog's only longer and rounder. They live in the mountains as far away as the Indus River. They are black and very just as are the rest of the Indians with whom they interact. They understand what the Indians say to them, but they can only respond with barking and hand and finger gestures as the deaf and mute do. The Indians call them the Calustoi, which in Greek is Cunocephaloi [Dog-Heads]. There are around 120,000 of this tribe.

Near the source of this river grows a purple flower from which is extracted a purple die that is not only no less intense than the Greek dye but is even brighter. In the same area also is an animal as large as a beetle and as red as cinnabar. It has extremely soft feet and a body soft as that of a worm. It spawns on the trees that produce amber and eats the fruit, destroying the trees. They are similar to the worm that destroys the wines in Greece. [48a] The Indians crush these animals and extract a dye used for cloaks, tunics, and whatever else they want. The dye is better than Persian dyes.

Ctesias writes that the Cunocephaloi who dwell in the mountains do not have occupations but live by hunting. Whatever they kill, they cook in the sun. They raise many sheep, goats, and donkeys. They drink milk and the whey from sheep's milk. They also eat the fruit of the siptachorus tree, from which amber comes. The fruit is sweet. They also dry the fruit and store it in large baskets just as dried grapes [raisins] in Greece. The Cunocephaloi make rafts and load them up with the fruit, a clean-smelling purple flower, 260 talents of amber, the same amount of the purple dye, and then 1,000 more talents of amber, and then ship it all to the Indian king. They bring their other goods to exchange with the Indians for bread, barley-meal, and robes.[259] They also trade for swords used for hunting wild beasts, arrows, and spears. They are very skilled archers and spear-throwers. The Cunocephaloi are impossible to make an attack upon, since they live in an impassable mountainous region. Every five years, the king sends them as a gift 300,000 arrows, the same number of spears, 120,000[260] shields, and 50,000 swords.

---

257. Inflammation of the eyes caused by infection or other trauma.

258. The mountains through which the Hyparchus River runs.

259. The text says "wooden" robes, and it is possible that Photius means cotton, since Indian cotton is from trees, but it is unclear.

260. The text says "twelve," but we must assume that *murias* (10,000) should be supplied as with the other numbers in the list. The numbers are them multiplied, not added.

The Cunocephaloi do not have houses but live in caves. They hunt with arrows and spears, and are able to pursue and overtake their prey on foot because they are very fast runners. The women bathe once each month when their menstrual period comes, but not at any other time. The men do not bathe at all, but wash their hands. Three times a month, they anoint themselves with an oil made from milk, and they rub themselves with skins. Both the men and women clothe themselves in fine, smoothed leather, not animal furs. The wealthiest among them, few in number, dress in linen. They do not have beds, but sleep on pallets made of rushes or leaves. Whoever has the most sheep is considered the wealthiest, and so on with other types of possessions. All of the men and women have a tail above their hip bones as dogs do, but the tails are larger and bushier.

72.48b. The Cunocephaloi have sex in the manner of dogs and think it shameful to do it in any other way. They are just and the longest-lived of all humans, for they live 170 years, and some even live 200 years. They say that beyond them above the river's source dwell other men who are black like the rest of the Indians. They do not have jobs, nor do they eat grain or drink water. They raise a lot of cattle, oxen, goats, and sheep. They drink nothing but their milk. When children are born to these people, they have no orifice in the buttocks and do not excrete waste. Instead, they have fleshy haunches at the hip and the orifice develops as they grow up. For this reason, they do not excrete waste. It is said that they urinate a substance similar to cheese that is not entirely solid but is thick. In the morning and again at midday, they drink milk. There is said to be a sweet root that prevents milk from solidifying in the stomach. In the evening, they nibble a bit of this root and it makes them vomit up easily everything they have ingested.

Ctesias says that there are wild asses in India as big or even bigger than horses. Their bodies are white, their heads are dark purple, and they have blue eyes. In the middle of their head is a large horn about eighteen inches long.[261] The lower part of the horn, about eight fingers width from the base to the middle, is completely white. The top, where the horn comes to a point, is a purplish-red color. The remainder of the horn, the middle portion, is black. Those who drink from the horn (for they make them into drinking cups) are not subject to convulsions or the sacred disease [epilepsy]. If they drink wine, water, or some other beverage from the cup before and after drinking poison, they are even immune to poisons. While donkeys and single-hoofed animals in other lands lack ankle joints and gall bladders, these creatures have both. Their ankle joints are the most beautiful I have seen. They are the same size and shape as those of oxen, and the skin covering them is the color of cinnabar. The creature is very fast and extremely strong. No horse or other creature can catch them in pursuit. It starts off its run rather slow, but as it continues to run, it picks up speed miraculously and runs faster and faster.

---

261. Some scholars have pointed to this description as the origin of the mythical unicorn. It is more likely a white rhinoceros, as the discussion of its strength, size, and the way it is hunted suggests.

72.49a. The animal can only be captured in the following manner: When it takes its young to feed, one surrounds it with many horses. The animal refuses to flee and abandon its young, but fights with its horn and by trampling and biting its attackers. It kills many horses and men this way, but the hunters subdue it by a continual shower of arrows and spears. It cannot be taken alive. The animal's skin is very bitter to taste and thus inedible. The only reason to hunt it is for its horn and ankle joints.

Ctesias tells us that a worm dwells in the Indus River similar in form to those found in fig trees. They are about 10.5 feet long, some longer, some shorter.[262] It is thick, supposedly so thick that a ten-year-old boy can hardly wrap his hands around it. They have two teeth, one on top and one on bottom, and they eat whatever they seize in those teeth. It passes the day in the mud of the river and emerges at night to seize whatever beast it happens upon, be it an ox or camel or whatnot. It then drags the prey into the river and eats all of it except the intestines. One hunts the beast with a large fishhook attaching a young goat or lamb to it by chains. After catching them, hunters hang them up for thirty days with jars placed underneath. A liquid drips from them, enough to fill ten Attic *cotulae*.[263] When the thirty days is up, they dispose of the worm and seal up the oil. They then take it to the king of the Indians, and only to him, since no one else is allowed to have it. This oil lights up and burns wood, animals, or whatever else it is poured over. It cannot be extinguished, except by covering it with a large amount of mud.

He says also that there are trees in India lofty as cedars and cypresses. The leaves of these trees are like palms only broader. Further, they have no shoots and flowers as the male laurel does. They have no fruit. The tree is called *carpon* in the Indian language. In Greek, it is called the *myrorodon*. It is rare. Drops of oil drip from it. These drops are then wiped off the tree with cotton and squeezed into alabaster containers. The oil is silky, reddish, and somewhat thick. It has an extremely pleasant fragrance that some say can be smelt nearly a mile away. Only the king and his family are permitted to have the oil. [49b] The king of the Indians sent some of it to the Persian king, and Ctesias, who saw the oil, says that to catch a whiff of it is like nothing he can describe or has experienced before.

Ctesias says that the cheese and wine of India are the tastiest of all he has had the experience of tasting.

Ctesias further writes of a spring in India about 30 feet in circumference and squarish. The spring lies below the water's surface about 45 feet down. The water itself goes even deeper, about 180 feet down. The most important Indians bathe in it, men, women, and children alike. They immerse themselves by jumping in feet first. When they leap in, the spring shoots them back out of the water. It throws into the air not only men but pretty much

---

262. Although the behavior Ctesias describes is similar to a mud snake, the size and diet suggest the "worm" may actually be an Indian python, which frequently lives in riverbanks and swims quite well.

263. About five pints.

every type of creature, dead or alive. It does not throw out iron, silver, gold, or bronze, which rest on the bottom of the water. The water is very cold and pleasant to drink. It produces a loud sound, just as does boiling water in a kettle. The water cures leprosy and scurvy. In Indian it is called *ballade*, in Greek *ophelime* [helpful].

There are in the Indian mountains where the reed plants grow a tribe of people about 300,000 in number. The women of this tribe give birth only once in their lifetime, and the offspring are born with beautiful teeth on both top and bottom. All, male and female, are born with grey hair on both their heads and brows. Up until the age of thirty, the men have white hair covering their bodies, but then it begins to turn black. By the age of sixty, the hair is completely black.[264] Both male and female have eight fingers and toes. They are extremely warlike, and 5,000 of their bowmen and spearmen serve the Indian king. Ctesias says that they have ears so large that they cover their arms down to the elbow and also cover the back. The ears also touch each other.

72.50a. Ctesias, in writing and telling these tales, says that he wrote only the truth. He says that he wrote of what he saw or what he learned from others who saw it. He also says that he left out many more marvelous things because those not seeing them would think that he wrote fiction.

3. Arrian, *Indica* 1–17 excerpted (1st/2nd century CE). *Arrian wrote his work based primarily on the works of Megasthenes, historian and satrap under Alexander the Great, Eratosthenes, the geographer and librarian at Alexandria, and Nearchus, a friend of Alexander's who circumnavigated the coast of India to the Tigris River. Much of the work, then, is compiled from firsthand accounts by contemporaries or near contemporaries of Alexander with some experience of India. (CSR)*

1. The Astacenians and Assacenians, Indian tribes, inhabit the area beyond the Indus River to the west up to the Cophen River, [2] but they are not as tall as those who live on the east side of the Indus River, nor are they as good-spirited nor as black as most Indians. [3] Long ago, they were subjects of the Assyrians, and then of the Medes, and then of the Persians. They paid tribute to Cyrus, the son of Cambyses, from their land, which Cyrus imposed. [4] The Nysaeans are not an Indian tribe but are among those who came to the Indians' land with Dionysus, and perhaps some were Greeks who became unfit for fighting in the wars that Dionysus fought against the Indians. [5] Others perhaps were some of the people who were neighbors

---

264. It is not unusual for the ancients to hear reports of ancient primates and transform these primates into human tribes by giving them typical attributes one would expect of a distant, strange people (see Hanno, Chapter 9, Selection 1). In this case, Ctesias is likely working from reports of the hoolock gibbon, a primate native to the mountains of northeast India that is born white. The males change from white to black over the course of their nine-year lifespan.

whom Dionysus settled with the Greeks. Dionysus named the land Nysaea and the city itself Nysa after the mountain Nysa. [6] The mountain near the city, on the foot of which Nysa was built, is also called Meros [thigh] because of an event that occurred there right when Dionysus was born. [7] The poets sing these things about Dionysus and let the Greek and barbarian writers interpret them. [8] Massaca, a large city, is set in Assacenian lands and holds sway over the Assacian land. There is also the city Peucelaetis, which is also large, not far from the Indus. These are the inhabited areas beyond the Indus River to the west up to the Cophen River.

2. The areas to the east of the Indus River are what I define as the land of India and the people who live there as Indians.

Arrian goes on to describe the boundaries of India and its major geographical features.

5. Whosoever wishes to discuss the reasons for the number and size of the Indian rivers, let him discuss it. It is for me to write down the things that I have heard. [2] Megasthenes has written down the names of many other rivers beyond the Ganges and the Indus, which feed into the eastern and southern sea, and he says that there are fifty-eight Indian rivers, all of which can be sailed. [3] But it seems to me that Megasthenes did not go to much of India, although, indeed, he saw more than did the men who came with Alexander the son of Philip. For he says that he was with Sandrocottus, the most powerful king of the Indians, greater even than Porus.[265] [4] Megasthenes says that the Indians did not make war upon any other men, nor did other men make war on them . . . [8] Alexander alone took an army into India. A popular report claims that Dionysus took his army into India before Alexander and conquered the Indians. A similar story about Heracles is not well attested. [9] The city of Nysa is a strong marker of Dionysus' campaign, as is Mount Meros and the ivy that grows on the mountain, as well as the Indians who prepare themselves for battle with drums and cymbals and their clothes that are spotted like those of Dionysus' Bacchants. There are not many records of Heracles. [10] But concerning the rock of Aornos, which Alexander took by force and Heracles was not able to capture, this seems to me to be a Macedonian boast, just like when the Macedonians call Parapamisus Caucasus, although it is nothing like the Caucasus. [11] When they discovered that there was a cave among the Parapamisadae, they said that this was the cave of Prometheus the Titan, in which he was hung for the theft of fire. [12] When they saw that the Sibae, an Indian tribe, were dressed in skins, they claimed that the Sibae were men who had been left behind from Heracles' campaign. Also, the Sibae carry a club and brand their cows with a club, and so the Macedonians claim that they carry a reminder of the club of Heracles. [13] If these tales are believable to anyone, then this was some other Heracles, not the Theban one but the Tyrian or Egyptian one, or some great king in the high lands not far from India.

---

265. Porus is the Indian king who fought Alexander and, although he lost the battle, became an ally of Alexander.

Arrian describes more of India's rivers and its climate. He begins a comparison between India and Ethiopia.

6.8. It is not outside of likelihood that it rains there as in India, since the Indian land is not unlike the Ethiopian land and Indian rivers, similar to the Ethiopian and Egyptian Nile, have crocodiles. In them there are fish and other water animals like the Nile has except for the hippopotamus, and Onesicritus at least says that they even have hippopotami. [9] The appearance of Indian and Ethiopian men does not differ very much. The southern Indians are especially like the Ethiopians in their black skin and black hair, except that they are not as flat-nosed or curly-haired as the Ethiopians. The more northern Indians are especially like the Egyptians in their physical appearance.

7. Megasthenes says that there are, in all, 118 Indian tribes. I agree with Megasthenes that there are many Indian tribes, but I cannot guess how he counted and wrote them down precisely, since he did not visit much of the Indian land and the races do not all interact with each other. [2] Megasthenes says that long ago the Indians were nomadic, like the Scythians who do not farm, who wander in their wagons and exchange one place for another, do not live in cities, and do not worship at altars to the gods. [3] Similarly, the Indians did not have cities and did not build altars to the gods. They wore the skins of wild animals they killed, and they ate tree bark. In the Indian language the trees were called *tala*, and something very similar to balls of yarn grew on them, similar to what grows on the tops of palm trees.[266] [4] They ate raw whatever wild animals they could catch, at least until Dionysus came to India. [5] When Dionysus came and when he became powerful in India, he established cities and gave laws to the cities. He also gave wine to the Indians, as he did to the Greeks, and gave them seeds and taught them to sow them in the earth. [6] Either Triptolemus did not come here when Demeter sent him out to sow the whole earth, or this Dionysus came to India before Triptolemus and gave them seeds of domesticated crops. [7] Dionysus first yoked oxen behind a plow and made many of the Indians farmers rather than nomads, and he armed them with weapons of war. [8] Dionysus also taught them to honor the other gods and himself in particular by playing on cymbals and drums. He taught them the dance of satyrs, [9] which the Greeks call the *cordax*, and he showed the Indians how to grow their hair long for the god. He taught them how to wear a mitre and put on oily perfumes. As a result, the Indians went into battle against Alexander still playing cymbals and drums.

8. Once he had established these practices, Dionysus left India and established Spatembas as king of the land, who was the most experienced of his companions in Bacchic rites. When Spatembas died, his son Boudyas succeeded to the throne. [2] The father was king of the Indians for fifty years, the son for twenty. Then Boudyas' son Cradeuas took the throne, [3] and after him the kingship changed mostly according to hereditary

---

266. Probably a coconut.

rights with the son taking it from his father. If hereditary succession failed, then the kings were established according to merit. [4] As for Heracles, the one who went to India, as the story says, the Indians themselves considered him indigenous. [5] This Heracles is especially honored among the Sourasenians, an Indian tribe, where they have two great cities, Methora and Clisobora. [6] The Iomanes, a navigable river, flows through their land. According to Megasthenes, the clothes and equipment that this Heracles wore were like the clothes of the Theban Heracles. The Indians also say this. He had very many wives and children in India—for this Heracles also married many women, but he only had one daughter. Her name was Pandaea, [7] named for the land where she was born and the rule of which Heracles handed over to her. She had 500 elephants, which she got from her father, 4,000 horsemen, and 130,000 infantry. [8] Certain other Indians say that Heracles traveled all over the land and the sea and cleansed it of evils and then discovered a new kind of womanly ornament in the sea. [9] Thus, even now, traders shipping goods out of India to us are eager to buy these things and bring them to us. [10] Wealthy and fortunate Greeks of old and Romans today buy with even more eagerness the sea *margarita*,[267] as it is called in the Indian language. This ornament seemed so beautiful to Heracles that he gathered the pearls from every sea and brought them to India to be an ornament for his daughter. [11] Megasthenes also says that the oysters are caught with nets, and that many oysters inhabit the sea, much like bees. For the pearl oysters also have a king or a queen, as bees do. [12] Whoever should happen to catch the king may easily throw a net around the remaining swarm[268] of pearl oysters. If the king should escape the nets, then the others are no longer catchable. Those who catch the oysters allow the flesh to rot away but use the shell as decoration. [13] For, among the Indians as well, the pearl is worth three times as much as refined gold, which is also mined in India.

9. In this land where the daughter of Heracles ruled, women are considered marriageable at seven years and men live to forty years at most. [2] A story is told about this among the Indians. When Heracles, after his daughter was born in his old age, learned that his death was near, he slept with her himself when she was seven years old since there was no man equal to him to whom he might give his daughter. He did this so that he might leave behind his own descendants to be kings of India. Heracles brought it about that she was the right age for marriage. [3] Out of this tradition the race, which Pandaea began, has this prerogative from Heracles. [4] It seems to me, however, that if Heracles was able to achieve such an unheard of thing, then he could have made himself live longer so that he could sleep with his daughter when she was the appropriate age. [5] But if this fact about the maturity of the girls is correct, then it seems to me to fit in with the idea of

---

267. A pearl; the term *margarita* is a Persian word.

268. Arrian deliberately uses a word here that is associated with bees, meaning beehive or swarm.

the age of the men, the oldest of whom die at forty. [6] For if old age comes that much more quickly and death comes with old age, then logically one's peak will develop more quickly relative to the end. [7] As a result, thirty-year-old men would be nearing old age, and twenty-year-old men would be young but beyond their youthfulness. The peak age of youth would be around fifteen years, and according to that logic the marriageable age for women would be seven. [8] Megasthenes also writes that the crops ripen more quickly in this land than other places and also rot more quickly. [9] The Indians number the kings from Dionysus to Sandracottus at 153, and count 642 years. < . . . >[269] [12] None of the Indians prepared for war outside of their home country because of their sense of justice.

10. These things are also said: That the Indians do not make memorials for their dead, but rather think that men's virtues, as well as songs sung for them, are sufficient as a memorial for those who have died. [2] It is not possible to write down the number of Indian cities correctly because of their great number. The cities next to rivers or coasts are built from wood, for if a city were built with bricks it would not last a long time because of water from rainfall, and because the rivers overflow their banks and fill the lowlands with water. [3] The cities, however, which are established in high places bare of plant life, are made from bricks and clay. [4] The greatest Indian city is called Palimbrothra. It lies in the land of the Prasians where the Erannoboas and Ganges Rivers meet. . . . [8] The following is a great thing in the land of the Indians: all the Indians are free; no Indian is a slave. It is the same for the Lacedaemonians as it is for the Indians. [9] The Lacedaemonians, however, have helots who do the work of slaves. The Indians, on the other hand, have no slaves at all, much less Indian slaves.

11. All the Indians are divided into seven groups. The Wisemen are one of these. Their numbers are smaller than the others, but they are the most elevated in terms of esteem and honor. [2] It is not necessary for them to do physical labor or put what they make toward the common interest. No necessity at all weighs on the Wise men, other than to make sacrifices to the gods on behalf of the Indians as a community. [3] Whenever someone sacrifices in private, one of the Wise men advises him on the sacrifices since, if they did otherwise, the sacrifices would not please the gods. [4] The Wise men are the only ones of the Indians who are expert in prophecy, and it is not allowed to anyone else to make prophecies unless he is a Wise man. [5] They make prophecies about the seasons of the year and about whether some misfortune will befall the community. They do not care to prophesy for people about private things, since prophecy is neither concerned with smaller matters nor is it worth their while to spend time on them. [6] If any-one should make three mistakes in their prophecies, no harm happens to him but he is compelled to be silent for the future. [7] No one may compel the man who has been sentenced to silence to speak. These Wise men live naked. In winter they live in the open air and sunshine; in summer, when

---

269. The text is corrupt here. It may describe political changes in India. Arrian does mention again that no one invaded India except Alexander.

the sun is oppressive, they live in the meadows and lowlands under large trees, whose shade Nearchus says reaches 500 feet on all sides. These trees are so large that one tree provides shade for 10,000 men. [8] The Wise men eat seasonal fruits and tree bark, which is no less sweet and nourishing than the fruits of a palm tree.

[9] The second group of Indians after the Wise men are the farmers, who are the greatest in number. They have no weapons of war nor do they care about warfare. Rather, they work the land and pay taxes to the kings and the independent cities. [10] If war occurs between Indian tribes, then it is considered wrong to attack those who work the land or to harm the land itself. Thus, while some fight and kill each other as they will, others nearby are plowing or harvesting or tending or reaping peacefully. [11] The third group of Indians are the herdsmen, who tend sheep and cattle. These men do not live in cities or villages; they are nomads and live in the mountains. They pay taxes out of their herds and hunt birds and wild animals throughout the land.

12. The fourth group consists of craftsmen and merchants. They serve in public offices and pay taxes on their work, except those who make weapons for war. These men take payment from the community. This group includes the shipbuilders and the sailors who sail the rivers. [2] The fifth group is made up of the warriors, who are second in numbers to the farmers. They enjoy the most freedom and contentment. They practice only military actions, [3] while other men make their weapons, provide them with horses, and serve in their military camps by taking care of the horses, cleaning their weapons, driving the elephants, and maintaining and driving their chariots. [4] They fight when they must fight, but when there is peace, they celebrate. Their pay from the community is so great that they easily support others with it.

The sixth group of Indians are called guardians or overseers. [5] They oversee what happens in the land and in the cities, and then they report this back to the king (where the Indians are ruled by a king) or to the magistrates (where the Indians are independent). It is not right to report anything false, and no Indian has ever been charged with lying.

[6] The seventh group of Indians are those who counsel the king about community affairs or, in the independent cities, who counsel the magistrates. [7] This group is small in number, but it is the most eminent in wisdom and justice. From this group, the rulers, provincial officials, lieutenants, treasurers, generals, admirals, stewards, and agricultural overseers are chosen. [8] It is not right or legal to marry outside one's group. It is not right, for example, for a farmer to marry a craftsman or vice versa. It is also not legal for one man to pursue two crafts or to change from one group to another. A shepherd may not become a farmer, nor a craftsman a shepherd. One can become a Wise man out of any of the groups, since life is not easy for the Wise men, but rather the most wretched of all.

Arrian describes elephant hunts and the habits of elephants. He then discusses tigers, ants, parrots, and snakes.

15.11. Of all the Greek doctors, no one has found a cure for someone bitten by an Indian snake, but the Indians themselves have cured those who were bitten. Nearchus says in addition that Alexander kept those Indians who were the most skilled in medicine gathered around him, and he had it announced throughout the camp that whoever had been bitten should visit the king's tent. [12] These same Indian men were also doctors of other sicknesses and suffering. There are not many diseases in India because the seasons are moderate there. If someone caught something worse, they would take council with the sophists, for these men seemed to cure what might be cured with the help of a god.

16. The Indians wear linen clothing, as Nearchus says. The linen comes from the trees which I mentioned earlier. It is lighter in color than all other linen, or maybe the linen appears brighter because the people are black. [2] They wear a linen tunic that falls between their knee and ankle, and one cloth wrapped around the shoulders, and another tied around their heads. [3] Some Indians wear ivory if they are very wealthy. Nearchus says that the Indians dye their beards with different colors. Some dye them white to appear as white as possible, others dye them blue, red, purple, or even spring green. [4] The Indians who are not heedless carry parasols for protection from the summer weather. They wear sandals made of white leather, which are strangely adorned. The soles of the sandals are worked in different colors and raised so that they seem taller. [5] The weapons used by the Indians are not of a particular type. The foot soldiers have a bow of about the same height as the shooter. They put this on the ground and stand on it with their left foot, then they shoot after drawing the string very far back. [6] The arrows they use are a little less than five feet long. Nothing resists an arrow shot by an Indian archer, not a shield or a breastplate or anything stronger. [7] The infantry hold a shield of untanned leather in their left hand. These shields are narrower than the people carrying them but not much shorter in length. Some carry javelins instead of bows. [8] Everyone carries a large, broad sword that is not much less than five feet long. When they fight at close quarters (although the Indians do not fight each other easily this way), they wield the sword with both hands, and the stroke is indeed strong. [9] Their cavalry carry two javelins, which are called *saunia*, and a shield smaller than the ones the foot soldiers carry. Their horses are not equipped with saddles, nor do they use a bridle similar to those the Greeks or Celts use. [10] Rather, the horses have a piece of stitched, untanned leather wrapped around their noses with copper or iron goads on it that are not very sharp. The wealthy use ivory goads. The horses have a piece of iron in their mouths, a sort of rod, to which the reins are attached. [11] When they pull the reins, the rod guides the horse. The goads attached to the bridle bother the horse so that he is not allowed to do anything other than obey the reins.

17. The Indians have lean and tall bodies more elegant than other men's bodies. Many Indians have camels, horses, or asses for riding; the wealthiest have elephants. [2] The elephant is a regal mount among the Indians, second in honor is the four-horse chariot, and camels are third. There is

no honor in riding a single horse. [3] Their women, who are very sensible, would not be indiscreet for any other price, sleeping only with a man who gives her an elephant. The Indians do not think it is shameful to have sex for an elephant, rather, it seems grand to them for women to have their beauty thought worthy of an elephant. [4] They marry without giving or receiving any dowry. Whoever of the women are marriageable are brought out into the public by their fathers and offered to the one who is victorious in wrestling, boxing, or running, or to someone who has proven their worth otherwise. [5] The Indians who do not live in the mountains eat grain and work the land. Those who do live in the mountains eat meat they get from hunting.

> **4. Strabo, *Geography* 15.1.57–60, 15.1.62–67, 15.1.69–71 (1st century BCE/1st century CE).** *Strabo discusses the various peoples at length, including the Indian philosophers, especially the Brahmins. Strabo bases his account on various contemporaries of Alexander the Great, who accompanied him on campaign. (RFK)*

15.1.57. Megasthenes,[270] exceeding even mythology, says that there are men who are forty-five inches and even twenty-seven inches tall, and some of them lack noses and have only two air-holes above the mouth. The twenty-seven-inch-tall people are the ones who fought with the cranes (which Homer describes)[271] and with the partridges, which are as large as geese. He says also that these people pick out the cranes' eggs and destroy them since the cranes lay their eggs there. Because of this, one finds neither the eggs nor the young of cranes anywhere around there. Most often the cranes escape the attacks with bronze spear tips stuck in them. Similar tales are told concerning men with ears large enough to sleep inside, wild savages, and other oddities. Megasthenes says that the wild savages and other odd peoples were not taken to Alexander's camp at Sandrocottus because they starved themselves to death. Some of these people have their feet reversed, with the heels in the front and the balls of their feet and toes in the back. He also saw some people without mouths, a gentle people, who dwell near the source of the Ganges. They nourish themselves with the vapors from roasting meats and fruits and with the scents of flowers, for instead of mouths they have an air-hole. Ill-smelling things, though, cause them harm. As a result, they had difficulty surviving, and things were even worse for them if they were brought into the soldiers' camps. Concerning other peoples, Megasthenes says that the Wise men described them to him. They tell of the Ocypodes [Swift-feet], who run as fast as horses, and the Encotocoitae, whose ears stretch to their feet and which are so strong they use them to pull up trees and snap bow strings. There are also the one-eyed people,

---

270. Philosopher who served as an ambassador and satrap for Alexander the Great.
271. See note for Chapter 12, Selection 4.

who have ears like dogs and a single eye in the middle of their forehead. They also have hair that sticks up on end and hairy chests. Then, there are the Amycterae, voracious eaters of raw flesh and short-lived men who die before they reach old age. Their upper lips are more prominent than their mouths.

Megasthenes agrees with Simonides, Pindar, and the other mythologists about the long-lived Hyperboreans. The story of Timagenes that bronze rains down from the sky in droplets in India is a myth. Megasthenes' statement is more believable. He says that the rivers carry gold dust, and from this gold tribute is taken away for the king. This is what happens in Spain also.

15.1.58. Megasthenes says about the mountain-dwelling Wise men that they sing the praises of Dionysus and point out as evidence of his presence that vines grow there wild. They grow of their own accord along with ivy, sweet bay, myrtle, boxwood, and other evergreens, none of which, Megasthenes says, grow to the east of the Euphrates, except, rarely, in gardens where they need much tending in order to survive. Also related to Dionysus are the clothes they wear, their Dionysian mitres, ointments, and floral dyes. Further, the king is accompanied by bell-ringers and drummers whenever he goes out. The Wise men of the plains honor Heracles. These stories of Megasthenes have been contested by many, especially the stories about vines and wine. Mesopotamia and Media as far as Persia and Carmania lie east of the Euphrates, and each of the peoples dwelling in those areas have good vines and wines.

15.1.59. Megasthenes makes another division concerning the Wise men, stating that there are two types. The first he called the Brahmins, the second, the Sramans. The Brahmins, he says, have a better reputation since their opinions are more agreeable to people. Immediately upon conception, their children have as teachers learned men who seem, while present, to speak charms to the mothers and the unborn child in order to bring about a happy birth. The truth is that they give the mothers some sound advice and counsel. Those who are especially receptive to their advice are thought to be happy in their children. After the birth, other teachers, one after another, care for the children, and the teachers become progressively better educated as the child gets older. He also says that these Wise men pass their time in groves in front of the city underneath an appropriately sized enclosure. They live frugally with only straw for sleep and hides for clothes. They abstain from eating meat and from sexual intercourse. They pay attention to serious speech, and themselves speak with anyone wanting to speak with them. They do not consider it right that anyone prattle on while listening to them. Nor should anyone cough nor clear his throat nor spit. If it happens, that person is removed from the company of the Wise men for the day, as if the person were contemptible. After living like this for thirty-seven years, the Brahmin withdraws to his own property and lives without worry and more freely. They then wear clothes made of fine linen and wear gold adornments (with moderation) on their ears and hands. They also then eat the meat of animals that are not useful to man, but still keep away from pungent or seasoned foods. They consider it best to marry as many wives as possible so as to produce as many children as possible since more children of serious disposition are likely to be born that way. Also, they do not keep slaves but use their children as attendants.

The Brahmins do not philosophize to their wives. First, this prevents their wives, if they become malicious, from telling things that should not be told to profane men. Second, if their wives become serious philosophers, they might leave their husbands because no one who despises pleasure and toil, and likewise life and death, is willing to be subject to another. Such are the serious-minded man and woman. The majority of the Wise men's talk is about death. In fact, they believe that life here is like being in the womb, while dying is, for those who study philosophy, like being born into real life and happiness. This is why they devote the majority of their training to preparing for death. They consider nothing of what happens to humans to be inherently good or bad. If it was, then never would the same things be vexations to some but joys to others, both having dreamlike qualities. Further, the same things would not be at one time vexatious and at another time pleasant to the same person. Concerning the nature of things, Megasthenes says that the Wise men demonstrate a naivety, for they are better at deeds than words and, especially, since they confirm many of their beliefs through myths. He also says that they agree with the Greeks about many things such as that the universe was born and can die, as the Greeks say. They also believe that the earth is a sphere and that the god who made and governs the world also encompasses it. They also say that the beginnings of all things vary, but that water is the ultimate source of creation. They also say that there is a fifth natural element beyond the four, from which come the heavens and the stars. Earth sits in the center of everything. Concerning the seed and the soul, and many other things, they speak as the Greeks do. They even weave myths as Plato does, concerning both the indestructible nature of the soul and judgment in Hades and other such things. This is what is said about the Brahmins.

15.1.60. With respect to the Sramans, Megasthenes says that the most honored are called the Hylobii. They live among the trees and sustain themselves by eating leaves and wild fruits. They wear clothes made of tree bark and avoid sexual intercourse and wine. They associate with kings who learn from them through messengers about the causes of things. The kings also consult the Hylobii concerning dealings with the gods. Second in rank of honor after the Hylobii are the doctors. They are philosophers concerned with humanity. They are frugal but do not dwell out of doors. They nourish themselves with rice and barley-meal, all of which they receive either through begging or as an offering of hospitality. Megasthenes further says that the doctors are able to make people more fertile and increase childbirths of both male and female children through the use of drugs. They accomplish cures primarily using grains, not drugs. Of their drugs, the most reputable are their ointments and poultices. The rest of their drugs are somewhat malicious. These men also practice endurance in both labor and perseverance. For example, they practice by remaining motionless in a single position for an entire day. He says that others among the Sramans are prophets and enchanters who have knowledge of spells and customs for the dead. They care for themselves by begging around the villages and cities. There are, Megasthenes says, men more graceful and clever among the Sramans, but even they indulge in the common chatter about Hades, since such talk reputedly increases reverence for the gods and piety. He says that even the wives of some Sramans practice philosophy and avoid also sexual intercourse.

. . .

15.1.62. Aristobolus[272] says of the customs of those who dwell at Taxila that they are peculiar and novel. Those who are unable to give their daughters in marriage because of poverty lead them into the market when they reach their youthful prime and summon a crowd with horns and drums (the type used to signal for battle). They then expose their daughter's backside all the way up to the shoulders to the first man who approaches. If she is acceptable to him and she allows him to persuade her, upon coming to terms, they marry. He says that among some Taxilans the dead are tossed to the vultures. It is common, as with other peoples, to have many wives. He also says that among some of these people the wives are burned willingly along with their husbands. Wives who are unwilling to submit are held in disrepute. This practice is noted among other peoples as well.

15.1.63. Onesicritus[273] says that he was sent to converse with these Wise men because Alexander heard that they were always naked and practiced endurance. The Wise men were held in great honor and did not attend to others when summoned, but ordered others to come to them if they wished to participate in the happenings and conversations of the Wise men. This was the situation, and Alexander did not think it fitting to visit the Wise men himself, nor would he compel them to do something contrary to their ancestral laws. Thus Onesicritus was sent. He said that he discerned fifteen men about 2.5 miles from the city, each sitting in a different position, standing, sitting, or lying naked and motionless until evening when each would depart into the city. Onesicritus says that it was most difficult to endure the sun, which was so hot at midday that no one else was able to easily endure walking with bare feet on the ground.

15.1.64. Onesicritus says that he engaged in conversations with Calanus, one of the Wise men who had followed the king[274] as far as Persis and there died according to ancestral custom, placed on a burning pyre. When Onesicritus first met him, Calanus happened to be lying on some rocks.

---

272. Historian of Alexander the Great who also served as an officer under him.
273. Head steersman of Alexander who took part in the journey to and from India.
274. Alexander.

Onesicritus walked toward him and greeted Calanus and said that he had been sent by the king to listen to their wisdom and then report back. If Calanus had no problem with this, Onesicritus was ready to listen. Calanus saw the short mantle, felt hat, and boots he wore and laughed. He then said to Onesicritus that in ancient times barley-groat and wheat-meal were everywhere, just as now dust is, and springs flowed everywhere, some with water, others with milk, or honey, or wine, or olive oil. Man, through his wantonness and overindulgence, fell into arrogance. Zeus, hating the situation, suppressed all good things and delivered to men a life of toil. When moderation and other such virtues arose in man once again, he reintroduced an abundance of good things. A situation of indulgence, Calanus said, is once again near, and there is a danger that the destruction of all living things is coming. After saying this, Calanus ordered Onesicritus to take off his clothes and lie naked on the same stones as he and thus have a share in listening if he wanted to listen. While Onesicritus was making to obey this command, Mandanis, the eldest and wisest of the Wise men, chastised Calanus for being arrogant even while he accused another of being so. Mandanis then summoned Onesicritus and said that he applauded the king, because he desired wisdom while governing such a large empire. The king was the only philosopher bearing arms he had ever seen. It would be, Mandanis said, most helpful of all if such men should be wise to whom the power was given to persuade the willing and compel the unwilling to practice moderation. Mandanis added that he would be forgiven if he should be unable to explain this knowledge in a useful way while talking through three interpreters, who understand nothing more than the mob itself except the language. It would be like expecting clear water to flow through mud.

15.1.65. At any rate, Onesicritus says that what Mandanis said amounts to this: The best teaching would be teaching that removes pleasure and pain from the soul. Also, pain and toil are different, since the former is an enemy and the latter a friend to men. Toil exercises the body, at least, so that through exercise one's opinions are made stronger, resulting in one's ability to put an end to strife and be on hand to offer good advice in both public and private matters. Indeed, Mandanis advised Taxiles to welcome Alexander because either, by welcoming a better man than himself, Taxiles would benefit, or, an inferior man would be bettered by Taxiles' welcome. After saying these things, Mandanis inquired if among the Greeks such teachings were common. Onesicritus responded that Pythagoras taught such things and ordered his followers to abstain from eating living creatures. Socrates and Diogenes, whom Socrates had heard speak, also taught these things. Mandanis replied that he thought the Greeks seemed reasonable in this and other ways, but erred in one thing—they placed custom before nature. Otherwise, they would not be ashamed to go about their daily business naked as he did, nor would they be ashamed to live simply. The best house, he said, is the one that needs the least repair. Onesicritus says that the Wise man Mandanis inquired further about Greek views on many natural phenomena, like prognostics, rains, droughts, and diseases.

The Wise men all then went away into the city and dispersed around the markets. Generally, if the Wise men happen upon someone in the city carrying figs or grapes, they take some fruit from them as a gift. If there is olive oil, they pour it over themselves and anoint their skin. The whole of wealthy households are available to them, even the women's quarters. They enter these homes and share dinner and their teachings. The Wise men consider bodily diseases the worst thing that can happen to them. If one suspects that he has a disease, he leads himself to fire, first building a pyre and then anointing himself with oil. Once he is seated on the pyre, he orders that it be lit, and he burns without moving.

15.1.66. Nearchus[275] speaks of the Wise men in the following manner: He says that the Brahmins participate in government and attend the kings as advisors. The other Wise men examine natural phenomena. Calanus was one of these Wise men. Their wives philosophize with them, and the lifestyle of all of them is austere. Nearchus states the following about the customs of the rest of the Indians: Their laws are unwritten, both public and private, and their customs are unlike those of others. For example, among some of the Indians, maiden girls are presented as prizes for boxing champions and thus are married without a dowry. Among other Indians, the crops are cultivated in common by kin groups and each man carries off only the amount equal to his household need during the year. The rest of the crops are then burned to ensure the need for toil thereafter and to avoid the urge to laziness. They arm themselves with 4.5-foot bows with arrows, or with a javelin, small shield, and 4.5-foot broadsword. Instead of bridles for their horses, they use something similar to a muzzle. The lips of the horses are pierced through with metal spikes to attach to the muzzle.

15.1.67. Nearchus also says that the ingenuity of the Indians was demonstrated with respect to sponges they saw the Macedonians using. They made imitation sponges by stitching hair, small ropes, and cords through wool. After compressing the wool into felt, they removed the cords and such and then dyed the remaining wool object. Among the Indians as well there are numerous makers of both scrapers and oil flasks. They write script upon tightly woven linen (though others report that they do not use an alphabet at all). They use melted bronze, both poured and beaten. Nearchus does not explain how they use it but says that the resulting objects are strange. The vessels shatter like clay tiles upon impact with the ground. Among other stories he tells of the Indians is this one: There is a custom of not bowing to kings and other people in positions of power or prominence. They offer prayers instead. He also says that the land produces precious stones like crystals, rubies, and even pearls.

Strabo next records a debate among historians concerning Calanus' death and the principle of suicide among the Indian Wise men.

---

275. Commander of Alexander's fleet. He circumnavigated the coast of India on a return voyage to the Tigris River.

15.1.69. The following things are also said by historians. They say that the Indians worship Zeus the Storm-Gatherer, the Ganges River, and local spirits. Whenever the king washes his hair, they have a great festival and send large gifts, each person's gift displaying his wealth in competition with others. They say that some of the gold-digging ants are winged and that gold dust is carried down the river, as happens also with the Iberian rivers. In parades during the festivals, there are many elephants adorned with gold and silver. There are also many four-horsed chariots and ox-carts. The army comes next, all decked out, and then large golden cauldrons and six-foot round craters are carried through. In addition, they parade tables of Indian bronze, thrones, drinking cups, and basins. The majority of the objects are set with precious stones like emeralds, beryls, and rubies. The people wear multicolored clothes woven through with gold, and they are accompanied by aurochs, leopards, domesticated lions, sweet-voiced and colorful birds. Clearchus[276] says that there are four-wheeled wagons that carry trees with large leaves upon which a type of domesticated bird rests, a most sweet-voiced bird, a type of orion, that has the most splendid and colorful appearance. It is called the catreus and looks most like the peacock. Clearchus can provide the rest of the description.

15.1.70. Regarding the Wise men, historians contrast the Brahmins and the Pramnae. The Pramnae are fond of strife and debate. The Brahmins practice physiology and astronomy, but they are mocked by the Pramnae as imposters and stupid. Some of the Pramnae are referred to as the Mountain Pramnae, while others are called the Naked Pramnae. There are also City Pramnae and the Neighbors. The Mountain Pramnae wear deerskins and have pouches filled with roots and drugs. They pretend to cure people with witchcraft, chants, and charms. The Naked Pramnae, as the name suggests, spend their time naked and mostly out of doors. As we said before, they practice endurance for up to thirty-seven years, have wives with whom they do not have sexual intercourse, and are generally admired.

15.1.71. The City Pramnae live in the city or in the country nearby and either wear linen clothes or fawn or deerskins. It is said that the Indians in general dress in white clothing, either in linen or flax, contrary to those who say that they wear colorful clothes. They all let their hair and beards grow long and then braid it in a turban.

5. Pomponius Mela, *Description of the World* 3.62–65 (1st century CE). *Pomponius describes the peoples living in India and further east. (RFK)*

3.62. India is fertile and bubbles with a diversity of human and animal kind. It supports ants no smaller than the largest dogs,[277] which are said to

---

276. Student of Aristotle who traveled throughout Asia Minor and wrote works that contained numerous anecdotes and "curiosities," especially concerning people of the far east.

277. Pomponius likely derives this story from Herodotus.

guard, in the manner of griffins, gold that is brought up from deep within the earth. They are the greatest danger to anyone who touches the gold. The land also supports monstrous serpents that can impair even an elephant with their venom and coils. The land is so rich in some places and the soil so fertile that honey there flows from leaves, trees produce wool,[278] and split bamboo shoots [are so large] they convey, as if boats, two or even three people at the same time.

3.63. The manner of dress and customs of the people vary. Some dress in linen or what we have called "wool," others in the skins of birds and wild animals. One group of Indians goes naked, while another covers just their privates. Some Indians are short and tiny, others have such tall and large bodies that they use elephants, even the largest in India, as easily and expertly as we do horses.

3.64. Certain Indians kill no animals and think it best to eat no meat, while fish alone nourishes others. Some kill their parents as one does a sacrificial animal before they fall into atrophy through illness and old age. They also think that to eat the innards of those killed is right and extremely pious. 65. But when old age or disease is allowed to come upon others, they go away far off from others and await death quietly and without fear. More prudent even than these people are those who devote themselves to the art and study of wisdom. They do not await death but seek it out joyfully and gloriously by throwing themselves into flames.

6. Pliny, *Natural History* 20.54–55, 24.84–91 (1st century CE).
Pliny discusses the Chinese, the people furthest from Rome with whom the Romans traded. He also addresses a land called Taprobone, an island nation near India in the Indian Ocean, identified with Sri Lanka. (MLG)

20.54. The first inhabitants of the far northeastern region are called Seres, notable for the thread obtained from their forests.[279] They soak the foliage with water and comb off the white down. This activity provides our women the two tasks of unweaving the threads and reweaving. So much work derived from so far away in order to provide our wives with translucent clothing for public view! The Seres are indeed gentle, but they are like wild animals in that they shun contact with other humans and let commerce come to them.

20.55. The first known river of their land is the Psitharas, the next is the Cambari, and the third the Lanos. From this arises the Chryse headland, the Cirnaba, the river Atianos, and the bay and people called Attacorae. Sunny hills protect them from every harmful wind, and they enjoy the same climate as the Hyperboreans. The Attacorae are the subject of a specialized

---

278. He is referring to cotton.
279. Silk.

treatise by Amometus, just as Hecataeus wrote on the Hyperboreans. Next to the Attacorae tribe are the Thuni and the Focari, and then the inhabitants of India: the Casiri who live in the interior toward the Scythians. These eat human flesh. Indian nomads also wander in this direction. Some say that these people share a northern border with the Cicones and the Brisari.

Pliny discusses Taprobone (Sri Lanka).

24.84. I acquired more accurate information than earlier reports when, during the reign of Claudius [41–54 CE], an embassy from that island arrived. It happened like this. Annius Plocamus acquired the rights to collect taxes from the Red Sea area, and his freedman sailed around Arabia. En route the north wind drove him beyond Carmania. Fifteen days later he reached the port of Hippuri, where the king kindly entertained him for six months. During that time, he became acculturated and responded to the king's inquiries with a narrative about the Romans and Caesar. During this report, the king was exceptionally impressed by Roman justice because the coins found on the captive were of equal weight, although the diverse symbols revealed that they were coined by many different rulers. 85. This so encouraged him to seek our friendship that he sent four ambassadors. The leader of this embassy was Rachia. The information obtained from this embassy is as follows: There are 500 towns and a south-facing harbor next to the most famous town Palaesimundus. This is the seat of the king, with a population of 200,000.

24.86. In the interior is the Megisba marsh. It is 375 Roman miles in circumference and contains islands that are suitable only for pasturage. This marsh is the source of two rivers. The Palaemundum flows past the city of the same name and runs to the harbor in three channels. It is a little more than a half mile at the narrowest point and 1.75 miles at the widest. The other river, the Cydara, runs north toward India. They say that India's closest promontory is the one called the Coliacum, a four-day sail that passes the Island of the Sun in the middle of the trip.

24.87. The sea there is green and filled with bushy trees. The tops of these underwater trees are grazed by the rudders of ships. The ambassadors marveled at our constellations, the Septentriones and the Vergiliae,[280] as if gazing on a new heaven. They confessed that they did not even see the moon rise above the land except from the 8th to the 16th of the month. Canopus, a large and bright star, shines there at night. What most surprised them, however, was that their shadows pointed north and not south, and the sun rose from the left and set on the right and not the other way round.

24.88. They also reported that the side of the island that lies southeast of India extends for 1,250 miles. They also claim that they face the Seres, who dwell beyond the Hemodos,[281] with whom they also trade. According to the ambassadors, Rachia's father traveled there often, and the Seres came

---

280. The Wain and the Pleiades.
281. Himalayas.

to meet them on their arrival. They say that these men are in fact larger than normal men, with red hair and blue eyes, who make harsh sounds with their mouths and use no language for trade. For the rest, the ambassadors' accounts agree with what our traders say. When the goods are laid next to the merchandise on the far shore of the river, they take the barter if it is sufficient. A more righteous hatred of luxury derives from a contemplation of those products, the manner of their acquisition and their purpose.

24.89. Although banished by nature beyond the edge of the world, our vices are found even in Taprobone. They value gold and silver and a tortoiseshell marble as well as pearls and gems. Their whole accumulation of luxury far exceeds ours. They claimed a great wealth but said that we make more a show of ours. According to them, no citizen has a slave. They get up at dawn and do not sleep during the day. Their buildings do not rise high in the air. The price of grain never rises. They have no courts or lawsuits. They worship Heracles. They choose their king from the people on account of his age, his mercy, and his lack of children. If he afterwards should have a child, he must abdicate in order to avoid an hereditary monarchy.

24.90. They say that the people elect thirty governors and that no one is executed without a majority vote. After this, they say, there is an appeal to the people and seventy judges are appointed. If these acquit the defendant, the thirty are no longer respected but are absolutely dishonored. The king wears the robe of Liber Pater, but everyone else dresses like Arabs.

24.91. If the king misbehaves, he is condemned to execution, but nobody kills him. Everyone turns away and refuses even to speak to him. They spend their holidays hunting. Their favorite quarry are tigers and elephants. They are diligent farmers, and, although they lack the vine, they have plenty of fruits. They also find pleasure in fishing, especially the turtle, whose shells serve as roofs for family homes, for they are very large. They say that the average lifespan is one hundred years.

7. Plutarch, *Life of Alexander* 60, 62–65 (2nd century CE).
Alexander has led his army into India. (CSR)

60. Alexander himself wrote about what happened with Porus in his letters as follows: The river Hydaspes flowed between the two camps. Porus stationed his elephants on the opposite bank of the river and continuously guarded the crossing. Each day Alexander made a great deal of noise and disturbance in his camp and in so doing convinced the barbarians opposite not to be worried by it. [2] Then, on a stormy and moonless night, he took some of his infantry and his strongest horsemen, went down the river from the enemy, and crossed to a small island. Terrible storms soaked them, and many fierce gusts and lightning strikes hit the camp. Even though some men had been killed or burned by the lightning, he led them off the island and to the opposing riverbank. [3] The river was rough and rising from the storm; its current caused a great rift in the bank and a large part of the river

flowed into it. The area between the branches of the river offered no steady ground to the men since it was slippery and broken in pieces. Onesicritus said that at this place Alexander said, "Athenians, would you believe that I endure such great dangers just so I might enjoy your good opinion?" [4] Alexander himself, however, said that they left their rafts and crossed over in their armor, getting soaked up to their chests in the process.

Alexander crossed over and rode with his cavalry more than a mile in front of his infantry. He reasoned that if the enemy attacked with his cavalry, he would win, but if they moved up their heavy infantry, then his infantry could join him quickly. The first of these two possibilities happened. [5] After he defeated 1,060 chariots that fought against him, he captured all the chariots and killed 400 of the horsemen. Porus realized that Alexander had crossed over and so moved against him with all his strength, except the men he left to block the Macedonians who were crossing the river. Alexander was afraid of the elephants and the large numbers of the enemy, and so he attacked the left wing while ordering Coenus to attack on the right. [6] After a rout on both wings, the enemy who had been forced out of position withdrew and crowded around the elephants. From then on, the battle was fought closely, and only in the eighth hour did the enemy surrender. This is what the victor of the battle, Alexander himself, said in his letters.

Most writers agree that Porus was over six feet in height, and the size and bulk of his body suited him to an elephant as most men are suited to a horse. [7] Indeed, his elephant was huge and showed amazing consideration and care for the king. It pushed men back and defended him from his attackers while he was still strong; when the elephant perceived that his rider suffered from many arrows and wounds, it feared that he would slip off and so it carefully lowered itself to the ground onto its knees and gently took hold of and drew out each spear from his body with its trunk.

[8] When Alexander asked Porus, who had been captured, how he should treat him, Porus said "in a kingly way." When Alexander asked what else he had to say, he said, "Everything falls under the 'kingly way' comment." Because of his answer, Alexander not only allowed him to rule where he had been king before and that was now named a province, he also included in addition the land of some autonomous tribes he had defeated. It included fifteen races, 5,000 cities that are worth mentioning, and many villages. They say that he conquered another land three times as big and gave the province to Philip, one of his companions.

> *After the battle, Alexander's horse Bucephalus dies. Alexander grieves and names a city in India after him.*

62. The battle with Porus, however, made the Macedonians less spirited and thus prevented them from going still further into India, for they had barely defeated Porus when he had brought 20,000 infantry and 2,000 horsemen to battle. They strongly resisted Alexander when he pressed them to cross the river Ganges, which they had found out was nearly 3.5 miles wide and 600 feet deep. The opposing banks of the river were hidden by a mass of

armored men, horses, and elephants. [2] The kings of the Gandarites and the Praesii were said to be waiting with 80,000 horsemen, 200,000 foot soldiers, 8,000 chariots, and 6,000 battle-elephants. This information was not a boast, for Androcottus, who was king there not long after this, gave 500 elephants to Seleucus and attacked and conquered all of India with 6,000 men in his army. [3] First, Alexander, out of anger and despair, shut himself into his tent and just lay there. He did not see any good in what they had accomplished if he did not cross the Ganges; rather, he saw a retreat as an acknowledgment of weakness. His friends tried to appease him, and his soldiers stood before his doors and begged him with much weeping and wailing. He relented and then began to break up his camp while plotting numerous tricky and clever things to do to enhance his reputation. [4] He equipped his camp with bigger weapons, larger stables, and heavier bridles; then he tossed them about and left them behind. He established altars for the gods, which even now the kings of the Praesii honor when they cross the river by making sacrifices in the Greek style. As a young man Androcottus saw Alexander, and it is said that he often claimed later that Alexander came close to conquering the country since their king was hated and scorned for his depravity and low birth.

63. Alexander was eager to leave there and see the ocean beyond, so he had a number of ferry boats and rafts built and was carried on the river at a leisurely pace, though the trip was not without toil or without war. He disembarked often, attacked many cities, and conquered everything. But in an attack against the Malli, who are said to be the most warlike of the Indians, he was nearly killed. [2] He caused the men on top of the walls to scatter by shooting at them with arrows. After that, he was the first to climb up the walls with a ladder. When the ladder shattered, he endured many blows from below from the barbarians stationed alongside the walls. He only had a few companions, and so he crouched up and launched himself from the wall into the midst of the enemy, fortunately landing upright. [3] As he shook his weapons, the barbarians thought that some kind of flaming apparition appeared in front of his body. At first, they retreated and scattered to the winds. When they saw that he was alone except for two armor-bearers, they ran back at him and kept trying to wound him through his armor with their swords and spears while he tried to defend himself. One man stood a little further off and shot an arrow from his bow that was so well aimed and forceful that it cut through Alexander's breastplate and pierced his rib cage. [4] He gave in to the blow and doubled over. The shooter ran up and drew his barbarian knife, but Peucestas and Limnaeus stood in front of him. Both of them were wounded—Limnaeus died, but Peucestas held his ground and Alexander killed the barbarian. Alexander took many wounds, though finally the side of his head was struck with a club. He leaned his body against the wall and kept watching the enemy. [5] Just then the Macedonians spread out around him, and he was picked up, unconscious of everything around him, and carried to his tent. Almost immediately a story of his death started going around the camp. Once they

had sawed off the wooden arrow shaft, though with difficulty and much effort, and only just had managed to loosen his breastplate, they then had to cut out the arrowhead that had penetrated one of his bones. The arrowhead was said to be three fingers wide and four fingers long. [6] Its removal made Alexander faint, and he was very close to death before he recovered. After he had escaped the danger, he was still weak and held himself to a strict diet and treatment for a long time. He recognized that the Macedonians making a racket outside longed to see him, so he put on his cloak and went out to them. He conducted sacrifices to the gods straightaway, and then sailed on and conquered many lands and great cities.

64. He captured the ten Naked Wise Men, who had persuaded Sabbas to rebel and caused the most problems for the Macedonians. They were thought to be clever in their answers and men of few words. Therefore, Alexander put some difficult questions to them and said that he would kill the one who first answered wrongly and the rest in order after that. He ordered the eldest one to judge the answers. [2] The first one was asked whether he thought there were more living or more deceased people. He said that there were more living people, for the dead no longer existed. The second one was asked whether the earth or the sea produced larger wild animals, and he said that it was the earth since the sea was part of the earth. The third was asked which animal was the smartest, and he said, "The one which man does not yet know about." [3] The fourth was examined about why he encouraged Sabbas to revolt, and he answered, "I wished him to live well or to die well." The fifth one was asked whether he thought day or night came first. He said, "day, by one day." He added, when the king stared at him, that difficult questions needed difficult answers. [4] Alexander went on to the sixth one and asked how someone could be especially beloved. He answered, "If he is the most powerful but is not feared." Of the three remaining, one was asked how he might become a god instead of a man, and he answered, "If he should do something that is not able to be done by man." The second was asked whether life or death was the stronger, and he replied that it was life, since life endures so many hardships. [5] The last one was asked what age it was good for a man to live until, and he answered, "Until he does not think that dying is better than living." Alexander turned to the judge and ordered him to declare his opinion. When he answered that each one spoke worse than the next, Alexander said, "Therefore, you will be killed first because you judged such things." "No indeed, king," he said, "as long as you did not lie when you said that you would kill first the man who answered the most badly." 65. He then gave the Naked Wise Men gifts and sent them away.

Alexander sent Onesicritus, who was a philosopher of the school of Diogenes the Cynic, to the men who were especially well respected and lived alone and in peace and asked them to speak with him. [2] Onesicritus says that Calanus arrogantly and roughly ordered him to take off his tunic and listen to their words while naked, or else he would not speak to him, not even if he came from Zeus. Dandamis[282] was nicer. After he had learned about Socrates and Pythagoras and Diogenes, he said that these men seemed to be naturally well disposed but to have lived with too much shame before the laws. [3] Others say that Dandamis said nothing other than this one question: "For the sake of what did Alexander come so far?" Taxiles, however, persuaded Calanus to go to Alexander. His real name was Sphines, but since when he greets people he happens to meet he greets them with "Cale" in the Indian language, he was named Calanus by the Greeks. He is said to have presented a model of empire to Alexander. [4] He put a dried and brittle hide on the ground and stood on one edge. It was held down on that side but lifted up on the other sides. He went around the hide in a circle and showed that this is what happened on each side when it was pressed. Finally, he stepped on the middle and held it down so that everything was pressed down. He wanted it to serve as an analogy for rule: Alexander ought to press down on the middle of his empire and not wander away to the edges for too long.

8. Philostratus, *Life of Apollonius of Tyana* 2.18 (2nd century CE).
Philostratus relates the flooding of the Indus and the Nile as Apollonius and company crossed the Indus. (MLG)

And so they sailed across the Indus at a point about five miles wide, so large is its navigable size. About this river, the following facts have been written. The Indus begins at the Caucaus, greater in size at its source than all the rivers of Asia. As it flows, it incorporates many navigable rivers. It behaves like a twin to the Nile: it pours over India, heaps soil on soil, and allows the Indians to plant in the manner of the Egyptians. I do not think it right in view of the authorities to contradict the opinion that the snows of Ethiopia and of the mountains of the first Cataract are the source of the Nile's flooding. But in contemplating the Indus, I reason that it accomplishes the same rising as the Nile without the land above it having snowfall. In addition, I know that god has revealed the extremities of the whole earth to be Ethiopia and India, whose inhabitants he darkened, the one from the rising and the other from the setting sun. How could this happen to people unless they were warmed even in winter? And if the sun heats the land all year, how could one think that it snows? How could one think that the snow discharges for the rivers the duty of causing them to overflow their portions? And if snow visits such sunny regions, how could it cause such a large flood? How could there be a sufficient amount for a river flooding Egypt?

---

282. This is the same man as Mandanis in Strabo.

9. Philostratus, *Life of Apollonius of Tyana* 3.6–9 (2nd century CE). *The description of a snake hunt in India. (MLG)*

3.6. As they descended the mountain, they said that they happened upon a snake hunt, which I should say something about. Especially when men who take notice of such things have said much about how the hare is captured and may be captured, it is quite absurd for me to leave out an account of a noble and miraculous hunt, a hunt not passed over by the man about whom I am composing this biography.

The whole land of India is, of course, swarming with snakes of unaccountable size.[283] They fill the marshes and the mountains. No hill is free of them. The marsh snakes are sluggish and around fifty-two feet long without standing crests. They are like female snakes, quite black on their backs and less scaly than the rest. About these, Homer has hit upon the wiser account than the other poets, because he calls the snake in Aulis who lived by the fountain "tawny-backed."[284] The other poets say that a similar snake in the Nemean wood has a crest, the very thing we would not find on the marsh snake. 3.7. The snakes from the foothills and mountain ridges come down into the plains for hunting. These have every advantage over the marsh snakes, especially since they greatly surpass them in length, are swifter than the fastest rivers, and nothing escapes them. These also have crests, which rise up moderately in youth but increase to a great size with age, when they become red and sawlike. These even grow beards and raise their necks high, and their scales glitter like silver. The pupils of their eyes are red-hot stones and are said to have extraordinary powers for many mysterious things. It is lucky for the hunters to find a plain snake when it is digesting some elephant, because this destroys both animals. Those who catch snakes are rewarded with the eyes, the skin, and the teeth. These last are in other respects like massive boar tusks, but they are finer, twisted, and with pristine edges like those of large fish.

3.8. The mountain snakes have scales that appear golden. They are longer than the snakes of the plain. They have curly, golden beards. They have larger eyebrows than the snakes of the plain, and the eyes set under these brows flash terribly and shamelessly. They sound like the clanging of bronze when they move wavelike over the ground. A fire larger than a torch blazes from their fire-red crests. These snakes catch elephants as well and are in turn captured by the Indians in the following manner. They weave golden letters into a scarlet robe, cast a sleeping spell on the letters, and place it before the snake's hole. This robe conquers the immovable eyes of the snake. They also sing to it many songs of secret wisdom, which lead it to lift its neck out of its hole and fall asleep on the letters. And then the Indians rush forward and fall upon the sleeping snake with axes. Cutting off its

---

283. Perhaps a source for later stories of dragons.
284. Homer, *Iliad* 2.308.

head, they plunder the stones within it. They say that within the heads of mountain snakes lie stones. These stones are formed like a flower flashing every color and with a mystical power like what is said about Gyges' ring.[285] Often the snake takes an Indian along with his ax and magic and drags him into his hole and disappears, nearly causing a mountain tremor. These mountains, they say, are located near the Red Sea [here, Indian Ocean] and one can hear their terrifying hissing. The snakes are said to travel down to the sea and swim far out to sea. Concerning the lifespan of this beast, it is impossible to discover and unbelievable to utter. So much for what I know about the snakes.

3.9. They say that there is a great city under the mountain called Paraca. In the center of this town are many snakeheads, because the local Indians train in this hunt from their youth. They are said to understand the speech and wishes of animals because they eat the heart and liver of a snake . . .

10. Philostratus, *Life of Apollonius of Tyana* 3.20 (2nd century CE). *The Indian Wise man, Iarchas, teaches Apollonius by comparing the Indian hero Ganges (his past incarnation) to Achilles. (MLG)*

Once upon a time, Iarchas said, there lived in this land the Ethiopians, who are an Indian tribe. Ethiopia did not yet exist, but Egypt extended its borders beyond Meroë and the Cataracts, the land containing the sources of the Nile and ending with its outlets. In this period, then, the Ethiopians lived in this land, subject to King Ganges. The land fed them sufficiently, and the gods took care of them. But when they killed this king, the rest of the Indians considered them impure, and the land did not allow them to remain, since it destroyed whatever seeds they planted in it before they flowered. The land made the children stillborn, gave their flocks poor food, and the land on which they placed a city collapsed in a sinkhole. The ghost of Ganges threw the crowd into confusion and drove them on in their flight, not stopping until they sacrificed to the land the murderers and those with bloodied hands. Ganges was over seventeen feet tall, more handsome than any mortal, the son of the river Ganges. The father used to flood India, but the son turned him to the Red Sea and reconciled the river to the land. As a result of this act, the earth fed him while he was alive and avenged him when dead. Homer takes Achilles to Troy on behalf of Helen and says that he sacked twelve coastal and eleven inland cities, and, when his war-prize was taken by the king, he was enraged, seeing how he was an unfeeling and savage man. Let us compare the Indian with this man. Regarding cities, the Indian founded sixty, and they were the most admired in the land. As to destroying cities, no one considers this more glorious than building them. He drove off a band of Scythians, who were invading this land from the

---

285. That is, it renders the bearer invisible.

Caucasus. The good man who frees his own land is clearly much better than the man enslaving a city for the sake of a woman and especially a woman who was likely willingly abducted. The Indian hero made an alliance with the king of the land now ruled by Phraotes. When this king in absolutely lawless licentiousness stole away Ganges' wife, he did not break the alliance but claimed that he had sworn such serious oaths and he could never think it just to break them.

CHAPTER 14

EUROPE: THE BLACK SEA REGION

In the Greek and Roman imaginations, the Black Sea was frequently a home to savages, magic, and horses. The Black Sea was the home of the Golden Fleece, the semidivine Medea, and the horse-lord Scythians. Perhaps the most influential of the fantastic peoples, the Scythians embody the myth of the Noble Savage, and, along with Tacitus' Germans, influenced modern representations of Native American culture. The Black Sea region was also one of the most well-known and necessary regions for the Greeks. It was a primary source of both precious metals and grain for the Greeks and, as a result, was heavily populated with colonies. Immigrants from this area were also numerous in Greece from the 5th century onward. The Romans recognized the centrality of this region as well, with the establishment in the 3rd century CE of one of the Roman administrative capitals in Split, in modern Croatia, and Constantine's decision to establish his own capital at Constantinople, modern Istanbul, located on the ancient Greek colony of Byzantium (which gave its name to the post-Roman Empire of the Byzantines).

1. Herodotus, *Histories* 1.215–216 (5th century BCE). *At the end of his description of Cyrus' expansion of the Persian Empire, Herodotus describes the habits of the Massagetai, the tribe whom Cyrus has just fought and who are often conflated in ancient sources with the Scythians or their women with Amazons. (RFK)*

1.215. The Massagetai share similar clothing and lifestyle with the Scythians. They are horsemen, infantry (they have some of both), and archers and spearmen. They also customarily carry axes. They use gold and bronze for everything. All spear points, arrowheads, and axes are made of bronze, while belts, girdles, and headgear are all made of gold. [2] In like fashion, they gird their horses' chests with bronze plating, but the bits, bridle, and faceplates are gold. They don't use either iron or silver since their land has none. The land, however, has unlimited supplies of gold and copper.

1.216. They have the following customs: each man marries a woman, but the woman is used in common. The Greeks say that this is a Scythian practice, but it isn't. The Massagetai do it. When a man desires a woman, he hangs his quiver on the front of her wagon and then has sex with her without fear. [2] The Massagetai set no limit on one's age, but whenever a man reaches extreme old age, his relatives gather and sacrifice him along with other beasts. They then boil him and feast on his flesh. This is considered the happiest death among them. [3] Those who die from disease are not eaten but are buried in the earth. They consider it a misfortune that he did not achieve being sacrificed. They also don't sow crops but live off livestock and fish, which the Araxes River supplies in abundance. [4] They are milk drinkers. Of all the gods, they worship only the sun and sacrifice horses to it. The reason they sacrifice horses is because they consider the sun the swiftest of all immortals and so offer the swiftest of all creatures to it.

> **2. Herodotus, *Histories* 4.2–3, 4.5–12, 4.17–27, 4.46, 4.59–76, 4.78–80, 4.93–96, 4.102–107 (5th century BCE).** *Herodotus gives a detailed account of the Scythian peoples. While Herodotus and the author of the Hippocratic* Airs, Waters, Places *(Chapter 3, Selection 1) are roughly contemporary and clearly share some information, there are marked differences between the two representations of the Scythians. Herodotus' account, unlike the Hippocratic one, has been shown by scholars to demonstrate accurate knowledge of many Scythian practices. (CSR)*

4.2. The Scythians blind all their slaves because of the milk they drink, which they get in this way: They take pipes made of bones, which most resemble our Greek pipes, and put these into the genitals of a female horse. Then they blow with their mouths, and one person milks while the other blows. They say that they do this for the following reason: After they are blown into, the mare's veins are filled and the udder comes down. [2] Once they get the milk, they pour it into hollow wooden vessels, put their blind slaves at the vessels, and have them stir the milk. After that they draw off the upper part of the liquid, which they think is the better portion, and then the lower part, which they think to be the lesser of the two. For these reasons the Scythians blind everyone they capture, for they are nomads not workers of the land.

4.3. The children born from these slaves and Scythian women grew up and, when they learned about their birth, began resisting the Scythians when they returned from Media. [2] First, they separated off their land by digging a wide ditch that stretched from the Taurian Mountains to the widest part of Lake Maeotis. They entrenched themselves and fought the Scythians who were trying to attack them. [3] There were many battles and, since the Scythians were not able to gain anything more from fighting, one of the Scythians said, "What are we doing, Scythian men? We are fighting with our slaves. By being killed we become inferior and by killing them we will rule fewer later. [4] Now it seems best to me to put aside our spears and bows, and for each of us to take up our horsewhips and approach them. For up to now they have seen us holding weapons, and so they have been thinking that they were our equals and born from people equal to us. But when they see us holding whips instead of weapons, they will learn that they are our slaves and, once they realize this, will not stand their ground."

. . .

4.5. As the Scythians say, their race is the newest of all the races, and this is their origin: The first man who came into this land, which was deserted at the time, was named Targitaus. They say that the parents of Targitaus are Zeus and the daughter of the Borysthenes River, although they seem to me to be saying an untruth. [2] Of such a lineage is Targitaus, and he had three sons—Lipoxais, Arpoxais, and the youngest Colaxais. [3] While these three were ruling, golden implements fell from the sky onto the Scythian plain—a plow, a yoke, a *sagaris*, and a cup—and upon first seeing them the eldest brother wanted to approach and take them, but the gold burned him as he approached. [4] When he got away, the second one approached, and the same thing occurred again. The burning gold pushed him back. But when the third and youngest approached, the burning gold stopped burning, and he took the implements back into his house. Because of this event, the elder brothers agreed to give the entire kingship over to the youngest son.

4.6. From Lipoxais came those of the Scythians who are called the Auchatai; from the middle son Arpoxais come the races called the Catiaroi and the Traspians; and the royal Scythians, who are called the Paralatae, come from the youngest brother. [2] The name given to all of them is the Scoloti, the Greeks call them Scythians. [3] The Scythians say these things about themselves.

4.7. They also say that all the years since they came into being, from the first king Targitaus up to the invasion of Darius, do not add up to more than 1,000. The kings' most important job is to guard the holy gold and appease it with great sacrifices and honor it every year. [4] Whosoever has the sacred gold and falls asleep in the open at a festival will not live out the year according to the Scythians. Therefore he is given as much land as can be ridden around on a horse in one day. Since the land of Scythia is large, Colaxais established three kingdoms for his children and made one of them the largest, and that is where the gold is guarded. [5] They say that in the lands of the inhabitants further northward one is not able to see very far or to cross it because feathers have covered it. The land and the air are full of feathers, and so these places are shut off from sight.

4.8. The Scythians say these things about themselves and the lands north of them, but those Greeks living on the Euxine Sea say the following. When he was driving the cows of Geryon, Heracles arrived in a deserted land, where the Scythians now live. [2] Geryon lives beyond the Euxine Sea, inhabiting an island the Greeks say is Erytheia, which is near Gedira by the Ocean and beyond the Pillars of Heracles. They say that Ocean begins in the direction of the rising of the sun and flows around the whole world, but they do not show this with evidence. [3] So when Heracles arrived in the land that is now called Scythia, he slept wrapped in his lion skin (for he found snow and icy cold there) and his horses were grazing near his chariot. And at that time they were taken off by divine happenstance. 9. When Heracles woke up, he sought them out, wandering the whole of the land until he finally arrived at the land called Hylaea. There he found in a cave a half-maiden, the dual-formed Echidna. Everything from her buttocks up was woman but below was snake. [2] He saw her and marveled. He asked if she had seen his horses roaming about; she said that she had them and would not return them until they had sex. Heracles had sex with her for this price. [3] She put off returning the horses, for she wanted to spend the most time possible with Heracles, while he, although taken care of, wanted to be set free. Finally she returned them and said, "I saved these horses for you when they arrived here, and you handed over a reward. I will have three sons by you. [4] Explain what ought to be done with these sons when they grow up. Should I settle them here (for I have power over this land) or send them to you?" She asked these things, and they say that Heracles answered in this way: [5] "When you see that the children have become men, do these things and do not make a mistake: see if they can draw this bow and put on this belt in this particular way. Whoever can, settle him in this land; but whoever should fall short in these deeds that I command, send him away from the land. By doing these things you will be cheered and you will complete my commands." 10. He drew one of his bows (for earlier on Heracles carried two) and showed her the way to clasp the belt. Then he handed over the bow and the belt, which had a golden bowl right where it joined. After he gave them to her, he went away. When the children were born and grown to manhood, she gave these names to them: Agathursus to one, Gelonus to the next, and Scythes to the youngest. Mindful of her orders, she did what Heracles commanded. [2] Two of her sons, Agathursus and Gelonus, were not able to attain the prize set before them, and so they lived exiled from their country by she who bore them. The youngest of them, Scythes, completed the task and remained in the land. [3] And from Scythes son of Heracles all the kings of Scythia have descended, and because of his bowl the Scythians still carry bowls hanging from their belts. His mother arranged this result for Scythes alone. Those of the Greeks living on the Euxine Sea say this.

4.11. There is another story, which I especially prefer, that goes as follows. The Scythians were nomads living in Asia and were hard-pressed in war by the Massagetai. They left and crossed the river Araxes into Cimmerian land (which the Scythians now inhabit but was said to belong to the Cimmerians long ago). [2] The Cimmerians took counsel about the Scythians' arrival and the greatness of the army invading, and their opinions were divided. Both sides felt strongly, but the better plan was that of the royalty. For the opinion of the people was that it would be best to leave and not run risks for a place that lacked many things; the opinion of the royalty was that they should fight the invaders for the land. [3] The people were not willing to be persuaded by the royalty, and the royalty was not willing to be persuaded by the people. The people wanted to leave the land and hand it over to the invaders without a battle, but the opinion of the royalty was that it was good to die in their own land and not to flee with the people, for they were reckoning up the good things that they had and how many evil things they would take up if they fled from their homeland. [4] And so they decided to do as follows. They divided up into equal numbers, and they fought with one another, and once they all had died the Cimmerian people buried them in their own land alongside the river Tyras (and their grave mound is still visible) and, once they buried them, they made their exodus out of the country and the Scythians entered into and took hold of an empty land.

4.12. Even now in Scythia there are Cimmerian walls, Cimmerian straits, and a section of land called Cimmeria—even the Bosporus is called Cimmerian. [2] Clearly, the Cimmerians fled the Scythians into Asia and populated the peninsula on which the Greek city of Sinope is now. And it is clear that the Scythians in pursuing them entered into Media because they made a mistake in their travels. [3] For the Cimmerians consistently fled along the sea, but the Scythians, keeping the Caucasus to the right in their pursuit until they entered the Median land, directed their path into the interior. This other story is told by both Greeks and barbarians.

. . .

4.17. Beginning from the trading place of the Borysthenites (for this is the exact middle point of the coasts of all Scythia), the Callippidae, who are Greek Scythians, are the first inhabitants you meet, and beyond them is another race called the Alizones. These people and the Callipidae practice many other customs that are the same as the Scythians, but they differ in that they are farmers and eat grain, onions, garlic, lentils, and millet. [2] Beyond the Alizones the farming Scythians live, who do not sow their grain for eating but rather for selling. North of these people live the Neurians, but the land to the north of the Neurians is empty of men, as far as we know.

4.18. These, then, are the peoples who live by the river Hypanis to the west of the Borysthenes. But for one crossing the Borysthenes and heading away from the sea, the first tribe is the Hylaia, and then beyond them to the north live farmer and herder Scythians, whom the Greeks who live by the Hypanis call the Borysthenites, while calling themselves Olbiopolites. [2] These farming Scythians inhabit an area that covers a three-day journey eastward, reaching to the river Panticapes, and an eleven-day sail northward up the Borysthenes. North of these people is a great empty area. [3] Beyond that the Androphagoi [Cannibals] live, who are a particular race and not at all like the Scythians. Beyond these people is an area that is truly empty and without any race of men as far as we know.

4.19. Traveling east from these farming Scythians and crossing the Panticapes River, one meets the nomadic Scythians who live there, who neither sow anything nor plow. This whole area except for Hylaia is devoid of trees. These nomads inhabit a land that is a fourteen-day journey to the east extending to the river Gerrhon.

4.20. Beyond the Gerrhon is what is called the Kingdom, where the best and most populous Scythians live who think that other Scythians are their slaves. Their territory extends to the Taurian land in the south, and to the east up to the trench, which the offspring of the blind slaves dug, and to the trade exchange on the shores of Lake Maeotis (which is called Cremnoi) and also all the way to the river Tanais. [2] To the north of the Scythian Kingdom live the Black Cloaks—a different race and not Scythian. North of the Black Cloaks are lakes and an area empty of men, as far as we know.

4.21. It is no longer Scythian land across the Tanais, but the first of the territories belongs to the Sauromatai, who inhabit the land starting from the tip of Lake Maeotis for a fifteen-day journey to the north; the whole area is bare of wild or cultivated trees. The Boudinoi, who have the next area of land beyond them, live in a land entirely thick with all sorts of forest life.

4.22. North of the Boudinoi is a wasteland for a seven-day journey, and after the emptiness and turning a little to the east the Thussagetai live, who are a large and particular race. They live by hunting. [2] In the same area and next to these people live the Iyrcae, as they are called. These people live by hunting as follows. They climb a tree and hide in it, for the trees are dense throughout the whole land. Each man's horse was trained to lie on its stomach so that it will be low down and ready, and a dog is there too. [3] When he sees a wild beast from the tree, he shoots it, gets down onto the horse, and chases it, and the dog comes too. Beyond these people and turning to the east other Scythians live, Scythians who rebelled from the Royal Scythians and for that reason live in this land.

4.23. Up until the land of these Scythians the ground is flat and has deep soil, but beyond them it is rocky and harsh. [2] Far off from this rugged land at the foot of high mountains live people who are said to be completely bald from birth—both men and women—and have flat noses and large chins. They speak a particular language, wear Scythian clothes, and live off trees. [3] The tree is named a *ponticus*, and it is the same in size as a fig tree. It bears a fruit like a bean, which has a stone in the center. When the fruit becomes ripe, they strain it through cloth and what flows through is thick and dark. They call this fluid *askhu*. [4] They lick this up and drink it mixed with milk, and from the thickest part of the dregs they make cakes and eat them. They do not have many herds because the pasturage is not good there. They each live under a tree. During the winter they wrap the tree with a white, waterproof felt cloth; they do without the felt in the summer. [5] No men are unjust toward them (for they are said to be holy), and they do not possess weapons for war. They decide on disputes for their neighbors, and when a fugitive flees to them, no one harms him. Their name is the Argippaei.

4.24. Up to this bald tribe much is clear about the land and the peoples around it, for Scythians travel to these groups. It is not difficult to learn about them, for the Scythians as well as the Greeks from the Borysthenite trading place and other trading places on the Euxine Sea visit them. The Scythians who go among them use seven interpreters and seven languages.

4.25. Up to these people the land and peoples are known, but beyond the bald people no one knows enough to speak with certainty, for the high and impassable mountains cut us off and no one has gone over them. The bald people say (and they do not seem to me to speak the truth) that goat-footed men live in the mountains, and over the mountain there are other people who sleep six months out of the year. I do not believe this at all. [2] To the east of the bald people the land is known for certain to be inhabited by the Issedones, but beyond them to the north of the bald people or the Issedones it is not known, except for whatever these tribes themselves say.

4.26. The Issedones are said to practice the following customs. Whenever a man's father dies, all his relatives lead their herds to him, sacrifice them, and, after cutting up the flesh of the cattle, they also cut up the dead father of the man who received them; then, mixing it all together, they lay out all the meat as a feast. [2] As for the man's head, they pull out the hair, clean it out, and cover it with gold. Then they use it like a religious statue and make great sacrifices to it yearly. The father's son does this, just as the Greeks practice the *genesia*.[286] Otherwise, the Issedones are said to be just, and the women share power equally with the men.

4.27. These people are known to us, but beyond them to the north the Issedones say that there are one-eyed men and gold-guarding griffins. The Scythians heard this from them and say it themselves. The rest of us learned it from the Scythians and call them, as in the Scythian tongue, Arimaspians, because the Scythian for "one" is *arima* and for "eye" is *spou*.

. . .

4.46. The Euxine Sea, where Darius invaded with his army, holds the most ignorant peoples of all the lands except the Scythians. For we do not have, of all those living on the sea, any people to put forth as especially wise, nor do we know any man who is learned outside of the Scythian people and Anacharsis. [2] The greatest single idea among humans and the wisest idea of all ideas we know of has been discovered by the Scythian race; there is nothing else I admire more. The thing they have discovered is so wonderful for them because no one who attacks them escapes, and no one is able to capture them if they do not wish to be found. [3] Since they do not have cities or walls that they have built, but rather they all carry their houses with them and are mounted archers, and since they do not live off of fields or from cattle, and their houses are carried on the backs of yoked animals, how are they not invincible and impossible to approach?

. . .

---

286. A festival day devoted to honoring the dead. The Athenian *genesia* was in September at the end of the military campaign season.

4.59. What follows are the Scythians' remaining customs. They sacrifice to these gods alone: Hestia especially, and then Zeus and Gaia, who they think is the wife of Zeus, and after them Apollo, heavenly Aphrodite, Heracles, and Ares. All the Scythians believe in these gods, but the Royal Scythians also sacrifice to Poseidon. [2] In the Scythian tongue Hestia is called Tabiti, Zeus (rightly so in my opinion) is called Papaios,[287] Earth is Api, Apollo is Goitosyros, Heavenly Aphrodite is Argimpasa, and Poseidon is Thagimasadas. It is not their custom to make statues or altars or temples to any of the gods except Ares; they do these things for him.

4.60. The same sacrifice is established for all of them and similarly for all rites, and it is done in the following way. The sacrificial victim stands there with its front feet tied together, and the one making the sacrifice stands behind the animal, pulls on the rope, and brings the animal down. [2] As the animal falls the one making the sacrifice calls on the god to whom he is sacrificing and then inserts a stick into the rope he has thrown around the animal's neck and twists it; this strangles the animal. He does not light a fire or consecrate the victim or pour a libation. After he strangles and skins the animal, he applies himself to cooking it.

4.61. Since the land of the Scythians is mostly treeless, they have found this way to cook their meat. When they have skinned the victims, they strip the bones of meat and then throw the meat into pots (if they happen to have them) that are customary in this country. These pots are similar to Lesbian mixing bowls, other than that they are much bigger. After they throw the meat in they cook it by burning the bones of the victim. If a pot is not to hand, they put all the meat in the stomachs of the victims, mix in water, and burn the bones underneath that. [2] These burn especially well, and the stomachs hold the meat that has been stripped off the bones without any trouble. Thus the cow or other sacrificial animals cooks itself. When the meat has been cooked, the one making the sacrifice offers up the first fruits of the meat and viscera and throws it in front of him. They sacrifice many other herd animals but especially their horses.

4.62. In that way they sacrifice to the others of the gods and use these animals, but they sacrifice to Ares this way. In each district of their realm a temple to Ares is built and bundles of sticks are gathered together so as to be about 1,800 feet long and wide, but shorter in height. A four-sided building is built on this with plain surfaces. Three of the sides are closed off, but the fourth is accessible. [2] Each year they pile up 150 wagonloads of sticks because the structure always settles in winter. On top of the sacred building an ancient iron *akinakes*[288] is placed by each group, and this serves as a representation of Ares. They make yearly sacrifices of cattle and horses to the *akinakes,* and they sacrifice more to it than to any other gods. [3] However many people they have captured in war, they take one man out of every hundred and sacrifice him, though not in the same way as they sacrifice

---

287. Herodotus connects the name Papaios to a Greek word for "father."

288. A Persian sword that is straight and short.

cattle. After they pour wine over their heads, they cut the mens' throats over a jar and then carry the jar onto the mass of sticks and pour the blood out on the *akinakes*. [4] While they carry the jar above, below they continue the rite this way: They cut off the whole right arm along with the hand of all the men who had their throats cut and throw all of them into the air. Then they finish off the other sacrifices and leave. The arms lie where they fell, separate from the bodies. 63. These sacrifices are established for them. They think pigs are worthless, and they do not wish to raise them in their country at all.

4.64. War-related matters are organized as follows. Whenever a Scythian kills his first man, he drinks his blood, and he brings all the heads of however many he kills in battle back to the king, for once he has brought the head back he gets a share of the plunder that they have taken, but if he does not bring a head back, he does not get a share. He skins the head in a particular way. After he cuts around the head at ear-level in a circle, he takes the skin and shakes it off the head. [2] He scrapes the scalp with a rib of a cow and softens the skin with his hands. Once it is softened the result is sort of like a towel. He attaches it to his horse's bridle and he exults in it. Whoever has the most scalps is judged to be the best man. [3] Many Scythians also make cloaks like peasants' clothes to wear out by stitching the scalps together. Many men also skin the right arms of their dead enemies up to their fingernails and make covers for their quivers. The skin of a human is both thick and bright white, brighter in whiteness even than almost all skins. Many Scythians may also skin a man entirely, stretch the skin on wood, and carry that around on their horses.

4.65. These things are established as customs for them. As for the heads, not of everyone but of their enemies, they do this to them. After they saw the top of the head right below the eyebrows completely off, they clean it out. If one happens to be poor, then one only stretches raw oxhide all around the skull, starting from the outside, and uses it as a drinking vessel; but if one is rich, then he also stretches the oxhide, but on the inside he gilds it. [2] They do this also when a dispute arises out of their own household, and they battle each other in front of their king. Then, when guests have come to visit, they bring out these heads and tell how although these men were of their household they brought war and how they themselves defeated them. They say that this is courage.

4.66. Once each year the head of each province according to the province's own custom mixes a crater of wine. Those of the Scythians who have killed an enemy drink from it. Those who have not accomplished this do not drink the wine; rather, they sit apart, dishonored. This is the greatest reproach among them. Whosoever of them who has killed an especially large number of men gets two cups and drinks them together.

4.67. There are many seers among the Scythians who seek divination using many willow sticks. Whenever they bring out large bundles of sticks, they put them on the ground and untie them. They put down one rod at a time and prophesy; while they are saying these things they bind the sticks back together again and place them in the bundle one by one. This is their inherited tradition of seeing, but the Enarees, who are hermaphrodites, say that Aphrodite gave them the gift of prophecy; they prophesy with the bark of the linden tree. First they divide the linden in three and then, while interweaving and then loosening it on their fingers, make their prophecies.

4.68. Whenever the king of the Scythians gets sick, he sends for three diviners who have an especially good reputation. They prophesy in the manner described above. In general, they usually say these things: that someone or other swore falsely by the hearth of the king, and then they usually name one of their countrymen. [2] It is customary among the Scythians to swear by the king's hearth when one wishes to swear a really great oath. Straightaway the man who they said swore falsely is seized and brought out; the seers question the man about how it appears through their prophecy that he swore falsely on the king's hearth and because of these things the king suffers. The man rejects the accusation, denies that he swore falsely, and complains loudly. [3] Since this man denies it, the king sends for another set of seers double in number. [4] Then, if they look into the prophecy and condemn the same man of swearing falsely, straightaway they cut off the man's head and the first set of seers divide up his property. But, if the seers who arrived later acquit him, and more sets of seers come and if most of them acquit the man, then it is established that the first set of seers should be killed.

4.69. They kill them in the following manner. First they fill a wagon with dry sticks and yoke oxen to it; then they bind the seers' feet together, tie their hands behind their backs, gag them, and enclose them in the middle of the dry sticks. Next they set the thing alight and send it away by frightening the oxen. [2] Many oxen are burnt with the seers, but many also escape merely scorched because the wagon pole burns through. They burn seers in this way for other reasons also, each time calling them false seers. [3] The king does not leave the children of those whom he killed free either; he kills all the male children, but he does not harm the girls.

4.70. The oaths the Scythians make to each other are performed as follows. They pour wine into a large ceramic mixing cup and mix in the blood of those sacrificing for the oath; they get the blood by striking themselves with an awl or cutting a small portion of their bodies with a knife. Then they dip an *akinakes*, arrows, a *sagaris*, and a spear into the cup. Once they have done these things, they pray a great deal, and then the ones making the oath and others of their followers deemed most worthy drink the mixture.

4.71. The graves of the kings are in the territory of the Gerrhians, as far up as the Borysthenes River is navigable. There, when their king has died, they dig a great, four-sided trench in the earth. Once they have made this ready they take the corpse (which is now covered in wax; its belly has been opened and cleansed and then filled with chopped herbs and incense and parsley seeds and anise, then it has been stitched up again) and carry it off on a wagon to another tribe. [2] These people receive and take care of the corpse, and then they do what the Royal Scythians do: they cut their ears, shave off their hair, cut their arms, tear at their faces and noses, and thrust arrows through their left hands. [3] Then they accompany the corpse in the wagon to another tribe whom they rule over. Those who follow the procession come from where the procession has already gone. When they have traveled everywhere in company with the corpse, they come to the Gerrhians who live the furthest out of all the tribes over whom they rule, and there also they come to the graves. [4] When they have put the corpse in his tomb on a pile of grasses, they plant spears here and there around the body and place wood over it, and then they cover that over with plaited grasses. In the remaining free space of the grave they strangle and then bury one of the king's concubines, a cup-bearer, a cook, a groom, a waiting man, a messenger, and horses, as well as the best portions of all his other things, most especially his golden cups. They offer neither silver nor bronze. [5] After they have done this they all pile up a great mound, striving eagerly to make the greatest possible heap.

4.72. Once a year has passed, they do the following. They take the most deserving of the king's remaining attendants (who are native-born Scythians, for these men attend when the king himself bids it, and there are no slaves bought for silver among them) [2] and strangle fifty of these attendants and fifty of the most beautiful horses. Then they pull out their innards, cleanse them, fill them with husks, and stitch them together again. [3] They then stand half a wheel upside down that is affixed upon two wooden posts and plant many of these things firmly in the ground in this manner. Then they drive stout posts into the side of the horses up to their necks and mount the horses on the wheels. [4] The forward wheels hold up the shoulders of the horses, and the back ones support their bellies near the thigh. Both sets of legs hang down in the air. They put bridles and bits on the horses and stretch the reins out in front of the horses and tie them to pegs. [5] After fifty of the young attendants have been strangled they mount each one onto a horse, and they do it this way: They drive a straight wooden spike through each corpse up to its neck, and then they stick the spike into a socket in the post that goes through the horse. They set up such horsemen as these for burial in a circle and then they depart.

4.73. That is the way they bury their kings. In regard to other Scythians who have died, their closest family and friends lay them in wagons and take them around to their friends. Each of them receives them willingly and entertains the crowd lavishly. They put before the corpse nearly as much as they give the rest. Regular citizens are carried around in this way for forty days, and then they are buried. [2] After the burial, the Scythians purify themselves in the following way. After they wash and anoint their heads, they make a structure for the cleansing of their bodies. They take three sticks, lean them against one another, and then stretch woolen cloths around them. Next they gather as many rocks as possible that have been made hot from a fire and throw them into a trench, which lies in the middle of the tent made from sticks and cloth.

4.74. There is a plant, cannabis, which grows in their land. Cannabis is a lot like flax but thicker and taller; actually, it is much taller. It grows wild or it can be farmed. The Thracians make clothes out of it that are like linen clothes. There is not much difference between flax and cannabis even if you were to test them. If you did not know about cannabis, you would think the clothes were made of linen.

4.75. The Scythians take the seeds from the cannabis, go into a tent, and throw the seeds onto rocks, which are red-hot from the fire. Once they are thrown on, the seeds burn and send out much more smoke than any Greek sweat bath produces. [2] The Scythians enjoy their smoke bath and howl while doing it. This is what they do in their place of a bath, for they never wash their whole bodies in water. [3] Their women do add water to a mixture of cypress, cedar, and frankincense after they have ground them down with a rough stone. Then they slather this thick substance all over their bodies and their faces. A sweet smell results from this, and when they remove it on the second day they are shiny clean.

4.76. The Scythians especially avoid using foreign customs, especially Greek customs. The stories of Anacharsis and later Scyles make this clear.

. . .

4.78. Many years later Scyles the son of Ariapeithes suffered similar things. For Scyles was born from Ariapeithes the king of the Scythians along with other children. He was born from an Istrian woman who was not at all a native. His mother taught him the Greek language and alphabet. [2] Some time later Ariapeithes died because of a trick by Spargapeithes the king of Agathursos. Scyles took the kingship and the wife of his father the king, whose name was Opoia. This woman was a citizen, and Ariapeithes had a son by her named Orikos. [3] Scyles was king over the Scythians but did not at all like the Scythian way of life; he tended rather more to Greek things, which he had learned from his childhood education. He did this: When he led the army of the Scythians against the city of the Borysthenites (who say that they are Milesians), Scyles would go among the Borysthenites and leave his army in front of the town. [4] He would go within the walls and close the gates, take off his Scythian clothes and put on Greek clothing, and with these on he would go around the marketplace with none of his spearmen or anyone else following him. They would guard the gates so that none of the Scythians would see him wearing these clothes. And so he would practice. [5] When he had spent a month or more there, he would put Scythian clothes back on and leave. He did this often, and he even built a house in the city of the Borysthenites and married a woman who was a native of the city.

4.79. It was inevitable that things go badly for him, and it occurred from the following cause. He desired to perform the Bacchic rites to Dionysus. A great sign came to him as he was about to perform the rites with his hands. [2] In the city of the Borysthenites he had a precinct of a large house and great walls (I made mention of these things a little while before), and all around it white stone sphinxes and griffins stood. The god sent a thunderbolt against it and the whole thing burnt down, but Scyles completed the rites despite this. [3] The Scythians do not approve of the Greeks concerning the practice of Bacchic rites, for they deny that it is right to seek a god who drives men to insanity. [4] But when Scyles completed the Bacchic rites, one of the Borysthenites went over to the Scythians and said, "You laugh at us, Scythians, because we practice the Bacchic rites and the god takes us, but now this god has taken your king, and he practices the rites and is made mad by the god. If you do not believe me, come, and I will show you." [5] The leaders of the Scythians followed him, and the Borysthenite led them in secret and put them in the citadel. When Scyles went past with the Bacchic revel and the Scythians saw him performing the rites, they thought it a very great disaster, and they left and told what they saw to the whole army.

4.80. When Scyles returned to his people, the Scythians had already set up his brother Octamasades in his place, who was born from the daughter of Teres. He rose up against Scyles. [2] After Scyles learned what had been done against him and its cause, he fled to Thrace. Octamasades learned of this and marched against the Thracians. When he arrived at the Ister, the Thracians opposed him. While they were about to meet in battle, Sitalces[289] sent a messenger to Octamasades who said these things: [3] "Why is it necessary for us to test one another? You are the child of my sister, and you have my brother with you. If you give him back to me, I will give Scyles to you. Do not risk your army and let me not endanger mine." [4] After these things were said, Sitalces agreed to negotiate. His brother was with Octamasades because he had fled to him. Octamasades agreed to their bargain and handed over his uncle to Sitalces and took his brother Scyles. [5] Sitalces took his brother and went away, and Octamasades cut off the head of Scyles. Thus the Scythians protect their own customs and give this sort of penalty to those who practice foreign customs.

. . .

4.93. Before Darius reached the Ister, he first captured the Getae, who think they are immortal. The Thracians, who hold Salmydessos and live north of the cities of Apollonia and Mesambria and are called the Cyrmianae and the Nipsaei, gave themselves over to Darius without a fight. The Getae, however, who became arrogant, were enslaved straightaway. They were the bravest and most just of the Thracians.

4.94. They hold themselves to be immortal for the following reason. They do not think that they die but rather that they go to a divinity named Salmoxis when they have been killed. Some of them name him Gebeleïzis. [2] After a term of five years, they send a messenger chosen by lot from among them to the god, given messages for the god about the things they each need. They send him in this way: They arrange three lances, which they hold, and others take the hands and the feet of the one being sent to Salmoxis. They then sway him back and forth above the ground and then cast him onto the lances. If he dies by being pierced through, the god seems

---

289. See Thucydides 2.96 (below, Chapter 14, Selection 7).

to them to be propitious. [3] But if he does not die, they blame the messenger, claiming that the man is evil, and they condemn him and send someone else. They command him to do this while still living. [4] These Thracians also shoot arrows up into the sky at thunder and lightning and threaten the god, thinking that there is no god other than their own.

4.95. So I learned from the Greeks living around the Euxine Sea that Salmoxis was a man and had been enslaved on Samos, and that he was a slave to Pythagoras the son of Mnesarchus. [2] When he was freed he gathered a lot of money and went back to his own land. The Thracians live a hard life and are somewhat stupid, and Salmoxis had learned the Ionian way of life and more complex customs than what was practiced among the Thracians, customs that he practiced while consorting with the Greeks and with Pythagoras in particular, who was not at all the weakest in wisdom of the Greeks. [3] Because of his experience, Salmoxis prepared a banqueting room in which he entertained the first men of the cities and, after treating them sumptuously, taught them that neither he nor his drinking mates nor anyone ever born from them would die, but would go into the earth where they would always enjoy all the good things they have. [4] While he was making these speeches and saying these things, he made a room in the ground at the same time. And when he had the room completely finished, he disappeared from the Thracians, went down into the underground chamber, and lived there for three years. [5] They longed for him and grieved for him as if he were dead. In the fourth year Salmoxis appeared to the Thracians, and in this way made what he had been saying plausible to them. [6] They say that he did these things. 96. I do not believe in this underground room, nor do I trust anything excessively. I do think that Salmoxis lived many years before Pythagoras. [2] Either there was a certain man named Salmoxis, or this is some divinity native to the Getae; but let us dismiss it. These people who consulted the god in this manner were defeated by the Persians and then followed their army.

. . .

4.102. The Scythians reasoned to themselves that they would not be able to push off Darius' army alone in a straight fight, so they sent messengers to the neighboring peoples. The kings of these people came together and made plans about the great army coming toward them. [2] Among those gathering were the kings of the Taurians, the Agathursians, the Neurians, the Androphagoi, the Black Cloaks, the Gelonians, the Boudini, and the Sauromatai.

4.103. The Taurians practice these customs. They sacrifice shipwrecked men and any Greeks whom they go out and capture to the Maiden Artemis in this way: [3] After they have prepared the victim they strike him on the head with a cudgel. Some say that they push the body from a cliff (for their shrine is established at the cliff) and affix the head to a stake; others agree about the head but say that the body is not pushed from the cliff but buried in the ground. The Taurians themselves say that the goddess to whom they sacrifice is Iphigenia the daughter of Agamemnon. [3] If they capture their enemies, they do this: Each man cuts off a head and takes it home to their house, and then he sticks it on a long wooden stake and stands it up so that it is held over the house, usually over the smoke hole. They say that these heads hanging over the house guard the whole household. They live off of plunder and war.

4.104. The Agathursians are the most luxurious of these peoples and wear gold much of the time. They have sex with their women in common, so that they will all be brothers and relatives of each other, and so that they not experience envy or hatred toward each other. Their other customs are like the Thracians.

4.105. The Neurians practice Scythian customs. One generation before the invasion of Darius they had to leave their entire land because of snakes. The land produced many snakes, and more snakes came upon them from empty lands to the north, until, feeling hard-pressed, they left their own land and lived with the Boudini. These men are likely to be sorcerers. [2] For, so it is said by the Scythians and the Greeks who live in Scythia, once a year each Neurian becomes a wolf for a few days and then is turned back again. Those saying these things do not persuade me, but they say it no less and swear to it.

4.106. The Androphagoi have the most savage practices of all men; they do not think about justice nor do they practice any customs. They are nomads, they wear clothes like the Scythians, they have the same language, and they alone of these peoples eat people.

4.107. The Black Cloaks all wear black clothes, and they get their name from this practice. They practice Scythian customs.

3. Herodotus, *Histories* **4.110–117 (5th century BCE).** *After an extensive description of the Scythians, Herodotus continues by relating the history and customs of a related people, the Sauromatai, a female-oriented society supposedly descended from the mythical Amazons. (RFK)*

4.110. The following is said about the Sauromatai. The Greeks fought with the Amazons (the Scythians call the Amazons the Oiorpata, a name that means "mankiller" in Greek from *oior*, man, and *pata*, to kill). The story goes that after the Greek victory in the battle of Thermodon they sailed away leading three ships loaded with as many Amazons as they could capture. The captive Amazons then attacked and killed the Greeks while the ships were at sea. [2] The Amazons, however, knew nothing of sailing and ships, not how to use the rudder, the sails, or the oars. Thus they were at the whim of the waves and winds. Eventually, they ran aground at the Cremnoi, cliffs that overhang Lake Maeotis. The Cremnoi are in the territory of the free Scythians. There the Amazons disembarked and traveled toward the inhabited regions. They seized the first herd of horses they happened upon and, riding all over, plundered the lands of the Scythians.

4.111. The Scythians were unable to understand what was happening, since they did not understand the language, clothing, or ethnicity of these women. They were completely puzzled as to where they had come from. They thought the women were actually men in their youthful prime and so engaged them in battle. The Scythians then learned from examining the corpses of those they had killed in battle that they were women. [2] It seemed best to them after that to avoid killing the women at all costs and, instead, to send their own young men to the women, as many young men as they guessed there were women. These young men were to take up position near the women and then mirror whatever the women did. If the women pursued them, the young men were not to fight but rather to flee. When the women cut off their pursuit, the young men were to return to their encampment nearby.

4.112. The young men who had been sent did what they were ordered. And when the Amazons realized that the men meant them no harm, they allowed them to remain unmolested. Each day, the Scythian camp moved closer to the Amazon camp. The young men had nothing except their weapons and their horses, like the Amazons, and they lived by hunting and pillaging, the same as the Amazons.

4.113. Every midday the Amazons did the following. They scattered either individually or in pairs and separated from each other for some comfortable time away. When they Scythians learned of this habit, they started doing the same thing. One of the Amazons wandered off on her own and drew near to one of the young men. He approached and the Amazon did not push him away. She let him have intercourse with her. [2] She did not speak to him (since they did not understand each other), but indicated by signing with her hand that he should return to the same place on the next day and, using the sign for two, indicated that he should bring another man and that she would bring another Amazon. [3] The young man then departed and relayed to the rest of the men what had happened. The next day, he went to the same place and brought both himself and another man. There he found the Amazon with another woman awaiting them. The rest of the young men, as they learned about it, followed suit, and thus tamed the rest of the Amazons.

4.114. After initiating sexual relations, the two groups begin dwelling in a single camp. Each young man had as his wife the woman he first had sex with. The men were unable to learn the Amazon language, but the women understood the men. [2] When they came to understand one another, the men said the following to the Amazons: "We have parents and property. Let's not continue this way of life any longer but let's leave and go live with our people. We will have you as our wives and no other." [3] The Amazons replied as follows: "We could not dwell among your women because our customs are not the same as theirs. We shoot bows, throw javelins, and ride horses. We did not learn womanly work. Furthermore, they remain in wagons and do not go out to hunt or even at all. [4] We could not get along with them. But if you want to have us as wives, go to your parents and obtain from them your portion of their property and then let us dwell together elsewhere."

4.115. The young men were persuaded and they did just that. When they had received the property allotted them and had gone off with the Amazons, the women spoke to them, [2] "Fear and horror are upon us about how we will live in this land now that we have robbed you of your families and have caused a great deal of damage to these lands. [3] But since you deem us worthy of being your wives, do the following with us at once. Come on and let's migrate from this land and cross over the Tanais River to dwell there."

4.116. The young men agreed to this. Crossing over the Tanais, they walked east about a three-days journey beyond the river and about a three-days journey north of Lake Maeotis. They arrived and settled in the land where they now dwell. The Sauromataian women have carried on their ancestral practices. They go hunting on horseback along with the men and even without them. They go out to war and carry the same equipment as the men.

4.117. The Sauromatai know the Scythian language, though they have spoken it badly from ancient times since the Amazons never learned it properly. Their marriage practices are as follows: no maiden is allowed to marry until she has killed a man from among their enemies. Some of the Sauromatai get old and die before they marry, if they are unable to fulfill this custom.

4. Herodotus, *Histories* 5.3–9 (5th century BCE). *Herodotus discusses the Thracians, a people considered by the Greeks either to be Greek or related to Greeks, depending on who is asked and when. The hero Achilles was from Thrace and many Athenians had property or mining rights in the region. The Macedonians, also variously considered Greek or related (see Chapter 5, Selection 5), had close ties to Thrace. Herodotus here considers them a separate people. (CSR)*

5.3. The race of Thracians has the largest population of all men after the Indians. If they were ruled by one man or had common intentions, they would be undefeatable and the most powerful by far of all races, in my opinion. But this will never be practical or possible for them, and because of this they are weak. [2] Each have many different names based on where they live, but they practice pretty much the same customs everywhere, except among the Getae, the Trausians, and those who live north of Crestonia.

5.4. I have spoken of what the Getae, who think they are immortal, practice. The Trausians practice all other customs the same as the other Thracians, but they use different customs at birth and death. [2] Family and friends gather around and mourn at a birth, at the number of bad things that will happen to the one born, and they recount all of human suffering. At a death, however, they play and rejoice as they bury the dead in the

322 Chapter 14 Europe: The Black Sea Region

ground, for they claim that the dead have been freed from a great many evils and are in a state of complete happiness.

5.5. The people who live north of Crestonia practice the following customs. Each man has many women, and when one of them dies, there is a great judgment of the wives and significant eagerness among their friends to find out who of his wives was the most loved by her husband. [2] She is picked out and honored, and then, accompanied by men and women, she is killed over his grave by her closest male relative and buried alongside her husband. The other wives hold this to be a huge misfortune for them, for they feel the greatest shame at not being chosen.

5.6. This is a custom among other Thracians. They sell their children for exportation. They do not guard their young women but rather allow them to have sex with whatever men they wish to. They do guard their wives severely and buy them from their parents for a lot of money. Being tattooed marks one as well-born, and being untattooed marks one as lowly. The best thing is not to work, and working the land is the most dishonorable. It is best to live off of war and plunder. These are their most notable customs.

5.7. They worship only Ares, Dionysus, and Artemis. Their kings, however, beyond the other people, worship Hermes especially of the gods. They swear only by him and say that they are descended from him.

5.8. Burials for their wealthy are as follows. They lay out the corpse for three days, sacrifice all sorts of victims and feast, but first they mourn. Then they either cremate and bury the ashes, or they just bury the body in the ground. Then they pile up a mound of earth and hold all sorts of contests; the greatest prizes are granted in single combat. This is the nature of Thracian burials.

5.9. As for the land to the north of the Thracian lands, no one is able to say for certain who the men are who live there, but the land beyond the Ister River appears to be empty and pathless. Of those people who live beyond the Ister, I have been able to learn only about the Sigynnae, who wear clothes like the Medes. [2] They have horses that are shaggy all over their bodies, and the length of their hair is up to five fingers long. The horses have short, flat-nosed faces and are unable to carry men, but they are very fast when yoked to a wagon, and so the natives ride in wagons. The Sigynnae's land stretches nearly to the boundaries of the Eneti by the Adriatic Sea. [3] They say that they are emigrants from Media. I am not able to figure out how they are emigrants from Media, but anything may happen in a large amount of time. The Ligues, who live north above Massalia, call retailers *sigynna*, and on Cyprus *sigynna* translates as "spear."

5. Euripides, *Medea* 1–8, 29–35, 223, 253–258, 534–541, 1323–1343 (5th century BCE). *Medea is often viewed as a paradigmatic barbarian, and in most texts about her from the late 5th century BCE onward her status as a foreigner is emphasized (cf. Hesiod* Theogony *992–1002), although in Euripides the term "barbarian" is used for her in very* *limited contexts. In later texts, Medea's homeland, along with Thrace, becomes a locus of magic and witchcraft. Euripides' play is set years after the journey for the Golden Fleece during which Jason and Medea met. They have settled in Corinth after and Jason is leaving Medea to marry the daughter of Creon, king of Corinth, while she and their children have been ordered into exile. (RFK)*

The Chorus enters and laments the voyage of the Argo and what it means to leave one's land, the root cause of the troubles Medea faces as the play begins.

1–8. Would that the Argo had not flown to the land of Colchis through the dark Symplegades,[290] nor had the pines from the Pelion grove ever been cut down and used to furnish oars for the hands of the noble men who went in search of the Golden Fleece for Pelias. For then my mistress Medea, driven by lust for Jason, would not have sailed toward the towers of Iolcus.

The Chorus continues.

29–35. Medea pays as much attention to the advice of friends as rocks or the waves of the sea would except when she turns her cheeks down toward her white neck and bemoans her beloved father, her land and home, which she betrayed when she came here with a man who now has dishonored her. The poor woman, compelled by misfortune, understands now what a good thing it is not to be bereft of one's native land.

Medea explains to the Chorus the difficulties of her situation given her status as "without a polis" since her husband Jason has left her to marry another.

223. Medea: It is a great necessity for a foreigner to comply with the demands of the polis.

253–258. You, however, have a polis and a paternal household, certain advantages of life and the company of friends. I have been outraged by that man while I am defenseless and without a city because he carried me away from a barbarian land. I have no mother, no brother, no kin with whom to seek refuge from these misfortunes.

534–541. Jason to Medea. Jason here rebuts Medea's claims that she was mostly responsible for the success of the Argo's quest to claim the Golden Fleece. Jason voices opinions that could probably be heard in Athens during the period, a reflection of the anti-barbarian rhetoric developed during the 5th and 4th centuries BCE and directed primarily toward the Persians. These opinions, however, should not be read as necessarily the view of the audience, since Jason is not a sympathetic figure within the play and much of his speech is given to justifying his poor treatment of Medea and oath-breaking. This should also be read within the context of the Chorus' sympathetic treatment of Medea above.

---

290. The Symplegades, the "Clashing Rocks," were considered the gateway between Europe and Asia in the north. Medea's long voyage to Greece is referred to by the Chorus at numerous points later in the play.

534–541. At any rate, you gained more from my safety than you gave, and I'll tell you how so. First, you now dwell in Hellas instead of a barbarian land, and you know justice and are subject to laws not force. Next, all the Greeks learned that you are wise and you gained a reputation. If you dwelt still on the furthest boundaries of the earth, there would be no mention of you.

> *Jason to Medea. Jason discovers that Medea has killed their two sons as revenge against him. Again Jason brings up the fact that he brought her to Greece from Colchis and wishes he had not. His claim that no Greek woman would have committed such a crime, however, is false—both Jason and King Creon are members of the house of Aeolus, which had a long tradition of mothers killing their children (such as Ino, Jason's and Creon's distant aunt, and Tyro, Jason's grandmother and a distant aunt of Creon's). The audience would not have been unaware of this context. Medea, having undergone a form of apotheosis, is already mounted on the chariot of the sun god Helios, her grandfather, while Jason shouts his harmless curses at her.*

1323–1343. Hateful woman. Most hated of all women, despised by the gods and by the entire human race! You dared thrust a sword into your own children! And now that you've done it, now that you've dared this most heinous crime, you still look upon the earth and sun? I'm lost. Now I understand [1330] what I didn't understand when I led you to Greece away from your home in a barbarian land—an evil deed. You are a betrayer of your own father and the fatherland that nourished you. The gods have cast the avenging demon meant for you at me! It all started then—you boarded the Argo (such a beautiful ship!) after you had killed your brother near the heart of your home. Then you married me and bore me children, and now you've killed them because of sex and a marriage! [1340] No Greek woman would dare do such a thing. And yet I chose to marry you instead of one of them—a destructive choice. You are no woman. You are a lion more savage by nature than Etruscan Scylla.

6. Euripides, *Iphigenia among the Taurians* 28–41, 179–185, 392–421, 1153–1175 (5th century BCE). *As the play (dated between 414 and 412 BCE) opens, Iphigenia explains the circumstances under which she came to Tauris. Although her father, Agamemnon, intended to sacrifice her at Aulis to appease Artemis and free the Greek fleet to sail to Troy, Artemis saved her at the last minute and took her away to the land of the Taurians beside the Black Sea. In this play "barbarian" is used as a negative characteristic that is distinctively "other" and "not Greek." The tale found in this play of a distant king who sacrifices foreign travelers is common in ancient Greece. In pre-5th-century images and stories, it was King Busiris of Egypt who did so, but by the 5th century, Egypt is a place that honors guests and the Black Sea inherits the barbarousness of inhospitality. (RFK)*

28–41. Iphigenia: But Artemis stole me away and gave the Achaeans a deer in exchange for me. [30] Through the bright air, she sent me and established me here in the land of the Taurians. The barbarian Thoas rules over the barbarians of this land, Thoas, whose feet are as swift as the birds and thus he is named for his swiftness. Artemis made me the priestess in this temple. Here I preside over a feast of sorts, customs the goddess rejoices in (though it is noble in name only; I remain silent about other things since I fear the goddess).[291] Others tend to the sacrifices, <*unspeakable acts within the temple of the goddess*>.

> *After Iphigenia's speech, she enters the temple and her brother Orestes and his companion Pylades appear. He has been sent to Tauris by Athena to steal a cult statue of Artemis and take it to Brauron in Attica. Iphigenia has not seen her brother since he was an infant and has just experienced a dream in which he has died. The Chorus of captive Greek women comforts her.*

179–185. Chorus: I sing harmonious songs and an Asiatic barbarian cry to you, mistress. I will speak out. Hades sings an unhappy song, in dirges for the dead, he sings no victory songs.

> *Iphigenia laments her lost family and then learns of the appearance of two Greek strangers on the shores of Tauris. She learns that one of the strangers, whose name they do not know (but the audience knows is Orestes), had a fit of madness before being captured by the Taurians. Iphigenia laments her fate again and prepares to complete the unholy sacrifice. The Chorus then sings, asking why men travel to barbarian lands in search of wealth.*[292]

392–421. Chorus: Dark, dark narrows of the sea where a gadfly from Argos flying went across the inhospitable waves < . . . > exchanging Europe for an Asian land. Whoever it was who once left behind well-watered Eurotas, green with reeds, [400] or the sacred streams of Dirce and came, came to this inhospitable land, where human blood wets the altars and the columned temples for the divine maiden. Did they sail the pine oars over the swelling sea with a double-beating roar, [410] a ship-chariot with sail-billowing breezes, augmenting their wealth for the competitions in their palaces? For hope is a friend, hope insatiable for men, to mortals a doom, a doom for those who carry a heavy weight of wealth upon the waves and look to sell it in barbarian cities with a shared expectation. For some men, however, the mark of wealth comes at the wrong time. For others, wealth is ever only middling.

> *1153–1175. The strangers are brought to Iphigenia for sacrifice. She asks them who they are and discovers that it is her own brother Orestes. She tells them her own tale in turn, and the siblings are reunited. Orestes then informs*

---

291. An emendation in the text notes, "For I sacrifice according to an old law of the city any Greek man who comes to this land." Since she has just said she remains silent about the "other things," it seems unlikely she would then tell it in the lines immediately following.

292. For similar songs see both Euripides, *Medea* this chapter, Selection 5, and Apollonius, *Argonautica* this chapter, Selection 9.

Iphigenia of his reason for traveling to Tauris. They concoct a plan to steal the goddess's statue and escape back to Greece together, agreeing as well to return the captive Greek women who make up the Chorus to their homes. Thoas, the king of the Taurians, then approaches the temple to check on the sacrifice.

Thoas: Where is the guardian of the halls, the Greek woman? Has she begun to perform the sacrificial rites over the strangers already? <*Are their bodies lit up by fire in the holy sanctuary?*>

Chorus: Here she is, King. She will tell you everything clearly.

Thoas: Oh! Why, child of Agamemnon, why are you moving with your arms the goddess' image from the base it is not to be removed from?

Iphigenia: King, stand there where you are away from here.

Thoas: [1160] What is it? What has happened in the temple?

Iphigenia: I spit. For I offer this word for purification.

Thoas: What is this novel invocation? Tell me clearly.

Iphigenia: The sacrificial victims you captured for me are not pure.

Thoas: How did you learn this? Or is this just your opinion?

Iphigenia: The statue of the goddess turned itself away from its seat.

Thoas: All by itself? Or did an earthquake move it?

Iphigenia: All by itself. It also shut tight its eyes.

Thoas: What was the cause? Was it the impurity of the strangers?

Iphigenia: Yes. There is no other reason. They have committed terrible deeds.

Thoas: [1170] Did they murder some barbarian here upon the shore?

Iphigenia: They left their home after they had already committed murder.

Thoas: What? I have developed a sudden desire to know their deed.

Iphigenia: They killed their mother together with a sword.

Thoas: By Apollo! This would never happen even among the barbarians!

Iphigenia: And they are driven, chased out, from Hellas.

7. Thucydides, *History of the Peloponnesian War* **2.96–97 (5th/4th century BCE).** *During the third year of the war (429 BCE), Sitalces, the son of the Odrysian king of Thrace, attacked Perdiccas, king of Macedon. The events of this region held great interest to the Athenians, especially since they had colonies near Thrace and relied on mines and grain shipments from the region. It will become a major theater of war for the Athenians and Spartans in later years of the war, and Thucydides himself will spend the majority of the war living on family property in Thrace after his exile in 424 BCE. (RFK)*

2.96. Beginning first then from the Odrysians, Sitalces recruited those Thracians living in the Haemus and Rhodope mountains, as many as he ruled as far as the sea [to the Euxine and the Hellespont]. Next, he recruited the Getae who live beyond the Haemus and as many others as he could from those who live on this side of the Ister River[293] and closer to the Euxine. The Getae and their neighbors share a border with the Scythians and are similarly equipped. All of them are mounted archers. [2] He also called up many of the mountain-dwelling Thracians who are autonomous and carry sabers. They are called the Dii,[294] who dwell mostly on Mount Rhodope. He enticed some of them with pay, and others came voluntarily. [3] He recruited both the Agrianians and the Laeaeans and many other of the Paeonian peoples whom he ruled. These were the most remote people in his empire. His empire was extended at this time as far as the Laeaean Paeonians and the Strymon River, which flows from Mount Scombrus through the Agrianians and Laeaeans. The autonomous Paeonians marked out the empire's limit. [4] The Trepes and Tilataeans near the Tribali, another autonomous people, also mark the limits of his borders. These people dwell to the north of Mount Scombrus and stretch out west along the Oscius River. This river flows from the mountains where the Hebrus and Nestus Rivers flow. It is a large and desolate mountain that touches Mount Rhodope.

2.97. The size of the Odrysian Empire was great, stretching as it did along the sea from the city of the Abderans to the Euxine as far as the Ister River. The sea voyage around the land is very short. If the wind stays up for the entire journey, it take four days and as many nights on a merchant ship. By road, the shortest trip an unencumbered man can accomplish is eleven days from Abdera to the Ister. [2] Such was the extent of the Odrysian Empire at that time that to travel up into the mainland from Byzantium to the Laeaeans and toward the Strymon (the longest path away from the sea inland) would take an unencumbered man thirteen days. [3] The tribute paid by all the barbarian and Greek cities at the time of Seuthes, who ruled after Sitalces and collected the greatest amount, was worth 400 silver talents, calculated in only the gold and silver collected. Gifts of gold and silver no less in value than the tribute itself were received by the king, which were separate from the goods he received that were embroidered, plain, or of another sort. It was not to the king alone that such gifts were given, but also to government officials and the Odrysian nobility as well. [4] They established a custom opposite of that found among Persian royalty; they receive gifts rather than give them. The same custom holds in the rest of Thrace, too (and shame comes not to the one refusing to give when asked, but for the one asking and not receiving). All the same, because of their wealth, the Odrysians practiced the custom to a great extent and nothing was done without the giving of gifts. In this way, the monarchy became powerful. [5] In revenues and other forms of prosperity, the Odrysian Empire was the greatest of all those in Europe between the Ionian Sea and the Euxine. In military strength, however, they were second by a large margin to the Scythians. [6] No one in Europe or even in Asia could stand against the Scythians if they united.

---

293. The Danube River.
294. The Godly.

However, they are not equal to others in soundness of judgment or in that intelligence a people uses to guide their way of life.

> **8. Thucydides,** *History of the Peloponnesian War* **7.27, 7.29 excerpted (5th/4th century BCE).** *In the nineteenth year of the Peloponnesian War (413 BCE), the Athenians hire Thracian mercenaries from the Dii tribe for the expedition to Sicily. The Thracians arrived too late to make the journey, so the Athenians, not wanting to pay them, sent them back to Thrace, and the Thracians caused much destruction along the way. (RFK)*

7.27. In the same summer, 1,300 light-armed peltasts of the Thracian Dii, a sabre-bearing tribe, arrived at Athens. They were supposed to sail with Demosthenes to Sicily. [2] The Athenians intended to send them back again to Thrace whence they came because they arrived too late. To keep them for the Decelean War seemed an expensive proposition, since each man cost a drachma per day to hire.[295]

. . .

7.29. Because they did not want to spend the money given their current economic difficulties, they sent back the Thracians they had hired to accompany Demosthenes. They appointed Diitrophes to watch over them and instructed him to harass the enemy, if possible, on the journey home (they were going to pass through the Strait of Euripus). [2] He first put them to shore at Tanagra, and they engaged in some quick pillaging. He then sailed them during the night from Chalcis in Euboea over the Euripus and, after putting ashore in Boeotia, led them against Mycalessus. [3] They passed the night unnoticed near a temple of Hermes (the temple sits about 1.75 miles from Mycalessus). At first light, they attacked the city, which was not a very large city, and seized it. They fell upon the city unexpectedly while it was unguarded. It never occurred to the Mycalessians that someone might attack them from the seaward side. Their walls were weak and collapsed in some places. They were also built low in some places, and the gates were left open because they felt safe. [4] The Thracians attacked Mycalessus and plundered the houses and temples. They killed everyone, sparing neither the young nor the old. They killed them all one after another, whomever they happened upon. They killed children and women, even the livestock and any other living creature they saw. They did this because the Thracians are extremely murderous, equal to the bloodiest barbarian, when they have no fear. [5] The city was in complete chaos and was overcome by every type of destruction. They attacked a school for young boys, the largest in the city, just when the children had entered it. The Thracians cut them all down. The misfortune the city endured was second to no other both in its unexpectedness and its terror.

---

295. This is one and a half times the pay rate for an Athenian hoplite, which was four obols (six obols = one drachma).

**9. Apollonius, *Argonautica* 2.317–406, 2.411–418, 2.962–1029
(3rd century BCE).** *Phineus tells the Argonauts how to complete their
journey. (MLG)*

2.317–406. Phineus: After you leave me, you will first see two dark rocks
with a narrow sea between. I affirm that no one has sailed through these
rocks because [320] no deep roots support them. They often collide against
each other, and the water, violently shaken, swells over them, and the rocky
shore all around echoes with a shrill clamor. Now follow my advice, if you
are in fact traveling with a shrewd mind and with respect for the blessed
gods. Do not be foolishly eager to choose self-destruction, obedient to youthful passion. No, first send a dove from the boat to make a trial and be an
omen. If she safely flies through the rocks to the sea beyond, then cease delay
and do not hold back from your course. Take the oars in your hands and,
rowing stoutly, cut through the narrows of the sea. Safety depends less on
prayers than on the strength of your arms. [330] And so forget about the rest
and toil boldly at what is most useful. Before this, I do not forbid you to pray
to the gods. If, however, the bird is destroyed as it flies through the middle,
take in your sails and return home since it is better to yield to the immortals. You would not avoid a wretched death, not even if the Argo was iron.
Miserable men, do not dare to transgress my prophecy, even if you think that
I am three times as hateful to children of Olympus as I am. Even if I am more
hated than that, do not dare to travel by ship contrary to the omen.

These things will be as they will be. If you should safely escape the clashing of the rocks, keep the land of the Bithynians to the right and avoid the
reefs while you are passing into the Black Sea [Pontus]. Sail on until you
pass the swift flowing Rhebas River and the Black Cape [350] and reach the
harbor of Thynias. Run the ship ashore at the land of the Mariandynians,
which lies a short distance across the sea. Here there is a steep path down to
Hades, and the jutting headland of Acherusia extends upwards, and eddying Acheron cuts through the bottom of this headland, pouring out a stream
from a deep chasm. Near to the headland you will pass by the many hills of
the Paphlagonians. Pelops from Enete was the first king of these men and
they boast that they come from his bloodline.

[360] Opposite the Revolving Bear is another headland, rising steeply
on all sides, which is called Carambis. This headland splits the north wind
into two currents because it rises so high above the open sea. After sailing
around this headland, one comes to the Long Shore. Past the Long Shore,
beyond a lofty headland, the river Halys belches out a terrible flow. Just
beyond, the smaller river Iris flows into the sea, twirling white eddies.
Beyond it rises a large, high bend of land. [370] Next, the mouth of the
Thermodon flows under the Themiscyrian headland into a calm bay, winding through the broad mainland. Here one can find the plain of Doeas
and the three Amazon cities that are nearby. Next are the Chalybes, most
wretched men, whose land is rugged and barren. They labor at ironwork-
ing. Nearby dwell the Tibarenians, a people rich in sheep, living just beyond

the Genetaean cape of Zeus of Hospitality. Bordering the Tibarenians are the Mossynoecians, [380] who live on a forested mainland before the foot of a mountain. They build their wooden homes on timber towers. They call these sturdy towers *mossynes*. This is where the people get their name.

After passing these, pull your ship ashore on the smooth island, after driving off in some way the numerous and ruthless birds that inhabit this deserted island. On this island a stone temple was built by Otrere and Antiope, queens of the Amazons, when they left to wage war. There you will have unexpected aid, which cannot be mentioned. It is because I am well disposed to you that I prophesy for you to stop. [390] What need is there for me to transgress a second time by using my prophetic art to reveal each thing in order.

Beyond this island on the opposite shore live the Philyres, and past them are the Macrones, and after them in turn are the countless tribes of the Becheirians. Next after them live the Sapeires, and then the Byzeres on their borders. And finally beyond them are the warlike Colchians themselves. You, however, remain in your ship until you reach the innermost sea. There on the Cytaean land the eddying Phasis, [400] flowing from the distant Amarantian Mountains and the Circaean plain, dashes its broad flow onto the sea. Drive your ship through the mouth of this river and behold the towers of Cytaean Aeetes and the shadowy grove of Ares. There a snake—a terrible monster to behold—wraps himself around a tall oak. Gazing all around, he guards the fleece. Neither by day nor by night does sweet sleep overcome his ruthless eyes.

Jason responds to Phineus' prophesy.

2.411–418. Jason: Old man, already you have recounted the completion of the labors relating to the voyage and you told us the sign, which we will have to trust in order to pass through the hateful rocks into the Pontus. I would love to learn from you if we will return to Hellas after having escaped these dangers. How will I do it? How will I make so long a return voyage over the sea? I am inexperienced and so is my crew. Colchian Aia is located on the far border of the Pontus and the world.

The Argonauts make their journey through the Black Sea.

2.962–1029. Carried by a swift wind, they left behind the Halys River and the Iris that flows near it, and the Assyrian delta. On the same day they rounded from far off the promontory of the Amazons, which encloses a harbor. Once upon a time in this place the hero Heracles lay in wait for the daughter of Ares, Melanippe, as she came out of her home. Hippolyte put her flashing girdle in his hands as a ransom, and he returned her sister unharmed. [970] The Argonauts beached their ship in the bay by the mouth of Thermodon. The sea was too rough to travel further. No other river is like the Thermodon. None divides itself and sends out so many streams over the earth. If one were to count each stream, he would reach ninety-six. But there is only one true source. This flows down to the lowlands from the high mountains, which are said to be called Amazonian. From there it spreads out over the steeper land opposite. This is the cause of its meandering streams. [980] They roll on this way and that, seeking out the easiest route to low land. One flows from afar; another from close by. Many streams lack a name where they dry out. The river, however, is openly mixed with the small streams and roars out at the curved promontory into the inhospitable sea. They would have remained there and mixed in battle with the Amazons, and the contest would not have been bloodless, because the Amazons living around the plain of Doeas were by no means gentle and paid justice no honor. Instead they are devoted to terrible violence and to the deeds of Ares. [990] Especially since they are a race descended from Ares and the nymph Harmonia, who bore to Ares daughters in love with battle, after she lay with him in the valley of the Acmonian grove. With these women they would have fought, but Zeus again sent breezes from the northwest. Using the wind they left the rounded headland, where the Themiscyreian Amazons were arming. They are not assembled in one city, but they live divided throughout the land according to the three tribes. In one part lived the Themiscyreians, who were at that time ruled by Hippolyte; in another part dwelled the Lykastians; in the last part, the dart-throwing Chadesians. [1000] Sailing through the next day and night they reach the land of the Chalybes. These people do not care to furrow the land with oxen nor to plant sweet fruit. They do not send sheep out to pasture in the dewy field. Instead they dig the harsh earth, which bears iron, and they sell this for a living. Never does dawn find them away from toiling, but black with soot and smoke they endure their heavy labor. Past these people, rounding the cape of Zeus Genetaeus, [1010] they hurried on beyond the land of the Tibarenians. In that land, when the women bear children for the men, the men fall on the bed groaning in labor pains, wrapping up their heads. The women tend to them, feed them, and prepare for the men the water for childbirth. Past them, they passed the sacred mountain and the land where the Mossynoecians live in their mountain *mossynae,* from which they are named. They have established unusual customs and laws. Everything it is customary for us to do openly before people [1020] or in public, all this is done by them within the home. Everything that we have come to do within the house, they do outside in the middle of the road without incurring blame. There is no shame in sex in public, but, like pigs in the pasture, they are not in the slightest upset by bystanders. Instead they join in intercourse with women right on the ground. Justice, however, is meted out to the multitude by the king, sitting on a lofty *mossyn.* Poor man! If ever he slips up in giving a judgment, the people lock him up and starve him for a day.

10. Diodorus Siculus, *The Library of History* 2.44–47 (1st century BCE). *Diodorus discusses the Amazons and Hyperboreans, the furthest known inhabitants of the Black Sea region, both of whom are shrouded in myth. (MLG)*

2.44. There have been powerful women who have ruled among the Scythians, where women train for fighting along with men and are not inferior in valor. When Cyrus was ruler of the Persians and at the height of his power, he marched into Scythia with a remarkable force. A queen of Scythia even destroyed a Persian army under Cyrus and crucified him. The tribe of the Amazons, after it was established, had such manly courage that it was able not only to overwhelm all the neighboring lands but also to subdue much of Europe and Asia to its authority. [3] Since I have mentioned the Amazons, I think it is appropriate to give an account of them, even if my surprising narrative appears like myth.

2.45. The reports are as follows. Next to the Thermodon River there was a powerful tribe where women ruled and where women took part in all belligerent activities in the same way as the men. One woman held the royal authority and was exceptional for valor and strength. She organized an army of women, trained it, and invaded some of their neighbors. [2] As she was increasing her military excellence and reputation, she waged continual wars against the peoples of the neighboring areas. As her fortune prospered, she was filled with pride and called herself Ares' daughter. To the men she assigned the spinning of wool and the household tasks of women. She established laws whereby the women marched out to the contests of war and the men were saddled with a humiliating slavery. [3] The male children were mutilated on their legs and arms, rendering them useless for any military use. The female children had their right breast burned so that the swelling of the female body at its bloom would be no hindrance. This is the reason why this tribe was called the Amazons [without a breast]. [4] In general, the queen was outstanding for sagacity and strategy. She founded a great city next to the mouth of the Thermodon River and built a famous palace. In her campaigns, she cultivated military discipline and she defeated all her neighbors as far as the Tanais River. [5] These are the acts told of this queen, who is said to have ended her life heroically, as she fought brilliantly in a battle.

2.46. When her daughter inherited the rule, she emulated the manly virtue of her mother and partly surpassed her in certain actions. For example, she trained the maidens in hunting wild beasts from a young age and drilled them daily in military arts. She introduced a magnificent sacrifice to Ares and to Artemis, called the Tauropolis. [2] Campaigning in the land beyond the Tanais River, she conquered all the tribes all the way to Thrace. Returning home with much war booty, she built magnificent temples to the already mentioned deities. Because of her just rule, her subjects had the greatest esteem for her. She campaigned across the Black Sea and conquered much of Asia, and her power stretched as far as Syria. [3] After her death, an unbroken royal succession of this family ruled with distinction and increased the power and reputation of the tribe of the Amazons. Many generations later, when the reputation of these women had extended throughout the inhabited world, Heracles, the son of Alcmene and Zeus, was given the labor by Eurystheus to retrieve the girdle of the Amazon Hippolyte. [4] For this reason he invaded and conquered them in a great conflict, cut down the Amazon army, captured Hippolyte and her girdle, and completely crushed this tribe. And so the neighboring barbarians, who despised the weakness of these women and remembered the suffering they caused, made continual war against that tribe to such a degree that not even the name of the Amazon race was left. [5] A few years after the campaign of Heracles during the Trojan War, Penthesileia was the queen of the remaining Amazons and a daughter of Ares. She killed a relative and so had to leave her native land because of the religious pollution. She fought with the Trojans after the death of Hector and killed many Greeks. Having proven her excellence in the battle, she died heroically at the hands of Achilles. [6] And so they say that Penthesileia was the last Amazon to be renowned for manly valor and from then on the tribe declined and was completely weakened. Therefore in later times, whenever their manly courage is related, the old stories about the Amazons are considered fictitious myths.

2.47. Since I have thought it worthy to record information about those parts of Asia that face the north, I think it not unreasonable to relate the marvelous tales about the Hyperboreans. Among those who have composed the ancient mythologies, Hecataeus and some others claim that in the regions opposite the Celts there is an island in the ocean no smaller than Sicily. This island, they say, is located in the north and is inhabited by the Hyperboreans, whose name comes from being situated beyond [*hyper*] the north wind [*Boreas*]. This land is fertile and produces everything since it has an excellent climate and produces crops twice a year. [2] The mythographers write as follows: Leto was born there and so they honor Apollo most of all the gods. The people are all like priests of Apollo, because they sing hymns to the god all day and especially honor him. On the island there is a sacred precinct to Apollo and a remarkable temple, spherical in shape and adorned with many statues. [3] There is a city sacred to this god whose inhabitants are generally kithara players and perform with their kithara in the temple continual musical hymns, hymns that glorify the god's deeds. [4] The Hyperboreans have their own individual language and have a most friendly predisposition to Greeks, but most of all toward Athenians and Delians, a goodwill inherited from ancient times. A certain Greek traveled to the Hyperboreans and left lavish offerings inscribed with Greek writing. [5] In the same way the Hyperborean Abaris came to Greece to reaffirm the goodwill and kinship with the Delians. The moon on this island appears very close to the earth and to have an earthlike topography. [6] It is said that the god visits the island every nineteen years, the amount of time it takes the stars to return to their starting point. Because of this, the Greeks call the nineteen-year period the cycle of Meton. [7] During the god's epiphany, he plays his kithara and dances in choruses all night long from the spring equinox until the rising of the Pleiades, rejoicing in his personal achievements. The rulers of the whole city and the caretakers of the sacred precinct are a clan called the Boreades, so-called because they are descendants of Boreas. The administration is always passed down through this family.

11. Ovid, *Heroides* 12.7–10, 12.21–28, 12.101–112, 12.121–124 (1st century BCE/1st century CE). *In* Heroides *12, Medea writes to Jason just after learning that he will end their marriage to marry the princess of Corinth and asks him to reconsider. Much of the lament is focused on the decision of Jason to roam to the distant lands of the Colchians and on Medea's decision to leave her native land for Greece. In every case, the land of Colchis is linked to mythical monsters. Ovid also hints at the ambiguous status of the region as only sometimes barbarian. (RFK)*

12.7–10 Woe to me! Why ever was the ship built of Pelian wood and driven by youthful strength to seek the Phryxian ram? Why ever did we Colchians look upon the Magnesian Argo? And why did your Greek crew drink the Phasian water?

12.21–28. There is some pleasure in reproaching an ingrate with the favors done, I will enjoy it; this joy alone will I gain from you. Ordered to turn your untested ship toward Colchis, you entered the blessed kingdom of my homeland. There, Medea was what your new bride is here; as wealthy as her father is, so was mine. Her father holds the two-shored Ephyre (Corinth), while mine holds all the land from the Pontus as far as snowy Scythia.

12.101–112. Behold! The unsleeping guardian bristling with rattling scales hisses and sweeps the ground with his coiling belly! Where was your wealthy dowry then? Where was your royal bride and her Isthmus that separates two seas? I, who now at last am made a barbarian to you, who now am poor, who now seem criminal to you, I subdued the flaming eyes with a sleeping potion. I gave you a secured fleece, which you then stole. My father was betrayed, and I fled my kingdom and homeland. My reward is the right to be exiled! My virginity has been made the spoil of a wandering pirate; the best sister left behind with a dear mother.

12.121–124. Would that the Symplegades had caught us and crushed us and that my bones were now clinging to yours. Would that violent Scylla had submersed us to be eaten by her dogs[296]—Scylla ought to cause harm to ungrateful men.

12. Ovid, *Tristia* 5.7.1–24, 41–68 (1st century BCE/1st century CE). *Ovid, relegated by Augustus to Tomi on the shores of the Black Sea, writes a verse letter to a friend about his life in his new home. (MLG)*

The letter that you are reading comes to you from that land where the broad Danube flows into the sea. If you are alive and have your sweet health,

---

296. Scylla was often pictured with a tentacle-like bottom half to her body. The tentacles ended in dogs' heads.

one brilliant part of my fortune remains. My dear friend, of course you are asking, as always, what I am doing. You can know this even if I stay silent. A short summary of my misfortunes: I am wretched. Whoever lives after offending Caesar will be wretched.

Who are the peoples of the region of Tomis? [10] Among what customs do I live? Do you care to learn about these things? Although there is a mix of Greeks and Getae, the hardly pacified Getae have more influence. A great crowd of Sarmatians and Getae travel back and forth in the middle of the road on horseback. None of them is without a quiver, bow, and arrows dipped in viper's gall. Wild speech, violent faces—the true image of Mars. No barber's hand has touched their hair or beard. Their right hand does not hesitate to plunge in the knife [20] that every barbarian carries on his side. Your poet lives, alas, among these people; he has forgotten all his playful love poetry. These are the people he sees, my friend. These are the people he sees. Would that he was not alive but had died among those he loves. He would be dead, it is true, but far from these hateful places.

> *Ovid responds to the popularity of his poetry back at Rome and laments that some of it caused him to offend Augustus. He still composes poetry, although fame is not the main reason he does it.*

What else can I do, alone on deserted shores? What else can I try to counter my misfortunes? If I look at my location, it is unloveable. No place on earth could be gloomier. If I look at the people, they are hardly worthy of the name human. They have more wild savagery than wolves. They have no fear of laws, but justice yields to force and rights lie conquered by a violent sword. They ward off cold with pelts and broad pants. [50] Their bristling faces are covered with long hair. In a few, traces of the Greek language remain, but even this is already rendered barbaric by Getan pronunciation. There is not a single person who could reply with a word of Latin. I, a famous Roman poet (forgive me, Muses), I am compelled to speak more in Sarmatic. I confess it, and it is shameful, that Latin words hardly ever come to me because of long disuse. There are perhaps some barbarisms even in this book. [60] It is not the fault of the writer but of this place. So as not to lose practice with my western language and to prevent my voice from becoming mute in my native language, I speak to myself and rehearse the unaccustomed words and repeat the dissimilar signs of my studies. In this way I pass my life and my time. In this way I restrain myself from contemplating my wretchedness. I seek in my poems oblivion from my wretched state. If I should obtain that reward from my studies, it is enough.

13. Seneca, *Medea* 42–54, 116–134, 203–216, 301–379, 397–414, 483–489, 670–739 (1st century CE). *Seneca's* Medea *opens with Medea having discovered Jason's betrayal. She already has decided how she will punish Jason and calls upon her grandfather, the Sun, to send his chariot to her, which he does to end the play. As with the representations in*

Ovid, the Colchians are also conflated with the Scythians and Medea herself is strongly associated with the monsters and demigods represented in Homer at the edges of the world. The characters of the individuals are also frequently linked to their ethnicity or to the geography of their homeland. (RFK)

42–54. Medea: Drive away womanly fear and in your mind assume the persona of the inhospitable Caucasus. Whatever wrongs the Phasis or Pontus saw, the Isthmus will see. Savage, unspoken horrors, my mind stirs up evils deep within to make both the earth and sky shudder: wounds, murder, and death wandering through limbs. But I have recalled events too trivial. I did them as an unwed girl. My grief grows more serious and greater crimes befit me now—I have given birth. Anger, make yourself ready and prepare to cause destruction with your all-encompassing rage. Let the tale of our divorce equal that of our marriage. How do you leave your husband? The same way you followed him.

Medea discusses what it means to be barbarian in a foreign land (see Euripides, Medea 223, 253–258, this chapter, Selection 5) and what she did to save the "Pelasgian" from destruction in Colchis.

116–134. Medea: I'm finished! A wedding hymn strikes my ears. Scarcely do I believe such a thing, scarcely do I believe this evil. How could Jason do this? After snatching away my homeland from me, my kingdom, how could he be so harsh and abandon me alone in a foreign land? Does he who saw flames [120] and the sea conquered by my crimes value my services to him so little? Does he believe I've used up all of my power to do wrong? Frenzied, uncertain, and unstable of mind, I am torn apart. Where shall I find my vengeance? Would that he had a brother! There is a wife: Let the sword be thrust into her. Is this satisfaction enough for the harm done to me? If the cities of the Pelasgians or the barbarians should know of some type of crime that your hands don't yet know, now you must be ready to do it. Your former crimes urge you, and they must be paid back: The renowned glory of my kingdom, stolen! The little companion of the criminal girl cut to pieces with a sword, his death cast at his father, and his body scattered in the sea. And let us not forget the limbs of old Pelias cooked up in a pot.

. . .

203–216. Medea to Creon: How difficult it is to turn away one's mind from anger once excited. How regal it appears to follow down the path once begun to someone whose proud hands are accustomed to touch the scepter. I learned this in my royal home. For although I am weighed down now by my pitiable injuries—exiled, a suppliant, alone, deserted, harassed on all sides—I once shone illustrious in my noble father's courts, [210] and I trace my brilliant race to my grandfather the Sun. Wherever the Phasis flows with its gentle path and whatever the Scythian Pontus gazes upon from behind, where the seas are sweetened by marshes, whatever lands that unwed cohort terrifies, restrained only by the Thermodon River and armed with crescent shields, all of this my royal father rules through his power.

. . .

The Chorus ponders the opening of the seas to travel and exploration. They bring up once again the voyage of the Argo and the impact of visiting foreign lands and, in turn, being visited by the inhabitants of such lands.

301–379. Chorus: Too daring was the man who first ruptured the treacherous seas with his boat, broken so easily, who, seeing his own land behind him, entrusted his soul to the fickle winds, and cutting the waves with an uncertain course, could put his faith in such tenuous wood—too thin was the line drawn between life and death. No one yet knew the constellations, the sky was adorned with stars for no purpose. Not yet could a boat avoid the Hyades soaked with rain, nor the lights of the Olenian Goat, nor the Great Bear, which the old, slow man Boötes follows and guides. Not yet did Boreas and Zephyrus have their names. Tiphys dared to unfold his sail to the vast sea and write new laws for the winds: [320] Now to pull taut the ropes with full sail, now to seize the travailing winds with sail extended, now to place the yards safely at the mid-mast when the sailor, too eager, hopes for whole breezes and the red topsails shake above the sails.

Our fathers saw splendid ages, far removed from crime. Reluctant, they touched only their own shores and became old men on their ancestral lands, rich in little, they knew no wealth [330] except what their native soil brought forth. A Thessalian pinewood ship dragged together an alliance of the well-dispersed world and ordered the sea to endure its lashes and made the sea, once unknown, become a part of our fears. [340] That wicked boat, paying a heavy price, was led through such enduring terrors, when the two mountain cliffs, barriers of the seas, crashed suddenly together and groaned with thunderous sounds. The sea crushed between them splashed even the clouds and stars. Daring Tiphys grew pale and let loose all the reins from his unsteady hand. Orpheus, his lyre stupefied, fell silent, the Argo itself lost its voice. [350] What of when the young maid of Sicilian Pelorus, whose womb is surrounded by raging dogs, opened all her mouths at the same time? Who was not horrified throughout every limb at the cacophonous barking of this single creature? What of when those dire threats calmed the Ausonian sea with their harmonious voice, when Thracian Orpheus, playing his Pierian cithara, [360] nearly compelled the Sirens to follow even though they were accustomed to hold ships with their song?

What was the prize won on this journey? A golden fleece and Medea, an evil worse than the sea and goods worthy of the first ship. Now the sea has yielded to man and suffers all man's laws. No need for an Argo, built by Pallas and carrying home its royal crew: any little boat that wants can sail the seas now. [370] All boundaries have been removed and cities have established walls in new lands. The world lies open, nothing remains where it once sat; the Indian drinks of the icy Araxes River, Persians drink the Albis and the Rhine. An age will come in later years when Ocean will loosen its chains and the vast earth will lie open. Tethys will show new worlds, and no longer will Thule be the furthest away of lands.

Medea compares her anger to the monsters at the end of the world.

397–414. Medea: If you seek, wretched woman, what measure you should establish for your hatred, mimic your love. Should I suffer unavenged that you make a royal marriage? Will this day, which I sought after [400] so aggressively and gained, pass unfruitful? So long as the earth in the center bears the balance of the heavens, so long as the glittering globe spins out its certain vicissitudes, so long as the sands are uncountable and the days follow the sun while the stars follow the night, so long as the pole keeps the Great Bear turning and the rivers flow into the sea, never will my anger cease in its quest for punishment. It will continue to increase its force. What monstrousness of wild beasts, what Scylla, what Charybdis swallowing the Ausonian and Sicilian seas? [410] Will Aetna, pressing down upon the roaring Titan, burn with such menace as I do? No whirling torrent, no stormy ocean nor sea made savage by the northeast wind, no force of fire aided by a breeze could hinder the progress of our anger. I will overturn and level everything.

Medea again recounts her losses and her status as foreigner. Once again, Colchis and Scythia are synonymous, while far off India pays tribute to Colchis.

483–489. Medea to Jason: Of all the wealth which the Scythians have seized from as far away as the burnt people of India and brought and which fills our halls to bursting (so much so that we decorate our trees with gold), of all this, I carried nothing away into my exile except the limbs of my brother. My fatherland gave way to you. My father, my brother, my sense of shame gave way to you. These are my dowry. Give the fugitive back what is hers.

The Nurse despairs at the force of Medea's anger and recounts Medea's magic rituals invoking the great constellation Draco to aid her in mixing the poisons she will use in her murders. The edges of the world as the Nurse imagines them are filled with monsters and are the source of all Medea's evils. Libya, India, Scythia, and Germany all yield up their treasures to Medea's anger.

670–739. Nurse: My soul is struck by fear, it bristles; great destruction approaches. How monstrous she grows. Her grief feeds itself on its earlier force and renews itself. I often saw her before raging and attacking the gods, dragging down the heavens. Greater than this and greater still is the monstrosity Medea now prepares. For just as she goes forth with her frantic step, she reaches her inner place of death and she pours out all her resources, even those she herself has long feared, and she exploits them all, a whole crowd of evils, hidden, secret, mysterious. [680] Praying at a mournful altar with her left hand, she calls down plagues and every monster: some created by the sands of burning Libya, others the Taurus restrains with its perpetual snow, frozen in the Arctic ice. Drawn by her magical incantations, the serpentine crows leave behind their desert lairs. Here a fierce serpent drags its massive body and flicks out its tri-forked tongue and seeks out those to whom it can bring death. It is stunned by the sound of her song and piles up its body, forcing itself coil upon coil into a ball. [690] "Too small," she says, "are these evils, too trifling a weapon forged deep in the earth. I will seek venom from the heavens. Already now, it is time to act at some loftier-than-average crime. [700] Let the serpent that lies as a great torrent descend to here, that serpent whose immense coils are felt by two beasts (Major, useful to the Pelasgians, and Minor, to the Sidonians). Let Ophiuchus release at last his grip and let the poison pour forth. Let Python who dared to challenge twin divinities come to my summoning song. Let the Hydra and all the serpents cut from it by the Heraclean hand return and repair itself with its own slaughter. May you too, unsleeping serpent first lulled by my songs, leave behind Colchis and come."

After she summons all the races of serpents, she gathers together the poisons of ill-omened plants: some the impassably rocky Eryx generates, some the Caucasus bear, sprinkled with the blood of Prometheus on its ridges that are trapped in perpetual winter. Still others the wealthy Arabs, warlike [710] Median archers, and swift Parthians use to anoint their arrows, or even those venoms that the noble Suebian women collect under the frozen axis in the famous Hercynian forest. Whatever the earth creates in nest-building spring or when the icy winter scatters the glory of the forests and constrains everything with its snowy frost, whatever plant blossoms with a death-bringing bloom, whatever dreadful sap is produced in its twisted roots as a source of injury, she lays hold of it. [720] Haemonian Athos volunteered some plagues, others the great Pindus provides. The ridges of Pangaeus deposited a tender shoot for her bloody knife. Other poisons the Tigris nourishes by suppressing her deep stream. Still others the Danube grows. Others the gem-bearing Hydaspes, which flows with its warmish waters through desert plains, gives, while others come from the land whose name is given by the Baetis, which strikes the Hesperian Sea with its limping current. One plant suffered her knife while Phoebus prepared the day. Another's stem was cut in the deep of night. Still another felt its stem sliced by her nails while she sang an incantation to it. [730] She grabs the deadly plants and presses out the venom of snakes and then mixes in also mournful birds, both the heart of an ill-omened horned owl and the entrails cut from a still-living screech owl. The maker of these crimes sets apart yet other poisons such as those with the searing force of fire from those with the freezing chill of the icy cold. She adds words to these poisons no less fearful than the venom itself. Behold! She sings and resounds with her frenzied step! The world groans with her first words.

14. Pliny, *Natural History* 4.89–91 (1st century CE). *Pliny discusses the Hyperboreans. (MLG)*

4.89. Past the northern mountains of Asia and Europe and beyond the north wind dwells a happy (if we can believe it) people called the Hyperboreans. Their lifespan is extremely long, and marvelous stories have collected about them. The belief is that this land is where are found the posts that support the heaven and where the stars end their circuit. There the sun does not rise for six months, but not, as the ignorant claim, from the vernal equinox until autumn. There the sun rises once a year on the summer solstice and sets once on the winter solstice. The region is pleasant and has a fortunate climate, completely lacking harmful winds. The inhabitants use forests and groves as their homes and worship the gods both individually and in groups. They know no discord and no sickness. They die only when they are tired of living: after banqueting and anointing their old age with luxury, they leap from a cliff into the sea. This is the most fortunate manner of burial.

4.90. According to some, these people dwell not in Europe but in the initial part of the Asian coast. This is because at that place a people called the Attaci live who have similar customs and location. According to others, they dwell between the sun's path between the Antipodal setting and our rising sun. This is quite impossible because of the large sea between. Some authorities locate the Hyperboreans in no specific place but just in a land with six months of sunlight, and these authorities report that the Hyperboreans do their sowing in the morning, reap at noon, pluck the fruit from the trees in the evening, and sleep in caves at night.

4.91. There can be no doubt that these people exist. So many authorities relate that the Hyperboreans are accustomed to send their first fruits to Apollo at Delos, a god to whom they are especially devoted. These offerings were, for many years, brought by young girls, who were honored and esteemed by many nations until a violation of trust caused them to deposit the offering on the border of their nearest neighbors, who in turn carried it to their neighbors, and so on until it reached Delos. Later, even this practice ceased.

CHAPTER 15

EUROPE: GAUL, GERMANY, AND BRITAIN

The Gaul, Germans, and Celts are a fixture in Roman writings, perhaps because it was the Romans, and not the Greeks, who first encountered the tribes of the north. They were viewed primarily through the lens of the sack of Rome by the Gauls in the 4th century BCE, becoming a northern boogey-man and perennial military threat. The level of civilization allotted to the European tribes varied based on their closeness and associations with Rome. The Gauls were civilized enough for some to be incorporated into the citizen body as early as the 1st century BCE by Julius Caesar. The Celts were seen as distant and strange. The Germans, however, held a special place in Roman thought as a pristine warrior culture, unsullied by the luxury and decadence of Rome.

1. Polybius, *The Histories* 2.17.3–12 (2nd century BCE). *In this section Polybius describes the Celtic tribes who settled in northern Italy. He provides a brief description of where they live and their way of life. (CSR)*

2.17.3. The Celts interacted with the Etruscans because of their geographical closeness and envied them because of the beauty of their land. From a minor pretext they unexpectedly went out against them with a great army, drove out the Etruscans from the land around the Po River, and held the plains there themselves. [4] The first people settling around the springs of the Po were the Laevi and the Lebecii, and after them the Insubres settled, who were the largest race of the Celts. Next to them the Cenomani settled near the river. [5] Another very ancient people hold the areas lying near the Adriatic: They are called the Veneti, who differ somewhat from the Celts in their way of life and dress and who use a different language. [6] The tragic writers have composed many a story about them and have arranged many fabulous compositions. [7] The first settlers of the land across the Po and around the Apennines were the Anares, and after them the Boii settled. Next to these the Lingones settled toward the Adriatic, and finally the Senones settled near the sea. [8] These are the most famous of the tribes settling the aforementioned areas. [9] They lived in villages without walls, and they settled in without having any extra furniture. [10] Because they slept in litters and ate meat, and did nothing other than make war and work the land, they had simple lives, and no other knowledge or skill was known to them at all. [11] Each man's property was made up of animals and gold, because these things alone can be carried easily around everywhere as the circumstances demanded and moved according to each man's choices. [12] They made friendship the greatest important thing, and he was considered the most feared and the most powerful among them who had the most attendants and companions.

2. Diodorus Siculus, *The Library of History* 5.27–32 (1st century BCE). *Diodorus' description of the Gauls, completed before Caesar's conquests of Gaul, seems to reflect the lost work of the writer Posidonius, upon whom Caesar and other later authors depended for much of their discussion of Gauls and Germans. (MLG)*

5.27. Gaul has absolutely no silver but much gold, which nature provides for the locals without mining or toil. As the rivers run through bends and twists and as they dash against the riverbanks, they break off chunks of the mountains, which are full of gold-dust. [2] The men responsible gather together these gold-dust-bearing clods of earth and grind them up. This ground soil is washed in water and placed in a kiln and melted. [3] They collect a mass of gold in this way, which they use for adornment not only for women but also for men. They wear bracelets on their wrists and arms and thick circlets of pure gold around their necks. They have remarkable gold rings and even gold corselets. [4] There is a certain idiosyncratic and unusual practice among the upper Celts concerning their sacred precincts. In their temples and areas consecrated to the gods, a lot of gold is placed as dedications to the gods and, despite the fact that the Celts are excessively greedy, none of the inhabitants steal it because of their reverence for the gods.

  5.28. The Gauls are tall and white, with flowing muscles. Their hair is not only blonde by nature, but they also seek to augment artificially this natural color. [2] They are always washing their hair with chalk dissolved in water. They wear their hair drawn up from their forehead over the top of their heads to the back of the necks so that their appearance resembles satyrs and pans. Their hair is like a horse's mane because their hair treatments make it coarse. [3] Some shave their beards and others let them grow a bit. The nobles shave their cheeks but let their moustaches grow so unrestrained that they cover their mouths. As a result, their moustaches get entangled with their food and act just like wine-strainers when they drink. [4] They dine sitting down, not on chairs but on the ground, after they have spread out wolf or dog skins. They are served by the youngest boys and girls who have reached maturity. Nearby are burning fire pits with pots and spits full of whole pieces of meat. They honor good men with the best pieces of meat in just the same way as the poet introduces Ajax being honored by the best men because he defeated Hector in single combat: "He honored Ajax with an unbroken cut of the loin."[297] [5] They invite even strangers to their feasts and, after the meal, they ask who they are and what they need. It is the custom even during the meal to look for any chance for verbal argument and to challenge each other to single combat, giving no consideration to death. [6] The view of Pythagoras prevails among them, namely that human souls are immortal and that, after the established time has passed, the soul enters into another body. For this reason, it is said that during funerals some throw letters written to their dead relatives into the pyre, believing that the dead will read them.

5.29. For journeys and battle, they use a two-horse chariot that carries a driver and a fighter. When they meet enemy cavalry, they throw their javelins and then leap off and begin sword fights. [2] Some of them think so little of death that they rush into danger naked except for a loincloth. They bring with them attendants selected from the free poor, whom they use as charioteers and shield-bearers in battle. When in battle order, they are accustomed to march in front of the line and challenge the bravest of their opponents to single combat while brandishing their weapons before them and seeking to astound their enemies. [3] Whenever someone agrees to combat, they sing a hymn to their ancestors' heroic accomplishments and boast of their own martial excellence. At the same time, they abuse and belittle their opponent and generally seek to diminish through words his boldness of spirit. [4] They cut off the heads of their fallen enemies and tie them to their horses' necks. To their servants they give the bloody spoils to take as plunder, singing paeans and victory hymns. They affix these first fruits to their houses just as men do who have overcome beasts in some types of hunts. [5] They embalm in cedar oil the heads of their most distinguished enemies, carefully preserving them in a box. These they show to strangers, solemnly asserting that some ancestor, either a father or himself, refused a large sum of money in exchange for the head. It is said that some of them boast that they have refused the head's weight in gold, revealing a certain barbarous greatness of spirit. I say this because it is noble not to sell badges of valor, but it is beastlike to make war against a dead man who belongs to one's own race.

5.30. They wear astonishing clothes: tunics dyed and embroidered in all sorts of colors, and pants which they call *bracae*. They buckle on striped cloaks, cloaks with fur in the winter and bare ones in the summer. The cloaks have a multicolored checkered pattern. [2] For their weapons, they use an oblong shield the length of a person, which they adorn after their own fashion. Some even have bronze embossed animal figures, which have been molded not only for adornment but also for protection. They put on bronze helmets that have large embossed figures that grant the wearer an appearance of great size. On some of these helmets horns have been attached, and on others there is a relief of the head of a bird or some four-footed animal. [3] Their trumpets are unique and barbarian. When they blow on them, the

---

297. Homer, *Iliad* 7.321.

trumpets produce a harsh sound, similar to the clash of battle. Some have iron-wrought chainmail for chest protection, while others are content with what nature has provided and fight without armor. In place of the short sword, they carry a long broadsword attached by a chain of iron or bronze and worn on the right side. Some tie their tunics with gold- or silver-plated belts. [4] They wield spears that they call *lanciae*, which have iron heads eighteen inches or more in length and a bit less than six inches in breadth. Their swords are not smaller than others' javelins, and the heads of their javelins are bigger than other's swords. Of these, some are forged straight, and others have a twisting spiral for the their whole length, so that a blow will not only cut the flesh but also destroy it, and so that the removal of the spear will tear the wound.

5.31. Their appearance is astonishing, and their voices are deep and quite rough. When they meet, they speak little and then in riddles and obscure metaphors. They say many things hyperbolically, boasting and threatening in dramatic style, in order to elevate themselves and diminish others. Yet they have sharp intelligence and are not unsuited to learning. [2] They even have among them lyric poets, whom they call bards. With a lyrelike instrument, they sing songs, some of praise and some of abuse. They have some especially honored philosophers and religious experts, whom they call Druids. [3] They even make use of diviners, whom they hold in high regard. These men foretell what is to come from examining the flight of birds or the sacrifices of holy animals, and in this way keep the whole multitude subservient. Whenever they seek a prophecy about some serious matter, they have an especially unexpected and unbelievable custom. After they have consecrated a person, they shove a dagger in the spot just above the diaphragm. When the victim falls, they know the future from the way the victim falls, by the spread of the limbs and even the flow of blood. They have come to trust in the ancient and time-honored observance of these matters. [4] It is their custom that no one performs a sacrifice without a philosopher. They say this is because it is necessary to perform thank-offerings through the agency of those skilled in the nature of the divine, in other words, men who speak the same language as the divine. They think it is necessary to seek good things through the agency of these men. [5] It is not only in the affairs of peace but also in wars that they put their highest trust in these singing poets, and both friends and enemies trust them. Often, when armies are approaching each other in battle array and have drawn their swords and are brandishing their spears, these men come between them and stop them as if enchanting wild animals. And so, even among the most savage barbarians, passion yields to wisdom, and Ares, the god of war, respects the Muses.

5.32. It is useful to distinguish a thing unknown to many: "Celts" is the name of those who dwell inland beyond the port town of Massilia, those who live beyond the Alps, and also those who live on this side of the Pyrenees mountains; "Gauls" is the name for all those who live past this Celtic land to the north, along the ocean and Mount Hercynia, up to Scythia. The Romans lump all these peoples together in a single name and call all of them Gauls. [2] The women of the Gauls are not only equal in size to their men but also match them in courage. Their children are generally born with grey hair, but it begins to change to match the color of their fathers as they approach maturity. [3] The most savage are those who dwell to the north, bordering on Scythia. They say that some of these men eat people, such as the Britons who dwell in the land called Iris.[298] [4] Since these people's valor and savagery has been widely reported, some say that these are the people that in ancient times overran all Asia and were called the Cimmerians, once time shortened the word into the name of those now called Cimbrians. They have indeed long been eager to invade the lands of others to pillage and to regard everyone with contempt. [5] In fact these are the people who captured Rome and stripped the sanctuary at Delphi, compelling much of Europe and no small part of Asia to pay them tribute. Having settled on the land of conquered peoples, they became called Helleno-Gauls through their mixture with the Hellenes. Finally, they shattered many large Roman armies. [6] As a consequence of their savagery, they are extraordinarily impious in their sacrifices. After keeping their criminals for five years, they impale them and offer them to the gods with many other first fruits, constructing huge pyres. And they even use captives as victims in honor of the gods. Some of them also slaughter or burn or destroy with some other punishment the animals captured along with the people.

[7] Although their women are beautiful, they pay very little attention to them; instead, they are extraordinarily mad for intercourse with men. They are accustomed to sleep on the ground on the skins of wild animals and to roll around with bedmates on both sides. The most surprising thing of all is that they do not care at all for their own reputation but easily give the ripeness of their body to others. They do not even think that this is shameful, but whenever someone offers this favor and it is not accepted, this they consider dishonorable.

3. Caesar, *Bellum Gallicum* 1.1 (1st century BCE). *Caesar begins his commentary on the wars in Gaul with a brief description of who the various tribes are and where they live. (RFK)*

Gaul as a whole is divided into three parts. The first part is inhabited by the Belgians, the second by the Aquitani, and the third by those people who call themselves Celts but whom we call Gauls in our own language. [2] All of these peoples differ from one another in language, institutions, and laws. The Garumna River[299] separates the Gauls from the Aquitani, while the

---

298. Perhaps Ireland.
299. The Garonne.

Matrona and Sequana[300] separate them from the Belgians. [3] The Belgians are the strongest among these peoples, because they are the furthest away from the province.[301] They also engage least often with merchants and do not import those goods that tend to soften the spirit. [4] They live nearest the Germans who are just across the Rhine and engage in constant battle with them. On account of this the Helvetians[302] precede the rest of the Gauls in virtue because almost daily they contend with the Germans in war, either when Germans keep the Helvetians back from their own borders or when they themselves wage war on the Germans' borders. [5] One part of the lands said to be held by the Gauls starts near the Rhone River and is enclosed by the Garumna, the Ocean, and the Belgians. It also touches the Rhine near the Helvetians and Sequani. It faces northward. [6] The Belgians originate in the furthest reaches of Gaul and extend to the lower part of the Rhine. They face north and east. [7] Aquitania stretches from the Garumna to the Pyrenees Mountains to the part of the Ocean near Hispania. It tends west and north.

Caesar then launches into a description of the tensions that brought him to Gaul.

4. Caesar, *Bellum Gallicum* 4.1–9, 4.13–15, 4.18–19 (1st century BCE).

Although Caesar was engaged in war with various Gallic tribes, he also engaged frequently with German tribes who were pressing the Gauls from across the Rhine. The events described here took place in 55 BCE. (RFK)

4.1. In the following winter, the year in which Gnaeus Pompey and Marcus Crassus were consuls, the German Usipetes and Tencteri tribes crossed the Rhine River with a great host of men where the Rhine empties into the sea.[303] [2] The cause of their crossing was that they, stirred up to war by the Suebi, were pressed for many years and were prevented from planting. [3] The race of the Suebi is by far the greatest and most warlike of all the Germans. [4] They are said to have 100 villages, from each of which they lead 1,000 armed men yearly from their territory for the sake of waging war. Those of the tribe who remain at home provide food for themselves and the warriors. [5] These men then take their turn the next year on campaign while the previous year's warriors stay home. [6] In this way, neither the agricultural cycle nor the strategy and practice of war are interrupted. [7]

---

300. The Marne and Seine Rivers.

301. Gallia Narbonensis, a Roman province established in 2nd century BCE.

302. Note that in Caesar's introduction, while the Helvetians are said to reside in Gaul, they are not, in fact, considered Gauls by Caesar. The Belgians and Helvetians are considered by Caesar to be non-Celtic who migrated into Gaul.

303. See Map 4.

But there is no such thing among the Suebi as private or individual property, nor is it permitted for anyone to remain on the same piece of land for more than a single year. [8] They do not have much use for grain but live mostly on milk and beef and spend most of their time hunting. [9] On account of this, as well as their general diet, daily exercise, and the freeness of their lifestyle (they are raised from boyhood without duty or discipline and do nothing against their will), their physical strength is increased and the men grow to great size. [10] They also accustom their bodies to wearing little except pelts and leave the majority of their bodies exposed even in the most frigid of places. They also bathe in the rivers.

4.2. They allow traders to visit them more so they can sell spoils captured in war than to satisfy a desire to import anything. [2] In fact, the Germans do not even import beasts of burden, which the Gauls favor and acquire at great cost. Instead, they train their native animals, though small and ill-formed, with daily exercise to bear even the heaviest burdens. [3] Often in cavalry battles, they dismount from their horses and fight on foot. They have trained the horses to remain in the spot they place them, and they can thus return to them quickly when necessary. [4] There is nothing more shameful or incompetent in their tradition than using a saddle. [5] Given this opinion, they dare to attack any sized party of saddled horsemen even when they themselves number only a few. They do not allow any wine to be imported, because they think its consumption renders a man soft and weak at enduring hardship.

4.3. They consider that greatest praise for people is that the land around their borders be uninhabited as far as possible. This signifies to them that a great number of states are unable to withstand their power. [2] Thus they say that the Suebi have no neighbors on one side for around 600 miles. [3] On the other side, the Ubii live. The Ubii were once a large and prosperous state, and they are slightly more civilized than their fellow Germans since traders visit them, and, being closer to the Rhine, they are accustomed to Gallic habits. [4] The Suebi made frequent attempts to dislodge them through numerous wars but did not succeed given the size and strength of the Ubii. The Ubii do, however, pay tribute to the Suebi and have become weaker and less influential.

4.4. The Usipetes and Tencteri mentioned above were in the same position. They withstood the strength of the Suebi for many years [2] but were driven from their land and wandered throughout various parts of Germany for three years before finally reaching the Rhine, specifically the territory inhabited by the Menapii, who had homes and buildings on both sides of the Rhine. [3] Greatly alarmed by the approach of such a large host, the Menapii deserted their buildings on the far side of the Rhine and then set up guards at intervals and tried to prevent the Germans from crossing. [4] The Germans tried everything they could to force a crossing, but since they had no ships and because of the garrisons set up by the Menapii, [5] they instead pretended to retreat to their own land. They followed the route for three days before turning around again. Their cavalry covered the whole distance in a single night and then fell upon the unaware and unsuspecting Menapii who, [6] having been informed through their scouts about the departure of the Germans, returned to their own villages across the Rhine without fear. [7] After killing these men and seizing their ships, the Germans crossed the river and occupied the Menapii's buildings before the part of the Menapii on this side of the Rhine were informed. They then supported themselves for the rest of the winter on the Menapii's provisions.

4.5. Caesar, having been informed about these events and fearing the weakness of the Gauls, since they are excitable in taking up plans and are generally eager for revolution, decided that nothing ought to be trusted to them. [2] For this is characteristic of the Gallic habit, both that they compel unwilling travelers to stand still and ask what anyone of them has heard or has learned about some matter, and the mob surrounds merchants in the town and compels each one to announce what regions he comes from and what he learned there. [3] Excited by what they have heard, the Gauls often enter into plans concerning the most important matters, of which instantly it is necessary that they repent since they are slaves to uncertain rumor, and since the majority of merchants and travelers respond with lies suited to the Gauls' desire.

4.6. Since he knew of this custom, Caesar set out earlier toward the army than was his custom so that he would not become engaged in a more serious war. [2] When he arrived there, he learned that the things that he had suspected beforehand would happen had happened: [3] embassies had been sent by some of the states to the Germans requesting that they depart from the Rhine and promising to pay whatever the Germans asked for. [4] The Germans, their hopes raised, wandered further into Gaul; they even ventured as far as the borders of the Eburones and Condrusi, clients of the Treveri. [5] When the leaders of the Gauls were summoned, Caesar decided that he ought to conceal what he knew, and with their minds soothed and encouraged and with the cavalry under orders, he determined to wage war with the Germans.

4.7. Once he had secured his grain supply and chosen his cavalry, Caesar began to approach each area where he had heard there were Germans. [2] When he was a few days away from the Germans, ambassadors came and said the following: [3] The Germans are not attacking the Roman people but would not refuse to take up arms if goaded, since it was a custom among the Germans to defend themselves from attack and never to run away. [4] Further, they noted that they had come to Gaul unwillingly after being ejected from their own lands. They went on to say that if the Romans should want their favor, they could be useful friends. Just let the Romans grant them some land or allow them to retain the land they had conquered. They admitted themselves inferior to the Suebi alone, whom not even the immortal gods could equal. Otherwise, there was no one else on earth whom they could not conquer.

4.8. Caesar replied to this as seemed best to him but ended his speech as follows: [2] There could be no friendship between Rome and them, if they remained in Gaul. Truly, he said, should a people unable to defend their own lands be permitted to occupy those of another? Further, there simply was no empty land in Gaul that he could grant to such a crowd without acting unjustly. [3] Ambassadors from the Ubii, however, were currently in his camp and were complaining about the harm caused by the Suebi and seeking help against them—he would order the Ubii to agree to allow the Usipetes and Tencteri to settle in Ubian territory if they wanted.

4.9. The ambassadors said that they would report this to their people and would return to Caesar after three days of deliberating the offer. [2] Meanwhile, they asked that Caesar not move his camp any nearer. [3] Caesar said that he could not agree to that. For he knew that a great part of their cavalry had been sent a few days before over the Meuse to the Ambivariti for the sake of plundering and foraging. He thought that they were expecting their cavalry and that they were interposing delay for this reason.

> *Caesar goes on to describe the Rhine River in this region, naming the tribes whose lands it cuts through as it makes its way to the sea. He then recounts a short skirmish between Caesar and the German tribes.*

4.13. When the battle was over, Caesar decided that he would no longer receive ambassadors nor accept conditions from these Germans who had used guile and treachery to seek "peace" while instead initiating war. [2] Indeed, he judged it the height of madness to wait while the enemy army increased and their cavalry returned. [3] And, knowing the infirmity of the Gauls, he sensed how much authority the enemy had gained among them after only one battle. He decided that he ought to grant them no time for making plans. [4] These decisions made, he told his plan of not losing a day to fighting to his legates and *quaestor*. Then a most opportune event occurred: The next day, the Germans, dishonest and grudging as ever, arrived at Caesar's camp with an entourage of their most senior leaders. [5] They had two goals: first, they sought to contradict any tales that they had participated in the fighting the day before contrary to their agreement and their own request; second, they sought to bring about a truce if they could by deceit. [6] Caesar was delighted that they had brought themselves to him and he ordered them detained. Then, he led his troops from the camp and ordered the cavalry, whom he thought had been shaken up in the previous day's battle, to take up the rear.

4.14. A triple column was formed and the army covered the eight-mile journey so quickly that they came to the enemy camp before the Germans could sense their danger. [2] Suddenly, they flew into a panic at the turn of events (specifically, our swift approach and the absence of their leaders). They had no time to plan or arm themselves and could not decide whether to lead their troops against the Romans, defend the camp, or make a run for safety. [3] When their fear had reached its peak (signaled by the noise and chaos), our soldiers burst into the camp, having been aroused by the previous day's betrayal. [4] Those in the camp who were quick enough to grab their weapons resisted our troops for a short while by fighting in between the carts and baggage. [5] The rest began to flee, mostly women and children (the Germans had left home and crossed the Rhine with their entire population). Caesar sent the cavalry to gather them up.

4.15. The Germans, hearing a clamor in the rear and seeing their own people killed, threw down their arms, abandoned their standards, and fled the camp. [2] When they reached the fork of the Meuse and Rhine Rivers with a great many dead or fleeing desperately, the rest threw themselves into the rivers and died having been overwhelmed by their fear, weariness, and the force of the waters. [3] Every one of our men survived and suffered few wounds. And now, freed from their fear of a long war with an enemy 430,000 in number, they returned to the Roman camp. [4] There, Caesar gave his German captives the option of departing, [5] but they feared reprisals from the Gauls whose land they had harried. Instead, they asked to remain among Caesar's men, and he granted them liberty to do so.

> *The campaign was over, but Caesar decided he should cross the Rhine in order to discourage more German incursions into Gaul. He goes on to describe in much detail how he built a bridge over the Rhine.*

4.18. The entire work was finished within ten days from when they had begun gathering materials. The army crossed. [2] Caesar left a strong garrison on both ends of the bridge and marched toward the borders of the Sugambri. [3] Meanwhile, ambassadors arrived from various tribes. Caesar responded courteously to their requests for peace and friendship and ordered them to present him with hostages. [4] The Sugambri, however, had been urged to flee by the Tencteri and Usipete among them from the moment construction had begun on the bridge. They had evacuated their land, carried away all their possessions, and had taken to hiding in the dark places in the forest.

4.19. Caesar, after delaying a few days in their territory, and once all the villages and houses were burnt and the grain cut down, proceeded into the land of the Ubii and, having promised them his help if they were pressed by the Suebi, learned these things from them: [2] that the Suebi, after they had learned through their explorers that the bridge was built, sent messengers into every region for a council meeting as is their custom, that they might move away from their towns and deposit their children, wives, and all their possessions into the woods, and that they might bring together into one place all those capable of bearing arms; [3] this chosen place was nearly in the center of those regions that the Suebi held. Here they awaited the arrival of the Romans, and there they had decided to fight. [4] When Caesar learned this, when all those things on account of which he had decided to bring his troops across [the Rhine] were accomplished—namely, to incite the fear of the Germans, to kill the Sugambri, to free the Ubii from siege—and with altogether eighteen days having been spent across the Rhine, he returned to Gaul and took down the bridge, since he thought that he had accomplished enough to satisfy both honor and usefulness.

5. Caesar, *Bellum Gallicum* 5.12–14 (1st century BCE). *In 55 BCE, Caesar decided to venture across the Channel to the land of the Britons in order to cut off assistance to the Gallic tribes from their British kin. The first crossing took place in 55 BCE. The second took place in 54 BCE and prompted Caesar's fullest description of the Celtic peoples he engaged there. (RFK)*

5.12. The interior part of Britain is inhabited by those who say that they, according to their tradition, are native-born. [2] The coastal regions are inhabited by people who came originally as raiders from Belgium. Nearly all of the tribes[304] have names that derive from their non-British origins. After invading, they settled permanently in Britain and began planting the fields. [3] The population is innumerable. Their buildings, rather similar to the Gauls', are set very close together. They also have a great many cattle. [4] They use either bronze or gold coins for money or, in place of coins, they use iron rods of a specified weight. [5] In the midlands, tin is produced. Iron comes from the coast, but only in limited quantities. They import any bronze they use. As in Gaul, every kind of timber is available except beech and pine. [6] They deem it wrong to eat hare, hen, and goose but keep them instead as "pets." The climate is more temperate than that of Gaul since the winters are milder.

5.13. The island is naturally triangular, and one side lies opposite Gaul. On this side, one angle, the one near Cantium,[305] faces the rising sun (this is where nearly all ships land from Gaul). The lower angle of this side looks to the south. This side stretches about 500 miles. The second side of the triangle faces Hispania and the setting sun. [2] In the same direction lies Hibernia, which is estimated to be half the size of Britain. The span of sea between the two islands is about the same as that between Britain and Gaul. [3] In the middle of that channel is an island called Man. There are also a number of additional smaller islands thought to lie near this island, some of which it is written have a midwinter night that lasts for thirty continuous days. [4] We were unable to confirm this through investigation, but we did discover through the use of a water clock that the nights are shorter on the island than on the continent. [5] According to the locals, the length of this side of the island is 700 miles long. [6] This side faces the north and has no land opposite it, though, for the most part, it faces toward Germany. The length of this side is estimated at 800 miles, [7] bringing the total circumference of Britain to about 2,000 miles.

5.14. Of all the peoples of Briton, the inhabitants of Cantium, an entirely coastal region, are the most civilized. They do not differ much in their customs from the Gauls. [2] The majority of those who live inland do not grow crops but live on milk and meat and wear pelts. All Britons dye their skin

---

304. Caesar uses *civitas*, a word often translated as "state" and used to denote a centrally organized unit of self-governed people.

305. Modern Kent.

with woad,[306] which makes them a blue color and thus a more terrifying sight to behold in battle. [3] They wear the hair on their heads long and, except for their heads and upper lips, shave their bodies. [4] Wives are held in common among groups of ten to twelve men, preferably brothers share with brothers or parents with children. [5] Any child born among the groups, however, is considered the child of that house into which its mother was first taken in wedlock.

6. Caesar, *Bellum Gallicum* 6.11–24 (1st century BCE). *In the midst of another invasion by the Suebi in 53 BCE, Caesar stops his commentary to give a somewhat detailed ethnography of the Gauls and Germans. (RFK)*

6.11. Since we have arrived at this point, it seems appropriate to relate the customs of the Gauls and Germans and how they differ among themselves. [2] In Gaul not only are there factions in every state, in every village, and every region, but there are factions even in nearly every single home. The leaders of these factions are those [3] who are thought in the opinion of others to have the highest authority and to whose judgment and justice the substance of all matters and councils is referred. [4] This seems to have been instituted in ancient times for this reason: lest someone of the plebs should lack help against a more powerful person. For no one allows his own people to be oppressed and cheated, nor, if he should do otherwise, does he have authority among his own people. [5] The same principle is held in all of Gaul, for every state is divided into two factions.

6.12. When Caesar came to Gaul, the leaders of one faction were the Haedui while the Sequani led the other. [2] Since the Sequani were less strong by themselves and because of the high reputation of the Haedui from ancient times, the Sequani had joined themselves with the Germans and Ariovistus, whom they won over with large bribes and promises. [3] In truth, as a result of the many battles that followed the alliance and the death of all the Haeduin nobility, the Sequani became so powerful [4] that they drew to them a great part of the Haeduin clients and received the sons of other leaders as hostages. They also forced their clients to take oaths in public stating that they would not initiate any plans against the Sequani. In addition, they occupied a part of their neighbors' territory by force and took over leadership of the whole of Gaul. [5] Prompted by such necessity, Diviciacus set out for the Roman Senate to seek help but returned with the matter unresolved. [6] After Caesar arrived a change in affairs took place. Hostages were returned to the Haedui, old clients were restored, and new ones were acquired through Caesar, because those who attached themselves to his friendship [7] saw that they enjoyed better conditions and a fairer rule, and in other respects, their influence and dignity were increased.

---

306. A blue dye made from vegetables.

Then, the Sequani lost their sovereignty and the Remi succeeded in their place. Those who were not at all able to join with the Haedui on account of old hatreds settled themselves into clientship with the Remi, because it was thought that they had equal influence with Caesar. [8] The Remi carefully protected them. Thus they held authority both new and suddenly gained. [9] Affairs were, at that time, in this state: the Haedui were considered by far the leaders; the Remi held the second position of rank.

6.13. In all Gaul there are two classes of men who are held in any esteem and honor. The plebs, who dare nothing on their own and are prevented from decision making, are almost the equivalent of slaves. [2] The majority of plebs declare themselves enslaved to the nobility since they either are weighed down by debt or heavy tribute or are oppressed wrongly by the more powerful. [3] Among these men, laws are the same as those of masters over slaves. But concerning the two classes noted above, the first are the druids, the second knights. [4] The druids are engaged in religious matters like the performance of public and private sacrifices and the interpretation of issues surrounding ritual. A great many young men join their ranks as students and hold the druids in places of high honor. [5] Druids commonly decide all public and private disputes. If there is a crime, perhaps a murder or a dispute over inheritance or property boundaries, they decide the case as well as rewards and penalties. [6] If any individual or group does not abide by their decision, the druids ban them from sacrifices. This is considered the most serious punishment among the Gauls. [7] Those so banned are thus considered impious criminals. Everyone avoids them and flees their conversation lest they become contaminated through contact. No justice is granted if such a one seeks it, nor are they granted a share in offices. [8] One man ranks first among the druids and has the highest authority among them. [9] Upon his death, whoever among them excels all others in worth succeeds as leader. If a number of men are equally qualified, they either hold a vote among the druids or may even decide by a contest of arms. [10] These druids gather in a sacred location within the borders of Carnutum (considered the center of all Gaul) at a certain time each year. Here men come from all around to have their disputes decided, and they agree to obey the judgments of the druids. [11] It is thought that druidism began in Britain and was imported to Gaul. [12] Thus nowadays those who want to embark on a more diligent study of the discipline tend to travel to Britain to study.

6.14. Druids abstain from war and do not pay into the war fund as the rest of the Gauls do. They are exempt from military service and hold privilege in all other matters. [2] Excited by such rewards, many men choose to study among the druids by their own choice or are sent to study by their family. [3] There they are said to learn by memory a great many verses. Thus not a few men remain at their studies for twenty years even. [4] Nor do they think it right that these things be put into writing. When [they must write] in other business, both public and private, they usually use Greek letters. They seem to me to have instituted this for two reasons: because they do not wish that the teachings be brought amongst the rabble nor do they wish those who learn to be less eager to memorize, relying on writings, because it almost always happens that with the assistance of letters they loosen their diligence in learning and in memory. [5] Their primary teaching is that the soul does not die but moves from one body to another after death. They believe that once the fear of death is removed, men can achieve the greatest courage. [6] In addition to this, they discuss and pass down to the young many things, such as the motion of the stars, the size of the earth and the universe, the nature of things, and the strength and power of the immortal gods.

6.15. The other class of note are the knights. Knights busy themselves with war whenever there is need and opportunity (which was generally every year before Caesar arrived, since they either instigated hostilities themselves or had to ward off such attacks from others). [2] Also, by however much each one of these men is distinguished in family history and wealth, by this much more does he have flatterers and clients around him. They know only this single type of influence and power.

6.16. The entire nation of Gaul is quite dedicated to ritual observance. [2] For this reason, those who are seriously ill or who occupy themselves with the dangers of battle either offer human sacrifices or promise to do so, and they use the druids to administer the rites. [3] They believe that it is not possible to appease the immortal gods without giving a human life for a human life. Sacrifices of this sort are practiced in both public and private matters. [4] Other men use sculptures of great size, the limbs of which are woven from twigs, which they then stuff full of men who are still alive. They then set the sculpture on fire, and the men are surrounded by the flames and killed. [5] They think that it is more gratifying to the immortal gods if they sacrifice those caught stealing or committing some other such crime. But if men of this sort are lacking, they stoop to sacrificing even the innocent.

6.17. Of all the gods, they revere Mercury most. There are images of him everywhere. They consider him the inventor of the arts, the guide on roads and journeys, and they believe he has the greatest power over money-making ventures and trade. [2] After Mercury come Apollo, Mars, Jove, and Minerva. They think the same way about these gods as other people do: Apollo dispels disease, Minerva gives rise to arts and crafts, Jove has dominion in the heavens, and Mars rules war. [3] To Mars they vow whatever spoils they might win when they have decided to engage in battle. . After their victory, they sacrifice all the captured animals and then pile up all the rest of the spoils in a single location. [4] In many states, one can go and look at the hills of spoils set up in sacred spots. [5] It rarely happens that a man ignores his religious duty and dares to take and hide in his own home any of the spoils. If he does, he receives the severest punishment and torture.

6.18. All Gauls state, and this is the tradition handed down by the druids, that they are descended from a single father, Dis. [2] For this reason, they reckon all periods of time by night, not day: they observe their birthdays and the start of months and years as if day follows night. [3] In other customs of life, they differ from others primarily in that they do not allow their sons to approach their fathers until they have grown to military age. They consider it disgraceful for a son to stand in his father's presence in public while they are still boys.

6.19. As much money as a man receives from his wife as a dowry, the same amount he adds to it from his own wealth. [2] An account is then kept of the shared money along with any profits earned during the marriage. Whichever of the couple outlives the other receives both shares of the dowry plus the profits of past years. [3] Men have the power of life and death over their wives as well as over their children. When the head of the family, one born to a noble house, dies, his relatives convene, and if they suspect the wife of foul play in her husband's death, interrogate her as they would a slave.[307] If they discover anything untoward, they execute her in flames and with all other sorts of excruciating tortures. [4] For a civilization like the Gauls',[308] their funerals are magnificent and extravagant: Everything a man held dear in life is burned with him in death, even his animals. Not more than a generation ago, slaves and clients who were known to be favored by the deceased were heaped up on the funeral pyre and burned along with his body.

6.20. Those states that are thought to administer their public affairs more favorably decree as law that anyone who hears reports or rumors from a neighbor about the state must report it to a magistrate, and that he should not share it with anyone else. [2] Men, often rash and inexperienced, are frightened by false rumors and are urged on to crime or to making decisions about the most important matters. [3] The magistrate, however, keeps hidden whatever seems to him best hidden and reveals to the public what he deems useful to them. Speaking outside of the council about a state matter is not permitted.

6.21. Germans differ much from this manner of living for they have no druids who preside over divine affairs, nor do they perform sacrifices. [2] They consider gods only those elements they can see and whose help they directly receive: the Sun, Vulcan [fire], and the Moon. The rest they do not welcome even in a story. [3] Their whole life is devoted to hunting and military activities, and from childhood they are all eager for hard work. [4] Those who preserve their chastity longest are granted the greatest praise by their kin. Some Germans believe that sexual purity increases one's height. Others think it increases strength or muscles. [5] They also consider it the most disgraceful thing to "know" a woman before turning twenty.[309] It is

---

307. That is, they torture her.

308. This phrase has a pejorative connotation that the Gauls' civilization is generally primitive.

309. Caesar uses here that well-known, cross-cultural euphemism for sex, "to have knowledge" of someone.

impossible to hide such activities anyway, since men and women all bathe together in the rivers, and they wear only small skins made of reindeer, leaving the greater part of the body bare.

6.22. They do not apply themselves to agriculture, and the greater part of their diet consists of milk, cheese, and meat. [2] No one holds any set amount of private property. Instead, the magistrates and tribal leaders assign each year as much land in whatever place they see fit to the nations and clans, and each year they compel them to move to another location. [3] They give many reasons for this practice: Perhaps people might form communities focused on farming instead of on waging war. Or, they might become eager for foreign territories, and so the more powerful might expel the weaker from their lands. Some think people might start building better structures to ward off cold and heat, or that a love of money might emerge and lead to the creation of factions and dissent. [4] On the whole, they think that the plebs are content when they see their own wealth as equal to that of the most powerful.

6.23. The greatest praise for these nations is to have deserted areas as far around them as possible and that territory laid waste. [2] They think it a mark of their courage when neighbors are expelled from and desert their land and then no one else dares to resettle there. [3] At the same time, they think they are safer when all fear of a sudden incursion is removed. [4] When the state either initiates war or defends against an attack, magistrates are elected to take command and are granted power over life and death. [5] In peacetime, there are no common magistrates, but leaders in various regions and districts declare laws locally and settle disputes. [6] Raiding outside the borders of one's state has no disgrace attached to it. Rather, they commend such activities for exercising the young and preventing laziness. [7] When any magistrate has said in assembly that he will be a leader and says, "Whoever wants to follow, let them declare it," the men who approve stand up and promise to aid him and thus earn the praise of the masses. [8] Whoever chooses not to follow is considered a deserter and a traitor and is distrusted in all future matters. [9] They do not think it right to harm guests; no matter the reason someone comes, they are protected from harm and declared sacrosanct. All homes are opened to them, and food is shared with them.

6.24. There was a time before when the Gauls surpassed the Germans in excellence and would wage war with them aggressively. Because of over-population and lack of land, the Gauls even sent colonies across the Rhine. [2] As a result, the most fertile places of Germany around the Hercynian forest (which I see was known by report to Eratosthenes and certain Greeks and was called the Orcynian forest) was occupied and settled by the Volcae Tectosages [a Gallic tribe]. [3] This nation holds these settlements to this day and continues to have the greatest reputation for justness and success in war. [4] Now, because they maintain the same poverty, want, and depra- vations as the Germans, they also follow the German diet and care for the body. [5] The other Gauls, however, because they are nearer our provinces and have become acquainted with imported luxuries, have become accustomed to defeat. [6] After losing so many battles, they no longer bother to compare their courage to that of the Germans.

> *Caesar goes on to describe the Hercynian forest and its creatures, including Eurasian elk (a relative of the North American moose) and the now extinct aurochs, ancient wild cattle that weighed nearly a ton. He tells us that the Germans used the giant aurochs' horns as drinking cups.*

7. Livy, *From the Founding of the City* 5.34–36, 5.38–39, 5.41, 5.48 (1st century BCE/1st century CE). *Livy describes the Romans' first meeting with Gallic tribes in Italy. The very successful Roman general Furius Camillus has been sent into exile. Soon thereafter, Gauls invade Italy. The Romans initially send ambassadors to find out who they are and what they want. The meeting does not go well and results in battle. The Gauls are victorious and march on the city of Rome. Some Romans stay in the city but most flee. (CSR)*

5.34. We have heard the following about the crossing of the Gauls into Italy. While Priscus Tarquinius was ruling in Rome, the Bituriges were the leaders of the Celts, who make up a third of Gaul's population. The king of the Celts came from the Bituriges tribe. [2] This man was named Ambigatus, and he was a leader of the people because of his excellence and his own luck, because during his rule Gaul was so rich in crops and men that such a large crowd seemed like it could be ruled only with difficulty. [3] He, in his great old age, wished to disburden his kingdom of the oppressive crowd and said that he would send Bellovesus and Segovesus, the sons of his sister and energetic youths, to settlements that the gods would point out through auspices. [4] They would lead as many men as were willing so that no tribe would be able to hinder them when they arrived. Segovesus was assigned the Hercynian woodlands by lot; the gods gave Bellovesus a much more pleasant road—to Italy. [5] He led out the excess population: the Bituriges, the Arverni, the Senones, the Haedui, the Ambarri, the Carnutes, and the Aulerci. He set out with a huge amount of infantry and cavalry and went into the land of the Tricastini.

[6] The Alps stood opposite them, which not surprisingly seemed impassable since they were crossed by no road, at least as far as memory held, unless it pleases you to believe stories about Hercules. [7] There the height of the mountains constrained the Gauls as if they were fenced in. They looked around for a way they might cross through passes that seemed joined to the sky and that might cross into another world. Scrupulousness also held them back, because it had been reported to them that some foreigners seeking land had been attacked by the race of the Salui. [8] The ones attacked were Massilians who had set out from Phocaea in ships. The Gauls thought that their situation was an omen of their own fortune, so

they helped the Massilians occupy and secure the place where they had first landed. The Salui allowed this. They themselves crossed the Alps through the Taurine passes and the pass of the Duria. [9] Then, after they had routed the Etruscans in battle not far from the Ticinus River and heard that the place in which they had settled was called the land of the Insubres, a name similar to a district of the Haedui, they accepted this as an omen about the place and established a city there, which they called Mediolanum.

5.35. Soon after this a band of Cenomani arrived—Etitovius was their leader—who had followed the footsteps of the earlier group. With the approval of Bellovesus, they crossed the Alps by the same pass and established settlements where the cities of Brixia and Verona are now. [2] After them the Libui came and settled, and then the Saluvii, who inhabited a place around the river Ticinus near the Laevi-Ligurians, an ancient race. Then the Boii and the Lingones crossed the Pennine pass, and, since the entire area between the Po and the Alps was already settled, they crossed the Po on rafts and drove out not only the Etruscans but also the Umbrians from the land. They kept themselves on the far side of the Apennine Mountains. [3] The Senones, the most recently arrived of the immigrants, settled lands bound by the Utens River and the Aesis River. I learned that this tribe went from there to Clusium and Rome; but it is not very certain whether they went alone or were helped by all the people of the Cisalpine Gallic tribes. [4] The people of Clusium were frightened by this foreign invasion. When they saw their numbers and the strange appearance of the men and the types of weapons they carried, when they heard that the legions of the Etruscans had been put to flight by them on both sides of the Po, and although they did not have any right of alliance or friendship with the Romans except that they did not defend their close neighbors the Veii against the Roman people, they sent an embassy to Rome to ask for help from the senate. [5] No help was obtained, although three sons of Marcus Fabius Ambustus were sent as ambassadors. They informed the Gauls in the name of the senate and people of Rome that they would accept no harm from them and that they should not attack allies and friends of the Roman people. [6] If the matter headed in that direction, the Roman people would keep her allies and friends safe through military means; but they told the Gauls that it seemed better if war itself were avoided, if possible, and that it would be better if they, who were a new race to the Romans, were met in peace rather than in war.

5.36. The embassy was not harsh, but it had impetuous ambassadors who acted more like Gauls than Romans. After they had set forth their demands in the council, the Gauls gave them this response: [2] that although they are first hearing the name of Romans, they nevertheless believe them to be brave men, whose aid had been sought by the men of Clusium in this fearful matter; [3] and since the Romans preferred to defend their allies by means of diplomacy rather than warfare, then the peace that they brought would not be spurned, as long as the men of Clusium, who possess more than they can farm, conceded a part of their territory to the Gauls, who need land. Peace would not be possible otherwise. [4] In addition, they wished to receive an answer from the Romans face to face. If land was refused to them, then they would fight in the face of these same Romans, so that they would be able to announce at home how much the Gauls exceeded the rest of mankind in bravery. [5] The Romans asked what law it was that said they could demand land from its possessors and threaten war and what business the Gauls had in Etruria. The Gauls fiercely replied that they brought the law in their weapons and that everything belongs to brave men. It was then that the spirits of both sides were fired up, and they ran to their weapons and began to battle. [6] There, since the fates were pressuring the Roman city, the ambassadors took up arms in a move that was contrary to the rules of war. This move was not able to be kept secret—not when three of the most noble and bravest of Roman youth fought before the Etruscan battle standard—because the bravery of these foreigners was strongly apparent. [7] Even worse, Quintus Fabius charged outside the battle line on his horse and struck the leader of the Gauls, who was charging fiercely against the Etruscan standards, in the side with a spear and killed him. The Gauls recognized Quintus Fabius when he was taking his spoils, and through the whole battle line a signal was given that it was the Roman ambassador. [8] They left behind their anger against the men of Clusium, sounded their retreat, and threatened the Romans. There were those who were for going to Rome immediately, but their elders convinced them to send ambassadors first to express the wrongs done to them and to demand that the sons of Fabius be handed over to them since they had violated the rules of war. [9] After the ambassadors of the Gauls had laid out these complaints and demands, as they were commanded, the senate did feel that the actions of the Fabii were wrong and that the barbarians seemed to be making a lawful request, but ambition in these men of such high nobility kept them from doing what they knew was right. [10] They put the demands of the Gauls up for consideration by the people so that the blame that might come from a potentially disastrous Gallic war would not fall on them. The Romans put such a greater value on political influence and wealth that the men whose punishment was being discussed were made military tributes with consular power in the following year. [11] Because of this the Gauls, who were enraged not at all less than the event merited, returned to their people after they had openly threatened war.

> *The Gauls and the Romans prepare to fight. What follows is a brief description of the battle and the Roman reaction to their defeat at the hands of the Gauls.*

5.38.3. Brennus, the chief of the Gauls, was very afraid of the Romans' strategy because their numbers were small. He thought that they had taken the higher ground so that, when the Gauls made a straight-on frontal attack against the lines of the legions, they would send reserve troops against the sides and the rear of the attack. [4] He turned his army to fight against the reserves and was not at all doubtful that victory would be easy on the level ground for his larger forces if he could drive them out of their place; and so not only luck but good reasoning was on the barbarians' side. [5] In the other line, there was nothing that still looked like Romans—not among the leaders, not among the soldiers. Fear and flight occupied their minds, and so great a fear of everything that a much larger portion of the army fled to Veii, an enemy city, even though the Tiber River hindered them, than the portion that fled by a straight road to Rome and their wives and children. [6] For a while their position protected the reserves, but in the rest of the battle line a great shout was heard at their side and at their rear at the same time. Nearly before they saw the foreign enemy, and even though they had not fought or returned the shout, they fled whole and unharmed. [7] There was no bloodshed among those who fought; but the backs of those who fled and were hindering others' flight were cut down in the crowd of fleeing men. [8] Near the bank of the Tiber River, where the entire left wing had fled after throwing down their weapons, great carnage occurred, and the river consumed many who did not know how to swim or who were weakened by their burden of corselets and other armor. [9] And yet the greatest part of the army fled to Veii unharmed, and from there they did not send aid or even a messenger to Rome to announce the defeat. [10] The soldiers of the right wing, which had stood far from the river and closer to the mountains, all sought Rome and fled into the citadel without even closing the gates of the city.

5.39. The miracle of the unexpected victory stunned the unbelieving Gauls into stillness at first; they stood transfixed by fear as if they were ignorant of what had occurred. Then they feared a trap. Finally, however, they took their spoils from the slaughter and, as is their custom, gathered together a pile of weapons. [2] Then, finally, after nothing at all hostile was observed, they set out on the road and reached the city of Rome just before sunset. The cavalry had gone ahead, and they reported back that the gates were not closed, no guard was stationed before the gates, and there were no armed men on the walls. Therefore another miracle, similar to the first one, held them up. [3] Since they feared the night and the site of the unknown city, they set up camp between Rome and Anio and sent out men to explore around the walls and the other gates to find out what kind of plan their enemy would have in such a desperate situation. [4] As for the Romans, since a greater part of their army had fled to Veii than had fled to Rome, no one thought that anyone remained except for those who had fled to Rome, and so they mourned the living and the dead equally and filled nearly the whole city with the sound of their weeping. [5] Then, after it was announced that the enemy was at hand, their public fear numbed their private grief, and soon they began to hear the dissonant cries and songs of the barbarians who were wandering around their walls in squadrons.

> The Romans who remained in the city make plans for a small force to defend the citadel and to evacuate most of the people. Many old men are left behind to allow the women, children, and younger men to leave easily. They choose to enclose themselves in their houses. The Gauls enter the city.

5.41.4. Because a night had passed since the fight, and because the battle had never been uncertain and they were not taking the city by attack or force, the Gauls had lost their battle energy and, without anger or firing of their spirits, they entered the city the next day. Since the Colline gate was left open they went straight into the forum and looked around at the temples of the gods and the citadel—this alone looked ready for war. [5] Then they left a small guard behind so that there would not be an attack on them from the citadel or the Capitoline Hill while they were scattered. They spread out to gather spoils on streets that were empty of men. Some rushed in a group into the closest buildings; others sought buildings that were further away, for they thought that they would be untouched and stuffed with spoils. [6] They became frightened, however, by the very emptiness of the streets and were afraid that some enemy trick would catch them as they were wandering around, so they gathered together and returned to the forum and the places close to it. [7] The houses of the common people were closed up, but the halls of the leaders were lying open. They felt a greater hesitation at invading an open house than a closed one. [8] And with the same spirit they honored the men whom they saw sitting in the front courts of their houses and, compared to their fine clothes and bearing, which seemed more venerable than human greatness, their appearance and the sternness of their faces made them seem like gods.

> One Roman who remained in his house strikes a Gaul, which rouses them to burn the city. Some besiege the Capitol, others march out into the country-side, where they meet Roman forces led by Camillus at the city of Ardea. The Romans attack and destroy the Gallic camp and move on to Veii, where they organize their return to Rome. The Gauls attempt to attack the Romans in the citadel but do not succeed. Livy goes on to discuss the effects of the siege on the Gauls and Romans.

5.48. That thing that is worse than all the evils resulting from the siege and the war, hunger, was beginning to press on each army, [2] and for the Gauls, disease as well, since they kept their camps between the hills in the lowlands that were scorched by fires, full of vapors, and even a little wind blowing through there would bring up ashes as well as dust. [3] The Gallic race is accustomed to wet and cold, and so they found this situation most intolerable. Since they were plagued with heat and suffocating air, like cattle they began to die from the diseases that wandered freely among them. Because they were lazy about burying their men individually, they piled up a heap of bodies all mixed together and burned them. That act marked the place with the name *Busta Gallica* or Gallic pyres. [4] Soon after they made a truce with the Romans, and the men talked with each other with the permission of their commanders. Again and again in these conversations the Gauls threw the Romans' hunger in their faces and told them to give in to their need and surrender. To show that they rejected the Gauls' advice, the Romans are said to have thrown bread from many places on the Capitoline hill down onto the enemy posts. [5] Soon, however, they could no longer hide or endure their hunger. Therefore, while the dictator Camillus was conducting a draft at Ardea, ordering his master of the horse, Lucius Valerius, to lead his army out of Veii, and preparing and organizing the army that would attack the enemy on equal footing, [6] the army on the Capitoline, which was tired out by their postings and watches and had survived almost all human miseries (since hunger is the only thing that nature does not allow us to conquer), was watching day in and day out for the help from the dictator to appear. [7] Finally, hope and food failed them. Whenever the guards went out, their weapons nearly overwhelmed their weak bodies. They demanded that they surrender or ransom themselves by whatever pact they would be able to make, since the Gauls were clearly letting it be known that they would be able to be convinced to lift the siege for only a little money. [8] The senate empowered the tribunes of the soldiers to handle the affair so that they might come to terms. The terms were arranged at a meeting between the tribune Quintus Sulpicius and Brennus, the chief of the Gauls. The price was set at 1,000 pounds of gold for a race of people who were soon to rule the world. [9] Shame was added to a matter already very horrible in and of itself: the weights brought by the Gauls were unfair and, when the tribune complained, a sword was added to the weight by the insolent Gaul with a saying that cannot be tolerated by Romans: *Vae victis!* (Woe to the conquered!)

>   **8. Livy, *From the Founding of the City* 23.24.6–13 (1st century BCE/ 1st century CE).** *As part of his discussion of the various battles of the Second Punic War, Livy provides a description of the fate of the Roman army under Postumius against the Gauls. The Gauls made clever use of their environment to defeat the Roman forces. (CSR)*

23.24. Just as these matters were being seen to, a new disaster was announced, for fortune was piling one bad thing on another this year. Lucius Postumius, the consul-elect, and his army were destroyed in Gaul. [7] There was a great forest called the Litana by the Gauls, through which he was going to lead his army. The Gauls cut the trees of this forest to the right and left around the road in such a way that they stood upright but would fall with a light push. [8] Postumius had two Roman legions, and he had conscripted a large enough force of allies from the area surrounding the upper sea so that he led 25,000 armed men into enemy land. [9] The Gauls circled the edge of the forest and pushed down the already cut trees from the outside when the army entered the forest. Since they were unstable and barely holding upright, these fell one against the other, and they buried weapons, men, and horses in destruction from all sides. Most of the men were killed by the trunks of trees and broken branches; scarcely 10 men escaped. [10] The armed Gauls, who were stationed around the whole forest, killed the remaining men, who had been terrified by the unexpected attack. Only a few were captured from such a large number of men—those who sought the bridge over the river were caught by the enemy who already held it. [11] Postumius fell there, fighting with all his strength not to be captured. The Boii, in triumph, brought the spoils from the body and the head of the leader to the temple that is the most sacred among them. [12] As is their custom, the head was cleaned out and then the scalp was covered with gold. This became a sacred vessel for them with which they pour out solemn libations and which the priest and the attendants of the temple use as a cup. [13] The plunder was as great as the victory for the Gauls, for although a great part of the animals had been buried by the destruction of the forest, nevertheless the rest of it, because nothing was spread out in flight, was found laid out along the entire length of the battle formation.

9. Pomponius Mela, *Description of the World* 3.18–19 (1st century CE). *A description of the Gauls between Spain and the Rhine. (RFK)*

3.18. The people are arrogant, superstitious, and at times so inhuman that they once believed the victim best and most pleasing to the gods was man. Vestiges of this savagery remain despite its now being abolished. Although they refrain from the ultimate bloodshed, they cull just the minimal amount from the faithful when they lead them to the altars. Despite this savagery, they have their own eloquence and druids, teachers of wisdom. [19] The druids profess to know the size and shape of the land and earth, the movements of the sky and stars, and what the gods want. They teach the most noble among their people many things secretly and over a long period of time [twenty years]. They teach either in a cave or in a hidden wood. One of their teachings has become common knowledge among the rabble (intended, perhaps, to make them better in war), that there is another life for the souls of the dead. For this reason, they cremate the dead and bury with them items appropriate for living. In times past, the calculation and collection of debt from business was deferred until death. Some people even freely threw themselves upon the funeral pile of their family members as if they would be living with them again after death.

10. Velleius Paterculus, *History of Rome* 2.118.1 (1st century CE). *Velleius stops his narrative of the defeat of Varus in the Teutoburg Forest (9 CE) by the Cherusci to demonstrate the Germans' treacherous nature. (MLG)*

The Germans are, and this is a fact that only someone who has experienced them can believe, not only very savage but also the most deceitful of men, a race born to lie. They invent one fake accusation after another and provoke each other into quarrels. Then they thank Roman justice for putting an end to them, for softening their savagery by this unknown new custom of legally deciding affairs that formerly required weapons to solve. These lies produced such carelessness in Quintilius that he believed that he was the Urban Praetor presiding over court in the forum and not a general in the middle of Germany.

11. Pliny, *Natural History* 16.249 (1st century CE). *Pliny is discussing the use of mistletoe for making bird-lime. (MLG)*

We must not fail to mention this plant that the Gauls venerate. The druids (this is the name for their sages) consider nothing more sacred than mistletoe and the tree it is growing on, so long as that tree be oak. They select groves of oak trees on this account, and they perform no sacrifice with these oak leaves. As a result, they may appear to be called druids from the Greek word *drues* [oak trees]. In fact they consider anything grown from oak trees to be sent from heaven and a sign of a tree chosen by god himself.

12. Pliny, *Natural History* 24.103–104 (1st century CE). *Pliny is discussing various herbs and their uses. (MLG)*

24.103. The herb called *selago* is similar to the herb *sabina*. It is harvested without iron, with the right hand covered by the tunic, and dug up with the left like a thief. While dressed in white and with washed bare feet, one makes a sacrifice of bread and wine before harvesting. It is carried away in a new napkin. The Gallic druids declare that this herb should be kept to ward off harm, and that its smoke is helpful for eye complaints.

24.104. The same authorities mentioned the herb *samolus*, which grows in wet areas. It is said that when this plant is plucked with the left hand by a fasting person, it is effective against swine and cattle illnesses; in addition, the person collecting should not look back or put it anywhere but in the trough, there crushed for the animals to drink.

13. Pliny, *Natural History* 29.52 (1st century CE). *Pliny discusses the variety of eggs known to the Gauls. (MLG)*

There is a type of egg that is very famous among the Gauls, but that the Greeks do not mention. It is made when many snakes intertwine in artful embrace and wind together an object out of their mouths' spittle and bodies' foam; this is called the "wind-egg." The druids say that the hissing of the snakes shoots the egg into the air, and it should be caught in a rough military mantle, so that it does not touch the earth. They say that the catcher must flee on a horse, since the snakes follow until they are prevented by some river. They say that the test of the egg is as follows: it flows against the current even if set in gold.

14. Pliny, *Natural History* 30.13 (1st century CE). *Pliny is discussing human sacrifice in Rome down to 97 BCE. (MLG)*

The Gauls performed such rites everywhere, even to a time within our memory. In his principate, Tiberius Caesar abolished the druids and this type of magician and doctor. Do I need to mention these things that have crossed Ocean and reached the empty void of nature? Britain today is full of superstitious awe and practices these rites with such ceremonies that it may appear that they gave them to the Persians. The nations show such unanimity in this practice, even when they hate or are ignorant of each other. It is almost incalculable how much the world owes the Romans for removing such monstrosities, in which it is a matter of religion to kill a man and where cannibalism is considered a quite healthy act.

15. Tacitus, *Agricola* 11–12, 15–16, 27, 37 excerpted (1st/2nd century CE). *Tacitus depicts British society, as well as his ideas about genetic inheritance and the influence of climate on the culture and physique of the Britons. (CSR)*

11. Little has been discovered about the people who have inhabited Britain from the beginning—either indigenous or immigrants—a common problem when it comes to barbarians. Their appearance is diverse, and from this some conclusions can be drawn. [2] The red hair and large limbs of the people inhabiting Caledonia [Scotland] are evidence of their Germanic origins. The Silurians have dark skin and curly hair (a common feature). This combined with the fact that Spain lies opposite their isle make it believable that the ancient Iberians crossed and inhabited this area. The people nearest the Gauls are similar to them, either because of the enduring strength of their roots, or because their lands are close to each other and the similar climate gives them a similar appearance. [3] In general, it is credible to assume that the Gauls occupied the nearby island. Observe that the Britons' sacred rites are akin to the Gauls' superstition and their speech is hardly different. They share the same audacity in seeking out danger and, when it comes, the same fear in their evasion of it. [4] The Britons, however, show more ferocity, as men do who have not yet been softened by a long peace. We acknowledge that the Gauls, too, had once been fierce in war, but soon laziness was introduced along with leisure. Their courage was lost at the same time as their freedom. This has happened to those of the Britons who have been conquered; the rest remain as the Gauls once were.

12. There is strength in the British infantry, and certain tribes also fight in chariots. The more distinguished men are charioteers while their subordinates make sorties. Once they obeyed kings; now their leaders draw them into factions and partisanship. [2] There is nothing more useful for us against such powerful races than that they do not make plans in common. A

united front from even two or three states against a common danger is rare, thus each tribe fights individually and is conquered universally.

. . .

15. Once their fear waned because the legate had left, the Britons debated among themselves the evils of servitude. They compared injuries and incited each other by the telling. They said: "Suffering achieves nothing except that even heavier burdens are imposed upon us than upon those who tolerate such things easily. [2] Once we each had one king over us, but now two rulers are imposed on us. Of the two, the military legate destroys our lifeblood, the tax collector our livelihood. Discord or concord among these leaders is equally hateful to us, their subjects. Centurions are the instruments of the legate; the tax collector's slaves mix force and insults together. Nothing now is exempt from their greed; nothing is exempt from their lust. [3] In battle the braver man wins the spoils, but now our houses are sacked mostly by ignoble cowards, our children are dragged away, and conscription is enforced as if on people who do not know about dying for their own country. Consider how relatively few soldiers came over to Britain, if we Britons should ever count ourselves? This is how the Germans shook off the yoke of subjection, and they are defended by a river not by the ocean. [4] We have country, wives, and parents. For them, avarice and luxury are their motivations for war. They will retreat, as the divine Julius retreated, should we only emulate the courage of our ancestors. Let us not get anxious about the outcome of one battle or another. There is more power in the fortunate, but a greater constancy and steadfastness in the wretched. [5] Already the gods pity the Britons—it is they who detain the Roman leader, who hold back the army on another island. We ourselves are already deliberating, which is the most difficult thing to do. Moreover, in such matters, it is more dangerous to be caught in deliberations than to dare to act."

16. Roused among themselves by such arguments as these, and with Boudicca for their leader, a woman of royal breeding (for they do not differentiate between the sexes among their leaders), they undertook the war united. They hunted down the soldiers scattered through the forts. The defenses breached, they invaded the Roman settlement itself since it was the locus of their servitude, and anger and victory caused them not to leave out any kind of savagery known among barbarian tribes. [2] If Paulinus had not come back quickly once he learned about the uprising of the province, Britain would have been lost. Yet the outcome of one battle restored their old enduring submission. Many retained their weapons—those who worried over the consciousness of their defection and their particular fear of the legate—in case this otherwise generous man should demand more from those who surrendered and decide on harsher revenge for the injuries committed as if they had been against his own person.

. . .

27.2. But the Britons did not think that they had been conquered by courage, but by the circumstance and the machinations of the Roman leader. They lost nothing of their pride; rather they lost so little that they armed their youth, moved their wives and children to safe locations, and sanctified the confederation of the states by treaties and sacrifices. Once they had done all this, they departed with spirits excited on every side.

. . .

37. And those Britons who were still uninvolved in the battle sat on the peaks of the hills and scorned our small numbers. Little by little they began to descend and go around to the rear of the victorious side. But Agricola, since he already feared this very action, sent four divisions of cavalry, which he had held back as insurance against an unexpected war, to meet them. However much more ferociously they attacked, that much more sharply did Agricola scatter them after they had been driven into flight. [2] Thus this plan of the Britons turned against them. The divisions, which Agricola with foresight had turned around from the front of the battle lines, infiltrated the line of the enemy from the other side. Then indeed a huge and horrible spectacle occurred on the open plains: The Romans pursued, they wounded, they captured, and then they slaughtered these same men as even more came to fight them. [3] Already, according to the character of each man, ever smaller crowds of armed enemies offered their backs to our men, and certain unarmed Britons rushed back and offered themselves up to death. Everywhere there were weapons and bodies and lacerated limbs and bloody earth; sometimes anger and courage roused even in the conquered Britons once they neared the forests. [4] They gathered together and were able to surround the first of their incautious pursuers because they had knowledge of the land. But Agricola seemed to appear everywhere and ordered the infantry cohorts and a part of the cavalry whose horses were unnecessary for the main battle to jump down and search wherever the forests were denser. At the same time he ordered the cavalry to pursue where the trees were more spread apart, otherwise there might have been injuries from overconfidence. [5] Moreover, when the Britons looked back to see the men following them in organized and well-formed lines, they turned in flight, not orderly as before, and not looking at each other. Rather, they were spread out and avoiding each other; each of them sought far-off and pathless places on his own.

16. Tacitus, *Germania* 1–9, 15–22, 27–46 (1st/2nd century CE).
Tacitus' account of Germany and German customs. (CSR)

1. All Germany is separated from the Gauls, Rhaetians, and Pannonians by the Rhine and Danube, and from the Sarmatians and Dacians by mutual fear or mountains. Ocean surrounds the rest of Germany, embracing wide bays and huge expanses of islands. Certain peoples and kings, who have been

introduced to us by war, are only recently known. [2] The Rhine, rising from an inaccessible and steep ridge of the Rhaetian Alps, turns slightly toward the west and mixes with the northern Ocean. The Danube flows from the moderate, gently sloping ridge of Mount Abnoba and passes many people until it breaks out into the Pontic Sea in six channels; the seventh channel is swallowed up by swamps.

2. I believe that the Germans themselves are indigenous, and the arrival and friendship of other races have resulted in very little mixing, because people who were seeking to change their homes came not by land but by ships. The Ocean beyond them is immense, as I would say, on the opposite side and is rarely approached by ships from our world. Moreover, not even considering the danger or the rough and unknown sea, who would leave Asia or Africa or Italy behind and seek Germany, which is wild in lands, harsh in climate, and unpleasant in habitation and in aspect, except if it was your homeland? [2] With ancient songs, which are the only kind of tradition or history they have, they celebrate as the origin and founders of their race the god Tuisto, born from the earth, and his son Mannus. They claim that Mannus had three sons; from their names those closest to the Ocean are called the Ingaevones, those in the middle the Hermiones, and the rest the Istaevones. Certain people, using the license granted by antiquity, claim more were born from the god and provide the names of more races—the Marsians, Gambrivii, Suebi, and the Vandilii—and say that these are true and ancient names. [3] Moreover, the word Germany is new, since those who first crossed the Rhine and expelled the Gauls are now called Tungri but used to be called Germans; thus the name of the nation, not of the race, grew little by little so that all were called by the made-up name "Germans"—first by the conquered out of fear and soon by themselves also.

3. They say that Hercules lived among them, and in battle the natives sing about him first of all brave men. They also have these songs, which they call "baritus," that they recite and in so doing ignite their spirits and foresee through the song itself the outcome of the upcoming fight; for they cause fear or they tremble based on how it sounds in the battle line. It seems to be not so much a coming together of voices but a coming together of courage. A harshness of sound and a broken murmur is brought about by holding their shields in front of their mouths so that their voices might swell more fully and heavily by the resonance. [2] In addition, some think that Ulysses, in his long and fabled wandering, was carried into the Ocean and approached the lands of Germany. Asciburgium, which is situated on the banks of the Rhine and is inhabited today, was established and named by him. They also say that an altar dedicated by Ulysses, with the name of his father Laertes added, was once found in the same place, and they say that monuments and certain *tumuli* inscribed with Greek letters still exist on the boundaries of Germany and Rhaetia. [3] It is not my intention to either confirm this argument or refute it; each individual may add to or subtract from their belief according to his own opinion.

4. I myself accept the opinion of those who think that the people of Germany have been infected by no marriages with other nations and exist as an individual and pure race that is similar only to itself. It is because of this that the build of their bodies is the same in all the people, even though the population is so large. They have fierce blue eyes, red hair, huge bodies, and they are strong only on impulse. At the same time they have no patience for labor or great works. They do not tolerate heat and thirst at all; rather, they are accustomed to cold and hunger because of their climate and soil.

5. The land varies somewhat in appearance; on the whole, however, it is bristling with forests or unhealthy with swamps. It is more humid near Gaul and windier near Noricum or Pannonia. It is fertile in grains but unable to bear fruit trees; it is good for herds, but they are mostly undersized. [2] There is no grace in their cows nor are there glorious horns on their foreheads. They rejoice in their number, for these are their only and most valued form of wealth. [3] I do not know whether the gods deny them silver and gold because they are pleased or angry. I would not assert that no vein in Germany bears silver or gold, for who has searched carefully for them? [4] They are not at all affected by the possession or use of them. One can see silver vases among them, given to their legates and leaders as gifts, but they do not use them differently from how they use earthenware. Those nearest to us have gold and silver in monetary form for commercial use, and recognize and choose out certain forms of our money. The groups in the interior practice barter more simply and in the ancient manner. [5] They approve of old money that has been known for a long time—coins notched on the edges and with chariots on it. They seek out silver more than gold, not because of a predilection for silver, but because the value of silver is easier for use for those who buy common and cheap materials.

6. Not even iron is in abundance there, as we can gather from the type of weapons they use. There are a few who use swords or larger lances, but for the most part they carry short spears or *frameae* (to use their own word) that have a short and narrow piece of iron attached, but one that is so sharp and handy to use that they can fight with the same weapon close at hand and at a distance as the situation demands. Horsemen too are content with a shield and *framea*, and foot soldiers also throw javelins. Each man, nude or lightly covered with a cloak, has many weapons that they throw over immense spaces. There is no boasting about apparel. They make their shields stand out with the choicest colors. There are breastplates for a few; scarcely one or two have metal or hide helmets. [2] The horses stand out neither in beauty or in speed. They are not taught to swerve in circles as is our custom; rather, they drive them straight or bending to the right in a circle joined so tightly that no one falls behind another. [3] On the whole you would say that the infantry has more strength. The infantry fights mixed up with their cavalry, and the speed of the infantry, whom they choose from all the youths and place in front of the battle line, is adapted to the cavalry and works in congruence with it. Their number is defined—one hundred from each

district—and they are called "the hundred" among themselves. What was at first a number is now a name and an honor. [4] Their battle line is organized in wedges. To cede a place, as long as you step up again, is thought to show good planning rather than fear. They carry back their dead even in battles with uncertain outcomes. The worst disgrace is to leave behind your shield; it is not right for one who has acted so ignominiously to approach sacrifices or to go into council meetings. Many survivors of battles end their infamy with a noose.

7. They choose kings by their nobility, war leaders by their courage. The kings do not have infinite or free power, and their leaders lead by example rather than by force. If they are energetic, if they stand out, if they lead the front of the battle line, then they are preeminent because of the people's admiration for them. Nothing beyond this is permitted to them—not to rebuke nor enchain, not even to beat men. This is permitted to the priests, and not in punishment or by the war leader's order, but if a god, whom they believe is present among the warriors, had ordered it. [2] They carry into battle effigies and certain standards brought out of sacred groves. The strongest incitement to bravery is this: neither chance nor a fortuitous grouping makes the company or the battle wedge but rather families and kin. An additional guarantee is nearby, for they keep their families close so that they can hear the shouts of women and the wailing of infants. These are the witnesses dearest to each man; these are the source of their greatest praise. They bring their wounds to their mothers and wives, and these women do not hesitate to count the wounds or examine them. They also provide the fighters with food and encouragement.

8. According to tradition, some wavering or uncertain battles were restored by women through the constancy of their prayers, the baring of their breasts, and the demonstration of the approach of slavery. Slavery in respect to their women is such an unendurable source of dread for them that states are most effectively bound when noble girls are also among the hostages. [2] They think that there is something holy and providential within women, and they do not look down on their advice or neglect their answers. Under the divine Vespasian we saw Velaeda, long believed among many to be a goddess. Also, long ago, they venerated Aurinia and many others more, but not with flattery nor as false goddesses.

9. They worship Mercury especially. On certain days they consider it right to sacrifice even human victims to him. They placate Hercules and Mars with approved animals. Some of the Suebi also sacrifice to Isis—I have not found out the cause and the origin of this foreign rite, except that the cult sign is fashioned like a Liburnian ship, which shows that the religion was introduced, not native. [2] Furthermore, they do not think it right to confine the gods within walls or to assimilate them into any aspect of human appearance because of the greatness of these heavenly beings. They

consecrate woods and groves and name that secret thing that they see only in worship with the names of the gods.

Tacitus details the political habits of the Germans. Each tribe, he states, has an assembly and a chief who keeps a group of sworn followers near him.

15. When they are not entering into wars, they pass much of their time in hunting but even more in leisure, dedicating themselves to sleep and food. The bravest and the most warlike do nothing; the house and the care of the hearths and field are handed over to women and old men and the weakest from the family. They themselves are dull because of a strange dissonance in their nature: they love idleness and hate quiet at the same time. [2] It is the custom for the citizens to give either flocks or fruits to their leaders, which are accepted as an honor, but they are also necessities. They especially delight in gifts from neighboring races—which are sent not only by each individual but also by the general public—such as select horses, great arms, military decorations, and torques. We have now taught them to accept money.

16. It is well enough known that the German people do not live in cities; they do not even allow their houses to be attached to each other. They live separately and are spread out, wherever a fountain, a plain, or a grove pleases them. They do not situate their villages in our manner, with connected and attached buildings. Each man surrounds his home with open space, either as a measure against the chance of fire or because they are ignorant about architecture. [2] They do not even use uncut stones or tiles; they use unshaped timber for all things without thinking about appearance or attraction. Certain places are carefully smeared with earth so pure and shining that it seems like a painting or bright splotches of color. [3] They often open subterranean pits and pile a lot of dung over them. This serves as a shelter from winter and as storage for produce, because places like this soften the harshness of the frosts. If an enemy ever comes, he ravages the things out in the open, but he either ignores or is deceived by what is hidden and buried because they have to be searched out.

17. Everyone wears cloaks attached with brooches or, if they do not have a brooch, thorns. When they are not wearing them, they spend the whole day uncovered near the hearth and fire. The richest are marked out by their clothes, which are not flowing like the ones the Sarmatians and Parthians wear, but are drawn tight and are tight-fitting. They also wear skins of wild beasts: the tribes near the river as casual clothes, the tribes further away as more formal wear, since nothing nice is available for them in trade. They hunt wild animals, and then they decorate the skins they've taken with the spotted skins of beasts that the furthest Ocean and the unknown sea bring forth. [2] Women's dress is not different from men's, except that more often women are cloaked in linens, which they decorate with purple dye. Also, they do not have sleeves on the upper part of their clothes. Their shoulders and arms are bare, and the area adjacent their arms is exposed.

18. Nevertheless, marriage is strict there, and you could not praise any other of their customs more. For they, almost alone out of all barbarians, are content with one wife each with a few exceptions, who are bound in multiple marriages not out of lust but because of their nobility. [2] The wife does not bring a dowry to the husband, but the husband to the wife. The parents and relatives are present and approve the gifts. Gifts are not given to satisfy womanly pleasures or to adorn the new bride. They include cows and a bridled horse and a shield with *framea* and sword. The wife accepts these gifts and, in turn, she herself brings some kind of weapon to her husband. They think that this is the greatest bond: these gifts represent the sacred *arcana*, the conjugal deities. [3] In case the wife thinks that she is beyond the considerations of courage and the fortunes of war, she is warned by these signs at the beginning of the marriage that she comes as an ally to her husband in both labor and danger. She is reminded that she will suffer and dare the same in peace as in war. This is what the gifts of yoked cows, the equipped horse, and arms announce. Thus she must live; thus she must die. What she accepts, she hands down inviolate and still valuable to her children; her daughters-in-law will take them and hand them down to her grandchildren.

19. Because of these customs, they live with their chastity well protected; they are corrupted by no enticements like spectacles and by no desires for banquets. Men and women are equally ignorant of secrets in letters. There are very few cases of adultery for so numerous a race, the punishment of which is immediate and granted to the husband. In front of her relatives, the husband drives his wife, naked and with her hair cut off, from their home and beats her as they go through the whole village. There is no pardon after a public revelation of a lack of chastity: her beauty, her age, or her wealth will not find her a new husband. No one laughs at vice there, nor is corrupting or being corrupted chalked up to "the times." [2] Even better still are those states in which only virgins may marry and so only once is she fixed by the hope and promises of being a wife. Thus they accept one husband just as they accept having one body and one life, so that there are no more stray thoughts, no drawn-out desire, so that they love not so much the husband himself but rather their marriage. The Germans consider it an outrage to limit the number of children or to kill any of their children. The good customs here are much stronger than good laws elsewhere.

20. In every house, naked and dirty children grow into those long limbs and bodies that we admire. A mother nurses her own child from her breasts; they do not pass them on to slave-women or wet-nurses. You cannot distinguish master and slave by any charms of education; they spend their time among the same herds, on the same land, until maturity separates out the native freeborn and courage distinguishes them. [2] The charm of youth lasts a long time, and puberty is not wasted. The maidens are not hastened; they wait until the couple is the same age and has come to a similar level of maturity. They marry as equals in age and strength, and the children reflect the strength of their parents. [3] The son of a sister has the same honor before his uncle as before his father. Certain people think that this bond of blood is more sacred and tighter and they demand hostages bound in this

way more often, as though they would hold their enemy's attention more firmly and his family more widely. A man's own children are his heirs and successors, and there is no will. If there are no children, brothers, paternal uncles, and maternal uncles are the nearest degree in succession. The more relatives and thus the larger number of connections make an old man that much more popular; there is no value in childlessness.

21. It is considered as necessary to take up the enemies of one's father or relative as it is to adopt their friendships; these hostilities, however, do not endure without end. Even homicide can be payed off by a set number of cattle or sheep and the whole household receives satisfaction. This is useful in public matters, because hostilities are more dangerous when mixed with freedom. [2] No other race indulges more effusively in parties or hospitality. It is held to be wrong to keep anyone from entering your house; each man gets well-prepared meals according to his fortune. If the host runs out of food, he becomes the guide and companion for more hospitality elsewhere: they go to the next house uninvited, but it does not matter, for they are received with equal generosity. No one distinguishes between known and unknown guests as far as the right to hospitality goes. It is customary to give the one departing anything he has demanded, and the host feels comfortable asking for something in return. They rejoice in gifts, but they do not make an account of what is given, nor are they bound by what is received.

22. Immediately after sleeping—an event that drags out into the day— they wash, more often in hot water, as you would expect among those who have such a long winter. After bathing they grab a meal: a separate seat and separate table for each man. Then, armed, they proceed to business no less often than they go to a feast. No one finds it disgraceful to drink continuously day and night. As among drinkers, frequent fights happen—seldom with abusive language, more often with death and wounds. [2] On the other hand, at these banquets they also make decisions about reconciliation with their enemies, about forming alliances, about appointing leaders, and finally about peace and war, as if at no other time is the mind so open to simple thoughts or more inspired to great ones. [3] Since they are a race neither astute nor shrewd, they open up the secrets of their hearts because of the freedom at their banquets. Therefore everyone's minds are uncovered and made plain. The next day ideas are reconsidered, and they remember the outcome of each discussion. They deliberate when they are unable to deceive, they decide when they cannot make mistakes.[310]

Funerals, and a tour of all the different tribes of the Germans.

27. In their funerals there is no showing off; the following rite alone is observed. The bodies of famous men are burned with a particular kind of wood. They do not add clothes or incense to the heap of the pyre; for some of them, a man's own arms and horse are added to the fire. The tomb is turf: they scorn the difficult and onerous honor of monuments that, in

---

310. Herodotus 1.33 tells us that the Persians, too, debate matters both sober and drunk (See Chapter 10, Selection 4).

their opinion, weigh on the dead men. They put laments and weeping aside quickly, grief and sorrow slowly. It is fitting for women to mourn, for men to remember. [2] We have received this information concerning the origin and customs of all Germans in general; now I will explain the institutions and rites of individual tribes, how they differ, and which nations migrated from Germany into Gaul.

28. The divine Julius, the highest authority, said that the affairs of the Gauls were once more noble; thus it is even believable that the Gauls migrated into Germany. The river barely stood in the way so that, as each tribe got stronger, they would occupy and exchange areas of control that were still uncertain and undivided by the power of separate kingdoms. [2] Therefore the Helvetians held the land between the Hercynian forest and the Rhine and Moenus Rivers, the Boii held the land beyond, each a Gallic race. The name of the Bohaemun still remains and marks an old memory about the place, although the inhabitants have changed. [3] But whether the Aravisci migrated from the Osi into Pannonia or the Osi from the Aravisci into Germany is uncertain, since they still use the same speech and established customs. For once they shared the same fortune and had equal amounts of poverty and freedom on either bank of the river. [4] The Treveri and the Nervii are ambitious in their affectation of German origins, as if through this glory of blood relations they could be separated from the shared weakness of the Gauls. The peoples inhabiting the banks of the Rhine are German without a doubt: the Vangiones, Triboci, and Nemetes. Not even the Ubii are embarrassed by their origins, although they earned the status of a Roman colony and are happy to be called Agrippinenses after the name of their founder. They once crossed the sea and, because of a proof of good faith, were settled on the bank of the Rhine, so that they might hinder others not so that they might be watched.

29. The Batavians are the foremost in virtue of all these races. They inhabit some land along the river and an island in the Rhine. They were once a people of the Chatti and, because of a domestic coup, crossed over into these settlements where they became part of the Roman Empire. The honor and marker of their ancient alliance remain, for they are not degraded by tribute nor does a tax man oppress them. They are exempt from these burdens and collections and set aside for use in battles; like weapons and arms, they are reserved for war. [2] The race of Mattiaci has the same kind of treaty. The greatness of the Roman people and regard for them goes forth beyond the Rhine and beyond the old boundaries of the empire. In terms of their location and boundaries they live on their own side; in mind and spirit they act with us. Moreover, they are like the Batavians, except that even now they are more sharply animated by the soil and climate of their land. [3] I would not count among the peoples of Germany those who work the tributary lands, although they have settled on the far side of the Rhine and Danube. The least consequential of the Gauls, daring because of poverty, have occupied this land of doubtful ownership. Soon thereafter, once our border was

set and the bulwarks were pushed forward, they were considered a small projection out of the empire's borders and part of the province.

30. Beyond these people the Chatti live. Their settlements start from the Hercynian forest, where it is not so low and swampy as it is in other areas into which Germans have spread. They live as far as the hills extend there; little by little the Chatti's presence fades as the hills do. The Hercynian forest attends its native Chatti until it and their settlements end. [2] This race has stronger bodies, tight limbs, a threatening face, and a greater strength of spirit. They employ a good amount of reason and ingenuity for Germans: They put forth elected people, then listen to those put forth. They know military order, understand opportunity, disperse their attack, divide up the day, fortify themselves at night, consider fortune to be among things that are doubted and virtue among things that are sure, and, what is the most rare and not granted except to Roman discipline, they put more faith in their general than in their army. [3] All their strength is in their infantry, which they load down with iron tools and baggage in addition to their arms. You might see others go to battle, but the Chatti always go to war. Raids and chance fights are rare. This is indeed characteristic of their cavalry, for quickly they win victory, and quickly they cede it. Speed is synonymous with fear, and delay is more like perseverance.

31. Among the other German peoples there is a practice adopted rarely and because of the private daring of each man. It has, however, become a common thing among the Chatti that when they first reach adulthood, they let their hair and beard grow and do not shave their beards, which they dedicate to courage, until they have killed their first enemy. They stand over the blood and spoils and reveal their faces, and then they declare at length that they have returned the price of their birth and are worthy of their country and their parents. Dirty hair stays on the faces of the cowardly and unwarlike. [2] Each of the bravest men also wears an iron ring (and this is an ignominious thing for these people) like a chain until he absolves himself by the slaughter of an enemy. This habit pleases most of the Chatti, and those men grow white-haired marked thus and conspicuous to the enemy and their own people. [3] The beginning of all fights belongs to these men. These are always the first ranks, a strange thing to see. Even in peace they do not grow tame, nor do they have a milder appearance. None of them have houses or fields or other concerns. Whenever they go anywhere, they are fed. They are prodigal about others' possessions and contemptuous of their own, until lifeless old age makes them unequal to such hardy courage.

32. Nearest to the Chatti on the Rhine, which now keeps to a sure channel and serves as a boundary, the Usipi and Tencteri live. The Tencteri, in addition to the customary distinction in warfare, excel in the art of equestrian discipline. The praise of the infantry among the Chatti is not more than the praise of the cavalry of the Tencteri. Their ancestors instituted it; their descendants imitate them. These are games for their infants, competition for their youths, and even the old persevere at it. In addition to slaves and household gods and the rights of succession, horses are handed down. A

son inherits, but not the eldest by birth as with other things, rather the one who is fiercer and braver in war.

33. Once the Bructeri used to be neighbors of the Tencteri; now it is said that the Chamavi and Angrivarii immigrated there and the Bructeri were pushed out and completely destroyed by the consensus of the neighboring nations. We do not know if this was done out of hatred for their pride or the sweetness of the booty or because the favor of the gods is toward us. They did not even deny us the spectacle of the battle. Above 60,000 died not by Roman arms and weapons but, what is more magnificent, as a delight for our eyes. [2] Let it remain, I beg, and may it persist for these races, if not love for us, at least indeed hatred of their own kind, since while the fates of the Empire progress, fortune can grant us nothing better than discord among our enemies.

34. The Dulgubnii and Chasuarii and other absolutely unmemorable races border the Angrivarii and Chamavi at their back and the Frisii at the front. They are called the greater and lesser Frisii from their respective strength. Each nation borders the Rhine as far as the Ocean and circles huge lakes that have been navigated by Roman fleets. [2] We have even tried the Ocean itself there. Rumor claims that the Pillars of Hercules are beyond that further still, because either Hercules himself went there or whatever is magnificent anywhere we agree to name after him. Drusus Germanicus did not lack daring, but the Ocean resisted research into itself and also into Hercules. Soon after no one tried the northern Ocean, and it now seems more holy and worthy of reverence to believe in the works of the gods than to know about them.

35. Up until now we have gotten acquainted with western Germany. In the north it recedes in a huge bend. The first race you meet is the Chauci. They start from the Frisii and occupy part of the shore; they border the sides of all the tribes that I have mentioned, until their land curves into the Chatti's territory. The Chauci not only hold such an immense space of land, they also fill it. They are the most noble race among the Germans; they prefer to guard their greatness by justice. [2] Without greed, without weakness, quiet and hidden away, they provoke no wars, and they are populated by no raiders or robbers. The foremost argument for their manliness and strength is this: they do not arrive at their superiority through harm to others. Their arms are ready for everything, and if the situation demands it, they have an army made up primarily of men and horses. Their reputation is the same in peace.

36. On one side of the Chauci and the Chatti, the Cherusci, who are never attacked, have long nourished an excessive and enfeebling peace. To do this was more pleasing rather than safe, because when you live between weak men and strong you only have false peace. Modesty and probity are names only for the stronger, where things are done by strength. Thus the Cherusci, who once were good and evenhanded, now are called indolent and stupid. When the Chatti are victorious, good fortune looks like wisdom. [2] The Fosi, a neighboring race, were also dragged down by the ruin

of the Cherusci. They are allies on equal terms in adverse events, although in prosperous times they are treated as the lesser of the two.

37. The Cimbri inhabit the same area of Germany, nearest to the ocean— a small state now, but huge in glory. Extensive traces of their ancient fame remain: camps and spaces on each bank. You may now measure the mass and strength of the race and the mark of so great a departure by the circumference of these areas. [2] Our city was going through the 640th year, when Caecilius Metellus and Papirius Carbo were consuls, when first we heard of the arms of the Cimbri. If we calculate from that time to the second consulship of the Emperor Trajan, it adds up to nearly 210 years. We have been conquering Germany for that long. [3] Throughout such a long era there have been many losses on each side. Neither the Samnites nor the Carthaginians nor the Spaniards nor the Gauls nor even the Parthians have caught our attention so often. Indeed, the liberty of the Germans is fiercer than the kingdom of the Arsaces. For what else is there, other than the death of Crassus, for the East to throw at us? The East itself was cast down by lost Pacorus and in front of Ventidius. [4] But the Germans beat and captured Carbo and Cassius and Aurelius Servilius Caepio and Maximus Mallius, and in the process took five consular armies from the Roman people. And they even took Varus and three legions from a Caesar. Not with impunity did Marius in Italy, the divine Julius in Gaul, and Drusus and Nero and Germanicus in their own countries beat them down. Later, the huge threats of Gaius Caesar [Caligula] were turned into games. [5] Then they were at leisure until, at the opportunity presented by our discord and civil war, they attacked the winter quarters of the legions and even turned their attention to Gaul. Again they were pushed back, but in recent times we have celebrated triumphs more times than we have actually defeated them.

38. Now we must talk about the Suebi, who are not one race, as the Chatti or Tencteri are. They hold a greater part of Germany and are distinguished by particular nations and names, although they are called Suebi as a group. [2] The mark of this race is that they twist aside their hair and tie it in a knot. In this way the Suebi are distinguished from the rest of the Germans and the native Suebi are distinguished from their slaves. Among other races, whether from some relationship with the Suebi or, which often happens, from imitation, this custom is rare and practiced among youths. Among the Suebi they twist back their hair until it is grey, and often they tie it on the very top of their heads. The chieftains have even more ornate hair. This is their concern for appearance, but it is harmless for they do not do it so that they may love or be loved; rather, they do it so that they may go into battle with a certain height and fearsomeness. They are adorned for the eyes of the enemy.

39. They claim that the Semnones are the oldest and noblest of the Suebi. This belief is affirmed by an ancient rite. At an established time, in a forest sanctified by the auguries of their fathers and by an ancient fear, all people of the same blood gather through representatives. They celebrate the horrible beginnings of their barbarian ritual by publicly slaughtering a man.

[2] There is yet another rite in the grove: No one enters unless he is bound in chains, so that he knows he is lesser and keeps the power of the divinity before him. If by chance he falls, he is not allowed to be lifted up or to get up himself; rather, he is rolled along the earth. The entire belief system looks to this belief: that such is the beginning of the race, and that there is a god who is ruler of all things and everyone else is subjugated and obedient. [3] The fortune of the Semnones adds authority to this belief. One hundred districts are inhabited by them, and their great population makes them believe that they are the head of the Suebi.

40. In contrast, the smallness of their population distinguishes the Langobardi. They are surrounded by many very strong nations. They are safe not because they are compliant but because they battle and show bravery in the face of danger. [2] There are also the Reudigni, the Aviones, the Anglii, the Varini, the Eudoses, the Suardones, and the Nuitones, who are protected by rivers and forests. There is not anything notable in each of them alone, except that they worship Nerthus, or Mother Earth, in common and think that she intervenes in the affairs of men and travels among the people. [3] There is a pure grove on an island in the Ocean with a sacred chariot on it that is covered with a cloth. One priest is allowed to touch it. He understands that the goddess is present inside and follows her with much reverence as she is drawn along by female cattle. In whatever area is honored by her coming and her visitation, the days are happy and the places are festive. During that time they do not go to war and they do not take up arms. All iron is put away; peace and quiet are known only then, and only then loved, until the same priest returns the goddess to the temple once she has been sated by conversation with mortals. [4] Soon after this the chariot and the cloth and, if you are able to believe it, the divinity herself are washed in a secret lake. Slaves do it, who are then immediately swallowed by the lake itself. From this belief there arises a secret terror and holy ignorance of that which only those about to die may see.

41. This area of the Suebi territory stretches into the more secret parts of Germany. Nearer to us (I follow the Danube now as I followed the Rhine a little while before) is the city of the Hermunduri, who are allies of the Romans. Thus, for them alone of the Germans, there is trade not only along the riverbank but within the province and even in the most splendid settlement of the Raetian province. They go everywhere without a guard. We only show other races our arms and our camp; to these men, who are not desirous of them, we open our homes and villas. [2] The river Elbe arises among the Hermunduri—a once famous and well-known river but now only a rumor.

42. Next to the Hermunduri live the Naristi and then the Marcomani and Quadi. The glory and strength of the Marcomani are outstanding, and their home was gained by courage once they had driven the Boii out. The Naristi and Quadi are also not degenerate. This is the foremost part of Germany, where it is enclosed by the Danube. [2] In our recent memory the kings of the Marcomani and the Quadi came from their own race—the noble

offspring of Maroboduus and Tudrus—but now they suffer foreign kings. But the kings have force and power from Roman authority. They are helped by our arms sometimes and more often by money, which is no less strong.

43. The Marsigni, Cotini, Osi, and Buri shut in the backs of the Marcomani and Quadi. Of these the Marsigni and Buri resemble the Suebi in speech and culture. The Gallic and Pannonian tongues expose the Cotini and Osi, respectively, as not German, and also because they pay tribute. The Sarmatians impose part of the tribute, and the Quadi impose another part as if on foreigners. The Cotini (all the more shameful) dig up iron. [2] All these people settle in places that have few plains and more woodlands and mountains. For a chain of continuous mountains goes through and divides Suebia. Beyond these more races live. The name of the Lugii is used extensively in many societies. It is sufficient to name the most valorous: the Harii, Helvecones, Manimi, Helysii, and Nahanarvali. [3] Near the Nahanarvali one can find a grove sacred to an ancient religion. The priest presides in womanly dress, but they claim to worship the gods Castor and Pollux following a Roman interpretation. These are the forces of their divinity, which they name Alx. There are no images or traces of imported superstition, yet they are honored as brothers and young men. [4] Moreover, the Harii, in addition to their strength, which surpasses the people listed a little earlier, are wild and their inborn ferocity is enhanced by artifice and time. Their shields are black and their bodies painted; they pick black nights for battles, and their feral armies incite fear through darkness and shadows. None of the enemy holds up against their strange appearance, like ghosts. The eyes are the first to be conquered in all battles.

44. Beyond the Lugii we find the Gotonoes, who are ruled by kings—a little more strictly than the other tribes of the Germans, but not without some liberty. Next, immediately bordering the Ocean, are the Rugii and the Lemovii. The shields of these peoples are round, their swords short, and they submit to kings. [2] After them one can find the cities of the Suiones, on the Ocean itself, that are strong in fleets as well as in men and arms. The form of their ships is different, because they have put a prow at each end so they are always prepared to be beached. They do not steer with sails nor have oars down the sides; the oarage is loose, as in riverboats, and flexible so that the boat can move from here to there as events demand. [3] They have respect for wealth, and for this reason one man rules them with no limitations and who claims a not uncertain right to obedience. And their arms are not out in the open, as among other Germans, but shut up under a guard, who is indeed a slave. The Ocean prohibits the sudden invasion of enemies, and bands of armed men easily become bad when they are at leisure. Because of this, it is indeed useful for kings for no one to be in charge of weapons, not a noble or a native or even a freedman.

45. Beyond the Suiones there is another sea, slow-moving and nearly motionless, which, you may trust, circles the lands. There, the last brightness of the setting sun stretches into sunrise so brightly that you never see the stars. Popular thinking claims that you can hear the sound of sun's rising

and see the forms of its horses and the rays of its head. Here is the boundary of nature, if the rumor is true. [2] On the right shore of the Suebian sea live the races of the Aestii, who follow the rites and habits of the Suebi, though their language is closer to the Britons. They worship the mother of the gods. They wear the mark of this belief in the form of a wild boar. This decoration stands in the place of arms and is a safeguard for men. It makes the keeper of the goddess safe even among the enemy. [3] The use of iron is rare, but the use of clubs common. They farm grains and other fruits more patiently than can be considered usual when one thinks of the customary laziness of the Germans. [4] They also search the sea and, alone of all people, gather amber, which they themselves call *glesum,* between the shallows and on the shore itself. It has not been sought out or investigated what accident of nature or for what reason it occurs, as is often the case among barbarians. Indeed for a long time it was just lying among the other flotsam of the sea until our luxury gave it a name. They have no use for it; it is gathered randomly, brought home without being worked on, and then they receive money for it and marvel at the pay. [5] You can gather that it is the sap of trees, however, because certain land animals and winged creatures appear throughout it, which were caught in it when it was wet and shut in once the material quickly grew hard. I believe that there must be more fertile groves and woods, as in the corners of the east, where incense and balsam sweat in the islands and lands of the west, because these things, which are acted on by the rays of the nearby sun and liquefied, float on the nearby sea and are washed up on opposite shores by the force of storms. If you test the nature of amber by holding a flame near it, it flares up in the manner of tinder and produces a fat and odorous flame; soon after it softens into pitch or resin. [6] The tribes of the Sitones connect to the Suiones. Although mostly similar they differ in one thing—a woman rules them. They have degenerated greatly not only from liberty but also from slavery.

46. This is the border of Suebia. I am uncertain whether to ascribe the nations of the Peucini, Veneti, and Fenni to the Germans or the Sarmatians. The Peucini, whom some call Bastarnae, live like Germans in their speech, culture, location, and homes. The filth and laziness of all of them is great, and with mixed marriages they are defiled not a little into the likeness of the Sarmatians. [2] The Veneti have borrowed much from the Sarmatians' customs. Whatever forests and mountains stretch between the Peucini and Fenni they wander in looting expeditions. Nevertheless they fit among the Germans more easily, because they settle in homes and carry shields and rejoice in the use and swiftness of their feet. All these things differ from the Sarmatians who live in wagons and on horseback. [3] There is a strange wildness to the Fenni and nasty poverty: they have no arms, no horses, no household gods, but there are herbs for food, pelts for clothing, and ground for their beds. Their only hope is in arrows, which have points made of bones because they lack iron. The hunt equally provides for the men and women; for the women accompany them everywhere and ask for a part of the spoils. There is no other protection for infants from wild animals

or storms than that they are covered in some weaving of branches. This is the home the youths return to, and this is the receptacle of the old. They, however, think that this life is happier than groaning in the fields, laboring in homes, and twisting their fortunes and others' in hope and fear. Secure against men, secure against gods, they have attained a most difficult outcome: they have no use for prayer. [4] The rest is the stuff of stories. The Hellusii and the Oxiones have the expressions and faces of men, and the body and limbs of wild animals; I will leave this as unknown.

17. Tacitus, *Annals* 14.30 (1st/2nd century CE). *The Roman general Suetonius Paulinus crosses over to the island of Mona (modern Isle of Man) in order to defeat a group of Britons who are taking refuge there. Tacitus describes what the Romans encountered. (MLG)*

Standing on the shore was the opposing army, bristling with weapons. Women ran about among the men, dressed like avenging demons in funeral clothes, hair falling over their faces. From all sides the druids, lifting their hands to the sky and pouring forth prayers, terrified our troops by the novelty of their appearance. As a result, our men stood unmoving as if their limbs were frozen and left themselves open to attack. Then, provoked by the general and encouraging themselves not to tremble before an effeminate and maddened enemy, they marched forward, scattered the opposing men, and spread fire. The conquered had guards set over them. The Romans destroyed the groves that had been dedicated to savage superstition. It was held religiously proper to offer the blood of captives on the altars and to consult the will of the gods with human organs. As Suetonius was engaged in these actions, he heard of the sudden rebellion in the province.

18. Plutarch, *Life of Marius* 11, 15–16, 18–20, 23, 25–27 excerpted (2nd century CE). *Marius is at a low point after the war with Jugurtha, because Sulla, his rival, has claimed credit for Jugurtha's surrender. The tide turns, however, when Italy is threatened by invading German tribes, the Teutones and the Cimbri. (CSR)*

11. Soon after that, however, the danger from the west that was oppressing Italy dispersed and shifted the envy, hatred, and slanders away from Marius. Right then the state needed a great general and was looking about for a pilot who might help it escape such a great wave of war. No one was chosen in the consular elections from a great clan or a wealthy house; rather, the people proclaimed Marius consul, although he was absent. [2] For immediately after the arrest of Jugurtha had been announced to them, rumors about the Teutones and Cimbri began to circulate. In the beginning the rumors about the number and strength of the attacking army caused disbelief, but later they appeared to have suggested too low a number.

Three hundred thousand fighters with heavy arms were moving in, and larger crowds by far of children and women were said to be with them. They were seeking land that would support such a great number and cities in which they might settle and live, just as before them, they learned, the Celts had taken the best part of Italy from the Tyrrhenians and settled it. [3] They themselves were not known to the Romans, because they rarely interacted with others and because they had traveled so far. It was not known who they were and from where they had come that they should fall on Gaul and Italy like a cloud. They were primarily compared to members of the German race, whose territory stretched to the northern ocean, because of the great size of their bodies and the bright blueness of their eyes, and because the Germans call robbers Cimbri. [4] There are those who say that Gaul, because of the depth and greatness of the land, extends from the outer Ocean and the northern slopes to the Maeotic Lake in the east where it borders Pontic Scythia; at that point the races mixed together. These peoples did not set out in one wave or all at the same time, but at the same time in the spring of each year they always set out and advanced by means of war. They came to our land after a long time. [5] They have many names according to the group they left with, but they call their army as a whole the Celto-Scythians.

Others say that the Cimmerians, who were first known by the Ancient Greeks, were not a great portion of all the people but rather some fugitives or factions who were overpowered by the Scythians, and because of this they traveled into Asia from the Maeotic Lake under their leader Lygdamis. The most warlike of them lived at the edges of the earth along the outer Ocean. They inhabit a land that is closely shaded, woody, and completely without sun because of the depth and density of the forests. [6] This land extends as far as the Hercynians. They have by lot an area under the portion of the sky where the pole takes a great elevation because of the incline of the parallels. It does not seem to stray far from the mark that is set by the spectator. Days equal in shortness and length with the nights divide the time there. This made it easy for Homer to set his story about consulting the dead there. [7] From this place, therefore, did these barbarians set out into Italy. They were first addressed as Cimmerians and then, not wrongly, as the Cimbri. These things, however, are said from guessing rather than after a firm inquiry. [8] Many discovered that their numbers were not less but more than what was said before. And since they were irresistible in their courage and daring (and in terms of the force of their blows), they fought battles with the sharpness and force of fire and no one held out against their attack. As many people as they came against were taken and carried off as spoils of war; as many great Roman armies and generals as were stationed in Transalpine Gaul were stormed (and carried off) ingloriously. [9] These armies drew them down to Rome because they contended badly, for since they had conquered those whom they met and gotten a lot of money, they decided not to settle themselves anywhere until they had overturned Rome and utterly ruined Italy.

Marius returns to Italy and quickly organizes his army to march north to face the invaders.

15.4. The barbarians divided themselves into two, and the Cimbri were chosen by lot to advance through Noricum in the interior against Catulus and force a passage through there; the Teutones and the Ambrones were to advance along the sea through Liguria against Marius. [5] The Cimbri wasted a great deal of time and suffered from delay, but the Teutones and Ambrones set out straightaway and, as they went through the intervening countryside, appeared to be boundless in number and horrible to look upon, and completely unlike anyone else in their speech or uproar. After they surrounded a great portion of the plain and set up camp, they called Marius forth to battle.

16. But Marius did not give them a thought but rather held his soldiers in their entrenchment. He bitterly upbraided those who were emboldened, and called men traitors to their fatherland whose courage made them head out and want to fight. For they should not fight out of ambition for triumphs and trophies, but only after considering how they might thrust back so great a cloud and thunderbolt of war and save Italy. [2] He said these things in private to his leaders and equals, but he stood the soldiers on the entrenchments by section and ordered them to watch the enemy. He got them accustomed to withstanding their appearance, enduring the sounds they made, which were totally unusual and beastlike, and learning their arms and movement. In so doing, he made what had seemed scary in their minds manageable from their observation. He thought that the newness of things to those fearful of them makes them seem to be something they are not, but after habitual interaction even things scary by nature lose their terribleness. [3] Not only did the daily sight of them take away something of his men's fear, but also, because of the boasts of the barbarians and their unbearable noise, their hearts perked up and warmed and then set fire to their souls, for not only was the enemy taking and carrying off everything around them, they were also attacking their entrenchments with so much violence and excessive boldness that indignant speeches of the soldiers were carried to Marius.

. . .

18. Since Marius was keeping quiet, the Teutones attempted to storm the camp; they were met by many missiles shot from the entrenchment and lost some in their number. They then decided to advance forward so that they might cross the Alps peacefully. They packed up and, as they were passing the camp of the Romans, then indeed the hugeness of their numbers became apparent from the time it took for them to pass. [2] For it is said that they marched past the entrenchments of Marius for six days while moving continuously. And they marched near, asking the Romans with laughter if they wanted to send anything to their wives, for they would quickly be with them. Once the barbarians had passed and advanced, Marius got

up and pursued them closely, always staying near them and setting up camp next to them. He set up strong camps and took up strong positions so that he might spend the night in safety. [3] They were going along until they reached a place called Aquae Sextiae, which was not too far a march from the Alps. Because of the location, Marius prepared to fight there, and he found a strong position for his camp, although it did not have a sufficient water supply, because he wanted to use this, so they say, to spur on his soldiers. [4] Indeed many were annoyed and claimed they would be thirsty. Marius pointed out with his hand a river flowing near the barbarian entrenchment and said that their water supply was right there and that the cost of the water was blood. "So why," they said, "do you not lead us against them straightaway, while we have liquid blood?" And he quietly replied, "First, our camp must be strengthened."

19. Therefore his soldiers, although annoyed, obeyed him. But the multitude of servants, since they had no water themselves or for their draft animals, went down in crowds to the river, some bringing battle axes, others common axes, and some swords and spears with their water jars so that they might get water even through battle. At first only a few of the enemy fought with these men, for most of them happened to be eating after their bath and some were still bathing. [2] Streams of hot flowing water broke out there, and around these springs the Romans attacked the barbarians while they were enjoying themselves and celebrating in the pleasure and marvel of the place. When more of the barbarians came running toward the shouts of their friends, it was difficult for Marius to restrain his soldiers who were afraid for their slaves. And the most warlike of the enemy, who had overpowered the Romans under Manlius and Caepio earlier (they were named Ambrones, and they numbered more than 30,000), sprung up and advanced to their arms. [3] Their bodies were heavy with eating, and they were exultant in their minds and scattered from unmixed wine, but they did not head out in undisciplined or manic paths or spout forth inarticulate cries; rather, they were striking their arms in rhythm and all leaping together as they were shouting their name: "Ambrones!" They did this either to encourage each other or to scare their enemies beforehand by their demonstration. [4] The Ligurians were the first of the Italians to go down against them; since they heard and understood their shouting, they shouted it back as their own ancestral name, for the Ligurians call themselves the same thing from their original race. Therefore there was frequent singing back and forth of the name in turns before they came together in close combat. And as they cried out in turn from the back of each force and competed with each other to be first in the loudness of their shouting, the clamor of the armies urged on and roused their spirits to the fight. [5] Then the spring split up the Ambrones, for they did not all manage to cross and set up a battle line, but the Ligurians fell upon the first ones straightaway with a rush and the battle was fought hand-to-hand. The Romans helped the Ligurians; they came in from above, constrained the barbarians, and turned them back. [6] Most of them were killed where they were all pushed together around the

stream, and so they filled the river with blood and corpses, and once the Romans crossed, they killed those who did not dare to turn around until they had fled to their camp and their wagons. [7] There the women opposed them with swords and axes while shrieking terribly. Angrily they fought off those who fled and their pursuers equally, the fugitives as traitors, and the pursuers as enemies. All mixed together with the fighters, the women dragged the shields of the Romans away with their bare hands and laid hands on their swords. They endured wounds and gashes to their bodies until the end; they were unbeaten in their hearts. They say that the battle at the riverside was by chance rather than by the intention of the general.

20. After the Romans had destroyed many of the Ambrones, they retreated back and darkness fell, but the army did not, as is usual after such good fortune, sing songs of victory, or drink in the tents, or have friendly meetings around dinner, or that sweetest thing of all for men who have fought with good fortune, sleep sweetly. Rather, they passed that night especially in fear and troubles. [2] For their camp was without entrenchment or walls, and many tens of thousands of barbarians were still undefeated, and as many of the Ambrones who fled were mixed in with them, and there was sorrow throughout the night, not like the weeping and sighing of men, but beastly howls and roars mixed with threats and laments were made by so great a number of them that the mountains and the ravines of the river echoed all around. [3] A shivery sound held the plain, fear held the Romans, and concern held Marius himself, since he was expecting some disorderly and troublesome night battle. But they did not attack that night nor the following day; instead, they continued to organize and prepare themselves.

> Marius surrounds and defeats the barbarians, divides the spoils, and celebrates. Meanwhile, Catulus is forced to retreat into the plains of Italy in preparation for his fight against the Cimbri.

23.3. These barbarians felt so much contempt and boldness toward their enemy that, for the sake of showing their strength and daring rather than doing what was necessary, they endured being snowed on while naked and went through the mountains and the deep snow to the peaks, and from up there they put their broad shields under their bodies, pushed themselves forward, and were carried down slopes that had both smooth slides and wide breaks. [4] After they had set up camp nearby and examined the pass, they began to block it. They broke up the hills around them, like the giants did, and carried trees ripped up with their roots and pieces of the cliffs and heaps of earth into the river, thereby narrowing the current, sending great heavy masses down the river against the foundations that propped up the bridge, and shaking the bridge with the blows. Most of our army became very fearful and retreated from the great camp. . . . [6] The barbarians attacked and took the fort on the other side of the Atiso. They admired the Romans there who were the best of men and who bore the brunt of the battle in a manner worthy of their fatherland. They discharged them under a truce, after swearing on a bronze bull, which later was taken after the battle into the house of Catulus and set up, so they say, as the topmost prize of the victory. But at this time the barbarians overran and ravaged the land, since the Romans had no reinforcements.

> Marius is summoned to Rome, but he quickly sets out to help Catulus. The Cimbri refuse battle until the Teutones arrive. When Marius tells them of the Teutones' defeat, they are skeptical until he shows them the kings in chains. The Cimbri then march upon the Romans, but Marius keeps quiet. The two sides arrange a day for battle, and Catulus and Marius deploy their forces.

25.6. The Cimbrian infantry advanced slowly from their bulwarks, as many men deep as the front line was long. Each side of the formation measured 3.5 miles. [7] Their horsemen were 15,000 in number, and they marched out all adorned, for they had helmets looking like the mouths or peculiar heads of fearsome wild animals, and on top of these they had feathered crests that made them appear greater in height. They were also adorned with iron breastplates, and they glittered with white shields. Each man had throwing lances, and they used big heavy swords when they fought the enemy in close quarters.

. . .

26.4. The heat and the sun shining on the Cimbri helped the Romans in the battle. For the Cimbri were good at enduring icy cold since they were brought up in shady and freezing places, as has been said, but they were overwhelmed by the heat. They poured out sweat and panted a lot and held their shields in front of their faces, because the battle occurred after the summer solstice, which the Romans claim occurs three days before the new moon of the month now called August but then called Sextilis. [5] The dust hid the enemy and contributed to the Romans' courage. For they could not see the enemy's numbers from far away, but each attacked the ones near him at a run, and they fought in close combat, not frightened by the sight of the enemy host. Their bodies were so hardy and they were so well-trained that none of the Romans were seen sweating or panting because of such great heat or after their running attack. They say Catulus himself remembered this in his praise of the soldiers.

27. The greatest portion and the most warlike of the enemy fell here. In order not to break their ranks, their vanguard was held together by great chains bound one to the next through their belts. They pushed the fugitives back to their entrenchments, and there they happened upon a truly tragic calamity. [2] For their women, wearing black clothing, stood at the wagons and killed the fugitives—their husbands, their brothers, and their fathers—then they strangled their infants with their hands and threw them under the wagons and the trampling feet of the animals, and finally they cut their own throats. They say that one woman was hanging from the tip of the wagon pole and her children were tied to her ankles, fastened to each leg by nooses. [3] The men, since there were not many trees, fastened themselves by the neck to the horns or the legs of cattle, and then, after whipping them,

they were dragged or trampled to death by the cattle as they darted away. Yet although they were destroyed thus, over 60,000 were enslaved; those who fell were said to be twice as many.

19. Athenaeus, *Deipnosophistes* 6.234a–c, 6.246d, 6.249a–b (2nd century CE). *During dinner conversation, the interlocutors share numerous stories they have heard about the people known as both the Celts and Gauls. (RFK)*

234a–c. A people of the Gauls called the Scordistai do not import gold into their lands, although when they plunder other lands and outrage them, they do not leave silver behind. This people is a remnant of those Gauls who invaded the oracle at Delphi with Brennis. A certain Bathanattus, their leader, settled them on land around the Ister < . . . > from whom they also call the road by which they returned home "Bathanattian," and even still they name the descendants of that tribe the Bathanatti. Those people disdain and won't remove gold to their own lands because of the many troubles it caused them in the past. They use silver, though, and commit many horrors for its sake. And yet, they should have limited not the type of plunder but their urge toward irreverent, temple-robbing behaviors. If they did not take silver home with them, they would commit outrages over bronze or iron, or, if these items were banned, they would go berserk over food and drink or other necessities.

. . .

6.246d. Posidonius of Apamea in the 23rd book of the *Histories* says that the Celts bring along with them companions whom they call parasites even when going to war. These men go around saying encomia at crowded assemblies and to anyone individually within earshot. The music of the Celts comes from men called bards whose job it is to sing their praises.

. . .

6.249a–b. Nicolas of Damascus (he was one of the Peripatetics) says in the 116th book of his many-volumed *History* (the whole thing was 144 books) that Adiatomos king of the Sotiani (a Celtic people) had 600 hand-picked men around him, whom the Gauls called in their own tongue *silodouroi*. In Greek this translates as "those bound by oath." Their lives are bound to the king's, since they have taken their oath to live and die with the king. In return, the king grants them a share of his power. They wear the same dress as the king, live the same lifestyle, and—this part is absolutely necessary— they die with him. This is the case whether the king dies from disease, in war, or in any other manner. No one has found a single one among them who shied away from or slipped out of death when the king died.

ABOUT THE SOURCES

The following list gives the texts used for the translations in this volume. We have attempted to use the most recent and accurate texts. A number of texts were accessed through the *Thesaurus Linguae Graecae* (*TLG*) or the *Biblioteca Teubneriana Latina* (*BTL*). We have also noted commentaries accessed as part of the translation process. Each author is listed with his general dates. Where no such information is available, we have listed the language in which the original text was written. For this anthology, all translations have been completed by one of the editors, whose initials are listed throughout the volume where appropriate. For bibliographic information on the ancient authors, please consult the *Oxford Classical Dictionary* (4th edition).

Achilles Tatius (2nd century CE) *Achille Tatius d'Alexandrie: le Roman de Leucippé et Clitophon,* ed. J.-P. Garnaud, Les Belles Lettres (Paris, 2002).

Aeschylus (d. 456 BCE) *Suppliants: Aeschyli Septem Quae Supersunt Tragoedias,* ed. D. L. Page (Oxford, 1972); *Persians: Aeschylus Persae,* ed. A. F. Garvie, with commentary (Oxford, 2009), and *Aeschylus Tragoediae,* ed. M. L. West, Teubner Classical Texts (Leipzig, 1998).

Apollonius (3rd century BCE) *Apollonius Rhodius: Argonautica,* ed. W. H. Race, Loeb Classical Library (Cambridge, MA, 2008).

Aristotle (384–322 BCE) *Aristotle: Politics,* ed. H. Rackman, Loeb Classical Library (Cambridge, MA, 1998).

Arrian (c.86–160 CE) *Arrian: Anabasis of Alexander Books V–VII; Indica,* ed. P. A. Brunt, Loeb Classical Library (Cambridge, MA, 1983).

Athenaeus (2nd/3rd century CE) *Athenaeus: The Learned Banqueters,* vols. 3, 6–7, ed. S. Douglas Olson, Loeb Classical Library (Cambridge, MA, 2006–2011).

Babrius (possibly 1st century CE) *Babrius and Phaedrus,* ed. B. E. Perry, Loeb Classical Library (Cambridge, MA, 1965).

Caesar (100–44 BCE) *C. Iulius Caesar, Bellum Gallicum,* ed. W. Hering, Teubner Classical Texts (Leipzig, 1997).

Catullus (c.84–54 BCE) *Carmina,* ed. R. A. B. Mynors, Oxford Classical Texts (Oxford, 1958).

Cicero (106–43 BCE) *M. Tulli Ciceronis Orationes,* ed. A. Clark, Oxford Classical Texts (Oxford, 1909).

Ctesias (c.441–394 BCE) *Photius: Bibliothéque,* vol. 1, ed. R. Henry, Les Belles Lettres (Paris, 1959).

Demosthenes (384–322 BCE) *Demosthenis Orationes,* vol. 1, ed. S. H. Butcher, Oxford Classical Texts (Oxford, 1903/1966).

Diodorus (1st century BCE) *Diodorus Siculus: Library of History,* 12 vols., ed. Oldfather et al., Loeb Classical Library (Cambridge, MA, 1933–1976).

Euripides (d. 405 BCE) Medea: *Euripides Medea,* ed. D. Mastronarde (Cambridge, 2002); all other plays: *Euripides Fabulae,* vols. 1–3, ed. J. Diggle, Oxford Classical Texts (Oxford, 1981–1994).

Hanno (5th century BCE) *Periplous,* ed. D. Roller, Appendix, *Through the Pillars of Herakles* (London, 1995).

Heliodorus (3rd/4th century CE) *Héliodore: Les Éthiopiques (Théagène et Chariclée),* 3 vols., eds. T. W. Lumb, J. Maillon, and R. M. Rattenbury, Les Belles Lettres (Paris, 1960).

Herodotus (c.480–428 BCE) *Herodoti Historiae,* 2 vols., ed. C. Hude, Oxford Classical Texts (Oxford, 1927).

Hesiod (8th/7th century BCE) *Hesiod: Works and Days,* ed. M. L. West, Oxford Classical Texts (Oxford, 1978).

Homer (8th century BCE) *Homeri Odyssea,* ed. P. von der Mühll (Basel, 1962).

Horace (65–8 BCE) *Q. Horati Flacci Opera,* ed. S. Borzsák, Teubner Classical Texts (Leipzig, 1984).

Hyginus (2nd century CE) *Hyginus: Fabulae,* ed. P. K. Marshall, Teubner Classical Texts (Leipzig, 1993).

Isocrates (436–338 BCE) *Panegyricus: Isocrate. Discours,* vol. 2, eds. É. Brémond and G. Mathieu, Les Belles Lettres (Paris, 1938/1967).

Josephus (b. 37/8 CE) *Jewish Antiquities: Flavii Iosephi Opera,* ed. B. Niese, vols. 1–4 (Berlin, 1892).

Juvenal (1st/2nd century CE) *Juvenal and Persius,* ed. S. M. Braund, Loeb Classical Library (Cambridge, MA, 2004).

Livy (54 BCE–17 CE) *Titi Livi Ab Urbe Condita,* vols. 1 and 3, ed. R. Ogilvie, Oxford Classical Texts (Oxford, 1974).

Lucan (39–65 CE) *Lucan: Civil War,* ed. J. D. Duff, Loeb Classical Library (Cambridge, MA, 1928), and *M. Annaei Lucani Belli Civilis Libri Decem,* ed. A. E. Housman (Cambridge, MA, 1927).

Manilius (1st century BCE) *Manilius: Astonomica,* ed. G. P. Goold, Loeb Classical Library (Cambridge, MA, 1977/1992).

Martial (40–c.104 CE) *Martial: Epigrams,* 3 vols., ed. D. R. Shackleton Bailey, Loeb Classical Library (Cambridge, MA, 1993).

Ovid (43 BCE–17/18 CE) *Amores, Medicamina Facieie Femineae, Ars Amatoria, Remedia Amoris,* ed. E. J. Kenney, Oxford Classical Texts (Oxford, 1961/1995); *Epistulae heroidum,* ed. H. Dörrie (Berlin, 1977).

Petronius (d. 66 CE) *Satyricon Reliquae,* ed. K. Müller, Teuber Classical Texts (Stuttgart, 1995).

Philo (20 BCE–50 CE) *The Works of Philo,* eds. F. H. Colson and G. H. Whitaker, 10 vols., Loeb Classical Library (Cambridge, MA, 1929–1953).

Philostratus the Athenian (d. c.245 CE) *Apollonis of Tyana,* ed. C. P. Jones, Loeb Classical Library (Cambridge, MA, 2006).

Philostratus the Lemnian (3rd century CE) *Imagines/Philostratus; Descriptions/Callistratus,* ed. A. Fairbanks, Loeb Classical Library (Cambridge, MA, 1960).

Pindar (522–443 BCE) *Olympian 9: Pindari carmina cum fragmenti,* ed. H. Maehler, Teubner Classical Texts (Leipzig, 1971); *Olympian 3: Olympian Odes/Pythian Odes,* ed. W. Race, Loeb Classical Texts (Cambridge, MA, 1997).

Plato (428–348 BCE) Menexenus: *Platonis Opera,* vol. 3, ed. J. Burnet, Oxford Classical Texts (Oxford, 1968), and P. Tsitsiridis, *Platons Menexenos: Einleitung, Text, und Kommentar* (Stuttgart, 1998); Timaeus and Republic: *Platonis Opera,* vol. 6, ed. J. Burnet, Oxford Classical Texts (Oxford, 1902/1992).

Pliny the Elder (23–79 CE) *Natural History,* ed. H. Rackham, 10 vols., Loeb Classical Library (Cambridge, MA, 1942).

Plutarch (c.46–120 CE) Pericles: *Plutarchi vitae parallelae,* ed. K. Ziegler, Teubner Classical Texts (Leipzig 1964); *On Superstition*: F. C. Babbitt, *Plutarch's Moralia,* vol. 2, Loeb Classical Library (Cambridge, MA, 1928/1962); *Dinner Conversations*: C. Hubert, *Plutarchi Moralia,* vol. 4, Teubner Classical Texts (Leipzig, 1938/1971).

Polybius (c.200–118 BCE) *The Histories,* eds. W. R. Paton, P. Walbank, and C. Habitch, Loeb Classical Library (Cambridge, MA, 2010).

Pomponius Mela (1st century CE) *Kreuzfahrt Durch die Alte Welt,* ed. K. Broderson (Darmstadt, 1994).

Pseudo-Scylax (fl. 330s BCE) *Pseudo-Scylax's Periplous: The Circumnavigation of the Inhabited World,* ed. G. Shipley (Exeter, 2011).

Ptolemy (2nd century CE) *Tetrabiblos,* ed. F. E. Robbins, Loeb Classical Library (Cambridge, MA, 1940/1980)

Sallust (86–35 BCE)   *Sallust,* ed. J. C. Rolfe, Loeb Classical Library (Cambridge, MA, 1921).

Seneca (4 BCE–65 CE)   *L. Annaei Senecae Tragoediae,* ed. O. Zwierlain, Oxford Classical Texts (Oxford, 1986).

Strabo (1st centuries BCE/CE)   *Strabonis geographica,* ed. A. Meineke, 3 vols., Teubner Classical Texts (Leipzig, 1877/1969).

Tacitus (d. after 118 CE)   *Annales: Coenelius Tacitus Annales XI–XVI,* ed. K. Wellesley, Teubner Classical Texts (Leipzig, 1986); *Histories* and *Agricola: Cornelii Taciti Opera Minor,* eds. M. Winterbottom and R. M. Ogilvie, Oxford Classical Texts (Oxford, 1975/1985).

Thucydides (c.460 BC–c.395 BCE)   *Thucydidis historiae,* 2 vols., eds. H. S. Jones and J. E. Powell, Oxford Classical Texts (Oxford, 1942)

Vegetius (fl. 380s CE)   *Epitoma rei militaris,* ed. A. Önnerfors, Teubner Classical Texts (Leipzig, 1995).

Vergil (d. 19 BCE)   *P. Vergili Maronis Opera,* ed. R. A. B. Mynors, Oxford Classical Texts (Oxford, 1969).

Vitruvius (c.75–15 BC)   *Vitruve: De l' Arcitecture,* ed. P. Fleury, Les Belles Lettres (Paris, 1969).

Xenophon (c.430–360s BCE)   *Xenophontis opera omnia,* vol. 4., ed. E. C. Marchant, Oxford Classical Texts (Oxford, 1910/1970).

THE FOLLOWING TEXTS HAVE NO KNOWN AUTHOR:

Airs, Waters, Places **(early 5th century BCE)**   *Hippocrates: Works,* vol. 1, ed. W. H. S. Jones, Loeb Classical Library (Cambridge, MA, 1923/2010).

[Apollodorus] *Library* **(1st or 2nd century CE)**   *Apollodorus: The Library,* ed. J. G. Frazer, Loeb Classical Library (Cambridge, MA., 1921).

Moretum **(1st century CE)**   *Appendix Vergiliana,* eds. W. V. Clausen, F. R. D. Goodyear, E. J. Kenney, and J. A. Richmond, Oxford Classical Texts (Oxford, 1966).

[Aristotle] *On Marvelous Things* **Greek (4th/3rd centuries BCE)**   *Aristotle: Minor Works,* ed. W. S. Hett, Loeb Classical Library (Cambridge, MA, 1936).

Prometheus Bound **(430–420 BCE)**   *Aeschylus Tragoediae,* ed. M. L. West, Teubner Classical Texts (Leipzig, 1998).

SELECT BIBLIOGRAPHY

Adams, C., and R. Lawrence, eds. *Travel and Geography in the Roman Empire*. London: Routledge, 2001.

Almagor, E. "Who Is a Barbarian? The Barbarians in the Ethnological and Cultural Taxonomies of Strabo." In *Strabo's Cultural Geography: The Making of a Kolossourgia*, edited by D. Dueck, H. Lindsay, and S. Pothecary, 42–55. Cambridge: Cambridge University Press, 2006.

Almagor, E., and J. Skinner, eds. *Ancient Ethnography: New Approaches*. London: Bristol Classical Press, 2012.

Bacon, H. *Barbarians in Greek Tragedy*. New Haven: Yale University Press, 1961.

Beagon, M. *The Elder Pliny on the Human Animal: Natural History, Book 7*. Oxford: Clarendon Press, 2005.

Bernal, M. *Black Athena: The Afroasiatic Roots of Classical Civilization*, 3 vols. New Brunswick: Rutgers University Press, 1987–2006.

Blok, J. L. *The Early Amazons: Modern and Ancient Perspectives on a Persistent Myth*. Leiden: Brill, 1995.

Boatwright, M. T. *Peoples of the Roman World*. Cambridge: Cambridge University Press, 2012.

Bonfante, L., ed. *The Barbarians of Ancient Europe. Realities and Interactions*. Cambridge: Cambridge University Press, 2011.

Bradley, M., ed. *Classics and Imperialism in the British Empire*. Oxford: Oxford University Press, 2010.

Braund, D., ed. *Scythians and Greeks: Cultural Interactions in Scythia, Athens, and the Early Roman Empire (Sixth Century BC–First Century AD)*. Exeter: University of Exeter Press, 2005.

Burkert, W. *The Orientalizing Revolution: Near Eastern Influence on Greek Culture in the Early Archaic Age*. Cambridge: Cambridge University Press, 1992.

Burnstein, S. *Ancient African Civilizations*, Princeton: Markus Weiner, 1985.

Calame, C. "Uttering Human Nature by Constructing the Inhabited World: The Well-Tempered Racism of Hippocrates," 135–56. In *Masks of Authority: Fiction and Pragmatics in Ancient Greek Poetics*. Ithaca: Cornell University Press, 2005.

Cartledge, P. *The Greeks: A Portrait of Self and Others*. Oxford: Oxford University Press, 1993.

Cole, S. "'I Know the Number of the Sand and the Measure of the Sea': Geography and Difference in the Early Greek World." In *Geography and Ethnography: Perceptions of the World in Pre–modern Societies*, edited by K. Raaflaub and R. Talbert, 197–214. Chichester: Wiley–Blackwell, 2010.

Coleman, J., and C. Walz, eds. *Greeks and Barbarians*. Bethesda: CDL Press, 1997.

Dee, J. "Black Odysseus, White Caesar: When Did 'White People' Become 'White'?" *Classical Journal* (2004): 157–67.

Dench, E. *Romulus' Asylum: Roman Identities from the Age of Alexander to the Age of Hadrian*. Oxford: Oxford University Press, 2005.

Derks, T., and N. Roymans, eds. *Ethnic Constructs in Antiquity: The Role and Power of Tradition*. Amsterdam: Amsterdam University Press, 2009.

Doughetry, C. *The Raft of Odysseus: The Ethnographic Imagination of Homer's Odyssey*. Oxford: Oxford University Press, 2001.

Dueck, D. *Geography in Classical Antiquity*. Cambridge: Cambridge University Press, 2012.

Dueck, D., H. Lindsay, and S. Pothecary, eds. *Strabo's Cultural Geography: The Making of a Kolossourgia*. Cambridge: Cambridge University Press, 2005.

Eliav-Feldon, M., B. Isaac, and J. Ziegler, eds. *The Origins of Racism in the West*. Cambridge: Cambridge University Press, 2009.

Garland, R. *The Eye of the Beholder: Deformity and Disability in the Graeco-Roman World*. 2nd ed. London: Bristol Classical Press, 2010.

Grafton, A. *New World, Ancient Texts: The Power of Tradition and the Shock of Discovery*. Cambridge, MA: Belknap Press, 1992.

Gruen, E. *Re–thinking the Other in Antiquity*. Princeton: Princeton University Press, 2011.

———, ed. *Cultural Identity in the Ancient Mediterranean*. Los Angeles: The Getty Research Institute, 2011.

———, ed. *Cultural Borrowings and Ethnic Identity in the Ancient Mediterranean*. Los Angeles: The Getty Research Institute, 2005.

———. *Diaspora: Jews Amidst Greeks and Romans*. Cambridge, MA: Harvard University Press, 2002.

Hall, E. M. *Inventing the Barbarian*. Cambridge: Cambridge University Press, 1989.

Hall, J. *Hellenicity: Between Ethnicity and Culture*. Chicago: University of Chicago Press, 2002.

———. *Ethnic Identity in Greek Antiquity*. Cambridge: Cambridge University Press, 1997.

Harrison, T. *Writing Ancient Persia*. London: Bristol Classical Press, 2011.

———, ed. *Greeks and Barbarians*. New York: Routledge USA, 2002.

Hartog, F. *The Mirror of Herodotus.* Translated by Janet Lloyd. Berkeley: University of California Press, 1988.

Isaac, B. *The Invention of Racism in Classical Antiquity.* Princeton: Princeton University Press, 2004.

Kurht, A., ed. *The Persian Empire: A Corpus of Sources from the Achaemenid Empire.* New York: Routledge USA, 2010.

Lape, S. *Race and Citizen Identity in the Classical Athenian Democracy.* New York: Cambridge University Press, 2010.

Lefkowitz, M. R. *Not Out of Africa: How Afrocentrism Became an Excuse to Teach Myth as History.* 5th ed. New York: Basic Books, 1996.

Lefkowitz, M. R., and G. M. Rogers, eds. *Black Athena Revisited.* 5th ed. Chapel Hill: University of North Carolina Press, 1996.

Levine, M. M. "Multiculturalism and the Classics." *Arethusa* 25 (1992): 215–20.

Levine, M. M., and J. Peradotto, eds. *The Challenge of "Black Athena."* Special Issue, *Arethusa* 22, no. 1 (1989).

Malkin, I. *A Small Greek World: Networks and the Ancient Mediterranean.* New York: Oxford University Press, 2011.

———, ed. 2001. *Ancient Perceptions of Greek Ethnicity.* Cambridge, MA: Harvard University Press, 2001.

McCoskey, D. *Race: Antiquity and Its Legacy (Ancients and Moderns).* Oxford: Oxford University Press, 2012.

———. "Answering the Multicultural Imperative: A Course on Race and Ethnicity in Antiquity." *Classical World* 92 (1999): 553–61.

Miller, M. C. "The Myth of Bousiris: Ethnicity and Art." In *Not the Classical Ideal: Athens and the Construction of the Other in Greek Art*, edited by B. Cohen, 413–42. Leiden: Brill, 2000.

———. *Athens and Persia in the Fifth Century B.C.: A Study in Cultural Receptivity.* New York: Cambridge University Press, 1997.

Momigliano, A. *Alien Wisdom: The Limits of Hellenization.* Cambridge: Cambridge University Press, 1975.

Munson, R.V. *Black Doves Speak: Herodotus and the Languages of Barbarians.* Center for Hellenic Studies, 9. Cambridge, MA: Harvard University Press, 2005.

Parker, G. *The Making of Roman India.* New York: Cambridge University Press, 2008.

Richlin, A. *Rome and the Mysterious Orient: Three Plays by Plautus.* Berkeley: University of California Press, 2005.

Roller, D. *Through the Pillars of Herakles: Graeco-Roman Exploration of the Atlantic.* New York: Routledge USA, 2006.

Romm, J. "Continents, Climates, and Cultures: Greek Theories of Global Structure." In *Geography and Ethnography: Perceptions of the World in Premodern Societies*, edited by K. Raaflaub and R. Talbert, 215–35. Chichester, UK: Wiley-Blackwell, 2010.

———. "Dog Heads and Noble Savages: Cynicism Before the Cynics?" In *The Cynics*, edited by R. Branham and M.-O. Goulet-Cazé, 121–135. Berkeley: University of California Press, 1996.

———. *The Edges of the Earth in Ancient Thought*. Princeton, NJ: Princeton University Press, 1992.

Rood, T. "Herodotus and Foreign Lands." In *The Cambridge Companion to Herodotus*, edited by C. Dewald and J. Marincola, 290–305. Cambridge: Cambridge University Press, 2006.

Shaw, B. "'Eaters of Flesh and Drinkers of Milk': The Ancient Mediterranean Ideology of the Pastoral Nomad." *Ancient Society* 13–14 (1982–1983): 5–31.

Skinner, J. *The Invention of Greek Ethnography from Homer to Herodotus*. New York: Oxford University Press, 2012.

Snowden, F., Jr. *Before Color Prejudice: The Ancient View of Blacks*. Cambridge, MA: Harvard University Press, 1983.

———. *Blacks in Antiquity: Ethiopians in the Greco-Roman Experience*. Cambridge, MA: Harvard University Press, 1970.

Thomas, R. *Lands and Peoples in Roman Poetry: The Ethnographic Tradition*. Cambridge: Cambridge Philological Society, 1982.

Thomas, R. *Herodotus in Context*. Cambridge: Cambridge University Press, 2000.

Thompson, L. *Romans and Blacks*. Norman: University of Oklahoma Press, 1989.

Tuplin, C. "Greek Racism? Observations on the Character and Limits of Greek Ethnic Prejudice." In *Ancient Greeks East and West*, edited by G. Tsetskhladze, 47–75. Leiden: Brill Academic Publishing, 1999.

Vasunia, P. *The Gift of the Nile: Hellenizing Egypt from Aeschylus to Alexander*. Berkeley: University of California Press, 2001.

Versluys, M. *Aeguptiaca Romana: Nilotic Scenes and the Roman Views of Egypt*. Leiden: Brill Academic Press, 2002.

West, M. *The East Face of Helicon: West Asiatic Elements of Greek Poetry and Myth*. Oxford: Clarendon Press, 1999.

Woolf, G. *Tales of the Barbarians: Ethnography and Empire in the Roman West*. Chichester, UK: Wiley-Blackwell, 2011.

INDEX